For the Freedom of Zion

For the Freedom of Zion

THE GREAT REVOLT OF JEWS AGAINST ROMANS, 66–74 CE

Guy MacLean Rogers

Yale UNIVERSITY PRESS

New Haven and London

Published with assistance from the foundation established in memory of
Amasa Stone Mather of the Class of 1907, Yale College.

Yale University Press books may be purchased in quantity for educational,
business, or promotional use. For information, please email sales.press@yale
.edu (U.S. office) or sales@yaleup.co.uk (U.K. office).

Set in Adobe Garamond type by Westchester Publishing Services.
Printed in the United States of America.

Library of Congress Control Number: 2021941137
ISBN 978-0-300-24813-5 (hardcover: alk. paper)
A catalogue record for this book is available from the British Library.

This paper meets the requirements of ANSI/NISO Z39.48-1992
(Permanence of Paper).

10 9 8 7 6 5 4 3 2 1

Dedicated to the Memory of

Fergus Millar

"A Man's a Man for a' That"

Contents

Acknowledgments

I would like to thank Jennifer Banks, senior executive editor of Yale University Press, for the many contributions she made to this project. The suggestions Jennifer made for how to improve this book were thoughtful and perceptive. I am fortunate to have worked with such an intelligent and sensitive editor. I would also like to express my thanks to the staff at Yale University Press and to Westchester Publishing Services for their work on a large, complex, and difficult manuscript.

Doing the research for this book and then writing up my ideas required time, effort, and perseverance. This book could never have been completed without the love and help of friends, colleagues, and family. I can never repay Pam Wiener, David Eisenberg, and Jon Imber for their selfless friendships. In Israel, Hannah Cotton, Jonathan Price, and Ben Isaac generously shared their scholarly expertise with me. Of course it should not be assumed that these distinguished scholars agree with any of the arguments or conclusions of this book.

The gods smiled upon me the night I met Dr. Nancy Thompson at the National Archives in Washington, DC, nearly 30 years ago. I have been honored to share my life with Dr. Thompson from Litchfield County to Riverside Drive to the Aventine Hill. I am grateful to Baxter, Wobble, and Fidget for making me laugh throughout 2020.

This book is dedicated to the memory of Sir Fergus Millar.

I met Fergus Millar by accident. In 1977 I was studying Classics at the University of Pennsylvania when I was awarded a Thouron Fellowship to continue my studies in Great Britain. I did not know a soul in Britain and had no idea where to go or even how to apply to universities. A friend recommended that I write to the Roman historian Robert Browning at the University of London to see if he could help.

I wrote to Professor Browning and was delighted to receive a quick response. He politely told me that it was impossible for me to study at his college (Birkbeck), which was for "mature" students, but that I should write to his friend, Professor Fergus Millar, who was teaching across the street at University College London (UCL), to see whether it would be possible for me to attend UCL.

I had no idea who Fergus Millar was. I wrote anyway and I immediately got back a short handwritten letter. I had trouble deciphering what the missive said. But I eventually decided that it offered me a place at UCL to study with Professor Millar. I told my professors at Penn. They were shocked. Did I have any idea who Fergus Millar was? Of course not. They referred me to a recently published book titled *The Emperor in the Roman World.* That was who Fergus Millar was.

Fergus and I stayed in touch after he went back to Oxford in 1984, and I started teaching at Wellesley College in 1985. In 1987 Fergus visited Wellesley to take part in a colloquium focused on the work of the Harvard sociologist Orlando Patterson about slavery in the ancient and modern worlds. With impeccable courtesy and his usual understated humor, Fergus critiqued Patterson's ideas about how Roman slavery developed and functioned in Roman society. Afterward all of the conference participants enjoyed a convivial dinner together at the Wellesley College Club. It was indeed true that Fergus knew how to disagree in ways that were polite and collegial.

But it would be very wrong to conclude that when Fergus politely disagreed about the answers to scholarly questions, he didn't think that he was right. He was sure of his judgments and he was unshakable, both with regard to scholarship and friendship. If Fergus was in your corner he was there, come what may. The sun would rise in the west and set in the east before Fergus would desert a friend. It was unthinkable. Fergus's personal loyalty and integrity were adamantine.

Conversely, if Fergus thought that the independence of individual scholars or of the humanities in general was under attack he did not hesitate to defend it, no matter what the potential consequences were to his own career. Winston Churchill said that courage was the foremost virtue because it was the one upon which all the others depended. Of Fergus's many virtues, his selfless courage was the one I most admired.

I was honored that Fergus asked me, along with Hannah Cotton of The Hebrew University in Jerusalem, to be the editor of his collected papers. It was a privilege to work with such renowned scholars and in some small way to repay Fergus for everything he had done for me over the years.

Why the gods chose to put Fergus and his strong, wise, and radiant wife, Susanna, in my path I will never understand. Everyone knows what a great historian Fergus was. He changed how we understand the role of the emperor in the Roman world; put democratic politics back into the study of Roman Republican history; sketched out the first mental "map" (a favorite Fergus word) of the Roman Near East; and projected that map forward to the time of Muhammad. Fergus was and is among the giants of ancient history, a different and worthy successor to Syme. Over the last few years of his life Fergus took to calling himself an extinct volcano. Some volcano.

And yet, Fergus told me point-blank in 1979 that what really mattered was character. Brilliant guys are a dime a dozen, he said. Character is what counts. How and why Fergus became a man of such generosity, integrity, and courage I do not know, and it does not matter to all of the people whom he so profoundly and positively affected over the decades. There will never be another Fergus Millar.

Thank you, Fergus, for everything you gave to us. "A Man's a Man for a' That."

Guy MacLean Rogers
Villa dei Gatti
5 September 2020

Maps

MAP 1. Herod's Kingdom, including major benefaction sites.
A.D. Riddle, RiddleMaps.com.

REGIONAL MAP
of the Roman Near East

COMMAGENE

Taurus Mts

CILICIA

Amanus Mts

Samosata

Edessa

Zeugma

Cyrrhus

Euphrates R

Antioch

Beroea

Mediterranean Sea

Laodicea

Bargylus Mts

Apamea

Epiphania/Hama

Arados

Orontes R

Palmyra

Tripolis

Byblos

PHOENICIA

Heliopolis-Baalbek

Berytus

Chalcis

Sidon

ITURAEA

Damascus

Tyre

Paneas/Panias/Caesarea Philippi

Raphanaea

Sea of
Galilee

Ptolemais

Tiberias

Hippos

Canatha

Syrian Desert

Dora

GALILEE

Gadara

AURANITIS

Caesarea

Scythopolis

Dion

Samaria/Sebaste

Pella

Bostra

Lydda

Gerasa

Iamnia

Jordan R

Philadelphia

Ascalon

Jerusalem

JUDAEA

Gaza

IDUMAEA

Dead Sea

Masada

NABATAEA

Wadi

Sirhan

Wadi Arabia

Negev Desert

North Arabian
Desert

0   30   60 mi
0   48   96 km

Created by A.D. Riddle

MAP 2. Regional map of the Roman Near East. A.D. Riddle, RiddleMaps.com.

MAP 3. The Roman empire during the early first century CE. A.D. Riddle, RiddleMaps.com

THE ROMAN EMPIRE
during the Early First Century CE

Borysthenes (Dnieper)

BASTARNAE   SARMATIANS

PANNONIA

DACIANS   GETAE   TAURI

irmium•

ILLYRICUM   Danuvius (Danube)   MOESIA

Pontus Euxinus

Hebrus THRACE

MACEDONIA   Byzantium•   Sinope•

chium   Thessalonica   Nicomedia   BITHYNIA   PONTUS
ollonia   Nicaea   Ancyra

Corcyra•   THESSALY   Troy• MYSIA   GALATIA   Halys   ARMENIA

m/Nicopolis   Aegaeum   •Pergamum   CAPPADOCIA

Delphi•   Mare   Chios•   Smyrna•   ASIA   Tyana•   •Melitene

Olympia•   •Athens   •Ephesus   Taurus M.   •Samosata

PELOPONNESE   Argos• Samos•   Aphrodisias•   Tarsus•   •Zeugma

          Sparta•   Delos•   LYCIA   CILICIA

          •Cos

          •Rhodes   Antiochia

          Cnossus   (Antioch)

CRETE   •Salamis   SYRIA

Mediterranean Sea   CYPRUS   Byblos•   •Emesa
                                   Berytus•

Cyrene•   •Damascus

Pentapolis   Caesarea•

          Alexandria•   Jerusalem•

CYRENE   Leontopolis•   JUDAEA

          Memphis•   ARABIA

AEGYPTUS

          Nilus (Nile)

          Sinus Arabicus

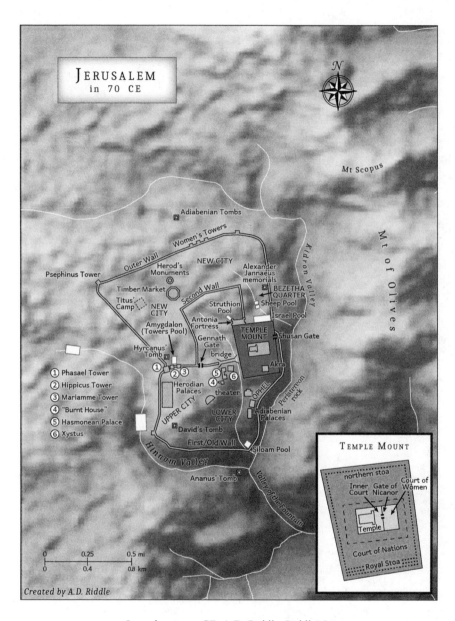

MAP 4. Jerusalem in 70 CE. A.D. Riddle, RiddleMaps.com.

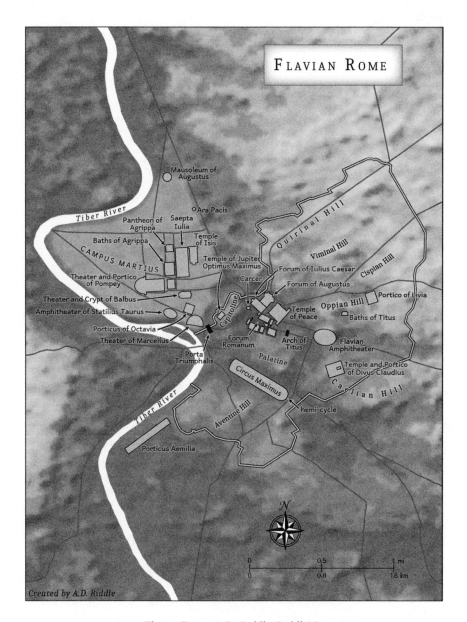

MAP 5. Flavian Rome. A.D. Riddle, RiddleMaps.com.

Introduction: A Small and Insignificant War?

THE SACRIFICE OF BIRDS

The fighting broke out in the spring of 66 CE over a sacrifice of some birds.[1] Somewhere, perhaps in the northwest quarter of the Mediterranean harbor city of Caesarea, Jews had a synagogue that abutted land belonging to a Greek.[2] The Jews had attempted to buy the Greek's property, offering him far more money than the plot was worth. In response, the Greek built workshops on the site. The workshops made access to the synagogue for Jews more difficult.[3]

Some of the younger Jews tried to halt construction of the workshops, but the Roman governor Florus intervened on behalf of the Greek. Some prominent Jews then gave Florus the enormous sum of eight talents to get the Greek to desist. Florus took the money, went off to the city of Sebaste to the north of Judaea, and let the work go on.[4]

The next day was the Sabbath. When the Jews were gathering around the synagogue, one of the non-Jewish Caesareans began sacrificing some birds on an upturned pot outside the synagogue. The sacrifice led to a confrontation between Jews and Caesareans.[5] A local cavalry commander intervened but to no avail. Some Jews who went to Florus in Sebaste to complain about the incident were arrested.[6]

News of what had happened in Caesarea was reported in Jerusalem. The reaction was muted at first. When Florus withdrew 17 talents from the Temple treasury for "imperial needs," however, protests broke out, and he was verbally abused by the crowd.[7]

After the leaders of the Jews did not surrender those who had mocked him, Florus let the troops under his command sack the Upper Agora of Jerusalem. More than 3,600 people were killed, including Jews who were members of the Roman equestrian order.[8] The murdered Jews who belonged to that order were among the wealthiest people in the Roman empire.

There was a second massacre when Jews from the city went out to greet two more cavalry squadrons that were approaching Jerusalem from Caesarea. The soldiers pursued the terrified residents back into the city, killing those they encountered as the cavalrymen tried to reach the fortress called the Antonia, located at the northwestern corner of the Temple Mount.[9] The fortress was linked to the Temple by porticoes. Florus too was trying to make his way to the bastion, but his route was blocked by the enraged populace. After the population cut off access to the Temple from the colonnades of the Antonia, Florus fled from the city, leaving behind one cohort of between 500 and 1,000 soldiers.[10]

When the fighting subsided, Cestius Gallus, the Roman governor of Syria, launched an investigation into what had happened in Jerusalem. The inquiry confirmed the loyalty of the people to Rome.[11] At a gathering of the populace held within the area known as the Xystus, which lay between the palace of Judaea's former Hasmonean rulers and the Temple Mount, the Jewish king, Agrippa II—who had been king of Chalcis in what is now southern Lebanon since 50 CE—urged the Jews of Jerusalem not to start a war with Rome that they could not win, to rebuild the porticoes that connected the Antonia Fortress to the Temple, and to pay the tribute owed to the Romans.[12]

At first the people heeded Agrippa's advice. But he was driven out of Jerusalem in a hail of stones after he urged the people to give obedience to Florus until a new Roman governor could be sent out.[13]

At that point the Temple captain Eleazar, son of the high priest Ananias, convinced the priests in charge of the Temple services not to receive any more gifts or sacrifices from any foreigner.[14] Such gifts or sacrifices might include those made by Romans, as well as ones offered by others on behalf of Rome and the emperor. Similar sacrifices had been made at the Temple since the time of the emperor Augustus.[15] Putting an end to the sacrifices on behalf of Rome and the emperor was, in effect, a declaration of independence from Rome.[16]

The war of Jews against Romans that began in Caesarea in the late spring of 66 CE was symbolically declared by this refusal to let sacrifices for Rome and the emperor continue at the Temple in Jerusalem. The conflict led to the destruction of the national site of sacrifice for the Jews, the beginning of a new imperial dynasty in Rome, and the Jews' loss of even nominal political independence for almost 1,900 years. When the unnamed Caesarean sacrificed some birds on an upturned pot next to the synagogue in Caesarea in 66, he bent the arc of history for Jews in the direction of unprecedented suffering but finally back to the promised land of freedom.

THE COSTS OF WAR

The fighting lasted for eight years, and many of the Jews who gathered in the Xystus of Jerusalem to hear King Agrippa's speech in the spring of 66 did not survive the war. Villages and towns in the Galilee were destroyed by the Romans and their inhabitants massacred or enslaved. A substantial number of Romans also died or were wounded. Over the better part of a decade Romans killed Jews and Jews killed Romans. Romans fought not only Jews but also each other after a Roman civil war broke out during the fighting in Judaea. But Jews also slaughtered each other as they fought over the question of whether to seek peace with the Romans or to fight to the very end. The war of Jews against Romans almost immediately became a war of Jews against Jews, Jews against their neighbors, and, according to Flavius Josephus, our main narrative source for the war, a war of Jews against their own God.[17] God himself, Josephus believed, intervened directly in the fighting, taking the side of the Romans.

In Jerusalem there occurred a civil war among three factions of Jews, widespread murder, a Roman siege, famine, cannibalism, combat of every kind, a conflagration, the destruction of the Temple, a massacre of the civilian population, and the razing of large sections of the holy city. Some who escaped from the Roman massacres in Jerusalem later committed murder or mass suicide rather than be slaughtered by the Romans. Josephus implausibly claims that there were 1.1 million casualties in the war, most of them Jews. That figure is difficult, if not impossible, to accept, since recent studies estimate that the entire Jewish population of Palestine was approximately 600,000 at the time.[18] Much more credibly, he also says that 97,000 were captured.[19]

Those who were not killed outright by the Romans during the fighting were used later as slave laborers on imperial work projects or were made to fight each other or wild animals in the amphitheaters of Rome's provinces. Some of the leaders of the revolt were brought to Rome, where they marched in the triumphal procession of Rome's conquering generals in the summer of 71. Simon bar Giora, or son of Giora, who was perhaps the most effective rebel leader of the Jews during the war, was ritually executed in Rome at the end of the Romans' triumphal celebration of their victory.

After the war was over the Roman emperors appropriated the land of Jews in Judaea and imposed an unprecedented punitive tax upon all 1.2 million Jews living within the Roman empire.[20] Rome's new Flavian emperors, Vespasian and his sons Titus and Domitian, also used the victory over the Jews to legitimate their claims to rule the empire. They saw to the building of monuments in Rome designed to memorialize their great triumph.[21] Some of the treasures that the Romans looted from the Temple in Jerusalem were displayed in buildings of the capital.

Archaeological excavations in Rome have revealed that the Flavian dynasty erected in Rome not one but two monumental triumphal arches celebrating their victory over the Jews and the destruction of Jerusalem: the famous Arch of Titus at the southeastern corner of the Roman Forum and a larger, though less well known, triumphal arch that led into the Circus Maximus from the southeastern side. On a daily basis for centuries these monuments and others reminded Romans and the large population of Jews living in Rome of the destruction of the Jewish Temple and of a large part of Jerusalem. Most importantly, as we shall see, the Flavian Amphitheater, or Colosseum, was financed at least in part from the spoils of the Roman victory over the Jews. The looted wealth of Jews paid for Rome's greatest monument, its most popular tourist attraction to this day.

Debate about the effects of the war upon the most prominent "schools" of thought (*haireseis* in Josephus's Greek) or sectarian groupings of Jews in Jerusalem and Judaea continues.[22] Years after the war's conclusion, the first-century CE Jewish Roman general and historian Josephus wrote as though there were Essenes and Sadducees still around, and Pharisees, whom he identified by name, such as Simon, the son of Gamaliel, are recalled as sages in later rabbinic sources.[23] A case therefore can be made that the destruction of the Jewish Temple in 70 did not cause a theological break or crisis within Judaism.[24]

But while individual Essenes may have survived the war, the community, or *yahad*, of about 4,000 ascetics known as Essenes (from the Hebrew, meaning "Those Who Do [the Law]") seems to have disappeared by the conclusion of the war, and after the Temple was destroyed, the Sadducees lost the physical focus of their activities and the base of their authority.[25] How and why this happened are matters of debate. The likeliest explanation for the disappearance of the sectarian communities, however, is not that their theological beliefs were falsified by what happened during the war. Rather, most of the Essenes and Sadducees disappeared because the Romans attacked and killed them at Qumran in June of 68 and in the Temple and the city of Jerusalem in 70.[26]

A reformulation of Judaism, meanwhile, was begun in the town of Iamnia (modern Yavneh) after and in light of the Temple's destruction and the cessation of sacrifices.[27] That was accomplished under the spiritual and intellectual leadership of Johanan ben Zakkai, who reportedly was secretly carried out of Jerusalem in a coffin by his students, met with the Roman general Vespasian, predicted Vespasian's elevation to the emperorship, and asked that Iamnia be given to him and the sages.[28] Eventually, the interpretation of Judaism espoused by Johanan ben Zakkai and his followers, who are called sages (*hakhamim*), elders (*zeqenim*), or rabbis (*rabbanim*) in later sources, became the most widely practiced form of the religion of their ancestors.[29]

The followers of Jesus of Nazareth somehow survived Jerusalem's siege and destruction too, and they spread out over the Roman empire and beyond to preach their message that the proclaimer was indeed the proclaimed. By the early second century CE, Roman governors called them Christians, thereby distinguishing them from Jews, at least in their minds. Two hundred and fifty years after Jesus's death, the Christians' appropriation of Abraham's and Moses's religion was made legal by the political heirs of those who had destroyed the Temple and Jerusalem, and it eventually gained imperial support and then legal sanction. The descendants of the Jews who survived the war's horrific conclusion, however, did not experience independent, sustained self-government again until the middle of the twentieth century.[30]

THE CAUSE, COURSE, AND INTERPRETATION OF THE WAR

What caused the war? Was there some long-standing enmity between Jews and Romans? Was the war incited by regional tensions? Is it true that the appearance of Roman armies led by Cestius, the governor of Syria, and later by Vespasian and Titus "manufactured" enemies of Rome? Or were there Jews willing to fight against the Romans before Rome's legions marched into the Galilee on their way to Jerusalem?

What was the Roman strategy for winning the war? How much resistance to Rome's legions was there? Did the Galilee and the Peraea, to the east of the Jordan River, submit to the Romans "immediately" in 67? Was there only minimal resistance to Rome's legions and allies?[31] Indeed, was there no real war at all?[32]

Was it primarily nonresidents of Jerusalem who provided the main impetus for fighting the Romans after 66, as Josephus claimed? Did the future Roman emperor Titus destroy the Temple as a matter of policy, or was it burned down by accident, as Josephus seems to imply?

Were the Jews who made their way to the fortresses of Machaerus, Herodeion (Herodium), and Masada, either before the war broke out or afterward, primarily freedom fighters, or were they just trying to avoid the Romans? Was there no real siege or heroic defense of Masada? Did Eleazar ben Yair and the *sicarii* (dagger-men) atop Masada really commit mass suicide and murder?

Why did the Jews lose? Was the outcome of the war a matter of divine providence, as Josephus argued? Or did they lose, as many modern historians have reflexively stated, because it was militarily inevitable? Why were the Romans willing to commit one-seventh of the approximately 150,000 legionaries spread over the entire 1.5 million square miles of their empire to capturing Jerusalem, at a time when imperial finances were stretched almost to the breaking point?[33]

Had God destroyed the Temple or allowed it to be incinerated because Jews had sinned, like Moses striking the rock to bring forth water instead of just commanding it?[34] Did the destruction of the Temple mean that God had broken off his covenantal relationship with the Jews? Had the Temple been destroyed because of fateful ordinances, such as the one that prohibited Moses from entering the promised land after he had lived the 120 years allotted to him?[35]

In his works Josephus repeatedly wrote that it was the impiety of Jews that led to the destruction of the Temple and much of Jerusalem: God himself had punished Jews for their sins.[36] By the end of the first century CE, the redactor of the book of Ezra had raised the question of why Israel had become a byword among the Gentiles and why the people beloved of God had been put at the mercy of godless nations.[37] The author of the book of Baruch answered those questions by claiming that God had brought disaster down upon the Jews because they had sinned and committed sacrilege by not following God's precepts.[38]

Some rabbis later argued that Jerusalem or the sanctuary or both had been destroyed because of the Jews' neglect of Torah; because they (the Jews) abandoned teaching schoolchildren or disrespected the sages; or because of the idolatry, immorality, and bloodshed that prevailed among them.[39] Others, it should be emphasized, challenged the idea that Israel was to blame for what happened. They argued that it was God himself who was responsible for Israel's suffering, either because he did not follow the law, had grown too old or too weak to defend Israel from its enemies, or had failed to keep his promises. Comparing God to the owner of a stronger and a weaker gladiator, the third-century CE rabbi and expert on oral law (aggadist) Isaac ben Nappaha criticized God for not protecting the weaker gladiator (Israel) from the stronger (the other nations).[40] Both for the sages who blamed Jews for what happened and for those who criticized God, the destruction of the Temple in 70 was a watershed event that raised questions about divine justice and the status of the covenant that could not be avoided.[41]

After this event influential Christian apologists, including Justin Martyr, Origen, and Eusebius, argued that the Temple's destruction by the Romans was punishment for the execution of Christ by "the Jews": it was the decisive historical proof "text" that Christians had replaced Jews within God's covenant.[42] Attempts by Jews to rebuild the Temple consequently were and are sacrilegious efforts to buck the will of God.[43]

Some influential Muslim leaders have gone further and argued that the historical proof text of Christian apologists is unnecessary. They have denied that there ever was any connection between Jews and the physical remains of the so-called Western Wall, the retaining wall of the Herodian-era Temple Mount.[44] Indeed, in 2015 the grand mufti of Jerusalem, Muhammad Ahmad Hussein, asserted that there never was a Temple of Jews on the site of the Temple Mount.[45] Since there was no Temple, it could not have been destroyed by Titus and the Roman legions in 70. Some scholars of Islamic history and philosophy, in contrast, have more generously understood the existence of the Al Aksa Mosque on top of the Temple Mount as an intensification of the sanctity of the spot where the Temple of the Jews once stood.[46]

Scholars thus disagree about the effects of the Temple's destruction upon Jews and their theologies.[47] But whatever they argue, more people alive today are invested in the meaning of the Temple's destruction than in any other event in ancient history.

Visitors to the site of ancient Ephesos in western Asia Minor (Turkey) are usually disappointed to find only one rather forlorn-looking, re-erected column of the once great Temple of Artemis still standing. Almost none of those visitors have any idea when and how the Temple of Artemis was destroyed, and so their disappointment when they see a solitary column from one of the ancient world's seven wonders does not affect the way they live their lives and think about their futures. The same is not true of the physical remains of the war of Jews and Romans. The remnants of no other ancient structure support as many fears and hopes about the present or future of humanity as those of the Western, or Wailing, Wall of the Temple. Many people today believe that the fate of humanity itself will be decided at the site of the destroyed Temple. Visitors to the Western Wall today are immediately aware that they are visiting not just another tourist site; they are at an active religious shrine and are witnesses to expressions of piety that are sometimes intended to have consequences for all of humanity.

The revolt of Jews from 66 to 74 was not the only rebellion against Rome during the first century CE, and it was not the most successful in purely military terms.[48] For example, in 9 CE a Roman citizen and former auxiliary soldier named Arminius and his fellow Germanic warriors wiped out three Roman legions and liberated from Roman rule all the territory east of the Rhine River.[49] For that reason a large part of what would one day become the modern nation-state of Germany lay outside the administration of Roman rule, with incalculable historical consequences. The Boudica revolt in Britain led to the deaths of tens of thousands of Romans in 60 or 61.[50] In another revolt in 70, Civilis and the Batavians in Germania Inferior destroyed nearly two Roman legions.[51]

Some scholars have argued that the revolt of Jews against Rome during the first century CE did not mark a turning point in Jewish or Roman history or that Jews responded to the cataclysmic outcome of the revolt more quickly and with greater resiliency than has usually been appreciated.[52] There is some truth to the latter claim at least. Yet, as we shall see, the Jews' revolt led to the longest siege in the history of the imperial period and arguably was the most significant revolt in the history of the early Roman empire both for the losers and for the winners.[53]

The army that the Romans ultimately mustered to crush the revolt was larger by far than the force Alexander the Great used to conquer the Achaemenid Persian empire during the fourth century BCE and also greater than the task force that the Roman emperor Claudius sent to invade Britain in 43 CE. To supply the forces that they gathered to defeat the Jewish rebels, the Romans drew upon resources from the provinces of Syria, Commagene, Cilicia, and Pamphylia; the scale of the logistical operation has never been plausibly estimated or appreciated. During the operations commanded by the future Roman emperor Titus, four of Rome's legions were actively engaged in Judaea and Jerusalem. It is somewhat puzzling that scholars have paid far more attention to the war's causes and effects than to the question of why the Romans were willing to devote such resources to crushing the Jews in 66. What was the strategic reason for fighting such a war, 1,500 miles away from Rome, in the way that they did?

The war between Jews and Romans was fought with great ferocity by both sides, and it led to suffering, death, and destruction on a scale for which we have no other comparable testimony in the history of the early Roman empire, even if Josephus, its historian, exaggerated casualty figures on both sides. Yet some scholars have downplayed the scale and significance of the war of Jews against Romans. This book will prove that the war was not small, short, or insignificant. Its outcome changed the course of Judaea's history, of Rome's history, and that of the world. Nor is the story over. The efforts to give the war meaning continue, and not only among the priestly courses of historians and archaeologists.

WHO SHOULD SPEAK FOR ZION?

Within the self-governing polity of Israel today, there are many who wish to rebuild the Temple of the Jews where it was, as it was, as the Venetian expression has it, and to resume the full order of sacrifices that were ended in 70.[54] Indeed, in the immediate aftermath of the Temple's destruction in 70 CE, many Jews expected it to be rebuilt and the sacrifices there to be resumed, just as Jews, under the civil leadership of King David's descendant Zerubbabel and the high priest Joshua, had built the Second Temple between the year 520 and 3 Adar of 516 or 515 BCE after the First Temple was destroyed in 586.[55]

Those who wish to rebuild the Temple today see this action as the key to Israel's—and the world's—redemption.[56] In 2017 on Tisha B'Av (31 July), the date when some Jews believe that both the First and the Second Temples were destroyed, more than 1,300 Jews visited the site of the Temple Mount, the most since Israel captured it during the Six-Day War in 1967.[57] Every year the numbers who visit the Temple Mount on that day increase.

Many others, including Theodor Herzl and David Ben-Gurion, have considered the idea of rebuilding the Temple undesirable, dangerous, and possibly blasphemous.[58]

There have been two Temples. Will there be a third? Should there be? To what end? Who should decide this question? Who has the authority to define what piety or obedience to the law is for Jews? Will a trumpeter some day stand again at the southwest corner of another Temple on the Temple Mount and blow his silver trumpet at the beginning and end of Shabbat, telling Jews when to cease their work and when to begin it again, as we know happened until the destruction of the Second Temple in 70?[59]

There are more than 7.8 billion human beings on the face of the earth today. The "people of the Book," or *ahl al-Kitab,* an Arabic expression that arose from a description of the legal status of Jews, Christians, and Muslims according to Islamic law, now constitute an absolute majority of the earth's population.[60] Whatever the theological and ritual differences among modern Jews, Christians, and Muslims (in all their diversity), both internally and externally, the destruction of the Temple and Jerusalem in 70 is for all of them an essential episode in their intertwined and often competitive histories. Countless people over the last two thousand years have drawn strategic, philosophical, spiritual, and personal lessons from the war of Jews against Romans based upon conclusions about its causes, course, and outcome. The story of the Temple's destruction is often seen as the paradigmatic, if not unprecedented, warning or lesson for Jews and others. Sin will be punished; great sin will be greatly punished.[61]

But what if the cause of the war was not impiety? Was the defeat of those who rebelled in 66 CE inevitable? What if the war's course and outcome were not determined by some divine plan, as Josephus argued? Or, if they were part of a divine plan, did Josephus misunderstand the plan? If these questions yield different answers today, how might that change how people understand the significance of the war for history and for their lives? To this day the idea of "chosen-ness" begs the question of chosen for what: Were Jews chosen for great rewards and an exalted and holy place among nations or for excessive, disproportionate suffering?[62]

When Titus and the Roman legions destroyed the Temple and brought to an end the sacrificial cult practiced there, they thought that they had defeated the God of Israel and won the war of Jews against Romans. Instead they had set the stage for God's victory, because destroying the Temple turned Jews and their theological heirs back to the word of God. Thus far God's word has never been successfully besieged. The Jews lost the war against the Romans and have often walked a road of sorrows since 70 CE. But they have won the peace. The sacrifices their ancestors made for the freedom of Zion have not been in vain.

To begin to understand how and why a war came to pass that influences the way so many people still understand themselves and the world, it is instructive to turn back to the reign of Herod the Great, when the forefathers of the man who first made that sacrifice of birds in Caesarea came to live in the city that Herod named after the Roman emperor.

PART ONE

The Breakdown of the Herodian Model

CHAPTER I

Herod Agonistes

HEROD THE HORRIBLE?

There were signs that King Herod of Judaea should repent as he prepared to meet God and receive his judgment in the spring of 4 BCE.[1] He was nearly 70 years old and desperately ill with a variety of appalling maladies. His fever was low but constant. His skin itched all over, and he had pains in his intestines. Pus oozed out of tumors on his feet. His stomach was inflamed, and worms crawled out of the gangrene on his genitals. He had asthma and his limbs convulsed. Unsurprisingly, he was depressed.[2] He was no doubt aware that the Seleucid king, Antiochus IV Epiphanes, who had profaned and pillaged the Temple, had been consumed by worms.[3] Being eaten alive by worms was a telltale sign of divine punishment.

Seeking relief, Herod crossed the Jordan River and traveled to Callirrhoe on the eastern side of the Dead Sea to soak in the warm waters of the site.[4] While Herod was there, his doctors recommended that his body temperature be raised by lowering him into a bath of hot oil. Herod followed his doctors' orders to the letter and passed out as soon as he was lowered into the bath. The shouts of the king's attendants brought Herod back from the brink.[5]

Having barely survived his doctors' prescribed treatment, Herod turned to his diviners. The king's seers interpreted his horrendous afflictions as divine punishment for the lawless actions he had committed as he ascended to his throne and then fought to stay on it. The list of misdeeds the diviners based their divine diagnosis upon was long, multigenerational, and bloodstained.

During the Roman civil wars, Herod's Idumaean father, Antipater II, had been a supporter of the Roman general Pompey the Great.[6] After Pompey's murder in Egypt in the late summer of 48 BCE, Antipater went over to the side of Pompey's enemy Iulius Caesar and, with an army of 3,000 Jews, provided Caesar with crucial military assistance in Egypt.[7] As a reward Antipater was given Roman citizenship and freedom from taxes. To please Antipater, Caesar also confirmed Hyrcanus II, who had been ethnarch, or leader, of the people of Judaea since 63 BCE, as high priest.[8] Antipater himself was made *epitropos*, or procurator, of all Judaea. Antipater in turn appointed his oldest son, Phasael, as general or governor of the Jerusalemites and his son Herod as general of the Galilee (47 BCE).[9]

Young Herod quickly proved his military ability. Tracking down the brigand chief Ezekias and his followers along the Syrian border, Herod had Ezekias and many of the brigands executed, though without a trial.[10] His successes, however, aroused the jealousy of the leaders of the Jews and the high priest Hyrcanus. Herod was called back to Jerusalem to stand trial for the brigands' unlawful execution.[11] Under Roman pressure Herod was acquitted of the charge and was then appointed by Sextus Caesar, the Roman governor of Syria, to be general of Coele-Syria ("Hollow Syria") and possibly Samaritis, the region to the immediate north of Judaea, in 46 BCE.[12] Coele-Syria probably refers here to the regions contiguous to the territory that Herod had already cleared of bandits, thus including southern Lebanon and the Upper Galilee; the area around Panias (now Banias); and parts of the Gaulanitis (the Golan) and Trachonitis, northeast of the Jordan River.[13]

After Iulius Caesar's assassination on 15 March of 44 BCE, Herod and his older brother Phasael became tetrarchs, or rulers of one-fourth of all Judaea, in 41 BCE by the decision of Iulius Caesar's right-hand man Mark Antony.[14] The Parthians, who ruled the territories on the eastern side of the Euphrates River, meanwhile appointed Hyrcanus's nephew Antigonus II Mattathias (or Matthias) as king and high priest in 40 BCE to replace his uncle, who had been favored by Herod's father, Antipater.[15] After Antigonus's appointment the Parthians invaded Judaea in 40 BCE on behalf of their appointee and deceitfully captured both Herod's brother Phasael, who committed suicide or was poisoned, and the former high priest Hyrcanus, whom they mutilated and took away into captivity. Herod himself was forced to flee from Jerusalem with only a few soldiers and his family members, with the Parthians in hot pursuit.[16]

Herod soon defeated the pursuing Parthians and their Jewish supporters near the hill where he later had built the self-named fortress palace of Herodeion. After installing his family members atop the rock fortress of Masada along the western shore of the Dead Sea, Herod himself pushed on toward Petra, now in Jordan.[17] When no help was forthcoming from the Nabataeans, Herod then moved on to Egypt and from there to Pamphylia, the island of Rhodes, and finally to Rome.[18]

Then only 32 or 33 years old, Herod was formally recognized as king of the Jews by the Roman Senate in Rome during his seven-day visit there in the winter of 40–39 BCE. Immediately after receiving his kingdom from the Senate, Herod made sacrifice in the Temple of Jupiter Capitolinus. His territory originally included Judaea, the Galilee, the Peraea to the east of the Jordan River, and Ituraea in southern Syria.[19] It was nevertheless only by late 37 or early 36 BCE, with the aid of Sosius, the new Roman governor of Syria, that Herod was able to capture Jerusalem and Antigonus (who was later beheaded in Antioch) and to take charge of his kingdom.[20] As soon as he was seated on the throne Herod exterminated some 45 of Antigonus's leading partisans.[21] Having had to fight for his crown, Herod decided that no one was going to take it from him.

Soon Herod became fearful that the *figura* cut by Jonathan Aristobulus III, the teenage brother of Herod's beautiful and brilliant Hasmonean wife, Mariamme, was a bit too *bella*. Herod had appointed Aristobulus high priest in place of the deposed Babylonian Jew Hananel, whom he had earlier elevated to that position, and the young man had made a sensational impression on the people when he officiated at the Temple altar during the Sukkot festival in 35 BCE. (See appendix E for the high priests appointed by Herod.) So Herod had the 17-year-old Aristobulus drowned in a swimming pool in Jericho—after which Herod arranged elaborate funeral rites for him.[22]

The septuagenarian former high priest Hyrcanus II, who had been carried off into captivity by the Parthians in 40 and then brought back at Herod's invitation in 36, was executed in 30 BCE for his alleged involvement in a conspiracy against Herod, instigated by Hyrcanus's daughter Alexandra.[23] His execution was probably a preemptive strike, designed to remove potential rivals to Herod's rule.

After the defeat of Herod's patron Antony at the Battle of Actium on 2 September of 31 BCE, Herod deftly transferred his friendship and loyalty to Antony's enemy Octavian during their meeting on the island of Rhodes the following spring.[24] When Herod, then 43 years old, came into the presence of Octavian, he took off his diadem. Pleased by this theatrical display of deference, the Roman placed the crown back on Herod's head after Herod promised to be as loyal a friend to Octavian as he had been to Antony.[25]

Both men had taken each other's measure. Large gifts to Herod's new patron Octavian, including no less than 800 talents of silver, followed, and Herod's kingship was once again confirmed by the Roman Senate.[26] After the deaths of Antony and Cleopatra in 30 BCE, Octavian (Gaius Iulius Caesar, later Augustus) gave Herod more territory and muscle: lands that Cleopatra had appropriated; the cities of Gadara and Hippos in the Decapolis, an administrative association of up to 10 cities located mainly in the area to the east of the Rift Valley between Syria, Iturea, Nabataea, and Judaea; Samaritis; the Phoenician (Sidonian)–influenced coastal cities of Gaza, Anthedon (Khirbet Teda), Joppa (Yafo), and Iamnia, and Straton's Tower (later Caesarea Maritima); as well as Cleopatra's personal bodyguard of 400 Gauls.[27] Deference paid dividends.

In the aftermath of his royal reconfirmation, between the summer of 30 BCE and 29 BCE, Herod authorized the minting of a coin series that featured a table on each coin's reverse side and a diadem on the obverse, or top. These iconographic images were intended to symbolize a cultic table in Jerusalem and the legitimation of Herod's royalty.[28] The gifts and honors that Herod bestowed upon the emperor and his friends bought him an expanded domain, great prosperity, and a deep well of imperial toleration for his ruthless responses to anyone who challenged his rule, thought about it, or even imagined a future without him.

In 29 BCE, Herod had his 25-year-old wife, Mariamme, the granddaughter of the former Judaean ethnarch and high priest Hyrcanus II, executed on the suspicion of adultery with his brother-in-law Joseph or, perhaps more likely, with an Ituraean named Soëmus—a charge that Josephus states was false.[29]

Hyrcanus's daughter Alexandra was executed in 28 BCE after she appeared to be making plans to seize power after Herod's death.[30] Around 27–25 BCE Herod did away with his sister Salome's husband Costobar and his friends for plotting revolution. The theophorically named Costobar was a descendant of the priests of the Idumaean-Edomite deity Cos, or Qos, and had served as governor of Idumaea, to the south of Judaea, and Gaza since about 37 BCE.[31]

After Costobar's execution there was a pause in the bloodletting until the children of those whom Herod had already put to death had grown up. As soon as they did, Herod turned his attention to them when they too were alleged to be plotting against him.

After Herod consulted the Roman emperor Augustus, in 7 BCE Herod's half-Hasmonean, Rome-educated sons by his already executed wife, Mariamme—Alexander and Aristobulus—were strangled in Sebaste for plotting to assassinate Herod.[32] It is possible that the execution of these young men lies behind the "Massacre of the Innocents" story that the apostle Matthew tells about the murder of all boys under two years old in Bethlehem and the surrounding region by Herod, after he learned that a king of the Jews had been born in Bethlehem.[33]

Herod then had his brother Pheroras and his wife, who was the sister of Mariamme (though we don't know her name), exiled to the Peraea for maligning his daughters and for paying the fine he had imposed on the Pharisees when they refused to swear a loyalty oath to him.[34]

Herod expelled his Jerusalemite wife, Doris, twice, the second time in 7 BCE, confiscating all of her finery before she was sent away. That "finery," probably referring to her wardrobe, may have been part of the indirect dowry given to Doris by Herod's family on their marriage.[35] Her son Antipater was put on trial and accused of planning Herod's murder, of ingratitude, of taking advantage of the king's indulgence, and of being a hypocritical schemer.[36] He escaped immediate execution only because Herod was preoccupied with his own worsening health.[37]

While he was trying to recover from his various ailments, on 12 March of 4 BCE, Herod had ordered that two "sophists," or experts in the interpretation of Mosaic law, Judas (Judah ben Sephoraeus) and Matthias (Mattathias ben Margalus), be burned alive. These legal experts had incited a group of young men to hack down the golden eagle that Herod had hung above the Temple Great Gate on the grounds that it was unlawful to put images, busts, or representations of any living thing in the Temple. In the middle of the day the young men had climbed up, detached the eagle from the outside wall, and, after letting themselves down with ropes, chopped up the eagle with hatchets. The 40 young men who were arrested for their part in destroying the eagle were put to death in Jericho.[38]

Herod probably had the gilded eagle hung above the Temple Great Gate sometime between completion of work on the Temple building in 18 BCE and 15 BCE, when Augustus's friend Agrippa visited Jerusalem and presumably saw that Herod had had Agrippa's name engraved on the gate.[39] It is possible that during the same time period Herod also had minted a bronze half-prutah coin type that featured a single cornucopia on the reverse side and a closed-wing, right-facing eagle on the obverse. The half-prutah eagle coin may have been intended to symbolize and propagandize Herod's temple project, to be discussed later in the chapter.[40]

Some Jews could have understood the golden eagle on the Temple Great Gate as a violation of the Second Commandment's prohibition against graven images or as a symbol of Herod's loyalty to Rome. Given the fact that eagles were depicted on the reverse side of the silver Tyrian shekels that Jews had used for many years to pay the half-shekel Temple tax, however, it seems unlikely that Herod thought that the presence of a golden eagle above the Temple Great Gate should have offended the religious sensibilities of most Jews. It is even possible that Herod intended the eagle to convey the message that as the Temple's rebuilder he was acting as God's agent or messenger. In the Hebrew Bible the eagle was a frequently cited symbol of God himself or of his might.[41]

The timing of the destruction of the golden eagle is probably the key to understanding its significance. The golden eagle had been perched above the Temple Great Gate for more than a decade before it was vandalized in 4 BCE. The young men who cut down the eagle did so in broad daylight when Herod was gravely ill, and they might have thought that he would die soon. Whether Herod believed that the eagle was a biblically warranted symbol of his piety or not, the two sophists and their young followers wanted to send a message to Herod and his potential successor(s). In their eyes Herod was not a messenger of God; he was a breaker of the law. Destroying the eagle in turn sent a warning to whoever would follow Herod. A repeat of Herod's violation of the law would be met with resistance.

Herod obviously disagreed with the legal experts and their acolytes. His execution of the learned teachers and the young men who cut down the eagle was not just the intemperate reaction of an old man near death. The golden eagle was a symbol of God. Therefore it was the sophists and the young men who were the blasphemers, not Herod. They deserved death for trying to turn God's eagle into a symbol of impiety.

HEROD'S PIG

Observing the Herodian familial carnage from Rome, the emperor Augustus—who knew a thing or two about family issues, having exiled his wayward daughter Iulia to the wine-less and man-less island of Pandateria in the Tyrrhenian Sea in 2 BCE—was quoted as saying that it was better to be Herod's pig than his son: "Melius est Herodis porcum esse quam filium."[42]

The point of this Augustan witticism seems to have been that whereas Herod kept kosher (laws of *kashrut*), observing the Jewish prohibition against killing and presumably consuming pigs' meat, Herod's son was not equally safe from his father's hands. Though the emperor was surely no expert on Jewish dietary law, Augustus's remark nevertheless indicates that he thought Herod was an observant Jew, at least when it came to a dietary restriction that distinguished Jews from most of the emperor's subjects. Yet the emperor seems to have undervalued the good fortune of the king's pig: it was better to be Herod's pig than any of his royal rivals or their supporters, the relatives of his rivals, at least some of his (10) wives or his brothers, his sister-in-law, most of his children, and anyone who challenged his adherence to Jewish law or who incited others to do so.

Augustus may have been right about the relative fortunes of Herod's pig and his son and many of his other relations. But was Herod's pig better off than the majority of the king's subjects? Was the lucky hog more fortunate than tens of thousands of Jews and non-Jews alike living outside Herod's kingdom who had benefited from his generosity? As death and possible judgment loomed, Herod could have argued plausibly that no other Jew or half-Jew, or even non-Jew for that matter, had done as much as he for both Jews and Gentiles in the eastern Mediterranean since Alexander the Great. At least some of Herod's generosity was self-interested or in the interest of his supporters in Rome. But the king also gave generously in support of the infrastructure and institutions of Graeco-Roman civic life at the same time as he looked out for the interests of diaspora Jewish communities.

HEROD THE HEROIC? THE EASTERN MEDITERRANEAN BENEFACTOR

In fact, Herod's desire to become known as an eastern Mediterranean benefactor was signaled even before he was first crowned by the Roman Senate. (See maps 2 and 3 for his benefaction sites.)

Though Herod was short of cash when he landed on the island of Rhodes on his way to Rome to seek Antony's help against Antigonus in the midwinter of 40–39 BCE, he gave money to the Rhodians to rebuild their city after it was damaged during the Roman civil war.[43] At some later point he also subsidized shipbuilding on Rhodes, and when the Temple of Apollo there burned down, Herod had it rebuilt on a greater scale.[44]

After the crown of Judaea was fixed firmly on his head, Herod distributed his largesse to cities and peoples northward into Asia Minor, the Greek

islands, and the Greek mainland. He had gymnasia built for the cities of Tripolis (Tripoli), Damascus, and Ptolemais (Acco); a city wall for Byblos; and
halls, porticoes, temples, and marketplaces for Tyre (Sur) and the Roman *colonia*, or colony, of Berytus (Beirut). Theaters were constructed for Sidon
(Saïda), and for Damascus, perhaps in the area just below the Suq Midhat
Pasha in the modern city; he also had built an aqueduct for Laodicea in Syria.[45]
For the Antiochenes in Syria, Herod had the main north-south street paved
in polished marble for about 2.5 miles and the entire street adorned with a
covered colonnade to protect those who walked along it from rain showers.[46]

In the spring of 14 BCE, Herod had a stoa built for the Greek island of
Chios after it was destroyed in the Mithridatic War, and he subsequently paid
the taxes that the Chians owed to the procurators of the Roman emperor.[47]
He provided the annual office of the gymnasiarch on the island of Cos in the
southeastern Aegean with a perpetual endowment, and grain was supplied to
all who applied for it.[48] An inscription of the assembly of Cos from around
14 BCE honoring Gaius Iulius Herodes—thus indicating that Herod bore
the standard *tria nomina*, or three names, of a Roman citizen—may refer to
that endowment or to another one.[49]

Herod made gifts to the Lycians who inhabited the southern coast of Asia
Minor, to the Samians, to the Ionians who lived on the west coast of Asia
Minor, and to the city of Pergamon in Mysia.[50] Herod and his adviser Nicolaus of Damascus, who likely joined Herod's circle after the Battle of Actium,
also interceded with Agrippa in 14 BCE on behalf of the Jews of Ionia.[51] The
Ionian Jews had complained that they were being forced to do military service
and perform other civic duties, that the Temple taxes they had collected were
being confiscated, that taxes were imposed on them, and that they were taken
to court and other places of business on holy days.[52] Agrippa subsequently
confirmed their citizenship rights and their right to self-rule (*isonomia*).[53]

Herod probably was also involved in persuading Agrippa to send edicts
to the magistrates, council, and assembly of Ephesos that ordered the secure
care and custody of the Temple tax and the exemption of Jews from court
appearances on holy days. In addition, Agrippa probably was prevailed upon
to write to the magistrates, council, and assembly of Cyrene in Libya, once
again securing the unmolested collection and transfer of the Temple tax.[54]

Through Herod's intervention, Ilium (Troy) was relieved of a fine imposed
upon it by Agrippa after Agrippa's wife nearly drowned in a flash flood of the
famous Scamander River.[55] Perhaps less ostentatiously, Herod himself light-
ened the tax burdens of the people of Phaselis in Lycia and of Balanaea (Banias

or "Baths") in the district of Arados on the Syrian coast, and of towns in the south coastal region of Cilicia in Asia Minor as well.[56]

On the Greek mainland, Herod gave gifts to the Athenians, for which Herod received two and possibly three honorary inscriptions; to the Lacedae-monians, or Spartans, in the Peloponnesus; and to citizens of Nicopolis in Epirus, on Greece's west coast, probably around 27 BCE.[57] The gift to the citizens of Nicopolis—perhaps to help with the building of the sanctuary of Apollo, the gymnasium, and stadium there—was another way for Herod to honor his patron Augustus, since Nicopolis, or "Victory-polis," was built as a kind of triumphal city commemorating Augustus's victory over Antony at the nearby Battle of Actium in 31 BCE.[58]

Herod also accepted the post of president of the Olympic games when they were having funding problems; he then endowed the celebrations with a per-petual fund so that his presidency would always be remembered. Herod made a point of attending the games in 12 BCE on his way to Rome, at the time of his third and final trip to the capital.[59] Herod no doubt relished playing the role of the Olympic games' savior.

Herod acted as the eastern Mediterranean benefactor because it was in his own self-interest, it was in the interest of his Roman benefactors, and it also benefited diaspora Jews who lived in the towns and cities that he supported, such as in Ephesos. The vast majority of his benefactions outside of his king-dom, however, clearly subsidized the construction of civic and sacred build-ings or social activities that originated and developed within Graeco-Roman culture.

THE REGIONAL BENEFACTOR

Self-interest motivated Herod's magnanimity within his own domain as well. Once his rule was reconfirmed by Octavian and the Roman Senate, Herod transformed the physical and cultural landscape of his domain in honor of his Roman friends, his family, and himself.

To the southwest of Jerusalem, perhaps during the early period of his reign in the 30s BCE, Herod had the site of Mamre (Ramet el-Khalil) in Idumaea—approximately 2.5 miles north of Hebron, where Abraham supposedly pitched his tent and built an altar—enclosed within a rectangular sanctuary wall. Then, at Hebron itself (Haram Ramet el-Khalil), he had a building constructed above the caves of Machpelah, which Abraham supposedly purchased as a family burial ground.[60]

Herod's early interventions at these sites could be interpreted as an attempt to emphasize the common patriarchal ancestry of Judaeans and Idumaeans. But they also may be linked to later constructions. Some of the architectural features of the Herodian structures at Mamre and Hebron, such as the use of large ashlar blocks in the walls and the kind of floor paving, foreshadowed features used later in the rebuilding of the Jerusalem Temple.[61]

The original Hasmonean-era defenses of the fortresses of Masada, overlooking the west coast of the Dead Sea, Hyrcania (Khirbet el-Mird), Cypros (Tell el-'Aqaba), Docus or Dok (Jebel Qarantal), and Alexandreion (Sartaba) in eastern Samaritis, were improved from about 39–38 BCE and over the next decade. (For Herodian-era construction at Masada across three temporal phases, see the detailed description in chapter 21 on the Roman siege of Masada during the war.)

Money and arms were stored at some of these fortresses. But they also were endowed with facilities, such as bathhouses at Cypros and Machaerus, that made them suitable for entertaining prominent guests. In addition, they served as burial sites for Herod's executed family members.[62] These multipurpose sites stood in a line from Alexandreion in the north to Masada in the south, on both sides of the Jordan River and the Dead Sea, like strong but elegantly attired sentinels keeping their eyes peeled for whomever might appear on the eastern horizon.[63]

At the primeval site of Jericho (Tell es-Sultan), some 17 miles south of Jerusalem, where Joshua had trumpeted down the walls of the Canaanites, Herod had three palaces constructed between the fortress of Cypros and the Hasmonean palaces of Hyrcanus I and Alexander Jannaeus. The first palace was built to the south of Wadi Qelt during the early years of Herod's reign. It was a rectangular structure with a colonnaded internal courtyard that surrounded a garden. The palace had two bathhouses and a dining room with a view of the courtyard's garden.

After the Battle of Actium, the second palace was raised up to the north of the wadi, over the earthquake-damaged remains of the previous Hasmonean-era palace on the site. The Herodian palace made use of preexisting Hasmonean swimming pools to create a much larger pool that was encircled by a garden. Two wings were built to the south of the large pool: the higher wing had a colonnaded garden and a dining room, and the lower wing had two more pools and a bathhouse. The overall effect was to create a kind of garden oasis surrounding the pools.

The third and most sumptuous palace was constructed adjacent to and over Wadi Qelt after 15 BCE. It had four large wings. There were two peristyle courtyards, as well as guestrooms, and a bathhouse in the wing to the north of the ravine. The enormous (approximately 95 × 62 feet) *triclinium* (dining area) of the northern wing remains the largest formal dining hall discovered in Israel datable to the Roman imperial period. A bridge across the wadi connected the northern wing to a large sunken garden, with walkways, water channels, and pools to the west; a man-made tell with a covered, round dining and entertainment hall built on top of it; and to the east, an approximately 295 by 138 feet swimming pool to the south of the wadi.[64] Two of this palace's wings were named for Augustus and Agrippa.[65] The comparisons with Caesar's Palace—in Las Vegas—are hard to resist.

North of the Herodian palaces a hippodrome or stadium complex was also created, just to the south of Tell es Samarat.[66] A theater with a wooden stage and seating for about 3,000 was also constructed there at the north end of the racetrack by 15 BCE.[67]

On the northern side of the road from Jericho heading eastward toward Philadelphia (modern Amman) in the Peraea, Herod had another royal palace erected at Betharamphtha (Tell er-Rama). The palace was later burned by insurgents, and subsequently the site was expanded into a city by Herod Antipas.[68] Along the road to Alexandreion, some 15 miles north of Jericho, Herod after 12 BCE named a foundation in the Jordan Valley Phasaelis (El Fasayli) after his older brother.[69]

Some 4.5 miles to the east of the Dead Sea on the border with Nabataea, beginning in about 30 BCE, Herod had renovated the Hasmonean-era fortress of Machaerus (Jebel al-Mishnaqa). The refurbished Herodian palace included a garden, a royal bath, with a large *miqveh*, or ritual bathing pool, outside for use by Herod and his family, a *triclinium,* and a peristyle courtyard.[70]

Starting in the mid-30s BCE, though some scholars prefer dating it from 23 to 15 BCE, Herod had constructed a self-named fortress-palace in the toparchy called Herodeion, now usually called Herodium in English.[71] The fortress-palace was sited on a hill (Jebel el-Fureidis) in Judaea some 7.5 miles south of Jerusalem, near where Herod had fought off Parthian supporters of Antigonus and some Jewish bandits as he was making his way to Masada from Jerusalem, as described earlier.[72]

Built up artificially on the crest of a breast-shaped mountain, the building complex of "Upper" Herodeion was crowned with a circular casing of two walls, each about 98 feet in height, with stone towers (three semicircular and one circular) at the cardinal points. Herod may have used the circular eastern tower as a kind of retreat and lookout. An abundant water supply was brought to the site from near Solomon's Pools, which were 3.7 miles away, although a system of cisterns to collect rainwater was also integrated into the layout of the Upper Palace.[73] The western part of the palace within the casing walls constituted the royal living quarters and included bedrooms, a Roman-style bathhouse, and a dining room. Depictions of waterfowl were painted onto the walls of the warm room of the bathhouse using the *secco* technique (painting on dry plaster).[74]

By the late 20s BCE, a small theater with a seating capacity of about 300 to 400 was built on the north slope of the hill. Architecturally the theater building followed Roman precedents, but also departed from them in creative ways.[75] A reception room, called the Royal Room by the excavators of the site (for receiving guests and for entertaining between performances), was constructed above the theater's cavea; it included paintings of "illusory" windows (*pinakes*) onto painted landscapes. The landscape scenes had images of animals and soldiers; a wall painted in the same room showed two ivy-crowned men reclining at a symposium.[76] A stucco-work entablature with a floral frieze divided the walls, on which the "windows" were hung from the ceiling.[77] It is possible that these scenes and the others that included figurative images at Herodeion were done before Agrippa visited the fortress-palace in 16 or 15 BCE.

If Agrippa spent any time in the easternmost room above the theater, he might have noticed a graffito, some three feet above the floor of the southern wall, that cited (not very accurately) line 264 from book 6 of the *Iliad,* in which Hektor refused honey-hearted wine offered to him by Hecuba before he met Andromache and Astyanax and then went off to battle. We have no idea who inscribed the graffito on the wall, but it remains the only citation of Homer found in the epigraphic record of Judaea or Palaestina.[78] In any case, however, the graffitist's effort to display classical erudition to posterity seems to have been in vain because the theater and its adjacent buildings were demolished as part of the preparation for the construction of Herod's mausoleum in the same area.[79] (See the later discussion in this chapter of the mausoleum.)

At the base of the hill, "Lower Herodeion" sprawled over approximately 37 acres.[80] On the site there was a large palace; a huge (230 by 148 feet) garden-enclosed swimming pool, with some kind of man-made island at its center; accommodations for guests and staff; and a large Roman-style bathhouse near the southwestern corner of the great pool. The rooms of the bathhouse were decorated with mosaics and wall paintings. A *labrum*, or three-legged marble basin, that perhaps on its handles had heads of Silenus, one of the companions of the god Dionysus, was placed in the niche of the *caldarium*, or hot room, of the bathhouse. The excavators of the site hypothesized that the basin may have been a gift to Herod from Agrippa after his visit to Herodeion in 16 or 15 BCE; it was for that reason that Herod could not reject this gift, even though it had figurative images on it.[81]

Herodeion would later serve as Herod's final resting place.[82] Herod's selection of a site for burial where he had fought off both Parthians and Jews perhaps was made with some sense of ironic self-understanding.

To the north of Judaea, in Samaritis, beginning in the spring or summer of 27 BCE, Herod had built up a city named Sebaste on the site of the town formerly named Samaria.[83] The word "Sebaste" was the Greek (feminine) equivalent of the Latin neologism "Augustus," and Herod's Sebaste seems to have been the first city to have been founded using it after the Roman Senate awarded Octavian the name Augustus in January of 27 BCE.[84]

In Sebaste Herod had constructed a temple dedicated to Augustus and Roma, apparently also the first of its kind.[85] (See figure 1.) The temple was built upon a raised platform on the acropolis of the site and was oriented toward the south. It may have been influenced by the plan of the Forum Iulium in Rome that Herod saw when he visited the capital.[86] Another temple in the rebuilt city was dedicated to Kore, the daughter of Persephone.[87] The city of Sebaste also included a stadium with a colonnaded racetrack for athletic contests, including wrestling and boxing, and a strong circuit wall 1.27 miles in length.[88]

The site of Sebaste earlier had been inhabited by Hellenized Samaritans and descendants of Macedonians, who settled there after Alexander the Great's conquest of the region in 332 BCE. The renamed Herodian foundation of Sebaste eventually (about 27–20 BCE) became (near) home to some 6,000 veteran colonists. Many of the veterans probably fought as allies of Herod when he was struggling to secure his throne; they seem to have been settled at *Pente Komai* (Fondaquma) just to the north of the city center. These colonial settlers were most likely non-Jews.[89] Soldiers recruited from the citizen body of the Herodian foundation played a major role in the outbreak of the revolt in 66 CE.

More veterans were settled inland in new military settlements or refortified sites, including Gaba (Sha'ar ha-'Amaqim) in the southwestern Galilee,

FIGURE I. Stairs leading up to the Herodian-era temple dedicated to Augustus
and Roma in Sebaste, Samaria. A.D. Riddle/BiblePlaces.com.

Bathyra (possibly As-Sanamayn) on the border between Batanaea and Trachonitis, Heshbon (Heshbonitis) in the Peraea, and in Idumaea.[90] These settlements were established to overawe the locals and to serve as recruiting
grounds if reserves needed to be called up.[91]

Herod had captured Sepphoris in the lower Galilee in the winter of 39–38
BCE during his struggles against Antigonus and eventually built a palace there
too.[92] After Herod's death, the palace was raided by Judas the son of Ezekias,
and the arms stored there were stolen.[93]

Farther to the north, after receiving the additional territories of Auranitis,
Batanaea, and Gaulanitis from Augustus, Herod had built and dedicated to
the emperor Augustus and Roma a temple of white marble at or near Paneion
(renamed Caesarea Philippi by Herod Philip), close to the sources of the Jordan
River.[94] As we know from the reverse side of coins minted from year 5 (1 CE)
of the reign of Philip the Tetrarch and later, the temple had a tetrastyle or four-
columned façade, with Ionic capitals and a Doric frieze, with some kind of
plant shown on its pediment, set upon a Roman-style raised podium.[95]

Herod's sense of piety about ancient shrines and deities seems to have extended beyond those to which he himself was attached by blood or religious

observance. Perhaps as late as 9 BCE Herod patronized the temple of the sky god, Ba'al Shamim, or Lord of the Heavens, at S'ia, near Canatha, modern Qanawat in Syria, in the Auranitis (the Hauran). He was also the recipient of an honorary statue with a dedicatory inscription to "Herod, master" by "Obaisatos, son of Saodos," created at his own expense. The inscription belonged to a statue base found in the area of the porch to the right of the Temple of Ba'al. From this it is possible to argue that Herod was in some way involved in the subsidization of the temple itself.[96]

To the northwest of Jerusalem, in honor of his father, Antipater, Herod around 9 BCE rebuilt Pegae (Springs) or the biblical Aphek on top of a Hellenistic-era settlement on the plain of Sharon along the road from Caesarea to Jerusalem, renaming it Antipatris.[97]

Near and along the Mediterranean coast more veterans were also settled in the rebuilt and renamed (in honor of Agrippa) city of Agrippias or Agrippeion (formerly Anthedon) that had been annexed to Judaea after the Battle of Actium.[98] Herod also subsidized baths, fountains, and colonnades for the old Philistine coastal city of Ascalon (Hebrew, *Ashkelon*), on the road from Alexandria north to Antioch.[99]

THE CROWN JEWELS

Most famously, however, along the coast, Herod re-founded the small Phoenician or Ptolemaic Greek settlement of Straton's Tower (or Strato's Tower) as a city named Caesarea, in honor of the Roman emperor. Straton's Tower supposedly was founded during the fourth century BCE by Straton (perhaps Abdashtart in Phoenician), king of Sidon, and perhaps subsequently was renamed as a polis called Demetrias. Herod's re-foundation was organized on an orthogonal street grid plan over a 10- or 12-year period (about 25–24/23–22 to 12 or 10 BCE) in "white stone"; it was provided with a magnificent harbor named *Sebastos limen* in Greek, which was larger than the harbor of the Piraeus in Athens.[100] In fact, by the time of its completion (15 BCE), Herod's harbor at Caesarea was probably the largest man-made harbor in the world.[101] (See figure 2.)

The new harbor of Herod's Caesarea had two breakwaters. The longer, southern breakwater extended some 2,000 feet out into the sea, to help protect ships from strong currents in the sea from the south. The northern breakwater was about 400 feet shorter. Towers at the ends of both breakwaters marked their endpoints. The tower on the southern breakwater was named

FIGURE 2. Aerial view of the remains of the Herodian harbor "*Sebastos limen*"
at Caesarea from the west. Todd Bolen/BiblePlaces.com.

Drusion in honor of Augustus's deceased stepson Drusus.[102] It was modeled
on the Pharos of Alexandria and served as a lighthouse like its famous architectural inspiration. To construct the harbor, Herod's architects and engineers
used massive 90-ton stone and concrete blocks made from volcanic ash (*poz-
zalana*), imported from the Bay of Naples, and also local sandstone (*kurkar*).[103]

On a platform raised almost 40 feet above sea level in Caesarea, with its
porch facing the harbor mouth—although diverted at an angle of about 30
degrees from the east–west orientation of the city's orthogonal street grid—
stood a Corinthian-order, hexastyle (six columns in front), and peripteral (with a
columned row) temple (93.8 by 152.2 feet) dedicated to Augustus and Roma.
The temple's colossal statue of the emperor rivaled that of Zeus at Olympia in
Greece, created by the famous Athenian sculptor Pheidias, and the personified
statue of Roma apparently was meant to recall the well-known statue of Hera at
Argos in Greece, carved by Polykleitos.[104] The temple and its statues would
have been the first objects people saw when they entered the harbor of the city,
and their placement and monumentality were indications of the Roman character of the Herodian foundation—although, as noted in the introduction,
there was a synagogue in the city, probably in its northwestern quarter.[105]

FIGURE 3. Aerial view of Herod the Great's promontory palace in Caesarea
from the southeast. After 6 CE the palace complex became the seat
of the Roman governor. William Schlegel/BiblePlaces.com.

Herod also had built two separate palaces on the promontory at Caesarea.
(See figure 3.) In the earlier and lower one there was a massive freshwater pool,
about 115 by 59 feet, surrounded by colonnades on the north, south, and west
sides, leaving the eastern side open to the sea. After Judaea became a Roman
province in 6 CE, Herod's double palace complex served as the physical seat
of the Roman governor (*praetorium*).[106]

The city was endowed with what Josephus calls an amphitheater, with
seating for 10,000, where horse and chariot races, as well as animal hunts
and gladiatorial combats, took place (figure 4); a semicircular Roman-style
stone theater with seats for somewhere between 3,500 and 4,000 spectators
and a unique background wall behind the stage; and marketplaces. Public
quadrennial games named after Caesar were instituted to celebrate Caesarea's
dedication, perhaps in 12 BCE, with generous prizes for first-, second-, and
third-place finishers. There were musical and athletic contests (common in
Greek cities), as well as gladiatorial combats and wild animals, horse races, and
other lavish shows like those put on in Rome.[107] Fresh, drinkable water was
brought to the city by an aqueduct that carried spring waters from the south
side of Mt. Carmel to Caesarea.[108]

References to the Caesarea project, the harbor, and the trade that came
from it were denoted by a coin series minted in Jerusalem on Herod's order,

FIGURE 4. Aerial view of the hippodrome of Caesarea from the north, where Roman-style spectacles were put on. Barry Beitzel/BiblePlaces.com.

which featured coins with an anchor on their obverse (with opposing cornucopias) and with a *caduceus* (the staff of Hermes, god of trade) on the reverse side. The anchor symbolized control of the sea, *cornucopiae* prosperity, and the *caduceus* trade. Herod may have authorized the minting of the coin type at least in part to pay workers involved in the Caesarea project, including constructing its harbor.[109]

Herod's first project in Jerusalem, perhaps dated to 37–35 BCE, seems to have been a fortress that allowed him to keep an eye on the Temple in Jerusalem and also to advertise his loyalty to his original Roman patron.[110] On an approximately 72-foot rock scarp in the vicinity of the Temple's northwest corner, a four-towered fortress was built at great cost and was named Antonia in honor of Herod's Roman patron Antony, clearly before Antony's defeat by Octavian at the Battle of Actium in 31 BCE.[111] The walls of the Antonia were 65 feet high, and the southeastern tower loomed above its rock base to a height of about 102 feet.[112] During the first century CE, the Antonia became the permanent barracks for a cohort of Roman auxiliary soldiers.[113]

Herod's signature project in Jerusalem, however, was the rebuilding of the Temple, supposedly at his own expense, although literary sources and inscriptions make clear that others made contributions to the project.[114] (See map 4.) The great bronze doors of the triple gate that separated the Court of Women from the Court of Israelites, for instance, were donated by Nicanor of Alexandria, and Alexander, the brother of the Jewish Alexandrian philosopher and polymath Philo, gave gold and silver plate for nine other gates.[115]

Before work on the project began Herod made a speech to the people.[116] In his speech Herod supposedly described the rebuilding of the Temple as an act of piety for the gift of his kingdom, made possible by the prevailing peace and prosperity and his friendship with the Romans.[117] Of course, successfully rebuilding the Temple complex on a massive scale would have brought the additional benefits of making Herod more popular with his people and drawing attention to his kingship.[118]

Perhaps to convince the skeptical people of the seriousness of his commitment, Herod assembled 1,000 wagons to carry the stones that would be used, hired 10,000 skilled workmen, and had trained 1,000 priests as masons and carpenters to work on the Temple itself, because only priests were allowed within the area of the inner sanctuary.[119]

The work on the Temple Mount began in 23–22 (or less likely 20–19) BCE by leveling, enlarging, and raising the (500 royal square cubits = 861 square feet) mount on which the earlier, pre-Hasmonean Second Temple was built during the late sixth century BCE: the new construction created a platform covering an area roughly twice the size of its third- or second-century BCE predecessor.[120] (See figure 5.) The Herodian platform was supported by the construction of subterranean corridors or passageways with vaulted arches (*cryptoportici* in Latin). The retaining walls built to support the platform were constructed out of square or rectangular cut stones laid in courses that comprised walls 15 to 16 feet thick.[121] These stone blocks weighed up to 300 tons

FIGURE 5. An aerial view of the Temple Mount from the south. Herod's royal stoa was built along the southern side (approximately 914 feet) of the enlarged Temple Mount. Across the Kidron Valley to the right is the Mt. of Olives. Ferrell Jenkins/BiblePlaces.com.

each.[122] All of this heavy construction work was done without the aid of mechanized earth-moving machines, trucks, or cranes.

The footprint of the completed Herodian platform encompassed more than 144,000 square meters, or almost 35 acres.[123] It was almost three times as large as the base of the Great Pyramid of Giza in Egypt.[124] It was also more than five times as large as the enclosure of the temple of Olympian Zeus in Athens and twice the size of the plot of land on which the White House in Washington, DC, sits.[125]

Double colonnades were erected on the eastern, northern, and western sides of the Temple Mount platform. Josephus claimed that the columns of the approximately 46-foot-high colonnades were made out of monolithic white marble; as elsewhere, it was probably the case, however, that the columns were carved out of some kind of local stone that was then covered with white plaster to look like marble.[126] Around the whole sanctuary were displayed spoils taken from the "barbarians." Herod dedicated these monuments, called *anathemata* in Greek, adding those he took from the "Arabs," no doubt meaning the Nabataeans.[127] Displaying such spoils in temples was a common practice in Greek cities.[128] Merchants and vendors subsequently sold their wares and changed money for people within the stoas of Herod's Temple, as we know from many references in the Gospels.[129]

On the southern side of the sanctuary a two-storied building called the Royal Stoa (*Basileia Stoa*) was built that extended the length of the southern wall, about 914 feet. Its architectural form was that of a triple colonnade, about 124 feet in width, built on two levels (in the center). Gilded Corinthian capitals capped the stoa's 162 columns.[130] The cedar ceilings of the structures were decorated with wood carvings of figures in deep relief.[131] It is likely that the Royal Stoa was planned and executed as Herod's personal imprint on the Temple Mount project, given the fact that he was barred from entering the Temple building itself.[132]

Josephus reports that work on the porticoes and the outer courts went on for eight years and that renovation of the earlier Temple of Zerubbabel and the High Priest Joshua itself took a year and a half—though later in the *Antiquities* he states that work on Herod's Temple was only completed during the governorship of the Roman procurator Albinus (62–64 CE).[133] Departing from previous organizations of the courts, the new Herodian Temple included a Court of Gentiles (Nations), as well as a Court of Women.[134] Opening up access to the Temple and participation in the Temple cult to Gentiles and women, even to a carefully limited extent, was a remarkable development, and it is surprising that there is little evidence of opposition.[135]

Elsewhere, in the Gospel of John, it is implied that the work on Herod's Temple had been going on for 46 years when Pontius Pilate was governor.[136] In an Aramaic inscription on an ossuary found at Givat Hamivtar in Jerusalem, a certain Simon, or *Shimon* in Hebrew, is named as the builder or, more specifically, as some kind of master craftsman or engineer of the sanctuary (*hklh*).[137] After the work on the sanctuary was completed, there were said to be 18,000 laborers out of work and pay.[138] No uncritical admirer of Herod, Josephus claimed that the cost of the entire project was incalculable, its magnificence never surpassed.[139]

The work on the Temple itself by 18 BCE was followed by a sacrifice of 300 oxen.[140] The daily sacrifice of two sheep and a bull for Caesar and for the people of the Romans was made in the morning and the evening at the Temple from the time of Herod's reign.[141] The annual cost of these sacrifices has been estimated at 87,600 drachmas or denarii.[142] According to Josephus, the nation of Jews subsidized these sacrifices, although the Jewish Alexandrian philosopher Philo claimed that the emperor picked up the bill.[143]

In 66 CE, when Cestius Gallus, the governor of Syria, came down to Jerusalem at Passover (*Pesach*), some three million pilgrims supposedly had already flocked there to celebrate the weeklong festival for which the Herodian
Temple was the sacrificial and cultic focus.[144]

Though Josephus and the later rabbis may have thought that the supersized
Temple platform was built by a sinfully cruel king, Herod's Temple should
have been one of the wonders of the ancient world, and perhaps not number
eight on the list.[145] There were first-century BCE precedents for sanctuaries
built on top of terraces and artificial platforms raised up on vaulted substruc-
tures, but not on the scale of the Herodian Temple.[146] When Herod considered covering the renovated Temple itself in gold, the local sages told him to
leave it alone, because the building's blue, yellow, and white marble (or polished limestone, according to some scholars) made it look like the waves of
the sea.[147] Later Jews claimed that the Herodian Temple was the building
against which the beauty of all others could not compare.[148]

Like Herod himself, Herod's Temple was a synthesis of Graeco-Roman
and indigenous elements on a scale meant to dwarf Solomon's Temple and to
be remembered forever. It is seldom appreciated by non-Jews that the sense
of loss Jews felt after the destruction of the Temple in 70 CE was not just
because of the elimination of the sacrificial center of their ancestral religion.
It was also because of the spectacular building that was destroyed: a home of
unique grandeur and beauty, a house designed and built to be worthy of their
one and only god. Amazingly, however, some did not consider the Temple to
be Herod's greatest architectural achievement.

Just to the east of the city's western wall, within the area Josephus calls
the Upper City, enclosed by walls that were 14 meters high (nearly 46 feet
high), Herod also had constructed for himself between 29–28 BCE and 23
BCE a rectangular-shaped palace complex, the remains of which lie beneath
today's Armenian Garden.[149] In Josephus's opinion no building surpassed
Herod's palace either in extravagance or construction. The complex covered
nearly 11 acres. The two wings of the palace were named Caesareion and Agrippeion, after Herod's two most important Roman patrons, Caesar Augustus
and Marcus Agrippa. The naming of the wings was perhaps connected to
Agrippa's visit to Judaea in 15 BCE. The palace wings had banqueting halls
and bedrooms for 100 guests.[150] Three towers protected the palace: those of
Phasael, Hippicus, and Mariamme. The Phasael Tower, which was dedicated
to Herod's eldest brother, was the highest at 90 cubits, or about 155 feet, tall
and was the westernmost of the three towers of the citadel that guarded

Herod's palace.[151] Behind the Phasael tower was the Hippicus Tower (about 138 feet high), dedicated to one of Herod's Roman friends.[152] The third and smallest tower of the citadel, at about 95 feet high, was erected in honor of Herod's beloved and executed Hasmonean wife, Mariamme.[153] Adjoining these towers to the south in Jerusalem was some kind of camp for Herod's soldiers.[154]

There was also a theater, probably made of wood, that was erected near or in Jerusalem—perhaps somewhere in the Upper City—for quadrennial "Isactian" games that Herod organized to honor Augustus on his birthday, 23 September, in 28 BCE.[155] Originally there were inscriptions all around the theater relating to Caesar, as well as gold and silver trophies (*tropaia*) of the peoples that Herod had conquered in war. When some Jews protested that the trophies presented forbidden images of men, Herod led the protestors into the theater and, having stripped the trophies of their ornaments, revealed the imageless wooden stands on which they were mounted. That satisfied most of those who had objected. But afterward 10 men who believed that Herod was forcibly introducing foreign practices conspired to assassinate him. The plot was revealed, and the conspirators were executed.[156]

A large hippodrome or unique combination hippodrome-amphitheater, possibly located in the Hinnom Valley to the south of the city center, was also constructed, where athletic and musical contests and horse races, as well as animal hunts (*venationes*) and combats between condemned criminals and animals (*damnatio ad bestias*), were put on. At least some Jews objected to these forms of combat on the grounds that it was impious to condemn men to be killed by animals to bring pleasure to spectators.[157]

In the towns and cities of his kingdom where non-Jews were in the majority, Herod subsidized the kind of public buildings that could be found all over the map of the Roman empire. Some had architectural or artistic elements or encouraged practices, such as gladiatorial combats, that challenged the tastes or offended the piety of some Jews, even if the overtly Roman temples were constructed on "foreign" ground in Caesarea, Sebaste, or Paneion (Panias): these were places where Jews were not in the majority. Where Jews were in the majority, Herod tried to avoid supporting projects that might offend the religious sensibilities of most Jews.[158] In places where Jews and non-Jews lived together, such as Caesarea Maritima, the juxtaposition of Jewish and non-Jewish buildings, institutions, and cultural activities became focal points of conflict. After Herod's death his model of how to be a benefactor of Jewish and Graeco-Roman culture and to serve both God and Caesar was explicitly and violently rejected by at least some Jews.[159]

HEROD THE ROMAN JEW

Some Jerusalem insiders—Josephus among them—never really accepted the half-Arab from Idumaea, even if Herod's mother, Cypros, belonged to the Nabataean royal family.[160] That was the wrong royalty. The Hasmonean high priest Matthias Antigonus sneered that Herod was a *hemiioudaios:* a half-Jew.[161] Many scholars have pointed out that, according to the widely accepted legal definition at the time, Cypros's marriage to Herod's father Antipater made her into a Jewess; therefore, Herod was legally a Jew.[162] But the point of Antigonus's slur was that, because Cypros was not born a Jewess, she never could be a proper member of the *ethnos* and neither could her son. Herod's parentage was an opening for attacks by his detractors.

Herod's Idumaean ancestry also might have raised eyebrows. It was true that in the Hebrew Bible Esau, the progenitor of the Edomites (later Idumaeans), was the son of Isaac and Rebekah, the grandson of Abraham, and the brother of Jacob. The Edomites and the (later) Jews therefore were related, at least according to literary tradition, and in reality many Idumaeans adopted the practices of their Jewish cousins.[163]

But there was another tradition that most Idumaeans had not become Jews until after their conquest by John Hyrcanus I (r. 135–134 to 104 BCE) and that their conversion to Judaism was not voluntary.[164] So Herod's Idumaean background might be another reason for some Jerusalemites to look down on him. Priestly pedigree and authority were problems too.

Herod was not even a priest, let alone a high priest, or even descended from "legitimate" (i.e., Zadokite) high priests.[165] So even if some Jews understood Herod as a Jew, he did not belong to the right tier of Jewish society. To compound that issue, most of the high priests Herod appointed did not come from the families of the Jerusalem elites. Rather, Herod preferred to appoint high priests from among extended family members or diaspora Jews, precisely because they did not belong to the Jerusalem-based families of high priests that looked down on Herod.[166] It was for that reason, among others, that at least some of the approximately 6,000 Pharisees around at the time disapproved of Herod, though he was careful to show them respect.[167] Some later rabbinic sources lamented the effects that the "houses" of Herod's high priests had upon them, but what these sources really disclose is that Herod created a new, non-Hasmonean priestly elite through gifts of land.[168]

In fact, Herod was a commoner, even if his family was prominent in Idumaea and later in Jerusalem. But from the time that Herod settled onto his throne, no Greek or Roman forced his way into the Temple's Holy of Holies (*devir*), as both the Seleucid king Antiochus Epiphanes and the Roman general Pompey the Great had done. Nor had anyone helped himself to the Temple's riches, as Crassus had in 54 BCE.[169] As far as we know, Herod himself never saw any of the inner spaces of the Temple.[170]

Judas Maccabaeus and his sons had managed to wrest control of the Temple away from the Seleucids, purified the sanctuary, and resumed the daily sacrifices there. Subsequently, during the reign of Simon Maccabaeus (167–160 BCE) the Jews of Judaea were essentially autonomous and free to take care of their families and to worship their God as they wished. Those were the things that really mattered to most Jews. Indeed, at no time since Alexander and the Macedonians had passed by the promised land had the Jews of Judaea enjoyed a longer period of uninterrupted freedom from violent outside interference than during Herod's long reign.

It is true that Herod ruthlessly pruned branches off his family tree, some of which he had done much to grow. Not all offshoots of those branches, however, had been strict observers of the Fifth Commandment.[171] And Herod had not hesitated to subsidize the building of polytheist temples and forums or palaces and fortresses in places that were not inhabited by a majority of Jews, perhaps influenced by the kinds of buildings he had seen in Rome during one or more of his (at least) three trips to the *caput mundi* in 40, 17–16, and 13–12 BCE.[172] Roman-type bathing facilities were built at palaces and fortresses that Herod had constructed or rebuilt, although these often included Judaean-style ritual immersion pools, implying attempts to maintain ritual purity; in addition, figurative art is largely absent in the palaces that Herod had built for himself all over Judaea.[173] The zoomorphic images from the bathhouse and the Royal Room at Herodeion are exceptions; their appearance may signify that Herod considered Herodeion to be essentially a private possession.

There were tensions among Greeks, other Gentiles, and Jews living within Judaea and in the surrounding regions between 37 and 4 BCE. Those tensions were born out of the conquests of mainly Greek or, at any rate, non-Jewish towns and cities by the Hasmoneans, as virtually all scholars acknowledge. But the same scholars sometimes fail to note that it was the region's invasion by Alexander the Great in 332 BCE that fundamentally changed the ethnic landscape. Herod's way of trying to release the steam from those tensions in the non-Jewish communities was through civic benefactions: an amphitheater here, games there.

Herod's patron Augustus claimed to have found Rome a city of brick (or clay) and left it a city of marble.[174] Lacking Augustus's funds and access to Carrara marble, Herod left a kingdom of white-plastered ashlar—and threw in some buildings for his regional neighbors for good measure. (See appendix C, "The Costs of Munificence," for a discussion of Herod's financial resources and expenditures.)[175] If Herod had an "edifice complex," it was one that benefited Jews and non-Jews alike from Jerusalem to Nicopolis.[176] Both Augustus and Agrippa, who were in a position to know, often said that the extent of Herod's rule matched the greatness of his soul (*megalopsychias*) and that he deserved the kingship of all Syria and Egypt.[177]

Herod's *megalopsychia* may have been part of an attempt to reconcile his own complicated identities and the pressures he operated under.[178] But he obviously coveted the attention that his benefactions brought. And it surely is at least arguable that those who benefited from Herod's benefactions, especially his building projects, probably had a far more positive view of the king than did his critics among Jerusalem's priestly elites.[179] Herod's ancient and modern critics have almost always overlooked the relief he gave to the poor and starving, who certainly outnumbered them.[180] Despite his obvious class contempt for Herod, Josephus makes clear that there was a recognizable group of supporters of Herod, the *herodeioi,* from the time of his war with Antigonus.[181]

Herod's son Alexander made fun of his father's age and dyed black hair. The Cappadocian princess Glaphyra taunted Herod's sister and wives for their low birth: his wives had been chosen because they were beautiful rather than noble, though Josephus points out that polygamy was permitted according to the ancestral custom among Jews and that at least some of Herod's marriages were part of a strategy to extend his family connections.[182] Voting by graffito, at least one contemporary—an unnamed, literate nomad—opined that Herod was certifiably "mad" (QATALA in Safaitic).[183]

The degree of Herod's adherence to the law(s) of the Jews and his moral "character" have been the focus of many modern studies.[184] Josephus himself set the terms of the debate, especially in his *Antiquities,* when he criticized Herod for departing from the customs of their forefathers and for adopting foreign practices that corrupted the ancient way of life.[185] The point of this argument seems to be to decide whether Herod deserved to be called "Great," as Josephus deemed the king in one passage.[186]

But often when Josephus criticized Herod for not observing the law or for changing it, his own account of the law is open to question. For instance, Josephus asserted that Herod contravened the law when he made being sold into slavery and deported the punishment for theft, rather than the biblically prescribed fourfold restitution.[187] In fact, in the book of Exodus the punishment for theft is four- or fivefold restitution in the case of a sheep, but if the thief had nothing, he should be sold for his theft.[188] Thus Josephus represents an interpretation of the law as a violation of it.[189]

Herod's piety and character are important topics. But if we are trying to explain the reasons for his success, how he kept his kingdom relatively free and prosperous, and what went wrong between Judaea and Rome after Herod's death, we should attend more closely to Herod's statecraft and his adaptability in both war and peace. Herod saw off the last of the Hasmoneans, found a way to be a friend first of Antony and then of Octavian—as he was officially proclaimed on stone weights dated to his reign—and outmaneuvered Cleopatra, never falling for her "fatal beauty" or, more likely, fending off her attempts to acquire his kingdom by staying as loyal as possible to his patron Antony.[190]

Herod won. He had stooped—often—but he had indeed conquered. He found a way to eliminate any of the Hasmoneans who threatened his position at the same time that he represented himself as the successor and political heir to the freedom that the Hasmoneans had brought to the Judaeans. Claiming to be the political heir of Jerusalem elites who despised him and whom he had systematically eliminated as political rivals was a stroke of self-advertising genius.

After the Roman Senate chose him to be king in 40 BCE, Herod sacrificed in the Temple of Jupiter Capitolinus. That was a clear violation of Jewish law, but it sealed his alliance with the ancient Mediterranean's world's only superpower: when in Rome, Herod did as the Romans did and gained the backing of Antony. In Judaea, Herod's choices were different and for the most part arguably consistent with the law or a scripturally warranted interpretation of it, and he avoided offending the religious sensibilities of Jews.[191]

Herod's choices and identity were contextual and time sensitive. When he was young, he was a calculated risk-taker who continually observed the actions of the other players around the high-stakes eastern Mediterranean table. After he had won the hand that mattered the most—kingship—almost everyone, both internally and externally, behaved or at least left each other alone, if only because they feared Herod and his backers in Rome more than each other. Both Antipater and Herod mastered the art of never letting their personal feelings get in the way of their political self-interest. They chose Rome, not individual Romans, and that choice ensured their people's safety.

Herod was neither horrible nor a hero, neither culturally Jewish nor Graeco-Roman: he was both Jewish and Roman. The mixture was the essence. Cultures are not hermetically sealed, and individuals can easily make choices in context that draw from traditions, mix them up, and then go beyond them in different situations. To set out to measure whether Herod remained a pious Jew or was "Hellenized" or "Romanized" misses the point. For Herod there was no contradiction between rendering unto Caesar and Rome a beautiful temple in Caesarea and building a house for God in Jerusalem that was larger and more beautiful than the pyramid at Giza.

It was probably his nature and was certainly consistent with his position as a benefactor—or client—of Rome (depending upon one's perspective) and a king of Jews and others to make such choices without thinking that his actions were contradictory. He worked with and for a politically astute and demanding emperor in a restive, dangerous neighborhood. Just as his Hasmonean predecessors were caught between Seleucids and Ptolemies, Herod had to operate between Romans and Parthians who had hungry eyes fixed on greater Syria. Herod kept the many wolves that circled Judaea, including the she-wolf of Rome, at bay.

Fear of Herod had also persuaded people belonging to different ethnic groups in the cities and towns of his kingdom not to push their enmities from words to deeds. Jews, or groupings such as the Pharisees who questioned his ethnicity or piety or who disagreed about the interpretation of the law, almost always knew not to press the point. Judaism was already pluralistic by the time Herod finally got to sit on his throne; Herod policed the boundaries of his subjects' actions, if not their beliefs. Attacking the king who was the inspiration and majority investor behind the rebuilding of the Temple on religious grounds would not have endeared the attackers to the masses who made a living (re)building the Temple.

Of course, Herod was an individual too, with a taste for wine (Italian whites), women (varietals), and large swimming pools (Jericho, Masada, Caesarea, and Herodeion). Herod's wandering eye and limited attention span brought complications into his life but never really threatened his regime. By the middle of his reign he was simply too well connected (to the right Romans), too successful, and too rich to be brought down by his domestic scandals. As so often for the rich and powerful, happiness and health were different questions.

Riches might not buy happiness or health, but they could build monuments with Herod's name on them and could help alleviate anxiety about how he would be remembered. Building allowed Herod to express his creativity and vision, his willingness to push beyond boundaries that others were more comfortable living within. His Hasmonean predecessors were also civic benefactors in the Hellenic style and had their own personal tastes.[192] But Herod outdid them. His Temple was bigger than Solomon's, his imperial reach greater than David's. Those who challenged him openly or laughed at him behind his back never considered what life without Herod might be like.

As soon as Herod was gone, unresolved questions and conflicts among the Jews, between them and their neighbors, and with Rome resurfaced. What kind of state should the Jews have? What was the proper relationship between priestly and royal power? Whose interpretation of the law should prevail? How far was it permissible for Jews to accommodate themselves to foreign customs and practices? Who should have which rights in towns and cities of mixed ethnicities? Could Jews have a master other than God? Herod had found the way to be both a Jew and a Roman. Could other Jews? Should they?

Thus, as he lived out his last days, Herod had reason to claim that after death he belonged in the company of Israel's patriarchs and prophets, not in Sheol's dreary democracy of the dead. And yet, despite the many blessings Herod had bestowed upon his people—not to mention the *goyim*—many were ungrateful. They were far better off than either his family members or the fortunate pig—but they refused to give the "half-Jew" his due.

Herod therefore planned one last coup de main against his enemies. It was a brilliant surprise attack from just beyond the grave, designed to ensure that the families of his opponents throughout Judaea would grieve when he died, like it or not. The plan was brilliant, ruthless, and just a touch savage: in a word, Herodian.

THE DEATH OF HEROD

Nearing the end, Herod gathered up the most distinguished men from every corner of Judaea and had them locked up in the hippodrome of Jericho (just south of Tell es Samarat). He then ordered his family to have everyone in the hippodrome struck down the minute that his own death was announced. That way, although his death might be a cause for celebration among his critics, every household in Judaea nevertheless would weep during his funeral. And Herod could die satisfied, if not happy, knowing that his final wish had been fulfilled.[193]

Having guaranteed that the Judaeans would be shedding tears after his death, Herod had the satisfaction of experiencing one last frisson of familial revenge—an unplanned but very welcome piece of bonus vengeance—before he died. Appropriately, it involved a close relative. After he failed to kill himself with an apple knife to put an end to his excruciating suffering, Herod learned that his imprisoned son Antipater thought he had succeeded and was trying to bribe his jailer to let him go, now that his hated father was finally dead.

Reacting with a fury that belied his grave condition, Herod ordered Antipater's immediate execution, and his bodyguards carried out his order at once.[194] Antipater's body was subsequently interred in the fortress of Hyrcania.[195] Herod then changed his will one last time, naming Herod Antipas, his son by his fourth wife, the Samaritan woman Malthace, as tetrarch, and Archelaus, the eldest of Malthace's sons, as heir to the throne.[196]

Five days later Herod died, probably in late March of 4 BCE, but possibly in the winter of 4–3 BCE, some 37 years after he had been declared king by the Romans.[197] Before the army discovered that Herod was dead, his sister Salome departed from the palace and freed all the prisoners whom Herod had ordered to be killed as soon as he died. Salome implausibly told the fortunate prisoners that Herod had changed his mind and that everyone could go home. No one apparently paused to ask why, as they no doubt hurried away to celebrate their unexpected deliverance.

Salome and her (third) husband, the Herodian courtier Alexas, then went to the amphitheater in Jericho and announced the news of Herod's death to the soldiers and the people. Ptolemy, to whom Herod had given his signet ring, gave a blessing upon the dead king and made an entreaty to the people. He also read out a letter that Herod had written to the troops, urging them to be loyal to his successor.[198]

After this, Ptolemy read the attachments (Herod's seventh and final will). These gave Herod's son Philip, by his fifth wife, Cleopatra, rule over Trachonitis and the neighboring districts of Gaulanitis, Batanaea, and Paneas, to the east and northeast of the Galilee; appointed Herod's son Antipas as tetrarch of the Galilee and Peraea; gave his sister Salome control of the cities of Iamnia, Azotus, and Phasaelis, along with 500,000 pieces of coined silver; and named Archelaus as king.[199]

To the Roman emperor Augustus were left 10 million silver coins, as well as gold and silver vessels and some expensive garments; to Augustus's wife, Livia, Herod left 5 million silver coins. The emperor therefore received a be-quest 20 times larger than Herod's beloved sister Salome. Archelaus was also instructed to bear Herod's ring to Caesar, along with the sealed documents related to the administration of his kingdom. Control of his arrangements and his will's ratification were left to Augustus. Archelaus was immediately hailed as king. The troops and the people promised allegiance, and God's blessing upon him was entreated.[200]

Archelaus gave his father, Herod, a magnificent funeral. The dead king's body was laid out on top of a golden bier studded with precious stones. It was wrapped in a purple cloth embroidered with various colors. A diadem, one of the most recognizable symbols of royalty of the Hellenistic world, encircled Herod's head, on top of which there was a golden crown. By his right hand there was a scepter.[201]

Around the bier stood Herod's sons and a mass of his relatives. After them followed the bodyguards, the cohort of Thracians, Germans, and Gauls (from Gaul or Galatians from Asia Minor), all armed as if for war.[202] The rest of the soldiers marched in front, led by their officers and their subordinates. Behind the troops were 500 of Herod's household servants and freedmen bearing spices.[203]

THE VIEW FROM HERODEION

Herod's corpse was carried about 25 miles to Herodeion, where he had fought off both his Parthian and Jewish enemies.[204] Herodeion now was to be Herod's eternal refuge, close to his Idumaean homeland, visible from Jerusalem, and closer still to Bethlehem, the birthplace of another warrior king and messianic figure, David. [205]

There, by his own directions, Herod was interred, halfway up the artificially built-up mount of Herodeion's northeastern slope, in a reddish-colored limestone (*mizi ahmar*) sarcophagus, decorated with three rosettes imposed upon each other on the short sides. A rosette of similar design once decorated part of the Doric frieze of the Royal Stoa of the Temple Mount, a building particularly associated with Herod.[206]

The sarcophagus was placed inside the circular (*tholos*) Ionic top story of a three-storied, pyramid-like white limestone structure that resembled the later "tomb of Absalom" in Jerusalem, although its architectural inspirations included Augustus's mausoleum in Rome, Alexander's tomb in Alexandria, and the Philippeion in Olympia.[207] The 82-foot-high pyramid with its conical roof

FIGURE 6. The view toward Jerusalem from behind the model of Herod's mausoleum at Herodeion. G. Rogers.

faced Jerusalem to the north, about 9.3 miles away—as if Herod wanted to keep a wary eye on the Jerusalemites after death.[208] (See figure 6.)

Within a few years at least some Jerusalemites understood that however Herod treated his family members or those who challenged his piety, it had been Herod the Roman Jew who had stood between them and the truly ungodly.[209] No such leader was found in 66 CE.

CHAPTER 2

The Little Revolt of 4 BCE

ARCHELAUS AND THE PASSOVER TEST

Herod's eldest son and heir, Archelaus, tried to present himself to the people as the anti-Herod. He soon proved to have inherited more than a kingdom from his father.[1] Herod's ability to keep his subjects in line while staying on the right side of the Roman emperor, however, was not passed on to Archelaus. That inability cost Archelaus his eparchy and then bought him a one-way ticket to early retirement along the banks of the *Rhodanus* (Rhone) in southern Gaul.

In accordance with the tradition of the Jews, Archelaus mourned his father's death for seven days.[2] Afterward he provided the populace with a funeral banquet. When the feasting was over, Archelaus went to the Temple and mounted a golden throne that was set up on some kind of platform. He then addressed the crowd that had gathered below.

He thanked them for the zeal they had shown for his father's funeral and for the marks of honor they had displayed toward him. He told them that he would eschew authority for the present. Indeed, he said that he would not assume the royal titles until his succession had been confirmed by Caesar (Augustus).

Archelaus's cautious approach to taking power was probably designed to reassure his potential subjects: he did not want to be accused of seizing the throne. It also signaled deference to Augustus. Archelaus was smart enough to know that if Augustus heard that he simply had assumed the kingship, his presumption could be used against him.

In his address to the crowd, Archelaus added that he would make an abundant return to the soldiers and citizens for their enthusiasm and goodwill as soon as his kingship was ratified by the supreme powers: the Roman emperor and Senate. He closed by saying that he would make every effort to treat them better in every way than his father had.[3]

The delighted population immediately made a series of demands. Some shouted out for a reduction of taxes, others for duties on sales to be abolished. Still others cried out for prisoners to be freed. In the *Antiquities* Josephus adds some details about the taxes and duties at issue, making clear that it was the annual poll tax that the people wanted relief from and that the duties were on public purchases. Not wanting to puncture the atmosphere of mutual goodwill, Archelaus agreed to all of their requests.[4] Whether Archelaus actually made good on his promises we do not know.

After making a sacrifice Archelaus then settled down to relax with his friends. Toward evening, however, a group gathered together and loudly began to lament the fate of those who had been executed by Herod for cutting down the golden eagle above the Temple's Great Gate. They demanded that those who had perished by fire in defense of the traditional laws and the Temple should be avenged by punishment of Herod's most honored friends. The first step, they asserted, should be to depose the high priest appointed by Herod. It was fitting, they said, to select a man of greater piety and purity.[5] Suddenly Archelaus was backed into a corner created by his father.

Archelaus, we are told, wanted to use persuasion rather than force against those who were calling for a new high priest. He also wished to avoid provoking a riot before being confirmed as king by Caesar. After that there would be time to negotiate about their demands. So he sent the general (*strategos* in Josephus's Greek, but perhaps in Hebrew *segan,* or temple captain) to beg those who were making these demands to stop. Before the officer could utter a word the demonstrators began throwing rocks at him. Those sent after him received the same reception.[6] The love fest between Archelaus and his would-be subjects was over even before he was officially seated on the throne. Too late Archelaus learned that generosity did not necessarily buy goodwill. Archelaus had received his first lesson in what it cost to wear his father's crown.

Soon the Passover feast came around. At a minimum the celebration of the festival would have brought about 15,000 pilgrims into Jerusalem, nearly half of the city's lowest estimated population.[7] The pilgrims brought not only lots of money with them for sacrifices and other kinds of expenses but also their own grievances and agendas, both public and private.[8] The festival thus became an occasion for agitation. A group of people who favored political change gathered together and stood in the Temple mourning the executed sophists Judas and Matthias. Food was provided to beggars, who also stirred up discord.

Archelaus was alarmed by what was going on, and so before the sedition spread to the whole crowd, he sent in a tribune (*chiliarchos* in Greek) at the head of a cohort (*speira*) of soldiers. Josephus's use of the Greek technical terms for the tribune and the cohort indicates that the soldiers belonged to the Roman auxiliary cohort stationed in the city. It is very likely that the soldiers came from the garrison stationed in the Antonia Fortress; they comprised the best-trained military force in Jerusalem. The cohort might have numbered 500 infantrymen.[9]

The tribune's orders were to constrain the leaders of the disturbance, if necessary by force. When the soldiers appeared the assembled crowd became agitated and pelted them with stones. Many of them were killed. The wounded tribune barely escaped. Then, as if nothing had happened, the riot was over and the people turned their attention to making a sacrifice.[10]

At this point Archelaus no longer believed that the crowd could be restrained unless he authorized a more aggressive, hands-on response. He therefore unleashed the whole army upon them. The infantry advanced together through the city, the cavalrymen coming by way of the plain.[11] The cavalry soldiers fell suddenly upon those who were sacrificing and killed about 3,000 of them. The rest of the crowd scattered into the adjoining hills. Archelaus's heralds followed them there and ordered them to go home. Abandoning the festival, the survivors of the massacre departed.[12]

As so often in Jerusalem's history, the celebration of one of the three main pilgrimage festivals (Pesach, Shavuot, Sukkot) had started with animal sacrifices and ended in human bloodshed.[13] Although he did not belabor this point, Josephus himself was surely aware of the irony. The Jews had come to the Passover festival with their sacrificial lambs, ready to commemorate their Exodus from Egypt. Instead they became the victims.

After leaving his brother Philip in the city to take charge of the palace and look out for his personal interests, Archelaus and his mother and his friends, including Poplas (or Ptollas), Ptolemy, and his adviser Nicolaus of Damascus, then went down to the coast, accompanied by Herod's sister Salome and her children. Archelaus's plan was to move on from Caesarea to Rome where he could get his succession confirmed.[14] Herod's nephews and sons-in-law were also in the royal traveling party, purportedly to support Archelaus's claim to the throne. In reality, Josephus claims, they were there to accuse him of violating tradition over what had happened in and around the Temple.[15]

Sabinus, the procurator or financial official of the province of Syria, who was on his way to Judaea to try to take command of Herod's estate, met Archelaus and his entourage at Caesarea. Quinctilius Varus, the governor (*legatus*) of Syria, who had been asked to come to Caesarea by Archelaus, prevented Sabinus from continuing his journey and carrying out his scheme. Varus wanted Sabinus to wait until he learned what Augustus wanted to do with Herod's kingdom and possessions. In deference to Varus, Sabinus promised to take no action until Caesar had made his decision about Herod's estate, and he remained in Caesarea.

But as soon as Varus returned to Antioch and Archelaus departed for Rome, Sabinus quickly went to Jerusalem and took possession of the royal palaces. Calling together the governors of the citadels and the treasury officials there, he attempted to look into the royal accounts and to seize possession of the citadels. But the governors were not unmindful of Archelaus's orders. They continued to guard the citadels and the treasury, diplomatically vowing to hold them for Caesar, rather than for Archelaus.[16] Not for the last time did a conflict among Roman governors set the stage for trouble down the road.

THE JOB INTERVIEW IN ROME

Unfortunately for Archelaus, despite what King Herod had specified in the last modification of his will, Herod Antipater or "Antipas," Herod's younger son by Malthace, now decided to press his claim to the throne of Herod's kingdom. He staked his case upon Herod's "original" will—actually, will number six, from 5–4 BCE—in which Antipas had been named as Herod's successor.[17] His claim was supported by Herod's influential sister Salome and many of the relations and friends of Herod who had sailed to Rome with Archelaus. They included Archelaus's and Antipas's mother, Malthace; Herod's ex-friend and accountant, Ptolemy, the brother of Nicolaus; Herod's former advocate, Irenaeus; and his relations in Rome. All of these people favored autonomy under a Roman governor rather than rule by Archelaus because of their hatred of him. Failing direct Roman rule, however, their preference was to have Antipas as king.

Antipas, they thought, would serve their interests better than Archelaus. Antipas was less like his father. The Roman procurator Sabinus too supported Antipas's cause. In letters sent to Rome, he accused Archelaus and praised Antipas. Before the emperor even had a chance to consider his case, Archelaus got a taste of the kind of situational loyalty and machinations that had led to his father's strained relations with his family.

After she arrived in Rome, Salome and her friends handed Caesar a letter indicting Archelaus. In response Archelaus wrote a summary statement of his rights. His father's ring and papers, meanwhile, were delivered to the emperor by Herod's ex-friend Ptolemy.[18]

Before holding his public hearing on the succession question, Caesar Augustus first privately considered the allegations from both sides, taking into account the size of the kingdom, the amount of its annual revenue, and the number of Herod's offspring. He also read the letters from the governor Varus and the procurator Sabinus. He then gathered up a council of prominent Romans, including his own grandson (the son of Marcus Vipsanius Agrippa and his daughter Iulia the Elder) and his own daughter Iulia.[19] Afterward he called upon the two parties to speak.[20] The professional orators led off.

Salome's son Antipater, the most skillful of the speakers on Antipas's side, spoke first. He accused Archelaus of assuming the kingship before he had been confirmed by Caesar, of feigning grief at the death of his father, Herod, and of massacring innocent, poor people who had come to the Temple merely to sacrifice. (He did not mention the stones they had brought with them.) Herod, he argued, had only named Archelaus as his heir after he had lost the ability to reason soundly. Antipater went on at great length, and after he stopped, most of the royal relatives came forward to support his accusations.[21]

The essence of Antipater's attack upon Archelaus was that he had usurped authority before it was granted to him by Caesar and had shown that he was morally unfit to sit on the throne of Judaea by his slaughter of the innocents during the festival. Archelaus lacked the right character to be king, in other words.

Herod's former adviser, ambassador, and all-around éminence grise Nicolaus of Damascus answered Antipater's speech on Archelaus's behalf. He explained that the military action in the Temple had been necessary because the victims had shown themselves to be enemies, not only of the kingdom but also of Caesar himself. In effect, Archelaus had suppressed a riot against Rome. As far as Herod's selection of Archelaus as his heir in the final codicil to the will was concerned, Nicolaus stated that the codicil's legal validity was confirmed by the fact that Caesar himself had been selected to stand as guarantor for the succession. One (Herod) who was sane enough to select the master of all things (Caesar) to surrender his authority to, Nicolaus argued, was surely mentally competent enough not to have made a mistake in his selection of an heir (Archelaus).[22] It was not for nothing that Augustus later named a date famous for its sweetness after Nicolaus.[23] Nicolaus knew that judges liked the taste of appeals to their own authority and vanity.

After Nicolaus concluded his defense of his client, Archelaus himself came forward and fell at Caesar's knees. Archelaus's dramatic gesture was less subtle than Nicolaus's verbal riposte to Antipater and less elegant than his father's display of submission to Octavian on Rhodes 26 years earlier, when Herod had presented himself to Octavian without a crown. But it nevertheless went down well for the moment.

Caesar lifted Archelaus up and intimated that he thought he was a worthy successor of his father. But he did not pronounce judgment at the time. After dismissing the council, the emperor retired to consider whether he should appoint as successor one of those designated in the wills or whether he should divide the rule among the family members.[24] By 4 BCE Augustus had long since learned when to step away from the orators' table of sweets and quietly digest. He probably also wanted to consult his friends and those who knew something about the individuals involved.

While Augustus was deliberating, Archelaus's and Antipas's mother, Malthace, died, and reports of a revolt of the Jews came to the emperor from Varus, governor of Syria. The responsibility for precipitating the revolt lay with the procurator Sabinus. The details are significant, because the news might have influenced Augustus's thinking about the succession, and the overall pattern of Roman administrative overreach and insensitivity leading to violent reaction prefigured the events of 66 CE and the outbreak of the great revolt.

The story was that after Archelaus sailed for Rome, Varus, who anticipated trouble while the succession was being sorted out, went up to Jerusalem with three legions to suppress the promoters of unrest. Because it was evident that the people would not remain quiescent, Varus left one legion in the city before he departed northward to Antioch.[25] One legion was not a massive force; it probably amounted to around 5,000 soldiers, the vast majority of whom would have been infantrymen.[26]

The visible presence of such a force might effectively intimidate the populace into submission. But it would not be capable of dealing militarily with a mass uprising of Jerusalemites and others who might have come into the city. A low estimate of the population of Jerusalem at the time was around 33,000.[27] Varus must have known this. Unfortunately for Varus and the population of Jerusalem, Varus's colleague Sabinus had a different agenda from the governor of Syria. Even within the same province a legate and another handpicked Roman administrator could differ openly on matters of policy, with unfortunate consequences for provincials.

THE PENTECOST REVOLT

After Varus departed to Antioch the procurator Sabinus arrived in Jerusalem and immediately pressured the governors of the citadels to surrender them to him. He also searched rigorously for the royal monies. To conduct the search he relied upon the soldiers left by Varus and also his own slaves, whom he had armed.

While Sabinus was doing whatever he could to get his hands on the royal treasury, the time of the *Shavuot* (Weeks) festival came around. Shavuot was a biblically mandated one-day harvest festival when Jews were ordered to bring the first fruits (*Bikkurim*) of their labor from the ground to a priest at the Temple (normally baked into two loaves of bread) 50 days after the feast of unleavened bread; hence its name in Greek, *Pentekoste,* or fiftieth.[28] Over time the festival became an occasion to celebrate the giving of the Torah on Mt. Sinai and the renewal of the covenant made with Noah and renewed with Abraham, Isaac, and Jacob on behalf of Israel.[29] At the time of this year's festival, masses of people had made their way to Jerusalem from the Galilee, Idumaea, Jericho, and the Peraea on the eastern side of the Jordan River, not only because of their piety, according to Josephus, but also out of indignation over Sabinus's high-handed insolence.

Both in terms of numbers and zeal, however, it was the native population of Judaeans that was preeminent. Some recent estimates of the population of the city during the late first century BCE at festival times range from tens of thousands to several hundred thousand, with the majority of scholars arguing for around 100,000 people.[30] Whatever the exact number, the sole Roman legion in the city at the time was vastly outnumbered by the city population and the festival participants from outside of Jerusalem. Dividing themselves up into three parts and then three camps—one north of the Temple, one on the south adjacent to the hippodrome that was probably built by Herod, and a third to the west, near the royal palaces also built by Herod—the indignant festival pilgrims sat themselves down and in effect besieged the Romans.[31]

Suddenly terrified by the large numbers of pilgrims, Sabinus sent messengers to Varus, requesting immediate assistance. He also warned the legate that if he did not send aid right away the Roman legion in Jerusalem would be cut to pieces. In the meantime he himself climbed up to the top of the Phasael Tower and signaled to the soldiers to attack their enemies. Obeying the order, the Romans made their way into the Temple and assaulted the Jews there.

As long as they were not attacked from above, the Romans' military experience gave them the advantage. But after some Jews mounted the porticoes surrounding the Temple's outer court and hurled stones at them from above—and archers next to them shot arrows at the Romans—the Romans did not find it easy to defend themselves against those above them or to hold their ground against those with whom they were fighting at close quarters.[32]

Attacked both frontally and from above, the Romans in desperation set fire to the Temple porticoes. The fires quickly reached the roofs, in which the woodwork was filled with highly combustible pitch and wax, presumably on the undersides. Some of the woodwork also featured gold smeared with wax; it must have burned as well. The roofs went up in flames immediately, causing them to fall down, along with the Jews who were on top of the porticoes. Many Jews perished there in the flames. Others jumped down from the roofs and were killed by the Romans. Some threw themselves over the rear wall. Still others killed themselves with their own swords. Any who made it down safely were easily dispatched by the Romans, because of their lack of weapons and dazed condition.

Having slain or scattered their enemies, the Romans then turned to plundering the Temple treasury, helping themselves to the sacred monies. Sabinus took what was not pilfered by the soldiers themselves—which amounted to as much as 400 talents.[33] Nothing like this had happened while Herod was still alive.

The Roman victory inside the Temple, however, had the effect of rallying the Jews in far greater numbers on the outside. The majority of the royal troops who were there and were Jews joined them, although not the 3,000-man contingent of so-called Sebastenians (non-Jews recruited from Sebaste [Samaria]) and another unit of cavalrymen, perhaps 500 men of unknown ethnic origins, who served under the royal cavalry commander Rufus and the royal infantry commander Gratus.[34] Nevertheless, the rebels and those royal forces that did defect surrounded the palaces to which the Romans had withdrawn and threatened to kill the Romans to a man unless they evacuated. They guaranteed safe conduct to Sabinus and his men. As they pressed the siege, they called upon the Romans not to stand in the way of men who, after such a long time, were on the way to recovering self-rule. Sabinus, however, did not trust their guarantees and was hoping for reinforcements from Varus.[35]

While this fighting was going on in the capital there was unrest in various districts of the countryside, though the center of the trouble was in the north.[36] The targets of attacks included the rich, Romans, and royalists.

Some 2,000 of Herod's veterans banded together in Idumaea to fight against the royal troops led by Herod's cousin Achiav, who avoided direct engagement with these veterans, preferring to fall back from the plain to stronger positions in the hills.[37]

At the city of Sepphoris in the Galilee the "brigand-chief" Judas, son of Ezekias, who had caused Herod difficulties during the 40s BCE before he was subdued and executed, also raised up a force of followers. They broke into the royal armory, and having armed his followers, Judas organized attacks upon others who aspired to power. Judas, we are told, had his own royal aspirations.[38]

In the Peraea, Simon, one of the royal slaves, crowned himself and, after collecting together another force of "brigands," went around burning down large homes and also the royal palace at Jericho. His activities were halted by the intervention of Gratus, the commander of the royal infantry. Joined by the Romans, Gratus, with the royal archers from Trachonitis (El Leja) and some of the best troops of the Sebastenians, engaged Simon's followers, killing many of them.[39] Gratus himself cut off Simon's head as the royal slave tried to escape up a ravine. However, another body of subversives in the Peraea burned down the royal palaces at Betharamatha (Betharamphtha/Tell er-Rama in Jordan).[40]

In Judaea a shepherd named Athronges, who also aspired to the throne and eventually would put on a diadem, and his four brothers launched a guerilla war. With their followers they not only killed Romans and royalists alike but also any Jews they encountered from whom they had something to gain. Near Emmaus (Nicopolis), they surrounded a Roman century (*centuria*) that was gathering grain and conveying arms to the legion in Jerusalem, killing 40 troops or about half of its paper strength, including its centurion Arius. The rest were saved by the intervention of Gratus and the Sebastenians.[41] Eventually three of the brothers were captured, and the fourth surrendered to Archelaus.[42]

It was only the governor Varus's direct intervention that at least temporarily put an end to this unrest. Joined by 1,500 auxiliary recruits from Berytus

(Beirut), Varus, with two other legions stationed in Syria and four squadrons of cavalry, marched down from Antioch.[43] The Romans used such locally recruited auxiliary soldiers, who often fought according to local practices with their own weaponry, to supplement and add tactical flexibility to the legions.[44] At this time the auxiliaries would have been non-Roman citizens. Only from the reign of Claudius were auxiliaries who completed 25 years of service given citizenship and the right to have their marriages legally recognized.[45]

At Ptolemais (Akko), the Roman army was joined by contingents of allies and Aretas IV, the Nabataean king, who brought with him a large body of cavalry and infantry. Aretas, we are told, contributed to the Roman rescue force at least in part because of his hatred for Herod the Great. One detachment of the army was then sent into the Galilee under the command of Varus's friend Gaius. Gaius routed all opposition and captured and burned Sepphoris. The population was enslaved.[46]

Varus himself marched into Samaritis and encamped near a village named Arous (Haris). Because the village was a possession of Herod's ex-friend Ptolemy, the Arabs who had joined up with the Roman army sacked the village. After advancing to another fortified village named Sappho or Sampho (possibly Saffa) they destroyed it too, along with the neighboring villages they fell upon. In revenge for the deaths of the centurion Arius and his men, Emmaus was burned to the ground on Varus's order, even though it had already been abandoned by its inhabitants.[47]

Varus then proceeded to the outskirts of Jerusalem, where his appearance led the Jews who had been besieging the single legion in Jerusalem to flee into the countryside. Varus and his soldiers were then met outside the city by Archelaus's cousin Joseph, with Rufus, the royal cavalry commander, and Gratus, the royal infantry commander, at the head of the royal army and the Sebastenians, and the Roman legionaries.[48] Sabinus meanwhile had fled to the coast.

Once Varus entered the city, he rebuked the people for what had happened. The inhabitants of Jerusalem who were left behind, however, refused to take any responsibility for what had occurred, claiming that they had not lifted a finger. On the contrary, they said that they had been forced to receive the crowd into the city because of the festival and that they had actually been besieged along with the Romans, rather than besieging them with the rebels.

Varus sent part of his army to search the countryside, looking for those who had been the leaders of the uprising. Many were captured, and those deemed less culpable were imprisoned. But 2,000 judged to be more blame-worthy were crucified.[49] This action did nothing for Varus's reputation or memory among Jews and may well have encouraged anti-Roman sentiment. But Varus's response in Jerusalem is probably an indication that he, at any rate, accepted the argument of the majority of Jerusalemites that they had not been responsible for the outbreak of the fighting.[50]

Having settled affairs in Jerusalem Varus turned his attentions to Idumaea. He had been informed that there were now 10,000 men (Jews) under arms there. No doubt at least some of them were ex-soldiers of Herod. Dismissing his Arab allies, who were judged to be making war for the sake of private re-sentment of Herod, Varus marched off to confront the rebels with part of the Roman legions.

But before there was any engagement, the rebels surrendered on the ad-vice of Achiav. Most of the regular soldiers were pardoned. But the leaders were sent on to Caesar to be tried. Caesar subsequently excused all but a few who were of royal blood. Among those were some relatives of Herod, who were punished for taking up arms against a member of the royal household. Leaving the legion previously quartered in Jerusalem in the city and with or-der restored, Varus then made his way back to Antioch.[51]

In some revealing ways what happened in 4 BCE during "Varus's War," as it was remembered by Jews, prefigured the events that led to the great revolt in 66 CE, and the fighting followed a similar pattern as well.[52] In both cases attempts by Roman officials to help themselves to the resources of the Temple during the celebration of one of the regularly scheduled festi-vals led to fighting. The actions of a single aggressive procurator could easily turn a festival into a fiasco or worse. Moreover, in both instances Jews fought not only with Romans but also among themselves. Disturbances in Jerusalem inspired unrest in the countryside. Finally, both in 4 BCE and in 66 CE, the Romans first snuffed out the main pockets of resistance outside of Jerusalem, especially in the Galilee, and then headed to the capital city of Judaea. A "Great Revolt" of Jews against Rome easily could have broken out in 4 BCE. Once the strong hand of Herod was removed from the scene, Judaea became a tinderbox at every change of power and during the times of the festivals in Jerusalem. Through quick and effective action in 4 BCE, Varus was able to put a lid on the box. In 66 CE the governor of Syria, Cestius Gallus, hesitated, was led to underestimate the opposition, and so fanned the flames of rebellion.

CAESAR'S DECISION

While Varus was putting out the fire that Sabinus had lit in Judaea, Archelaus was being forced to defend himself once again before Caesar in Rome. With the permission of Varus, 50 Jewish representatives had come to Rome to plead for the autonomy of their people. Eight thousand Jews in Rome supported their case.[53]

Caesar gathered together another council of prominent Romans and his own friends in the Temple of Apollo on the Palatine Hill. (See map 5.) At least some of Rome's Jews stood next to the representatives of the Jews from the homeland. Archelaus with his friends were positioned opposite them. His relations' friends did not appear on one side or the other. Out of hatred for Archelaus, they did not wish to be seen as being too close to him. But they also were ashamed to appear in front of Caesar next to his accusers. As ever, where people stood indicated what they stood for.

Also present was Archelaus's brother Philip, sent by Varus with an escort to support Archelaus—or to get a piece of the kingdom, if Caesar decided to divide up Herod's kingdom among the great king's descendants.[54]

The professional persuaders Antipater and Nicolaus had put in their performances. Now it was the amateurs' turn. The representatives of the Jews spoke first and tore into the dead king Herod and his living son Archelaus. Herod had been buried with honors. But as soon as he was safely sealed up in his sandy-pink sarcophagus at Herodeion his subjects counterattacked.

They began by accusing Herod of tyranny, of torturing not only individuals but even whole cities, of crippling his own possessions while adorning those of others, of pouring out the blood of Judaea on other communities, and of sinking the nation into poverty and the furthest limit of immorality. The misfortunes that Herod had wreaked upon the Jews, they said, surpassed all the others that their ancestors had endured since they left Babylon. Informed listeners would have understood that those earlier misfortunes included the Seleucid king Antiochus Epiphanes's profanation of the Temple. Herod by implication had been worse than Antiochus.

And yet, so used to misfortune had they become, they asserted, that at Herod's death they had agreed to make their slavery hereditary and to choose the heir themselves. They had acclaimed Archelaus king and mourned for Herod. Yet Archelaus, apparently not wanting to be mistaken for an illegitimate son of Herod, had initiated his reign with the massacre of 3,000 citizens in the Temple at the festival.

They begged the Romans, therefore, to have pity upon the remains of Judaea and to join their country to Syria and to assign its administration to governors from among them. Although disparaged as seditious and warlike, the Jews would demonstrate that they knew how to obey fair rulers, they told the emperor and his council.[55]

In response to this assault upon the characters of the dead king and his son, Nicolaus of Damascus rose up yet again and mounted a defense of both Herod and Archelaus. It was unfair, he said, to bring charges against Herod, now that he was dead, that had not been brought against him while he was alive. As for Archelaus, he had only taken action against men who had slaughtered those who had tried to prevent them from acting in violation of the law—and now these men were complaining about the punishment.

Nicolaus also answered the ambassadors with an attack upon the national character of the Jews, who were by nature seditious and insubordinate to kings, he argued—a clear warning to Caesar himself. Lastly, he criticized the relatives of Archelaus who had sided with the accusers.[56] After listening to both sides, Augustus discharged the council.

A few days later the emperor's resolution was announced. The emperor sided with his dead client Herod in part but rendered a judgment that Solomon himself might have appreciated if not approved, perhaps because the news from Judaea showed how quickly the situation there could deteriorate and there already were alarming indications that Archelaus lacked his father's combination of utter ruthlessness and disarming flexibility. So Herod's baby was divided up into three unequal pieces. (See maps 1 and 2 and appendix D for the Herodian rulers.)

Approximately half of Herod's kingdom was given to Archelaus as an ethnarchy, along with the title of ethnarch (*ethnarches*, or ruler of a people).[57] Augustus also promised to make Archelaus king (*basileus* in Greek) if he showed himself worthy of the title. Archelaus's ethnarchy included all of Idumaea, Judaea, and Samaritis, the last of which had its tribute reduced by one-quarter because it had not taken part in the recent unrest. The cities made subject to Archelaus included Straton's Tower/Caesarea Maritima, Sebaste, Joppa, and Jerusalem. The (ethnically) Greek (and indigenous) towns of Gaza to the southwest—Gadara (Umm Qeis) and Hippus/Hippos (Susita) in the Decapolis to the east of the Jordan—were separated from the ethnarchy and annexed to the province of Syria, an indication that Augustus was not sure that Archelaus would be able to keep these cities quiet. Altogether, the territory given to Archelaus could be counted upon to generate either 400 or 600 talents of revenue yearly.[58] In effect Augustus had given Archelaus a kind of starter kingdom. Archelaus cannot have been overjoyed by Caesar's decision, but neither would have been his critics.

The other half of Herod's kingdom Augustus split up into two tetrarchies, which were bestowed upon two of Herod's other sons, Philip and Herod Antipas, who became tetrarchs, or rulers of one-fourth. Herod Antipas's tetrarchy, which he would rule from 4 BCE until 39 CE, when he was deposed by the emperor Gaius, included the Peraea, the area east of the Jordan River between the Decapolis and the Nabataean kingdom, and the Galilee; this tetrarchy produced an annual revenue of 200 talents. Philip essentially received what had been his father's northeastern or Syrian territories: Batanaea, Trachonitis, Auranitis, and parts of the territory of Zenodorus, the hereditary tetrarch and high priest of Ituraea near Panias that together annually produced a revenue of 100 talents.[59] His reign over these areas, where few Jews lived, would last from 4 BCE until 34 CE.[60] The differences in the revenues from the inherited territories revealed a hierarchy of authority, resources, and honor: (1) Archelaus (600 talents); (2) Antipas (200 talents); and (3) Philip (100 talents).[61] The totals also give us some idea of how much money Herod was deriving from these parts of his unified kingdom before his death.[62]

Herod's sister Salome was proclaimed ruler of the cities of Iamnia, Azotus, and Phasaelis, the last one named after her deceased oldest brother.[63] She also received a palace in Ascalon. Her revenues totaled 60 talents. Archelaus was given legal jurisdiction over her so-called toparchy (*toparchia*).[64] A toparchy was essentially a district comprising a number of villages, with one town or large village serving as its administrative center (*metrokomia* or *komopolis*). The division of villages into toparchies in this region had its roots in the transition from Persian to Greek rule following the conquests of Alexander the Great.[65]

The other members of Herod's family received the legacies specified in his will. Herod's two unmarried daughters, Roxane and Salome, in addition to their father's legacies, each received 250,000 drachmas of silver from Augustus and were given in marriage to sons of Herod's brother Pheroras. After dividing up Herod's estate in this way, Augustus then gave back to Herod's family the cash legacy Herod had left to him. This amounted to 1,000 (or 1,500) talents. When all was said and done, the emperor only kept for himself a few of the vessels that had been given to him in memory of the king.[66]

Herod probably had left the money to Caesar as an expression of loyalty but also to buy imperial goodwill. Roman wills were family umbrella insurance policies. By returning the money, Augustus publicly rewarded the dead king and reminded everyone who was the patron and who was the client.

DIVIDE AND WEAKEN

By dividing rule over Herod's once unified kingdom into three territories among the dead monarch's sons, Augustus had effectively weakened all of them politically. No doubt this was intentional, though it was based upon the main lines of Herod's seventh and last will. Augustus himself probably recognized that Herod was uniquely suited to promoting Roman interests over the whole of his kingdom. On the one hand, Herod ruled with an iron fist; on the other, he was totally loyal to Augustus and Rome.[67] He could work with at least some of the families of the priesthoods and sects, as well as with the wealthy landowners who were associated with them. Herod also never made the mistake (like his Hasmonean predecessor, Judah Aristobulus I) of trying to be high priest and king. Herod's family members, however, were untested, his sons were young (Archelaus age 19, Antipas 17, and Philip about 16), and at least some of them had manifested signs of disloyalty and instability. So Augustus took precautions. Despite the measures Augustus took, the seven decades that followed before the outbreak of the great revolt were not completely peaceful: there was spasmodic opposition to Roman policies and eventually rule (both in 6 and in 66 CE).[68] Yet in 4 BCE Varus and Augustus successfully turned what could have been the great revolt into a little revolt.

CHAPTER 3

From Ethnarchy to Province

THE CREATION OF THE PROVINCE OF JUDAEA

After Archelaus took charge of his ethnarchy, the multitude demanded a man of greater piety and ritual purity as high priest. Archelaus obliged them, replacing the serving high priest, Joazar, with his brother Eleazar. He purportedly made the change because Joazar had supported the rebels who caused unrest during the succession struggle.[1] Josephus does not make clear which rebels the high priest was supposed to have backed. But, in any case, the reason why Archelaus deposed Joazar was probably because the high priest was tainted in the eyes of many Jews by his association with Herod. Archelaus was determined to show that he did not want to be associated with his father and his legacies. But he could not help himself.

Having appointed a new high priest, Archelaus embarked upon a building program that recalled his father's ambitions, if not their scope, scale, and grandeur. He rebuilt the palace at Jericho that had been burned by the royal slave Simon and his followers and redirected Neara's water source to the plain north of Jericho, which he planted with palms. He then had a village constructed or built up on the road from Jericho to Scythopolis (Beth Shean). Keeping up the family tradition, he named the new town Archelaïs after himself.[2] Self-deprecation had never been the primary Herodian virtue.

He also divorced his first wife, Mariamme, and then married his executed half-brother Alexander's wife, Glaphyra. Glaphyra was the daughter of Archelaus, the king of Cappadocia. Under unknown circumstances Archelaus (the ethnarch) had developed a great passion for her.[3] Since Glaphyra had had children with her first husband, Alexander, Archelaus's marriage to Glaphyra violated Levite law.[4] The unlawful marriage did not last long, for Glaphyra died in Judaea, not two days after Alexander supposedly came to her in a dream, upbraided her for marrying his brother, and promised to reclaim her.[5]

As Herod's shade observed his son, what he saw must have brought a smile to the dead king's lips. Archelaus protested that he was not his father's son. But his flexible attitude toward the law when his passions were aroused and his relations with his subjects told a different story.

After nine years of alleged mistreatment, the Jews and the Samaritans, who disagreed about almost everything—starting from where Yahweh wanted his temple built (Mt. Moriah in Jerusalem versus Mt. Gerizim in Samaritis)— found Archelaus's rule to be intolerable. Both peoples therefore sent delegations to Augustus condemning Archelaus. Archelaus was then summoned to Augustus for another hearing.

Augustus listened to both sides but finally had heard enough. Archelaus's critics had been right. Herod had been ruthless but was focused and precise and did not cause much collateral or nonfamilial damage. In contrast, Archelaus was indiscriminate and too quick to unsheathe the sword. He was not a victim of unrest; he was creating and uniting it. That was not in Rome's interest.

In 6 CE Augustus therefore banished Archelaus to Vienna (*Vienne*), at the confluence of the Rhône and the Gère Rivers in Gaul.[6] His "house" and other possessions were taken over to be liquidated.[7] The city of Archelaïs was handed over to Herod's sister Salome, the friend of the empress Livia.[8] In less than a decade the Archelaus experiment was over.

In his earliest work describing the background to the great revolt, Josephus tells his readers that Archelaus's ethnarchy was converted into a Roman province (*eparchia* in Greek). Coponius, a man of equestrian status among the Romans, was sent out immediately as prefect, receiving from Caesar Augustus the power to inflict capital punishment.[9] (See appendix H for more information on the Roman province of Judaea and appendix F for the names of the Roman governors of Judaea.)

With the exception of the years from 41 to 44 CE, when Agrippa I was made ruler of all of Palestine by the Roman emperor Claudius, Judaea thereafter remained part of the Roman provincial system up to the outbreak of the great revolt in 66. The rest of the territory that once belonged to Archelaus's ethnarchy was added to the province of Syria.

Because of the personal nature of power within the Roman state, after Archelaus's ethnarchy was absorbed into the Roman provincial administration, the personalities and policies of the individual Roman emperors and the governors sent out to Judaea inevitably affected the lives and experiences of those they governed in the province. While some emperors and governors went out of their way to understand the traditions and sensitivities of their Judaean subjects and to adjust their policies to them, others did not and thereby strengthened the hand of those who rejected accommodation to Roman rule.

Finally, events that occurred elsewhere pushed enough Jews over into the rejectionist camp so that not just a little revolt but instead a great revolt broke out in 66. As with all wars, there was nothing inevitable about its outbreak. It came about as a result of decisions and choices made by individuals, most of which we will never know, because they left no record of why they made the choices they did. What we do know, however, is that from the beginning of the province's creation there were Jews who objected strongly to having the Romans as their masters. It would take almost exactly 60 years for the rejectionists to convince enough of their fellow Jews that the unthinkable—a war against Rome—was first thinkable and then desirable.

THE EARLY ROMAN GOVERNORS

To keep order within the province, Coponius and his successors commanded non-Roman citizen auxiliary troops.[10] Josephus does not provide specific details about the origins or ethnic composition of this force in 6 CE. What we do know is that at the death of King Agrippa I, ruler of Judaea from 41 to 44, there was one squadron of cavalrymen from Caesarea and Sebaste and five infantry cohorts.[11] During his procuratorship (48–52) Ventidius Cumanus used the squadron called the Sebastenians and four cohorts of infantry to attack Jews in the wake of a Samaritan assault upon Galilaean Jews who had passed through Samaritan territory on their way to the (or a) festival in Jerusalem.[12] Later, during the governorship of Felix, Josephus reveals that most of those who had taken military service under the Romans were from Caesarea and Sebaste.[13] When Vespasian assembled his invasion force at Ptolemais in 67, he was joined by five infantry cohorts or perhaps 2,500 men, plus one squadron of around 512 cavalrymen from Caesarea.[14] These troops were stationed in Caesarea Maritima.[15]

It is a reasonable inference that at least by the time of the governorship of Felix, if not before, the majority of auxiliary solders in the cohorts serving under the Roman governors were non-Jews. Such a force was sufficient for policing actions such as riot control but not for major military operations. It was for that reason that, if anything happened that escalated beyond rioting, legions from Syria would have to be brought down into Judaea to restore order.

Coponius was sent along to be the prefect of the province with the new legate (*legatus Augusti pro praetore*) of Syria, Publius Sulpicius Quirinius. Quirinius was instructed by the emperor to make an assessment of the property of his province's inhabitants.[16] It was this assessment that the author of the gospel of Luke, writing toward the end of the first century CE, mistakenly associated with the birth of Jesus around 10 years earlier.[17] An inscription from Apamea confirms that the census was carried out in Syria by a certain Q. Aemilius Secundus.[18]

Quirinius, however, also visited Judaea to make an assessment of the property of the Jews.[19] Although Josephus is not explicit on the point, based upon evidence from Roman practices in nearby provinces, including Egypt and Arabia, some scholars argue that Quirinius and the Romans conducted the census in order to register property, for payment of a land tax (*tributum soli*), and persons, for payment of a poll or head tax.[20] Whatever the purpose of the census was, the Jews reacted with hostility to the news of the imposition of a direct tax, though the reinstated high priest, Joazar, the son of Boethus, convinced most but not all of them to declare the value of their property.[21]

JUDAS THE GALILAEAN

Though we do not know exactly what were the rates of taxation that the Romans imposed upon the inhabitants of the province, the imposition of the property assessment stirred up a resistance movement.[22] Josephus says that a Galilaean named Judas called his fellow countrymen cowards and reproached them for paying tribute to Romans and, after God, accepting mortal masters (*thnetous despotas* in Josephus's Greek text); in his later version of events, Josephus writes that Judas and the Pharisee Zaddok said that the property assessment implied a status amounting to slavery (*douleian*), and they called upon the nation to make a bid for independence (*eleutherias*).[23]

This Judas is almost certainly the one whom Josephus identified as the son of the executed bandit-chief Ezekias.[24]

In his account of the great revolt of 66, Josephus called Judas a "sophist" who founded a school or sect of his own that had nothing to do with the others. Later in the *War* Josephus admitted that Judas persuaded "not a few" Jews not to register for the Roman census.[25] We know, however, that some Jews went further than simple tax evasion. They not only defied the Romans but also turned on those who complied with the Roman census.

Indeed, Josephus says that dagger-men (*sicarii*) banded together at that time (*tote gar*) against those who wished to submit to Rome and in every way regarded them as enemies. They seized their homes, stole their cattle, and set fire to their houses, claiming that they were in no way different from foreigners who gave up Judaea's freedom and admitted that they chose slavery under the Romans.[26]

From this statement it arguably follows that "dagger-men" existed as early as 6 CE in Josephus's view, and from what Josephus says about their motives at the time it is hard to draw any other conclusion than that they opposed Roman rule of Judaea, if it entailed the imposition of a census and tribute— even if, in the passage Josephus is talking about, their actions were taken against fellow Jews. The manifestation of Roman rule was thus the imposition of a census. The dagger-men of this period, in other words, were ethnic, nationalist rebels against Roman rule of the kind imposed in 6 CE and against those who submitted to it. Thus there were Jews who opposed Roman rule on nationalist, ideological grounds from the very beginning of the imposition of the first equestrian governor, no matter how and why Josephus used the term *sicarius* later.

Josephus goes on to write that the population responded happily to the appeals of Judas and Zaddok, who sowed the seed from which civil discord and the murder of fellow citizens arose. They started a "fourth philosophy," and after they won a mass of followers they filled the state up with tumult and planted the seeds of the troubles that overtook it. It was, according to Josephus, particularly the zeal they fostered among the younger men that led to the public ruin.[27]

Judas's influence is verified by another first-century CE source. According to the author of the Acts of the Apostles, who quotes the Pharisee Gamaliel, Judas did draw many people to him. But he perished, and then as many people as had been persuaded by him were dispersed.[28] In 66, however, Judas's son Menahem became one of the leaders of the revolt against Rome, and Judas's descendant Eleazar, possibly his grandson, was the leader of the rebels and, it turns out, of others on Masada.[29] Indeed, Josephus explicitly connected the resistance movement that Judas started to the later dagger-men through Judas's descendant Eleazar, who was the leader of the *sicarii* who occupied Masada in 73–74, though Josephus does not say that Judas himself was a *sicarius*.[30]

Some scholars have argued that the resistance movement that Judas inspired should not be seen as specifically anti-Roman. Rather, it was a reaction to the removal of Archelaus from Jerusalem and the annexation of his territory to Syria. That change had the effect of making Jerusalem just another polis within the large province of Syria, and not the capital of a kind of Judaean mini-empire.[31]

This is a clever and intriguing hypothesis. But some explicit evidence undermines it. First, Josephus says specifically in the *War* that Judas reproached his countrymen (*epichorious*) for paying tribute "to Romans."[32] He does not say that these countrymen lived only in Judaea. Second, nowhere does he say that at this time "Jews" or "the Jews" protested the removal of Archelaus or the supposed annexation to Syria. On the contrary, as we have seen, Josephus makes clear that Archelaus was unpopular with at least enough Jews and Samaritans to lead to his dismissal by Augustus. His removal would have been no cause for protest among the Jews whom Josephus was talking about, at any rate. Nor does he say that anyone protested the change in Judaea's or Jerusalem's status from being a separate province to becoming part of Syria, as some have contended.[33] In fact Josephus does not say that Judas's followers came from Jerusalem in particular; he only writes that he and Zaddok attracted a mass of followers. It is worth pointing out and remembering that Judas, like Judas Maccabaeus, apparently did not come from Jerusalem. The epicenter of the resistance in 6 CE was in the north. That was where Judas came from anyway.

Even if we do not know exactly which "countrymen" supported Judas and his partner, can we say more about their message that will help us understand its target and audience?

We can probably assume that the inhabitants of Archelaus's ethnarchy paid taxes to him during his brief reign. But we do not know how they registered to pay taxes, how taxes were calculated, or what was the rate of taxation. Nor do we know whether Archelaus, unlike his father Herod, paid tribute to Rome, though of course it is a likely inference. Therefore, it is impossible to know whether Quirinius's registration in 6 CE represented an administrative innovation or, after it was completed, whether the taxes assessed and gathered to make up the tribute represented an increase, decrease, or any change at all from what had been extracted from the population before. Josephus does say, however, that Judas upbraided his countrymen for paying tribute to the Romans—not that the tribute represented some vast increase over what Archelaus had collected. The natural sense of the sentence is that his objection was to paying tribute to the Romans at all. Why, beyond the obvious transhistorical fact that no one enjoys paying taxes to anyone?

Judas's reproach seems to have been based upon an idea enunciated in the books of Deuteronomy, Joshua, and elsewhere in the Hebrew Bible and repeated in Josephus's work *Against Apion,* that although Israel might set a God-chosen king over itself despite the warning of the prophet Samuel, it was forbidden to place a foreigner over itself as king. All sovereignty and authority were understood, at least by the lawgiver Moses, to be placed in the hands of God.[34] Israel, in other words, should be, at least in theory, a theocracy, albeit one in which the commands given to the lawgiver by God were thereafter mediated or interpreted by a literate priestly aristocracy.[35] The only real king of Israel was God, as Moses, the people of Israel, Gideon, Samuel, Asaph and his brethren, the singers of the Psalms, and the prophet Isaiah repeatedly reminded the Jews.[36] It should also be noted that a similar argument was made by representatives of the people to Pompey when John Hyrcanus II and Aristobulus II were vying for the throne.[37] The fact that the Jews had submitted to censuses in the past and no doubt paid taxes to mortal masters in no way alters the crucial point that there was scriptural warrant for Judas's position.[38]

Whatever we make of Josephus's claim about the introduction of a "fourth philosophy" by Judas and Zaddok, what is clear is that the essential idea of having God alone as lord or master could be traced back in the history of the people to the book of Exodus. In Exodus it is written that, when Moses was on Mount Sinai to receive the commandments, he was told that he and the Israelites should have no other gods before him (God).[39] The only real master of the people was and must be God.

Later in the book of Exodus and elsewhere, including in Deuteronomy, the injunction against tolerating other masters, bowing down before other gods, or making covenants with other peoples or their gods is often repeated.[40] Judas and his followers could have found an intensification of the idea that Jews should have no other master than God in the source known to scholars as Deutero-Isaiah. In that sixth-century BCE text, which arose out of the experience of conquest, subordination, and the Babylonian exile, not only should Jews not have any other master or god but also the prophet of Deutero-Isaiah quotes God himself telling the Jews that there is no other god: he is the first and the last, and there is no god beside him.[41]

Josephus wants to present Judas as the founder of some new and different "school." But Judas and his followers were neither scriptural innovators nor theological revolutionaries, at least as far as the central point about God's sole mastery over the Jews was concerned.[42] Rather, they identified one of the most important doctrinal ideas in Judaism and insisted upon a rigorous adherence to it. Judas therefore was not a sophist but a "rigorist" or a textual literalist. Those who agreed to pay the tribute to Romans and to accept them as masters were guilty of transgressing the covenant with God and therefore the law.[43] It is a frequently overlooked fact that nowhere in any of his writings about Judas and the revolt does Josephus, who claimed to have studied all of the major strands of scriptural interpretation, as he proudly tells his readers, say that Judas was wrong about his central theological argument. The reason why was because he could not.

Putting up with a Hasmonean or Herodian master who was a Jew or half-Jew and paying taxes to him was problematic enough for some Jews and arguably a violation of the covenant; accepting a Roman master and paying taxes to him was unacceptable.[44] Whatever we think of the way that Judas and his followers chose to act after adopting his theological position, it should be accepted that the position itself could be scripturally justified. Judas and his followers therefore were not theological revolutionaries, as Josephus himself seems to have understood very well. Nor were they founders of some kind of millenarian movement. There is no evidence that Judas, his family members, or their followers envisioned some apocalyptic moment of transformation, to be followed by the establishment of a new, utopian society. Rather they primarily seem to have wanted to be left alone from outside (i.e., foreign) interference. Their concerns were with the here and now, not the there and then.

Indeed, Judas and his supporters agreed in all other ways with the teaching of the Pharisees, we are told, except that the followers of the "sophist" had a passionate desire for freedom under God alone that was unconquerable. This extraordinary passion was based upon their belief that God was their sole, indeed the only, master. This may have been an absurd platform saddled upon Judas by Josephus. But if so, it was a theological absurdity ultimately attributable to none other than the God of Abraham and Moses himself.[45]

COPONIUS AND THE SAMARITANS

After helping instigate a rebellion of at least some Jews, Coponius then got caught up in the on-again, off-again conflict between Samaritans and Jews.[46] Those conflicts could be traced back to at least the mid-fifth century BCE, when Nehemiah's rebuilding of Jerusalem's walls was opposed by Sanballat of Horon, perhaps to be identified with the village of Huwara at Mt. Gerizim.[47] When Alexander the Great passed through the region in 332 BCE, Samaria's governor, another Sanballat (possibly III) took Alexander's side against the Persian king Darius III, and Alexander supposedly granted him permission to build a temple.[48] The Jewish high priest Jaddus reportedly refused to betray Darius.[49]

While Coponius was prefect, perhaps in the spring of 7 or 8 CE, some Samaritans who had managed to enter Jerusalem and the Temple precinct scattered human bones in the porticoes and the Court of Nations (Gentiles) during Passover.[50] This intentional act of defilement made it necessary for the priests to clear the Temple during the celebration of one of the most important religious festivals of the Jews and then to purify the sanctuary. The interruption of the celebration would have caused religious anxiety and a loss of revenues for the Temple and the city if the festival had to be canceled (because of the pollution to the sanctuary) and the pilgrims sent home.

In the aftermath of the attack, the Jews took additional steps to protect the sanctuary. It is possible that it was in response to what happened at this time that the office of the Temple captain, which was to figure prominently in the outbreak of the revolt in 66, was instituted to supervise the Temple guards.[51]

Coponius himself seems to have been called back to Rome after this incident (in 9 CE); perhaps his recall was connected to this episode.[52] Whether Coponius's recall was linked to the Samaritan raid or not, its occurrence was an indication of tensions, if not outright hostility, between at least some Samaritans and Jews almost from the inception of the province.

AMBIVULUS AND ANNIUS RUFUS

Coponius's replacement was a man named Marcus Ambivulus (or Ambibulus). We know virtually nothing about what happened during his administration from 9–12 except that Salome, the sister of King Herod the Great, died in 10 while he was governor. In her will the king's sister left her toparchy and the cities of Iamnia, Phasaelis, and Archelaïs, the last of which was famous for its palms and dates, to Augustus's wife Livia (Iulia).[53] Even less is known about the prefecture of Ambivulus's successor, Annius Rufus, whose governorship is usually dated from 12 to 15.[54] It was, however, during Rufus's prefecture that Augustus died at the age of 77 on 19 August 14 CE. It is probably a positive sign about relations between these two Roman governors and the Jews of the province that we know virtually nothing about what happened during their governorships. Apparently there were no major scandals or outbreaks of violence in Judaea.

Tacitus claims that Tiberius feigned reluctance to succeed Augustus, but whatever the case, the transfer of sovereignty to the new emperor was made without effective opposition or bloodshed.[55] Because power had become officially personal since Octavian's victory over Antony at Actium in 31 BCE, it was inevitable that decisions made by Tiberius and his successors about how to manage Judaea and the surrounding region would affect the lives of both Jews and non-Jews living there. Arguably the apogee of cooperative relations between Judaea and Rome already had been reached when Herod the Great and Augustus sat on their respective thrones in Jerusalem and Rome.

HEROD ANTIPAS AND PHILIP THE TETRARCH

Outside of Judaea, after the death of Augustus, the tetrarchs appointed by him continued to rule, rebuild, and found new cities in their tetrarchies.[56] It was within several of these towns and cities that fighting took place during the great revolt of 66. A brief sketch of some of the major developments in these places during the mid–first century CE will help us understand what happened and why. (See maps 1 and 2 and appendix D for the rulers and their territories.)

Herod Antipas, the son of Herod and Malthace, fortified Sepphoris, which he renamed Autocratoris or "Emperorville," though the new name was not widely used; he also had a wall built around the village or town of Betharamphtha in the Peraea (renamed Iulias or Livias).[57] An increase in the population of Sepphoris, perhaps to 12,000 inhabitants—though some scholars have argued for much lower numbers—was made possible subsequently by the construction of an aqueduct.[58] Archaeological evidence for the existence of ritual baths (*miqva'ot*) in some houses in one section of the new city during the first century CE also suggests that some of the Jews in the city attempted to adhere to rules about ritual purity.[59] By 66 Sepphoris would become the leading population center of the Lower Galilee and a bastion (*proschema*) of support for Rome.[60]

Antipas had a new port city or polis built, by 19 to 21 CE based upon the numismatic evidence, on an approximately 17-acre site between Mt. Berenice and Lake Gennesaret (Hebrew, Kinneret; hereafter the Sea of Galilee), which he named Tiberias in honor of the Roman emperor.[61] Josephus alleges that the new polis was built on the site of tombs that had been destroyed, a violation of law and tradition. The population of the new foundation was made up of Galilaeans forcibly brought to the city, but it also included magistrates, poor people, and possibly ex-slaves.[62] Its population range during the first century has been estimated between 4,500 and 15,000.[63] Though Jews made up a large majority of the population in the Galilee, the exact ethnic mix of the Tiberias foundation is not known.[64]

During the first century CE the polis included a council or *boule* of 600, a chief magistrate or *archon,* a board of 10 overseers called *dekaprotoi,* a citizen assembly or *demos,* and a market supervisor or *agoranomos.*[65] It was unmistakably organized according to one model of a Greek polis's institutional structure.[66]

Antipas had a palace built for himself at the site of the new foundation, and there also were a building for prayers or *proseuche,* hot baths, and a stadium.[67] A first-century CE theater was discovered at the site in 1980; subsequent excavations revealed that its eventual seating capacity was about 7,000.[68] Later, after Josephus was selected as the general for the Galilees and Gamala during the revolt, he claimed to have been commissioned by the Jerusalem assembly to destroy Antipas's palace there, with its representations of animals, but he was beaten to the job by his enemy, Jesus, the son of Sapphias, and his followers.[69]

Although the economic effects of Antipas's building programs in his tetrarchy are disputed, there is less doubt that the construction of new cities with at least some structures characteristic of Graeco-Roman cities, such as stadia, would have raised the public profile of Graeco-Roman urban culture in the region.[70] It was not a coincidence that there was ethnic and cultural conflict in Tiberias during the great revolt.

Philip the Tetrarch minimally made improvements or perhaps was responsible for establishing an administrative center at Paneas (Panias)/Caesarea, which he called Caesarea Philippi, combining his own name with that of Caesar. Bethsaida (El-Araj/Beit Habeck or et-Tell), then on the northern shore of the Sea of Galilee, was raised up to the status of a polis named Iulias (after

Augustus's wife Livia, called Iulia after 14 CE) by adding inhabitants and strengthening its fortifications.[71] Philip's reign, ending in 33–34, was otherwise most notable because, apparently beginning from year 5 of his reign or in 1–2 CE, he was the first ruler of Jewish ethnicity to have coins minted with an image of himself on them.[72] Having such coins minted at Caesarea Philippi probably tells us at least something about the population of the town. At the beginning of the first century CE that town was populated by non-Jews who were accustomed to seeing human images of their rulers on coins. It is perhaps just as revealing that none of Philip's coins have been found in Jerusalem or Judaea and that the vast majority of them seem to have circulated within his tetrarchy.[73]

VALERIUS GRATUS AND PONTIUS PILATE

Annius Rufus's successor as governor, Valerius Gratus, who was appointed early in the reign of Tiberius (14–37), deposed the high priest Ananus and then appointed no less than four high priests during his 11-year administration from 15 to 26: Ishmael, son of Phabi (or Phiabi); Eleazar, son of Ananus; Simon, son of Camith; and Joseph, son-in-law of Ananus and also known as Caiaphas.[74] The rapid turnover was a sign that Gratus was dissatisfied with the performance of the high priests during his governorship, though we do not know the details.

After Gratus returned to Rome, his replacement was Pontius Pilate, the only governor of the province whose prefecture is epigraphically attested. From line 3 of the famous Pilate inscription, discovered in Caesarea in 1961, we know that the office Pilate held was that of *praefectus,* and we infer that it was the office held by the rest of the Roman governors from 6 until 44.[75] According to the restorations of the fragmentary inscription suggested by Alföldy, the full text referred to Pilate's restoration of a lighthouse for sailors at Caesarea, known as the Tiberieum.[76]

Pilate's prefecture, perhaps starting from 18–19, or more likely taking place during the years 26 to 36 CE, is infamous, because it was while he was prefect that Jesus was accused and then crucified by his order, probably in early April of 33, leading to the creation, spread, and ultimate triumph of Christianity within the Roman empire.[77] But in addition to overseeing the execution of the "christos" or anointed one, as Josephus or the Christian interpolator of Josephus's later work, the *Antiquities,* calls Jesus,[78] and securing for himself a permanent place in later world history, it is less widely appreciated that

Pilate nearly managed to incite a full-scale revolt of Jews against Rome at the time—and it was these incidents, and not Jesus's life and death, that almost led to the revolt on which Josephus and Philo of Alexandria focused.

The earlier story appears in Philo's *Embassy to Gaius,* a text that was written after Philo took part in the embassy to Rome, probably in the late winter or spring of 39, decades before Josephus wrote the *War* or the *Antiquities.*[79] In Philo's story, Pilate, to deliberately anger the multitude, dedicated some gilt shields in the palace of Herod (in Jerusalem). The shields had no form or anything else forbidden on them, only some necessary inscription. The inscription mentioned the name of the person who put the shields there and the person in whose honor they were so placed.[80]

When the multitude heard what had been done, they put forward four sons of the king and his other descendants, as well as magistrates, who begged Pilate to remove the shields.[81] After Pilate refused their petition, the Jews wrote a letter to Tiberius asking the emperor to intercede.[82] When Tiberius read the letter, he threatened Pilate and wrote him a letter commanding him to remove the shields and take them to Caesarea, to be set up there in the Temple of Augustus.[83]

Since the shields, according to Philo, had no image or anything else forbidden on them, it is possible that the inscription itself was what gave offense to the Jews. A dedicatory inscription such as the one described by Philo would have included the name of the dedicator, Pontius Pilate, and then the name of the dedicatee, in this case the emperor Tiberius. But it was also standard practice to include the name of the emperor's father and perhaps grandfather: the father would be Augustus, who had been deified upon his death in 14, and the grandfather was Iulius Caesar, also deified after his assassination in 44 BCE. The inscription on the dedicated shield(s) might therefore have read, "To Tiberius Caesar Augustus, son of divine Augustus, grandson of divine Iulius, Pontius Pilate, Prefect of Judaea." The sticking point for the Jews may have been the references to the divinity of both Augustus and his adoptive father, Iulius Caesar.[84]

Josephus then reports a second, similar story, but one probably related to another incident indicating Pilate's attempt to get around Jewish religious scruples. In the second story Pilate had military standards (*semaiai*) with representations of Caesar (*kaisaros eikonas*) brought into Jerusalem, albeit at night and under cover.[85] Bringing the standards in during the evening and under wraps suggests that Pilate understood that their introduction into the city might cause unrest. In his later account of the incident Josephus calls the offending objects on the standards *protomas kaisaros,* possibly meaning busts of Caesar.[86] Pilate was forced to remove the military standards after a massive five-day protest by the Jews in the stadium of Caesarea.[87]

Another indication of Pilate's lack of sensitivity to issues of iconography within Judaea was his minting of coins in Caesarea while he was governor that included images of a ladle used during Roman religious ceremonies called a *simpulum* and the staff or *lituus* of Roman augurs, who traditionally interpreted the will of the gods by studying the flight of birds. The coins on which these symbols appeared circulated widely within Judaea, and they too might have offended some Jews.[88]

In any case, unabashed by the emperor's rebuke over the images he tried to introduce into Jerusalem, Pilate caused further offense by using money from the Temple treasury's offerings, or *qorban* fund, to build an aqueduct for Jerusalem that brought water to the city from either 400 or 200 furlongs, or at least 23 miles, away. The money in the offerings fund came from fines paid to the Temple for offenses such as robbing tombs.[89] The Jews were compelled to accept the construction of the aqueduct, but only after a riot involving tens of thousands took place. During the riot, Pilate's soldiers, disguised as Jews, cudgeled to death and wounded large numbers of those who presumably opposed the use of the sacred monies for the project, though perhaps not the project itself.[90]

More trouble from another quarter ensued in 36 CE when an unnamed man, characterized overtly as a liar by Josephus, who implied that he had false, messianic pretensions, persuaded some Samaritans to follow him to Mt. Gerizim, site of the Samaritan Temple that had been destroyed by the Hasmonean ruler John Hyrcanus I.[91] There he promised to show them sacred tabernacle vessels supposedly buried there by Moses.[92]

The man's promise may have been connected to the story in Deuteronomy that God would raise up a prophet from among the Israelites and that he would uncover the vessels of the Temple—though the two oldest versions of a story about the hiding of sacred vessels seem to have come from the second book of Maccabees, dated between 163 and 160 BCE, and the work of Eupolemus during the mid–second century BCE and are connected not to Moses, but to Jeremiah. The difficulties and problems of connecting this story to the Samaritans—for instance, Moses never entered the promised land and therefore could not have hidden anything on Mt. Gerizim—cannot be used to rule out the possibility that there was a contemporary tradition connecting Moses and hidden vessels to the Samaritans' sacred mountain.[93]

Perhaps alarmed at the great multitude that gathered to make the climb up the mountain and presumably to witness the discovery of the sacred vessels, Pilate sent cavalry and heavy infantry to block their ascent. A battle broke out during which the soldiers slew some of those who had come to the nearby village of Tirathana or Tire, some 3.7 miles southwest of Shechem or Duwara, at the foot of Mt. Gerizim; other Jews were induced to flee. The soldiers also took many prisoners. Pilate put the leaders among them and the fugitives to death.[94]

The council of the Samaritans went to Vitellius, the legate of Syria, and accused Pilate of the murder of those who were killed.[95] Vitellius decided to send a friend of his named Marcellus to undertake the governorship among the Jews and to send Pilate back to Rome to render an account before the emperor Tiberius of the things with which the Samaritans had charged him.[96] We know virtually nothing about the governorships or administration of Marcellus from 36–37 and of his successor, possibly the cavalry commander Marullus, from 37–41.[97] Before Pilate reached Rome, however, Tiberius died, on 16 March of 37.

Any assessment of Pilate's governorship must take into account its long duration—at least 10 years.[98] It is difficult to believe that Pilate could have lasted as long as he did if he had not cooperated with influential figures in Judaea, especially in Jerusalem. The crucifixion of Jesus could be interpreted as an attempt to mollify some of those figures, with Pilate taking ultimate responsibility for the execution order, and it was probably not Pilate alone who came up with the idea of bringing the military standards or images from them into the palace in Jerusalem at night. It seems likely that Pilate tried to introduce the standards into the sanctuary and had the coins, with their Roman ritual iconography, minted during his prefecture after consulting Jews who shared interests with him. Yet Pilate's actions clearly did offend the religious sensibilities of some Jews, and he managed to alienate Samaritans as well.[99]

VITELLIUS

Vitellius, the Roman legate of Syria, on the other hand, repeatedly seems to have gone out of his way to avoid offending Jews. While Pilate was still prefect, probably in 36 CE, Vitellius made a trip up to Jerusalem when the Passover feast was being celebrated. Having been splendidly welcomed by the populace, Vitellius wanted to make some gesture of thanks for his reception. He therefore canceled all taxes on agricultural produce for the inhabitants of the city, probably applying to the time while the festival was being celebrated, and when the people apparently asked that the sacred robe of the high priest be put under their authority, the governor of Syria agreed to write to Tiberius about the request.[100] What is probably meant by the sacred robe is the high priest's ephod or apron, the breastpiece attached to it that had four rows of stones with the names of the tribes of Israel on them, and the high priest's turban that had some kind of rosette on it with the inscription, "Holy to the Lord."[101] Control over the robe was an important issue because, by tradition, the high priest had to wear the robe, originally made for Aaron, the first high priest, while he was performing his duties within the Temple.[102] Since the high priest could not carry out his sacrificial duties without the vestments, whoever controlled the high priest's vestments in effect could control the high priest and what went on in the Temple.

As he awaited Tiberius's reply about control of the robe, Vitellius was nearly dragged into a war between Herod Antipas the Tetrarch and Aretas IV, king of Petra, now in Jordan. Vitellius's actions during the conflict revealed his desire to avoid provoking Jews if possible.

The war had arisen out of a family feud. Herod Antipas had married Aretas's daughter Phasaelis but then had fallen in love with Herodias, the wife of his own half-brother Philip, the son of Herod the Great and Mariamme II, daughter of the high priest Simon. Herod the Tetrarch promised Herodias that he would divorce Aretas's daughter and then marry her after he went to Rome and transacted some business there. Herodias, however, insisted that he get rid of Aretas's daughter right away. The smitten tetrarch agreed. This was the scandalous divorce and marriage to a brother's wife that had led John the Baptist to tell Antipas that it was not lawful to have Herodias, leading to the "pleasing" dance of Herodias's daughter Salome and John's beheading.[103]

Phasaelis somehow found out about Herod's plans and asked to be sent to Machaerus, the fortress to the east of the Dead Sea. The redoubt was situated conveniently on the border between the territories of Herod and her father. After reaching Machaerus, Phasaelis, by pre-arrangement with the governor, contrived to continue her journey to Arabia and her father. As soon as she reached her father, she reported Herod's plot to him. Aretas made his daughter's humiliation and a dispute over the boundaries of Gabalis (probably meaning Gamala) the pretexts for declaring war on Herod Antipas in 36.

Both rulers delegated the prosecution of the war to commanders. A battle ensued in which Herod's forces were destroyed. Herod then sent a report of what had happened to Tiberius. The emperor ordered Vitellius to declare war on Aretas and to bring the Arab king to him in chains or to send him his head.[104]

Vitellius duly gathered together two legions of heavy infantry, as well as light-armed infantry and cavalry, and brought them to Ptolemais. As he was preparing to march down through Judaea on his way to confront Aretas, however, some men of the highest standing among the Jews went to the Roman commander and begged him not to bring his army through their territory bearing biblically forbidden images on their military standards.

Vitellius acquiesced to their request and ordered that the army be led through the great Jezreel Plain, probably the Jordan Valley, rather than through Judaea proper. Meanwhile, along with Herod and his friends, the governor separated from the army and went up to Jerusalem to sacrifice to God during the Passover festival then being celebrated (37 CE).

While he was in Jerusalem Vitellius announced that Tiberius had granted the Jews' request about the supervision of the sacred robe, giving custody of the high priest's vestments and ornaments to the priests in the Temple; he then deposed Caiaphas, the high priest, who was replaced by Jonathan, the son of Ananus.[105] Caiaphas's deposition may be an indication that he was closely associated with the disgraced Pilate.

It was also while Vitellius was in Jerusalem during the Passover celebration of 37 that he received news of the death of the emperor Tiberius on 16 March of that year. Vitellius promptly administered the oath of loyalty to the new emperor, Gaius, whose accession probably became official on 21 April, and suspended his campaign against Aretas. Vitellius presumably wanted to make sure that the war against Aretas had the blessing of the new emperor. Vitellius then returned to Antioch. Coincidentally, Aretas, after receiving an ambiguous sign from his consultation of the flight of birds, also decided to suspend his prosecution of the war.[106] We are not told how Phasaelis took her father's decision.

CHAPTER 4

The Owl and the Golden Chain

THE ADVENTURES OF YOUNG AGRIPPA

The Roman emperor Tiberius's death on 16 March of 37 CE and Gaius's accession to the purple in Rome led to a reversal of fortune for Herod the Great's grandson, Marcus Iulius Agrippa I (b. 10 BCE). Agrippa's good fortune and success as the last king of Judaea were equally implausible, given the nearly unblemished record of irresponsibility and poor judgment that he established as a young man.

Agrippa I was the son of Aristobulus IV, who was executed by Herod in 7 BCE for plotting the king's assassination.[1] After his father's death Agrippa was taken to Rome when he was six by his mother Berenice, the daughter of Herod's sister Salome. There she and young Agrippa became friends of Antonia Minor, the younger daughter of Mark Antony and Octavia Minor and the niece of the emperor Augustus. While he was in Rome, Agrippa also befriended Drusus, the son of the future emperor Tiberius.[2] From boyhood, then, Agrippa was close to men and women at the center of power in Iulio-Claudian Rome.

As long as his mother was alive, Josephus tells us, Agrippa kept his natural tendency toward profligacy in check. Following her death, however, he indulged his own tastes and was free with his gifts to others. As a result, Agrippa fell into debt to some of the emperor's freedmen and then lost his strongest connection within the imperial family when Drusus perhaps was poisoned by the praetorian prefect Sejanus in 23 CE. In debt and depressed, Agrippa, now an adult, did what debtors do. He skipped town and fled back to Judaea.[3]

The change of scene did not alter his habits or his fortunes. So he considered suicide while sequestered in a tower at Malatha in Idumaea. Agrippa's wife Cypros staged an intervention, securing for him an allowance from the tetrarch Herod Antipas, husband of Agrippa's sister Herodias, and also got him a job as market commissioner (*agoranomos*) of Tiberias. Market commissioners made sure that the weights and measures used to determine the value of items traded in markets adhered to a known standard, and they also had responsibility for the quality control of products.[4] Becoming a market commissioner put the office's holder on a fast and easy track to financial security and at least local influence. Agrippa now appeared to be on his way to a more stable future. Unfortunately, after living *la dolce vita* in Rome in the company of the imperial heir apparent, Agrippa wasn't well suited to spending his time regulating the price of fish from the Sea of Galilee. After arguing with his brother-in-law, Agrippa moved on again, this time north to Antioch, where he was put up by an old friend from his Roman days, the governor of Syria, Lucius Pomponius Flaccus.[5]

The renewed friendship didn't last very long. Agrippa soon alienated his host. He did so by accepting a large sum of money from the Damascenes to influence Flaccus to take their side in a case about a boundary dispute with the city of Tyre that Flaccus was supposed to adjudicate. When Flaccus heard about the payment to Agrippa, he broke off the friendship. His suddenly unwelcome guest packed up and headed south to Ptolemais.[6]

Once he was settled in Ptolemais, Agrippa pressured his own freedman Marsyas into borrowing money from Protos, a former freedman of Berenice, to pay for his return trip to Italy. He got the money, but before he could get away, while he was in Anthedon (Agrippias), Gaius Herennius Capito, the procurator of Iamnia, sent soldiers after Agrippa to collect the 300,000 drachmas that he owed the imperial treasury.[7] Although he promised to stay put and face the charges against him, Agrippa promptly fled to Alexandria in Egypt, a short voyage ahead of Capito's tax collectors.[8]

In Alexandria, Agrippa was saved once again by his wife. Cypros borrowed money to send her husband back to Italy from the alabarch or customs superintendent Alexander Lysimachus, the father of Tiberius Iulius Alexander (later Titus's chief of staff), after he refused to lend any money to Agrippa personally. The alabarch supposedly gave Cypros the money because he was so impressed by her deep love for her husband. Flush again, Agrippa hopped a ship to Puteoli, while Cypros returned to Judaea with the children.[9]

In Italy the emperor Tiberius at first welcomed Agrippa back into his sphere of friends and acquaintances on the island of Capri, where the emperor lived to get away from Rome. But once Tiberius found out from Capito about the money Agrippa owed to the treasury, he banned him from his company.[10]

Undaunted and unabashed, Agrippa turned to Antonia. For the sake of her friendship with Agrippa's mother, Berenice, Antonia loaned Agrippa 300,000 drachmas to pay off his debt to the imperial treasury.[11]

Welcomed back into the circle of Tiberius, Agrippa became a friend of Antonia's grandson Gaius (Caligula). The friendship was enhanced by means of a loan of one million drachmas that Agrippa got from a good, and better still rich, Samaritan freedman of Tiberius, which he used to pay back Antonia the money he owed her and to entertain her grandson.[12]

Yet Agrippa retained his talent for scoring goals against himself just when victory was in sight. While he was out for a spin in a chariot with his young friend Gaius, Agrippa seized upon the occasion to make a prayer that Tiberius would give up rule as soon as possible in favor of Gaius who, he added, was more able in every way. The prayer no doubt was meant to flatter Gaius. That was easy to do, as Agrippa would soon find out, because Gaius had delusions not just of grandeur but also of divinity. Unfortunately, however, Agrippa's prayer was also overheard by his chariot driver, a freedman named Eutuchus, who reported it verbatim to Tiberius after getting into a spat with his employer over some clothes he stole from Agrippa. Tiberius was not amused. Agrippa was put in chains and sentenced to prison in 36 CE.[13]

THE OWL AND THE GOLDEN CHAIN

As he stood in front of the palace in iron chains on his way to jail, Agrippa, still dressed in crimson, leaned against a tree upon which lit a horned owl. Another prisoner, a German, informed Agrippa that the owl had been dispatched by the gods to foretell that he would be released from his irons and advanced to the height of honor and power. But when Agrippa saw the owl again, he was warned, he would die within five days.[14] In exchange for revealing what the gods had in store for Agrippa, the unnamed German prophet only asked Agrippa to help him gain release once Agrippa was free.[15]

Soon after Gaius became emperor, the first part of the prophecy came true. A few days after Tiberius's funeral ended, Gaius freed Agrippa and made him the king of the tetrarchy that had belonged to Philip. The tetrarchy had Panias (renamed Caesarea Philippi) as its focal point. Gaius added the tetrarchy of Lysanias, farther to the north, to Agrippa's realm. Taking a cue from the new emperor, the Senate bestowed the *insignia* of a praetor upon the new king.[16] These included the right to wear the Roman toga with the broad purple stripe indicating senatorial rank (*latus clavus*), to be preceded by lictors bearing bundles of rods and axes (*fasces*) as he walked about, and to sit on the folding ivory seat used by higher Roman magistrates, the *sella curulis.* To symbolize Agrippa's reversal of fortune, Gaius also gave the new king a golden chain equal in weight to the iron one with which he had been bound.[17]

Areas in the Galilee, including Tiberias, where Agrippa later would have coins minted, and the Peraea, across the Jordan to the east, were joined to Agrippa's kingdom in 39 after his brother-in-law Herod Antipas and his wife Herodias, in a fit of jealousy over Agrippa's acquisition of a kingdom and the royal title, went to Rome to petition Gaius for a kingdom and crown of Antipas's own. But Gaius—after learning that Herod Antipas kept arms for 70,000 heavy infantry in store, supposedly had conspired with Sejanus to overthrow Tiberius, and was conspiring with the Parthians—instead took away Herod's tetrarchy and then exiled Herod and his wife to Spain or Lugdunum (Lyons) in Gaul.[18] Gaul seems to have been the preferred exile destination for out-of-favor Herodians.

Against his own track record and long odds, Agrippa had somehow come right. The German prisoner turned out to be a reliable source for what the gods had in mind for Agrippa. Circumstances were now favorable for a prolonged period of good relations between the Jews of the region Agrippa ruled and Rome. Agrippa was the emperor's personal friend and had the ear of a ruler who was easy to flatter and therefore to manipulate. Soon, however, Gaius's pretensions to divinity nearly led to the outbreak of war.[19]

At Gaius's suggestion, Agrippa traveled to his new kingdom by way of Alexandria in Egypt, primarily to take advantage of the midsummer Etesian winds that would make for a quick trip across the sea.[20] Agrippa also was given the job of delivering the new emperor's instructions (*mandata*) to Flaccus, the Roman governor of Egypt, while he was in Alexandria and seeing to the renewal of Flaccus's ruling authority or *imperium,* which had lapsed at the death of Tiberius.

Carrying out the emperor's instructions should have been easy, and Agrippa probably anticipated a pleasant stay in Alexandria. What he found there, however, was a city seething with interethnic enmity. Soon after he left, that hatred gave rise to open violence, partly because of the failure of the Roman governor and the Roman emperor to protect Alexandria's Jews from their neighbors. Almost the exact same sequence of events played out later in Caesarea, leading to the outbreak of the great revolt in Judaea in 66.[21] It was no historical accident that, even after the destruction of the Temple and a large part of Jerusalem in 70, after Titus's and Vespasian's triumph in Rome in 71, and after the fall of Masada in 74, ethnic violence in Alexandria continued. Regional conflict between Jews and non-Jews that sympathetic Romans could not control and that unsympathetic Romans had no wish to alleviate provided the kindling for a war of Jews against Romans.

GAIUS AND THE JEWS

Agrippa arrived in Egypt by the end of July or in early August of 38 CE.[22] (See map 3.) At some point after his arrival in Alexandria Agrippa paid a visit to the gymnasium where a crowd was celebrating Flaccus's reappointment as governor. During the celebrations a street beggar named Carabbas was brought into the gymnasium dressed up in faux royal attire and surrounded by a bodyguard. It is possible that the gymnasiarch (head of the gymnasium) Isidorus, a Greek well known as an opponent of Alexandria's Jews, organized the charade.[23] Whoever was behind the skit, it would have been difficult for people to miss the point that Agrippa was being satirized as a phony, beggar king.

Agrippa's reception from the Jews of Alexandria was more respectful. They requested that he send along their decree honoring Gaius's accession, which Flaccus apparently had refused to transmit a year before, and they also asked Agrippa to forward to the emperor a longer supplication about their suffering, perhaps related to lawsuits dated to early in 38.[24]

At some point after Agrippa moved on from Alexandria, Alexandrians (non-Jews) assembled in the theater at dawn and began to agitate to have images or *eikones* erected in the prayer houses (synagogues) of the Jews. These images might have been representations of the emperor Gaius. But any representation of a living being would have constituted a violation of the biblical injunction against graven images.[25] The Jews of Alexandria resisted but apparently to no effect.[26] The incident led Flaccus to publish an edict, probably on Gaius's authority, that denounced the Jews as foreigners and immigrants who did not have the right to speak and who could be sentenced without a judgment.[27] In effect, by this edict Flaccus changed the status of the community of Jews from legal residents of Alexandria to foreigners. This change in status had immediate consequences.

It became clear subsequently that the terms of the decree compelled the Jews of the city to live in one quarter of the city's neighborhoods, rather than in many, as they had in the past, on pain of death.[28] It is very likely that the neighborhood to which they were legally confined was the so-called Delta Quarter of the city, where the Jews of the original, late-fourth-century BCE Macedonian military settlement made their homes.[29]

Even so, a mob entered into the Delta Quarter, attacked the meeting houses there, and in the houses they did not destroy they set up images of Gaius; they also installed a statue of Queen Cleopatra (which Cleopatra we do not know), mounted on an old chariot in the largest synagogue.[30] Jews who were found outside of the Delta Quarter were attacked, tortured, and killed, and their possessions and property were stolen.[31] Thirty-eight members of the council of elders or *gerousia* of the Jews who had refused to leave their homes outside of the Delta Quarter were arrested, tried, and executed in the theater during the emperor's birthday celebrations (which lasted until 31 August).[32]

In the aftermath of this massacre Flaccus was arrested in the autumn of 38, though not as a result of failing to protect Jews or their property. Rather, he was relieved of his duties for allowing the Jews to be despoiled while the *iustitium,* or suspension of judicial operations, during the official mourning period for the death of Gaius's sister Drusilla was supposed to be in effect. The appointment of Flaccus's replacement, Vitrasius Pollio, did not materially change the Jews' legal situation.[33]

In the spring or early summer of 39 delegations of five prominent Jews and five Alexandrians assembled in Rome before the emperor Gaius.[34] The Jews seem to have been summoned to Rome for a hearing about their civic rights.[35]

The Greek grammarian and sophist Apion was the leader of the delegates sent to Rome on behalf of the gentile Alexandrians.[36] The aristocratic Jewish Alexandrian philosopher Philo was the head of the delegation of Jews.[37] Apion was famous for his learning, his self-love, and his energy. Gaius's predecessor Tiberius referred to the Alexandrian as the *cymbalum mundi,* or gong of the world; the emperor did not intend this sobriquet as a compliment. Apion was apparently a bit too noisy, perhaps about himself, for Tiberius's tastes.[38] Apion was also no lover of Jews or Judaism. After completing his

Antiquities of the Jews, in fact, Josephus felt compelled to compose a comprehensive refutation of Apion's slanders against the Jews (*Against Apion*).[39]

When he appeared before Gaius, Apion asserted that while all the subject peoples of the Roman empire had dedicated altars and temples to Gaius and in all other ways had paid him the same respect as they did to the gods, the Jews alone disdained to honor him with statues or to swear an oath by his name.[40] Apion and his Alexandrian colleagues thus were in Rome essentially to accuse the Jews of being unwilling to acknowledge Gaius's divinity.[41] Gaius was impressed by Apion's presentation and no doubt accepted its fundamental premise, as is clear from what followed.

According to Philo's account of what happened next, during the hearing Gaius's questions to the Jews were directed toward finding out if they believed he was a god or not. When the Jews protested that they had made sacrifices at his accession, a second time when he recovered from a disease, and a third time when he defeated the Germans, the emperor answered that they had not sacrificed to him.[42] Gaius also asked the Jews why they didn't eat pig's flesh and what their constitution's principles of justice were. As they were replying Gaius cut them off and ran into another house to deal with the hanging of some pictures. When he returned he announced that the Jews were not so much wicked as unfortunate and foolish because they did not believe that he had been endowed with God's nature.[43]

When he was out of the emperor's earshot Philo reportedly said to the Jews who accompanied him that they needed to take courage, for Gaius's anger against them was a matter of speech. But indeed the young emperor already was lining up God against himself.[44]

Philo was right. But, as so often, God decided to take his time before moving against the divine pretender, and before that happened, his chosen people in Judaea nearly found themselves on the wrong side of Rome's famed and feared legions.

PUBLIUS PETRONIUS

Gaius's first deed was to replace Vitellius as the governor of Syria. The Jews of Judaea probably did not welcome the change. During Tiberius's reign, as we have seen, Vitellius literally had marched his army far out of its way to avoid offending the Jews in Judaea. To replace Vitellius, Gaius sent out Publius Petronius (who served as governor from 39–42). Gaius probably assumed that Petronius would be less sympathetic to the Jews than Vitellius had been and at least would follow direct orders without hesitation.[45] He was proved wrong on both counts.

In the summer of 39 Gaius directed Petronius to lead a large force into Judaea and, if the Jews received him willingly, to set up a statue or statues of Gaius as Zeus in the Temple. This was, of course, a clear violation of the biblical prohibition against the erection of such images by Jews anywhere, above all in the Temple.[46] But if the Jews resisted, Gaius commanded, the governor was ordered to set up the statues by force.[47]

Philo of Alexandria may supply the background to understanding Gaius's order. In his work on *The Embassy to Gaius* Philo tells his readers that in the city of Iamnia some non-Jews, who had learned about how eager Gaius was for deification and his hostility toward Jews, had constructed a mud-brick altar. The Jews in the city, considering the altar to be a defilement, destroyed it. Their opponents then wrote to Capito, who was the collector of imperial revenues in Judaea, and he reported the incident to the emperor. Gaius then ordered the statue of himself as Jupiter (Zeus) to be set up in the Jerusalem Temple in retaliation.[48] The non-Jewish residents of Iamnia may have dedicated the altar to Gaius; building it in any case was an assertion that Iamnia belonged to them. The reaction of the Jews there represented their claim that Iamnia belonged to Judaea. Gaius's reaction to all of this was his response to a challenge both to Roman authority and to his own self-identification.[49]

Taking over the governorship, Petronius set about carrying out Gaius's orders. After gathering up a large force of auxiliary soldiers from Syria, he led two or three of the four legions stationed in Syria down to Ptolemais.[50] His plan was to winter in Ptolemais and then, toward the spring, to wage war. Meanwhile, he wrote to the emperor informing him of what he intended to do. Gaius praised Petronius for his zeal and ordered him not to hold back but to make war with vigor if the Jews continued to be disobedient.[51]

While Petronius was still in Ptolemais, however, tens of thousands of Jews came to the plain in front of the town and petitioned him not to use force to make them violate their ancestral law. Petronius quickly realized that it would be impossible for him to carry out Gaius's order without causing much blood to be shed. So gathering up his friends and an entourage of attendants, he left the statues he had brought along with his troops in Ptolemais and made his way to Tiberias in the Galilee.[52] After arriving in the Galilee Petronius began to assess the situation of the Jews there. The analysis did not require deep thought about the potential consequences of following Gaius's orders.

Once again tens of thousands of Jews came to Petronius. They urged him not to put them under such necessity nor to pollute the city of Jerusalem by putting a statue up in it. Petronius asked the Jews if they would go to war with Caesar regardless of Petronius's military preparation and their own weakness. The Jews reminded Petronius that they sacrificed twice daily for Caesar and the Roman people and told him that they would not fight. But they would die rather than violate their own laws. Falling on their faces they then bared their throats and declared that they were ready to die right there and then. These demonstrations went on for 40 days.[53]

Further pressure not to enforce Gaius's order was brought to bear upon Petronius by Aristobulus, the brother of King Agrippa; Alexas Helcias the Elder, prefect or army commander, not Roman governor, and friend of King Agrippa; powerful members of Agrippa's house; and civic leaders. All these men appealed to Petronius to write to Gaius and inform him of their opposition to receiving the statue. They asked the governor to tell the emperor how they had left their fields to sit and protest, that they did not wish to make war, since they were not able to, but that they too would die with pleasure rather than breach their laws.[54]

Petronius convened some kind of assembly of the petitioners at Tiberias. At the meeting he announced his intention to send a letter to Gaius explaining the opposition to the emperor's order and setting out his own case for respecting the Jews' resistance. In his letter Petronius first made the eminently practical point that if the Romans killed all the Jews who refused to carry out his order then he (the emperor) would be robbed of their revenue. On top of that, he added, Gaius would be placed beneath the ban of a curse in perpetuity.[55]

Although there had been a drought that year, at the end of Petronius's speech there was a heavy rain shower. Petronius understood the downpour as a sign of divine favor. It too was noted in his missive to the emperor.[56] Learned Jews such as Philo may have seen the providential shower as a sign that their lord was stirring.

Before Gaius received Petronius's letter, Gaius's boyhood friend King Agrippa I, who was in Rome at the time, already had persuaded the emperor to abandon his attempt to enforce his original order or, at least, not to force the Jews to accept the erection of the statue, if it had not already been erected. He did so by explaining to Gaius why Jews did not allow any figure made by the hands of men to enter the sanctuary of God.[57] Agrippa's argument was an attempt to persuade Gaius that the Jews' resistance to his order was nothing personal. If Romulus himself came back to life and ordered them to put his own statue in the Temple, the Jews still would not do it.

When Gaius received Petronius's missive he somehow wrongly concluded that the Jews were about to revolt. He therefore wrote an angry, threatening letter to Petronius. The letter informed the governor that all men in the present and the future would cite him as *the* example that the orders of the emperor were never to be contradicted. He then ordered Petronius to be a judge in his own case.[58] Since the anger of the emperor was understood as death for its recipient (*ira principis mors est*), such a suggestion usually was taken by upper-class Romans as an invitation to do the honorable thing and commit suicide. Doing so would spare the emperor the expense and public embarrassment of having to send someone out to do the job.

Because of inclement weather the bearers of the emperor's letter were held up at sea for three months. In the meantime Petronius received another letter. This one bore more congenial news for both Petronius and the Jews.

Gaius had been assassinated on 24 January 41 CE by the military tribune Cassius Chaerea, Cornelius Sabinus, and others at the Palatine Games that Livia had established in honor of Augustus.[59] Gaius apparently had insulted Cassius Chaerea's manhood by instructing him to use names such as Priapus and Venus as the daily passwords of the praetorian guards. Statues of the fertility god Priapus usually featured his super-sized, erect penis. Chaerea apparently took the passwords as none-too-subtle references to his erotic prowess—or perhaps lack thereof. Gaius's sense of humor was difficult to understand and dangerous to interpret.[60]

Gaius's assassination saved Petronius from having to commit suicide and the Jews of Judaea from having to endure the profanation of their Temple. The learned Alexandrian Philo had been right, or at least partly right: Gaius had been lining up God against himself. Chaerea arguably was his chosen instrument.

CLAUDIUS AND THE KING

The new emperor Claudius, the youngest brother of Germanicus and uncle of the assassinated emperor Gaius, was urged to seek the throne by King Agrippa after Gaius's death. Agrippa also played a key role in persuading the hesitant Roman senators to accept Claudius as the next emperor. Not coincidentally, after Claudius became emperor he published an edict, subsequently engraved on bronze tablets deposited on the capitol, that confirmed Agrippa's rule over his grandfather Herod's core kingdom (comprising Judaea and Sa-maritis). To his kingdom were added Trachonitis, Auranitis, Abila (Abela) in the tetrarchy of Lysanias (in Syria, northwest of Damascus), and land within the mountain area of Lebanon (the Anti-Lebanon). (See map 2.) A treaty be-tween Agrippa and the Roman Senate and people later was celebrated by Claudius with Agrippa in the middle of the Roman Forum.[61] Agrippa subse-quently had coins struck in Caesarea commemorating the signing of the treaty.[62]

At the stroke of a stylus Claudius had transferred a Roman province back into the hands of a king, adding new territory for good measure, though not the Greek cities Herod the Great had ruled over.[63] Who was emperor mat-tered, and Claudius's action, the implications of which have never been fully appreciated by scholars, shows that it was not inconceivable for Jews in Ju-daea and elsewhere to aspire to live within a polity that was not ruled directly by foreigners. Agrippa was also given the rank of a Roman consul, and his brother Herod, ruler of Chalcis, was elevated to the rank of a praetor.[64] Why did Claudius take these actions?

After Gaius nearly incited a war in the region, perhaps Claudius thought that it would be better to return to the model of Herod the Great's rule, hop-ing that Agrippa, like his grandfather, would be able to keep the peace in the neighborhood without compromising Rome's interests. It was a bet, probably based on Agrippa's recent record of diplomatic success in the capital. And it might have worked but for the unfortunate reappearance of that owl.

STRIFE IN ALEXANDRIA (AGAIN)

At the same time, strife broke out again between the Jews and Greeks living in the polis of the Alexandrians in Egypt. At the death of Gaius, the ethnos of the Jews in Alexandria, which had been degraded and outraged during his reign, was encouraged and immediately took up arms, according to Josephus. Claudius ordered the prefect of Egypt to snuff out the unrest.

After he was petitioned by Agrippa and Herod, the emperor also report-edly issued an edict both to Alexandria and Syria. The edict concluded that none of the rights should be lost to the ethnos of the Jews because of the madness of Gaius, but that their former privileges should be safeguarded to them as long as they adhered to their own customs. Claudius also instructed both the Jews and the Greeks to take the greatest foresight to prevent any upheaval after the publication of the decree.[65]

A second decree was sent to "the rest of the world." In the decree Claudius ordered that the same privileges were to be guarded for the Jews throughout the empire under the Romans as those in Alexandria, not only because he had been petitioned by Kings Agrippa and Herod but also because of the Jews' loyalty and friendship toward the Romans. He went on to say that it was just that no Greek city be deprived of such rights and privileges that had been assured to them during the time of divine Augustus. He also stated that it was right that the Jews throughout the whole world under Roman rule should be permitted to observe the customs of their fathers without obstruction. He nevertheless charged Jews to take advantage of his philanthropy in a more moderate way and not to set at nothing the beliefs about the gods held by other peoples but to observe their own laws.[66] The second decree, in other words, was an admonition by the emperor for Greeks and Jews alike to respect each other's legally granted rights and protected beliefs.

Scholars have raised serious questions about the authenticity of these edicts based upon their style and content. Some have considered them to be authentic imperial documents that Josephus nevertheless manipulated, most importantly, to show that Claudius restored the rights to all the Jews in Alexandria that had been recognized by Augustus. Others have argued that at least the first edict is essentially a forgery. The case for it being a forgery is supported by the evidence from two papyri that shows that Claudius did not restore the legal rights of all Alexandrian Jews in 41.[67]

From a fragmentary papyrus dated to the first century CE we know that some kind of embassy from the Alexandrians was sent to Claudius and met with the emperor before 1 May of 41, when Claudius ordered that Isidorus, one of the Greeks who had been involved in activities against the Jews in 38, be put to death.[68]

In the aftermath of that embassy, Isidorus's sentencing, and another initiative from the Alexandrians (non-Jews), Claudius sent a letter to Alexandria that was posted in the city by the prefect on 10 November of 41.[69] In the last part of the letter Claudius addressed the "war" between the Alexandrians and the Jews.[70] He ordered the Alexandrians not to disturb Jews who had lived in Alexandria for a long time and to allow them to follow their religious customs.[71] The Jews were told not to busy themselves with anything beyond what they previously had, never to send two delegations again as if they lived in two cities, not to intrude upon the gymnasium, and not to invite immigrants from the rest of Egypt and Syria.[72]

What Claudius's order to the Alexandrians probably meant was that they should not interfere with the religious rights of the longtime inhabitants of the Delta Quarter of the city.[73] As far as the Jews were concerned, Claudius's ruling implied that he would not restore political rights taken away by Gaius from those Jews who lived outside the Delta Section. The separate embassies referred to by Claudius is probably an allusion to two sets of representatives: one group representing the Jews who had lost their rights from outside the Delta Quarter and a second group representing Jews of the Delta Quarter whose property had been destroyed during the governorship of Flaccus. It is possible that Claudius's admonition about intruding upon the gymnasium was connected to Jews' interfering with it because of the anti-Jewish activities that had arisen there previously. Finally, Claudius's order to Jews not to invite immigrants from Syria and Egypt affirmed Flaccus's edict against the immigration of Jews to Alexandria. Overall, Claudius's letter confirmed the status quo established by Gaius and Flaccus.[74]

It may well be correct that Josephus interpreted or misinterpreted Claudius's letter to the Alexandrians to put Claudius's response to the situation in Alexandria at the time in the best possible light with respect to all the Jews who had lived in Alexandria and were living there in 41.[75] Claudius, we should recall, for reasons that scholars have never been able to persuasively account for, at the very same time issued an order expelling Jews from Rome.[76] It is possible that the expulsion was related to the strife in Alexandria and the worry that there could be trouble between Jews and other ethnic groups in Rome.

Whatever the explanation for that expulsion decree, Claudius did not give back to the Jews who had lived outside the Delta Quarter of Alexandria legal residency or the political rights that Gaius had taken away from them, breaking with the policies of Augustus and Tiberius. Gaius made those Jews into immigrants and foreigners and prohibited more "foreigners" from immigrating to the city legally. The legal rights of Jews to worship were restricted to one small quarter of Alexandria.

Not far from Agrippa's new kingdom then, the civic status and legal rights of Jews were subject to legal challenge and violence, and Claudius, often seen as sympathetic to the rights of Jews, at best recognized the rights of only one group of Jews living in one district of Alexandria. A similar dispute over territory and legal rights in Caesarea fanned the flames of ethnic conflict between Greeks and Jews during the reign of Nero and put Rome and the Jews on a collision course.

THE REIGN OF AGRIPPA I

Once Agrippa reached Jerusalem he made sacrifices, leaving out nothing of the things stipulated to be performed according to the law. He then ordered a considerable number of Nazirites to be shaven.[77]

The Nazirites were Jews, both men and women, who signaled their consecration to God for a specified time by abstaining from all products made from grapes, by avoiding contact with corpses, and by not cutting their hair: hence, the origins of their name, from the Hebrew noun *nazir,* or someone who is separate (that is, consecrated).[78] After the period of their "separation" was completed the Nazirites purified their bodies by immersing themselves in a *miqveh* and then made gifts to God of a lamb for a burnt offering, a ewe as a sin offering, a ram as a peace offering, and a basket of unleavened bread, along with grain and drink offerings. These offerings would have been brought to the Court of the Nazirites at the southeast corner of the Court of Women in the Temple complex, where a priest presented them to God.[79] After making these gifts the Nazirites shaved their hair and put the hair in the same fire under the peace offering (the ram). Once they had fulfilled their vows and made their offerings the Nazirites were allowed to drink wine.[80]

What Agrippa probably did for the Nazirites was to subsidize the cost of the offerings they made. From this it might be inferred that what Agrippa was trying to do was to make it possible for poorer Jews to express their piety. But we know that such "separations" or consecrations appealed to wealthy people as well; Queen Helena of Adiabene, for instance, was later reported to have undertaken a vow to live as a Nazirite for seven years if her son Izates returned safely from a war.[81] Agrippa's generosity is more plausibly interpreted as an attempt to gain a general reputation for piety, perhaps to help balance whatever people had heard about his profligate lifestyle in Rome.[82]

The flip side of that piety and the desire to display, it according to the author of the Acts of the Apostles, was Agrippa's treatment of Jews who perhaps appeared to him to deviate too energetically from standard teachings and interpretations of the law.[83] For instance, he had the apostle James, son of Zebedee, beheaded in 44, and he executed the guards who let Peter escape after he had imprisoned him.[84] The way that the Acts' author relates the story, it was precisely Agrippa's impiety that led to his death, described later in this chapter.

Agrippa also hung up the golden chain, which had been presented to him by Gaius, over the treasure chamber within the Temple precincts. The dedication of the golden chain was supposed to be a symbol to show all men that

Agrippa had once been thrown into prison and stripped of his former status but that, not a long time afterward, had come out of his chains and been up-lifted to rule as king.[85] Agrippa no doubt meant the display of the golden chain to convey a message of hope to his subjects. But he also took more prac-tical steps to make his point.

Agrippa displaced Theophilus, the brother-in-law of Caiaphas, from the high priesthood and gave the office to Simon Cantheras.[86] The tax on every house in Jerusalem was revoked, and Silas was appointed to be head of the whole army. Later, Silas would be removed from his position and impris-oned after reminding the king a little too persistently how often he (Silas) had previously suffered hardships on the king's behalf.[87]

Afterward, at some time during the early 40s, Agrippa was compelled to deal with certain young men of the Sidonian-influenced coastal city of Dor (Tel Dor now in Israel, nine miles north of Caesarea), who had set up a statue of the emperor Claudius in a synagogue there. Since introducing a graven im-age of the emperor into a space set aside for reading holy scripture would defile the synagogue, the young Dorians presumably were not any of the Jews who lived in the city; what they did was a deliberate provocation, similar to what the non-Jewish residents of Iamnia had done when they built the altar to Gaius there. Reading beneath the lines of Josephus's report about the incident, what the young Dorians were trying to do was to assert that Dor belonged to non-Jews. The significance of their action was recognized immediately.

Without delay Agrippa went to see Petronius, who was still serving as the legate of Syria. Agrippa's intervention indicates that at the time Dor fell under the administrative authority of the governor of Syria. Petronius wrote a letter to the leading men of Dor ordering that those who had placed the image in the synagogue be brought to him by the centurion Proclus Vitellius. The legate reminded the Dorians that Jews were allowed to follow their own customs and had equal status in the community, as ordered by an edict of the emperor himself. The Syrian governor also implied that the reason why the young men had placed the statue in the building was to incite strife, and he warned the leaders of Dor to seek no excuse for sedition or public upheaval but for each to follow his own customs.[88]

Whatever we make of the contents of the letter Petronius supposedly wrote, the greater significance of the episode is what it reveals about relations between the king and the governor of the province of Syria and the role played by the king in bringing the traditional rights and customs of Jews to the gover-nor's attention.[89] Just as governors of Syria could and did intervene in Judaea and indeed south of Judaea, so too Rome's client king Agrippa thought it was appropriate for him to intercede with Syria's governor far away from Jerusalem to protect the rights of Jews. Modern historians want clear and transparent definitions of jurisdictions among Roman governors and local rulers. The reality on the ground was that both sets of administrators acted in ways that were consistent with their jurisdictions as they understood or interpreted them. Those interpretations were often personal and subject to dispute and revision. By far the best example of this from the region during the era was the non-existent "trial" of Jesus.[90]

Once the situation in Dor had been resolved, Agrippa moved to replace Simon Cantheras as high priest for reasons that are not specified.[91] Originally Agrippa wished to reappoint Jonathan, son of Ananus, but after Jonathan demurred, on his recommendation his brother Matthias was appointed to the position. (Later in Agrippa's reign Matthias would be replaced by Elionaeus.) At around the same time (42 CE), Petronius was replaced as governor of Syria by Vibius Marsus.[92] Again, we are not sure why this change was made. It was not a fortuitous change of personnel for Jews.

Some time after Marsus took up his post, Agrippa set about building a new north defensive wall for Jerusalem. (See map 4.) The northern side of the city was the only side not at least partially defended by the deep valleys surrounding Jerusalem on its other sides (Kidron to the east, Tyropoeon and Hinnom to the west and south). Had the wall been completed as planned, it would have made Jerusalem invulnerable to any subsequent siege, according to Josephus. But Agrippa's activities were reported to Claudius by Marsus, the new governor of Syria, and the emperor, fearing or, more likely, being led to fear some kind of revolution wrote to Agrippa charging him to cease building the wall. The king decided it was best not to disobey such a direct order from Claudius, even though Claudius arguably owed his position to Agrippa.[93] Agrippa was a king and a "Friend of Caesar," as inscriptions on coins minted during his reign proclaimed him.[94] But he was still a subject, and it was better not to provoke a confrontation over a construction project.

Although Claudius ordered Agrippa to cancel his work on the new north wall of Jerusalem, the emperor did not prevent the king from endowing other cities with monuments and spectacles, following the Herodian model of what ambitious kings did. Thus Agrippa had built a theater, amphitheater, baths, and porticoes for Berytus. At the dedication of the theater he exhibited spectacles, including all kinds of musical entertainment, and in the amphitheater, he arranged for no less than 700 "malefactors" to fight another 700 to entertain the spectators.[95] Among other construction projects associated with the reign of Agrippa I were the renovation of the hippodrome/stadium in Caesarea Maritima and a road station (some kind of guarded checkpoint) at Archelaïs.[96]

Josephus tells us that from the territories he ruled over Agrippa derived 12 million drachmas, but still had to borrow money because his expenses exceeded his means.[97] Old Herodian habits died hard. These expenses presumably included the cost of the construction projects and benefactions made outside his own kingdom.

As a patron of buildings, art, and events in cities outside his own realm that could not be traced back to any traditions of the Jews, Agrippa followed in the footsteps of his grandfather Herod the Great. When, like Herod, he tried to play a larger role in regional politics, however, the limits of his power and political skill were made clear to him. Claudius apparently thought that one Herod the Great had been enough.

While he was in Tiberias Agrippa was visited by Antiochus IV, king of Commagene (in southern Turkey); Sampsigeramus, king of Emesa (Homs), along the Orontes River in Syria; Cotys, king of Armenia Minor; Polemon, king of Pontus (along the Black Sea coast); and his own brother Herod, who ruled over Chalcis. (See maps 2 and 3.) Agrippa entertained all of these five Roman client kings royally. As Agrippa was feting them, however, Vibius Marsus, the governor of Syria, approached the city. We do not know if Marsus's appearance was a coincidence or if he somehow had got wind of the meeting and came to the lakeside city for that reason.

In any event, at Marsus's approach, Agrippa, accompanied by the other kings in his carriage, went out about one mile from the city to meet the Roman governor, very likely as a sign of diplomatic courtesy and respect. Marsus, however, seeing the group of regional kings all together, became suspicious and somehow concluded that their meeting was a threat to Roman security. He therefore sent out subordinates to the kings, telling each of them to set off without delay to his own territory.

Under the circumstances Agrippa could hardly have understood Marsus's order as a vote of confidence in his loyalty. This incident seems to have poisoned relations between the two men.[98]

THE DEATH OF AGRIPPA I

At the end of the third year of his reign over Herod's kingdom and the lands added to it by Claudius, Agrippa traveled to Caesarea. There Agrippa celebrated spectacles in honor of Caesar.[99] Attending the festival were a large number of men who had held offices in the kingdom or had advanced to worthy positions. At daybreak on the second day of the spectacles Agrippa entered the theater of Caesarea wearing a garment of woven silver. His flatterers raised their voices from various directions, addressing Agrippa as if he were more than mortal.

The greeting was surely prearranged and indicates that Agrippa somehow wished to receive the kind of honors that had been bestowed upon Greeks or even Romans in the past but never upon Jews, though it is no doubt wrong to understand such honors as implying that Agrippa sought divine worship. The physical setting of the episode is crucial; it took place in Caesarea, the city Herod the Great had built as an urban center in which extraordinary honors were routinely paid to living Roman emperors. Agrippa wasn't the emperor. But he also wasn't just another petty king either, as the Alexandrians had implied.

In confirmation of his aspirations, Agrippa did not reject the flattery of the sycophants as impious. But shortly thereafter he looked up and saw an owl roosting on a rope above his head. Agrippa immediately recognized the owl's appearance as a sign of his impending doom, just as the owl's epiphany when Agrippa had been imprisoned by Tiberius was a harbinger of a reversal of fortune. We are told that the king was suddenly seized by a stabbing pain in his heart and by an ache in his stomach. After five days of agony Agrippa died in the palace of Caesarea at the age of 54.[100] Although he could not know it, Agrippa would achieve, if not the kind of contemporary honors he desired, lasting fame. Agrippa was the last king of Judaea.

Before the populace became aware that the king had died, Herod, the king of Chalcis, and Helcias, the prefect of the army, sent a man named Ariston to slay Agrippa's imprisoned general, Silas, pretending that this was done by the king's order. After it became known that Agrippa had passed away, the people—clearly non-Jews of Caesarea and Sebaste—forgetting the king's benefactions, hurled insults at Agrippa and his daughters, celebrated feasts, made libations to Charon, the ferryman of the dead, and toasted the king's death.

Those who had been serving in the auxiliary military went to their homes, and taking hold of statues of the king's daughters—Berenice, Mariamme, and Drusilla—brought them into the brothels where they were set up on the rooftops and insulted obscenely. Josephus passes on relating exactly how this was done. In doing so, however, Josephus writes, the soldiers were heedless of the generosity not only of Agrippa but also of his grandfather Herod the Great, who had constructed their cities and had built harbors and temples for them at enormous expense.[101]

HEROD THE GREAT AND HIS GRANDSON

Although Josephus does not remind his readers in this context, Herod and his grandson had kept a lid on communal and intercommunal tensions and conflicts between and among Jews and non-Jews, at times by stern measures. The auxiliary soldiers probably believed that those measures had worked to their disadvantage. Their response to Agrippa's death was their way of giving a thumbs down or up, to be consistent with ancient Roman gestures of condemnation in the arena, to a king whom they saw as favoring the Jews, despite the clear evidence for his support of Greek customs and traditions up to and including games and bloody spectacles in amphitheaters, at least outside places where Jews were in the majority. In those locations Agrippa, like his grandfather, had indeed tried to be careful about not offending Jews. But just as had happened after the death of Herod, as soon as Agrippa was gone, the tensions among people and groups that he had tried to contain ignited into open conflict almost immediately.

CHAPTER 5

Procurators, Prophets, and Dagger-Men

When the Roman emperor Claudius learned of Agrippa's death and the insults the people and the soldiers of Sebaste and Caesarea had heaped upon him, he felt sorry for the king. But he was also incensed by the dead king's ungrateful subjects. That could only be non-Jews in Caesarea and Sebaste, since they were the ones who had insulted Agrippa and his daughters.

At first Claudius was inclined to send out Agrippa's young son Agrippa II (who was in Rome at the time) to take over his father's kingdom. But his freedmen and friends persuaded Claudius that it was risky to entrust such a position to a 16- or 17-year-old, who would not be able to bear up under the burdens of governing, not to mention deal with the evident ingratitude of the population toward his father. Even for a grown man, they said, the kingdom was a weighty responsibility. Claudius agreed.[1]

So according to Tacitus, after the deaths of Agrippa I and Sohaemus of Ituraea, an area around Mt. Lebanon to the northeast of the Sea of Galilee, Judaea and Ituraea were added (*additi*) to the province of Syria.[2] Tacitus, however, does not explain to his readers exactly what he meant by writing that Ituraea and Judaea were "added" to the province of Syria, and in his *Histories* he clearly states that in 69 Antioch was the capital of Syria and Caesarea was the capital of Judaea.[3] The latter statement seems to imply that Syria

98

and Judaea were understood as separate administrative units. If Judaea was added to Syria why did it need a capital?

Whatever Tacitus meant, we know that the administrative arrangement in Judaea was more complex than the legate of Syria simply taking over effective responsibility for all aspects of administration in Judaea. Josephus, who was born and raised there, unlike Tacitus, tells us that after the death of Agrippa I the emperor again (*palin*) reduced the kingdoms to a province (*eparchia*) and sent out procurators (*epitropoi*), beginning with Cuspius Fadus.[4] Indeed, in his later account of the administrative change Josephus wrote that Cuspius Fadus was sent out to be procurator of Judaea and the whole kingdom.[5] In addition, we know that even after Judaea was "added" to the province of Syria and procurators began to be sent out from Rome, supervision over the Temple and the sacred vessels and the right to appoint the high priest were given over to King Herod of Chalcis (situated in the Beq'aa Valley in Lebanon), rights that he retained until his death in 48.[6] The articulation of authority and power over and in Judaea therefore was not nearly as simple and clear as might be understood from Tacitus's statement. (See appendix H.)

From 44 onward governors in Judaea were designated as procurators rather than prefects (as they were called before 41). After three years of royal rule, Judaea was brought within the Roman provincial administration in 44: it was placed by the emperor under the jurisdiction of a procurator whose day-to-day, on-the-spot administration could be watched over and supervised, although at times belatedly, by the legate of Syria in Antioch. The key difference between the position of the legate in Syria and the procurator in Judaea was that the former had overall command of a number of legions stationed in Syria, whereas the latter did not command legions.

Claudius also honored the memory of the dead king Agrippa I by not making Marsus, with whom Agrippa had argued, governor over Agrippa's former kingdom. In fact, Marsus was replaced as governor of Syria by Cassius Longinus, a clear sign of Claudius's displeasure.[7]

The new procurator, Fadus, was first instructed to chastise the people of Sebaste and Caesarea for their insults to Agrippa and his family. He was also ordered to send the cavalry squadron of troopers from Caesarea and Sebaste along with the five auxiliary infantry cohorts to Pontus in the Black Sea region. It was soldiers from these units who had celebrated Agrippa's death and insulted his daughters' statues. These men were to be replaced with the same number of (probably auxiliary) soldiers attached to the Roman army in Syria.[8] The idea behind this change was not just to punish the unruly soldiers.

Claudius wanted to lessen tensions and prevent future conflicts between these locally recruited non-Jewish soldiers and the Jews of the province. This policy change shows that Claudius understood that there was a problem of ethnic animosity in the region.

The troops who were to be transferred, however, sent an embassy to Claudius, and somehow the emperor was persuaded to let them remain in Judaea.[9] Josephus offers his readers no explanation for why Claudius changed his mind. He does say, however, that Claudius's reversal proved to be a source of the greatest misfortune for the Jews.[10]

The presence and actions of the auxiliary soldiers from Caesarea and Sebaste who were allowed to stay on in the province sowed the seeds of the war that broke out in 66.[11] Their hostility toward the Jews of the region eventually made armed conflict much more likely. But they exhibited more than just passive enmity. In 66 the auxiliaries were responsible for spilling the blood of many Jews, including both poor and wealthy civilians. Once that happened and the Jews responded in kind, it became much more difficult to restrain those on both sides who wanted war.

Claudius made a determined effort to clarify, define, and protect the rights of both Jews and non-Jews in the eastern Mediterranean and to check those who wanted violence and war. As we have seen in Alexandria, his efforts were not always to the advantage of Jews. But there is no doubt that Claudius tried to understand the situation and provide rules of conduct. Unfortunately, his efforts failed. After Vespasian became emperor, he transferred the problematic auxiliaries out of the province.[12] It was a generation too late.

THE FIRST PROCURATORS

Cuspius Fadus

As soon as Fadus arrived in Judaea in 44 he was confronted by a dispute between Jews living in the Peraea and the people of Philadelphia (Amman) across the Jordan. It had to do with the boundaries of a village named Zia, located around 15 miles west of Philadelphia. Zia apparently was serving as some kind of base for men who were hostile to the Jews. In response, the Jews had attacked the Philadelphians.[13] Josephus doesn't say so explicitly, but the logical inference must be that the Philadelphians had been supporting the villagers of Zia in their dispute against the Peraean Jews.

Fadus was angry that the Jews of the Peraea had taken up arms before he had made any kind of judgment about an issue involving his jurisdiction. For that reason he imprisoned three of the Jews' leaders named Annibas, Amaranus, and Eleazar, one of whom, Annibas, he subsequently had put to death. The two others were exiled.[14]

The incident provided a preview of the interethnic violence that flared up and then burned out of control in the region in 66. At the same time it underscored the significance of local village politics outside the main urban centers.[15] Fadus's intervention also exemplifies the essentially reactive character of Roman power in a regional landscape characterized more by villages than major urban centers. With the limited resources and soldiers available to him Fadus and his successors could only react to such conflicts and unrest in the countryside. When they did so the soldiers they dispatched tended not to act with restraint. Heavy-handed punitive operations produced short-term results but built up long-term resentment and the desire for revenge.

Not long after the Zia episode in the Peraea, an "arch-brigand" or *archilestes* named Tholomaeus, who apparently had wreaked havoc in Idumaea and among the Arabs too, was brought to the governor in chains. We do not know who brought him in or how he was captured. He too was put to death. The whole of Judaea, Josephus claims, thenceforth was cleansed of bands of robbers thanks to Fadus's attention.[16]

Like other Roman governors in Judaea before him, Fadus nevertheless could not avoid running afoul of local religious sensibilities. For reasons that are not explained, at some point during his tenure as governor Fadus decided that the tunic and robe that the high priest alone of the Jews was permitted to wear should be stored in the fortress of the Antonia, attached to the Temple in Jerusalem, where they had been kept from 6 to 36 CE. It is possible that Fadus thought that by controlling the high priests' garments he could control the high priests and, by extension, the Temple.

In response to the procurator's decision the chief priests and some of the local leaders petitioned Fadus and the Syrian legate Longinus, who had come down from Syria with a large force in case of trouble.[17] In their petition the Jews asked the governors to grant them permission to send a delegation to the emperor Claudius to ask for the authority to keep the vestments in their own hands and to wait until they knew Claudius's answer before they complied with Fadus's decision. Fadus and Longinus agreed to let the Jews send the delegation, as long as its intended members gave their children as hostages. The Jews complied and the embassy was sent off.[18] The fact that Fadus insisted that hostages be given before that embassy would be allowed to leave does not suggest a high level of trust between the governor and even some of the most distinguished Jews.

Once the delegation had made its way to Rome, young Agrippa II intervened with Caesar on the Jews' behalf. He asked Claudius to let the Jews store the robes of the high priest and to send a letter to Fadus announcing his decision. Claudius granted the request, taking care to point out to the delegates that he had done so at Agrippa's behest.[19] As ever within the Roman imperial system of governance, personal access to the emperor and individual relationships were crucial factors in resolving disputes over policy initiatives that otherwise could have provoked a violent reaction. The reverse side of this truism was the predictable outcome of disputes in which either access to the emperor or his closest associates was limited, there were no personal relationships, or both. Or, as would be the case in 66, there would be trouble when the government—Nero—doubled down on a policy that was initially resisted.

In his letter of 28 June of 45 CE to the Jews about the embassy, Claudius cited the precedent set by his friend, the two-time consul Vitellius. As we have seen in the case of the dispute between the Greeks and Jews in Alexandria, Claudius preferred to base his decisions on citable precedents. He claimed that he had granted the petition because of his own piety and his wish to see everyone continue practices according to their ancestral traditions. Of all the Iulio-Claudian emperors Claudius was perhaps the most receptive to appeals based upon ethnohistorical traditions, being himself an antiquarian historian of Etruscan and Carthaginian traditions.[20]

In addition, the emperor wrote that he yielded to the Jews' request to please King Herod of Chalcis and Aristobulus the Younger, the son of Herod of Chalcis. Finally, he informed the Jews that he was writing to his procurator Cuspius Fadus.[21] At this time or shortly thereafter Herod of Chalcis also wrote to Claudius, asking to receive authority over the Temple and its holy vessels and over the choice of the high priests. Claudius granted these requests, and Herod soon replaced the serving high priest with Joseph, the son of Camei.[22]

By granting Herod these privileges, however, Claudius may have complicated rather than simplified the structure(s) of authority within the province, over which the governor of Syria also exercised some overall supervisory authority that no ancient source clarifies.[23] Apparently it did not trouble Claudius that the governor of Syria, the procurator of Judaea, and a local king all felt that they could and should intervene in matters that were central to the religion and culture of Jews. This was not a system of governance designed to satisfy those who wanted precise definitions of the parameters of authority. The reason for those blurred lines of authority was something that all of the parties knew but hesitated to put into writing at the very least, unless you were an emperor like Gaius (Caligula): power was ultimately unified in the person of the emperor, and because of the distances involved it might take some time before the emperor's consideration of issues and then his decision could be known.

Fadus's governorship was notable for one more popular disturbance. A man named Theudas, called by Josephus a *goes* (magician), persuaded a mass of followers (400 according to Gamaliel in the Acts of the Apostles) to gather up their belongings and to travel with him to the Jordan River. He told them that he was a prophet and that at his order the waters of the river would part and there would be an easy way across it. What would happen after that is not made clear, but Theudas may have had some kind of latter-day "Exodus" in mind. To the east of the Jordan lay desert, if not the Sinai. The plan in any case implies that there needed to be some kind of physical withdrawal from a situation of distress.

Unfortunately for Theudas's disciples, however, whether he was a magician or a prophet, parting rivers—let alone seas, Red or otherwise—was not within his power. Before his followers could get safely across the Jordan by one means or another, a squadron of cavalry sent off by Fadus caught up with them and slaughtered a great many of them. Others were taken prisoner. Theudas himself was among the captured. Fadus's soldiers cut the magician's head off and brought it back to Jerusalem.[24] Cutting off the head of one charismatic, however, would not affect the causes that led hundreds or even thousands of locals to follow such figures, as successive Roman governors would soon discover.

Tiberius Iulius Alexander

In 46 Fadus's successor as governor, probably with the title of *praefectus* rather than procurator, was the Alexandrian Jew Tiberius Iulius Alexander. He was the son of the alabarch (head customs collector on the Arabian side of the Nile) Alexander of Alexandria and nephew of the renowned philosopher Philo. Tiberius Iulius Alexander had become *epistrategos* of the Thebais in Egypt several years earlier, in 42. The office of the *epistrategos* was a junior-level equestrian position within the Roman provincial administration of Egypt, but its holder had administrative authority over at least one-quarter of the province.[25] Tiberius's uncle Philo, as we have seen, was distinguished enough to be selected to head up an embassy sent to the emperor Gaius. But Tiberius's father, Alexander, was even more renowned in his day. Both in ancestry and wealth the father outclassed his fellow citizens, according to Josephus; in fact, Tiberius's father was famous for the gilded gates he subsidized for the Temple in Jerusalem. His piety toward God also surpassed that of his son, for Tiberius Iulius Alexander did not maintain the ancestral practices of his fathers, according to the same source.[26]

Exactly what can be inferred from Josephus's statement about Alexander's piety is not clear. It is often assumed that he meant that Tiberius was an apostate. Yet he could just as easily be read as implying that Tiberius Iulius Alexander was simply nonobservant.[27] Perhaps because Tiberius was known to be a nonobservant Jew during his governorship, he was upstaged by one of the most remarkable and memorable women in Jewish history, Queen Helena of Adiabene.

Helena was the daughter of Izates, the king of Adiabene, a small, semi-independent kingdom in northern Mesopotamia, with its capital at Arbela (Erbil in Iraqi Kurdistan).[28] After Izates's death he was succeeded by his son Monobazos. Following local traditions Monobazos married his sister Helena.[29] Around the turn of the millennium Helena gave birth to a son also named Izates, a Persian word that could be translated as "genius."[30] Because of the jealousy of Izates's half-brothers, Monobazos sent his son Izates away to live at the court of King Abennerigus (or Abinerglos) of Charax Spasinou in lower Mesopotamia (located between the mouths of the Tigris and Euphrates), site of a city foundation by Alexander the Great in 324 BCE.[31] While Izates was away Monobazos died and was succeeded by Helena's eldest son, Izates's older brother Monobazos II.[32]

During the period when he was living in Charax Spasinou, Izates met a Jewish merchant named Ananias who taught him to worship God, following the Jewish tradition. At the same time, in Adiabene Izates's mother, Helena, met another Jew who brought her over to obedience to the laws of the Jews.[33] After returning to Adiabene and taking over the throne from his brother, against his mother Helena's advice, Izates was circumcised.[34]

At some point Helena conceived a desire to go to Jerusalem and worship God there in the Temple. Izates gave her leave to go and provided her with a large sum of money.[35] Helena arrived in Jerusalem during a famine in 46 or

47. She sent some of her attendants to Alexandria in Egypt to buy grain for large sums and also to Cyprus to bring back a cargo of dried figs. When the food reached Jerusalem she distributed it to the needy. Izates also sent a great deal of money to the leaders in Jerusalem.[36]

The queen garnered still more attention, from later sages anyway, by having a golden candelabrum set over the door of the Temple (*heikhal*) and also a golden tablet (*sotah*), on which was inscribed the story of the suspected adulteress.[37] What this probably means is that Helena had engraved on the tablet a copy of the passage in the book of Numbers where God instructed Moses about the testing of a woman alleged to have committed adultery and the curse put upon her if she were found guilty.[38] Why Queen Helena chose the passage is unclear. Her choice, however, helped establish her reputation for piety among the authors of the Mishnah.

The generous queen also had a palace complex constructed on the southeastern hill of Jerusalem in the Lower City for herself and her family.[39] Remains of this complex have been excavated beneath the modern Givati parking lot (in the City of David).[40]

Helena's son Izates meanwhile had become involved in a war against the Parthian king Vologaeses. Vologaeses had been incited to fight by Adiabenians who resented Izates's conversion and the popularity of Judaism among his kinsmen.[41] Helena probably took her vows as a Nazirite to help ensure Izates's safety during this war. It seemed to have worked. Vologaeses supposedly had to call off his war against Izates after Dahae and Sacae nomads invaded his kingdom.[42]

Monobazos became king after his brother Izates's death. Around 56 CE Helena returned to Adiabene, where she died shortly thereafter. Monobazos sent her bones along with those of Izates to Jerusalem where they were interred in three pyramids, which stood north of the city's third wall.[43] The tomb, known today as the Tomb of Kings (Wadi Joz in the Upper Kidron Valley), became one of Jerusalem's most notable landmarks and tourist attractions.[44] During the great revolt members of the Adiabenian aristocracy who lived in Jerusalem after Helena's death conspicuously remained within the city of Jerusalem throughout the Roman siege, thereby declaring their loyalties. If Herod the heroic and horrible deserved an *opera buffa,* Queen Helena of Adiabene merited an *opera seria.*

It was while Tiberius Iulius Alexander was governor (perhaps from 46–48) that James (or Jacob) and Simon, the sons of the Galilaean Judas who had led the popular resistance movement when Quirinius imposed the census of

Judaea, were tried and crucified.[45] Josephus does not specify what the charges against the two sons were. Perhaps they were involved in the conflicts that broke out after the death of Agrippa I. If that were so, it might indicate that the two sons had issues with the auxiliary soldiers. But we do not know.[46] Another possibility must be that the brothers were punished for activities related to Judaea's reintegration into the Roman provincial system.

During the same period King Herod of Chalcis dismissed Joseph, the son of Camei, from the high priesthood, and replaced him with Ananias, the son of Nedebaeus.[47] Josephus does not explain the reason for the change. Ananias subsequently became a figure of controversy. In the Acts of the Apostles he is depicted as the high priest who ordered Paul to be struck in the mouth by his attendants after Paul said that he conducted himself before God with a clear conscience; Ananias then accused Paul before the Roman governor.[48] In the Babylonian Talmud Ananias was said to have eaten 300 calves, drunk 300 barrels of wine, and eaten 40 *se'ah* of young birds at one sitting.[49] The unsubtle point the author was trying to make was that Ananias was a wealthy glutton. At the beginning of the great revolt, however, as we shall see, Josephus presents him as an opponent of Menahem and later as his victim.[50] It is at least possible that Herod of Chalcis appointed Ananias to the high priesthood because of his perceived political, if not culinary, moderation.

At some point after Tiberius Iulius Alexander left his position and after King Herod of Chalcis died, in 50 Claudius then gave both rule over Chalcis and care of the Temple, including the right to appoint and dismiss high priests, to the 20-year-old Agrippa II (the Younger). Thereafter Agrippa II appointed six of the last seven of the 83 high priests that Josephus reported to have served since the time of the first high priest, Aaron.[51] No doubt this was Agrippa's way of trying to assert some sort of control over operation of the Temple. The last high priest, as we shall see, was appointed according to a very different selection process.

Ventidius Cumanus

The procuratorship (48–52) of Tiberius Iulius Alexander's successor, Ventidius Cumanus—Tacitus claimed he was governor of the Galilee, with Felix governor of Samaritis and Judaea, whereas Josephus wrote that he was procurator in Judaea—was eventful and troubled. Josephus reports three major incidents. The first occurred during the celebration of Passover, either during the late 40s or early 50s. The incident revealed how trivial, if vulgar, acts could quickly escalate into major civic disturbances.

On the fourth day of the festival one of the auxiliary soldiers who was standing guard on the roof of one of the Temple porticoes turned his back-side to the crowd below, lifted his cloak, and mooned the pious who had gathered below. He then farted or produced a convincing imitation of a fart, or flashed his genitals. Whatever he did, the offending soldier apparently was not wearing any underwear (*subligar*) at the time, and the people below got either an earful or an eyeful or both. Those who witnessed the soldier's juvenile display went into a rage, claiming that it had been done not to insult them but to blaspheme God.[52] Given the physical setting of the soldier's obscene performance, they may have been right.

Some of the observers reproached the governor, Cumanus, himself, alleging that the soldier had been egged on by him. That seems far-fetched. It is hard to believe that Cumanus had the time or inclination to incite soldiers on guard duty to indulge in such embarrassing and potentially incendiary behavior. In any case, some Jews called for the offending soldier to be punished. Others started to throw rocks at the soldiers. Cumanus was incensed by what was going on but only warned those who were escalating the situation. He then ordered them to stop agitating for revolution and creating disturbances during the festival. That was a not very convincing attempt to transfer blame for what had happened onto the victims.

Cumanus's words had no effect, and the people continued with their reproaches. Fearing a mass attack, the procurator ordered the entire army to come to the Antonia Fortress in full battle gear. From there the soldiers advanced into the porticoes of the Temple, where large numbers of people who had come to the city to make their sacrifices and celebrate the Passover were congregated. The crowd of pilgrims, seeing the soldiers coming, became frightened and began to flee in a panic. The exits from the porticoes, however, were narrow, and as the Jews tried to force their way out, thinking that they were being pursued by Cumanus's soldiers, they pressed up against each other in the narrow passages. Those who had the misfortune to fall down were trampled to death. Josephus puts the number of those who died up to 30,000, all because one soldier had exposed himself.[53]

Josephus's casualty figure must be wildly exaggerated; we should be skeptical about such large, imprecise, and rounded-off figures. But the incident itself is indicative of the continuing tensions and conflicts between the population and the auxiliary soldiers, especially during the three major festivals in the city. It was usually at these festival times, when the population of Jerusalem vastly increased, that such tensions erupted into violence. But incidents in the countryside could escalate quickly too.

A slave of Caesar's named Stephanus was robbed by some brigands (*lestai*) as he was traveling along the public road to Beit-Horon about 12 miles northwest of Jerusalem. When Cumanus heard about what had happened, as Josephus tells us in his earlier version of the episode, he sent troops out to the villages in the neighborhood, with orders to bring the inhabitants to him in chains. The villagers were chastised for not pursuing or arresting the robbers.[54] In his later account Josephus says that Cumanus ordered the soldiers to plunder the villages in the area where the robbery had taken place and to bring the most eminent men from the villages to him in chains, either because they had not bothered to pursue the robbers or because Cumanus simply wanted to get revenge.[55]

While the soldiers were rounding up the villagers, one of the soldiers seized a (scroll) copy of the laws of Moses that was kept in one of the villages. The soldier brought the scroll out into the open, tore it into two pieces (*dieschisen* in the Greek version of the episode reported in the *Antiquities*), and then threw the remains into the fire.

After hearing about the soldier's actions the Jews gathered in great numbers and went to Caesarea, where Cumanus happened to be at the time. There they entreated the governor to avenge God, whose laws had been so outraged (in the version given in the *Antiquities*). Fearing another revolt and after consulting his friends, Cumanus had the offending soldier beheaded.[56] Cumanus thereby defused the anger of the Jews.

The memory of the incident in which the slave was robbed and the resulting collective punishment meted out either to the villagers or to the most eminent men can hardly have been quickly forgotten.[57] The significance of the event, however, may extend beyond the ill feeling it caused about the punishments. The so-called brigands may only have targeted Caesar's slave Stephanus for his possessions, though we do not know what they were. But it is hard to believe that Stephanus's identity was not known to those who robbed him. He no doubt spoke Greek and probably was better dressed than a traveling villager. The fact that Stephanus was robbed, but not killed, increases the probability that the robbers had time to identify him.

A known slave of Caesar was a symbol of Roman power in Judaea, and the attack upon Stephanus may have been a targeted act of defiance or resistance. Understanding the robbery as a form of resistance to Rome perhaps helps explain why Cumanus punished so severely the local villagers who did not try to apprehend the robbers. Cumanus understood their lack of enthusiasm as support for an assault upon someone associated with Roman authority. If this reading of the incident is correct, even if the crime against Stephanus was not specifically anti-Roman, the unenthusiastic reaction of the villagers was. Who cared if a slave of the emperor was robbed?

Enmity between some Samaritans and Jews in 52 eventually led to Cumanus's recall to Rome.[58] It was the custom among the Galilaeans at the time of festivals to pass through the land of the Samaritans on their way to Jerusalem. Once, while the Galilaeans were on their way to "the" festival or "a" festival, some of the inhabitants of a village called Gema or Ginae, clearly Jenin, at the top of the plain of Esdraelon (Jezreel), having joined battle, killed one (*War*) or a great number (*Antiquities*) of the pilgrims. Learning what had happened, the leaders of the Galilaeans went to Governor Cumanus and entreated him to avenge the murder of those who had been killed. Cumanus, who allegedly had been bribed by the Samaritans, did nothing.[59]

The Galilaeans then exhorted the mass of Jews to take up arms and assert their freedom. Slavery, they said, was bitter in itself. But it was unbearable when it also involved insolence. When their principal men, presumably local magistrates of some kind, sought to calm them down, promising to try to persuade Cumanus to punish the murderers, they paid no attention. Taking up arms, they invited the help of the "brigand" Eleazar, son of Deinaeus, and an otherwise unknown man named Alexander. These men led the Galilaeans into the region bordering on the toparchy of Acrabatene, located southeast of Shechem, where they proceeded to burn and sack villages of the Samaritans, massacring the inhabitants without respect to age.[60]

Cumanus soon heard what had happened. His response was to gather together a force of Sebastenian cavalry and four cohorts of infantry to go out and hunt down the attackers. After arming the Samaritans, he marched out against the Jews and slew many of them. More, however, were taken alive as prisoners. At that point the leaders of the Jerusalemites urged their fellow Jews to throw down their arms, to return to their homes, and to lead a quiet life. Most were persuaded by their leaders to disperse and return home. Many, however, returned to lives of brigandage or took it up. From this time onward Judaea was full of robbers, according to Josephus.[61]

The Samaritans did not let matters rest. Rather, the leading, most distinguished, or most powerful Samaritans went to Ummidius Quadratus, the Roman governor of Syria, who was then in Tyre, and accused the Jews of burning and ravaging their villages. Later Josephus claimed that the Samaritans made the point that the Jews had taken the law into their own hands before they had appealed to their Roman governors to redress any injustices. For their part, the Jews—Josephus does not specify exactly who they were—said that the Samaritans were the cause of the strife and warfare. But they blamed Cumanus especially, insisting that he had been bribed by the Samaritans to ignore the murder of those who had been killed by them on their way to the festival.[62]

After listening to both sides, Quadratus at first said that he would defer judgment until he had reached Judaea and inquired further into the case. (Note again the willingness of the governor to march down to the south and intervene there.) After he reached Caesarea, or Samaritis in *Antiquities,* and held a full hearing, Quadratus decided that the Samaritans had been the cause of the public upheaval. He then crucified both the Samaritans and the Jews who had taken part in the mini-rebellion and were being held prisoner by Cumanus.[63]

From Caesarea Quadratus traveled to Lydda (Lod), where he heard the case of the Samaritans for the second time. There he was told by a certain Samaritan that a leader of the Jews named Doetus, together with four others, or 18 in the *War,* had incited the mob to revolt against the Romans. Quadratus ordered those accused Jews to be put to death too.[64]

The high priests Jonathan and Ananias, Ananias's son Ananus, the Temple captain, and some other prominent Jews—all in chains—as well as some Samaritan notables were then sent to Rome. At the same time Quadratus ordered Cumanus and the military tribune Celer to go to Italy to give an account of their actions. He then visited the city of Jerusalem, where the Passover festival was taking place. Satisfied that no revolution was about to break out he then went back to Antioch.[65]

In Rome the emperor Claudius assigned a day for Cumanus and the Samaritan leaders to plead their cases. Josephus claims that the freedmen and friends of Claudius provided such strong support for Cumanus and the Samaritans that they would have prevailed over the Jews but for the intervention of Agrippa II. Seeing that the leaders of the Jews were losing the case, he urgently appealed to the emperor's wife Agrippina to persuade Claudius to give the case a comprehensive hearing and to punish those who had caused the strife.

Persuaded by his wife's appeal Claudius dug down a bit deeper into the stories about the incident. Learning that the Samaritans had been the first to incite trouble, he ordered at least three of the most notable Samaritans who had come before him to be put to death. Cumanus was sent into exile. The military tribune Celer was ordered to be sent back to Jerusalem in shackles, to be dragged around the entire city in front of all, and then to be beheaded.[66] We do not know what the tribune had done that led Claudius to order such an extraordinary punishment.

In reviewing this episode some scholars have represented it as a case of Judaean vigilantism that, if it had escalated at the time, could have turned into "the Jewish revolt" against Rome. The reason why it did not in the early 50s was because of the response of the sitting emperor, Claudius. Ten years later Nero's reaction to a similar incident would be very different.[67] It mattered who the emperor was.

Identifying interethnic conflict—that is, if the Galilaeans and the Samaritans really were "ethnically" different—as one of the causes of the war that did break out in 66 is persuasive. Designating the response of Jews to the murder of Galilaean Jews after Cumanus refused to respond as "vigilantism" and leaving it at that, however, obscures the more salient points. In the *Antiquities* Josephus no doubt went out of his way to represent the Samaritans' actions in the episode more unfavorably than he had done in the *War;* in any case Josephus was interested in demonstrating that Agrippa II was a peacemaker.[68]

But in both accounts Jews took up arms against Samaritans only after Cumanus, who allegedly had been bribed, refused to do anything about the murder of their fellow Jews. Arguably in 52 Jews were simply defending themselves when the Roman governor refused to protect them. That is the pattern worth highlighting. Jews resorted to violence when the Roman government refused to provide them with protection from their neighbors. That violence ineluctably brought the legate of Syria down from Antioch by way of Ptolemais.

It was no accident at all that during the last few years of Claudius's reign Ptolemais was re-founded as an official Roman colony, known in Latin as *Colonia Claudia Stabilis Germanica Felix Ptolemais,* and was repopulated at least in part by veterans from the legions previously stationed in Syria. An approximately 250-mile road built along the coast from Antioch to Ptolemais during Claudius's reign facilitated communications and transportation between the capital of the Syrian province and the veterans' colony.[69] It was a road along which many Roman legionaries would soon be marching on their way south to put out even larger fires. But already by the early 50s, firefights were breaking out between Jews and auxiliaries in Jerusalem; among Jews, auxiliaries, and those identified with Rome in the countryside; and between Jews and their neighbors just to the north of the holy city. The strategy of the governor whom Claudius chose to replace Cumanus with was allegedly to extinguish the smaller fires by starting a much larger conflagration.

Felix

Cumanus's departure after a series of troubling incidents led to major changes in the administration of the province and the region. Marcus Antonius Felix, the brother of Claudius' freedman adviser Pallas and husband of Agrippa I's daughter Drusilla, was sent out as the new procurator of Judaea, Samaritis, the Galilee, and Peraea (around 52 to 58–60).[70] In 53 the former tetrarchy of Philip that included Gaulanitis, Trachonitis, Auranitis, and Batanaea was granted to Agrippa II, along with the tetrarchy of Lysanias (anchored by Abila in Syria) and the former tetrarchy of Varus, located somewhere in Ituraea. He was stripped of the small kingdom of Chalcis that he had been awarded in 50 after ruling it for four years.[71]

In the first year of Nero's reign (54 CE), Azizus, the ruler of Emesa (Homs in modern Syria), died and was succeeded by his brother C. Iulius Sohaemus. Nero then placed the government of Armenia Minor in the hands of Aristobulus, son of Herod, the king of Chalcis. In 54–55 or 55–56 Agrippa II then was given a part of the Galilee, the polis of Tiberias and the large village and toparchy capital of Tarichaeae (Magdala/Migdal), the poleis of Abila (Tel Abil in Jordan) and Iulias in the Peraea, and the 14 surrounding villages.[72]

These complicated administrative arrangements no doubt were designed to reward the emperor's supporters, to quell unrest, and to help secure Rome's border area facing the Parthian empire. They did not succeed. Indeed, the legacy of Cumanus's administration lived on in the form of brigandage, wizardry, and then organized violence directed against the local rulers.

At first Felix captured and put to death many of those who were involved in the brigandage, especially those operating in Judaea outside Jerusalem. Among them was Eleazar, the son of Deinaeus (called a bandit-chief by Josephus but considered to be a Zealot by some scholars) who, along with many of those associated with him, was persuaded to give himself up by a promise of safety. Once he was in Felix's hands Eleazar and his supporters were imprisoned and then sent to Rome.[73] Getting rid of agitators by breaking promises cannot have increased trust in the Roman government.

Having cleared the countryside of such brigands for the time being, Felix then began to make use of the so-called *sicarii* or dagger-men, who supposedly appeared first in Jerusalem.[74] They were called dagger-men because of the small daggers (*sicae*) with which they dispatched their victims, whether Jews or Romans.

The procurator apparently had taken a dislike to the high priest Jonathan, the son of Ananus, because of the high priest's frequent requests to improve the administration of matters in Judaea. Vexed by these requests, Felix bribed Jonathan's friend Doras, a native of Jerusalem, to hire some of the dagger-men to kill the high priest.[75] This method of assassination was widely copied.

Hiding their daggers under their clothes, the paid assassins insinuated themselves into the company of those around Jonathan. Once they gained access to their target the assassins stabbed the high priest to death and vanished.[76] The high priest's murder was not punished. Thereafter, the dagger-men, or brigands as they are called in the *Antiquities,* mingled among the crowds during the festivals with impunity, concealing the daggers with which they stabbed their victims. After Jonathan's death such murders were carried out on a daily basis. Some they killed for personal reasons. Others they were bribed to kill, not only in the city but also within the Temple itself.

The murders created panic within the city. Men eyed their enemies at a distance and did not trust their friends when they came near. Even though they kept up their guard, some still were struck down due to the swiftness of the conspirators and their ability to escape detection.[77]

Josephus later claimed that it was because of the impiety of these assassins who murdered people within the Temple that God turned away from Jerusalem. God now regarded the Temple as an unclean dwelling place for himself, brought the Romans in to purify the city by fire, and inflicted slavery upon the Jews. By these misfortunes God punished the Jews.[78] Josephus's theological explanation leaves out one important chronological fact: the Roman governor himself was one of the dagger-men's first and then most regular customers. If God therefore decided to use the Romans to cleanse the Temple and Jerusalem, he had made the previous decision to have the Romans take part in murder-for-hire terrorism.

While the dagger-men were murdering their enemies, there also appeared in Jerusalem a number of prophets who promised to give the people signs of their freedom (*semeia eleutherias*) if they followed them out into the desert. Most notable among them was an Egyptian "false prophet" (*pseudoprophetes*) who, having attracted a following of 30,000 (or 4,000 as reported in the Acts of the Apostles), led them out to the Mount of Olives, the highest ridge in Jerusalem and its ancient necropolis, where, at his command he claimed, the walls of Jerusalem would come tumbling down. The Egyptian prophet seems to have fancied himself as a kind of latter-day Joshua. Once the walls had tumbled, he promised that his followers would have an entrance into the city. After the Roman garrison had been overpowered, he would set himself up as tyrant there, with his adherents acting as his bodyguard.[79]

When Felix heard about what was going on, he armed his soldiers and went out from Jerusalem to find the Egyptian and his followers. Felix's cavalry and heavy Roman infantry soon caught up with them and, joined by "the whole people" in defense, managed to kill 400 of them while taking another 200 prisoners. The Egyptian himself escaped and disappeared as quickly as he had appeared.[80]

The participation of the whole people—presumably the population of the area to which the Egyptian and his followers had gone—in defense against the Egyptian and his followers indeed suggests that not everyone in Judaea at the time was interested in overthrowing the Roman garrison in Jerusalem.[81] But the numbers involved in the incident, anywhere between 4,000 and 30,000, also indicate that by the 50s there were thousands of Jews who were willing to listen to revolutionary appeals against Rome. Central to the Egyptian's message was the elimination of the Roman fortress in Jerusalem. Indeed the Roman garrison in Jerusalem became one of the first targets of the rebels in 66.

Although the movement led by the Egyptian was eradicated, Josephus claims that afterward a number of "sorcerers/cheats" (*goetes*) banded together with brigands and went around inciting many to revolt and to stand up for freedom, or *eleutheria*. These men threatened to kill any who submitted to the hegemony of the Romans and to suppress by force those who willingly accepted slavery. Forming companies, they robbed the houses of the well-off, killed their owners, and burned the villages of those who refused to go along with their calls for resistance.[82]

The actions of the brigands and their followers have been interpreted as manifestations of class warfare within Judaean society during this period rather than as reactions to Roman rule.[83] Indeed, for this period and throughout the duration of the revolt itself, Josephus does provide evidence of conflict not only between the rich and the poor within Judaean society but also among the different tiers of the rich.[84]

Yet it is also clear from Josephus's accounts of the episode involving the Egyptian "false prophet" and the formation of bands of magicians and brigands that, whatever tensions and conflicts there were between the poor and the rich, and between the rich and the richer, in mid-first-century Judaea, and however Roman rule through the wealthy might have exacerbated those problems, from the time of Judas the Galilaean to the outbreak of the fighting in 66, there were Jews who opposed the Roman imperial presence in Judaea on ideological or theological grounds. Some of those who opposed Rome were poor, as we shall see. But others were well-off. The war of Jews against Romans in 66 was not the simple outcome of a class struggle. Among those who took up arms against Rome were well-off Jews, poor Jews, and those in the middle.

SPIRALING OUT OF CONTROL

With the considerable assistance of some incompetent, greedy, corrupt, and at times malevolent Roman administrators, those Jews who wanted the Romans out of Judaea eventually convinced enough of their fellow Jews of their point of view to incite a full-scale rebellion. Although we cannot reconstruct an unbroken history of anti-Roman, rejectionist resistance from 6 to 66 CE, Josephus provides evidence of at least some Jews in the region rejecting Roman rule and advocating rebellion periodically, from the very beginning of the creation of the province to the outbreak of the revolt itself.

Ethnic strife was also a factor, and it enflamed the situation within the cities of the province and beyond. Although the majority of the population of Caesarea Maritima were "Hellenes," the Jews claimed "precedence," or that the city belonged to them, or equality of citizenship (*isopoliteias*), because the founder of Caesarea, King Herod, had been a Jew, even if his mother was a Nabataean Arab.[85] What this probably means is that the minority of Jews living in the city wanted Caesarea to be officially recognized as a *polis* that would follow the law of the Jews and their customs. The "Syrians" of Caesarea acknowledged Herod's ethnicity but claimed that before there was a Caesarea there had been a town on the site named Straton's Tower. There had not been a single resident of the town who was a Jew, they said. Moreover, they argued, not completely implausibly, that if Herod had meant for Caesarea to be a city for Jews alone, he never would have put up statues or temples there. Soon street fighting between the two sides broke out.

The magistrates of the district heard about the quarrel and, after arresting those on both sides who were responsible for it, had them beaten or incarcerated. This response quieted things down but not for very long. Some of the Jews in the city, who were wealthier than the Greeks, abused the Greeks, according to Josephus, thereby hoping to provoke them. The Syrians, who took pride in the fact that most of the soldiers who were serving there under the Romans were non-Jews recruited from Syria or Caesarea or Sebaste, at first only responded with insults. But soon both sides, following time-honored regional practice, started throwing rocks at each other, and many were wounded.

Seeing that he had a kind of war on his hands, the governor, Felix, called upon the Jews to desist after they won one of the street battles. When they did not he turned his soldiers loose upon them. Many were killed; more were taken alive. The houses of some of the wealthy Jews were plundered with Felix's acquiescence. Some of the more moderate Jews eventually prevailed upon Felix to call off the attack in exchange for their repentance. When the ethnic quarreling within the city persisted, however, Felix selected the most notable men of the two parties and sent them to Nero as ambassadors to argue about their rights.[86] Despite his close connections to those at the very center of power and politics in Judaea, Felix finally was not up to the job of keeping peace there.

In Jerusalem the strife took a different form, arising as it did not out of ethnic hatred but from intracommunal rivalry and economic disparities. The faction heads gathered around themselves bands of revolutionaries. When their factions engaged they insulted each other and then started hurling rocks. While these gangs were fighting, the high priests sent slaves to gather the tithes from the threshing floors that were due to the priests. Apparently they kept so much of what was collected from the tithes that some of the poorer priests, who lived off of what was gathered, died of starvation.[87]

The biblical warrant and history of tithing was complex and changing in practice, but the story Josephus tells about what was going on during Felix's governorship indicates that there was a struggle over who should benefit from the system at the time. In the book of Deuteronomy farmers were ordered to bring the tithe of all they produced at the end of three years to their town and lay it up to be consumed by the Levites, the sojourner, the fatherless, and the widow, because they had no portion of inheritance (i.e., land).[88] In Leviticus it was specified by God to Moses that the tithe of the land belonged to God and that every tenth animal of the herd was holy to God.[89] Speaking to Aaron and Moses in Numbers, God gave every tithe in Israel to the Levites, who in turn were ordered to give one-tenth of the tithe to the priests.[90]

By the Hasmonean period Jews were paying three tithes: a first tithe to the Levites or priests based upon the tradition elaborated in Numbers, a second tithe for personal expenses in Jerusalem that found its warrant in Deuteronomy, and a third tithe (every third and sixth year) for the poor, widows, and orphans. Altogether that added up to 14 tithes over a seven-year period, since they did not pay the first or second tithes during the seventh or sabbatical year and only paid the third tithe in years 3 and 6. From the time of Caesar the distinction between Levites and priests as beneficiaries of the first tithe seems to have disappeared.[91]

It may be that the tithing system had always been a way for a priestly elite to live off the sweat and produce of the majority of Judaeans. The anecdote that Josephus reports about the high priests confiscating tithes that traditionally had been earmarked for all priests, and not just Levites, indicates, however, that the system was exacerbating inequalities of wealth between high priests and other priests at the time. What had once been an instrument to make sure that those whose time and energies were devoted to serving God had societal support had become a tool for accumulating greater wealth. A struggle, and eventually a war, not only of Jews against Romans but also of Jews against other Jews, was coming into focus.

CHAPTER 6

The Fuse

NERO'S RESCRIPT

When Porcius Festus was appointed by Nero to succeed Felix as procurator of Judaea, the leaders of the Jews in Caesarea traveled to Rome to make accusations against the former governor, Felix, before the emperor. The appeal to Nero by the rich freedman Pallas on his brother's behalf saved Felix.[1]

Meanwhile, the legal question of who had what rights in Caesarea came up again, this time pressed by the non-Jews. The two leaders of the Syrians in Caesarea appealed to the emperor for a rescript canceling the existing grant of the Jews' equal civic rights with the Syrians and giving the Syrians rule of the city.[2]

Nero might have been biased in favor of those citizens of Caesarea who identified as Greek either ethnically or culturally anyway because of his philhellenism.[3] It could also have been the case that Nero ruled in favor of them because they made up a majority of the population. But the emperor apparently was decisively influenced to rule in favor of Caesarea's Syrians by Beryllus, his former tutor and current secretary for Greek correspondence, who, according to Josephus, had received a large bribe from the Syrians in Caesarea. Whatever his motivation was, Nero ruled in favor of the Syrians, probably in 61. The legal issue therefore was settled, at least for the time being.[4]

The case of Alexandria, discussed in chapter 4, shows however that such rulings might be revisited, relitigated, and resisted. Nero's rescript therefore was not the end of the struggle. Rather, it marked the beginning of a new phase in the conflict.

After Nero issued his rescript, the Jews of Caesarea, who clearly were a minority within the city, carried their quarrel with the Syrians further and further, wrote Josephus, until they finally ignited a war.[5] Josephus's text, however, suggests that it was a Caesarean Greek who deliberately provoked Caesarea's Jews and set in motion the events that led to the war.

PORCIUS FESTUS

During his governorship (from about 60–62), Festus supposedly captured and put to death large numbers of the "brigands" who were active in Judaea. Among them, Josephus specifies that the *sicarii* were particularly numerous and that they carried out their assassinations not only during festivals in Jerusalem, as previously described, but also in the villages of their enemies, which they ravaged and then set on fire.[6] At least some of the *sicarii* were not just robbers, as we have seen. They were enemies of Rome and of Jews who, from their point of view, collaborated with the Romans.

Festus also felt compelled to send out a force of cavalry and infantry to deal with the followers of another "sorcerer/cheat" who had promised his disciples "salvation and an end of evils" if they followed him out into the desert.[7] Josephus does not tell us exactly what the evils were from which the followers of the magician were trying to escape. Minimally we can deduce that they were dissatisfied with the current situation. The troopers that Festus sent out destroyed both the unnamed leader and his followers.

Meanwhile, within Jerusalem Festus intervened to resolve a dispute between King Agrippa II and some of the most eminent men in the city. The conflict involved the king literally trying to keep an eye on what was going on in the Temple. While he was dining in the evening, from a large chamber adjacent to one of the colonnades of the Hasmoneans' palace the king enjoyed looking out over what was happening in the city, including sacrifices being made in the Temple.[8]

Realizing that they were being watched, those who were being spied upon within the Temple compound erected a high wall on the arcade within the inner Temple facing west. The wall blocked the king's view. But it also impeded the view from outside the Temple's western portico, where the Romans posted their guards during festivals to keep watch over things. So both King Agrippa and Festus were upset about the erection of the wall.

The procurator therefore ordered that the offending wall be torn down. In response, those involved in erecting it requested that they be allowed to send an embassy to Nero about the matter. Their request was granted. The embassy included 10 of the most distinguished men in the city, along with the high priest Ishmael, son of Phiabi, and Helcias, the Temple treasury keeper.

Nero heard the case and not only allowed the wall to be left standing but also ruled that the whole building should be left untouched. His reason for doing so seems to have been personal. Josephus reports that Nero's beautiful and intelligent mistress and later wife, Poppaea, to whom he was very devoted at the time, was a *theosebes,* or sympathizer with the beliefs and practices of the Jews. Poppaea apparently had interceded on behalf of the Temple officials, persuaded by their argument that the wall was part of the Temple itself and should not be tampered with. Nevertheless, when she and presumably the emperor sent the 10 men of the embassy back to Jerusalem, Helcias and Ishmael were detained in her house in Rome as hostages. King Agrippa, learning that Ishmael was being kept in Rome, then appointed Joseph Kabi, the son of Simon, as high priest.[9] Once again the incident and its outcome highlight the importance of access to the emperor and those near and, at least temporarily, dear to him.

LUCCEIUS ALBINUS

Festus died in Judaea while still holding the governorship. When Nero heard the news of Festus's death in 62, he appointed Lucceius Albinus as the new procurator of Judaea. A conflict involving the high priest, however, broke out in Jerusalem even before Albinus could reach Judaea.

The Sadducee high priest Ananus, the son of Ananus who had been appointed by King Agrippa II, had assembled the judges of the Sanhedrin (*sunhedrion*). Though the later rabbis conceived of these judges as a council of 71 clerical and lay sages presided over by a *nasi* or patriarch that had the authority to try people for various offenses, Josephus seems to have understood this body to constitute a kind of ad hoc advisory council to the high priest.[10] At the meeting the high priest accused James, the brother of Jesus, and others of transgressing the law. We are not told exactly what their crime was supposed to have been. But they must have been judged guilty because the accused were stoned to death.[11] James's body was subsequently buried "by the Temple."[12]

The execution offended some within the city, who secretly petitioned King Agrippa II to order Ananus to desist from such actions. They objected to what Ananus had done on procedural grounds, arguing that the high priest had convened the judges without the required prior consent of the procurator Albinus, who had not yet arrived.

Some of those who were angry with Ananus also went to Albinus, who was on his way from Alexandria, and told him what the high priest had done. Albinus promptly wrote a threatening letter to Ananus. But before Albinus could make good on his threat, King Agrippa II, who had responsibility for appointing the high priests at the time, dismissed Ananus from the high priesthood only three months after he had taken up the position. Jesus, the son of Damnaeus, was appointed in his place.[13]

Josephus later claimed that after Albinus finally made his way to Jerusalem he made every effort to bring peace to the land by wiping out the daggermen.[14] But in his earlier presentation of Albinus's governorship he paints a very different picture of what happened during his administration. That picture is circumstantially supported by evidence from elsewhere in the earlier account.[15]

In his monograph on the great revolt Josephus tells us that Albinus stole and plundered private property and burdened the whole nation with taxes. No doubt these taxes were levied to help Nero pay for his program of entertainments in Rome and for the costs of maintaining security along the eastern borders of the empire at a time of such financial duress in Rome that Nero had been compelled to appoint three former consuls (Lucius Piso, Ducenius Geminus, and Pompeius Paulinus) to oversee contributions to the state treasury. Distributing free grain to somewhere between 150,000 and 200,000 people in the capital city, a practice that began during the reign of Augustus, was an entitlement that could not be easily withdrawn.[16] Moreover, for reasons of security and Nero's own safety, the army, which accounted for two-thirds of the state's expenditures, had to be paid, no matter what.[17] Nero publicly blamed the dire economic situation on previous emperors who had drained the imperial revenues with their ruinous expenditures. He also claimed to have been making the state a yearly present of 60 million sesterces.[18] But the emperor's lavish generosity (*munificentia*) was not enough to balance the books or make up for the cash shortfall. So pressure was applied to governors such as Albinus to find additional sources of revenue.

Albinus turned out to be an imaginative generator of cash. Ransoms were taken from the relatives of those who had been imprisoned by local councils or the previous procurators. The only people left in prison were those whose relatives couldn't afford to pay Albinus off. The influential and wealthy among those who wanted change secured immunity from Albinus for their practices by means of bribes. Albinus thus cleverly created two revenue streams from the same shakedown racket.

Meanwhile, among the general population, those who were not satisfied with peace attached themselves to those who made common—if criminal—cause with Albinus. Peaceful citizens were plundered by the bodyguards of self-elected brigand-chiefs or "tyrants" who stood above their companies. Out of fear the victims of the robberies kept their grievances to themselves, while those who had escaped them groveled before one who was worthy of punishment: the governor himself.[19] In his later description of Albinus's regime, Josephus makes clear that the climate of intimidation, fear, and corruption extended to the very top of Judaean society and the local Roman government.

The ex–high priest Ananias bought goodwill and an honorable reputation among the citizens by giving out money. He also supplied Albinus and the serving high priest, Jesus, with gifts. His resources, though, had to come from somewhere.

One source was the Temple. His servants went to the threshing floor of the Temple and forcibly laid their hands on the tithes of the priests. Those who resisted were beaten. Deprived of the tithes the priests starved to death. Josephus tells us that other high priests had engaged in the same practices with the same results.[20]

Josephus may not have been right that some priests starved to death because of the greed of priestly elites in Jerusalem. But even if that is an exaggeration, the story's intended effect upon readers depends upon accepting that a wealth gap had opened up between richer and poorer priests by this time. The tithing system therefore contributed to the fracturing of society.[21]

Ananias also became involved with the dagger-men. During an unspecified festival a group of the dagger-men kidnapped the secretary or scribe of the Temple captain, Eleazar, the son of Ananias, at night. (This was the Eleazar who would soon play a key role in the outbreak of the revolt against Rome.) The dagger-men then contacted Ananias and told him that they would return the scribe to him if he would persuade Albinus to free 10 of their colleagues who had been captured. Ananias convinced Albinus to make the exchange. The concession, of course, encouraged more kidnappings. Soon "the brigands" kidnapped some of Ananias's own staff and held onto them in exchange for the release of some of the dagger-men.[22]

While these kidnappings were taking place King Agrippa's popularity was declining, at least among the Jews, in part due to his benefactions to largely Gentile cities. He built up Caesarea Philippi (Panias) and renamed the expanded city Neronias in honor of the emperor Nero, as we know from coins minted there bearing the new name of the city.[23] For Berytus (Beirut) he had constructed a theater at great expense and then arranged for annual spectacles. That project cost tens of thousands of drachmas. Distributions of grain and olive oil were also made. The city was adorned with statues, including copies of ancient sculptures. Agrippa's own subjects felt that they were being stripped of their possessions to decorate a foreign city.[24]

Agrippa's replacement of the high priest Jesus, the son of Damnaeus, by Jesus, the son of Gamaliel, led to further strife and infighting. The deposed high priest and his successor each collected bands of supporters who first exchanged insults and then showers of rocks. The influential ex–high priest Ananias meanwhile used his wealth to attract those who were susceptible to bribes.[25]

Imitating the high priests, two prominent brothers named Costobar and Saul, who were related to King Agrippa, also organized gangs to advance their interests. Those interests included plundering the property of those who were weaker.[26]

By the end of Albinus's governorship these gangs, or small private armies, once again had competition from the "brigands." For Albinus, having heard that his replacement Gessius Florus was coming from Rome to take his place, decided that he wanted to leave a name for himself as someone who had done something on behalf of the Jerusalemites—and to line his own purse (*sacculus*). He did so by putting to death all prisoners who had been marked for execution and then, for some kind of personal consideration, releasing the rest of the prisoners who had been thrown into prison for small and common offenses. A number of brigands or dagger-men must have been included among the latter if Josephus is correct that after Albinus's gesture, while the prison was empty, the land was once more infested with brigands.[27]

The situation near the end of Albinus's administration could not have been improved by the sudden unemployment of more than 18,000 workers who at last had completed their work on the Temple complex. Josephus's rounded-off figure of 18,000 men laid off may be an exaggeration, but there is no reason to doubt the basic story and its significance, which can be inferred from King Agrippa's response. Although King Agrippa considered putting the men back to work raising the height of the Temple's eastern portico, in the end he decided against it. Some of the unemployed workers might have been hired to pave the streets of the city in white stone. But not all of them can have found work on that project.[28] The sudden unemployment of thousands of men who had been working for years on the Temple project cannot have been a positive development for the economy or welfare of Jerusalem.

Toward the end of Albinus's governorship, for reasons that are not made clear, Agrippa then replaced Jesus, the son of Gamaliel, as high priest with Matthias, son of Theophilus. Matthias would be the high priest when the war with Rome began in 66.[29]

The high-handed actions and corrupt practices of former and current high priests, the collusion of the Roman governor, the lawlessness of gangs, the expenditures of the king, and the end of workfare projects in Jerusalem should have set off alarms in Rome. However, we have no idea whether what was going on in Judaea was even reported to the emperor. If it had been, perhaps Nero would have sent out a capable and incorruptible governor to replace Albinus. Instead he dispatched Gessius Florus.

GESSIUS FLORUS

Florus's tenure as governor soon made Albinus's procuratorship seem like halcyon days. Even Tacitus, no admirer of Jews or Judaism, seems to have understood that Florus was not a good choice to become governor of Judaea.[30] A native of the Greek city of Klazomenai in Asia Minor, Florus obtained the office of Judaea's procurator through the influence of his wife Cleopatra. Cleopatra had been a friend of Nero's murdered and mourned wife, Poppaea Sabina. Thus Florus had a personal connection to the imperial family. That connection gave him license to do his job as he saw fit. His job was to get money.

According to Josephus, Florus despoiled the country and punished people without restraint. The context for Josephus's idea that Florus thought that his main duty was to lay his hands on as much money as possible, however, had to be Nero's need for cash to help rebuild Rome after three of Rome's 14 urban districts had burned to the ground and seven others were left as smoldering ruins as a result of the great (nine-day) fire of July 64.[31]

Nero previously had depended upon his own liberality to help keep Rome's population fed, entertained, and quiescent. But now he literally had incalculable additional expenses, since one-third of Rome's population was homeless and hungry.[32] Under these circumstances the free distributions of grain to adult male citizen-residents of Rome had to be "suspended"—time-honored officialese for ended.[33] But even that cost savings would not rebuild the city. Nero suddenly needed a huge amount of cash. How much we do not know. According to one estimate, however, clearing the site of the burned-out city and dumping the rubble in the Ostian marshes, purchasing and transporting materials needed to rebuild, and paying those who were required to work on the reconstruction cost the equivalent of billions and billions of dollars.[34] Not even the emperor had that kind of cash. One place to get money was from the provincials, including the Jews of Judaea, whose world-famous Temple had a well-known treasury conveniently attached to it.

Nero's responsibility for setting in motion the sequence of events that led to the outbreak of the war between Rome and the Jews in Judaea has seldom been adequately emphasized. Nero may have wanted to burn down the city of Rome and rebuild it according to his own tastes, as alleged by his many prominent critics, including Pliny the Elder, Suetonius, and Cassius Dio.[35] But whether that was his motive or not, once a large part of the city was reduced to ashes, the rebuilding had to be paid for, and the Jews of Judaea, among many other provincials, were put on the hook to help pay the bill.[36]

From Nero's point of view, Judaea and the Temple represented a perfect revenue source. There was already a regular collection system of cash in place, so no new administrative system needed to be organized. The collection of the Temple tax ensured that there would be cash available every year. The way Nero's personally selected tax collector, Florus, went about collecting the revenues that the emperor demanded provoked the population of Judaea. But it was Nero who gave Florus permission not to be too gentle about how he got his hands on the needed revenues.[37] Nero probably did not want a war with the Jews in 66. But his actions made a rebellion not only conceivable but also predictable. For tax-burdened Judaeans, Nero was closer to zero than hero.[38]

Almost inevitably, Florus became a partner of the very brigands that his predecessors at least initially had attempted to control or exterminate. They were the ones, after all, who knew how to acquire large quantities of money without working too hard to get it. Under Florus the brigands were allowed to go about their business as long as the procurator received his share of the plunder. As a result, when Caius Cestius Gallus, the governor of Syria since 63, visited Jerusalem during Passover in April 66, three million people (according to Josephus's impossibly high reckoning) gathered together and reviled Florus as the destroyer of the country.[39]

Florus, who was standing at Gallus's side, dismissed their outcry. Gallus merely promised to secure more moderation from Florus. He then left for Antioch. Although he had already achieved consulates under three emperors (Tiberius, Gaius, and Claudius), Cestius Gallus, who was in his late sixties at the time, perhaps wanted to avoid a conflict with Nero's procurator—and tax-revenue producer—as much as he wanted to keep the peace in Jerusalem.

Florus, who traveled along with the governor of Syria as far as Caesarea, was already thinking about a war with the nation of the Jews, according to Josephus, because it was the only way to cover up his misdeeds. If peace prevailed he expected to be charged before Caesar. Therefore he attempted to bring about a revolt to cover up his lesser crimes.[40]

This is undoubtedly a wild overstatement, if not an outright fabrication on Josephus's part. Florus wanted to raise money, not a war. He would have been satisfied if the Jews just gave him whatever he wanted. But from what followed it does seem clear that Florus was looking for someone to blame for the ensuing violence and chaos. Blaming Nero was out of the question; that left the Jews.

In Caesarea, meanwhile, the Greeks had received from Nero official confirmation of their (the Greeks') government or legal possession of the city. It was at this time, in May 66, Josephus writes, that the war broke out, in the 12th year of Nero's reign.[41] This judgment perhaps was clearer in hindsight. As we have seen, there had been conflict and sometimes open fighting between Greeks and Jews in Caesarea for decades before 66. What seems to have changed in the spring of that year is that the strife that began there spread, and no one was willing or able to put a stop to it until a full-scale war erupted.

THE FUSE

The fighting that intensified into a war in 66 arose out of the intercommunal conflict between Jews and Hellenes or Syrians in Caesarea, briefly summarized in the introduction to this book.[42] The Jews in Caesarea, it will be recalled, owned a synagogue adjoining a plot of land belonging to a Greek. The Jews tried to buy the land from the owner, offering him far more money than the land was worth. The owner refused and then built workshops on the site, making access to the synagogue even more difficult for the Jews.

Some of the young men among the Jews had set upon the builders of the workshops and tried to put a stop to their construction. Florus suppressed their violent obstruction, whereupon some notable Jews, and with them the tax collector (*telones*) John, offered Florus eight talents to see to it that building came to a halt. John was probably a collector of local civic taxes rather than of imperial taxes on land or the poll tax.[43] Eight talents was an enormous sum of money. Divided up into silver Roman coins, eight talents would have been enough to pay the wages of a skilled laborer for more than a century. Florus pocketed the bribe and promptly left for Sebaste. The construction work continued.[44] For Florus the bribe was just business as usual.

The next day, when the Jews gathered together at the synagogue to observe the Sabbath, they found that a pot, turned upside down, had been put up outside the entrance to the synagogue by some Caesarean. On the upturned pot the Caesarean was sacrificing some birds.[45] We don't know what kind of birds were being sacrificed. But the sacrifice presumably was being made to or for some unnamed deity or deities.[46] The fact that only one person was making the sacrifice suggests that some kind of individual concern was being addressed, as opposed to a communal sacrifice carried out to enhance social and political cohesion among a group.[47] Making the sacrifice next to the synagogue in any case was the point. It was meant to further insult and outrage the Jews next door. It succeeded.

Some Jews wanted to refer the matter to the authorities. Those who didn't mind taking matters into their own hands and mixing it up a bit, along with some of the young men, were now spoiling for a fight. For their part, the Caesareans who also were inclined toward confrontation had sent the man to make the bird sacrifices in the first place. They too were itching for action. Soon the two sides were exchanging blows.[48]

In Florus's absence a cavalry commander named Iucundus intervened.[49] After getting rid of the offending pot, he tried to end the fighting between the two sides. However, not even he could cope with the violence of the Caesareans.

Since the Roman government was incapable of protecting them, the Jews gathered up their laws—presumably their sacred scrolls—and retired to the town of Narbata, some six to seven miles southeast of Caesarea. Twelve of their leading men, along with John the tax collector, went to see Florus in Sebaste to complain about what had happened. There they gently reminded the governor about the gift (or bribe) of eight talents they had lavished upon him. Instead of addressing their complaint or giving the money back Florus clapped the distinguished members of the delegation into irons because they had removed the laws from Caesarea.[50] Why the

Roman governor considered the removal of the laws to be a crime is not known precisely. Most likely Florus was simply looking for an excuse to silence the delegates.

News of what had happened in Caesarea quickly made its way to Jerusalem. The reaction there was restrained at first, even after it became clear that Florus had no intention of taking any action against the Greek who had instigated the incident in Caesarea. But then Florus had 17 talents of silver removed from the treasury of the Temple.[51]

Florus may have seized the money to make up for back taxes that were owed.[52] But that was not the motive imputed to Florus by Josephus. Florus claimed that the money taken was needed "for the sake of imperial service." What Florus probably meant by that rather vague phrase was that Nero needed cash from the Temple treasury to help mitigate Rome's financial crisis.[53] An emperor whose popularity was based upon his ability to entertain and feed Rome's masses could not afford to have the matinees canceled and the grain dole permanently halted. Whatever Florus's motive was, his timing did not hit the note.

The people in Jerusalem were very unhappy about the withdrawal of the Temple funds. A governor failing to punish a Greek for insulting some Jews in Caesarea was one thing and may not have stood out against a general background of interethnic conflict; pillaging the Temple was another matter entirely. The response was immediate and vehement but essentially peaceful and not without an element of humorous street theater.

Some Jews rushed to the Temple and, after invoking Nero's name, begged the emperor to free them from Florus's tyranny. Others excoriated and then mocked Florus. Going around with a basket, they begged for spare change for Florus, as if the Roman governor were destitute.[54] Florus didn't see the humor. He proceeded to gather together a force of cavalry and infantry and advanced upon the city, determined to get what he wanted by means of arms and intimidation.[55]

The citizens of the city, who wished if possible to preempt Florus's assault, went out of the city to meet the troops and got ready to give Florus an obedient reception. Florus, however, sent a centurion named Capito with 50 cavalrymen ahead of the army with orders to tell the Jews to go back into the city and not to mock with a show of friendliness someone that they had insulted so recently. If they were courageous and so fond of speaking freely, he continued, they should insult him to his face and show their love of freedom, not only by means of words but also by arms.

Florus's words and the sight of Capito's cavalry unnerved the multitude. Before they had a chance to acclaim Florus, as they had planned to do, or to show the soldiers their desire to obey orders, the people dispersed to their homes. They spent an anxious night beset by fear and depression.[56]

After Florus entered the city he took up residence in the palace(s), surely the Herodian palace in the Upper City on Jerusalem's western hill. The next day Florus had a *bema,* or tribunal seat, set up in front of the palaces. The chief priests, the nobles, and the most distinguished citizens came forth and appeared before the seat. Florus ordered them to surrender those who had abused him and told the assembled dignitaries that if they did not they would feel his vengeance.

They answered that the people wanted peace, and they sought forgiveness for those who had spoken disrespectfully. They told the procurator that it was not surprising that in such a large crowd there should be a few reckless and thoughtless individuals, on account of their age. But it was impossible to pick out those who were at fault. Everyone was now remorseful, and out of fear for what had been done would deny it anyway. If Florus was concerned about peace for the nation and wanted to save the city for the Romans, they said, he ought to forgive the few who had given offense for the sake of the many who were blameless.[57] It should be noted that the leaders in Jerusalem—so often pilloried for their failures—at this crucial moment, operating under great pressure from different quarters, stood up for their people and tried to do the right and sensible thing for them.

Florus, who obviously was rather thin-skinned and didn't like being told how to do his job, responded in a way that was far from forgiving or temperate or showed any desire to defuse the situation. Rather, he shouted at the soldiers to sack the so-called Upper Agora, one of Jerusalem's four markets, located just to the east of Herod's palace in the Upper City.[58] Thus on 16 Iyyar/ April–May of 66, the troops under Florus's command plundered the Upper Agora of Jerusalem and also broke into private houses and killed their inhabitants. A fight within the narrow alleys ensued, and there was a massacre of all those who were caught. There was pillaging of every kind.

Many of the moderate citizens who were caught were brought before Florus. They were scourged and crucified. The victims included women and children and numbered 3,600. Among them were Jews of the Roman equestrian order.[59] Membership in this Roman socioeconomic order, from which many of Rome's military officers and imperial officials were drawn, was based upon a substantial property qualification.[60] Provincials who qualified for inclusion were locally prominent, wealthy people. The execution of Roman citizens of any rank without trial was illegal under Roman law, at least in principle.

While this massacre was going on, King Agrippa II was away in Egypt congratulating Tiberius Iulius Alexander on his appointment to the governorship of Egypt (*praefectus Aegypti*). But his slightly younger sister, Berenice, who later had a long affair with none other than Titus, was in Jerusalem to fulfill a vow and witnessed the massacre.[61] As it was taking place Berenice repeatedly tried to intervene with Florus to put an end to the bloodshed.[62] But the Roman governor ignored her pleas. Indeed, prisoners were tortured and killed in front of her very eyes, and she herself was forced to seek refuge in the palace, protected by her guards, lest Florus's soldiers attack and kill her too.[63]

The next day the mass of the city's inhabitants made their way into the Upper Agora where they lamented what had happened. But they also cast aspersions upon Florus. The leaders of the Jews and the high priests begged the crowd to desist and not to provoke Florus further. The people complied out of respect for those who implored them. But they also did not want to give Florus an excuse to commit further atrocities.

Florus then sent for the chief priests and the leading men. He told them that the people had only one way to prove that they intended to desist from further revolutionary activity: that was by going out to meet the two cohorts of soldiers from Caesarea that were approaching the city (somewhere between 1,000 and 2,000 soldiers). By this demand Florus clearly intended to humiliate the Jews, who already had been the victims of his violence.

Florus then sent instructions ahead to the centurions leading the cohorts. He ordered the soldiers not to return the traditional salute of the Jews when they came out to greet them. If there were any word of disrespect uttered about him, he added, he ordered the soldiers to use their arms.[64] The order not to return the Jews' salute was a deliberate provocation, and under the circumstances can only be understood as an excuse to use violence.

Despite what the people had already suffered, the high priests urged the people to comply with Florus's orders and when they met the cohorts outside the city to give them a polite reception. Some refused to listen to the high priests altogether. They were now committed to insurrection. In light of the massacre that had just taken place the majority of the crowd also favored a less conciliatory reception of the troops.[65] Having seen so much of their own people's blood already spilled, many of the city's inhabitants wanted blood for the blood of their fellow Jews.

Understanding what might happen if the crowd gave the cohorts a hostile greeting, the priests and servants of God, dressed up in their priestly robes
and carrying the holy vessels in procession, fell down on their knees and
begged the people to safeguard the sacred ornaments, and not to incite the
Romans, thereby giving them an excuse to pillage the treasures of the Temple.
Heaping dust upon their own heads, tearing their garments, and exposing
their chests, the priests appealed individually to the most notable citizens and
to the people as a whole not to give offense over such a small matter and
thereby hand their fatherland over to those who wished to sack it.

They asked how the Roman troops would profit by receiving a salute from
the Jews and what recompense the Jews would get for past events (i.e., the
massacre) by refusing to go out from the city? But if they welcomed the Romans with their accustomed courtesy, they said, they would cut the ground
from beneath Florus for further hostilities and gain for themselves their fatherland and freedom from further suffering. It was feeble, they concluded,
to be persuaded by a few insurrectionists when they, being such a large body,
ought to coerce even those who were not content to join in their own well-
reasoned policy.[66]

By these arguments the leaders of the Jews in Jerusalem calmed down
the masses. They then led them out of the city in a well-ordered way. When
they met the troops, the Jews immediately saluted the Romans. As ordered by
Florus, the soldiers did not return the salute. In response, some among the
Jews started to shout out things against Florus. That was the cue for Florus's
soldiers to attack.

Right away the soldiers closed upon the Jews and struck them with clubs.
The cavalry pursued those who fled and trampled them. Many who were
wounded by the blows of the Romans fell down. More pressed up against each
other. People pushed each other as they tried to get back into the city through
the gates. The pushing and shoving of individuals only impeded the flight of
all. What happened to those who stumbled was horrible. Suffocated and man-
gled by the mob trampling upon them, they were crushed. Their bodies were
so mutilated that afterward they could not even be recognized by their relatives for burial.[67]

The soldiers pursued those who were fleeing, beating those they caught
up with. The Jews who made it in back within the city gates were driven into
the suburban area called Bezetha, the new city, to the north of the Temple
Mount. (See map 4.) The pursuing Romans meanwhile were trying to push their

way through the crowds and take control of the Temple and the Antonia Fortress. With the same objective in mind, Florus led his men out from the palace's court and struggled to reach the fortress. He failed because the Jews turned upon him and blocked his advance, while those standing on the rooftops also threw things at the Romans. Overwhelmed by the missiles from above and unable to cut a way through the masses that blocked the narrow alleyways, the Romans were forced to make a retreat to their camp next to the palaces.[68]

The rebels, who feared that Florus might attack again and capture the Temple through the Antonia, quickly climbed up to the porticoes that connected the two buildings and destroyed them. The Temple was thus cut off from the Antonia Fortress. This decisive action arrested Florus's greed. It had been the Temple treasures that he wanted to get his hands on. Now that the porticoes were broken, his desire was blunted.[69] The Temple treasures were literally out of his reach. The situation had been reversed in an instant. Minutes before, Florus and the cohorts from Caesarea had been massacring Jews, most of them unarmed civilians. Now they were outnumbered and effectively besieged by a numerically superior, enraged populace. Florus's deliberate provocation had backfired catastrophically.

As soon as it was possible, Florus sent for the chief priests and the council and informed them that he intended to depart from the city. He added that he would leave them a garrison such as they thought necessary. They replied that they would assume complete responsibility for order in the city and also forestall any revolutionary activity if he would leave a single cohort, provided that it was not the one that had been engaged in the fighting. The crowd held a grudge against that cohort because of what they had suffered from it.

Florus changed the cohort and then departed for Caesarea with the rest of the force.[70] Behind him he left a city in which the unthinkable—war against Rome—had become not only thinkable but even desirable and not only for dagger-men, false prophets, and magicians.

PART TWO

The War in the North

CHAPTER 7

The Regional Cleansing

CESTIUS INTERVENES

After fleeing Jerusalem, the procurator Florus sent a report to Cestius, the governor of Syria. The report accused the Jews of rebellion. He portrayed them as the initiators of the fighting. The officials of the Jerusalemites did not keep silent in response. They and Agrippa's sister Berenice wrote to Cestius about the harm that Florus had inflicted upon the city.

Cestius read the letters and talked the matter over with his officers. It seemed to the officers that Cestius should go south to Jerusalem personally with an army, either to put an end to the rebellion, if one had broken out, or else to confirm the loyalty of the Jews. Cestius did not follow his officers' recommendation, at least immediately.[1]

By the norms of Roman life expectancy Cestius was very old and had been favored by the gods. Although good nutrition and wealth increased the chances of surviving longer, the average life span of most Romans was somewhere in the range of 20 to 30 years.[2] Most adults died by their mid-forties, and less than 15 percent of the population lived to 60. Cestius was probably 69 or 70 years old in 66, and he had been a Roman consul three times before he was appointed governor of Syria in 63.[3] Other than emperors very few Roman citizens held the consulate three times. So the gods had been kind to Cestius. Unfortunately his warranty on the gods' favor was about to expire.

It would be expensive, time consuming, and tiring to lead an army some 300 miles south from Antioch to Jerusalem. Cestius would have to gather together the army and its supplies. At the time of Passover (Nisan/Xanthicus/ April), just a few months before, he had visited Jerusalem.[4] Sooner or later the expedition would also come to Nero's attention. Inevitably the emperor would ask questions. No doubt Cestius thought it would be safer and wiser to gather more information before acting decisively. Cestius decided to follow one of the emperor Augustus's favorite bywords: *Speude bradeos* or "Make haste slowly."[5]

THE MISSION OF NEAPOLITANUS

So Cestius decided to send the tribune Neapolitanus to Jerusalem. The tribune must have been decades younger than Cestius. Neapolitanus's orders were to investigate the state of affairs in the city and then to bring back to Cestius an accurate report about the attitude of the Jews there.[6] A young tribune's report would be subject to interpretation and could be cited later as evidence either for action or inaction.

But Neapolitanus did not go directly to Jerusalem. Rather, for diplomatic reasons, he first went to meet King Agrippa II at Iamnia (Yavneh) to inform the king about his mission and the reasons for it. Agrippa had gone to Iamnia on his way back from Alexandria.[7] The meeting indicates the degree of coordination and cooperation that existed between Rome's regional representatives and the king.

The high priests, leading citizens, and the council from Jerusalem also traveled to Iamnia to greet Agrippa. After doing homage to the king, the dignitaries gave Agrippa a full account of the misfortunes that had befallen them and of Florus's cruelties.

Agrippa believed what he was told and was aggrieved by it, according to Josephus. But in the interests of diplomacy, he affected to disbelieve what he had heard. He did this to divert the Jews from taking revenge. The priests and leaders understood Agrippa's tactics and intention, Josephus reports, but the rest of the population was less than impressed with the king's diplomatic maneuvering.[8] Some of them may have been asking themselves whose side Agrippa was on. Others probably knew. Agrippa did not owe his crown to them.

To make their point about Florus, the people came out some nine miles from Jerusalem to greet Agrippa and Neapolitanus as they approached the city. The widows of those who had been killed during the massacre ran forward and uttered ear-splitting cries. The rest of the people responded to their shrieks with wailing, begging Agrippa to aid them and recounting to Neapolitanus what they had suffered at Florus's hands.[9]

After entering the city they showed the king and the tribune the desolate Upper Agora and their plundered homes. Neapolitanus was given a tour as far as Siloam, the pool or reservoir located on the southeast side of the walled city, to show him their willing subordination to all Roman officials—except for Florus, that is.[10]

Neapolitanus then went up to the Temple, where he called the people together. Because Neapolitanus was a non-Jew this can only mean that he and his audience must have assembled within the Court of Gentiles, which was separated from the areas of the sanctuary restricted to Jews, between the outer wall of the pre-Herodian Temple platform and the *hel* or terrace. The line between the two areas was demarcated by the *Soreg*, a stone balustrade that Josephus reports was about 5 feet, 2 inches high. The *Soreg* probably functioned as a barrier on the eastern, southern, and western sides of the Herodian sanctuary.[11] At intervals of the balustrade there were inscriptions written in Greek and Roman letters (i.e., Latin) warning non-Jews not to proceed into the restricted area. Two of the surviving Greek examples read, "No foreigner shall enter into the balustrade of the Temple or within the Temple. Whoever is caught doing so will have himself to blame for his own death that will follow as a consequence."[12]

There is no record of anyone undergoing capital punishment for not heeding the warning. What is more significant about the prohibition itself, however, are the assumptions, first, that its Greek and, at one time, Latin texts could be read by visitors, and second, that "foreigners" visited the Temple. The Temple, in other words, might be an object of interest to non-Jews.[13] In fact we know that the Roman emperors were included among such interested parties because they probably had subsidized sacrifices at the Temple since the time of Augustus or at least benefited from them.

Neapolitanus complimented the Jews for their loyalty to the Romans and entreated them to keep the peace. After paying his devotions to God from the area permitted to non-Jews, Neapolitanus went back to Cestius to make his report about the situation (in late June 66).[14] Whatever the details were, the conclusion of the report cannot have been that the Jews of Jerusalem had been or were in revolt from Rome.

If what Josephus tells us about Neapolitanus's mission and its outcome is true, there was still time to head off a major confrontation between Jerusalem and Rome in the early summer of 66. What happened next, however, further provoked those who already had suffered at Florus's hands. Despite King Agrippa's intentions, too much blood had already been spilled.

THE SPEECH OF AGRIPPA

While Neapolitanus apparently was conveying to Cestius the news about the Jews' loyalty to Rome, the mass of Jews was pressuring King Agrippa and the high priests to send ambassadors to Nero denouncing Florus. They refused to keep silent after such a massacre, thereby leaving themselves open to the false charge of rebellion. They realized that they would be blamed for resorting to arms unless immediate action was undertaken to identify and make plain who had started the hostilities.[15] The motive that Josephus ascribes to the people for urging Agrippa and the high priests to send the embassy has been doubted. But it seems logical under the circumstances and fits into an empire-wide pattern of provincials appealing to emperors to redress wrongs committed by governors.[16] But whatever their motive, they did not get the response from the king that they wanted or perhaps anticipated.

Agrippa immediately recognized how disagreeable would be the task of appointing a group of representatives to denounce Florus to the emperor; it also might compromise his own reputation and position and call into question his loyalty to Rome. Agrippa no doubt understood that ultimately it was Nero who had been responsible for Florus seizing the Temple monies "for imperial service." Florus would claim that he was just following orders. At the same time, the king also could see the danger, even to himself, of letting the flames that were already burning among the Jews burst out into open warfare. The Romans had not given Agrippa his kingdom to heat up a pot that was on the brink of boiling over. His job was to keep a lid on it. If he couldn't do it, the Romans would find someone else who could. He could then join Archelaus and the other failed Herodians in southern Gaul. Agrippa obviously had no intention of being rusticated.

So, after seating his sister Berenice on the roof of the Hasmonean palace, Agrippa called the people to the Xystus and spoke to them. In Greek, *xystus* was an architectural term for the covered portico of a gymnasium or exercise area; in Jerusalem the area called the Xystus was also used periodically for informal assemblies.[17]

Agrippa began by saying that he would not have made his speech at all if he knew that everyone favored the worse policy. But he knew that the most honest and single-minded citizens were in favor of keeping the peace, he said. Those who preferred war did so because they were young and inexperienced, or they hoped to regain independence or to enrich themselves during the general tumult. He, on the other hand, would tell them what was in their self-interest.

He then talked about the pretexts for going to war. The first was revenge for injustice, the second, servitude. He said that these objectives were mutually exclusive. If they desired revenge, he asked, what good was it to extol freedom? And if they really wanted freedom, what good was it to complain about their rulers?

If the pretexts were considered on their own merits, the weakness of the reasons for going to war were apparent, he asserted. Although the actions of the individual Roman governors were harsh, he conceded, it did not follow that all Romans were unjust, and the actions of the unjust few did not justify going to war against Rome itself.

As far as liberty was concerned, Agrippa said that it was too late to strive after it; that should have been done when Pompey invaded the country. He then cited examples of others who had submitted to Rome, including the Athenians, the Lacedaemonians (Spartans), the Macedonians, and many others who had been far more powerful than his listeners.

He invited his audience to compare their own military resources with those of the Romans. Citing examples of peoples who had been defeated by the Romans, such as the Gauls, he asked what inspired their confidence that they could defy the Romans?

Agrippa spoke of liberty and how a long list of noble and proud peoples and cities had bowed before Roman governors and their soldiers. These included not only the Athenians and the Macedonians but also 500 cities in Asia, the Thracians, the Illyrians, the Dalmatians, the Gauls, the Iberians, the Germans, the Britains, the Parthians, the Carthaginians, the Cyrenians, indeed the third part of the inhabited world bounded by the Atlantic Ocean and the pillars of Hercules, and right up to the Red Sea, the countless Ethiopians. All had been subdued by the Romans and paid tribute to them. The Thracians, who lived in a country far more rugged and stronger than Judaea, were kept in check by two legions, the Dalmatians by one, the Gauls by 1,200 soldiers, and the Iberians over their vast land by one legion.

Closer to the home of his listeners, he brought up the example of Egypt, with a population of 7,500,000, apart from Alexandria, which did not disdain to submit to Roman domination. Alexandria, he said, paid more tribute to Rome in one month than did Agrippa's audience, and fed Rome for four months each year by the grain it sent to Rome; Alexandria, protected by deserts and by seas without ports, by rivers and lagoons, was no match for the fortune of Rome.

He then asked what allies they expected to have for their war. Perhaps they were expecting help from their fellow tribesmen in Adiabene beyond the Euphrates? But their Parthian master would not allow them to do so and thus endanger his truce with the Romans.

Their only hope was divine assistance. But the vast size of the Roman empire was proof that God was on the side of the Romans. Moreover, fighting the war itself would inevitably cause them to compromise their laws. They should not fight on the Sabbath, whereas they could be sure that the Romans would, just as Pompey had done. If they violated their laws to fight the war, how would that be consistent with the justification for going to war, which was to uphold the institutions of their fathers? How could they invoke the aid of God after deliberately omitting to pay him the service owed to him? There would be no assistance from man or God in this war, and the aggressor therefore was going to certain disaster with eyes wide open.

Nor would there be any mercy. There perhaps were some who expected that the Romans would fight them under special terms and treat them with some kind of concern. On the contrary, the Romans would make an example of them to the rest of nations. They would burn down the holy city and wipe out their race. Those who survived would have no place of safety because the whole world had the Romans as their masters or dreaded having them. Moreover, the Jews who inhabited foreign cities would also be imperiled. If they went to war they would be butchered by their enemies.

He urged them to take pity, if not on their children and wives, then at least on their mother city and its sacred enclosures. He begged them to spare the Temple and to save for themselves the sanctuary with its sacred places. For the Romans, seeing that their self-control in the past had only been met with ingratitude, would restrain their hands no longer.

Agrippa closed his speech by calling upon the sanctuary, God's holy angels, and their common city to bear witness that he had held back nothing conducive to their salvation. If they decided rightly, he said, they would enjoy peace. But if they let themselves be swept away by passions, they faced tremendous danger without him.[18]

After finishing his speech, Agrippa and his sister Berenice both burst into tears. The crowd shouted in response that they were not making war against the Romans but against Florus, because of the things they had suffered. Agrippa replied that the things they had done already were acts of war against the Romans. They had not paid the tribute to Caesar, and they had cut off the porticoes of the Antonia to the Temple. He told them that if they wanted to clear themselves of the accusation of rebellion they needed to restore the porticoes and to pay the tax. The fortress did not belong to Florus, and it was not to Florus that the tax monies went.[19] If Agrippa did make this last point, it shows that even he understood that it was none other than Nero who was responsible for the collection of the taxes to which at least some of the Jews had objected in 66.

The people were persuaded by these arguments, and along with the king and Berenice, they went up to the Temple and started rebuilding the stoas. The officials and the councilors meanwhile went to the villages and began to levy the tribute. What was owed amounted to 40 talents, and it was collected quickly.[20] For the time being Agrippa prevented the outbreak of war.

Afterward, however, he tried to persuade the people to obey Florus until Caesar sent out a successor. This upset the people, Josephus tells us, and they abused the king and banished him from the city. Some of them threw stones at him.[21]

The king now supposedly realized that the ardor of the revolutionaries could not be extinguished by words. Angry at the insults and stones directed toward him, Agrippa sent some of the most influential men and leading citizens to Florus in Caesarea, from whom he could choose some to collect the tribute in the countryside, and then the king went back to his own kingdom (mid-Tammuz/Panemus 66).[22]

Josephus does not tell us to what location in his kingdom Agrippa retreated, though Caesarea Philippi must be a strong possibility. Later on, after Vespasian's conquest of Iotapata, it would be to Caesarea Philippi that Vespasian would go with his troops for rest and recreation at the king's invitation.[23] In any case, it was while he was in his kingdom in mid-Tammuz that Agrippa appointed Noarus or Varus to be his deputy while he went off to see Cestius Gallus either in Berytus or Antioch.[24] Berytus, of course. was closer to Agrippa's kingdom and Jerusalem than Antioch. Noarus was a relative of King Sohaemus of Emesa and a member of the Ituraean nobility (in Lebanon).

There was wisdom in the speech Agrippa made to the Jews assembled in the Xystus in the summer of 66, as Josephus reports it. The justifications for going to war apparently given by some Jews were different and arguably contradictory, and the war would be fought, not against a single procurator, but against Caesar and ultimately all the forces he needed to muster. The list of the peoples that Agrippa cited who had submitted to the Romans, while not exhaustive by any means, certainly included nations that had much larger populations, greater lands, and far more resources than the Judaeans possessed. It was also true that the Judaeans at the time had no army or navy with which to fight Rome. Moreover, there was no reason at all to think that the Romans would treat the Jews any more generously if they defeated them than they had the Carthaginians or the Gauls or anyone else.

But did Agrippa say to the Jews assembled in the Xystus in Jerusalem exactly what we read in Josephus's text?[25] There are reasons to think that the speech as reported in the *War* was at least revised by Josephus later when he was in Rome and had access to official Roman documents. It also was probably reshaped to make it consistent with Josephus's own views about the causes, course, and outcome of the war after its conclusion.

For example, the exact figures that Josephus has Agrippa give for the numbers of soldiers and legions that the Romans used to keep in check the Dalmatians, the Gauls, the Iberians, and the other provincials, for the population of Alexandria, and for how much grain it supplied to Rome all suggest that the text of the speech is based upon some official Roman government sources or conversations with Roman officials. How would Agrippa have known how many soldiers there were in Gaul at the time or how much grain Alexandria sent to Rome?

Much more importantly, what Agrippa supposedly told the Jews about God being on Rome's side of history is similar to what Josephus himself later wrote about God and whose side he was on, both in the *War* and the later *Antiquities*. According to Agrippa in 66 the proof that God was on the side of the Romans was the size of their empire.[26] Throughout the *War* and the *Antiquities* Josephus consistently claimed that God had taken the side of Rome in history and had decided to punish the Jews because of the impiety of (some) Jews.[27] If we read Agrippa's speech in its present form as a Josephan reflection upon the events of 66–74 rather than as a contemporary warning about the potential consequences of a revolt against Rome, the message of the speech was that Agrippa told the Jews what would happen if they revolted and that is (almost) exactly what happened. The Romans did not wipe out the *ethnos* or nation of the Jews in 70 or 73–74, but almost everything else that Agrippa predicted occurred.

The speech in effect exculpates Josephus's Roman friends and Agrippa and makes the rebellious Jews themselves responsible for the destruction of the

Temple and Jerusalem. The speech blames the Jewish rebels for the sake of Josephus's Greek-reading Roman audience, including the emperors.[28] The Jews chose war and suffered the consequences. The speech amounts to a rhetorically polished "I told you so!"

Agrippa was Rome's local point man. No one present in the Xystus that day would have been surprised to hear him give a speech advising the Jews not to go to war with Rome. But what Josephus reports Agrippa to have said has distracted historians from focusing on what Agrippa actually advised the Jews to do and why his final piece of advice was rejected and led many Jews to choose revolution and war.

Agrippa told the Jews to pay their taxes, to rebuild the porticos that connected the Temple to the Roman fortress of Antonia, and to obey Florus. Advising the people to take the first two actions amounted to telling them to put Roman chains back on themselves and on the Temple. Yet they did it. What they would not do was to obey Florus. Why?

Florus was responsible for ordering two massacres of unarmed Jews. Perhaps Josephus exaggerated the numbers of those who had been killed. But in a relatively small city everyone must have known someone who was murdered by Florus's soldiers. They would not obey such a man. Not being willing to give obedience to such a man was not irrational. Agrippa was both right and wrong. Taking on Rome was no trifling matter, but neither was the grievance.

THE END OF SACRIFICES ON BEHALF
OF THE ROMAN PEOPLE AND CAESAR

Meanwhile, to the south, around this time some of those who reportedly were keen on stirring up a war went and made an assault upon the fortress at Masada. Having taken it by a kind of stratagem or surprise attack (*lathra* in Greek), they killed the guards of the Romans there and stationed a garrison of their own upon the plateau.[29] Josephus, unfortunately, does not identify precisely who the insurgents were.

In Jerusalem at the same time, in the late summer of 66, Eleazar, who held the position of Temple captain and was the son of the former high priest Ananias, persuaded those who supervised the Temple services not to receive a gift or sacrifice from any foreigner or outsider; that is, a non-Jew.[30] Despite opposition from many of the chief priests, "the notables," and other experts, the priests remained adamant, and the sacrifices on behalf of "these" (*touton* in Greek) and Caesar were stopped.[31] Josephus claimed that the cessation of the sacrifices was the foundation (*katabole*) of the war against Romans.[32]

Some historians have argued that the cessation of the sacrifices was a declaration of war on Rome by Eleazar and those who supported him; others that stopping the sacrifices was not even directed against Rome, much less a declaration of war with Rome.[33] To understand the significance of putting an end to the sacrifices we have to consider the context of Eleazar's action, exactly what Eleazar did, and what the point of the sacrifices had been.

At least according to Josephus, Eleazar convinced the priests in charge of the Temple services not to accept gifts or sacrifices from foreigners after the two massacres of Jews outside and then inside Jerusalem by the Roman auxiliary soldiers commanded by Florus, Florus's retreat from Jerusalem, Neapolitanus's mission, and Agrippa's speech in which he urged the Jerusalemites to give obedience to Florus.

It is true that Eleazar apparently urged the priests not to accept a gift or sacrifice from any foreigner. He did not specify that they should not accept gifts or sacrifices from Romans alone. At the time, however, there is no evidence of gifts or sacrifices being accepted from foreigners other than Romans or for them. It could be argued that the way that Eleazar formulated his recommendation was designed to make not accepting the gifts or sacrifices a matter of general principle. That might have given some cover to priests who did not wish to come out as anti-Roman. But no one would have doubted who the principle was aimed at: the Romans.

Was not taking gifts or sacrifices from foreigners—specifically the Romans—a declaration of war against the Romans?

Earlier in the *War* Josephus implied that Jews sacrificed twice daily for Caesar and the Roman people. Philo of Alexandria reported that it was Augustus who had subsidized the sacrifices of two sheep and a bull to the God of the Jews for Caesar and the Roman people in perpetuity.[34] Some scholars have argued that the accounts of Josephus and Philo are inconsistent because they seem to disagree about who subsidized the sacrifices. But the two accounts might be consistent if we hypothesize that while Augustus and his successors paid for the sacrifices, the sacrifices at the Temple were nevertheless performed by Jews. The more important point is that the two accounts are entirely consistent about the purpose of the sacrifices.

They were made for the sake of the welfare of Caesar and the Roman people. No other purpose is plausible, and highlighting that purpose helps to explain why the sacrifices were stopped by Eleazar and what the significance of halting them was. After Roman auxiliary soldiers under the command of Florus, the emperor's handpicked governor, murdered thousands of Jewish civilians both outside and inside Jerusalem, and it was clear that no Roman or Roman-appointed official was going to do anything about it, it is inconceivable that Eleazar or anyone else in his position would have been willing to take part in making sacrifices on behalf of an emperor who countenanced such acts or the Romans (or auxiliaries) who carried them out. Making sacrifice to their God for the welfare of foreigners who killed their countrymen was too much for Eleazar and the priests he convinced. It was not, however, a declaration of war.

What stopping the sacrifices did was to deny the Roman emperor and the Romans (implicitly) access to the God of the Jews through sacrifice by Jewish priests at the Temple.[35] If the Romans were unwilling to protect their Jewish subjects, indeed were willing to kill large numbers of them, the Jews would cease to serve as intermediaries between the Romans and their God. Denying the Romans access to their God was a declaration of theological and political separation and independence from Rome.

The inscriptions and iconography on the coins minted by those who controlled the Temple and access to the silver needed to produce the silver shekels, half-shekels, and quarter-shekels from the time of the cessation of the sacrifices through the fifth year of the war are consistent with this interpretation of what stopping the sacrifices meant; they help us understand how those who were in control of the coins' production wanted their actions to be understood.

From the spring of 66, on the obverse side of the silver shekels was inscribed the legend "Shekel of Israel" in Paleo-Hebrew. Beneath the legend was inscribed one of the first five letters of the Hebrew alphabet, from *aleph* to *he*. These letters doubled for the numbers 1 through 5 and dated the coins. In the center of the obverse side was a representation of the vessel used to gather up and measure the first-fruit offering at the Temple during the Passover celebration. On the reverse side of the coins the legend read, "Jerusalem is Holy" or "Jerusalem the Holy," and in the middle of the coin there was an image of a blooming pomegranate or perhaps the staff of the high priest.

Over the course of five years there were changes in the coinage; after the first year, for instance, in addition to the Paleo-Hebrew letter signifying the year, the letter *shin* for year is added to make clear during which year the coin was minted. Other variations are attributable to the actions of the individuals who created the coin dies and struck the coins, just as we would expect.

The *omer* (measuring vessel) on coins from year 1 has slightly different shapes.[36] But overall, there is a remarkable consistency, at least with respect to the legends and the images, remembering that our conclusions are based upon a sample of all the silver coins that once existed.

Using the phrase "Shekel of Israel" was a choice and signified a desire on the part of those who authorized these coins to be associated with the name and story of Jacob, who received the name of Israel after striving with God, and from whom God promised that a nation would be descended.[37] The silver shekels of Israel therefore were the coins of a nation given to the descendants of Jacob/Israel by God. The numbers beneath the legend numbered the years of the nation. The writing in Paleo-Hebrew was another significant choice; using an older version of Hebrew was a linguistic archaism designed to connect the coins and their producers to the ancient past of the Hebrews/ Israelites. It is probable that few of the people who saw or used the coins could have read the legends in the ancient language of the people. That was the point: using Paleo-Hebrew was a deliberate attempt to identify Israel with its ancient biblical foundations. The *omer* was a reminder of the sacrifices made to God at Passover after he had liberated his people from Egypt. No historically informed Jew could have missed the analogy between the liberation from Egypt and the liberation from Rome.

The legend "Jerusalem is Holy" (on year 1 coins) or "Jerusalem the Holy" (years 2–5) on the reverse referenced the ancient sacred capital of the Jewish state. If the image on the reverse is a stylized pomegranate, it evoked the fertility of Israel; if the high priest's staff, the role of the high priest as an intermediary and guide of the people.

The inscriptions and images on the silver coins minted by those in charge of the Temple linked the Jews to the ancient beginnings of their nation and to the promise that they would rule over their land. They were reminders of their special relationship to God. There was no Rome in that relationship.

The bronze coins date themselves in Paleo-Hebrew in fully spelled-out words to years 2–4 of the war on their obverse side. The image in the middle of the reverse side is that of a wine jar. On the reverse side the legend, in a semi-circle around the edge of the coins, reads "For the Freedom of Zion" surrounding a vine leaf during year 3 and "For the Redemption of Zion" during year 4. Zion was the name of the hill to the south of Mt. Moriah in Jerusalem, but it became synonymous with the Temple, the city of Jerusalem, and Israel or the land of Israel.[38] The letter shapes change between years 3 and 4, and they proclaim their denominations. From year 4 the denominations include "Year 4, Half," "Year 4, Quarter," and just "Year 4" for the smallest coin, clearly one-eighth of a shekel. The image on the reverse of the smallest coin may be that of the *omer* but also possibly a cup of some kind.[39]

Scholars continue to debate the questions of who produced the bronze coins, where they were produced, and especially what is the significance of the difference between the legends reading "For the Freedom of Zion" and "For the Redemption of Zion." Some have argued that Simon bar Giora (for whom see below) was behind the change in the year 4 legend and that it signified his messianic mission and message.[40] Others have claimed that the transition shows that freedom had been achieved by year 4 and that the new goal was the larger one of redemption.[41] Meshorer contended that the change was due to the rebels' increasingly desperate position. By year 4 their only hope was God's divine intervention.[42] Rappaport argued that all of the bronze coins were produced by Simon or those around him and that the differences were a function of where they were produced—outside of Jerusalem in years 2 and 3, and in the Upper City for year 4.[43] Others have questioned how significant the difference between "Freedom" and "Redemption" was, since the meaning of redemption (*ge'ula*) in contemporary sources was very close to that of freedom or liberation (*herut*).[44]

Discussion and debate about who authorized or produced the silver and bronze coins during the war and to what end(s) no doubt will continue. But thus far no one has argued that any of the coins constituted a declaration of war upon Rome. The cessation of sacrifices in the spring of 66 and the coins minted thereafter were not declarations of war; rather they were assertions of independence and ancient nationhood that had been promised to the Jews supposedly before Rome even existed. The real foundation of the war of Jews against Romans was not the cessation of sacrifices or the minting of coins proclaiming the freedom of Zion: it was the slaughter of the civilian population of Jerusalem by Roman auxiliary soldiers on the order of Florus, the handpicked governor of Nero.

Nero apparently had pressed first Albinus and then Florus to squeeze as much money as he could out of the Temple and the Jews of Judaea to help ease his own financial problems.[45] The emperor thus bears a heavy burden of responsibility for the outbreak of the revolt in the spring and summer of 66. The reason why Nero is not more closely associated with the war is that he did not live to see its terrible results—or to capitalize upon them. That was left to Vespasian and his sons.

THE LEADERS OF THE JEWS INTERVENE

After Agrippa's speech, the most powerful citizens came together with the chief priests and the most eminent of the Pharisees to consider the state of affairs. Deciding to make an appeal to those who were causing the strife, they called an assembly of the people. The assembly took place within the confines of the sanctuary in front of the Nicanor Gate, where women were purified after giving birth and lepers were cured. It was a massive triple gate with doors made of Corinthian bronze that provided access from the Court of Women to the east, up to the Court of Israelites, and from there to the inner sanctum of the Temple.[46] Although it was called the Court of Women both men and women were allowed within it.

The Jewish leaders first expressed their outrage at the recklessness of the revolt and at bringing the threat of such a war to the fatherland. Like Agrippa they then sought to refute the war's pretext. They said that their forefathers had decorated the sanctuary from the wealth of people from other tribes for the most part and always had received gifts from outside nations. Not only had they never forbidden sacrifices but, around the Temple, they had set up the offerings that had been dedicated. These offerings were to be seen to this day and had remained there for a long time.

Now there were those who were challenging Roman arms and were inviting a war with them while instituting a religious innovation. Besides putting the city in danger, the leaders said, they were opening it up to the charge of impiety, if Jews alone among peoples did not allow anyone else to sacrifice or worship. If someone should introduce such a law in the case of an individual, they would be aggrieved at its inhumanity, they claimed. Yet they had no regard that the Romans and Caesar should be put outside of the accepted practice.

It was to be feared, however, that once sacrifices were denied to the Romans such sacrifices might not be allowed for themselves. The city might then be placed beyond the pale of Roman hegemony unless, coming to their senses quickly, the priests renewed the sacrifices and set right the act of arrogance before news of it reached those they had treated disrespectfully.[47]

As they said these things, the leaders brought forward the priests who were most experienced about their traditions. These men said that all of their forefathers had received sacrifices from foreigners. What they were referring to presumably included the gifts made to the Temple by a long list of foreign kings: the Persian king Cyrus II (animals for burnt offerings and wheat, salt, wine, and oil for the priests); Artaxerxes I (silver and gold to buy animals, cereal, and drink offerings for sacrifice, vessels, wheat, wine, oil, and salt); Ptolemy II (gold and silver, precious stones, vials, a table, libation cups of gold and silver, a large golden table, gold and silver mixing bowls, and a maeander); Antiochus III (allowance of sacrificial animals, wine, oil and incense, flour, wheat, salt, and timber for work on the Temple); and Seleucus IV (all expenses for the sacrifices).[48] In the letter of Artaxerxes specifying his gifts, the Persian was quoted as commanding that everything should be done for the house of God lest his anger be against the realm of the king and his sons.[49] It was presumably to gain the favor of the Jews' God and avert his wrath that sacrifices were paid for by the Romans since the time of Augustus or were made on their behalf.

None of those who wished for revolution listened to a word spoken by the most prominent Jews. Nor did the Temple ministers (*leitourgoi*) come to their support. They too were preparing the foundation for war according to Josephus.[50]

The leading citizens now understood that it was beyond their power to check the momentum of revolutionary movement, and they recognized that the danger from the Romans would come to them first. They therefore prepared to avoid blame for the war by calling in the Romans and by resorting to force against their fellow citizens. They sent out ambassadors to Florus, led by Simon, son of Ananias, and to Agrippa, perhaps by the end of Tammuz/Panemus/10–11 July. Among the ambassadors were eminent men including Antipas and the brothers Saul and Costobar. All these men were members of the royal family. (Saul and Costobar, it will be recalled, had gathered together gangs to protect their interests during the procuratorship of Albinus.) These emissaries begged the Roman governor and the king to come to the city along with an army and to eradicate the rebellion before it was unstoppable.[51]

To Florus this desperate message was good news, since he had resolved to fan the flames of war, according to Josephus's undoubtedly biased judgment.[52] Florus simply did not reply to the ambassadors. Agrippa, on the other hand, who, we are told, cared equally about the rebels and those against whom the war was being raised, sent 2,000 horsemen from Auranitis, Batanaea, and Trachonitis, led by the cavalry commander Darius and the general (*stratopedarches* or Latin, *praefectus castrorum*) Philip, son of Iacimus, perhaps around 1 Lous/Av.[53]

Assuming that these cavalrymen were based within Agrippa's kingdom, it seems likely that the plea of the ambassadors from Jerusalem reached Agrippa while he was still in his kingdom or before he had set out to see Cestius in Berytus or Antioch.[54] Rounding up and sending cavalry from Auranitis, Batanaea, and Trachonitis south from Caesarea Philippi would have been much easier to arrange than doing so from Berytus or Antioch.

Wherever Agrippa issued the order from, his cavalrymen seem to have been in Jerusalem by 7 Lous/Av.[55] The force's composition, 2,000 cavalrymen and no infantry, indicates that it was put together as a rapid reaction force: cavalry could get to Jerusalem more quickly than a substantial infantry force. Agrippa sent his cavalry down to Jerusalem hoping that its presence might shock the rebels into thinking again until an army equal to the task of putting an end to the insurrection could be mobilized and sent south.

Tactically, however, 2,000 horsemen could not be effective as a fighting force within an urban area such as Jerusalem. Its narrow streets and alleys were not ideal grounds for cavalry maneuvers. So the cavalry force was sent to get to Jerusalem as quickly as possible and to show Agrippa's flag in the city. Agrippa probably hoped that the rebels would be intimidated by the show of force and also wanted to support his friends within the city. He should have known better, or perhaps he wanted to be able to tell his Roman friends that he had not done nothing at the time.

FIGHTING BREAKS OUT IN THE CITY OF JERUSALEM

The "leading citizens," along with the high priests and the people who favored peace, were encouraged by the king's intervention and occupied the Upper City. By the mid–first century CE the Upper City (roughly today's Jewish Quarter) was where many, though not all, of Jerusalem's priestly elites lived in "mansions" that were decorated with Graeco-Roman-style frescoes, mosaics, and expensive luxury items.[56] The most widely known of the houses in this area was associated with the Kathros family, who seem to have been connected to the infamous early first-century CE high priest Caiaphas. (See the following discussion and map 4 for the destruction of the so-called Burnt House associated with the Kathros family.)[57]

The party in favor of rebellion held the Lower City and the Temple. Fighting between the two factions soon broke out, marking the real beginning of the war of Jews against Jews after the cessation of sacrifices and Agrippa's attempted intervention. Both sides used slings and stones, and missiles flew from each side. The lead "bullets" used in such slings sometimes had inscribed on them pithy examples of ancient trash talk, such as "take this!" or "taste it!"[58]

Sometimes companies ventured out and fought each other in hand-to-hand combat. The rebels were superior in daring, the royal troops in skill. For the royal troops the objective was to take the Temple and to drive out those who were seen as polluting the sanctuary. The goal for the rebels led by Eleazar was to capture the Upper City in addition to what they already held. For seven days there was much slaughter on both sides, and neither surrendered the parts of the city they held.[59]

The eighth day of the fighting coincided with the festival of the wood carrying (15 Lous/Av).[60] That was the day when, by tradition, people brought wood to the Temple, first to be inspected at the Chamber of Wood. If the wood was declared to be pure, it was then used to keep the altar fire burning continuously.[61] We know that 350 oxcarts of wood, each one weighing 1,200 Roman pounds, were needed to supply all the whole burnt offerings and other sacrifices made in the Temple each year, with another 513 carts needed for the daily sacrifices to Caesar and Rome. The cost of the wood alone would have been about 5,200 denarii, or enough to pay the wages of a skilled artisan for more than a decade.[62]

Although those who held the Temple prevented their enemies from taking part in this ceremony, some of the dagger-men nevertheless managed to make their way into the sanctuary by force. These men were conscripted into the service of those who held the Temple. The reinforced rebels now pursued their attacks with greater boldness and finally took the Upper City from the royal troops.[63]

Having captured the Upper City the victorious rebels proceeded to the house of Ananias, the ex–high priest, and the palaces of Agrippa and Berenice. These they set on fire.[64] Next the public archives were set alight.[65] This was done to destroy the records of the moneylenders that were kept there. By this act of arson the rebels hoped that the poorer citizens would rise up against the richer ones without fear.[66] This is the first tangible indication that there were tensions between some creditors and some indebted people in Judaean society at the time and that the rebels hoped that those tensions could be exploited to broaden the base of the rebellion—despite Josephus's near silence about the attitude of the indebted toward creditors and Rome in the run-up to the rebellion.

What the episode does not prove is that there was a surge of indebtedness at the time that can be cited as a cause of the revolt. First, the beginning of the revolt predated the burning of the archives in Jerusalem, and second, there is no evidence that debt was a greater problem in 66 than it had been earlier in the first century CE or earlier.[67] Then as now, debt was a fact of life. Debt relief was not the primary motive of those who took up arms against Rome in 66. Nor did it become a slogan of any of the various rebel groups during the war.

As the rebels advanced against their foes, the leading citizens and chief priests escaped. Some hid in the drainage tunnels. Others fled with the royal troops to the palace of Herod and shut the gates. Included among these were Ananias, his brother Ezekias, and other members of the embassy that had been sent to Agrippa.[68]

The next day the rebels attacked the Antonia Fortress and, after a short, two-day siege, captured it. The garrison there was killed to a man and the fortress set afire.[69] Although the ethnic origins of the soldiers who comprised the garrison are not known, their massacre can only be understood as an anti-Roman action, since the unit as a whole was part of the Roman auxiliary force of the province.[70] The rebels then attacked Herod's Palace in the Upper City, to which the royal troops, some of the city's notables, and chief priests had retreated. Although they attacked relentlessly the rebels were unable to capture the palace.[71]

MENAHEM BECOMES THE LEADER OF THE REBELLION

While the rebels were taking control of the city neighborhood by neighborhood, Menahem, son of Judas the Galilaean, who had criticized Jews in 6 CE for having the Romans as masters, went off with some of his friends to Masada, broke into Herod's armory there, and came back to Jerusalem with arms for his fellow townsmen and the other "brigands."[72] Josephus does not specify exactly what these weapons were, but the episode itself is revealing. From the beginning the rebels lacked weaponry and armor, and as Josephus's subsequent descriptions of battles between the Romans and the Jews make clear, throughout the rebellion Jews usually fought with light arms, especially swords and knives. Rocks, then as now, were plentiful, cheap, and effective.[73]

Since Josephus had informed his readers that some of those who were most desirous of war had taken Masada from its Roman guards earlier that summer, Menahem must have gained access to Herod's armory on Masada while it was being held by fellow insurrectionists—perhaps supporters of Menahem's younger relative, Eleazar ben Yair.[74] That might explain at any rate how Menahem gained access to Masada and its armory.

In any case, after his successful raid and return to Jerusalem, Menahem became the leader of the revolution and took command of the siege of the royalists in the palace of Herod. The besiegers did not have siege engines and found that it was not possible to undermine the walls of the palace, since they were vulnerable to missiles cast down from above. They therefore began to dig an underground tunnel, starting at some distance from the wall. When the tunnel reached one of the wall's towers, they shored it up and then set its supports alight. The tower fell down after its props were burned up. When it did, the rebels found that behind the collapsed tower was another wall that the besieged royalists had constructed to deal with such a development.

The rebels were dismayed by their failure. But the mood within Herod's palace was more desperate. Soon the besieged in the palace sent a message to Menahem and the other leaders of the rebellion requesting permission to depart from the city under treaty. This permission was granted, but only to the royal troops of Agrippa and to those who were natives of the country. Romans were excluded from the agreement.

After the royal troops and the natives had come out, the Romans were left alone inside, now in dire straits. Outmanned and having no faith in the word of their enemies, the Romans retired from their camp up into the royal towers of Hippicus, Phasael, and Mariamme at the northwest corner of the city's "First Wall" and on the north side of the palace precinct. Menahem's followers promptly broke into the palace, killed anyone they encountered, plundered the baggage that had been left behind, and set the Roman camp on fire (6 Gorpiaeus/Elul/15 August).[75]

THE DEATHS OF ANANIAS AND MENAHEM

The next day some of the rebels, undoubtedly followers of Menahem, caught up with the wealthy, former high priest Ananias near the canal on the palace grounds. They killed him there, along with his brother Ezekias (7 Gorpiaeus/Elul/about 16 August).

At this point, Ananias's son Eleazar and his followers, who found Menahem's conduct of affairs to be intolerable, decided to get rid of him. Eleazar's men reasoned that, after revolting against the Romans for love of freedom, they should not give it up to one of their own and endure a master who, even if he personally refrained from violence, was still inferior to them.

Coming upon Menahem in the Temple where he had gone to worship, dressed in a royal robe and accompanied by his armed disciples (*zelotas*), Eleazar and his men attacked Menahem.[76] They rushed upon Menahem and his followers, and the rest of the people there also began throwing rocks at Judas's son. At first Menahem resisted. But soon he and his followers fled in all directions. All who were caught were killed. Eleazar's men found Menahem hiding at the place called Ophlas in the Lower City. (See map 4.)[77] He was captured, tortured, and then put to death. His lieutenants, including Absalom, shared his fate. One of the few who escaped was Menahem's relative Eleazar ben Yair. This Eleazar subsequently made himself "tyrant" of Masada by some kind of deception (*dolo* in Greek) by August 66.[78]

From the summer of 66, then, part of the pattern of the war for the next eight years had already been set in place. The war of Jews against Rome was intertwined with a war of Jews against Jews. This civil war among Jews arguably was a major reason why the Jews were unable to prepare for an effective resistance against the Romans when they finally came to Jerusalem in numbers in 70.

THE SURRENDER OF THE ROMAN GARRISON

Josephus claims that the people wanted the siege of the Roman garrison in the royal towers to be abandoned, but it was pressed on instead. Realizing that further resistance was futile, the Roman commander (*praefectus*), Metilius, sent representatives to the rebel leader Eleazar, the son of Ananias, asking for terms of surrender. The Romans asked only for their lives, offering to leave behind their arms and their possessions. The rebels sent three representatives— Gorion, son of Nicomedes; Ananias, son of Sadok; and Judas, son of Jonathan—to the Romans to give guarantees of security and to take oaths.

After the surrender terms were agreed upon by both sides, Metilius and his men marched down from the towers. As long as they kept their arms, the Romans were unmolested. But as soon as they laid down their weapons in fulfillment of their oaths, Eleazar's men surrounded and massacred the soldiers. All were killed except for Metilius himself, who begged for his life, promising to convert and even to be circumcised. The massacre took place on the Sabbath.[79]

The slaughter of the Roman soldiers drew Josephus's censure, especially because it took place on the Sabbath, a day when Jews for religious reasons abstained from the most innocent actions.[80] What he might have added is that

Eleazar and the rebels, who, unlike the soldiers under Florus's command, had theretofore refrained from killing the unarmed, had in some sense given up the high moral ground in the conflict by killing the defenseless Romans. It was also a strategic mistake. After news of what happened reached the Romans, no Roman would ever lay down his arms based upon a pledge of security from the rebels. They would fight to the death no matter what. Jews who surrendered to Romans were also subject to the same treatment that the soldiers of the garrison received. That also meant that Jews would fight to the death. Those were now the rules of engagement. The duplicitous murder of Metilius's men made achieving the strategic objective of freedom more difficult for Jews.

THE MASSACRE OF THE JEWS OF CAESAREA

On the same day and at the very same hour of the garrison massacre, according to Josephus, the Caesareans (the non-Jews) of Caesarea massacred the Jews who lived among them in the city. Twenty thousand were murdered within an hour.[81] Again, such a large, rounded-up number prompts suspicion of gross exaggeration. In any case, the Caesareans emptied the city of Jews. Florus had arrested and brought to the docks in chains those who somehow escaped the ethnic cleansing.[82] The man who made the bird sacrifice next to the synagogue and those who put him up to it finally had what they wanted. Caesarea now belonged exclusively to the Syrians.

WAR SPREADS THROUGHOUT THE REGION

News of the massacre in Caesarea spread quickly and led to more ethnic violence. Dividing themselves up into bands, groups of Jews sacked the villages of the "Syrians" and the neighboring cities, especially those of the Decapolis to the east of the Jordan, including Philadelphia, Heshbon and its territory, Gerasa, Pella, and Scythopolis. (See map 2.) These cities were probably targeted because their populations were mostly descended from ethnic Greeks or Macedonians, and many of them were local bastions of Greek culture, though many of them also had Jews living among them as a result of their conquest by the Hasmonean Alexander Jannaeus (r. 103–76 BCE).[83] In some cases, such as Gerasa and Gadara, archaeological evidence seems to confirm destruction of public buildings at the time.[84]

Next, falling upon Gadara, Hippus (Hippos), and Gaulanitis, the Jews destroyed these and then set fire to everything in their path, advancing to Kedasa

(in the Upper Galilee), Ptolemais, Gaba, and even Caesarea.[85] Nor did Sebaste or Ascalon, noted for its wine, its onions, and the enmity between Jews
and non-Jews in the city, withstand their furious assaults.[86] The enraged
Jews burned these places to the ground and then laid waste to Anthedon and
the trade center of Gaza, with its connections to Arabia Felix and the lucra-
tive frankincense trade. Many of the villages around these places were also
destroyed, and the number of people captured and killed was immense.[87]

The Syrians retaliated and killed no fewer Jews. They slit the throats of
those they took in the cities, not only out of hatred, as in the past, but now
to avert the danger to themselves. All of greater Syria was a scene of terrible
upheaval. There were two camps in every city, and the only salvation for each
side lay in anticipating the actions of their enemies. The Syrians spent the days
in blood and the nights in fear. For though they thought that they had got
rid of the Jews, the non-Jews in each city also suspected those who were
thought to be sympathetic to the Jews. They hesitated to kill these people
whose loyalties were seen as ambiguous. But they also feared them.

Greed induced even those who had reputations for being mild-mannered
to carry out murder. After they dispatched their victims they plundered their
property and, as if returning from a battle, brought the spoils of those killed
to their own homes. The man who acquired the most things had the reputation as having prevailed over the most, Josephus claims. It was possible to see
cities filled with unburied bodies, and the bodies of infants lay next to old men
and uncovered women.[88]

Josephus draws his readers' attention to the image of the unburied bodies
because of the strong imperative to bury the dead among the Jews. In the book
of Deuteronomy one of the harshest curses placed upon those who do not obey
the voice of God and do all of his commandments is to be defeated by enemies
and for their dead bodies to be the food for all birds and for the beasts of the
earth.[89] Burying someone was seen as a signal act of kindness, since the dead
cannot bury themselves; according to a precept attributed to Raba in the tractate Megillah, between the study of the Torah and burying the dead, attending
to the burial of the dead took precedence.[90] The ethnic violence that followed
the massacre in Caesarea led to the abridgment of a sacred command.

THE END OF THE JEWS OF SCYTHOPOLIS

In some cities, Jews who believed that they had been accepted by their neighbors and were even willing to fight for them paid a terrible price for their naiveté.

When the rebellious Jews advanced against Scythopolis (Beth Shean) they found that the Jews living there had taken up arms against them. However, the non-Jews of Scythopolis became suspicious that the Jews of their city might attack the city by night to somehow make up for their disloyalty to their fellow Jews.

The Scythopolitans therefore instructed their allies among the Jews within the city to take themselves and their families to a grove to confirm their allegiance and loyalty. The Jews obeyed and for two days were left unmolested. On the third day, when some of the Jews were off guard and others were asleep, the Scythopolitans attacked and killed upward of 13,000 Jews. They then plundered all of their goods.

Among those to die was a certain Simon. Simon had fought bravely for Scythopolis against his fellow Jews. Finding himself attacked in the grove by those he had fought for and with, Simon killed the members of his own family first, including his parents, his wife, and his children, and then took his own life, but not before cursing himself for having put his faith in aliens.[91] In hindsight Simon's desperate and drastic destruction of his family foreshadowed what would happen at the last bastion of Jewish resistance to Rome in 74 CE.

Following the treacherous slaughter at Scythopolis, there were more attacks upon Jews in other cities. In Ascalon 2,500 were slain; in Ptolemais, where a colony for veterans of Syria's legions (III, VI, X, XII) had been established, 2,000 were murdered. The Tyrians killed a large number but imprisoned the majority. The people of Hippus and Gadara killed the most daring of the Jews in their towns and kept the more faint-hearted under guard. And so it went within the rest of the Syrian cities, depending upon whether there was hatred or fear of the Jews among them.[92] Up on the Golan Heights it was apparently the destruction of Gischala by the inhabitants of Gadara, Gabara, Soganaea, and Tyre at this time that motivated John of Gischala to see to the rebuilding and fortification of his town.[93]

Only the Antiochenes, Sidonians, and Apameans had mercy upon the Jews who lived with them, refusing to kill or imprison any of the Jews. These peoples may have discounted the possibility that the Jews represented any kind of threat because they outnumbered them by so many in each city. But, in Josephus's opinion, the real reason why they spared the Jews was their pity for people who showed no sign of being revolutionaries. The people of Gerasa, in fact, went so far as to escort to the border those Jews who wished to emigrate.[94] But Josephus's explanation for why these Jews were spared is not completely convincing. For elsewhere, equally loyal or pacific Jews were slaughtered.

POGROMS IN THE KINGDOM OF AGRIPPA

There were at least small-scale pogroms even within Agrippa's kingdom. These attacks affected Jews who had no wish to be included in the rebellion.

While Agrippa was away in Berytus or Antioch visiting Cestius and no doubt reporting on what had happened in Jerusalem, a group of 70 of the most distinguished Jews from Batanaea (Nuqrah, to the west of Trachonitis) came to Noarus or Varus, a relative of King Sohaemus of Emesa and a member of the Ituraean nobility (in Lebanon) who had been put in charge of the government by Agrippa.[95] The Jews asked for a body of soldiers to be sent to Batanaea to deal with trouble that might arise out of the activities of the rebels. Clearly these Jews wanted no part of the revolt or the massacres being carried out by Jews. Instead of assisting the Jews, by night Noarus sent out some of Agrippa's hoplite infantrymen, who promptly killed all 70 of the Jews from Batanaea. Although Agrippa had not been consulted about this action, Noarus continued his mistreatment of Jews until he was finally removed by Agrippa.[96] It is hard to reach any other conclusion than that Noarus and his henchmen simply wanted to kill Jews.

While Agrippa was struggling to maintain control over his own friends, the rebels captured Herod's rebuilt Hasmonean fortress of Cypros, slaughtered the garrison, and pulled down its defenses. The Jews of Machaerus also managed to prevail upon the Roman auxiliary garrison to leave. Once they had done so, it too was occupied by troops (66 CE).[97]

STRIFE IN ALEXANDRIA

In Alexandria, roughly a generation after Claudius affirmed Gaius's disastrous policies toward the Jews there, fresh strife between the Jews and the Greek citizens of the city led to another bloody outcome for the Jews.

At a public meeting during which the Greek Alexandrians were discussing sending an embassy to Nero, a great number of Jews entered the amphitheater where the meeting was taking place. Seeing the Jews, some of the Alexandrians shouted out "Enemies!" and "Spies!" and rushed forward to seize them. Most of the Jews fled in different directions. But the Alexandrians got hold of three men who were taken off to be burned alive. In response, the city's entire population of Jews came to their rescue and rushed to the amphitheater with torches in hand, threatening to burn alive everyone there.

The Roman governor of Egypt, Tiberius Iulius Alexander, sent some of the leading citizens of the city to calm the Jews down. These citizens begged the crowd of Jews to stop and not to give the Roman army an excuse to take action. Those who were determined to fight unfortunately made fun of Tiberius's exhortation and abused the governor by name.[98]

Tiberius Iulius Alexander thereupon let loose upon the Jews the two Roman legions stationed in the city, together with 2,000 other soldiers who had arrived from Libya. They were given permission not only to kill those who were rioting but also to pillage their possessions and burn their homes.[99]

The soldiers advanced into the Delta District of the city where most of Alexandria's remaining Jews lived and conducted a systematic attack upon the Jews there.[100] The Jews defended themselves but were no match for a trained Roman army. The number killed reached 50,000, we are told. The few survivors were left to ask for quarter.[101]

Tiberius Iulius Alexander finally gave his soldiers the order to desist, which the Romans obeyed as soon as it was given. It was with difficulty that the native Alexandrians were torn from the corpses of the dead Jews.[102] More Jews were killed in Alexandria than in either Caesarea or Jerusalem in the summer of 66.

From Caesarea to Sythopolis, Ptolemais to Alexandria, death and destruction spread out over the region at this time. As so often in the history of war, the problem was not motivating people to kill. The challenge was getting them to stop once they began.[103]

CHAPTER 8

The Clades Cestiana *(Cestian Disaster)*

After King Agrippa fled from Jerusalem, he went to visit Cestius Gallus, the Roman governor of Syria, in Antioch.[1] During his visit he must have told the Roman legate what had happened in the holy city. Cestius therefore knew that Agrippa had been stoned out of Jerusalem after he prevented the Jews from sending an embassy to Nero and then had urged them to obey Florus.[2] He also discovered that the Temple priests were no longer accepting foreign gifts or sacrifices.[3]

Furthermore, the Roman legate must have become aware that, in response to the request by some of Jerusalem's leading citizens, Agrippa had sent 2,000 cavalrymen to the city.[4] He may even have learned that Agrippa's royal cavalry had lost the battle to take control of the Temple and had been forced to evacuate the Upper City.[5] To Cestius this news must have seemed like a reversal of Neapolitanus's positive report about the situation in Jerusalem.

In light of these developments, but before he heard news about the internecine warfare in greater Syria, Cestius Gallus decided, probably in early Av/Lous (July), that doing nothing was no longer an option. He had to take action.[6] Open warfare in Jerusalem was unacceptable, especially if it resulted in the defeat of forces commanded by Romans or those serving under them. The governor of Syria had overall responsibility for security in the region even if there was a Roman procurator sitting by the seaside in Caesarea. Not acting in support of Nero's handpicked revenue collector could be dangerous. Even from Antioch Cestius had to look over his shoulder toward Rome or, closer still, Achaia in Greece, where by now Nero was on a concert tour with his entourage.

Before he could do anything in Jerusalem, however, by mid-July Cestius had to come up with a strategy to quell the unrest and then to assemble a force adequate to carry out his plan. He also needed to gather up the equipment and supplies required to support the campaign and the animals and wagons that would be needed to haul everything. From the size and composition of the force that Cestius put together in Antioch we can draw inferences about the kind of campaign Cestius anticipated. Because Cestius's intervention in the south resulted in a famous disaster, he has often been criticized for inadequate planning and poor leadership. But, as we shall see, the situation on the ground in the region changed dramatically after Cestius left Antioch in the summer of 66, and the Roman commander was not accurately apprised about the scale and intensity of the hostility to Rome by that time.

CESTIUS'S ARMY

As the violence in Jerusalem and elsewhere escalated, Cestius had Legio XII Fulminata, the "Thunderbolt," brought up to Antioch in Syria from its base at Raphaneae on the road south of Apamea, in full strength, or 4,800–6,000 men.[7] (See appendix G for the size and organization of Roman legions.) Fulminata was a legion with a venerable history, dating to its recruitment by Iulius Caesar in 58 BCE for his war against the Helvetii, who lived in part of what is now modern Switzerland. More recently, however, under the incompetent leadership of L. Caesennius Paetus, in 62 CE it had been defeated and humiliated at Rhandeia in Armenia by the army of the Parthian king Vologaeses.[8] One of the reasons why Cestius may have chosen the Thunderbolt to anchor his expeditionary force was because, among the Syrian legions, its base was the closest to Jerusalem, the ultimate objective of the operation. Cestius may have been hoping that the legion could live up to the reputation it had won originally under Caesar's command.

In addition, Cestius detached 2,000-man infantry vexillations or brigades from the three other legions stationed in the Roman province of Syria to join his force.[9] Vexillations took their name from the *vexillum,* or flag, that such brigades served under when they were separated from their legion. The vexillations Cestius called up came from Legio IIII Scythica at Zeugma (Belkis) on the Euphrates, Legio VI Ferrata at Laodicea (Latakya) or Samosata (Samsat), and Legio X Fretensis at Cyrrhus.[10] Cestius no doubt decided to take 2,000-man vexillations from each of the three other Syrian legions so that no legionary encampment in Syria would be left without a sufficient deterrent force.

The legionary core of Cestius's force thus numbered at least 10,800 or perhaps as many as 12,000 Roman citizen infantrymen: the 4,800–6,000 soldiers of Legio XII plus the 6,000 selected legionaries from the three other Syrian legions. Either way the paper strength of Cestius's army was at least two legions.[11]

Cestius also gathered up six non-Roman citizen auxiliary cohorts of infantry and four squadrons or wings (Latin *alae,* Greek *ilai*) of cavalry.[12] At this time auxiliary infantry cohorts included at least 500 and perhaps as many as 1,000 infantrymen.[13] The officers of these units were Romans of equestrian status.[14]

The total number of legionaries and auxiliaries that Cestius mustered for the operation thus numbered at least 15,800, though possibly as many as 22,000. The real strength of both types of units, citizen legions and noncitizen auxiliary cohorts and wings, may have been lower because, when the force was pulled together, some soldiers were probably sick, recovering from wounds, seconded, on leave, or in the process of retiring.[15]

In addition to the citizen soldiers and auxiliaries there were allied troops supplied by the Roman client kings from north and east of Judaea. From about 400 miles away to the north, Antiochus IV of Commagene, which controlled the crucial Euphrates crossings of Zeugma and Samosata, contributed 2,000 cavalry and 3,000 infantry, all bowmen, while Agrippa II provided the same number of infantrymen (3,000) and less than 2,000 cavalry, perhaps 1,667.[16] King Sohaemus, or "Little Dagger" in Arabic, of Emesa (modern Homs) on the Orontes River, came later with 4,000 soldiers, one-third of whom were cavalry, or 1,333 cavalry and 2,667 infantry. The majority of the rest were archers.[17] The allied kings thus furnished around 13,667 soldiers in total. Most of these were archers.

The entire force that Cestius assembled at Antioch to deal with the problems in the south in 66 numbered at least 29,467 and perhaps as many as 35,667 soldiers. There also would have been a large number of military slaves who served the legionaries and the auxiliaries. By one estimate at this time there would have been one military slave for every four Roman soldiers.[18] Thus, somewhere between 3,950 and 5,500 military slaves for the legion and vexillations were also part of Cestius's force. The allied armies must also have had servants, but we have no idea how many.

SUPPLYING CESTIUS'S ARMY

Cestius's army had to be fed and supplied. Anything the soldiers could not carry had to be hauled by animals on their backs or carried on wagons. All of the animals had to be fed and hydrated too. To feed, hydrate, and supply an army of 29,467–35,667 legionaries, auxiliary, and allied soldiers, plus thousands of pack animals, must have been a challenge. How big a challenge was it?

To stay fit and effective, each one of Cestius's approximately 5'7", 145-pound, 18- to 45-year-old legionaries needed to ingest about 3,000 calories from 2.85 pounds of food per day and to drink at least 2 liters of water or other liquids.[19] Somewhere between 60 to 75 percent of those pounds of food would have come from the wheat ration of the Roman soldiers, which was the staple of the Roman military diet.[20] For the 4,800–6,000 men of Legio XII Fulminata and the 6,000 men of the other Syrian vexillations, that alone would add up to somewhere between 30,780 and 34,200 pounds of food and 21,600–24,000 liquid liters that had to be carried or found and distributed daily.

Even if we assume less generous food rations for the auxiliary (2.5 pounds?) and allied soldiers (2 pounds?), though with the same liquid requirements, we still arrive at 70,614–86,534 pounds of food and 58,934–71,334 liquid liters that Cestius had to come up with every day to supply his 29,467- to 35,667-man army. (See appendix I for the size and supply requirements of Cestius's army.)

Finding food (*frumentatio*) on the march usually required a large-scale operation performed by soldiers, who used the sickles noted by Josephus among their equipment to reap grain.[21] The timing of such operations was also important; the availability of wheat and other foodstuffs was seasonal. Cestius probably hoped to take advantage of a May–June harvest of wheat planted three months earlier in the areas through which he would march during that summer of 66.[22]

The soldiers could have carried up to 17 days' worth of rations and water along with their personal gear. Water also seems to have been carried in leather bags, water skins, and wooden barrels, which leaked the least.[23] A relief on the Column of Trajan in Rome shows oxen and mules drawing a two-wheeled cart with such barrels on them.[24] The rest of the legion's equipment, along with their tents, the unit's grain-grinding mill, and the light and heavy artillery, would have to be carried by pack animals.

By one estimate one pack animal was needed to carry the unit equipment of every three legionary infantrymen and of every two cavalrymen. Most of the pack animals that Cestius brought with him were mules or asses.[25] We know that every mule required 2 kilograms (kg) of hard fodder, 6 kg of dry fodder, and 20 liters of water per day. Every horse of every cavalryman needed 2.5 kg of hard fodder, 7 kg of dry or green fodder, and 20 liters of water daily.[26] Some of that fodder would be carried by the pack animals themselves. But inevitably grazing would have to make up for what could not be carried.[27]

If we use these estimates as a rough guide we can conclude that to haul the equipment, food, and water of Cestius's army, somewhere between 10,989 and 13,389 pack animals were needed, depending upon estimates of unit sizes.[28] To take care of the needs of the pack animals and horses, Cestius had to have between 39,478–49,278 kg of dry fodder, 114,934–143,334 kg of green fodder, and 359,780–447,780 liters of water each day.[29]

To put some of these daily needs into perspective it is worth considering that the weight of the food Cestius needed to feed his army every day (70,614–86,534 lbs.) probably would reach the 80,000-lb maximum that 18-wheel trailer trucks are allowed to carry in the United States by law. The liquids required for his men and animals in liters would fill up at least two five-feet-deep, 30-by-50-feet backyard swimming pools. Where would these supplies have come from?

The cost of the food for the Roman legionaries was pre-deducted from their wages of 225 denarii per year.[30] But the food, water, and fodder for the soldiers and animals that had not been paid for in advance or carried had to be acquired by foraging, requisition, or pillaging.[31] Even the animals themselves were often requisitioned. None of these methods of supplying Cestius's army on the march would have endeared the governor or the Romans to the locals; no doubt they would have adversely affected the economic well-being of the people whose lands or crops were appropriated. This would be especially true if the main method of resupply was requisition; that is, simply taking what was needed without compensation. The impact of such an army passing through a region would have been disruptive at best, devastating at worst. The sudden introduction of a large army of men and animals into the region also must have created sanitation issues. Getting rid of the enormous amounts of human and animal waste each day is a subject Josephus and other Graeco-Roman sources evade but could not be avoided by the soldiers themselves.[32] Roman soldiers on the march were dirty locusts with swords.

The army Cestius put together at Antioch was not huge numerically. Nor was it a rapid reaction force: it was heavy and slow. Pack mules moved along at 3 mph carrying lighter loads, while oxen could pull heavier weights but at even slower speeds.[33] Cestius's army was not going to surprise anyone on its way to Jerusalem.

Two further points about the force stand out. First, the majority of the 29,467–35,667 soldiers were non-Romans: there were 10,800–12,000 Romans compared to 18,667–23,667 non-Romans. And of the non-Roman soldiers, between 7,000 and 9,000 were cavalry of one kind or another. This would suggest that if there were real fighting to be done Cestius expected the brunt of it to be waged by mounted auxiliaries and allies in open spaces, not by Roman infantrymen.

Second, although 29,467–35,667 soldiers constituted a substantial force, it was not a large enough army to besiege and capture a city the size of Jerusalem. Cestius, who had been to Jerusalem, must have known that. Four years later, when the future Roman emperor Titus besieged Jerusalem, he brought four Roman legions, 20 auxiliary cohorts, eight cavalry wings, and allied troops.

From all of this information it follows that in 66 Cestius never planned to besiege and capture Jerusalem, because he did not think he had to. The army he took south was organized to overwhelm isolated pockets of resistance out in the open and to intimidate everyone else into submission. Based upon what Cestius knew before he set out from Antioch, this was not an unreasonable plan. Unfortunately for Cestius and the Romans, by the time he got to Ptolemais the military challenges ahead of him had been dramatically transformed.

THE ROAD SOUTH

At the latest Cestius and his army set out from Antioch by 10 Elul (about 19 August) to the port city of Ptolemais (Akko), some 250 miles to the south.[34] A substantial army with a large, slow baggage train must have taken at least two weeks to complete such a march.

Ptolemais, which had been renamed after the Egyptian king Ptolemy II Philadelphus, was an ideal base for Cestius's campaign in the western Galilee. In 39 BCE Ptolemais was the starting point for Herod when he came back from Rome to fight for his kingdom against Antigonus.[35] Supplies, including food, could be brought directly to Ptolemais's port by sea and stored there if necessary, along with baggage, money, documents, extra weapons, and armor.

Ptolemais's Phoenician-descended population also could be counted upon to provide labor if necessary and would not be sympathetic to the peoples against whom Cestius was marching.[36]

Before Cestius reached Ptolemais he probably found out about the massacre of the auxiliary garrison in Jerusalem, the slaughter of the Jews of Caesarea, and the revenge attacks carried out by Jews described in chapter 7.[37] That news should have caused Cestius to reconsider the campaign and its objectives. Suddenly, fighting within the streets of Jerusalem was a very real possibility. Cestius was bringing a large contingent of cavalry with him, but it would not be very effective in the urban environment of Jerusalem. Its narrow streets and hills were not ideal terrain for using mounted troops. He would have to rely upon his infantry, and his artillery became much more important. He at least had to think about some kind of siege and how he would supply his army during such an operation. Yet the sources tell us nothing about any reconsideration of the mission.

All we know is that when Cestius reached Ptolemais, a large number (2,000?) of auxiliaries (*epikouroi*) joined his army from unspecified cities. What these auxiliaries lacked in terms of combat experience, Josephus tells us, they made up for by their zeal and hatred of Jews.[38] The advantage of adding such enthusiastic allies would have been balanced by at least two disadvantages: first, more soldiers of any kind meant more mouths to feed for Cestius, and second, soldiers who were motivated to kill Jews just because they hated them might be hard to control.

Josephus also informs us that from this point on King Agrippa II accompanied Cestius, acting as a guide for the route of the march and providing supplies needed by the army, as client kings often did for the Romans.[39] The latter would have been helpful to Cestius. If Agrippa chose the army's route to Jerusalem, however, Cestius would have been better off finding another guide.

OPERATIONS IN THE GALILEE

The news of the Jews' attacks upon the Syrian villages and Greek towns after the massacre in Caesarea may help explain the severity of Cestius's tactics after he established his operational base in Ptolemais. As we shall see, centers of uncertain loyalty were sacked and burned and their populations put to the sword even if there was no evidence of support for the rebels in Jerusalem. Loyalists were spared.

Taking a part of his force, Cestius first marched southeastward against a strong city in the Galilee called Chabulon (perhaps the Arab village of Kabul in the foothills of the west Galilee). The city was located on the western edge of the Galilee on land between territory where Jews lived and Ptolemais. Cestius found the town deserted. No doubt anticipating the arrival of Cestius and his army, the population had fled up into the hills. The city, however, was filled with all kinds of possessions, which the Roman governor permitted the soldiers to plunder. Cestius, we are told, wondered at the beauty of the town, which had houses built in a fashion similar to those in Tyre, Sidon, and Berytus. What Josephus may mean by this is that the houses were built according to a peristyle plan, with an interior courtyard surrounded by a colonnaded porch. Cestius's appreciation of Chabulon's domestic architecture did not stop him from ordering the town to be burned.[40]

Cestius and his soldiers then surged through the surrounding district and ravaged everything in their path. After they burned all the villages, Cestius and his men returned to Ptolemais, probably to resupply. While some of the Syrians, especially those from Berytus, were involved in plundering what had not been burned, the Jews, who discovered that Cestius had departed for Ptolemais, made a surprise attack on the troops that he had left behind and killed about 2,000 of them.[41]

Cestius then marched for two days from Ptolemais to Caesarea, some 32 miles to the south.[42] A part of his army was also sent on to Joppa (Yafo), Jerusalem's port on the sea. The soldiers sent to Joppa were instructed to garrison the city if they took it by surprise. But if the residents of the city anticipated their approach, the soldiers were told to wait until the main body of the army came.[43]

The troops sent to Joppa advanced by sea and land. The inhabitants of the city had no time to prepare for battle or flee. When the soldiers burst into the town they simply killed the Joppans where they were, along with their families, and then devastated and burned the city. The number of those killed was 8,400.[44] The relatively precise number that Josephus provides for these casualties lends some credibility to his figure.

The Joppans, who had played no role in the violence instigated by the rebels according to Josephus, seem to have been victimized by the Romans simply to serve as a warning to the rebellious Jews. It does not seem to have occurred to Cestius that killing Jews who were not part of the rebellion might have increased the numbers of rebels and hardened attitudes toward Rome.

The other side of hoping to intimidate a population into submission by such atrocities might be that it actually widened and deepened the resistance.

Cestius similarly sent a strong cavalry force to the toparchy of Narbata. Narbata was located some six to seven miles southeast of Caesarea. This cavalry unit devastated the countryside, killed a very large number of the inhabitants, plundered their possessions, and burned down the villages.[45]

Cestius then dispatched Caesennius Gallus, the legate of the Twelfth Legion, into the Galilee with a vexillation force considered large enough to stamp out resistance there.[46] Sepphoris (Zippori), the strongest city in the Galilee, received Gallus enthusiastically and thereafter served as his base of operations. Friendly Sepphoris, which looks northward over the Beit-Netofa Valley today, was left unbloodied by Roman swords, though Josephus mentions elsewhere that hostages were taken from Sepphoris and placed in Dora (Dor) on the coast, no doubt by Gallus.[47] The taking of these hostages suggests that Gallus and, by implication, Cestius were not completely certain where all loyalties in Sepphoris lay or else they were taking precautions to ensure that the Sepphoreans chose the right side. It also indicates that Cestius considered Dor to be a place friendly to Rome. Jews lived there, as we have seen, but the archaeological remains of the city show that it was built on a Hippodamian plan, and while it had a synagogue, it also had a number of polytheist temples and a theater.

Responding to what Josephus then calls the "good council" (*euboulian*) of Sepphoris, the rest of the cities in the Galilee followed suit and made their peace with Rome. All of those who favored unrest or were "brigands," however, fled up the mountain in the middle of the Galilee called Asamon (Atzmon in the central Galilee). Asamon was situated across the valley from Sepphoris, a few miles to the south of Iotapata. At a height of about 1,730 feet above sea level Asamon was much higher than Iotapata (about 1,345 feet). Gallus led his soldiers against the rebels on Asamon.

Initially, because they held the higher ground, those who had fled up the mountain easily beat off the Roman attacks and killed 200 soldiers. But when the Romans outflanked them, using classic Roman attacking tactics, and captured the high ground, the rebels were quickly defeated by Gallus's soldiers.[48] The lightly armed rebels could not withstand a sustained attack by heavy infantry, nor, after being routed, could they successfully flee from cavalry. Only a few managed to avoid detection in the broken ground of the surrounding countryside. More than 2,000 were killed.[49]

No longer seeing any sign of revolution in the Galilee, Gallus went back to Caesarea with his force. Thereafter Cestius with his entire force advanced southward toward Antipatris (Aphek, 66.4 km or 41.3 miles away).[50] His entire force should mean 29,467–35,667 legionaries, Roman auxiliary soldiers, allied soldiers, and the unknown number of auxiliaries from the cities, minus casualties from the earlier operations. With them would have been approximately 10,989–13,389 pack animals carrying their equipment, plus their cavalry horses.

If Cestius's army marched in rows of six across, as Josephus claimed was the norm for Romans on the march, the absolute minimum length of the road they occupied would have been three miles, although that number excludes the length of road taken up by the auxiliaries from the cities and the animals.[51] When we figure in the auxiliaries and the pack animals, the overall length of Cestius's column could easily have been six to nine miles long.[52] With a baggage train moving at 3 mph, the march from Caesarea to Antipatris probably took at least two or, more likely, three days.

THE AMBUSH

After sending a detachment of troops to deal with a group of Jews who had assembled around a tower named Apheku (Aphek Turris/Migdal Afeq), from which the Jews fled in fear at the soldiers' approach, Cestius then marched on to Lydda (Lod), some 22 km or 13 miles away.[53] Lydda occupied a key position on the road from Joppa to Jerusalem. That march could have been completed in one day. Cestius arrived in Lydda during the month of Tishri/Huperberetaeus (early September to early October of the Julian calendar) of 66. (See map 1 for what follows.)

Cestius discovered that Lydda was nearly deserted, since the entire (*pan*) population had gone up to Jerusalem to celebrate the biblically mandated harvest festival of Sukkot, or Tabernacles.[54] If Josephus is right about this, it should mean that at least the majority of the inhabitants of Lydda were Jews.

According to the lunar calendar of the Jews, that celebration would have begun on the evening of 15 Tishri. If "all" the Jews of Lydda who decided to attend the festival left in time for the beginning of Sukkot, then Cestius could have arrived in Lydda a few days before 15 Tishri, since it is 50 km or 30 miles from Lydda to Jerusalem. Families could have taken at least three days to make the walk from Lydda to Jerusalem. So Cestius might have been in Lydda on 11 or 12 Tishri.[55] Fifty people who did appear in Lydda while Cestius was there were killed, and the town was burned down.[56] From Lydda, Cestius then led his army eastward, headed for Gabaon.

Since all routes from Lydda to Jerusalem would have required making an ascent up the Judaean hills onto the plateau, Cestius probably took the road from Lydda to Gabaon that passes just south of Modein, the hometown of the Maccabees, because it was the most direct of all alternatives and involved a steep climb (some 755 feet) along a narrow road only from Lower Beit-Horon (Beit Ur al-Tachta, "Lower House of Straw") to Upper Beit-Horon (Beit Ur al-Fawqa, "Upper House of Straw") about two miles away, following roughly the route of the modern Highway 443 in Israel.[57] It was obviously in Cestius's interest to make sure that the column spent as little time as possible marching along the most vulnerable section of the route.

Cestius therefore confidently ascended some 755 feet up through the narrow and steep pass between Lower Beit-Horon and Upper Beit-Horon. In places the pass was less than 10 feet wide before Roman military engineers widened it.[58] After reaching Upper Beit-Horon Cestius then proceeded about 5.6 miles southeastward to the hill of Gabaon (modern al-Jib, elevation approximately 2,600 feet) where he encamped on the evening of the day after he left Lydda.[59] Gabaon had the considerable advantage of possessing an excellent natural water supply, noted already in the book of Samuel.[60] Jerusalem lay another six miles to the south/southeast.[61] That would be another half-day march for Cestius's army. By now it was five days since Cestius had left Caesarea.[62]

If Cestius's column was at least six miles long that would mean that when its forward ranks reached Gabaon, its rear still would have been in Upper Beit-Horon or perhaps even farther back. The rear of Cestius's column was brought up by the baggage mules.[63]

The Jews, who by now had seen that the war was indeed coming to the metropolis, ceased celebrating the festival of Sukkot and took up arms.[64] Disregarding the Sabbath and the assertions that Agrippa II had made in his speech in Jerusalem before the war broke out, they went out to meet the Romans with great confidence in their numbers, we are told, and they succeeded in breaking into the Roman lines and capturing the legion's eagle standard (probably that of Legio XII Fulminata).[65] But for a timely wheeling intervention by the cavalry and by a part of the infantry that was not as hard-pressed, Cestius and the entire Roman army would have been endangered, Josephus claims. Five hundred and fifteen Romans—400 infantry and 115 cavalry—were killed in this first engagement between the Romans and the rebels.[66] The Jews lost but 22 men. Among those who fought most bravely for the Jews were Niger of Peraea; Silas the Babylonian, who had served before with the royal cavalry of Agrippa; and Monobazos and Cenedaeus, relatives of Monobazos, the king of Adiabene.[67] The identities of these fighters suggest that, contrary to what Agrippa told the Jerusalemites assembled in the Xystus, at least some Adiabenians were willing to take up arms along with the rebels.

After their frontal attack was repulsed the Jews withdrew back into Jerusalem. However, as the Romans were making their way up through Beit-Horon, they were set upon by Simon, son of Giora, who cut up their rearguard and captured many of the mules that were carrying the Romans' baggage. These pack animals were then brought into Jerusalem.[68]

Simon's patronymic Giora meant "foreigner" or "convert" in Aramaic. This probably means that Simon's father was a gentile who observed Jewish law.[69] Later on we learn that Simon and his family probably came from Gerasa, possibly in the Decapolis (Jordan), though they may have hailed from Gezer (Gazara) or Jureish in the toparchy or district of Acrabatene.[70] One thing is certain, however: the foreigner-convert and his son did not come from Jerusalem.

Soon the elites of both Jerusalem and Rome would learn that their methods and goals were very different from those of Simon. They believed in compromise. Simon bar Giora did not. Though Jewish proselytes were far from rare during this period, perhaps the greatest irony of the war was that the leader who displayed the greatest commitment to the freedom of Zion was a first-generation Jew or observer of Jewish laws who hailed from outside the holy city.[71]

While Simon was leading the captured Roman mules into Jerusalem, Cestius remained in his former camp for no less than three days. During this time Cestius's doctors presumably were tending to his soldiers' wounds, and the soldiers themselves were wondering how they were going to get back to Antipatris safely. Meanwhile the Jews occupied the heights and defiles along the road from Beit-Horon to Antipatris, on the lookout for Roman counterattacks.[72]

Such is the opening scene of the confrontation between Cestius and the Jews that Josephus presents. It is dramatic. It is stirring and inspiring, especially for the rebels. And it seems to be convincing, until we think carefully about the chronology of the events Josephus describes and the distances involved.[73]

Josephus tells us that the Jews abandoned their festival and took up arms after Cestius reached Gabaon and encamped. It was after the Romans had pitched camp that the Jews rushed out from Jerusalem, attacked Cestius's lines, and penetrated their ranks.[74] Meanwhile Simon attacked the Romans in the rearguard as they were ascending Beit-Horon and carried off many of their pack mules to Jerusalem.[75]

The fundamental problem with Josephus's version of what happened that October day is that it does not explain how the Jews in Jerusalem learned of Cestius's presence in Gabaon after he was already encamped there, mustered an army, marched almost six miles to Gabaon, and then fought the Romans—all before the Roman baggage train had made it into Gabaon and was attacked by Simon while still climbing up Beit-Horon.

Even if the entire Roman column with soldiers and baggage train was nine miles long, which assumes that the soldiers were compelled to march three abreast at least through the narrow pass from Lower to Upper Beit-Horon, marching at 3 mph, it would have taken less than three hours for the entire column to march the 5.6 miles from Upper Beit-Horon to Gabaon. Thus, an attack upon the Romans at Gabaon after they had set up camp, followed by an attack upon the baggage train by Simon before it reached Gabaon, is not plausible. The slowest, least cooperative mules in the Roman army on the hottest day in October in the Judaean hills could have walked from Upper Beit-Horon to Gabaon and back in the time it would have taken for the Romans to have built the camp on Gabaon and the rebels to have heard of it, assembled and armed themselves, made their way from Jerusalem to Gabaon, and attacked. According to one estimate, pack mules, bearing 200-lb loads, still could have struggled along at 3 mph or slightly faster.[76]

The crucial point is that Josephus tells us that the Jews in Jerusalem only knew of Cestius's presence after he was already encamped at Gabaon. Building such a marching camp once enough soldiers reached Gabaon would have taken at least three hours.[77] Meanwhile, it would have taken the Jews at least several hours to muster a force and march out to confront the encamped Romans at Gabaon. By then the rear units of Cestius's column should have had plenty of time to make it from Upper Beit-Horon to Gabaon. Yet Josephus has Simon attacking the Roman baggage train still ascending up Beit-Horon (*epi ten Bethoran*)—but only after the attack on the already encamped army at Gabaon.

What really happened at Beit-Horon and Gabaon in early October 66? One possibility is that Cestius somehow disconnected his infantry from the mule train and that Simon attacked the rearguard as Cestius was being attacked.[78] But Josephus does not tell us that Cestius separated the two parts of his column, and there is no plausible tactical reason why he would have done so. In fact, if Cestius left the baggage train behind in Beit-Horon to get though the pass by itself, he was a far more incompetent commander than even Josephus later makes him out to be.

A more plausible scenario is as follows. The mustering, march, and operations of the large Roman-led army from Caesarea to Antipatris, then to Lydda, and from there to Beit-Horon took at least five days and could not have gone unnoticed by locals. This information must have been relayed both to Simon, wherever he and his men were, and to the rebels within Jerusalem. As soon as Cestius embarked upon the road to Antipatris it would have been obvious where he was heading. The time and distances involved in bringing the Roman army from Caesarea surely would have given Simon enough time to gather his band together and plan an attack upon the Romans at the most vulnerable point along their route—where the path was narrow and the terrain was suitable for surprise attacks from soldiers holding the high ground—and for Jews to assemble a force and march out from Jerusalem and attack Cestius's lead units *before* he set up his camp. An attack upon the front of Cestius's column before it had a chance to set up camp makes far more sense tactically.

Indeed, the attacks on the lead and rear units may have been planned and executed to take place simultaneously.[79] The fact that Simon brought the captured mules into Jerusalem after the attacks perhaps hints at some sort of coordination or cooperation between himself and the Jerusalemites. But however the attacks were planned, the time to attack the Romans was not after they made their way through the pass and encamped but before it.

But that is not what Josephus reports: he has the Jews from Jerusalem attacking Cestius only after the Romans had pitched camp at Gabaon.[80] So either Josephus got wrong what happened or, in the interests of showcasing the rebels' successes against Cestius and the infantry formations (*taxeis*) of the Romans, he reported what happened in a way that fundamentally confuses and distorts the timing and sequence of events.[81] For Josephus what was important was that the rebels bloodied Cestius's army even before it got to Jerusalem. Josephus probably got this essential point right, but how it happened was a bit more complicated.

This inference about Josephus's purpose is supported by what he tells his readers happened after the attacks. Cestius remained in his camp in Gabaon for three days while the Jews occupied the high ground and guarded the passes.[82] The delay makes sense in light of Cestius and Agrippa now realizing that they were in a dangerous situation, up against fighters who would not shrink from attacking Roman legions frontally. Less than a week out from Caesarea, Cestius's assumptions about his ability to intimidate the rebels into compliance were already demolished.

CESTIUS IN JERUSALEM

The questions for the governor and the king at this point were how to extricate themselves from the tactical situation they were in and to see whether those Jews who wanted to fight could still be isolated from those who did not. That helps explain their next move.

King Agrippa sent two friends named Borcius and Phoibus to negotiate with the Jews. Among the king's intimates these two men were especially well known to the Jews. Their selection therefore was intended to build trust; Agrippa and Cestius probably thought that the two men would be treated well and listened to because of their association with Agrippa. On Cestius's behalf Borcius and Phoibus were instructed to offer a treaty and pardon for the rebels' deeds in exchange for laying down their arms and returning to their allegiance to Rome. It should be noted that the offer implied that the actions of the rebels were seen by Agrippa and Cestius as specifically anti-Roman and rebellious.

Fearing that the entire population would respond positively to the proposal, the rebels, according to Josephus, attacked Agrippa's ambassadors. Phoibus was killed before he could utter a word. Borcius was wounded but managed to escape. Anyone who protested against what had been done to Agrippa's and Cestius's emissaries was driven into the town with stones and clubs.[83]

Cestius no doubt was disappointed by the failure of the negotiations but reportedly saw that the conflict among the Jews presented an opportunity for attack. He brought forward his force, routed the Jews, and followed them right up to Jerusalem. He made his camp on Mt. Scopus, which looked down over the city center from around 0.87 miles away. There he waited for three days, no doubt hoping that the defenders would surrender. But he also sent parties out to the countryside to collect grain.[84] Collecting grain was a sign that Cestius now understood that he was not going to march into Jerusalem and settle the situation just by trooping his colors.

On the fourth day (30 Tishri/Huperberetaeus) Cestius arrayed his force in battle order and led it southwestward into Jerusalem. At his advance the rebels retreated into the inner city and the Temple. After he entered the city

Cestius set fire to the district known as Bezetha or the New City and the Timber Market, located outside today's Damascus Gate. (See map 4.) The purpose of the fire was to terrorize the population into submission, not to prepare the ground for a siege. Cestius then made his way to the Upper City and set up camp opposite the royal palace.[85] It was a little over two weeks since Cestius had arrived in Lydda.

At that point, Josephus writes, if Cestius had attacked, he would have captured the city, and the war would have been over before it had begun in earnest. But Florus had bribed Cestius's camp prefect Tyrannius Priscus, who would have been involved in planning a siege, and most of the cavalry commanders. These men deflected Cestius from pressing home his advantage, so the opportunity was missed.[86]

Cestius may have hesitated because his cavalry officers were bribed by Florus. Florus wanted there to be a war to cover up his own crimes, according to Josephus.[87] But there is a more convincing explanation for Cestius's hesitation.

Although Cestius had been to Jerusalem before, now that he had brought a large army into the city he must have understood more clearly the tactical challenges he faced.[88] Burning down the New City and the Timber Market were easy enough to do but produced no real tactical advantage. These actions were probably taken to intimidate and terrorize the population. After that, however, if Cestius chose to pursue the rebels into the inner city, the difficulties increased exponentially.

The rebels, who already had inflicted casualties upon his army, would be fighting within an urban area they knew. In contrast, most of Cestius's troops would have been unfamiliar with the cobbled streets and alleys of Jerusalem's Upper City. Moreover, even if the Romans defeated the rebels within the Upper City, they still had to reckon with the Jews who were holed up behind the walls of the Temple Mount itself. Cestius must have known too that, although the force that he had with him was formidable, much of the population of the city was hostile to him after what had happened in the city at Florus's direction. Once he was inside the city, Cestius was confronted by a recently successful and motivated enemy that was preparing to fight on its own turf, supported by at least a sizable proportion of the civilian population. Some kind of siege was the obvious military solution to the situation. But conducting a siege at the time involved insurmountable problems.

Cestius and his army were in no position to carry out a successful siege of the Temple and the city. Cestius did not have enough boots (*caligae*) or *ballistae* (catapults) with him to conduct a siege in October 66. That was the wrong time of year to begin a siege that inevitably would require securing material and food resources from the surrounding area. Soon enough it would be winter, a time of rain and cold on the Judaean plateau.

The camp prefect Priscus may or may not have been bribed, as some historians have speculated. If he were bribed, it was a bribe that supported a well-reasoned conclusion. Cestius paused in Jerusalem for sound tactical, strategic, and logistical reasons.

At this point, persuaded by Ananus, the son of the high priest Jonathan, many of the most notable men went to Cestius, telling him that they would open the gates to him. In response, Cestius, partly out of anger and scorn (supposedly) but also because he did not trust the Jews, procrastinated further. He also may have had the massacre of the Roman garrison on his mind. The rebels, meanwhile, who had discovered the attempt to surrender the city to Cestius, pulled Ananus and those around him from the walls and with showers of rocks drove them back into their homes. Then, standing up on the towers, they repulsed those Romans who then were trying to climb the walls.[89]

With a siege out of the question, Cestius played the last military card he was holding: frontal assault. He probably did so in full knowledge that the chances of such an attack succeeding were very low. But it was inconceivable that a Roman legionary army would simply retreat in the face of an enemy that recently had killed hundreds of its soldiers. If it did, its commander would not be its commander for very long. The gods might also smile once again upon Cestius. An assault might cause divisions among the Jews and lead to the city being opened up to the Romans. It was worth the risk.

Once Cestius gave the order to attack, it was pressed for five days but without success. On the sixth day Cestius himself led a large contingent of hand-picked men and archers in an assault upon the long north side wall of the Temple compound, measuring at least 300 yards, with the Antonia Fortress at the northwest corner. From the portico of the Temple the Jews fought and drove back those who had come up to the wall. But at last, overwhelmed by the sheer quantity of Roman missiles, they retreated. The Romans, raising their shields up over their heads and locking them together to form a kind of protective shell that the Romans called the tortoise (*testudo*), proceeded to work at undermining the wall and to set the gate of the Temple on fire. That gate attacked by the Romans in 66, which no longer exists, probably was located between the eastern wall of the Antonia Fortress and the Pool of Israel.[90] A famous relief panel from the Column of Trajan shows Roman legionaries employing the *testudo* while assaulting a Dacian fort near the Dacian capital of Sarmizegethusa during the first Dacian War.[91]

Once again, Josephus claims, if Cestius had pressed the attack, he could have ended the war on the spot. The revolutionaries were already trying to flee, and the rest of the population was ready to open the gates to Cestius and welcome him in as a benefactor. But Cestius suddenly called his soldiers back from the attack and withdrew from the city. Meanwhile the "brigands," taking advantage of Cestius's unanticipated withdrawal, attacked the rear of the Romans and killed a large number of cavalry and infantry.[92]

Josephus never explains why Cestius called off the attack at this point, other than to assert that the opportunity missed by him was a sign that God had turned away from the holy places and did not want that day to be the end of the war. He does admit, however, that Cestius was unaware that the rebels were on the verge of breaking and that the city populace wanted him to press his attack.

Cestius's withdrawal can be explained without reference to divine intervention or ignorance of the rebels' state of mind. Nowhere in his description of the Romans' attack upon the north wall of the Temple Mount does Josephus mention whether the Romans had with them adequate equipment to conduct a siege or that October was not the time of year to begin what would probably turn out to be a lengthy operation. Romans generally commenced military campaigns in early March; Cestius began his intervention during the mid- to late summer because that was when he was able to gather up his force after hearing about what was going on in Jerusalem.[93] Moreover the attack against the north Temple wall, in the space between the Antonia Fortress to the northwest and the Pool of Israel to the northeast, was tactically challenging, even with adequate siege equipment. In fact, it funneled soldiers into a kill zone with walls to the west and south and the waters of the reservoir to the east.[94]

Cestius broke off the attack on the Temple wall because he did not have the equipment or the logistical preparation to complete a mission that his army had not been put together to execute. Feeding an army of more than 30,000 and supplying fodder for its horses and mules during a siege would have required the creation of a large-scale, ongoing resupply operation. The fact that Cestius had not made provision for any such operation indicates that he never anticipated that a siege would be necessary. Perhaps influenced by Agrippa, Cestius may have hoped that a large show of force at the north wall of the Temple would bring the Jews in Jerusalem to their senses. But Florus and his auxiliaries had already shed too much blood: they had made Cestius and his army into enemies of enough of the population of Jerusalem. In Jerusalem during the summer of 66 Cestius learned that what he and the Romans were facing was not civic unrest or even an extended riot. It was a war and one the Roman commander was not militarily prepared to fight at the time.

Because of what happened during Cestius's retreat from Jerusalem, readers of Josephus usually have formed an impression that it was a strategic error.

Cestius's withdrawal from Jerusalem was not a mistake.

If Cestius made an error, it was not anticipating the hostility he would face in Jerusalem and what it would take to overcome it. That was an error of intelligence. Agrippa may well have been the source of that faulty intelligence. But once Cestius fully comprehended the situation, leaving Jerusalem as quickly as possible was by far his best option. Resupply issues had forced none other than Caesar to retreat from Gergovia and elsewhere.[95] Unfortunately for Cestius and his men, the retreat itself was not effectively carried out, and the subsequent disaster gave Josephus an opportunity to suggest historical parallels between the Roman retreat from Jerusalem in 66 and the Athenians' famously disastrous retreat from Syracuse in 413 BCE, as described by Thucydides.

CLADES CESTIANA

Cestius spent the night after his withdrawal from his attack on the inner city at his camp on Mt. Scopus. The next day the Romans retreated farther from Jerusalem, inviting attacks upon themselves. The rebels, meanwhile, dogged the heels of Cestius's retreating army, inflicting casualties among its rear units. They also lined up on both sides of Cestius's retreat route and showered the flanks of the Roman force with missiles.[96]

The Roman soldiers in the rear supposedly did not have the courage to engage those that were attacking them because they thought that they were being pursued by an enormous host. More likely they had been ordered not to waste their time and energy fighting pointless rearguard actions. Meanwhile, those attacked on the sides offered no resistance because, heavily armed as they were, they were worried about opening up their files to attacks by lightly armed men. As a result the Romans offered very little resistance while they themselves suffered gravely. Among the casualties were Priscus, the commander of the Sixth Legion; a tribune named Longinus; and the cavalry commander Iucundus, whom we met before in Caesarea. With great difficulty the beleaguered Roman column finally reached Gabaon, the site of its camp on the way to Jerusalem, but only after leaving behind most of its baggage.[97]

Cestius and the Romans rested there for two days. But seeing that while they were resting the Jews were growing stronger, on the third day Cestius gave orders that all impediments to further retreat were to be left behind. Thus all the remaining asses, mules, and pack animals were killed, except those to be used to carry the missiles and war engines. Those animals were spared because the Romans needed the expensive missiles and engines and wanted to keep them from falling into the hands of their enemies. Cestius then led the army away along the road toward Beit-Horon.[98]

While they passed through open ground the Romans suffered less at the hands of the Jews. But once they were inside the defiles, one group of their enemies went ahead and blocked off the exit point. A second band drove Cestius's rearguard into the gorge. The main body of the Jews meanwhile lined the high ground above Cestius's men and rained arrows down on them. While the infantry had a hard time defending itself, on the uneven and precipitous ground the cavalrymen were virtually defenseless, and many of the horses and their riders slipped off the path and fell to their deaths into the steep ravines. Only the onset of night saved Cestius and his army from annihilation or capture and allowed them to find their way out to Beit-Horon.[99]

Once he reached Beit-Horon Cestius resolved upon a night retreat. Picking out 400 of his bravest men he posted them up on rooftops and ordered them to shout out the password throughout the night to deceive the Jews into thinking that the whole Roman army was still there. Then with the majority of his soldiers he slipped away, advancing about 30 furlongs, or 3.75 miles.[100]

At dawn the Jews discovered they had been tricked and quickly dispatched with javelins the brave soldiers whom Cestius had left behind. They then hastened on after Cestius and the main Roman force. Cestius and his men, who knew that they would be followed once the Jews discovered that they had been deceived, shed everything that might slow them down, including the battering rams, catapults, and most of the other war engines.[101] Since Cestius brought with him a force with the strength of at least two legions, that might mean that he lost at least 130 artillery pieces. Later on in the war Josephus claims that the rebels made use of 300 bolt-throwers and 40 stone-throwers.[102] Some of these artillery pieces presumably came from among those left behind by Cestius, though others perhaps were captured when the Antonia Fortress was taken at the beginning of the war.

The rebels pursued Cestius and his men all the way to the city of Antipatris, where the Romans finally found refuge. At that point the Jews gave up their pursuit of Cestius and turned back homeward. Along the way they captured the Romans' abandoned war machines, plundered the corpses of the dead, and collected booty. Among the booty was probably money, perhaps the pay or *stipendium* for the legionaries, left behind by Cestius.

Later on, in his history of the war Josephus mentions that Cestius's money was taken into possession by Eleazar, the son of Simon, the leader of the Zealot faction in Jerusalem.[103] Since it is hard to imagine how Eleazar could have got Cestius's money unless it was captured by his followers, it is likely therefore that Eleazar's "Zealot" disciples took part in the plundering of what the Romans had left behind. They may even have participated in the attacks upon Cestius's column as he retreated from Mt. Scopus to Antipatris.[104]

The Jews then returned to Jerusalem, singing a song of triumph. Few Jews had lost their lives during the pursuit of Cestius. By the time the action was over, on 8 Cheshvan/Dius, the Romans and their allies had lost 5,300 infantry and 480 cavalry.[105] The time between Neapolitanus's report to Cestius in late June and the ambush of Cestius's army was perhaps a little more than two months. Within that period of time about three weeks elapsed between Cestius's march from Lydda up to Beit-Horon to his reentry into Antipatris.

THE DISASTER OF CESTIUS: A FAILED TACTICAL BLUFF

Scholars have raised a number of questions about Josephus's description of Cestius's retreat from Mt. Scopus to Antipatris and have compared the ambush at Beit-Horon to another disastrous Roman retreat, the infamous Varian disaster of 9 CE. During that earlier retreat, Herod's friend and former governor of Syria, Publius Quinctilius Varus, and three Roman legions (nos. XVII, XVIII, and XIX), plus six cohorts of auxiliaries under his command and three wings of cavalry, were ambushed and wiped out in the Teutoburg Forest (Kalkriese) by Arminius and a group of Germanic tribes.[106]

Some historians have suggested that the length of the retreating Roman column from Mt. Scopus to Gabaon creates problems for Josephus's account of the rebel attacks upon it. But we have no idea how long the column was or even how many soldiers there were in it. Moreover, simultaneous harassing attacks upon the rear units of the column, as well as upon the more forward ranks, make perfect tactical sense. The rebels surely would not have wanted to get into a stationary, set-piece confrontation with retreating legions.

More problematic is Josephus's description of the ambush of the Roman army as it retreated from Gabaon to Beit-Horon, in particular the topographical details he reports. Nowhere along that route today can a gorge, truly precipitous grounds, or steep ravines be found corresponding to Josephus's language. The simplest explanation for the mismatch between Josephus's language and the actual topography is that Josephus exaggerated the topographical details for the sake of dramatic effect. But exaggeration does not mean that attacks did not take place along that part of the retreat route. And no scholar thus far has disproved the accuracy of Josephus's Roman casualty figures of 5,780, or 5,300 infantry and 480 cavalry. The precision of those numbers should give us some confidence in their accuracy.

These were very significant losses, greater than the equivalent of a legion's effective mustering strength plus a cavalry wing, though they were hardly Varian in scale. They possibly represented one-fifth or one-sixth of the army Cestius had brought with him from Antioch. A modern commander who lost 20 to 30 percent of his men in a battle would be sacked immediately. But Roman casualties in the Teutoburg Forest in 9 CE have been estimated at 15,000–20,000, or up to 100% of the force Varus led, and ultimately led the Romans to abandon attempts to project their imperium across the Rhine River. Suetonius says that the emperor Augustus was so distraught at what had happened in the German forest that he used to bang his head against a door shouting "Quintili Vare, legiones redde!" or "Quintilius Varus, give back legions!"[107]

Cestius's defeat cannot be compared to the Varian disaster (*clades Variana*) of 9 CE in scale or effects. Varus lost more than three times as many soldiers as Cestius. Cestius's expedition to Jerusalem, defeat, and retreat—or flight—over three weeks in the late summer–early autumn of 66 was nevertheless one of the most inglorious in early Roman imperial history. And it did help further inspire and energize a full-scale rebellion against Rome. If anything, the success of the rebels against Cestius probably gave them an undeserved and ultimately dangerous sense of overconfidence. But, as we shall see, it did not lead the naturally theatrical emperor Nero to dent the walls of his residence with his large head or to retreat from Judaea. In fact, Nero doubled down on his military response to what was going on in Judaea.

The *clades Cestiana* was a tactical defeat that cost the Romans thousands of lives, an unknown amount of money, their baggage train, the artillery they had brought with them, and their pack animals.[108] Assuming that it would take some time to find and train new recruits to replace the legionaries and auxiliaries, there is no doubt but that what happened to Cestius and his army during its retreat from Jerusalem was a major setback. But it was not a strategic defeat. The Cestian disaster did not affect Rome's ability to fight on, and Rome still possessed most of the military advantages.

The tactical defeat occurred not because Cestius and his army had "manufactured" new enemies among the Jews during their operations between Antioch and Antipatris. The word "manufacture" implies that Cestius and his soldiers literally made the Jews into their enemies. Agrippa and Cestius did not comprehend the depth of the rebels' hatred of Florus and those auxiliary soldiers he commanded. Before Cestius torched his first village in the Galilee, there were already more than enough Jews willing to fight to the death to make a full-scale confrontation in or around Jerusalem a very likely outcome when Cestius got to the city. The actions of Cestius's soldiers in the north and at Joppa must have enflamed passions further. But they were not the cause of those passions.

After the massacre of the auxiliary garrison, the destruction of the Jews of Caesarea, and the reprisals, large-scale resistance to Cestius should have been anticipated. Cestius's campaign in 66 may have helped create more committed enemies of Rome. But there were enough enemies of Rome before Cestius set out from Antioch to guarantee that there would be mass violence— in other words, a war.

Cestius and his army scored early and easy points against small groups of Jews in the Galilee. But the campaign in the north was in essence a kind of bluff. By carefully selected demonstrations of violence, Cestius's Galilaean campaign was an attempt to intimidate the rebels into giving up before a more serious, expensive, and comprehensive response had to be organized. None other than Varus himself had adopted a similar strategy in 4 BCE at the time of Herod the Great's death and the unrest during the accession period. Varus made it work. Cestius's bluff failed.[109]

Round one of the real war between the Jews and the Romans, however, was decided in the pass between Upper and Lower Beit-Horon, and it went to the Jews. Neither Cestius nor Agrippa apparently had heard or read about Seron, the governor of Coele-Syria, and his defeat by Judas Maccabaeus along the same route some 230 years earlier, and they underestimated the fighting spirit and quality of the rebels. In fact, during the rest of the war Roman commanders consistently underestimated the morale of their adversaries. The rebels meanwhile seem to have misunderstood the significance of their victory over Cestius.

Throughout their history the Romans had lost most of the battles at the beginning of wars. In many wars they had lost almost all of the early battles. But they almost always won the last and decisive battle. The Roman response to defeat was defiance, and in victory they were not magnanimous.

CHAPTER 9

John of Gischala

THE EFFECTS OF CESTIUS'S DEFEAT

The failure of Cestius's mission was the signal for many prominent Jerusalemites to flee the city. Among them were the Herodian royal brothers Costobar and Saul. The prefect of Agrippa's army, Philip, the son of Iacimus, also left.[1] These men made their way to Cestius, who received them and at their request sent Saul and his friends on to Nero in Achaia. Cestius reportedly instructed the group to tell the emperor about their own sorry state but also to put the responsibility for the war squarely upon Florus. Cestius did so to lessen the risk that he would be blamed.[2]

Cestius probably sent these prominent men to Nero to report what had happened so that he would not have to be the one who denounced Florus to the emperor. Cestius perhaps calculated that if Nero received critical reports about Florus from royal, pro-Roman Jews they might carry more weight.

While Nero was getting an earful about Florus, there was another pogrom in Syria. The men of Damascus determined to do away with the large number of Jews who lived in their city.[3] They kept their plan secret, according to Josephus, because most of their wives had become converts to Judaism.[4] Lest anyone betray the plot and the Jews escape, the Damascenes took the precaution of shutting the city's Jews up in the local gymnasium. Although Josephus is not specific about which gymnasium the Jews were herded into, it was probably the one that Herod had built for Damascus.

Then, apparently deciding that their wives' sympathies didn't matter, the Damascenes suddenly fell upon the unarmed Jews and killed 10,500 of them in an hour.[5] That number may be inflated. But there is no reason to doubt that some kind of ethnic cleansing took place.

THE REBELS' WAR STRATEGY

In Jerusalem, meanwhile, Josephus says that those who pursued Cestius back to Antipatris led Rome's supporters over to their side either through force (*bia*) or persuasion (*peithoi*).[6] We probably should understand this claim as an example of Josephan literary *hommage;* the literary coupling of contrasting means by which one party brought another over to its point of view in historical writing went back to Herodotus's invention of the historical genre, and Josephus himself used the topos of contrasting means of persuasion throughout his own writings.[7] A neatly coupled antithesis was hard to resist, especially for someone who wanted to show his Roman readers that he too had read at least some of the Greek masters. But we have no way of disproving that some people were actually forced and others were persuaded.

The rebels who had chased Cestius and his army back to Antipatris then assembled within the Temple and appointed generals to conduct the war. Joseph, the son of Gorion or Gurion, a Pharisee, and Ananus II, the Sadducee ex–high priest who had been deposed by Agrippa II after he had presided over the execution of Jesus's brother James, were elected to have supreme authority within the city. They were given special responsibility to raise the height of the city walls.[8]

The significance of their appointment should not be passed over. Their election meant that the "war party" in 66 included at least some members of Jerusalem's priestly elite, including Joseph and Ananus II but, as we find out later, also Simon, the son of Gamaliel; Joshua, the son of Gamala; and, of course, Josephus. It is not true therefore that only "brigands," radical dagger-men, or Zealots were willing to assert independence and go to war in 66. By that time at least one ex–high priest and an expert on the law were willing to lead the defense of the city against a Roman counterattack that was sure to come after Cestius's defeat and humiliation. The fact that Joseph and Ananus were put in charge of raising the height of the city's walls can have no other meaning.[9] Moreover, it is important to highlight that the plan to raise the city's walls was not directed against the Zealots or the dagger-men. They were already inside the city. Raising the walls was made a priority to keep out the Romans and their allies.

A number of other generals were picked to see to the defense of six territories outside of Jerusalem. Jesus, the son of Sapphas, one of the chief priests, and Eleazar, the son of the high priest Neus (possibly a mistake for Ananias), were given command over Idumaea, with the current governor, Niger the Peraean, given instructions to serve under them. Joseph, the son of Simon, was given authority over Jericho, and the Peraea was assigned to Manasseh. John the Essene or Essaean was given command of the toparchy of Thamna (Khirbet Tibne), including Lydda, Joppa, and Emmaus.[10] John, son of Ananias, was appointed chief of the toparchies of Gophna (Jifna, about 12.5 miles north of Jerusalem) and Acrabetta or Acrabatene (Khirbet Ormah, about nine miles southeast of Shechem). And finally, to Josephus, the 30-year-old son of Matthias, was given command of the two Galilees, as well as Gamala on the Golan Heights.[11] (See map 1.)

The assignment of these villages, towns, and territories to the designated individuals was a sign that the rebellion and the potential Roman reaction to it were conceived of as reaching outside of Jerusalem and Judaea. The rebellion extended to the southern borders of Idumaea, into the Peraea on the eastern side of the Jordan River valley, and up to the top of the Galilee and the Golan in the north. This was not only a Judaean war geographically; it was regional and extra-Judaean. The list of who got appointments and who did not also helps us understand the rebels' conception of what kind of war they thought it would be.

Overlooked was Simon bar Giora, despite the fact that he and his followers had fought effectively against Cestius. In fact, he may have fought too well. Before too long the new government decided to send a force out against him, perhaps thinking that he was a more immediate threat than the Romans.

Eleazar, the son of Simon, who had played a key role in Cestius's defeat and controlled most of the Roman spoils and the public treasury, was also not given any official office or command position at the time. Because Eleazar became famous as the leader of the Zealot faction during the siege of Jerusalem, his exclusion from any office or command at this time has led some scholars to hypothesize that the real goal of the elected group of leaders (Joseph and Ananus) in Jerusalem was to stamp out, or at least limit, the Zealot insurrection to give the appointed authorities time to reach some kind of accommodation with the Romans.[12]

As we shall see however, the actions of those who were appointed to lead the resistance, including Josephus, belie the theory that the goal of the first rebel government was to seek an accommodation with Rome. And Josephus unfortunately provides no other information about the strategic thinking of the rebel leaders at the time. To the extent that we can understand what their plan was, it can only be inferred from the identities of those appointed to prosecute the war from the beginning and how they began to execute it.

It is noticeable that at this crucial moment, just after the mauling of Cestius's column, responsibility for the prosecution of the war was handed over not to Zealot leaders or to military men but to those who had been high priests, came from high priest families, or belonged to other prominent priesthoods or schools of thought, beginning with the Sadducee ex–high priest Ananus and the Pharisee Joseph. The rest of the appointments support this pattern.

With the single exception of Niger the Peraean, none of the men given leadership positions, including Josephus, had any experience of general command and possibly even combat, as far as we know.[13] Eleazar, the son of the high priest Ananias, was a Temple captain—a security expert—not an experienced combat officer. The generals of the revolt in 66 were apparently selected on the basis of their status, not on account of their military records or skills. As far as we can tell, in 66 the war of Jews against Rome for the freedom of Zion was a war led by civilians.[14] The simple and obvious reason for that was that Judaean society in Jerusalem was dominated by priests, not soldiers.

Even more importantly, at least in the case of one of those civilians, Josephus, the son of Matthias, the way he chose to fulfill his duties would have fateful strategic implications for the kind of war that would be fought by the Jews. In his autobiography Josephus later claimed that he and two other priests named Judas and Joazar were sent out to persuade the disaffected to lay down their arms and let men picked by the people take up that responsibility if it was needed in the future. Meanwhile he was supposed to wait and see what the Romans did.[15]

In his work on the war written 20 years earlier, however, Josephus's decision to spend his time and energy trying to create a large army in the Galilee from scratch, and to fortify the towns in his territory, implied that he intended to fight the Romans from within those fortified population centers with an army created in the mirror image of Rome's legions. That is exactly what he ended up doing at Iotapata.[16] The leaders in Jerusalem later chose to do the same. Perhaps it was because of the demonstrated folly of fighting Rome in

Rome's way of war that Josephus, in his old age, remembered the original goal of the war so differently.

There were other indications that the rebels underestimated their foe and overestimated their own abilities in the aftermath of Cestius's defeat. Before the newly appointed generals had gone out to their posts the rebels sent out an army of their best fighters, led by Niger the Peraean, Silas of Babylon, and John the Essene, against the town of Ascalon. Ascalon was a traditional enemy. It was a walled city but was defended by a single cohort of infantry and one cavalry wing. Its commander was named Antonius. His name suggests that he was a Roman officer.[17]

Apprised of the impending attack, Antonius got his cavalry out of the city before the Jews arrived. After beating off an attack against Ascalon's walls Antonius let his cavalry loose upon the enthusiastic but disordered and poorly armed Jews. His mounted troops routed the Jewish infantry, dispersing them all over the plain. The Jews regrouped and attacked again, only to be ambushed by the cavalry. Eight thousand of the rebel soldiers were killed, including John the Essene and Silas, before Niger and the other survivors managed to escape to Idumaea.[18]

At Beit-Horon the Jews had used the topography to their advantage. Exposing infantry to cavalry on an open plain outside of Ascalon was a tactical error. More importantly, the attack upon Ascalon revealed that the rebels had not thought through a strategy that would lead to victory in the war. Attacking and capturing the city of an old enemy would have been satisfying but was not part of a coherent plan to defeat the Romans. Settling regional scores was not a strategy. In addition, soldiers lost in the effort were soldiers who could not fight against the Romans when they came to avenge Cestius, as the rebels surely knew they would. More strategic errors were evident as soon as Josephus took up the post assigned to him by the leaders of the revolt in Jerusalem.

JOSEPHUS'S (IMAGINARY) GALILAEAN LEGIONS

The strategic choices made by Josephus and his colleagues helped determine the course and perhaps even the disastrous outcome of the war. Josephus's retrospective recasting of what he was sent out to do in the Galilees and Gamala was a tendentious attempt to recast his failure as the successful completion of an entirely different mission. In his earlier account of his command, which was read by contemporaries who took part in the events themselves, Josephus, however, does make clear that he was preparing to face the legions of Rome, not the Zealots of Jerusalem.

In his first account of the war, Josephus tells his readers that after he was appointed to his generalship he first addressed issues of internal governance. He appointed 70 men of mature years and some discretion as magistrates for all of the Galilee. This council of magistrates seems to have been modeled upon the Sanhedrin in Jerusalem. In addition, he selected seven individuals within each city to judge petty disputes. These groups of seven were supposed to refer more important issues and any capital cases to Josephus and the 70 super-magistrates. In his *Life,* which was published in 93 CE, at least in partial response to criticism of the *War* by Justus of Tiberias, the secretary of Agrippa II, Josephus wrote that these Galilaean authorities in reality were hostages for the loyalty of the district.[19]

Having dealt with internal regulations, Josephus then turned to security concerns. Understanding, as he tells us, that the Galilee would be the first area to be attacked by the Romans in response to what had happened to Cestius, Josephus fortified the 18 most useful places, including Iotapata (Yodefat), Bersabe (Beer-Sheva in the Galilee), Selame (Salameh on the Zalmon River), Caphareccho (Kefar Ata), Iapha (Yaphia, 1.85 miles southwest of Nazareth), Sigoph (Sachnin), Mount Itaburion (Mt. Tabor), Tarichaeae, and Tiberias. In the neighborhood of the Sea of Galilee in the Lower Galilee he fortified the caves with walls (the caves of Arbela), and in the Upper Galilee the rock called Acchabaron (the caves opposite Akhbara in the Upper Galilee). Seph (possibly Safad, Tzefat), Jamnith (Khirbet Yamnit), and Mero (Maruss in the Upper Galilee). Seleucia (possibly Seluqiyeh), Soganaea (possibly Siyar es-Sujan), and Gamala in the Gaulanitis (the Golan) were also fortified.[20]

The people of Sepphoris received permission to erect their own walls because of their affluence and zeal for the war, he says, though elsewhere Josephus makes clear that the Sepphorites were consistently pro-Roman.[21] John, the son of Leios, spelled as such in his *War*, also fortified Gischala (Gush Halav/Jish) at his own expense but at Josephus's order.[22] In his autobiography, however, Josephus writes that John, son of Levite (*Leoueis*) of Gischala, actually took the initiative in the building of Gischala's fortifications.[23] Josephus tells us that he personally supervised and assisted in the building of the fortifications elsewhere and also raised in the Galilee an army of 100,000 young men, the equivalent of around 20 Roman legions, or 10 times the number of legionaries whom Cestius had brought to Jerusalem. All of these young men were equipped with old arms.[24]

Josephus then addressed issues of obedience and arms training. He recognized that the Romans owed their invincible military power primarily to their discipline and military training. He knew that he could not inculcate these qualities in his own soldiers in a short period of time. These attributes could only be fully acquired through long experience. But he also attributed the Romans' discipline to their well-organized system of what we call "command and control." He therefore organized his army along Roman lines.[25]

He increased the number of officers, established various ranks of soldiers, and put over them decurions—a Roman Republican title for officers in charge of allied troops—centurions, tribunes, and generals. In other words he copied, more or less exactly and accurately, the command structure of the Roman legions. He taught his new soldiers about giving signals, trumpet calls for charges and retreats, wing attacks and envelopments, how those who were victorious in battle should relieve those who were being hard-pressed, and how to give aid to those who were in trouble.

In his addresses to the soldiers, he talked about everything that contributed to the bravery of the soul and bodily stamina and repeatedly emphasized the good order of battle kept by the Romans. He urged his charges to abstain from malpractices, such as stealing and robbery, and told them that the armies that were most successful in war were those that fought with a clear conscience. Those that were depraved had to struggle, not only with their enemies but also with God.[26]

It has sometimes been overlooked, but Josephus's (imaginary) creation of a Galilaean army based upon the organization and tactical doctrines of the Roman army is not consistent with his later contention that his primary objective at the time was to reach an accommodation with the Romans. Rather, he was putting together, at least on paper, an army to fight them.

The army that Josephus trained to fight Rome's legions totaled, according to the account presented in *War*, 60,000 infantry and 350 cavalry. These 60,000 were presumably the recruits from among the 100,000 who managed to make it through Josephus's Roman-style boot camp. They were supplemented by 4,500 mercenaries. Josephus's own bodyguard comprised 600 handpicked men.[27]

If Josephus's numbers are accurate, the Galilaean army he recruited and trained after Cestius's disaster was far larger than the one Vespasian himself would muster at Ptolemais during the summer of 67, let alone the army Alexander the Great used to conquer the entire Persian empire from 334 to 327 BCE. Most historians think that Josephus was writing about the papyrus strength of the force. A Galilaean army of 60,000 infantrymen was a figment of his literary imagination—recruited, marshaled, and lectured to by Josephus at his desk in Rome during his retirement there. The simple reason why historians argue that Josephus's Galilaean task force never existed is that it does not appear during any of the subsequent engagements with the Romans or with anyone else for that matter. Building a Galilaean army in imitation of Rome's legions flattered Josephus's Roman readers and proved to them that Josephus had done his research about the famous Roman legions. Unfortunately, paper armies were less effective when it came time to fight. There may have been 60,000 young men in the Galilee; 60,000 trained infantrymen there were not.[28]

The Galilaean cities supposedly provided for all these troops, with the exception of the mercenaries. One-half of each city's levy was routinely sent off on military duty, Josephus tells us, while the other was kept back within the city to furnish them with supplies, especially grain rations.[29] Such a system of supply obviously depended, at least in theory, on the continued control and security of the cities themselves. If the cities were taken, the soldiers lost their source of food and therefore their ability to fight. The contrast with the logistical system of the Romans, with its strategic, operational, and tactical bases, all connected by protected supply lines, and described by Josephus as he told the story of Vespasian's invasion of the Galilee, is telling.

From the very beginning, then, at least in the Galilees, the rebel strategy was to hold on to and fight from behind the walls of the cities and towns that Josephus and others had fortified. Although he wrote his history of the war, and other works that dealt with aspects of the war, many years after its conclusion, nowhere in any of his reflections on the great revolt is there any indication that in hindsight Josephus questioned the wisdom of trying to supply his soldiers from the towns and cities that the Romans were most likely to attack and capture. It is perhaps not surprising that, in the sole surviving history of the war of Jews against Rome, the primary historian of the war should never acknowledge the failure of his own strategy. Rather, what Josephus was concerned with was shifting responsibility for what went wrong onto the shoulders of his nemesis—and doppelgänger—John of Gischala.

JOHN OF GISCHALA

At this point in the war Josephus informs his readers that he began to have conflicts with John of Gischala. As we have seen, John had been deputized or had seized the initiative to rebuild the walls of his native city of Gischala.

Assigning responsibility for the problems between Josephus and John is complicated. At the beginning of Josephus's description of his interactions with John he says, without qualification, that John was an unscrupulous, crafty, lying, ambitious brigand who somehow managed to muster a band of 400 accomplices from the region of Tyre and the neighboring villages to help him plunder the Galilee.[30]

John of Gischala may have been all of those things. But this paragon of vices and faults also turned out to be one of the most influential leaders of the rebellion in Jerusalem.[31] We need to remember that in Josephus's works we are seeing John, who fought to the end in Jerusalem and beyond and who marched in Vespasian's and Titus's triumphal procession, from the perspective of someone who did not. A "brigand" or unscrupulous wheeler-dealer John may have been. A turncoat he was not.

What do we know about John before he played a leading role in the siege of Jerusalem? According to Josephus, John had bribed Josephus's colleagues to get permission to seize hold of and then sell the imperial grain stored in the villages of the Upper Galilee to subsidize the building of Gischala's walls. Josephus supposedly wanted to keep the grain safe for the Romans or for his own use. Somehow or other John also managed to make a profit off the project, at the expense of the city's wealthy citizens.[32]

Josephus's implication that John seized the grain for the sake of making a profit deflects his readers' attention from the more important chronological point: seizing the Roman grain put John on the anti-Roman side well before the Romans responded to Cestius's defeat and, as we shall see, before John made his way to Jerusalem. Commandeering the imperial grain supplies in the villages of the Upper Galilee was another kind of declaration of independence.

John next obtained approval from Josephus to supply oil to the Jews of Syria or to those who had been shut up in Caesarea Philippi and only had access to Greek olive oil, supplied by their own countrymen. Until a ruling by Judah ha-Nasi and his court made at some time during the early third century CE, Jews refrained from using Gentile olive oil, though there was no prohibition against doing so in the Hebrew Bible.[33] John then bought up all the olive oil in the Galilee that he could lay his hands on at a rate of one 97-percent-pure silver Tyrian tetradrach (the equivalent of one Judaean shekel) for four amphorae. He then sold the oil at eight times the price, selling a half-amphora for the same price to those who needed it. He thereby made an enormous profit.[34] From these stories we can gather that John was an opportunistic businessman, with a sharp eye for how to make money out of people's piety, and that at first Josephus was willing to work with the Galilaean entrepreneur.

Afterward John directed the band of 400 "brigands" that he commanded to prosecute raids within the Galilee more vigorously. If Josephus tried to put a stop to the raids after he came onto the scene, John would ambush him. If he did not intervene, John would accuse Josephus of negligence: this was all according to Josephus. Either result would help John achieve his goal, which was to replace Josephus as commander of the Galilee. John also spread the rumor that Josephus was planning to betray the country to the Romans. That was a rumor that would be damaging only if people thought there might be some truth to it—for which Josephus shortly thereafter provided supporting evidence.[35] Josephus furthermore accuses John of having sought to take advantage of another dangerous problem that arose, though his retrospective account of the incident leaves his readers with a somewhat less confident estimation of his own reliability and loyalties.

THE KING'S OVERSEER

A group of young men from the village of Dabaritta at the foot of Mt. Tabor in the Lower Galilee had ambushed Ptolemy, the financial overseer of King Agrippa II, and his sister Berenice (or his wife in Josephus's autobiography) and robbed them of their baggage. Their bags included many rich robes, silver goblets, and 500 or 600 gold coins.[36] Because they could not get rid of such valuable booty secretly, the young men brought the loot to Josephus, who was in Tarichaeae.[37] Tarichaeae was the toparchy capital and port village on the northwestern side of the Sea of Galilee, famous for its prosperous fish-pickling industry and for a large pre–70 CE synagogue located in the northern section of the city. In that synagogue archaeologists found a decorated ashlar or square-cut stone, known today as the "Magdala Stone," that perhaps served either as a base for reading the Torah or as some kind of table for making offerings.[38]

Dabaritta's enterprising young thieves must have thought that the man appointed to lead the resistance in the region to Rome and its ally Agrippa would be pleased by their efforts and the haul they brought to him. Instead of congratulating the young men, however, Josephus reprimanded them for what they had done to servants of the king. Josephus then turned the valuables over to a man named Annaeus, the leading citizen of Tarichaeae. Josephus intended, he tells us, to return what had been stolen to the king's overseer, Ptolemy, when the opportunity arose, because Jews were forbidden by law to rob even their enemies.[39]

To the young men he said that the goods had to be put up for sale to help subsidize the repair of Jerusalem's walls, though Josephus openly admitted that he had already sent for two friends of the king and ordered them to return the stolen goods to Agrippa.[40] It is possible that by this intended return of the goods Josephus was hoping to gain the goodwill of Agrippa in case it was needed later, which it was.

The young highwaymen did not buy Josephus's explanation for his actions. They thought that what he had done was not consistent with the attitude of a man who was committed to the fight against Rome and its royal ally. The young men therefore went around the villages at night calling Josephus a traitor. They also created disturbances in the neighboring cities, including Tiberias. Soon 100,000 men (!) had gathered together in arms against Josephus, an equally fanciful match for the size of Josephus's Galilaean legions, at least on paper.[41]

JOSEPHUS LIVE

This angry mob made its way to the hippodrome of Tarichaeae, where some called for Josephus the traitor to be stoned to death. Others favored burning him alive. They were egged on by John of Gischala and Jesus, son of Sapphias, the chief magistrate (*archon*) of Tiberias.[42]

Nearly all of Josephus's friends and bodyguard fled as the crowd bayed for the blood of the general from Jerusalem. Only four brave souls remained with him. Josephus, we are told, was somehow sleeping while this was going on and only woke up as his enemies were about to set fire to the house he was in. His last four friends urged him to flee at once.[43]

Undismayed, Josephus went out to face the crowd and put on a performance that Thespis, the very first prizewinner at a Greek dramatic festival, would have applauded. He appeared before the mob as a supplicant, with his cloak ripped open, ashes strewn on his head, and his sword hanging from his neck. The crowd expected a full confession of his crimes. But Josephus, given permission to speak, did nothing of the sort. Instead he lied to sow dissension among those who wanted to spill his blood.[44]

He told them that he had had no intention either of sending the money to Agrippa or of keeping it for himself. Since he feared that the people of Tiberias—the rival city of Tarichaeae—and other cities had their eyes on the cash, he had decided to quietly keep the money, which would be used to pay for the building of Tarichaeae's walls. He then told the crowd that if this plan didn't meet with their approval, he was willing to deliver what had been brought to him and let them plunder from it. If, however, his rebuilding plan did meet with their approval, they should not punish their benefactor.[45]

The people of Tarichaeae bought his story and cheered Josephus. The natives of Tiberias and the other towns and villages cursed him and shouted threats. The opposing sides then fell to arguing among themselves, just as Josephus had intended. Even then Josephus understood that the issue of loyalty to Rome or resistance was divisive. But it could be used both to score rhetorical points and to manipulate people.

With the Tarichaeaens won over to his side, Josephus now addressed the assembled multitude more freely. He scolded them for their rashness, promised to build Tarichaeae's wall with the money he had, and also pledged to furnish protection for other cities as well. There would be money coming in, he told them, if they agreed upon who the real enemy was, against whom it was necessary to provide security, instead of attacking the man who was furnishing it.[46] Josephus had brilliantly turned the situation around. It was the Tarichaeans who were at fault, not their generous benefactor.

After this the majority of the crowd, though still agitated and doubtless a bit confused, dispersed. But a large group of armed men (either 600 or 2,000), who apparently were not bamboozled by Josephus's lies and sophistry, made for the speaker. Josephus managed to make it back into his lodgings with his small coterie of friends and 20 soldiers, leaving the angry crowd outside uttering threats.[47]

Cornered, Josephus came up with a second, even more devious deception. Making his way up to the roof of the building, he told the crowd down below that he had no idea what they wanted, because their shouting prevented him from understanding them. He said that he would give in to their demands if they would send in a delegation to talk things over quietly with him. When they heard this, the most notable citizens, along with the magistrates, went into the house. Josephus led them into the most secluded part of the building and shut the door. He then had the distinguished representatives of Tarichaeae scourged to the bone.[48]

The rest of the crowd, meanwhile, was still loitering around the building, thinking that their representatives were involved in some kind of extended negotiation. Suddenly Josephus had the doors of the house thrown open, and the bloody victims of his duplicity were revealed to all. His shocked foes dropped their weapons and fled.[49]

In the version of the story that he would relate later in his autobiography, Josephus reported that only one man was allowed into the house, supposedly to take possession of the stolen money. After the poor man entered the house Josephus had him whipped and one of his hands cut off. The severed hand was then hung from his neck before he was sent back out to his compatriots. It was the sight of this mutilated man that convinced Josephus's enemies to run away.[50]

THE HOT BATHS OF HAMMAT

Undeterred, or rather inspired by the failure of this plot against Josephus, John of Gischala immediately went to work on another gambit. Pretending that he was ill, John wrote to Josephus, asking permission to avail himself of the hot baths in Tiberias for the sake of his health. No doubt the waters John had in mind were the warm springs of Hammat, situated a few minutes' walk south of the city. Josephus, who wanted his readers to believe that he had not quite ticked over to John's irredeemable enmity, wrote to his subordinates in Tiberias, ordering them to treat John as a guest and friend and to provide what was suitable for his needs.[51]

John availed himself of the soothing waters for two days and then, using deception or bribery, began to try to persuade the citizens of the city to rebel against Josephus. Josephus learned what was going on in a letter sent from one of his city guards, a man named Silas.[52]

Josephus immediately made his way to Tiberias and hastened to address the Tiberians in the stadium built for the city by Herod Antipas. It is not known how many of the city's population of approximately 12,000 could have been seated in the stadium.[53] John, meanwhile, who had claimed that he could not come to meet Josephus due to his illness, had sent soldiers to the stadium to assassinate Josephus.

As Josephus was beginning to address the crowd about the news he had received, from behind him John's soldiers raised their swords up to cut Josephus down. Tipped off by the cries of the crowd in front of him, Josephus turned around in the nick of time and immediately fled down to the shore with two of his guards. Jumping into a boat, Josephus and his guards escaped first into the middle of the lake and, from there, on to now-friendly Tarichaeae.[54]

There Josephus's soldiers quickly armed themselves and got ready to take action against those who had been plotting against him. Fearing the consequences for the city of a civil war, Josephus ordered his soldiers to defend themselves but not to kill anybody or expose those who had been responsible. His soldiers obeyed these orders. But the inhabitants of the area, having learned who was responsible for the whole affair, put together a force to attack John, who had fled to his hometown of Gischala.[55]

Josephus restrained the anger of the Galilaeans who wanted to march against John. Instead of taking up arms, Josephus resorted to diplomacy combined with threats. From each city he got a list of the names of all those who took part in John's revolt. He then had it publicly proclaimed that those who did not desert John within five days would have their property taken and their homes burned down. This proclamation led three or four thousand of John's supporters to come to Josephus and throw down their weapons. Some 2,000 followers of John, we are told, nevertheless continued to engage in covert plots.[56]

JOSEPHUS'S RECALL

John now secretly sent messengers, including his brother Simon and Jonathan, son of Sisenna, with about 100 armed men to Jerusalem to complain about Josephus.[57] Once they reached the capital his agents denounced Josephus. Josephus held too much power, they claimed, and soon would appear in the metropolis as tyrant if he were not checked.

Of course, it was in Josephus's interest to represent the move to have him replaced as a personal attack, rather than an indication that he was considered to be incompetent or tyrannical. However, the status and influence of those who backed his recall suggest that poor performance was the real issue, or perhaps they too recognized that Josephus's 60,000- or 100,000-soldier vanguard of the Galilee was purely fictitious.

The leaders in Jerusalem—including Simon, the son of Gamaliel, who was a prominent Pharisee of the House of Hillel, the head of the Sanhedrin, and an old friend of John of Gischala; the high priests Ananus and Jesus, son of Gamaliel; and some of the magistrates—were prevailed upon, supposedly by means of bribery, to secretly furnish John with money to collect mercenaries and to make war upon Josephus. They also passed some kind of decree in the national assembly of the Jerusalemites (*koinon*) relieving Josephus of his command and recalling him. The passing of the decree suggests that dissatisfaction with Josephus's performance was not limited to John of Gischala and his friends among the leaders in Jerusalem, even if we accept that the institutions of the rebel state at the time were not completely stable or perhaps even functional.[58]

In addition, these Jerusalem leaders sent out a force of 2,500 men under the leadership of Joesdrus or Joazar, the son of Nomicus: Ananias, the son of Sadok; Simon; and Judas or Jonathan.[59] A Galilaean named Jesus, who happened to be in Jerusalem at the time with 600 armed followers, was sent for, given three months' pay for his soldiers, and told to accompany the relief force and do as ordered.[60]

According to Josephus, this force's mission was to undermine his popularity and, if he were prepared to come back to Jerusalem without a fight, to allow him to give an account of his actions. But if he refused, they were instructed to consider him a public enemy and to act accordingly. In his autobiography Josephus later asserted that these men had orders to bring him back to Jerusalem alive if he laid down his arms voluntarily but to kill him if he offered any resistance.[61]

Friends of Josephus or his father, who had been tipped off by the high priest Jesus, warned him in advance about the sending of the troops but not about the objectives of the force, since those had been conceived in private. Unprepared, Josephus could do nothing when Sepphoris, Gabara, Gishala, and Tiberias went over to his enemies' side after the force from Jerusalem arrived. Soon, however, with the exception of Gischala, these cities were brought back under Josephus's control without any military action.

How this happened Josephus does not really explain in detail, though in his autobiography he makes the point repeatedly that the Galilaeans begged him not to deprive them of his leadership; he also cites a dream he had while he was in Asochis (near Sepphoris), in which he was told that the things that grieved him at the time would bring him to greatness and good fortune in all things and that he must even fight the Romans.[62] This dream, which inspired Josephus to fight to keep his command and fulfill his destiny, prefigures the vision he soon would have at Iotapata that would justify his switching sides in the war. Subsequently, through some kind of stratagem that he does not describe in the *War,* Josephus managed to get the four leaders of the force who had been sent to recall him, with the best of their troops, sent back to Jerusalem, where they would have been killed by the people had they not fled.[63]

For the moment, fear of Josephus kept John within the walls of Gischala. A few days later, Tiberias, having appealed to King Agrippa for aid, revolted again. The king himself did not appear on the day they apparently had agreed upon. But when a small detachment of Roman cavalry happened to arrive on the same day, the Tiberians issued a decree prohibiting Josephus from entering the city.[64] This can only mean that the sponsors of the decree considered Josephus to be an enemy of Rome at the time.

TIBERIAS AND CLEITUS THE RIGHT-HANDED

Josephus got the news while he was in Tarichaeae. Ordering the gates of Tarichaeae to be shut, Josephus decided to try to trick the Tiberians into opening their gates to him. He assembled 230 boats on the lake and placed no more than four men in each. Josephus then led his phony armada within sight of Tiberias, but not close enough for the Tiberians to recognize that it was not a fully manned fleet. He disembarked and with seven of his bodyguards walked up to the city walls. The Tiberians, convinced that he had brought a huge force with him, threw down their arms and begged for peace.[65]

Josephus threatened and reproached the Tiberians, first for their foolishness in raising a war up against the Romans and then for expending their strength in civil strife. That was what their enemies wanted the most. In addition, they had tried to seize upon the one man who had provided for their safety—Josephus, of course—and had not been ashamed to close the city to him, the one who had built their city walls.

Nevertheless, Josephus agreed to receive those who might make some kind of defense for their actions and to help secure the city. The Tiberians obviously had not heard about the trick that Josephus had played upon his enemies in Tarichaeae. The 10 most prominent citizens of Tiberias came down immediately and were put on ships that sailed some distance from the land. Josephus next instructed the 50 most notable men of the council to come down to him. They received similar treatment. And so on, one party after another appeared and was taken onto the ships, supposedly to ratify the agreement with Josephus. In the end Josephus managed to get hold of all 600 members of the city council and 2,000 other citizens of Tiberias. All of these were brought to Tarichaeae and locked up.[66] Josephus's incarceration of Tiberias's council perhaps indicates that the primary support for the revolt against Roman rule in the city came from people below the socioeconomic status required to serve in the town council.[67]

Those who were left in the city testified that the instigator of the revolt had been a young man named Cleitus. Josephus was determined to punish the young man for fomenting rebellion. But he thought that it was impious to kill one of his own people. So he ordered the poor young man's hands to be cut off by one of his own bodyguards, a man named Levi. Levi, however, balked at going ashore among so many potential enemies and performing such a gruesome task.

Josephus, concerned about the impression that his guard's squeamishness might make upon the Tiberians, berated Cleitus for his ingratitude and then ordered him to be his own punisher or face a still graver punishment. When Cleitus begged Josephus to leave him one hand, Josephus agreed reluctantly, as long as he cut off the other hand himself. Cleitus complied, cutting off his own left hand.[68]

Josephus's troubles with Tiberias were not over, however. Tiberias revolted yet again, as did Sepphoris. This time Josephus gave the city to his soldiers to plunder. When they had finished, he turned around and gave the people their possessions back. Sepphoris received the same treatment. Josephus tells us that he did this to these cities first to teach them a lesson and then to regain their affection.[69] It is hard to believe that the majority of the residents of either town could have had much affection for Jerusalem's general of the Galilees and Gamala.

JOSEPHUS AND JOHN IN THE GALILEE

The complicated and at times conflicting stories Josephus tells us about the civil war in the Galilee and his rivalry with John of Gischala, first in the *War* and subsequently in his autobiography, cannot be taken at face value, in part because in the earlier work Josephus was more concerned with emphasizing his military preparations. Later Josephus had every reason to impugn John's character and actions and to stress that the objective of his leadership in the north had been essentially to quiet the revolutionary forces. So the two accounts had different emphases. But behind both of Josephus's accounts of events in the Galilee and his personal rivalry with John, some valuable information about the situation in the Galilee after the outbreak of the war but before the Roman campaign there nevertheless emerges.

First, both in the cities and the villages apparently there were Roman loyalists, those who favored revolt, and probably many more people who just wanted to be left alone. The political situation in the north, in other words, replicated the state of affairs in Jerusalem. As in Jerusalem in the summer of 66 people were divided on the question of whether to remain loyal to Rome or to take up arms. To complicate matters and our understanding of the situation, people also changed their opinions and sides.

Second, although Josephus did his best to represent his rival as a polar opposite to himself politically, personally, and morally, when it came to the vital issue of strategy there was no difference between the young general from the family of priests in Jerusalem and the sharp businessman from Gischala. Both men anticipated and prepared for a war against Romans that would be fought by Jews from behind the walls of fortified villages and towns. Both used their time and resources to build those walls. In doing so it apparently did not occur to either one of them that they were constructing traps for the people they presumably were hoping to protect. These conclusions about the strategic plans of Josephus and John of Gischala are unsurprising. Josephus was a priest, a product and representative of Jerusalem, of its priestly hierarchy, and of his own self-education. John of Gischala was a northerner, an outsider to Jerusalem, an operator, and a salesman. Neither of them had any real military command experience, and strategic military thinking was unfamiliar to both of them.

PREPARATIONS IN JERUSALEM

Thus were the internal disturbances in the Galilee quieted down. Among the Jerusalemites, Ananus the high priest and as many of the leading citizens who were not pro-Roman readied the wall and the war engines. Although Josephus does not specify which wall was put into shape, it is likely that it was the third or outer wall on the north side of the city. (See map 4.) That was the wall that Claudius had ordered Agrippa I to stop working on.[70] Claudius gave his order because he or his advisers or both knew that past successful attacks upon Jerusalem had been initiated from the high ground to the north of the city. Ananus's attention to the north wall shows that he took seriously his job as one of the leaders of the city's defense.

Throughout the city, missiles and suits of armor were made, and the young men were engaged in irregular military training.[71] Effective use of weapons, of course, was a different matter, and training is not the same thing as experience in combat. These preparations, however, indicate that Ananus understood that fighting within the city was likely. Nevertheless, Josephus claims that Ananus still intended to turn the rebels and the so-called Zealots to a more beneficial course of action.[72]

Moderates—those who objected to Florus's actions but wanted to avoid war with Rome—were in a state of dejection. Many who foresaw the approaching misfortunes lamented, according to Josephus. There were numerous omens that were variously interpreted. To those who loved peace the omens indicated evil, whereas those who kindled the war interpreted them favorably. Josephus claims that the atmosphere of the city before the Romans came was that of a place already doomed.[73]

Around the same time, in the toparchy of Acrabatene, on the border between Judaea and Samaritis, Simon, son of Giora, with a large band of revolutionaries—having been snubbed by the leaders of the revolt—was carrying out a campaign of systematic robbery. Ananus sent out an army to confront him. Simon and his women followers, however, made their way to the rebels at Masada during the winter of 66–67, where they stayed until Ananus and his allies were killed. Before that happened, Simon and his friends from Masada wreaked such havoc in Idumaea that the local magistrates were forced to raise up an army and put garrisons in the villages.[74]

Meanwhile, across the sea, command of the Roman response to Cestius's humiliation was being turned over to a general who could not stay awake while the emperor was trying to show the world what a truly great artist he was.

CHAPTER 10

Cometh the Hour

ENTER VESPASIAN

While the young men of Jerusalem were taking a crash course in combat tactics, the Roman emperor Nero was in Achaia from August 66 through December 67 practicing his musical scales. Distracted from his exercises by the news of Cestius's humiliating defeat, Nero at first affected an air of arrogant irritation. In public, and perhaps with some justification, he attributed what had happened to poor generalship rather than to the courage of Rome's enemies.[1] That can only mean that Nero blamed Cestius for the disaster. But privately, Josephus tells his readers, he was deeply disturbed.[2] Beyond consideration of its human and material losses, Cestius's disastrous intervention meant that Nero's plan to squeeze money out of the Temple and the Jews to help relieve his financial problems had to be put on hold.

While he was in Corinth in the winter of 67, the emperor selected an experienced 57-year-old military commander and ex-consul named Titus Flavius Vespasianus to take command of the war against the rebels and to prevent the rebellion from spreading.[3] Vespasian, as he is usually called in English, having had the inflected ending of his Latin cognomen lopped off, was born in the village of Falacrina (beyond Reate, modern Rieti, near Cittareale) in the Sabine hill country northeast of Rome on 17 November in 9 CE.[4] His father, Flavius Sabinus, had been a tax collector in Asia.[5] Coming from a rather modest socioeconomic background Vespasian took the tried-and-true path to advancement for ambitious Romans (and others): he went into the military. Vespasian became a military tribune by the age of 18 and rose to command Legio II Augusta during the Roman invasion of Britain in 43, when he was still in his early thirties. That is probably an indication that he had shown an aptitude for leadership. His efforts in Britain helped win triumphal honors for Claudius.[6] In 51 Vespasian became a consul at the age of 42 and went on to become a governor of the province of Africa in the early 60s.[7] The African governorship was an important position in a wealthy and peaceful province, although, for unknown reasons, during a riot in Hadrumentum (in modern Tunisia) he somehow got pelted with turnips.[8]

Since there was no military war college for officers in Rome, Vespasian, like all other Roman commanders, learned his job by doing it.[9] Some Roman commanders apparently were slow or no learners. The fact that Vespasian rose to the top from a humble background indicates that he was one of those who proved to be up to the job of leading men in battle.

At the time of his appointment to the Judaean command Vespasian was with the emperor in Greece. He received the imperial appointment despite either leaving frequently while Nero was singing or nodding off.[10] Vespasian's relatively modest socioeconomic pedigree probably counted in his favor with the emperor, despite his social gracelessness.

Vespasian's appointment took place just after Nero had forced his most successful general, Gnaeus Domitius Corbulo, to commit suicide.[11] Corbulo came from a senatorial family, and his half-sister Milonia Caesonia had been married to Caligula. He had achieved notable successes against Parthia and Armenia in the 50s CE, but afterward he was implicated in a plot against Nero's life, allegedly through his son-in-law Lucius Annius Vinicianus.[12]

Vespasian was chosen to pacify Judaea because he was an experienced and competent commander but not a man calculated to be a threat to the emperor.[13] He was connected but not too well connected, able but not too able, unlike Corbulo. Nero may also have thought that anyone who lacked the nous or ambition to stay awake during one of his recitals surely did not have the imagination to become a danger to him even after being put in charge of a legionary task force. The socially inept provincial tax-collector's son would do nicely.

Vespasian was a safe choice. He would get the job done. But he was not the kind of socially well-connected, charismatic general that Romans who did not fancy artist-emperors might rally around. Vespasian would avenge Cestius, put out the Judaean fire, and then could be sent off to a distinguished retirement in the Sabine hills from which his family descended. Cestius had had his chance to snuff out the unrest and failed spectacularly, leaving the bodies of hundreds of Roman soldiers to bake in the sun along the road from Jerusalem to Antipatris. Now it was Vespasian's turn. If all went well Nero could then count upon making regular withdrawals from the Temple treasury.

Before leaving Greece in January 67, Vespasian sent his 27-year-old elder son (by Flavia Domitilla), Titus Flavius Vespasianus, commonly called Titus, ahead to Alexandria in Egypt to take command of Legio XV Apollonaris.[14] "Apollo's Legion" probably had been given its name by Augustus after the Battle of Actium in 31 BCE, a victory that he publicly attributed to the god's intervention on his behalf.[15] In 62 Apollo's Legion had been transferred by Nero from its longtime base at Carnuntum on the Danube to the east to take part in Corbulo's operations in Armenia. After seeing action there, it was posted to Egypt.

Unlike his father, Titus did not grow up in the Apennines' shadow. Born on 30 December 39 CE, Titus had been brought up at the court of the emperor Claudius in the company of Claudius's son Britannicus. When he was young Titus was noted for his easy mastery of both Latin and Greek verse and his musical gifts. He was a good singer and cithara picker. But like his father before him and many other aspirants to higher offices in Rome, when he reached manhood Titus set aside his cithara and pursued a military career, serving as a military tribune both in Germany and Britain.[16] Apollo's loss, it turned out, was Mars's gain.

VESPASIAN'S ARMY

After crossing the Hellespont, Vespasian senior made his way by land to Antioch in Syria, perhaps by February 67.[17] There he found King Agrippa II waiting for him with all his troops, and Vespasian began to marshal forces for the impending campaign. From Antioch Vespasian marched south, reaching Ptolemais by mid-April.[18] Ptolemais was the perfect place for Vespasian to assemble his army for the invasion of the Galilee. It had a harbor into which supplies could be brought to the army by sea. There was also a defensible hill, Mt. Toron or Turon (Tell Akko), a little more than one-half mile from the harbor. To the south of the hill flowed the Belus River (Na'man), another useful resource.[19] From Ptolemais to Tiberias in the Lower Galilee it was less than 40 miles or a vigorous two-day march. Ptolemais also sat astride the

north–south road from Antioch to Caesarea. Ptolemais was an ideal operational base for the first phase of Vespasian's campaign.

In Ptolemais Vespasian was greeted by some emissaries who had come to
him from Sepphoris, less than 20 miles away.[20] Before Vespasian's arrival Sepphoris apparently had asked for and received some kind of Roman garrison.
The garrison was commanded by Caesennius Gallus, who had been the commander of the Twelfth Legion under Cestius.[21] Recognizing the strategic
value of the city because of its size—estimated by archaeologists to have been
somewhere between 30 and 100 hectares, or 74–247 acres—and position,
overlooking the Lower Galilee valley some 440 feet below it, Vespasian decided to strengthen that garrison. A vexillation force of 1,000 cavalry and
6,000 infantry, drawn from different units, if not legions, was sent under the
command of the tribune Placidus to help protect the city from rebel attacks.[22]

Of the known instances where such vexillation forces were sent off by
commanders to perform specific tasks during this period, the size of the force
sent to Sepphoris places it among the largest.[23] Its infantry strength alone was
greater than that of any known legion in the region. Clearly Vespasian understood that it was vital to encourage and reinforce the loyalty of Sepphoris, the
largest city in the Galilee and occupying a strategic position in the valley of
the central Galilee. Sepphoris would be the bastion of loyalty to Rome in the
Galilee around which Vespasian would build his northern security structure.

By 67–68, under the direction of Agrippa II, Sepphoris was minting coins
bearing inscriptions on the reverse side that read, "In the days of Vespasian in
Neronias-Sepphoris city of peace."[24] Such coins were intended as an expression of Sepphoris's loyalty and subservience to the emperor and Rome. A more
practical indication of the attitude of the 8,000–12,000 Sepphoreans was their
decision to tear down the fort on the western summit of the city that had
stood there since the Hellenistic period.[25] The Sepphoreans apparently did
not want the Romans to think that they were preparing for a siege.

After the request from Sepphoris was addressed, Vespasian's son Titus arrived from Egypt, bringing with him Legio XV Apollonaris. Under his immediate command Vespasian now had three Roman legions: Legio XV
Apollonaris; Legio V Macedonica, the Macedonian Legion; and Legio X Fretensis, or Legion of the Straits, because it originally guarded the straits of
Messina between Italy and Sicily. Vespasian's Roman legionary army thus
comprised at least 14,400 Roman citizen soldiers and possibly as many as
18,000. These legions were accompanied by 10 cohorts of 1,000 infantry and
13 cohorts of 600 infantry (7,800) plus 120 cavalry per cohort (1,560 total).[26]

One cavalry squadron joined them from Caesarea (500 or 1,000 riders) and five from Syria (2,500 or 5,000 in total). The auxiliary cavalry wings of Vespasian's task force therefore included 3,000 to 6,000 cavalrymen.[27]

Regional, dependent client kings also provided forces. Antiochus IV of Commagene, Agrippa II, and Sohaemus of Emesa each sent 2,000 infantry archers and 1,000 cavalry. Malchus II of Nabataea provided 1,000 cavalry and 5,000 infantry, mainly archers.[28] Cestius had not chosen to call upon the Nabataeans for help, probably because he knew that their presence would enflame the situation further. The allied client kings thus supplied a total of 15,000 soldiers (11,000 infantry and 4,000 mounted).

Without exactly enumerating the slaves or servants who followed this army, Josephus calculated the total strength of Vespasian's force as 60,000; this number seems to be based upon a "high" legionary calculation of 6,000 soldiers per legion.[29]

The mixed structure of Vespasian's force, including legions, auxiliaries, and allies, meant that his army bore striking similarities to the force Cestius had brought from Caesarea in Elul 66. But Vespasian's army was far larger than the legate's: at least 51,760 potential combatants compared to 29,467, plus city auxiliaries. Notably, its legionary core of at least 14,400, and very likely 18,000, was one-third larger than Cestius's total of 10,800. Vespasian's army also had four times more auxiliary soldiers than Cestius's force: at least 22,360 versus 5,048. Cestius's army had about 14,000 allied soldiers, Vespasian's 15,000.

Because Vespasian's army was larger than that of Cestius, its supply requirements were proportionately greater. Altogether Vespasian's army needed at least 126,940 pounds of food and 103,520 liters of water daily, excluding what was required for all the military slaves and free servants. Josephus tells us that the number of such servants was vast.[30] The (at least) 8,560 horses of Vespasian's cavalrymen (auxiliaries and allied soldiers included) plus at least 18,680 pack animals would have required at least 58,760 kilograms (kg) of dry fodder, 172,000 kg of green fodder, and 544,800 liters of water daily.[31]

The daily supply requirements of Vespasian's army thus were enormous. (See appendix J for the detailed calculations.) Every day the soldiers and animals of his army would have consumed about 634,612 pounds of food and 648,320 liters or 171,268 gallons of liquids. Every four days Vespasian's force would have drunk dry an Olympic-size (660,253 gallon) swimming pool of potable water—assuming anything that could hold that much water could be found in the hot, dry climate of the Galilee or Judaea.[32]

What kind of military operation was Vespasian's needy army mustered to carry out? The blend of different kinds of forces underscores the flexibility characteristic of the Roman army during this period.[33] Vespasian's army, with its heavy infantry, light infantry, infantry archers, and heavy and light cavalry, was capable of fighting different kinds of enemies in different kinds of engagements. The size of the Roman and allied army assembled to quell the rebellion in the spring of 67 was greater by far than the Pan-Hellenic host of about 40,000 that Alexander the Great had led through the region in 332 BCE or the force of 40,000 legionaries and auxiliaries the Romans themselves had sent to invade Britain in 43 CE. Nor can its size have been a function of the availability of Roman troops in the region, reduced by recent Roman campaigns against Armenia and Parthia led by Corbulo.[34] That alone would not explain why Legio XV Apollonaris was brought up from Egypt to join Vespasian's army or why such a large and diverse allied contingent was mustered.

The Romans must have considered that it was necessary to assemble such a large, diverse, and expensive force because of the anticipated size of the opposition and the difficulty of the campaign. The smallest of the villages in the Galilee had more than 15,000 inhabitants according to Josephus, who later claimed that the rebel army recruited in the region totaled 100,000.[35] That number most generously represents a paper strength estimate, or it could just be a wild exaggeration. But even if we divide Josephus's number in half the total would still be formidable.

More verifiably, the Romans would have been well aware of the challenges that the war was likely to pose. Roman soldiers and administrators had been actively engaged in the region of greater Syria since the time of Pompey. They knew the difficult topography of the region, especially in the Judaean hills and along the western coast of the Dead Sea. They were aware of the existence of the Herodian fortresses and recognized that keeping the peace in Judaea had been far from easy for a succession of Roman governors. Above all, they had the recent memory of Cestius's disastrous experience in mind.

The Romans put together such a formidable army because, after Cestius's humiliating defeat, they were determined to crush the rebels and thereby to make an example of them. They controlled their empire with a citizen army of roughly 150,000 soldiers, supported by another 150,000 auxiliary soldiers and an indeterminate number of allied troops. That works out to one legionary soldier for every 10 square miles at least nominally subject to Roman jurisdiction.[36] But those soldiers were not evenly distributed. During the reign of Tiberius almost half of Rome's legions were stationed on the Rhine and in greater Syria up to the Euphrates River.[37]

Because it was impossible for the Romans to maintain boots on the ground everywhere, they had to rely upon the threat of force to maintain control and keep the peace. It was particularly important to meet and deal with internal threats to their power and authority. Otherwise they would lose the psychological edge they held over their subjects. External threats could be dealt with by punitive raids and diplomacy; internal rebellions had to be crushed. Half-preparations and half-measures simply would not do. Vespasian brought overwhelming force with him in the spring of 67. If he could intimidate everyone into submission merely by the threat of using such a force, so much the better and cheaper. But if he could not, Vespasian brought a large hammer.

PLACIDUS: THE QUIET TRIBUNE

While Vespasian was in Ptolemais marshaling his forces, the tribune Placidus, whose name in Latin meant "quiet" or "serene," did not sit passively behind the city walls. Instead he launched a series of harassing attacks by infantry and cavalry against Josephus and his men in the Galilee.

Placidus's forays led Josephus to respond by making an assault upon the city of Sepphoris itself. The attack not only failed. It prompted the Romans to devastate the plains and to pillage the property of those who lived in the countryside. Those capable of bearing arms were killed. Those who were not were enslaved.[38]

The only escape for the people pursued by the Romans was to the cities or villages fortified by Josephus, as the historian informs his readers with some self-satisfaction. As further proof of this point and the effectiveness of the preparations he had made, Josephus tells us that when Placidus attempted an attack upon Iotapata (Yodefat), some seven Roman miles northwest of Sepphoris, the Romans were met by a large and well-prepared body of combatants. The inhabitants of Iotapata repulsed the Roman assault, killing seven and wounding a large number. Placidus was forced to retreat.[39] Some historians have questioned whether this action took place. But the specificity of the small number that Josephus gives for the Roman casualties militates against doubts. There was a skirmish and some Romans lost their lives. They were not invulnerable.

This small success against the Roman advance force in no way affected the rebels' prospects. For Vespasian soon set out from Ptolemais with the rest of the army, deployed to provide security en route but also to intimidate.

TROOPING THE EAGLE

In advance of the Roman column were lightly armed auxiliary troops and archers. Their job was to fight off any sudden attacks and look out for ambushes. Roman archers used composite bows, and the effective range of the arrows they shot has been estimated at anywhere from 55 to 190 yards, depending upon the strength and skill of the individual archer. Men hit by such arrows were more often wounded than killed.[40]

The archers were followed by heavily armed Roman infantry and cavalry and then a detachment of 10 men from each century who carried their own packs and equipment for measuring out a camp. After these came the military engineers, who were responsible for straightening out the army's route, leveling the ground, and cutting down blocking woods.

Vespasian's personal equipment and that of his officers were borne along next, protected by cavalry. After the equipment rode Vespasian himself, amidst handpicked soldiers of infantry, cavalry, and his bodyguard of lancers. The cavalry units of the legions, each 120 strong, followed. In their wake came mules carrying the components for siege towers and the rest of the machines of warfare, no doubt including bolt-throwers and stone-throwers.

The legates, prefects, and tribunes marched along next, with their own picked troops, followed by the ensigns surrounding the legionary eagle, which was borne before every Roman legion. Exactly such a scene is shown on one of the relief panels of Trajan's Column in Rome.[41] Trumpeters came next and then the legionary column of infantry soldiers, marching six abreast. Centurions marched along with the column, keeping all in order. Thousands of mules and other animals, supervised by servants, came after, carrying the soldiers' equipment. A mass of mercenaries followed. Light and heavy infantry and cavalry brought up the rear of the column, providing security.[42]

This order of march indicates that Vespasian understood the threat level to be high, and he was taking no chances. Auxiliary troops and archers led the column and were expected to assess the terrain and watch out for ambushes. The mules carrying the siege equipment were placed in the middle where they could be protected by the preceding cavalry. Light and heavy armed infantry and cavalry provided force protection at the rear. Vespasian would not invite a repeat of the Cestian disaster.[43]

The appearance of this ordered column meant that the rebels were no longer going to be facing the approximately 500-man units of locally recruited auxiliary soldiers, whose main motivation apparently was their hatred of Jews. Rather, they were about to meet one of Rome's rigorously trained, carefully organized, and harshly disciplined legionary armies. This was the kind of tactically flexible professional force that Rome had developed over centuries of warfare and then used to conquer and rule the Mediterranean world and beyond.

The core of the legionary army was its heavy infantry, at full strength divided up into 10 cohorts of at least 480 men per legion. Although new recruits to the cohorts might have been 18 years old or even younger, the average age of Rome's early imperial infantrymen seems to have been closer to 30.[44] Most of them, therefore, would have been veterans by the time they began the campaign in the Galilee.

To each of the 10 cohorts of the legion were assigned six centurions. These centurions usually came from the families of wealthy Roman citizens who lived in the towns and cities of Roman Italy. Each of the infantrymen in the cohorts wore a bronze or iron helmet and a cuirass made out of mail or scales, and carried a semi-cylindrical, rectangular (approximately 3.3 feet long, by 2.75 feet wide) shield (scutum) made of wooden strips that were glued together.[45] Such shields usually had metal bindings and a boss at the center. They seem to have weighed up to 16 pounds.[46] Roman infantrymen used their shields to protect themselves but also as an offensive weapon. Roman soldiers were trained to use their shields to knock their enemies off balance and then to stab them with their swords.

The legionaries under Vespasian's command probably wore "Coolus" pattern helmets. These helmets had wider cheek pieces than previous models, affording more protection for soldiers' faces, and metal strips affixed to the front to deflect blows to the helmets' bowl. A rim protruding out from the back of the helmet gave protection to the soldiers' necks.[47] Nevertheless, these helmets left soldiers' faces and ears more exposed than helmets worn by traditional Greek hoplites because Roman legionaries needed to hear orders and see the battlefield.[48]

The legionaries' shoulders, chest, and stomach area were protected by body armor of mail, scales, or segmented iron plates (lorica segmentata). This body armor could weigh up to 33 pounds.[49]

All of the infantrymen carried a slender, approximately seven-foot-long missile weapon known as a pilum (pila in the plural). The small (about two inches long) pyramid-shaped head of the pilum formed the point of an approximately 22-inch iron shank that was attached to a wooden shaft. Roman infantrymen threw their pila at their enemies before making physical contact with them.

The maximum effective range of such missiles seems to have been 100 feet, although Roman legionaries usually threw their *pila* at their enemies when they were much closer. Because all of the force of the *pilum* was projected upon its small head, *pila* could penetrate both enemy shields and metal body armor. *Pila* that struck enemy shields could be difficult to remove and would have made using shields for defense awkward at best. Although earlier legionaries carried two *pila* into battle Josephus describes the legionaries during the great revolt as only equipped with a single *pilum*.[50]

Roman legionaries at this time used their short (about 16.5–20 inches long) sword (*gladius*) as their primary fighting weapon in combat. The *gladius* had a straight blade and a short point. Although Roman infantrymen wielded their swords to slash and cut, their main use was as a thrusting weapon in close quarters.[51] Slashing wounds were often survivable; puncture thrusts that pierced vital organs were not. Perhaps as a weapon of last resort, legionaries also were equipped with a dagger (*pugio*).[52] Few of the peoples whom the Roman army had encountered in combat over the course of the early first century CE came out of their battles against Roman infantrymen unscathed.

The Roman army was also largely devoid of Jews. Because Jews ordinarily were prohibited from bearing arms on the Sabbath and had dietary restrictions as well, Jews with Roman citizenship seem to have been exempted from serving in the Roman army (if they did not wish to join). This is implied in a series of letters issued by Roman generals, including Iulius Caesar, and governors during the mid-first century BCE, though Jews in the city of Rome itself were pressed into military service on Sardinia during a crisis in 19 CE.[53] By this time period fewer than half of the recruits into Rome's legions were Italians; increasingly, recruits came from the regions in which the legions were regularly stationed.[54] Jews were not necessarily popular among their neighbors in the eastern provinces abutting Judaea. Thus there would be no feeling of sympathy or ethnic kinship between the Roman soldiers and the people they were about to fight in the Galilee.

ADVANCE TO CONTACT

As soon as Vespasian reached the borders of the Galilee he halted, established his camp, and began to prepare for sieges of the towns in the Galilee that Josephus had fortified. Roman armies on the march set up such camps every night as they moved along through enemy territory. Such "marching" camps were intended to provide the Romans with security at night, but their regimented spatial organization and character also sent out a message to Rome's enemies about the professionalism and inexorable advance of Rome's armies.[55]

These preparations were intended to intimidate not only the Galilaean civilians but also the troops under Josephus's command. They had an immediate effect. As soon as the troops that Josephus had brought up to the village of Garis, which was located about 2.5 miles to the east of Sepphoris, realized that a confrontation with Vespasian's army was imminent, they fled before they even set eyes upon the Romans.[56] Josephus's 60,000-man army of the Galilee vanished into the hot thin air, if it ever existed. Left without a force sufficient to confront the Romans, and already fearing the outcome of the war, Josephus decided to retire behind the fortifications of Tiberias, well away from Vespasian's advancing army.[57]

JOSEPHUS'S LETTER

Safely ensconced in Tiberias for the time being, Josephus wrote a letter to the leaders of the rebellion in Jerusalem, providing them with his assessment of the strategic situation. Josephus did not have to be a military genius to appreciate what that situation was. Vespasian was in the Lower Galilee at the head of a real 60,000-man-strong army. Josephus was virtually alone in Tiberias.

In his letter Josephus presented his superiors in Jerusalem with two choices. If they wanted him to negotiate with Vespasian, he wrote, they should instruct him to do so without delay. But if they wanted him to continue the war, they should send to him a force capable of contending with the Romans.[58]

Some scholars have interpreted Josephus's presentation of sending this letter as a thematic *topos*. As a responsible aristocrat Josephus did what he was supposed to do, which was to act honorably and look out for the people's interest.[59] But in its historical context, if the letter was actually sent, the missive surely would have been interpreted by its recipients as a sign of a lack of enthusiasm for the struggle by the Galilee's appointed general. It was also an implicit admission that Josephus's 60,000-man army no longer existed as a fighting force—if it ever had—and a preemptive excuse for flight or failure if Jerusalem did not give Josephus the army he said he needed. Josephus may have been declaring his allegiance to aristocratic leadership values by sending his letter to Jerusalem, but he was also covering his back. Even as he wrote his letter to Jerusalem, he knew that no adequate reinforcements would be forthcoming. No army capable of confronting Vespasian's force existed in Jerusalem or anywhere else for that matter, except to the east of the Euphrates. And the Parthians were not interested in crossing the Euphrates and taking on Vespasian to save Josephus.

THE ROAD TO IOTAPATA

Vespasian meanwhile had led his army eastward to the small city of Gabara (Arabah).[60] Empty of real defenders, the town was taken in the first assault. All males, including the young and the elderly, were slain, we are told, because of the Romans' hatred of the Jews and the memory of what had been done to Cestius and his men. Josephus says that Vespasian then set fire to the city, as well as the surrounding villages and towns. Some of these were deserted. The inhabitants of those that were not were enslaved.[61] Scenes of Roman auxiliaries burning villages and enslaving their women and children on Trajan's Column in Rome vividly evoke such operations.[62]

After Gabara was burned it became Vespasian's tactical base for his next objective, the fortress-town of Iotapata, located about six miles south-southwest of Gabara. Most of Rome's enemies (*pleistous ton polemion*) had fled to Iotapata when Vespasian reached the borders of the Galilee.[63] That was Vespasian's motive to move his army on to the city. Exactly who Rome's enemies were Josephus does not inform his readers. Josephus's later description of men, women, and children being massacred after the final Roman assault on Iotapata does perhaps imply that among Rome's enemies in the neighborhood were not just brigands or dead-end "never Romers": the resistance to Rome at Iotapata was conducted by local, family men.

Iotapata was an ancient town, built up on a hilltop about 1,345 feet above sea level. Josephus claimed that Iotapata was constructed almost completely atop sheer cliffs, surrounded by ravines on three sides that were so deep that the bottoms could not be seen.[64] Access to the town was only feasible from the northern side, Josephus writes, though he had enclosed the whole of the town with a wall when he strengthened the defenses of Iotapata and of the other towns in the Galilee.[65]

Indeed, although there was an impressively solid fortification wall around the highest part of the summit, excavations of the site reveal that a casement wall was hastily built to protect at least the lower northwestern part of the town in 67.[66] A casement wall included two walls with a space or spaces in between (usually connected by perpendicular walls at intervals) that could be used either as residences or filled up with earth or other materials that would help the walls absorb blows from battering rams.

In reality, however, Josephus's description of Iotapata exaggerated some aspects of its topography. On the eastern side of the relatively small (about 12.5-acre) hilltop the drop down to the valley below is so steep that from the top of the site the valley indeed cannot be seen, and the gradient could be described generously as cliff-like. No doubt this is why the eastern side of the city was protected by a single wall in 67.

On the other sides of the hill, especially from the north-northwest, the grade is more gradual, though still steep enough to present a tactical challenge to an assaulting force.[67] The late fourth-century CE military historian Vegetius would immediately have recognized that attacking up the northwestern hill of Iotapata would put the Romans at a disadvantage. They would have to fight both the Jews and the topography.[68] Presumably that was the reason why Josephus had a casement wall built on that side. Vespasian, an experienced besieger, would choose to mount his siege of the town from this direction.

Before he received any reply to his letter from the leaders of the revolt in Jerusalem, Josephus himself made his way from Tiberias to Iotapata on 21 Iyyar/Artemisius (April–May 67), joining back up with the soldiers at least nominally under his command.[69] From information about his interactions with the townspeople in Iotapata that Josephus included in his autobiography, we know that he had considered the town to be loyal to him and reliable when he was contending with John of Gischala.[70] Perhaps that is why Josephus went to the city, even though Vespasian's army was already nearby.

Roman infantry and cavalry meanwhile spent four days leveling the rocky, mountainous six-mile road leading from Gabara to Iotapata, opening it up for the army and the transport of provisions to it as it began the siege of Iotapata.[71] Learning that Josephus was within the city, Vespasian sent Placidus and the decurion Aebutius ahead of the main army with 1,000 cavalry to invest the city and make sure that Josephus did not escape.[72] The scene was now set for what would turn out to be one of the most dramatically recorded sieges in the annals of Roman and Jewish history.

CHAPTER 11

"I Go, Not as a Traitor, but as Your Servant"

THE SIEGE OF IOTAPATA

Josephus's description of the siege of Iotapata gives readers a unique insider's view of what it was like to be besieged by a Roman army during the early Roman empire.[1] When we read Josephus's account of what happened there, however, we need to keep in mind that he composed it years later, in part to justify his own actions during the siege in the early summer of 67. Josephus's "Siege of Iotapata" is a work of considerable historical value and artistry but it is also apologetic.

On the day after Placidus and Aebutius invested the city with their cavalry force, Vespasian himself arrived in the evening with the rest of the army. Encamping on a hill less than a mile north of Iotapata the Roman commander surrounded the city with two lines of infantry by late May. Outside those lines patrolled cavalry. These cordons blocked all avenues of escape, though not communication, as we shall see.[2] The view of these developments from the summit of Iotapata must have been intimidating and frightening, as intended.

The Romans launched an attack the next day, possibly against a body of rebel soldiers who were camped outside the city walls for some unknown reason. In keeping with typical ancient tactics, Vespasian first sent archers, slingers, and other marksmen into action against the Jews.[3] Josephus and the majority of the Jews promptly counterattacked. The two sides skirmished all day. Thirteen Romans were killed, and many were wounded in the engage-ments. Seventeen Jews also lost their lives, and no less than 600 were wounded, a bloody testament to the skill of Vespasian's specialty troops and the Jews' apparent lack of adequate defensive armor. Similar attacks and counterattacks continued for five days.[4] Clearly both sides were feeling each other out, prob-ing for weaknesses, and seeing if their opponents had the stomach for the com-ing siege.

VESPASIAN'S SECOND PLAN

At this point Vespasian held a meeting with his officers to consider a plan of attack. Roman generals often held such meetings (*consilia*) with their leg-ates, tribunes, prefects, and centurions before launching major operations, to discuss and debate tactics, though the commanders made the final decision about what to do and then issued orders to their subordinates.[5] Both Vespa-sian and Titus convened many such meetings during the course of the war.

Vespasian resolved to have earthworks or artificial banks of soil, stones, and timber raised up against the most accessible part of the city's defensive wall. The excavators of the site have identified the section they chose as Io-tapata's north wall. The gradient of the hill up to the wall on the northwest-ern side, while still steep, especially near the defensive wall, was far less severe and the distance shorter than on the other sides. So it was from the level ground below this sector of the wall that the Romans began to build their ramp.[6] (See figure 7.)

Roman legions had vast experience building such earthworks. Every sol-dier knew exactly what to do. Timber from surrounding mountain forests and masses of stones were immediately gathered up. Screening hurdles were put up over palisades by Vespasian's soldiers to protect the Romans while they built up the earthworks.[7] The effort involved in constructing such protective screens and the earthworks was enormous and should not be overlooked. Ro-man legionary soldiers were trained to fight but also to dig and build. In ad-dition to his weapons and armor, in his kit every legionary carried a saw, a basket, a pick, and an axe.[8] One of the distinctive characteristics of Rome's legionary infantrymen was that they were simultaneously warriors and com-bat engineers.

From the ramparts of the city wall the Jewish defenders meanwhile threw large boulders down onto the Roman screens.[9] Vespasian then had his esti-mated 160 artillery machines moved into a circular formation, and he ordered

FIGURE 7. View up toward the summit of Iotapata from the level ground
on the northwestern side. G. Rogers.

the soldiers who manned them to shoot at the rebel soldiers who were defending the walls. All at once the catapults (*catapultae*) shot arrows or bolts
and the stone-throwers (*ballistae*) hurled stones weighing upwards of 75 pounds
toward the Jews. Brands of fire and a great number of arrows also filled the
air. The barrage not only made the wall uninhabitable by its defenders but it
also cleared the spaces directly behind the wall. A mass of Arab archers, javelin throwers, and slingers discharged their weapons at the same time as the
artillery barrage.[10]

Although they were unable to defend the ramparts under this deadly bom-
bardment, assault teams of Jews nevertheless rushed out from Iotapata,
pulled off the protective screens that the Romans had put up, and attacked
the exposed workmen. When the workmen retreated, the Jews destroyed the
earthworks and set the palisades and hurdles on fire. These lightning raids
were stopped only after Vespasian ordered that all the hurdles were to be united
and defended by soldiers who had closed up together.[11]

No longer harassed by raiding parties, the Romans soon raised their embankment wall almost up to the level of the town's battlements. In response
Josephus ordered his masons to increase the height of the town's defensive wall.

To protect those involved in this task, palisades were attached to the wall with oxen hides fixed over them. These snared the stones hurled at the Jews from the Romans and deflected other projectiles. Working under this leathern screen the workers elevated the height of the wall by some 30 (?) feet, adding towers and a parapet for good measure. Having built up the wall, the town's defenders went back to making sallies, pillaging, and burning Roman works.[12]

PLAN NUMBER THREE

At this point Vespasian realized that the siege was not succeeding, so he changed tactics again. Like Iulius Caesar at Alesia in Gaul in 52 BCE, he ordered a total blockade of the city. Such a blockade, he believed, would eventually force the city's inhabitants to sue for mercy or to starve to death.[13]

Vespasian's belief that the blockaded city could be starved into submission was a miscalculation based upon inadequate intelligence. Apparently Josephus and his soldiers had seen to it that an abundant supply of grain had been brought within the walls of Iotapata before the Romans showed up. What the town lacked, however, like Uxellodunum in Gaul in 51 BCE, was an adequate supply of fresh water. There were no natural springs on top of Iotapata. For drinking water the residents had to rely upon rainwater, collected in cisterns, the remains of which are visible to this day. During the summer they could not expect much, if any, rain. For that reason, from the beginning of the siege, Josephus had rationed water within the town.[14]

Vespasian was aware of the Jews' lack of water because, from the slopes of the hills surrounding the town, he could see the Jews assembling at one spot to receive water rations. Thus Vespasian expected that the Jews would soon be forced to capitulate. To undermine that expectation, Josephus had a number of dripping wet garments hung from the city's battlements. The impression he hoped to convey by hanging out the laundry was that the city was overflowing with water.

The trick worked. After getting a good look at Josephus's laundry drying in the sun, Vespasian went back to the tactical drawing board and decided that he had been right the first time. The city had to be captured by main assault.[15]

The success of Josephus's ruse and the consequent shift in Roman tactics did not affect logistical necessities or intelligence requirements within the city itself. The defenders of the city were running short of supplies, and they also wanted to be able to communicate with the outside world. To keep lines of communication open to Jews outside the city and to bring in supplies, Josephus sent messengers down the ravine on the western side of the city along a gully that was so difficult to cross that the Romans had left it unguarded—a surprising, though not crucial, mistake by Vespasian. For a time these messengers enabled Josephus to send out letters from the city and for some provisions to be brought in. At night Josephus's messengers crept along the gully on their hands and knees, wearing fleeces on their backs so that they would be mistaken for dogs. Eventually, however, the Romans figured out what was going on and sealed off the gully.[16] Iotapata was now completely cut off from the outside world.

Josephus thereafter concluded that the situation was hopeless. So he consulted with the city's leading citizens, but not about surrender. Instead, he wanted to discuss his own flight from the city. Hearing of his intention to flee, the Iotapatans begged Josephus to stay and not to abandon them. If he stayed, they said, everyone else would put his heart into the struggle. If they were captured, it would at least be a consolation that he was still with them. They added that it would be unworthy of him to flee from his enemies and abandon his friends.

To this moving appeal Josephus responded that it was in their interest that he should leave the besieged city. His presence in the town could not help them if they were saved, he said, and if the city were taken, it would serve no end for him to perish with them. If he managed to escape from the city, he told them, he could benefit the city by stirring up the Galilaeans and drawing the Romans away from the city. Because the Romans attached so much importance to his capture, he argued, his presence in the city was causing them to press the siege more vigorously. If he left, they would slacken the attack.[17]

The populace was not won over by these arguments. Children, old men, and women carrying infants begged him to stay and share their fate. Out of compassion for their distress, and because he knew that he now would be watched, Josephus informs his readers that he decided to stay. He provides no information about how the disclosure of his desire to leave affected the morale of the Iotapatans.

Having made his choice, Josephus then led a series of raids against the Romans. He and some of his best fighters made their way down the hill, got within the Roman lines, tore the skin covers off their embankments, and set fire to some of their earthworks.[18]

Rather than using the legionaries to repel these attacks Vespasian made use of the allied Arab archers, Syrian slingers, and stone-throwers. Artillery was also put to constant use. The Jews nevertheless fought back ferociously, without regard for their personal safety.[19] But these hit-and-run raids could not break the siege itself.

THE RAM

As soon as the Romans rebuilt the earthworks nearly to the level of the raised ramparts, they brought up a ram (*krios*) to batter against the wall. The ram consisted of a large wooden beam with a mass of iron in the shape of a ram's head covering one of its ends. The beam was held up at its midpoint by ropes that were attached to a second beam. This in turn was supported at both ends by posts dug into the ground. The ram worked by men first drawing the wooden beam back and then pushing it forward with all of their might until its head crashed into the wall. The ram was hauled up to the wall after the Romans put into action catapults and other artillery to clear the ramparts of defenders. Archers and slingers provided additional covering fire. Iotapata's wall shook at the very first blow of the ram.[20]

To lessen the impact of the ram butting its head against the wall, Josephus devised another stratagem. He directed his men to lower sacks filled with chaff by ropes down to the places on the wall against which the ram was positioned. Once the sacks were in position they softened the force of the ram's butts. Not to be outdone, the Romans quickly devised their own countermeasure. Attaching scythes to long poles, the Romans cut the ropes that the Jews used to lower the sacks. The ram's battering of the wall then continued unimpeded.[21]

THE JEWS' COUNTERATTACK AND THE ARISTEIA (FINEST MOMENT) OF ELEAZAR, SON OF SAMEAS

Unable to stop the ram from weakening and inevitably breaking through the wall, Josephus and his soldiers made one last desperate attack upon the Romans' war engines. Gathering up all the dry wood they could find, they rushed out from the town and set fire to the engines, shelters, and props that held up the earthworks. In a single hour the fire from the dry wood—accelerated by the addition of bitumen, pitch, and sulfur—destroyed the works.[22] During this fighting three of the defenders of Iotapata distinguished themselves: Eleazar, the son of Sameas, from Saba in the Galilee, and two brothers, Netiras and Philip, from the village of Ruma (Rumah), also in the Galilee.[23]

Apparently standing atop the wall, Eleazar lifted up an enormous rock and then threw it down upon the battering ram, breaking off its head. Leaping down from his position, Eleazar then picked up the broken ram's head and carried it triumphantly to the foot of the ramparts. Archers from the Roman lines immediately began to shoot arrows at him. Pierced by no less than five arrows, he nevertheless climbed up the wall and stood momentarily with his trophy for all to see, until he pitched over, still holding the ram's fractured head.

Netiras and Philip, the brothers from Ruma, charged out against the soldiers of the storied Tenth Legion, putting to flight those whom they encountered.[24] Perhaps inspired by the examples of these men, Josephus and the rest of Iotapata's defenders then charged out of the town again and set fire to the war machines, shelters, and earthworks of the Fifth and Tenth Legions.[25]

These heroic individual feats did not put an end to the Roman attacks. Toward evening the Romans brought the ram, which presumably had been repaired by the specialty legionaries known as *architecti,* who were responsible for maintaining artillery pieces, back to the spot where it had weakened the wall earlier.[26]

The Romans did not keep their grip on their empire by giving up after suffering setbacks. Indeed, it was precisely their willingness to keep fighting after taking casualties and even losing battles that made them so formidable. As the ram went back to work an incident occurred, however, that might have changed the outcome of the siege and perhaps even the war.

From somewhere on top of Iotapata's wall an archer shot an arrow at his Roman enemies below. Either by luck or skill the arrow found a Roman target, striking him in the sole of his foot or the knee. Though the arrow drew blood, the man's wound was only slight. The man's wounding nevertheless caused great consternation among the Romans. They knew that if the archer had aimed just a bit higher Vespasian would not have been struck in the foot but might have suffered a mortal wound.[27]

Vespasian's wounding at Iotapata was a reminder of the war's unpredictable nature. If Vespasian had died beneath Iotapata's walls there is no way of knowing how the siege of Iotapata or even the outcome of the war might have turned out. Alexander the Great was very nearly killed during his first major battle against the Persians. If he had died on the banks of the Granicus River in 334 BCE, his army probably would not have overthrown the Achaemenid Persian dynasty. Considering the poor record of Roman military leadership in Judaea before the arrival of Vespasian, it can be argued that he and Rome just avoided an arrow potentially fatal both to Vespasian and to Rome's effort to quell the unrest among the Jews. If Vespasian had been killed at Iotapata, of course, Nero would have appointed someone else to crush the rebellion. Whether his replacement would have proved to be as effective a commander as Vespasian was we will never know.

THE NIGHT OF TERROR

As it was, Vespasian's brush with death only enraged the Roman troops and encouraged them to take risks and assault the ramparts yet again. These attacks led to a night of warfare memorable for its sights and sounds of horror and terror. Josephus tells his readers about a man whose head was ripped right off his torso by a stone; a pregnant woman who was struck by another stone, which tore her unborn infant out of her womb; whole files of soldiers laid low by missiles from Roman catapults and the "quick-fire" machines; the whizzing buzz of the stones in flight; the thudding of the dead as they hit the ground after being knocked down from the wall; and the fearful cries of the women within the town, mixed up with the moaning of the dying.[28]

Josephus included these stories in his account of Iotapata's siege to heighten the drama of his narrative and to affect his readers' emotions. But recognizing Josephus's literary objectives should not distract us from appreciating the collective terror that the Iotapatans must have felt during such an attack, even if the bolts fired from the Roman artillery hit and killed individuals alone. Because the momentum and force of the bolts were so powerful, they penetrated whatever body armor people wore and tore into and right through bodies. The sight of even a few people killed by such weapons must have spread terror among all the defenders of the town.[29]

THE WALL BREACHED

At just about the hour of the morning watch (6 A.M.) a breach was finally made in the city wall. The Jews there were left to defend the gap with their bodies and hand weapons before the Romans could position gangplanks across the opening.[30]

After giving his troops a little rest, Vespasian assembled them soon after dawn for what the Romans hoped would be the final assault on the town. The Roman commander knew that the defenders of Iotapata would concentrate their forces at the point where the wall already had been broken. So he ordered his troops to bring up ladders and to lay them all along the walls to draw the town's defenders away from the point where the wall already had been breached. At that point the bravest of dismounted Roman cavalry, wearing body armor, were lined up three deep to begin the assault once gangways were laid down. Behind the picked cavalry stood the best of the infantry. Archers, slingers and artillery gunners were arranged in a semicircle behind the infantry, ready to launch a covering barrage of missiles.[31]

THE BATTLE ON THE GANGPLANKS

Josephus anticipated Vespasian's tactics. He understood that what would matter was what happened at the wall's breach point. So he stationed the old and exhausted along the rest of the wall but positioned his best remaining fighters where Rome's elite warriors would try to force their way into the city. The Jews, including their commander, drew lots to determine who would meet the Roman assault force.

The lottery winners were ordered to stop up their ears so that they would not be frightened by the shouts of the advancing Roman legionaries and to crouch beneath their shields when the Romans launched their missiles. As they assaulted enemy towns during the war, the Romans often began attacks with a frightening war cry. Shouting just before an attack was a standard way for soldiers in the ancient world to encourage themselves and intimidate their foes.[32] Fearing that the women of the town might unnerve his soldiers by their wailing, Josephus ordered them to be locked up in their houses before the combat began.[33]

After the horns of the military trumpeters (*tubicines*) sounded and the troops gave a shout, the Roman assault began with a mass volley of arrows from all around. The defenders on the rampart kept their heads down until the Romans began to lay down the planks to make their way onto the ramparts of the wall. When the Jews saw them putting down the wooden boards, they dashed up and engaged the Roman soldiers. As the Romans struggled to get up on the planks the combat was waged hand to hand and the outcome of the individual battles was either victory or death. Because the Romans could replace those who lost their lives in these mortal struggles with fresh replacements, the Romans at first gained the local tactical advantage. Gradually the Roman soldiers managed to link up with each other side by side, and after raising their locked shields over their heads to provide protection from missiles, they pushed the defenders back from their wooden bridge onto the ramparts.[34]

At this critical juncture Josephus resorted to chemical and herbal warfare. He ordered boiling oil to be poured down upon the shields of the advancing Romans. The oil instantly penetrated beneath the armor of the Roman soldiers and began to boil them alive like cooked lobsters. Writhing in agony, the Romans fell or leapt down from the gangplanks or tried to make their way back down the ladders they had climbed up. The way back, however, was blocked by their fellow soldiers, who were formed into the second assault wave.

The soldiers in the second wave struggled forward to get past their retreating comrades, only to encounter a second problem. After the first Roman assault team was driven back by the scalding hot oil, the Jews poured boiling fenugreek upon the planks themselves. Fenugreek was a liquid extract from the local plant *Foenum Graecum*. The distilled juice of the plant was as slick as Pennzoil spilled upon new blacktop on a hot day. After the boards were covered in the fenugreek, it was impossible for anyone to stand up on them, let alone to advance or retreat. Those who tried simply fell down and were crushed underfoot or fell off the gangplanks altogether. Jewish archers dispatched anyone who tumbled down below. The Romans suffered many killed and more wounded during the battle on the gangplanks; six Jews were killed and 300 wounded.[35] The assault on 20 Daisius had failed in a memorably disastrous way.[36]

THE ROMANS REGROUP

Undeterred by this setback, Vespasian, like any good commander, consoled his troops and then devised a new plan. Recognizing that another frontal assault would lead to more lives lost and morale sapped, Vespasian ordered the embankment to be raised up even higher and the construction of three 50-foot-high siege towers, covered entirely with sheets of iron. The iron siding would increase their stability and also make the towers impervious to fire.

Once the siege towers were finished, they were hauled up on the raised earthworks with artillery, javelin throwers, archers, and slingers mounted on top of each one. The defenders of the city walls could no longer see the Romans, let alone retaliate against them. The Romans now could rain missiles down freely upon their heads. The Jews were consequently compelled to abandon the walls and henceforth only could make intermittent sallies against those who were attempting to reestablish the bridge across the breach in the wall.[37]

THE END OF IAPHA

While the Roman soldiers and their allies on the siege towers were forcing Josephus's men to lie low, Vespasian sent Marcus Ulpius Traianus, or Trajan, the commander of Legio X Fretensis from 67–69 CE and the father of the future emperor of the same name (Trajan), to deal with the town of Iapha (Yaphia). Iapha was a large, densely populated village located directly 16 kilometers, or almost 10 miles, south of Iotapata. Emboldened by the example of Iotapata's resistance, Iapha too had revolted.[38] If Josephus's chronology is correct, the Iaphans had done so before laying eyes on any Roman or royal soldier. The Iaphans were not newly created enemies of Rome. Their issues with Rome predated the Romans' siege of their town.

Iapha was built up on an elevated, naturally defensible position. The village was also surrounded by two sets of stone circuit walls. Perhaps placing too much trust in these fortifications, after Trajan and his men arrived the Iaphans ventured out beyond their outer wall and attacked the Romans. They were quickly routed, however, and chased back within the first walled circuit. After the Romans breached the first wall, the Iaphans retreated back to the gates of the inner fortification wall. With the Romans in hot pursuit the Iaphans desperately sought entry back into their city, only to have their own sentinels refuse to open the city gates to them. Perhaps the guards were worried that if they kept the gates open the Romans would enter the city too. Caught out in the open ground between the two sets of walls, the Galilaeans fought bravely but were massacred to a man. No less than 12,000 died, Josephus says, perhaps within a few hours, certainly beneath the eyes of their fellow townsmen on the ramparts of the inner wall. Without qualification Josephus attributed the fate of the Iaphans slaughtered outside the gates to God.[39]

Before the inevitable all-out assault on Iapha was ordered, Vespasian's son Titus arrived, having been summoned by Trajan so that he would get some credit for the anticipated victory. Perhaps Trajan anticipated that Titus's father was a man with a future in Rome. Titus brought reinforcements, including another 500 cavalry and 1,000 infantry. After posting Trajan on the left, Titus and his troops took up a position on the right and the attack commenced. Soldiers brought up ladders and began to scale the city walls at every point. Unlike the combat in Iotapata, the Romans soon were up the wall and masters of the ramparts, which were quickly abandoned by the Iaphans. Street fighting then began within the town and continued for six hours. By the end of that time another 3,000 Galilaeans were dead. All the male inhabitants of the city, excluding infants, were slain. The infants, along with the captured women, were sold into slavery. Fifteen thousand died during the brief siege and destruction of Iapha. By 25 Daisius, 2,130 also had been made captive.[40]

Again, these casualty numbers are no doubt unreliable though Josephus's number for those enslaved may be more credible. It could be based upon some sort of record kept by the Romans. Accurate records of the number of people enslaved after battles were important to the Romans because slaves were often auctioned off to slave traders who bought in bulk. After Iapha was destroyed Titus rejoined the Roman army at Iotapata. Before the Roman army launched its final assault on Iotapata, however, another pocket of fanatical resistance was eliminated.

THE SAMARITANS' LAST STAND

A large group of Samaritans had gathered themselves on their sacred mountain of Gerizim, some 3,100 feet above sea level, where the remains of the temple destroyed by John Hyrcanus I around 112–111 BCE were located.[41] (See figure 8.) The Samaritans were undeterred by the knowledge of what had happened to their neighbors. They knew. But they decided to fight anyway.[42]

No doubt the Samaritans had not entirely forgotten about Pilate's attack upon the Samaritans at the foot of Mt. Gerizim and Claudius's execution of the three Samaritan leaders involved in the incident during the governorship of Cumanus.[43] Many middle-aged Samaritans must have been young men when their leaders were executed in Rome. Samaritans also must have known that they were despised by Jews such as Josephus. But that knowledge did not imply that they were friendly to Rome.

Vespasian dispatched Cerialis, the commander of the Fifth Legion, along with 600 cavalry and 3,000 infantry, against the Samaritans on Gerizim. Those relatively small numbers suggest that Vespasian was not anticipating a major confrontation. Perhaps he knew that the Samaritans had no walls to protect them and had even less water than the Iotapatans. That was a huge disadvantage in the middle of summer.

Some of the thirsty deserted to the Romans after they appeared, and Cerialis promised to spare the lives of those who laid down their arms.[44] But the vast majority of the Samaritans refused to surrender, choosing to make their last stand on the ridges of their mountain. Perhaps only a few days after the annihilation of Iapha, by 27 Daisius, 11,600 had perished.[45]

FIGURE 8. Mt. Gerizim from Mt. Ebal. It was on Mt. Gerizim that some 11,600
Samaritans died in the summer of 67 fighting the soldiers of the Roman Fifth Legion.
William Schlegel/BiblePlaces.com.

Because Josephus nowhere mentions women and children enslaved after the massacre, as he does in other cases, it follows that the 11,600 Samaritans who died essentially constituted the male fighting force of Samaritans at the time.[46] Josephus and many other first-century CE Jews considered the Samaritans to be heretics. If so, the Samaritans who perished on Mt. Gerizim were anti-Roman heretics.

THE END OF IOTAPATA

Even as the Samaritans were dying on Mt. Gerizim, the Iotapatans were experiencing their last few days of freedom and life. Exhausted by the continuous fighting and with their numbers reduced, the Iotapatans became even more vulnerable to the Romans' relentless pressure. On the 47th day of the Roman siege a deserter advised Vespasian to begin an assault during the night's pre-dawn last watch, at a time when the city's guards apparently could no longer stay awake and alert.

Vespasian was not sure whether to believe the man's story, since the Iotapatans were famously loyal to each other. Another man captured earlier, for instance, had been tortured and then crucified without uttering a word about what was going on within the city. He was said to have died silently with a smile upon his lips. In the end, however, Vespasian decided to take a chance and act on the traitor's information, largely because of its inherent plausibility. It stood to reason that the guards would be exhausted by dawn after the long siege. Vespasian therefore ordered the assault.

Advancing to the city wall in total silence at the appointed hour, soldiers of the Fifteenth Legion, led by Titus and the tribune Domitius Sabinus, mounted the wall, quickly killed the dozing sentries there, and entered the city. Behind the initial assault team followed the tribunes Sextus Calvarius and Placidus with their troops. Before the Iotapatans had rubbed the sleep out of their eyes on that misty morning their fates had been sealed.[47]

After it became clear that the Romans were inside the city, some of the guards at the wall managed to make their way up into one of the towers along the northern side of the city wall. Hopelessly outnumbered by their Roman enemies, they finally surrendered and willingly offered themselves up to be killed by the Romans. But not everyone surrendered without making the Romans suffer as well.

One Jew who was hiding in one of Iotapata's numerous caverns, which still can be seen at the site, extended his hand to a Roman centurion named Antonius. When the Roman officer put out his own hand to help the man out of the cavern, the rebel stabbed the centurion below the groin, killing him on the spot. Such actions would hardly have endeared the population to the Romans.

On the first day the Romans slew all the Iotapatans who showed themselves. During the following days they searched all the hiding places within the city, including the vaults and underground caves. At least some of Josephus's picked men were said to have committed suicide rather than fall into Roman hands. All who were found hiding by the Romans were killed, except 1,200 women and infants who were made prisoner. The total number who died during the siege was calculated by Josephus at no less than 40,000.[48]

Based upon the size of the site—about 12.5 acres within the walls—the chief excavator of Iotapata has estimated that the number of those killed from among its approximately 7,000 inhabitants was more like 2,000, with another 1,200 taken into captivity.[49] These modern estimates seem plausible and suggest that all of the adult males found by the Romans were put to death.

Although the archaeologists did not find skeletal remains of thousands of casualties, the bones of two adults and one child were found in one cistern, and in the southern section of the city's residential area there were also discovered the skeletons of 20 more people. Some of these showed signs of having suffered violent traumas. These unfortunates presumably were victims of the Roman massacre that Josephus describes.

After the killing was over, Vespasian ordered the city to be razed and its forts burned.[50] By the early summer of 67 (1 Panemus), after a siege that lasted 47 days, Iotapata no longer existed.[51]

Why was Iotapata destroyed? Was Iotapata besieged and destroyed by the Romans only because the tribune Placidus had suffered a minor setback when he encountered some of the Iotapatans outside the city walls while Vespasian was still in Ptolemais with his army?[52] Was the siege only a "hiccup" during the Roman operations in the Galilee?[53]

Vespasian may have destroyed Iotapata to soothe Placidus's wounded pride. But Josephus tells us that Vespasian made the decision to besiege Iotapata because he knew that most of his "enemies" were holed up in the town.[54] Vespasian's job was to find and destroy the enemy, not to restore the pride of his officers. Everything we know about Vespasian suggests that he was a cautious commander who made decisions based upon calculations of interest and effectiveness, not emotion. Unless the Jews in Jerusalem spontaneously surrendered at some point, Vespasian had to head south to deal with the kinetic epicenter of the revolt in Jerusalem. Leaving a town unconquered that he knew to be a center of resistance at his rear (to the north) and near his supply line to Ptolemais, Antioch, and even farther to the north would have been strategic folly. That is why Vespasian was willing to expend enormous material and human resources upon the siege.

A 47-day (or 38- or 42-day) siege might not sound like a vast investment of time and effort. But if our calculations are even close to accurate—and they are based upon the lowest possible number of soldiers per Roman legion—during the seven weeks that Vespasian and his army were occupied with the sieges of Iotapata, Iapha, and Mt. Gerizim, his army would have required at least 5,966,180 pounds of food and 4,865,440 liquid liters for his soldiers, as well as 2,761,720 kg of dry fodder, 8,084,000 kg of green fodder, and 25,605,882 liters of water for his pack animals and horses.[55] These supplies were used up to capture and destroy one small village, one well-defended hilltop town in the Galilee, and a small army of Samaritans.

Nor was the siege of Iotapata only a strategic interlude for the Romans. Almost seven weeks of hard, frustrating fighting constitutes more than a spasm of violence. Vespasian himself easily could have lost his life during the siege, and even if we radically discount Josephus's casualty figures, it is obvious from the evidence cited in his account that Iotapata was a bloody encounter for both sides, especially of course for the Jews. Even though the summit of Iotapata was not surrounded by steep cliffs on all sides, the way up to the town, even on its northwestern side, under fire was no Sunday stroll up Primrose Hill.

Iotapata's fall was followed by a massacre. But the tactical difficulties the Romans encountered at Iotapata also should have served as a warning to the Romans about the siege of Jerusalem. The fighting in the Lower Galilee, though not in the north altogether, as we shall soon see, was over. The real war, however, was just beginning. We would know precious little about the details of that war but for the unlikely and controversial survival of the war's chronicler, Flavius Josephus.

THE ESCAPE OF JOSEPHUS

When Iotapata was about to fall, instead of choosing eternal sleep with his fathers, Josephus had jumped down into a deep pit.[56] At the bottom of the pit, off on one side, there was a large cavern that could not be seen from above. Within the cavern 40 other "distinguished" people were hiding, with enough supplies to last them for a long time.[57] The accumulation of such provisions suggests advance planning. Apparently at least some of the Jews trapped in Iotapata anticipated the outcome of the Roman siege and wanted to survive. So too did Josephus, it turned out.

For two days Josephus hid in the cavern with his new friends. At night he climbed out of his hiding place and looked for an escape route out of the occupied and heavily guarded city. None was found. The next day a woman from among Josephus's companions, who also must have crawled up out of the hole, was captured and betrayed his hiding place to the Romans.[58] The Romans, who had been scouring the city for Josephus, no doubt were thrilled to learn where Josephus could be found.

Wanting to take Josephus alive, Vespasian sent two tribunes named Paulinus and Gallicanus, along with some soldiers, to the pit's opening to offer Josephus his life if he would give himself up. (The location of the pit has not been identified.) Fearing punishment for his actions during the siege Josephus initially refused the Roman offer. A third messenger, a tribune named

Nicanor, who had been a friend of Josephus and Titus, then arrived and once again gave Josephus Vespasian's assurances of personal safety.[59] Vespasian's intention, Nicanor informed Josephus, was not to punish Josephus, which he could do whether he came up out of the cave or not, but to save a brave man.[60]

While Josephus was mulling over Nicanor's proposal he could hear soldiers agitating to set the cave on fire. Their commander, who surely must have had orders to take Josephus alive if possible, was trying to restrain them. At this moment of hesitation and crisis, Josephus tells us that he recalled nightly dreams he had had, in which God had told him of the impending fate of the Jews and the destinies of the kings (*basileis*) of the Romans. Since he claimed to be an interpreter of dreams and skillful at understanding the words spoken ambiguously by God, as well as a priest and the descendant of priests, Josephus then made a silent prayer to God (later recorded for posterity by him). The prayer went as follows:

> Since it pleases you who created the nation of Jews to break it, and since all fortune has passed to the Romans, and since you have made the choice of my spirit to announce the things about to be, I willingly give hands (surrender) to the Romans and live: but I call you as a witness that I go, not as a traitor, but as your servant.[61]

And thus, by this silent prayer to God, recalled decades later, Josephus absolved himself of his betrayal of his people. None other than God was his witness that he did so as his servant and not as a traitor to his people.

Josephus's fellow cave dwellers, who had not shared in his dreams and had not been selected by God as his servant and voice, had a different view of his decision to surrender. Crowding around him, they asked him if life was so dear to him that he could endure to see the light of day as a slave. They reminded him of how many times he had urged them to be willing to die for freedom. They also told him that if he died voluntarily he would die as a general of the Jews; but if unwillingly, as a traitor. They then pointed their swords at him and threatened to kill him if he gave himself up to the Romans.[62]

Fearing an attack and reporting that he believed it would be a betrayal of God's commands to die before he delivered his messages (about the destinies of the Roman kings), during this emergency Josephus began to reason philosophically with his companions. Answering arguments implied to have been made by his companions, Josephus argued that while it was indeed honorable to die in war or for liberty, that was so on the condition that one died fighting, not when the enemy was coming neither to fight nor to take lives. Nor was it noble to destroy oneself. Rather, suicide was abhorrent to the nature of all living animals. It was also impious toward the God who created us, he argued—ignoring the obvious example of Israel's first king Saul, who committed suicide after his defeat by the Philistines on Mt. Gilboa.[63] That was why the body of someone who had committed suicide was left unburied until sunset, he said, though the Jews believed it was proper even to bury the bodies of their enemies. That was why the crime was punished by the wisest legislator (meaning Moses).

In sum, there was nothing dishonorable about accepting the Roman offer. If the Romans killed them after they gave themselves up, they would die honorably, at the hands of their conquerors. Moreover, if the Romans killed him after he surrendered, breaking their promises of his safety, he would die content, knowing that they had compromised their triumph by perjury.[64]

The invocation of Jewish funerary practices and the allusion to Moses allow us to locate Josephus's speech squarely within the social and theological thought-world of late first-century CE Judaism. Whether the speech as we have it was made in that cave at Iotapata or was a product of Josephus's recollection or perhaps was a mixture of both, it did not play upon Hellenic tropes about death or the afterlife; it follows that it was directed primarily to appeal to Jews. This speech was made and composed to convince Jews why suicide was wrong under the circumstances Josephus found himself in and why his actions were justified.

The general's fellow cave dwellers were not persuaded by his arguments, philosophical, traditional, or otherwise. Calling him a coward, they rushed at him with swords in hand, intending to make sure that he would never be judged guilty of the impiety of suicide. Only the reverence they had for him as their commander saved Josephus's throat from their blades, so he tells us.[65]

Caught between the Romans and his own people, Josephus now entrusted his protection to God. He rolled the dice or rather decided to put his faith in the lottery. Feigning to agree, despite his earlier arguments, that they should all commit suicide rather than surrender to the Romans, he suggested that they all draw lots to establish the order in which they should kill each other in turn. The one who drew the first lot should be killed by the one who drew the second, and so on to the last survivor, who alone would be forced by necessity to commit the impious crime of suicide.[66]

Josephus's proposal was readily accepted, and all of those who were in hiding drew lots in turn. After each one drew his lot he gave over his throat to be cut by the next man. Eventually only two men remained alive, Josephus and another unnamed man. Not wishing to be condemned by the lot or to stain his hand with the blood of a fellow survivor of the massacre at Iotapata, under a pledge Josephus persuaded the other man to live and let live. The holders of the last two lots ended the game before it reached its conclusion. With a little luck or divine intervention and a last-minute change of the rules, Josephus thus survived the death lottery. At that point he and presumably his fellow survivor surrendered to Vespasian's soldiers.[67] We are not told what happened to the other man.

Ever since the fall of Iotapata, Josephus's manipulation of the death lottery and his survival of the Roman siege have tainted his reputation. He has been condemned as a coward and a traitor by his fellow Jews, and his actions at Iotapata have led many to conclude that his account of the war in general cannot be trusted because he needed to justify his conduct.[68] It is true that Josephus's prayer and justification for surrendering after the fall of Iotapata are conveniently consistent with his often-stated position that God himself decided to side with the Romans during the war to punish the Jews for their impiety. That does not mean, however, that Josephus did not sincerely believe that his actions were consistent with God's plan, which he claimed to be able to understand because of his skill as a priest and a descendant of priests. That skill supposedly was based upon his ability to interpret prophecies in the sacred books.[69]

Yet it has been rightly pointed out that Jewish priests were not particularly renowned at the time for their interpretation of the sacred books of the Jews. Therefore Josephus's claim to be an expert interpreter of dreams and prophecies would have been taken with a grain of salt by his fellow Jews. That does not imply, however, that Josephus simply made up the justification for his actions at Iotapata. On the contrary, all of the evidence suggests that Josephus really did believe that what he did at Iotapata was not a betrayal of his fellow Jews; rather, he was helping enact God's plan. His survival and Jerusalem's destruction were God's will. God let Josephus survive to become his prophet of Rome's victory and then afterward of the defeat of the impious among the Jews. The fact that this was the first time that Josephus seemed to claim for himself such a prophetic role, of course, raises suspicions about his motives and sincerity, though, as we shall see, others apparently did ascribe prophetic powers to him.[70]

At least some of us may not find any of this to be convincing, let alone attractive. We may be more sympathetic to the arguments of Josephus's companions in that cave on Iotapata. Josephus was their general and had urged the Iotapatans to fight to the death for their freedom. They had done so and suffered the consequences. Yet he refused to follow their example and fight to the end. Generals worthy of their positions do not urge their soldiers to sacrifice their lives and then refuse to sacrifice their own. Sacrifice on behalf of others is the essence of leadership. Minimally, therefore, Josephus was not an effective or admirable general and probably never should have put himself in the position of leading others, particularly in a war that he had expressed ambivalence about previously. However he justified it, in the end Josephus wanted to live. No leader worthy of the name can be in a position where his or her life is more valuable than those who follow him or her. But was Josephus a coward? The evidence does not support such a conclusion.

If we can believe Josephus's narrative at all, he had already faced large numbers of people who wanted to kill him in Tarichaeae and Tiberias, and he had returned to Iotapata after he learned that the Romans were in the vicinity in force and surely were likely to besiege the city. And Josephus had fought during the siege, risking his life against Rome's legionaries, auxiliary soldiers who hated Jews, and allies who hated them even more. He also had no guarantee that once he was brought to Vespasian after surrendering he would not be executed or worse. Josephus may have been a traitor to the anti-Roman cause and his followers in Iotapata. A coward he was not.

THE AUDIENCE WITH VESPASIAN

The tribune Nicanor brought Josephus to Vespasian. Some of those in attendance shouted for his blood. Titus, however, argued for his life, citing Josephus's courage during misfortunes. He was also said to have been moved to pity by Josephus's youth. Probably against the wishes of the majority of Romans present, Vespasian spared Josephus. But he ordered him to be closely guarded until he could be sent along to the emperor Nero, no doubt for trial and almost assuredly for execution.

Having learned of his fate, Josephus then asked for a private audience with Vespasian. For reasons that Vespasian took to his grave the request was granted.[71]

Before the Roman commander, his son, and two other friends, Josephus announced to Vespasian that he had been sent to him as a messenger of greater things. He should not be sent to Nero, he told the Roman commander, because Nero and those who succeeded him would not continue to rule. Rather

Vespasian would become emperor along with his son and would rule the land, the sea, and all the races of men.[72]

At the time Vespasian did not seem to put too much stock in this prediction. He believed, with some plausibility, that the prophecy was a trick on Josephus's part to keep him from being sent to Rome and to an almost certain, painful death. Yet Vespasian also did not forward Josephus along to Nero immediately.

Perhaps this was because at the interview, in response to questioning by one of Vespasian's friends in attendance, Josephus disclosed to the Romans that he had predicted to the Iotapatans the fall of their city after 47 days and also his own capture by the Romans. When other prisoners were questioned by Vespasian about these predictions and verified that they indeed had been made, Vespasian, we are told, began to believe the prophecies that Josephus had made about his own future. And so, while he was not released from custody or his chains, neither was Josephus sent to the emperor for the ultimate exit interview.[73]

Did Josephus really predict Vespasian's elevation to the purple after the fall of Iotapata in the summer of 67? If so, was the prophecy a moment of divine inspiration or was it just an educated guess? Why didn't Vespasian execute Josephus on the spot or send him along to Nero?

We can never know whether Josephus had some kind of divine inspiration that led him to make his prediction to Vespasian. What Josephus probably knew by 67, however, was that there had recently been a number of conspiracies against Nero in Rome and that Vespasian was connected to the friends and allies of powerful Romans such as the general Corbulo. With his life and his future on the line Josephus very plausibly could have identified Vespasian as "a" or "the" coming man in Rome and, with everything both to lose and gain, decided to give the prophecy about Vespasian's future a shot. So Josephus rolled the dice, and they came out "dogs" or double ones in Rome—what we call "snake eyes" in craps.[74] With one lucky throw Josephus won two pots: he saved his own life and also gave himself further evidence and justification for his actions after the fall of Iotapata. Against long odds Josephus needed to be spared to become the proclaimer of Vespasian's ascendancy and later to explain why the Temple was destroyed.

But why would the Roman general have spared someone who had used chemical weapons against his soldiers? Perhaps he wanted to believe Josephus's prophecy about his own future, or perhaps he was stunned into inaction by Josephus's amazing ingenuity and audacity under the circumstances, like the residents of Tarichaeae before him. But it is also possible that Vespasian and Titus saw an opportunity.

Both Romans undoubtedly were familiar with the story about how Herod the Great had switched allegiances from Antony to Octavian and had become a useful and loyal ally to Rome. A living former commander of the two Galilees and Gamala who already had given indications of a certain situational flexibility might be useful to the Romans. Killing Josephus would have been easy. But it would not have helped the war effort or the Flavian family. Josephus might be used to encourage other Jews to give up. He could be put to work. And so he was, as we shall see, being used to try to persuade the rebels in Jerusalem to give up and even to interview deserters (perhaps taking advantage of his language skills).[75] Indeed, it is doubtful whether Vespasian and Titus at the time could possibly have appreciated just how useful to Rome and the Flavians Josephus would turn out to be.

Especially in the case of a man who came from a relatively humble background, such as Vespasian, it also might not hurt to begin to gather up stories and storytellers about his divine pre-ordination, no matter the divine quarter from which it came. As Vespasian's successes piled up, omens from more familiar gods could be found. So Josephus lived to become the apostle of Vespasian's and Rome's god-ordained triumph, first to his fellow Jews and then to history.

CHAPTER 12

Vespasian the War Criminal

SOUTHBOUND

On 4 Tammuz/Panemus/mid-July 67, Vespasian led his victorious army by way of Ptolemais southwestward to Caesarea. Herod's dream city henceforth became Rome's operational base for the rest of the time that Vespasian was in charge of the war.[1] Its mainly Greek or "Syrian" population welcomed the Roman army enthusiastically. Their friendliness toward the Romans motivated them, we are told, but not as much as their hatred of the conquered Jews.

The Fifth and Tenth Legions were settled in Caesarea, where they would spend the winter. The Fifteenth Legion was ordered to march about 35 miles eastward (along the later route of Highway 90) to Scythopolis (Beit Shean) in the Decapolis, where it could keep watch on the Lower Galilee.[2] (See map 1.) Although Scythopolis had been captured by the Hasmoneans in 104 BCE, it had been retaken and at least partially rebuilt by Pompey in 63 BCE.[3] A sizable population of Jews lived there during the first century CE, though non-Jews made up the majority of the population, and they had turned upon the minority of Jews who lived in the city in 66, as we have seen.

THE CAPTURE OF JOPPA

The Roman commander also sent a combined force of cavalry and infantry five or six miles down the coast to Joppa. Its mission was to deal with a group of Jews who had taken up piracy there. Some of these Jews had been forced out of their towns by civil strife. Others were refugees whose homes had been destroyed. Having joined together, the two groups had rebuilt Joppa after Cestius had left it in ruins and then conducted a series of raids on the shipping traffic that passed along the coast from Syria to Egypt. The maritime trade route had become impossible to navigate because of the Jews' piratical raids. The pirates thus constituted a potential threat to Vespasian's seaborne supply lines.

At the approach of the Romans during the night, the novice pirates had taken to their ships and spent the night out on the sea beyond arrow range.[4] Unfortunately for them, in the morning a fierce north wind, known locally as a "Black Norther," blew up. The strong winds caused some of the vessels to collide. Others were dashed against the rocks of the coast. Towering waves swamped the ships that made for the open sea. Some of the Jews opted for suicide over drowning. The bodies of some 4,200 of these unfortunates eventually washed up on the shore.

The pirates who survived the winds and the waves and somehow made it to the shore alive were promptly cut down by the Romans. The Romans then razed the empty town again. To prevent its future use as a pirate base, Vespasian left cavalry and a small contingent of infantry at a camp on the former town's acropolis. This small force spent its time devastating the other towns and villages in the vicinity.[5] Joppa had been eliminated as a threat to Vespasian's western flank.

REPORTS OF JOSEPHUS'S DEATH
GREATLY EXAGGERATED

Meanwhile news of Iotapata's annihilation had made its way to Jerusalem. At first the report was not credited because the story of the calamity was not based on any eyewitness account. No one had escaped from the city to tell the tale. We do not know how, but the truth was eventually revealed in full and accepted as established beyond any doubt by everyone.

It was also initially reported that Josephus had been killed during the capture of the city. That news, according to Josephus, filled the city with great grief. The lamentations went on for 30 days.[6] Sorrow soon turned to rage, however, when it was discovered that, in fact, not only was the commander of the two Galilees and Gamala not dead, he was very much alive. Indeed Josephus was alive and living quite well in the company of the enemy's highest-ranking officers.

Some in Jerusalem then abused Josephus as a coward. Others branded him a traitor. The city was full of vexation and slanders against him. Incapable of doing anything about Iotapata's destruction and Josephus's treachery, the Jerusalemites dedicated themselves to taking revenge upon the Romans with even greater fury, since that would simultaneously include vengeance upon their former general.[7] By the end of 67 Josephus was probably the most hated man in Jerusalem, if not in all Judaea.

VESPASIAN ON HOLIDAY

In the meantime, presumably to get away from the summer heat, Vespasian, accompanied by some of his soldiers, had gone up to Caesarea Philippi (also known as Neronias, Irenopolis, and Panias) to visit King Agrippa II in the administrative capital of his kingdom.[8] Although its cave sanctuary of Pan at the springs of the Jordan had been noted by Polybius several centuries earlier, Panias was not built up into a recognizable polis cum administrative center until about 3 BCE, during the reign of Philip the Tetrarch.[9] Thereafter Agrippa II had expensively embellished Panias, adding temples, colonnaded streets, a forum, theaters, bathhouses, nympheia, administrative buildings, aqueducts, and a huge royal palace.[10] The mostly gentile population that lived either within Caesarea Philippi or in the surrounding countryside probably would have been the main beneficiaries of these characteristically Graeco-Roman urban amenities, though we know that many thousands of Jews also lived in the area.[11] What Caesarea's Jews thought of Agrippa's making his capital into a recognizable Graeco-Roman city we have no idea.

Agrippa had invited Vespasian and his men to Caesarea Philippi not only to entertain them and to give them some rest and relaxation but also to get their help in putting down the disorders that plagued his kingdom. Even for a Roman general handpicked by the emperor there was no such thing as a free vacation.

While the soldiers rested for 20 days the Roman commander himself was sumptuously entertained. Vespasian, we are told, also used this time to give thanks to God for his successes, although Josephus does not say that either

Vespasian or anyone else thought that the war in the north, let alone in the south, was over.[12] Indeed, as soon as he learned that at least some Tiberians were making revolutionary noises and that the people of Tarichaeae already had revolted, Vespasian determined to undertake a campaign against them. Both cities were now part of Agrippa's kingdom, having been given to him as gifts by Nero, probably during the first or second year of his reign (54–55 or 55–56).[13] The objective of Vespasian's new operation was to crush "the Jews" wherever they rose up and to pay Agrippa back for his hospitality by bringing the towns back to their loyalty to him.[14]

It could be argued that Vespasian's subsequent campaigns against Tiberias and Tarichaeae had nothing to do with Rome's war of revenge for what had happened to Cestius, because the towns were located outside Judaea. But this argument begs the question of the rebels' motivation in these towns. It also ignores the fact that Agrippa owed his very kingdom, with the parts added to it, to the Romans. A revolt against Agrippa was simultaneously a revolt against Agrippa's Roman masters. Tiberias and Tarichaeae were literally gifts of Nero to Agrippa. Agrippa was Nero's client; Nero was Agrippa's patron.[15]

It is impossible to believe that Tiberians and Tarichaeans did not understand the political implications of being given as a gift to the king by the Roman emperor. Some of the residents of these towns might have been satisfied, even happy, about the situation. But others clearly were not. Josephus's complicated and tendentious reconstruction of the background to the unrest in these cities supports this hypothesis.

THE STRUGGLE IN TIBERIAS

There were in fact three factions in Tiberias. The first was led by Iulius Capellus and favored continuing the city's loyalty to Agrippa and Rome. A second faction, comprising "the most insignificant people" in Josephus's judgment, was inclined toward war. The third faction, spearheaded by Ioustos, or Justus in Latin, the son of Pistus, favored revolution while feigning caution.[16] Pistus, according to Josephus's diagnosis, was simply crazy, or *epimanes*. His son Justus attempted to convince the Tiberians to revolt by reminding them that they had been handed over to Agrippa as a present by Nero and that it was time to take up arms and join with the Galilaeans, whose hatred of Sepphoris for its allegiance to Rome would make them willing recruits.[17]

Justus's revolutionary appeal thus was predicated upon anti-Roman sentiment among the Galilaeans. It is hard to see how such a feeling could have been leveraged if the Tiberians' issues were only with Agrippa. It is much more likely that some Galilaeans and Tiberians saw Agrippa and Rome as a connected problem and a common enemy.

To deal with the restive Galilaeans, Titus was sent back westward by Vespasian to Caesarea Maritima to gather up the Roman troops stationed there and then to bring them to Scythopolis, where Vespasian would be waiting.[18] After Vespasian, Titus, and their army reunited at Scythopolis, the three Roman legions and their commanders marched northward toward Tiberias, encamping some 3.7 miles away from the town, at a place called Sennabris (Khirbet el-Karak/Beth Yerah) on the southern shore of the Sea of Galilee.

Hearing that the people as a whole wished for peace but were being compelled to fight by the few who favored sedition, Vespasian sent a decurion named Valerianus with 50 horsemen to make peaceful propositions to those in the city and to exhort them to give assurances of faithfulness.[19] When Valerianus rode up to the wall of the city he and his escort dismounted so that those inside the city would not think they had come to engage in combat. But before Valerianus could make his proposals, Jesus, the son of Saphat or Sapphias—whom Josephus called the head man of the swarm of bandits in Tiberias but is also identified as the chief magistrate (*archon*) of Tiberias's council of 600—rushed out from the town with a band of armed followers. The fact that Jesus was the chief magistrate of Tiberias suggests that opposition to Agrippa and the Romans could be found within the governing body of the polis itself and not just among the poor or "insignificant."

Valerianus recognized that it would be dangerous to engage a numerically superior enemy. So he fled on foot, along with five of his fellow cavalrymen. Their mounts were left behind. That was usually a capital offense for a Roman cavalryman. Jesus and his followers triumphantly brought the abandoned horses back into the town.[20]

Fearing the consequences of what had happened, the elders of the people and those of "principal authority" in Tiberias promptly bolted to the Roman camp. Accompanied by King Agrippa II himself, they threw themselves down before Vespasian as suppliants and begged him not to overlook them nor to ascribe the madness of a few to the city as a whole. They pleaded with Vespasian to spare a people ever friendly to the Romans and to punish the authors of the sedition, under whose watch they had been kept.[21] Just as the elders' plea implied that they were friendly to the Romans, the attitude of those who had revolted was assumed to be the opposite.

Vespasian was angry with the whole city about the incident involving Vale-rianus and the seizure of the horses. But he also saw Agrippa's concern for the town, proving incidentally that Agrippa was with Vespasian during this phase of the operation. He therefore accepted the supplications made on behalf of Tiberias. Meanwhile, Jesus and his followers, understanding that they were no longer safe within Tiberias, fled to Tarichaeae, almost four miles to the north.[22] It may also have been at this point that some of the inhabitants of Tiberias, whom we know later died during the siege of Jerusalem or were taken prisoner after its capture, fled the city, and made their way to Jerusalem.[23]

The following day Vespasian sent Trajan with horsemen to the ridgetop of one of the nearby hills to find out if the majority of the townspeople of Tiberias were indeed peacefully inclined; that is, were friendly to Rome. Ap-parently assured that they were, Vespasian brought the army up to the walls of Tiberias. The population opened the gates of the city and went out to meet Vespasian, making acclamations and hailing him as a savior and bene-factor. The Roman troops marched into the city through a breach made in the southern part of the city's walls because the passage through the city gates was too narrow.

To gratify Agrippa, the soldiers were ordered to abstain from pillage and violence. The rest of the wall was spared destruction for the same reason. On the town's behalf the king took an oath of future allegiance.[24] Unlike the Gab-arans, the Samaritans on Mt. Gerizim, and the Iotapatans, the Tiberians lived on. From Vespasian's point of view, sparing compliant Tiberias was a wise policy for the sake of encouraging others.

TARICHAEAE AND THE MASSACRE ON THE LAKE

After the capitulation of Tiberias Vespasian set out for Tarichaeae. He stopped en route to pitch a well-constructed marching camp. It was to Tar-ichaeae (modern Migdal), the hometown of Mary Magdalene, that Jesus, the magistrate and rebel leader from Tiberias, and the whole body of revolution-aries had headed. At the beginning of the revolt Josephus had seen to it that Tarichaeae was fortified on all sides, except for the one facing the lake. In addition to these fortifications, the inhabitants of the town maintained a siz-able fleet of ships.[25]

While the Romans were still working on the wall for their camp, Jesus and his followers launched a raid against them, scattered the workmen, and destroyed part of the wall. After they saw the heavily armed Roman infantry soldiers collecting together to counterattack, however, Jesus and his raiders retreated toward their ships.

Having boarded their vessels, the rebels rowed out onto the waters of the lake just far enough to keep their Roman pursuers within range of whatever weapons they could throw or shoot at them. Casting anchor, they then brought their crafts close together, forming a kind of battle line, and from their ships they fought the Romans who were on the land. In the meantime, Vespasian, learning that a great multitude had gathered on the plain in front of Tarichaeae, dispatched Titus there with 600 picked cavalry, presumably to disperse them.[26]

After scoping out the size of the enemy force, Titus sent a message to his father saying that he needed more troops. Although most of the cavalry were eager to go into action before help could arrive, Titus noticed that some were secretly alarmed by the multitude of Jews. Taking up a position where he could be heard, he rallied his soldiers, making a speech that Josephus reports.

In his speech Titus supposedly compared the Jews' lack of training and experience in warfare with the discipline and long martial experience of the Romans. He went on to remind his men that wars were not won by numbers alone but by courage. He also argued that they were fighting for a higher cause than the Jews. The Jews fought for the sake of freedom and country while they (the Romans) fought for glory, so that it might never be said that the Jews were able to confront them.[27]

Though the war of Jews against Romans was a conflict of tactics, strategy, and logistics it was also a war of ideas. In this war of ideas freedom and ethnicity were pitted against imperialism and martial pride. Or this was what Josephus thought his Roman patrons and readers wanted to read about themselves and the justification for their actions after the fact.[28]

While Titus was making his speech a demonic fury supposedly fell upon his men. Trajan's arrival with a reinforcement of 400 horsemen was no longer welcomed. Rather, it annoyed Titus's men because the glorious reputation for the victory would now be lessened by being the common possession of so many. Or so it flattered Titus's veterans to remember when they read about how they felt at the time years later.

While this was going on, Vespasian sent Antonius Silo with 1,000 archers to a firing position on a hill opposite the city. From that spot they could keep the ramparts of the town clear of defenders who might provide any assistance to the army of Jews on the plain.[29]

Titus now marched his own horse toward the enemy. The rest followed with a great shout, extending themselves across the plain as widely as their enemy. For a short time the Jews absorbed the attacks. But after the Romans stabbed many of them with their lances and they were overpowered by the rushing noise of the cavalry, many of the Jews fell down and were trampled. Soon there were bodies lying all over the plain, and the survivors ran toward the city as fast as they could.

Titus pressed upon the stragglers among the fleeing Jews and dispatched them. During ancient battles it was usually when troops were fleeing that they took the most casualties, and it was part of Roman military doctrine to follow up tactical breakthroughs with attempts to rout and destroy their enemies.[30] Soldiers had a very difficult time defending themselves individually while running away.

Cutting lanes through those Jews who had managed to collect together, Titus rode out to their other side and charged them frontally. These too were trampled as Titus tried to push the Jews back onto the killing ground of the plain and prevent them from making their way back to the city. Only superior numbers allowed the remnants of the Tarichaeans to gather together into a group, force a passage through the Romans, and make their escape back into the city.[31]

A terrible discord within the city greeted the survivors. The native Tarichaeans had not been disposed to fight from the beginning and were even less inclined to do so after the army's decisive defeat outside the walls. But the multitude who had come into the city from outside were all the more determined to continue the struggle. A shouting match and disturbance ensued such that the two sides were on the verge of fighting each other instead of the Romans.[32]

Josephus's account of the conflict between the two sides is obviously meant to make the point that, left to their own devices, the Tarichaeans would not have fought against the Romans. The problem was created by outsiders. As we shall see, however, Josephus makes a similar argument about the battle for Jerusalem. In his retrospective view it was almost always "outsiders" who caused the troubles. It turns out, however, that at least in the case of Jerusalem, the outsiders were all Jews too. They just happened not to be native Jerusalemites.

Hearing the hubbub from his position near the city wall, Titus quickly seized upon the opportunity. Mounting his horse, he led his troops around to the side of the city facing the lake and, riding through the waters, entered the city first, followed by the rest of the Romans. Terrified by Titus's boldness, the defenders of the walls did not even attempt to fight with the Romans or hinder them. They just abandoned their posts.

After the Romans entered the city, Jesus's followers in the town made for open country. Others headed for the lake and were met by the Romans. Some of them were killed as they tried to board their ships, others as they swam out to overtake the vessels that already had launched. Within the city there was an indiscriminate slaughter, both of those who resisted and those who did not, until Titus had killed all the instigators of the revolt in the city. Only then did Titus take pity upon the inhabitants of Tarichaeae and stop the massacre. Those who had fled the city out onto the lake, seeing the city captured, sailed as far away as possible from their enemies.[33]

A cavalryman was dispatched by Titus to inform his father of the victory. Vespasian was delighted by his son's success, Josephus says, because he thought—wrongly, as would soon become clear—that the greatest part of the war was now over. Coming straightaway to Tarichaeae, Vespasian ordered soldiers to guard the city and to see to it that no one escaped from the town. Anyone who tried was to be killed.

The next day the Roman commander went down to the lake and ordered rafts to be fitted out and then launched on the lake to hunt down those who had fled over the waters. The crafts were quickly prepared due to the abundance of wood and the multitude of skilled workers.[34]

Vespasian put as many troops on the rafts as he thought necessary to defeat the rebels who had escaped to the lake. He then set his new fleet afloat. The rebels who had been driven onto the lake during the battle could not escape to land since the entire shoreline was now in Roman hands. Nor could they fight on equal terms out on the water. Their ships were small and designed for piracy and thus were no match for the Roman rafts. Moreover, those on the rebel ships were so few that they were afraid to approach the great number of Romans who attacked them.

Despite these disadvantages, Josephus tells us, as the Jews sailed around the Roman rafts and periodically approached them, they threw stones at the Romans or fought against them when they came closer. But in both cases they suffered more harm themselves. The stones they threw bounced off the Romans' armor ineffectively, whereas the stone-throwers were exposed to the arrows of the archers on the Roman floats. And when the rebels dared to come up close to the Romans, they and their ships were engaged by a better armed and more numerous enemy. Those who tried to break through the line of rafts the Romans killed with lances, or they leaped onboard their ships and stabbed them with their swords. In other cases the Romans encircled the rebels and captured both the crews and their ships.

Any of the rebels who fell overboard were either killed by arrows as soon as they lifted their heads up out of the water or were caught by the soldiers on the rafts. If, in desperation, they swam toward their enemies to board their vessels, the Romans chopped off their hands or heads. Thus the rebellious Jews were slaughtered in various ways until the survivors, being thoroughly routed, were forced to put to shore. Many were speared by the Romans while they were still in the water. Others who made it onto dry land were slain there.

The lake soon turned blood red and was filled with floating, dead bodies. Over the next few days shipwrecks washed up all over the shores of the lake, and the corpses of the rebels swelled up in the sun and putrefied. The stench of the bodies was such that it corrupted the air. All told, the fighting at Tarichaeae and during the battle of the lake claimed 6,700 lives.[35]

VESPASIAN'S WAR CRIME

When the slaughter on the lake was over, Vespasian sat down upon a judgment seat at Tarichaeae. Separating the indigenous population of the town from the crowd of "foreigners" who allegedly had instigated the war, he consulted his officers about their fates. His officers unanimously urged Vespasian to do away with the foreigners one and all because, the officers argued, they would never stay at rest and would compel others to take up arms against the Romans.[36] Vespasian agreed with his officer's arguments, another indication that this was a revolt against Rome, at least by the "foreigners" themselves. But Vespasian feared the reaction in Tarichaeae if the Romans simply executed those who had asked for mercy on the spot. It is worth noting that Vespasian's fear of the Tarichaeans' potential response suggests some sympathy for the rebels among the city's population. Vespasian therefore granted to the prisoners an ambiguous amnesty.[37]

The amnesty included permission to leave the city, but only by way of one road to Tiberias. Roman troops, meanwhile, were lined up along the entire route to prevent any of the refugees from leaving the road. Once they reached Tiberias the captives were shut up inside the city. Vespasian soon arrived and had all of the survivors brought into the stadium. He then ordered the old and "useless" to be killed without delay.[38] His friends supposedly helped him to overcome whatever scruples he had about breaking his promise by telling Vespasian that in the case of the Jews there could be no question of impiety (*asebeia*) and that he should prefer what was expedient to what was proper when the two were in conflict.[39] Suetonius informed his readers that Vespasian never took any pleasure in anyone's death and even wept over those who suffered justifiable punishments.[40]

There is no evidence in Josephus, Suetonius, or any other writer that Vespasian felt any remorse for ordering the murder of the prisoners. Nor is there a hint in his history of the war that Josephus expects his readers to be appalled by Vespasian's action. At the time the legal concept of a war crime did not exist. Nor was there any internationally recognized tribunal to investigate such crimes. Later, back in Rome, Vespasian and Titus would be celebrated for their actions during the war, not prosecuted.

At the same time, the fact that Josephus reports what Vespasian did is evidence that his work was not just a piece of Flavian propaganda. Josephus does not try to hide his own actions or those of the Roman commanders during the war. Although he does not openly condemn Vespasian and Titus for killing prisoners of war or civilians, he does hold them responsible to history for what they did.

The number murdered in cold blood was 1,200. Six thousand of the strongest young men were selected out of the refugees and sent to Nero at the Isthmus of Corinth, where they were set to work on the canal that Nero had decided to have dug there. To Agrippa, Vespasian made a present of those who were inhabitants of his kingdom. These the king sold into slavery. The rest, numbering 30,400, Vespasian himself sold as slaves.[41] The relatively precise totals for those enslaved and sold suggest that they may be based upon official Roman records.

Among those who had apparently come to Tarichaeae and joined the insurrection were people from Trachonitis, Gaulanitis, Hippus (Hippos), and Gadara, whom Josephus calls mostly revolutionaries and refugees. Later Josephus recalled that when he was in Tarichaeae he had spoken of others who had departed from their homes and thrown in their lot with the Tarichaeans. If this is correct, Josephus wanted his readers to believe that the majority of those involved in the fighting at Tarichaeae were not Tarichaeaens.

By 8 Gorpiaeus (September 67), some two months after the fall of Iotapata, Tarichaeae was in Roman hands.[42]

CHAPTER 13

The Camel's Hump

Tarichaeae's capture was the signal for most of the Galilaeans who had chosen to keep fighting Rome, even after Iotapata fell, to surrender. The exceptions were the Gischalans, the band that occupied Itaburion (Mt. Tabor), and the Gamalans.[1] It is important to draw attention to those who continued the fight. It is untrue that resistance to Rome collapsed in the north after the fall of Iotapata.

At the beginning of the revolt, Gamala in the southern Golan remained loyal to Rome. (See map 1.) Later the town switched sides, as numismatic evidence shows, despite ongoing arguments about the exact interpretation of the coins minted there.[2]

After the rebels gained ascendance in Gamala, they had large bronze coins (*prutot*) minted bearing images of a chalice-like vessel, with an inscription in Paleo-Hebrew or Hebrew block letters "Of the Redemption" on the obverse side and "Holy Jerusalem" on the reverse.[3] The chalice on the Gamala coins was probably copied from representations of a similar, though more detailed, object shown on coins minted by the rebels in Jerusalem during the early years of the revolt.

Some scholars have argued that the chalice-like image on the Jerusalem coins represented the golden vessel that held the *omer*, or first grain harvest measure, that was offered in the Temple every year on 15 Nisan. The 15th of Nisan, or Gregorian calendar April/May, was the day when Jews celebrated the covenant God made with Abraham bestowing lands upon Abraham's seed from the river of Egypt to the River Euphrates after being enslaved for 400 years, and when the exodus began from Egypt.[4]

The *omer* vessel image on the Gamala coins therefore was a reference to redemption or freedom given by God. It could be understood as drawing an analogy between the situation of the Hebrews enslaved in Egypt and the Jews under Roman rule, and the inscription referring to the redemption of Jerusalem the holy declared the Gamalans to be part of the holy war for the liberation of Jerusalem.[5]

Other scholars have disputed the reading of the inscriptions on the few bronze coins minted in Gamala at the time, claiming that the inscriptions on the obverse side read, "In Gamla," and therefore the coins did not have anything to do with a national war of liberation. A revised reading of the iconography of the coins and their inscriptions has convinced some historians that the coins were intended to make statements about Gamala and its independence, not from Rome but from Agrippa II.[6]

But the iconography and short epigraphs of the coins in question, whatever their correct reading is, do not have to imply that their minters saw revolt from Agrippa as separate from revolt from Rome. Rome had confirmed Agrippa II as a king and given him a territory. His rule was backed by Roman arms or the threat of their use, and the king had led Cestius into Judaea at the beginning of the war. Agrippa was Rome's point man on the ground in the region during the early stages of the war. No one in Gamala would have had any doubt whose side Agrippa was on as the Romans approached their town in the early autumn of 67.

Visual references to the Temple vessels were declarations of the minters' connections to Jerusalem.[7] Using Paleo-Hebrew or Hebrew or both for the inscriptions on the coins was an attempt to connect Gamala and its history with that of the ancient and free state of the Jews' ancestors.

THE CAMEL'S HUMP

Gamala was sited upon a rough ridge of a mountain. The form of the ridge resembled a camel—hence its name Gamala or Camel in Aramaic—with a rocky hump in the middle that rose to a summit of some 919 feet on the north. (See figure 9.)

FIGURE 9. Aerial view of Gamala from the east, where rebels fought against the army of Vespasian in the late summer of 67. Todd Bolen/BiblePlaces.com.

The sides and face of the ridge were split by ravines, and the houses of the town were built on the flank of the ridge, one above another. The residential town faced the south, and its southern point formed its citadel. Gamala possessed a large synagogue or meeting area on the southeastern side of its residential area, built of basalt stone blocks probably during the early first century BCE.[8] Unlike the Iotapatans, Gamalans had the advantage of having a natural spring within the walls of their city.[9] At least initially water would not be a decisive issue for the Gamalans. An adequate food supply, however, was another question.

Josephus himself claimed to have walled the city and fortified it further by ditches and mines, though according to the Mishnah, Gamala had been fortified since the time of Joshua. The modern excavators of the site have argued that what Josephus actually did was to close up the gaps that existed between houses and other buildings along the eastern border of the town and possibly to have had constructed a second wall beyond some sections of the first wall.[10]

Gamala had come within the gravitational pull of Jerusalem's influence when it was captured during the reign of the bellicose Hasmonean king

Alexander Jannaeus (103–76 BCE).[11] At the time of the Jewish revolt, however, Gamala was located within the territory of Agrippa II.[12]

There were far fewer fighting men in Gamala than there had been in Iotapata. But its inhabitants had confidence in Gamala's natural strength, and
they did not think that they would be too greatly outnumbered because the
city had been filled up by all the people who had fled to it for safety. For this
reason they already had been able to hold out for seven months against a force led
by Aequus Modius that had been sent to besiege the city by King Agrippa II.[13]
That siege probably had been broken off after the cavalry commander Philip,
the son of Iakim (or Iacimus)—who had holed up in Gamala after escaping
from Jerusalem and then was falsely accused of having gone over to the rebel
side by Agrippa's henchman Noarus—was able to convince Modius and
Agrippa of his loyalty and that of the town or its leadership to the royal and
Roman cause.[14]

After the siege ended, Joseph, the son of Yair, induced a number of Gamala's
young men to join him, and together they assaulted the magistrates of the
town and pressured them into taking up arms against Agrippa. In fact, the
territory of Gaulanitis right up to the village of Solyma, along the eastern
border of the region, also revolted from Agrippa's rule.[15] Josephus dated the
beginning of the revolt to 24 Gorpiaeus/Elul (27 September), only a few weeks
after the end of operations at Tarichaeae.[16]

THE COMING OF THE ROMANS

After resting with the army amidst the baths at Ammathus (Hammat) in
front of Tiberias, Vespasian now advanced up to Gamala on the Golan
Heights.[17] Although the distance from Tiberias to Gamala was only about 25
miles, the march up onto the heights for a large army during the late summer
could not have been easy; that Vespasian made the march at all is an indication of his determination to wipe out all pockets of resistance in the
north. Vespasian had not brought 60,000 men and 20,000 pack animals
and horses from Ptolemais merely to make a show of force. He intended to
use that force, even if it meant making a difficult march up onto the Golan
Heights. Along with Vespasian came Josephus. He therefore was an eyewitness
to the Roman siege.

Because of Gamala's topography it was impossible simply to encircle the
town with a guard. Where it was practical, however, sentries were stationed,
and the mountain that hung over the town was taken by the Romans. This is

likely the hill where the site entrance and ticket office for visits to ancient Gamala are located today.

While the legions were fortifying their camps on the mountain, Vespasian had earthworks built up. Near the bottom, at the part toward the east, where the city wall was no less than 20 feet thick and where stood the highest tower of the city, the Fifteenth Legion encamped and worked. The Fifth Legion performed their duties near the middle of the city, also on the east side, and the Tenth Legion filled in ditches and ravines.[18] Some of those ditches may have been among those that Josephus claimed to have had dug.

While the Roman legions were laboring on these earthworks, King Agrippa II ventured forth to negotiate about surrender with those up on the city ramparts. He received his answer when he was struck on his right elbow by a rock cast by one of Gamala's slingers.[19] That put an end to further negotiations.

The Romans finished building the earthworks quickly, both because of the multitude of hands devoted to the task and their experience at such work. Catapults were then brought up into position, probably onto a plateau about 1,000 feet to the east of the city's synagogue, to judge by the nearly 2,000 stone *ballista* balls later found in the area around the town's eastern wall.[20]

THE BATTLE OF GAMALA

Chares and Joseph, two of the rebel leaders within the town, drew their troops up into order, though they had become dispirited, Josephus writes, by the lack of water and other necessities.[21] Their leaders encouraged the Gamalans, however, and led them out onto the wall. There for a little while they managed to hold off the Romans who were bringing up the machines. But soon they were driven back into the city by fire from the catapults and stone-throwers.[22] Thousands of Roman arrowheads and ballista balls discovered along the town's eastern wall indicate where the artillery barrage apparently was most intense.[23] The Romans then brought the battering rams up to three positions and used them to make the walls shake until they collapsed.[24] (See figure 10.)

The Romans poured in through the parts of the walls that had been knocked down, shouting their battle cry as the trumpets sounded and their armor clattered. Once inside, the Romans engaged Gamala's defenders. At that point, however, the advantage went over to the Gamalans. No doubt because of their knowledge of the town's layout, Gamala's rebels stopped the Romans from advancing any farther than the entry points for a while and even succeeded in beating them back.[25]

FIGURE 10. The breach point in the wall of Gamala made by the Romans in 67.
Todd Bolen/BiblePlaces.com.

However, attacked violently by so many from every direction, some of the townsmen eventually fled, running to the upper parts of the city. Once they reached that section of the town they suddenly turned upon the pursuing Romans. Catching the Romans by surprise, the rebels managed to push the Roman soldiers back to the lower parts of the town, where the Romans were further discomfited by the narrowness and difficulty of the space. Many Roman soldiers were killed there and then. The surviving Romans, who were not able to fight off those who were pursuing them from above or to force their way back through their fellow soldiers, who were pressing forward behind them, climbed up on the low roofs of the Gamalans' houses.[26]

Because the wooden roofs of the houses had not been built to bear the weight of large numbers of soldiers in heavy armor, many of them suddenly collapsed. In addition, since the houses of the town had been constructed one above another on the slope of the hillside, when one house collapsed, it brought down those dwellings built directly beneath it. Many Romans were killed or pinned down by the debris in these building collapses. The dust that arose from the collapsing structures suffocated others.[27]

The Gamalans took what was happening to be a sign of God's assistance and pressed the attack. Romans who were not killed outright in the collapse of the houses were finished off by (human) stone-throwers. The ruins were a plentiful source of boulders for Gamala's defenders; the dead Romans in turn became a source of iron weapons. The rebels used the swords they took from the Romans to stab to death those who were still struggling for life. Other Romans died after throwing themselves from the tops of the collapsing houses.

Fleeing the scene of destruction was not easy. Because of their ignorance of the streets and the thick dust, the surviving Roman soldiers wandered around, having a hard time recognizing each other. Discovering the exits from the city by luck, out of the many soldiers who had entered the city, few made their way out safely.[28]

Vespasian meanwhile had gradually advanced to the highest section of the city, staying close to his suffering troops. In doing so he seems to have lost track of where he was. Suddenly he was left in the middle of danger with only very few followers. Josephus tells us that the Roman commander, recognizing that it was neither safe nor proper simply to turn and flee, linked up with a handful of his followers underneath the shields that protected their bodies and bore up under the attacks of their enemies, who had come running down from the top of the town.

When those attacks slackened, walking backward step by step, Vespasian and his comrades retreated from the city, never turning their backs upon their assailants until they were outside the city again. Yet even Vespasian's courageous withdrawal was not accomplished without losses. During his retreat many Romans fell, including the auxiliary officer Aebutius, who had played an important role in the siege of Iotapata.[29]

After he managed to escape from immediate danger, Vespasian saw that his troops were despondent and ashamed because they had let their general face such perils virtually alone. So he rallied his men in typical Roman, upper-class fashion—by making a speech that is duly reported by Josephus.

He reminded his men of the nature of war itself, which never granted victory without blood, and of how fortune came back to one's side. Attributing their defeat to the difficulty of the topography and their own ardor for battle, which had driven them to advance beyond the safe ground of the lower city, Vespasian urged his men to fall back upon their native virtue and for each man to look for consolation from his own hand. In that way, he said, they would avenge those who had been killed and punish those who had killed them. As for his own reaction to the disaster, as he had done during the battle itself, in every engagement Vespasian promised to be the first into battle against their enemies and the last to retreat.[30] Josephus's version of Vespasian's speech no doubt was patriotic music to the ears of his later Roman readers and patrons.

The people of Gamala had been encouraged by their unanticipated success. Sober reflection, however, had brought about a change of mood. Both surrender and escape were now impossible. Provisions were also running out. For these reasons, despite their success, the Gamalans were disheartened. Nevertheless, they did what they could to ensure their safety. The bravest soldiers guarded the places where the wall had been knocked down, and the rest stood guard on the sections that were still standing.[31]

When the Romans raised up the earthworks and tried to enter the city a second time, many of the Gamalans fled out of the city along trackless clefts and through underground caverns. Others, who stayed behind for fear of being caught, died for want of food. Whatever food could be found was given to those who were still able to bear arms.[32]

THE CAPTURE OF ITABURION

While the people of Gamala began to starve, Vespasian was planning the subjugation of those who had occupied Itaburion (Mt. Tabor). Itaburion was located southwest of Tarichaeae. Its summit rose to a height of some 1,843 feet above the plain of Esdraelon and its platform (the plain upon the summit) was around 3,000 feet long and 1,300 feet wide. Josephus had built the wall surrounding the summit's platform in 40 days, provided from below with every necessary material and water. The summit itself had no water source except for scarce rain showers.[33]

Vespasian sent his tribune Placidus with 600 horsemen to capture this summit, where a vast multitude had assembled. Since it was impossible for Placidus to ascend the mountain, he tried to lure the mass of people into making peace by offering surrender terms. In reality, Placidus wanted to draw the refugees down onto the plain below the mountain where he could attack them with his cavalry. Those who were up on the summit descended from the mountain, appearing to accept Placidus's offer. But they too were plotting. Perhaps they were familiar with Placidus from his past exploits. Their plan was to attack Pacidus when he was off-guard.[34]

Placidus's cunning duplicity, however, was superior. When the Jews attacked, in accordance with their stratagem, Placidus and his men pretended to flee. When the Jews followed the Romans far out onto the plain, Placidus suddenly turned his cavalry around and routed the pursuing Jews. A great many were killed. The rest were intercepted and prevented from going back up the mountain. Those who had not been killed or captured by Placidus's cavalry abandoned Itaburion, fleeing to Jerusalem. The rest of the indigenous population, who were pressed by the lack of water, gave up the mountain and themselves to Placidus.[35] We do not know their fate.

THE END OF GAMALA

At Gamala, meanwhile, somehow evading the Romans, the bolder spirits were able to flee. Those too weak to flee died from hunger. What was left of the effective fighting force resisted the siege until 22 Huperberetaeus/Tishri (mid-October). On that date, around the time of the morning watch, three soldiers of the Fifteenth Legion sneaked up under a high tower near them on the northeast side and began to undermine it. Since it was night the Romans were not detected by the guards on the tower.[36]

Without making a sound the three soldiers rolled away five of the towers' strongest stone supports and then leaped back. The tower suddenly collapsed with a great roar, and the guards fell down headlong along with it. Confused by the tumult, the other guards fled from their posts. Those who dared to break through the Romans killed. Among them was their leader Joseph, who was struck by a dart as he was escaping over the broken part of the wall.[37]

Thrown into confusion by the sound of the tower's collapse, the people in the town ran to and fro through the streets in great fright, thinking that the entire enemy force had fallen upon them. At that moment Chares, the other leader of the resistance, who had been bedridden and under a doctor's care, passed away, apparently stricken by a terror-induced heart attack.[38]

The Romans, remembering their previous misfortune, did not follow up their success immediately. Rather, presumably after reorganizing themselves, they waited to enter the city en masse until the next day, 23 Huperberetaeus/Tishri.[39]

On that day Titus himself, after selecting 200 cavalry and a body of infantrymen, cautiously made his way into the town. The guards, learning of Titus's entry, seized their weapons with a shout. When his presence became known to those inside the city, some took hold of their children and wives and, dragging them along, fled up to the citadel. Others, who went out to meet Titus, fell in continuous combat. All those who were hindered from running up to the citadel died fighting among the Romans. The blood of the dying deluged the whole city, flowing down the steep hillsides.[40]

As the streets of the town turned red with the Gamalans' blood, Vespasian brought his full force up against those who had fled up to the citadel. The citadel, everywhere rocky and inaccessible, was elevated to a great height and was surrounded by precipices on all sides. From there the Jews shot missiles at the Roman attackers and rolled boulders down upon them, wreaking havoc. Because of their elevated position the Gamalans were hard to reach by any Roman missile.[41]

At that point, however, there arose opposite the Jews a demonic wind (*thuella daimonios*) that seemed to be sent by heaven to assure their destruction.[42] The wind carried the Roman missiles up to the defenders on the citadel but checked and turned away at an angle the Gamalans' darts aimed at the Romans. Moreover, because of the force of the wind, the Jews no longer could stand on the precipices. Nor could they see the advancing Romans.[43] Josephus hardly needed to spell out for his readers who was the real force behind the wind: only God was capable of such an intervention, and for Josephus this was a specific example of God intervening in the war at a critical juncture on behalf of the Romans.

After the Romans made it up to the summit they surrounded the Jews and then killed both those who defended themselves and those who tried to surrender. The memory of their fellow soldiers who had been killed during the first attack upon the town increased the Romans' fury. Abandoning all hope of salvation, the defenders of the citadel threw first their children and wives and then themselves headlong from the citadel into the ravines below.[44] Josephus claims that more than 5,000 men, women, and children perished in this way rather than be slaughtered by the Romans. The Romans also killed 4,000 Jews, including infants, throwing them from the citadel as well. It was actions such as these by the Romans during the war that inspired third- and fourth-century CE rabbis such as Amora R. Abba b. Kahana and Amora R. Judah b. Simon to argue that the violence used by God's instrument (the Romans) during the war was not according to God's law.[45]

Only two women survived this massacre. They were nieces of King Agrippa's chief general, Philip, the son of Iakim (Iacimus). Thus was Gamala taken on 23 Huperberetaeus/Tishri/ (19–20 October) after a revolt that Josephus says began on 24 Gorpiaeus/Elul, roughly within six weeks of Tarichaeae's fall.[46] The siege had lasted less than a month. Like Iotapata, Gamala too ceased to exist as a human community. The divine assistance the Gamalans had invoked on their coins had not come. Instead, Josephus described the Jews' own God fighting against them. Gamala was never rebuilt.

Today the ancient site of Gamala is part of a peaceful, pristine nature preserve, the home of Syrian rock hyraxes, wild boars, and numerous species of raptors. The raptors swoop and glide freely in arcs over the black stones of the town.

THE CAPTURE OF GISCHALA

After the destruction of Gamala, the Tenth Legion was sent off to winter quarters in Scythopolis. Vespasian himself, with the two remaining Roman legions, returned to Caesarea Maritima to rest and train for the impending battle for Jerusalem.[47] In the north (close now to the border of modern Lebanon), only the small town of Gischala (Gush Halav/El-Jish) remained unconquered. Gischala was the hometown of Josephus's bête noire, John.

The Gischalans for the most part were peaceful farmers who were mostly concerned with tending their crops that grew easily in the rich local soil. However, a considerable "brigand" band had corrupted them, according to Josephus. The people of the town, who otherwise would have sent ambassadors to the Romans to negotiate about surrender instead, under John's influence and that of his faction, awaited the coming of the Romans on a war footing. To subdue the Gischalans, Vespasian sent his son Titus with 1,000 cavalrymen.[48] The small size of that force suggests that Vespasian and Titus were not expecting Gischala to be much of a tactical challenge, if the Gischalans decided to resist at all.

Once he brought his force up to Gischala, Titus instantly recognized that Gischala could be taken easily by frontal assault because its walls were far weaker than those of Iotapata or Gamala. Wishing to avoid the inevitable slaughter that would ensue once the Romans had breached the walls, Josephus tells us, Titus attempted to persuade the Gischalans to surrender.[49]

John took it upon himself to negotiate with Titus on behalf of the Gischalans. From this it could be argued that John was not deeply committed to the revolt or that Josephus has portrayed John's actions in Gischala as a kind of preview of his allegedly treacherous and self-serving behavior later in Jerusalem.[50] The two interpretations are not mutually exclusive, however, if we understand John as a leader whose attitudes changed according to circumstances—like Josephus, but with a very different denouement. After seizing the imperial grain stores in the north and putting himself on the wrong side of Rome, John had by now learned what had happened at Iotapata and Gamala. So he negotiated on behalf of the Gischalans.

Agreeing to Titus's peace offer, John promised to persuade or compel any opponents of the proposal. He asked, however, for one day of rest before the treaty was concluded. Apparently it was the Sabbath, presumably a Friday afternoon, from what follows in Josephus's narrative, and John pointed out to Titus that it was against the law for Jews either to conclude a treaty or bear arms on the Sabbath.[51]

Titus granted John and the Gischalans their respite. Josephus claims that Titus did so because God had decided to save John so that he could subsequently bring destruction to Jerusalem.[52] So Titus camped not close by the town but at some distance from it, at the Tyrian village of Kedasa (Qedesh) some six miles away to the northeast on the road to Tyre.[53] Perhaps logistical or supply requirements influenced Titus's decision. He had to look after the welfare of his cavalrymen's mounts, and there may have been good grazing land around Kedasa. Given the fact that Kedasa was a Tyrian settlement, it is also possible that Titus might have assumed that Kedasa's inhabitants would be friendly, if not active allies against the Jews.[54] Titus presumably knew that the Tyrians had taken part in the earlier attack upon Gischala.[55]

Titus's otherwise inexplicable decision not to stay put and keep a close eye on John and the Gischalans also may be explained by Josephus's literary and political agenda. Writing in Rome and sending an advance copy of his work to Titus himself for personal review, Josephus wanted Titus to be seen (and to see himself) as a generous and honorable commander, who occasionally was a bit too trusting for his own good.

Taking advantage of Titus's goodwill gesture, that Sabbath evening John led his armed followers and a large number of noncombatants with their families out of and away from Gischala. Those who could not keep up, especially women and children, were left behind.[56]

The next morning Titus came back to Gischala to finalize his agreement with John. He found the gates of the town wide open. After Titus entered the city, the townspeople who had remained behind told Titus of John's flight from the city the night before.[57]

Titus immediately sent a detachment of cavalry in pursuit. But John had already put too much distance between himself and the Romans, and he eventually made his way safely to Jerusalem. Some of the rest of his followers were not as fortunate. The Romans killed 6,000 of them and brought back some 3,000 women and children to Gischala.[58] Josephus' rounded-off numbers again give pause. John's trick had worked, but at a heavy cost, paid for by those who could not keep up with him. Of course, because John was Josephus's rival and enemy, Josephus was only too happy to emphasize John's duplicity and its consequences for those too slow to escape and for the women and children of Gischala.

A small section of the city wall of Gischala was pulled down by the Romans as a symbol of the city's conquest, and a garrison was installed there.[59] But there was no massacre of Gischala's inhabitants, as there had been at Iotapata and Gamala. Titus presumably understood that slaughtering yet more innocent civilians would do nothing to enhance his military glory and also would make future resistance even more determined.

THE FAILURE OF JOSEPHUS'S STRATEGY

From the fall of Tarichaeae to Gischala's capture roughly six weeks elapsed. By the end of 67, less than a year after Vespasian had set out from Ptolemais, all of the Galilee and parts of northern Judaea and Samaritis had been retaken by the Romans.

Josephus's strategy of fortifying the villages and towns of the Galilee and Gamala and encouraging the inhabitants of his area of responsibility to resist the Romans from behind those walls had been a bloody and complete failure. It had led to the deaths of a significant, though unquantifiable, percentage of the male population of the region and the enslavement of thousands of women and children.

It is not true, however, that there was no fighting in the Galilee and the Galilee did not submit to the Romans instantly.[60] At least some Galilaeans fought Vespasian's army with great courage. In hindsight we may judge it to have been a mistake for Jews living in the Galilee to resist Rome or the Romans at all. That may be. But their second and perhaps more decisive mistake was putting their trust in the strategy of an inexperienced young general who was responsible for advising them to follow a deeply misguided strategy.

Josephus's strategy invited, perhaps even ensured, that the Romans would pursue an "enemy-centric" strategy that not only suited their particular strengths with respect to siege warfare but also allowed them to finish off the first phase of the war within a year. During that phase Vespasian took his time, distinguishing between friends and foes. Most of his friends belonged to the elites in the big towns such as Sepphoris that had benefited the most from Roman rule. We know far less about the identities of Rome's foes in the rest of the Galilee and the Golan. But if Josephus's account of the fighting in both regions is at all reliable there certainly were thousands of them, and at Iotapata, Iapha, Itaburion, and Gamala they fought the Romans, their client Agrippa, and their allies with their wives and children clustered around them.

Vespasian destroyed his foes not only because they were foes and somebody had to pay for what had happened to the auxiliary garrison in Jerusalem in 66 and to Cestius. He also wanted to see if he could frighten the rebels in Jerusalem into submission without having to go there, besiege the city, and fight the rebels wall to wall, street by street. If that was Vespasian's strategy for bringing Jerusalem to heel, it failed, much to the later grief of both Romans and Jews. With the Galilee pacified, however, Vespasian's supply lines north of Judaea were secured, and he could proceed to the next phase of the operation: stamping out resistance in Judaea.

PART THREE

A Tale of Two Temples

CHAPTER 14

"Now You Have Our Vote"

CIVIL STRIFE AMONG THE JEWS

John of Gischala and his followers probably entered Jerusalem by early November 67. They supposedly represented their departure from Gischala to those who greeted them in the city as a strategic retreat. It had been pointless, they said, to risk their lives for Gischala and other such insignificant towns. They went on to tell their listeners that they ought to marshal their arms and energies together for the defense of the metropolis of Jerusalem.[1] Josephus clearly meant his readers to understand that what the Gischalans told the Jerusalemites about their departure from Gischala was hot air. Yet their advice about the defense of Jerusalem made sense, as Josephus himself knew well.

Most of those present understood that the retreat from Gischala had been flight pure and simple, Josephus wrote. When the Jerusalemites learned about the fates of the prisoners taken by the Romans, they became alarmed. They foresaw their own destinies in the Gischalans' misfortunes. But John went around to the various parties in the city and encouraged their hopes about the war. He asserted that the preparations of the Romans were weak, and he exalted the Jerusalemites' own power. Scoffing at the ignorance of those with no experience, he said that even if the Romans had wings, they would never make it over the wall of Jerusalem.[2]

Josephus says that the older men and anyone else who had any common sense saw what would happen if they went to war. All of them began lamenting, as if the city were already ruined. But most of the young men were corrupted and stirred up for war by John's harangues.[3]

Some scholars have found it hard to reconcile Josephus's presentation of John's willingness to negotiate with Titus before the walls of Gischala with the hard, anti-Roman line he took once he arrived in Jerusalem. But this underestimates the consequences of John's actions. First, whatever his view of the Romans and the question of resistance had been previously, John had tricked Titus at Gischala, taking advantage of the Roman commander's credulity, naiveté, or just plain incompetence. After duping the Roman commander, John could expect little mercy from him. Second, 6,000 Gischalans allegedly lost their lives as a direct result of John's successful deception of Titus. Again, that number is probably unreliable. Gischala was not a large city, and the rounded-up number is suspect. Whatever the number of casualties, however, at least some Gischalans died because John had betrayed Titus's trust. For John that would mean that he had nowhere to go and no one to go back to after what he had done. The surviving Gischalans would not be holding any homecoming parades in his honor. It was not an accident that by the time he got to Jerusalem John was ready to become a leader of irreconcilables.

After his escape from Gischala and Titus's humiliation, John must have realized that he was a marked man and that his personal enemy Josephus would be whispering into the ear of Rome's avenger. Even before Titus showed up at Gischala John had made himself into a figure of at best dubious loyalty in Roman eyes by stealing their stores of grain in the north. But the war as it developed turned John into an uncompromising enemy. Before John got a chance to meet Titus for the second time, however, he had the opportunity to test his martial skills against closer enemies.

The fighting in 66 had arisen out of conflicts among Jews, Greeks, and Syrians in Caesarea and then developed into a war between Jews and Romans. But by the winter of 67 Jews were fighting a third war in Judaea and Jerusalem: against each other.

STASIS *IN JUDAEA*

Even before armed conflict broke out in Jerusalem it had spread throughout the countryside. In every town there was civil strife between those who supported going to war against Rome and those who wanted peace. The second that the people enjoyed a respite from the Romans, they turned upon each other. The conflict first split up friends and then relatives. Strife (Greek, *stasis*) was everywhere.[4]

Influenced by the Athenian historian Thucydides's famous description of civic strife on the island of Corcyra (Corfu) during the Peloponnesian War (431–404 BCE), Josephus portrays the factional strife among Jews in 67 as something new and extraordinary.[5] But there had been conflict and mass violence among the Jews ever since they entered the promised land, and, as we have seen, even during the reign of the fierce and widely feared Herod there were conflicts among Jews that sometimes resulted in bloodshed and executions. Intercommunal strife and violence among the Jews were nothing new. Josephus knew that better than most Jews and probably all Romans.

Whatever the sources of internecine conflict had been earlier in the history of Israel, Josephus tells us that because of the youth and boldness of the revolutionary party, those who wanted war in late 67 usually overcame the older, more cautious men.

Outside Jerusalem the country dwellers turned to pillaging and banded into companies for robbery throughout the land. Those who suffered at the hands of the robbers supposedly found little or no difference between the savagery and lawlessness of the Romans and that of their fellow tribesmen. The garrisons in the cities did little or nothing to help the oppressed because they did not want to take any risks. Josephus adds that they hated the *ethnos,* or nation, of the Jews in any case. What that statement implies is that the garrisons were made up mostly of non-Jews.

After they were fed up with pillaging the rural areas, we are told, the brigand leaders among the Jews banded together and made their way into Jerusalem. Jerusalem was a city without a commanding general and one that, according to the custom of the Jews, was traditionally open to all of common tribal inheritance. Josephus notes with intentional irony that all who poured into the city at the time were welcomed, because it was universally assumed that they were allies of the Jerusalemites.[6]

The "brigands" from the countryside, after joining forces with those who were even more powerful within the city, now openly attacked people whom Josephus calls the most eminent. What made them eminent in his eyes?

Josephus makes clear that they were all proponents of making peace with Rome. The first target of the war enthusiasts was Antipas, a member of the Herodian royal family, and, not coincidentally, the man in charge of the public treasuries. Antipas was arrested and then imprisoned, followed by Levias and

Syphas, son of Aregetes. Both also were of royal blood. The principal men of the country were similarly treated.

The revolutionaries then sent a certain Yochanan ben Tzvi (Hebrew, gazelle), along with 10 others, to the jail where those who had been arrested were being held. There Tzvi's son and his colleagues proceeded to kill all of the prisoners by sword. Afterward they alleged that their victims had been negotiating with the Romans about the surrender of Jerusalem and were traitors to the common freedom.[7] The first of these charges may have been true; in fact, it was likely under the circumstances. But of course the accusation could not be challenged by dead men.

PINCHAS THE HIGH PRIEST

The leaders of the rebellion then decided to take upon themselves responsibility for the election of the high priest. Abandoning recent practices, the revolutionaries arranged for the high priest to be elected by means of a lottery limited to the members of one clan, called the Eniachin. The winner of the first lottery was a man named Pinchas (in Hebrew; Phanni in Aramaic; Phannias in Greek). Pinchas was the son of Samuel, from the village of Aphthia.[8] According to later sources Pinchas was a stonemason by trade.[9] Josephus says that the new high priest was not only not descended from any high priests. He had no idea what the high priesthood was.[10]

Dragged from his home, Pinchas was dressed up in the priestly vestments and told what to do by those who had arranged his election. At the same time that the rebels changed the method by which high priests were chosen, they also made the Temple into a fortress and its inner sanctum into the headquarters of their rule.[11]

What Josephus did not tell his readers in his condescending description of Pinchas's selection and background is that since the first half of the second century BCE, at any rate, the high priests of the Temple had not always been selected from among the Zadokites, that is, the descendants of Zadok, the high priest appointed by Solomon to officiate at the Temple built during his reign. Menelaus, who came from a priestly family but was not a Zadokite, usurped the high priesthood from Jason and his brother and predecessor as high priest, Onias III, in 172 BCE.[12] The Hasmoneans, who were of priestly descent, were not descendants of Zadok, though that did not prevent Jonathan from being appointed high priest in 152 BCE by Alexander Balas. Subsequently, Herod, Archelaus, Syria's and Judaea's Roman governors, Agrippa

I, Herod of Chalcis, and Agrippa II all had deposed and appointed high priests from among families they favored to advance their interests.[13] (See appendix E.) Therefore the families from which the high priests had been chosen since the second century BCE were no more qualified by blood descent from Zadok for the office than were other families of priests.[14]

The rebels' takeover of the process of appointing high priests is the most obvious indication that what the leaders of the second phase of the revolt had in mind was something more than just casting off Roman rule. Rather, they intended to carry out a thorough restructuring of authority and economic patronage within the state itself. As noted, in addition to their sacrificial duties high priests were in charge of collecting and then redistributing priestly tithes. Appointment and control of the high priests was a way of managing, distributing, or redistributing wealth.[15] The civil war of Jews against Jews thus had morphed into an internal socioeconomic revolution.

This revolution provoked resistance. Specifically, we are told, the new method for the appointment of the high priest roused the people. Gorion (or Gurion), son of Joseph, Ananus's co-leader of the rebellion in 66, and Simeon, son of Gamliel, urged the people to punish those who had destroyed freedom and to purge the sanctuary of its bloody polluters. The most eminent of the high priests—Jesus, the son of Gamala, and Ananus, the son of Ananus—who initially had resisted John of Gischala's attempt to have Josephus replaced as commander of the Galilee, also reproached the people for their sluggishness during their meetings and incited them against the "Zealots."[16] But who were these so-called Zealots at this time?

THE ZEALOTS

Many prominent historians have understood the Zealots (Greek, *zelotai*) to be religious purifiers or members of a unified freedom movement that drew its original inspiration from the biblical figure of Phineas (Pinchas). Phineas, it will be remembered, had displayed his jealousy on God's behalf by running his spear through the Israelite Zimri after Zimri had brought a Midianite woman named Cosbi into his family.[17] A second inspirational figure for the purifiers was Matthias or Mattathias, the founder of the Maccabean resistance during the second century BCE. At the time of the Seleucid king Antiochos Epiphanes (r. 175–64 BCE), the author of 1 Maccabees, writing in Greek, tells us that Matthias had burned with zeal (*ezelosen*) for the law, just as Phineas did against Zimri, the son of Salu.[18]

Other scholars have argued that Josephus uses the Greek word "zealot" ironically here, recounting events in late 67 and after, to describe people who historically had been imitators of virtue or moral exemplars, but in the case of the Zealots during the rebellion were "disciples" of immorality or tyrants. These different kinds of disciples became enemies of Rome not because they were anti-imperialists. Rather, it was regional strife that led them to take up arms on God's behalf.[19]

Neither of these explanations for the appearance of the Zealots and the role they played in the early stages of the rebellion is entirely convincing. Who the Zealots were and what they wanted up to the point when the method for the selection of the high priest was changed are more persuasively reconstructed from what we can know most plausibly about their actions.

The Zealots made their first appearance as an identifiable group or faction during this period as supporters of Menahem, the son of Judas the Galilaean, after he became leader of the revolution in the late summer of 66. After his followers besieged the royal troops and the Romans in Herod's Palace and murdered the high priest Ananias and his brother Ezekias, Menahem was attacked by the followers of Eleazar inside the Temple, where he had gone with his disciples (*zelotas*) to make his devotions.[20]

The first Zealots mentioned in Josephus's account of the war therefore were disciples or, more neutrally, followers associated with a descendant of the man who had chastised the Jews for submitting to the Romans when they had God as their master. These Zealots served as Menahem's bodyguard after he became the first leader of the rebellion. It is hard to believe that these followers of Menahem were unaware of Judas's resistance to the Romans in 6 CE.

After Menahem was murdered in August 66, the Zealots make their next prominent appearance as supporters or the bodyguard of Eleazar ben Simon after the ambush of Cestius and the election of Joseph, son of Gorion, and Ananus to be the leaders of the war. As we have seen, Eleazar was not given an office or leadership position at the time because of his tyrannical nature, according to Josephus. Thus his disciples (*zelotas*) conducted themselves like personal bodyguards.[21]

Before the influx of "brigands" into Jerusalem and before Ananus rallied the Jerusalemites against them, the Zealots therefore were followers of men who clearly were associated with anti-Roman ideology and actions. Josephus may have used the Greek word "zealot" to describe the Zealots sarcastically or ironically. Because he considered Menahem and Eleazar ben Simon to be murderous tyrants, Josephus's Zealots could not be emulators of the positive virtue of Phineas or Matthias. But their actions show them to have been enemies of Rome. If these Zealots were also enemies of those who submitted to Rome or who were allied to the Romans, that does not make them any less anti-Roman. Nor did Josephus create their anti-Roman stance by applying the Greek word "zealot" to them. Their actions made them anti-Roman.

THE ARISTEIA OF ANANUS

Although he was not there and therefore could not have heard what was said, Josephus then reports that at a general assembly Ananus admonished the populace for fostering the "tyrants" through their forbearance. No one had lifted a finger when the nobles were massacred without trial. The rebels now had taken control of the sanctuary and had made it into a citadel or fortress. He reminded his audience of their struggles for independence from the Egyptians and the Persians. He then asked why, if the pretext for the war was liberty, the people had submitted to slavery beneath villains of their own country?

He portrayed the Romans as the upholders of their laws because they had not entered into the inner parts of the sanctuary, while their fellows, still with the blood of their countrymen on their hands, walked about freely within its holy places. At the end of the speech Ananus urged his listeners not to be over-awed by the numbers and audacity of their foes (the Zealots), but to fight them and be willing to die, if not for their wives and children, then for God and for the sanctuary.[22]

Ananus's speech awakened the populace, and they shouted for him to lead them against their enemies—not the Romans but their fellow Jews. But as Ananus was enlisting and mobilizing those suitable for warfare, the Zealots, learning about the preparations for attack, became furious and rushed out from the sanctuary. They spared no one they encountered, Josephus reports. The hastily assembled city force led by Ananus counterattacked immediately. The two sides opened the fighting with an exchange of stones around the city and in front of the Temple. Next they began to heave javelins at each other from a distance. Finally, they engaged in hand-to-hand combat with swords. Superior numbers gradually gave the city populace an advantage and the Zealots were forced back into the Temple. Ananus and his men followed in hot pursuit.[23]

Having lost control of the outer court of the Temple, the Zealots were compelled to seek safety within the inner sanctuary. As soon as they were safely ensconced there they barred the gates. The Zealots continued to hurl missiles at Ananus and his fighters from above, but Ananus refused to press the attack using men who had not been purified for entry into the inner court. By law, access to the various courts within the Temple was restricted according to ritual purity, ethnic identity, gender, and religion: the high priest alone was allowed to enter the Holy of Holies, and only on Yom Kippur or the Day of Atonement.[24]

Ananus therefore selected by lot 6,000 men to serve as guards of the stoas that surrounded the sanctuary. These guards were assigned to fulfill their sentry duty in rotation, though we are told that many from the upper class, with permission from officers, hired poorer citizens to take their places at guard.[25]

The Zealots thus were blockaded inside the sanctuary, and it seemed as if the city populace led by Ananus had gained the upper hand. Their undoing, however, came about as the result of John of Gischala's duplicity and scheming, according to Josephus.

JOHN OF GISCHALA IN JERUSALEM

Having escaped from Gischala and roused the young men of Jerusalem to war, John now (allegedly) pretended to take the populace's side in the struggle with the Zealots. He accompanied Ananus as he consulted with the popular leaders by day and at night when he visited the guards. Afterward John revealed the popular party's secrets to the Zealots, so that every plan of the people was made known to their enemies.[26]

Josephus claims that John's obsequiousness to Ananus and the leaders of the people made him an object of suspicion. But his own narrative suggests a different estimation of the man by Ananus and his supporters. Ananus and the popular leaders took the precaution of trying to bind John to the popular cause by having him swear a loyalty oath not to betray any plan or action and to assist them in defeating those who attacked them. Only afterward did they give him access to their consultations and subsequently send him as an ambassador to the Zealots about a settlement. Ananus and the popular leaders sought such a settlement, we are told, because of their desire not to cause any pollution within the Temple and to make sure that none of their fellow tribesmen should fall there.[27]

So Ananus clearly was suspicious of John and worried about where his true allegiances lay. If that were not the case, a loyalty oath was unnecessary. It turned out, however, that Ananus either overestimated John's integrity or underestimated his cunning opportunism.

Once he was inside the sanctuary, instead of conveying the proposal about the settlement to the Zealots, John told their leaders that Ananus had convinced the people to send an embassy to Vespasian asking him to come immediately and assume control of Jerusalem. He furthermore informed them that Ananus was preparing a service of purification for the next day so that his followers might gain entry to the Temple and then use the opportunity to attack the Zealots. His advice to the Zealots was either to give up or to seek outside assistance. To alarm the Zealot leaders still further, he added that Ananus's threats were particularly directed against the Zealot leaders. Among these were Eleazar ben Simon (though Gion in some manuscripts), who earlier had taken possession of the money captured from Cestius, and Zacharias, son of Amphicalleus. Both these men were members of priestly families.[28]

Josephus may have made up the story of this threat to the Zealot leaders. But under the circumstances it was not implausible. That was the point. Threats are more effective if they are credible.

ENTER THE IDUMAEANS

Josephus says that the Zealots deliberated for a long time about what to do. But they could not have hesitated for too long, because we know that before any attack took place, they decided to send messengers to the Idumaeans, who lived in villages and towns about 10 miles south of the city.[29] (See map 1.) According to Josephus the Idumaeans had been conquered by John Hyrcanus I (r. 135–104 BCE), who allowed them to stay on their land as long as they were willing to undergo circumcision and agreed to live under and observe the laws of the Jews.[30] The Zealots therefore appealed to people who had become Jews by choice, though under duress.

The messengers were instructed to tell the Idumaeans that Ananus was about to betray the metropolis to the Romans, that they themselves, who had revolted on behalf of freedom, were imprisoned within the sanctuary, and that there was only a small time during which their safety would be decided. If they (the Idumaeans) did not give aid to them quickly, they would be overcome by Ananus and their enemies, and the city would be taken by the Romans.[31]

The two men selected to deliver the message, both of them named Ananias, were fleet runners and supposedly persuasive speakers. Though the Idumaeans' ancestors had been brought under Macedonian rule without significant resistance in 332 BCE at the time of Alexander's conquest of the region, the contemporary inhabitants of the hill country south of Jerusalem were at least locally famous for their independence and bellicosity.[32] Because of the latter, Herod had sent some 3,000 Idumaeans to Trachonitis to suppress bandits there.[33] Some of the Idumaeans who remained in their homeland may have been descendants of the veterans whom Herod had settled in Idumaea as a kind of reward for their loyal service.[34]

The Idumaeans seem to have decided to respond to the Zealots' plea right away. In no time at all 20,000 Idumaeans were mustered to march upon the capital and to lend their arms to the Zealots. They were led by four generals: John and James, sons of Sosas; Simon, son of Thaceas; and Phineas, son of Clusoth.[35]

Ananus and the guards around the Temple did not know that the Zealots had managed to contact the Idumaeans. But they were warned about the Idumaeans' approach, and Ananus therefore took precautions. The gates of the city were shut and guards positioned on the walls.[36]

Ananus had no desire to fight the Idumaeans. Rather he hoped to persuade them before more internal fighting broke out. Jesus, who was the eldest high priest alive after Ananus, therefore was sent forth to speak to the Idumaeans. Taking up a position on the tower opposite where the Idumaeans were gathered, Jesus addressed them. In another speech quoted at length by Josephus, though again he could not have heard it since he was still chained up in Vespasian's camp, Jesus refuted the charge that the popular leaders or the people themselves had been negotiating for the surrender of the city to the Romans. He pointed out that there was no evidence of such negotiations.

Three courses of action were open to the Idumaeans, the high priest asserted: to join the popular party and wipe out the Zealots because of the crimes they had committed; to lay down their arms and enter the city as arbitrators; or to leave the two parties to themselves and neither insult the popular party nor join up with those who were conspiring against the mother city.[37]

Jesus's speech pleased neither the Idumaean rank and file nor their generals. The soldiers were enraged that they had not been granted immediate entry into the city, and the generals had no desire to sheath their swords. One of the officers, a man named Simon, son of Cathas, replied to Jesus. Simon accused Jesus, the popular leaders, and their followers of closing the city, which was common to all, against the nation itself, of preparing to admit the Romans into Jerusalem while denying entry to their fellow countrymen, and of attaching the stigma of tyranny to the victims of their tyranny, namely the Zealots.

Near the end of his speech, Simon asserted that the Idumaeans would preserve the house of God and defend their common country against invaders from outside and traitors from within. Finishing with a flourish, he said that the Idumaeans would remain before the walls under arms until the Romans grew tired of waiting for them or they (meaning the people), having thought it over, came over to the side of liberty.[38] The mass of Idumaeans heartily acclaimed Simon's words.[39] The Idumaeans thus had concluded that John of Gischala and the Zealots were the true defenders of Zion's freedom against Rome.

That night in the winter of 67–68 there was a terrible storm. There were strong winds with violent thunderstorms, deafening thunderclaps, and tremendous rumblings of the earth. Josephus says that both the Idumaeans and Ananus understood the storm as an indicator of God's judgments upon their actions and also as a portent.[40] But whose actions were being judged and how?

The Idumaeans believed that the storm was a sign of God's anger against them for their expedition and that they would not escape punishment for bearing arms against the mother city. Ananus and his followers thought that they had achieved victory without a fight and that God was acting as a general on their behalf.[41] What happened in Jerusalem soon thereafter showed that the Idumaeans were right and Ananus was wrong, as Josephus surely intended his readers to recognize.

The Idumaeans spent the night huddled beneath their shields, trying to keep warm and dry. The Zealots meanwhile were meeting and considering how to help their allies outside the walls. Some argued for an all-out attack upon those guarding the Temple, a rapid movement through the city, and then a quick approach to the gates, which they would open to the Idumaeans. Others were more cautious. They pointed out that it was not only the Temple that was guarded but also the city wall itself.

In the end, late at night, the Zealots, using saws stored within the Temple, cut through the bars of one of the gates while the guards of the popular party who were posted at the colonnade slept. The noise of the winds and the thunder cracks prevented the sounds of the sawing from being heard by their foes. Escaping from the Temple unseen, they made their way to the city wall, and using their saws once again, they succeeded in opening up the gate closest to the Idumaeans.

At first, the Idumaeans thought they were under attack from Ananus's men and prepared to defend themselves. But after recognizing those who had come to open the gate, they hurried into the city. Although they might have taken the city as a whole, at the urging of those who had let them into the city, the Idumaeans made straight for the Temple.[42]

As soon as the majority of the Zealots realized that the Idumaeans had arrived, they advanced out from the inner Temple and, banding together with the Idumaeans, attacked the sentries. Some were slain in their sleep. The majority, however, aroused by the cries of those who had awakened, picked up their weapons and prepared to defend themselves. As long as they thought they were fighting only the Zealots, they pressed on, hoping to overwhelm their enemies by their superior numbers.

When they realized, however, that the Zealots had been joined by the Idumaeans they lost heart, threw down their weapons, and gave way to sobbing. Only a few of the younger men strapped on their armor and engaged the Idumaeans. By a shout these young men signified their misfortunes to those throughout the city. But no one dared to come to their defense when they recognized that the Idumaeans had broken into the city. Instead they simply wailed back in answer, and the women too let out a great shriek. The Zealots joined in the war cry of the Idumaeans, and the storm made the shout from all together even more fearful.

The Idumaeans spared no one. Josephus says that they treated suppliants and those who defended themselves in the same way—thrusting their swords right through many—even as their victims were reminding them of their kinship and begging them to have regard for the Temple that they had in common.

There was no place to flee, no hope of safety. Driven together upon each other, the supporters of the high priests were cut to pieces. The greater part of them, with nowhere to run and their murderers right upon them, threw themselves down headfirst into the city. The whole outer Temple was then stained by blood; 8,500 perished.[43] According to Josephus's reckoning, more Jews were killed by Jews that night than the combined number of Jews and Romans who died during the *clades* Cestiana. Focused as he was on the idea of *stasis* or civil war leading to destruction and defeat, Josephus obscured the more important point about the Idumaeans and their entry into the city. It was the Idumaeans who tipped the balance of force and power in favor of those who were not interested in a compromise with the Romans.

THE DEATHS OF ANANUS AND JESUS

Turning upon the city, the Idumaeans then began plundering houses and killing everyone they came across. Soon, thinking this to be a waste of their efforts, they sought out the high priests Ananus and Jesus. Captured quickly, the priests were slain. Standing on their bodies, the Idumaeans upbraided Ananus for his goodwill toward the people and Jesus for the speech he made to them from the wall. In violation of Jewish burial custom, which required that the dead be buried before sunset except under extraordinary circumstances, the bodies of the dead were cast out unburied.[44]

In his history of the war Josephus composed encomia for the ex–high priests Ananus and Jesus.[45] Of Ananus, he wrote that the high priest knew that the Romans could not be defeated. But by necessity providing for war in the event that the Jews would not come to terms with the Romans, he at least took care that it should be carried out with skill. Had he lived, Josephus claims, he would have persuaded the people to make peace with Rome, or at least he would have delayed Rome's victory. Jesus, while left behind by Ananus in comparison, nevertheless was head and shoulders above the others.

Josephus then goes on to account for the murder of two such men, whose bodies were left unburied to be eaten by dogs and beasts of prey. God, he concluded, having condemned a polluted city to destruction and wishing by fire to purge the holy places, cut off those who were their defenders and tender lovers.[46]

THE REIGN OF TERROR BEGINS

After the deaths of Ananus and Jesus, Josephus tells us that the Zealots and the Idumaeans descended upon and slaughtered the people the way a butcher fell upon a flock of ritually impure animals. Ordinary people were killed where they were caught. Nobles and young men were bound and put into prison. Their destruction was put off in the hope that some might come over to the side of the Zealots. None did, however. All preferred painful deaths rather than siding with the Zealots against their own fatherland. Terrible tortures were inflicted upon them for this refusal. They were whipped and tormented to such a degree that their bodies were no longer able to withstand the abuses, until the time that their murderers reluctantly thought them to have earned death by the sword.[47]

Those who had been arrested during the day were killed at night, and the dead bodies were carried out and thrown away so that there would be room for other prisoners. No one dared to weep openly for their dead relatives or even to bury them. Tears were shed behind the walls of homes. Even groans were uttered cautiously. Those who mourned suffered things equal to those who were mourned for. At night some mourners would take a little dust up in their hands and spread it on the bodies of the dead. If anyone were very bold, he did it by day. Twelve thousand young noblemen died in this way.[48] Disbelieving such figures, some historians have suggested that we divide the casualty figures by 100.[49] So far though, no one has claimed that there was not a reign of terror of some scale.

Having grown tired of this slaughter without any form of restraint, the Zealots eventually set up courts and trials, by which they hoped to clothe their executions in legal garb. In a kind of imitation of the Sanhedrin court, 70 of the leading citizens were ordered to play the role of judges in these revolutionary courts. Their first target was a man named Zacharias, the son of Baris, a rich man, known for his love of freedom. Zacharias was accused of betraying the realm to the Romans and having sent some kind of communication to Vespasian concerning his treason.

Zacharias, who realized that he had already been found guilty and was marked for execution, stood up and scoffed at the probability of the accusations. He then quickly refuted the charges against him. Turning his speech against his accusers, he used the opportunity to give a full account of all their legal transgressions and went on to lament many things about the confused state of public affairs.[50]

Against the Zealots' expectations, the 70 judges unanimously acquitted Zacharias, whereupon two of the Zealots set upon him in the middle of the Temple and killed him anyway. Jesting as they stood over the fallen man, they said, "Now you have our vote and a more sure release." Zacharias's body was thrown from the Temple into the ravine below. The 70 judges were then driven from the temple at sword-point.[51]

(SOME) IDUMAEANS THINK AGAIN

Josephus tells us that it was now that the Idumaeans began to regret coming to Jerusalem and giving their assistance to the Zealots. One unnamed Zealot went to the Idumaeans and greatly increased those regrets. He pointed out that they had allied themselves with the Zealots because they believed the charge that the high priests were betraying the mother city to the Romans. But there was no evidence to support that charge. On the other hand, if their actions were justified by the gates of the city being closed to them, Ananus, whose policy it was to close the city to them, was dead. Yet the atrocities in the city mounted, and although it was the Zealots who primarily perpetrated such atrocities, their actions would also be laid on the doorstep of the Idumaeans.[52] The Idumaeans were complicit in the reign of terror.

Appalled by what they had seen and persuaded by these arguments, the Idumaeans decided to depart from the city, though not all of them, including their leaders, as we shall see.[53] Before taking their leave, however, they freed around 2,000 citizens from the city's prisons. These men immediately fled from Jerusalem and joined the ranks of Simon, son of Giora.[54]

The departure of the Idumaeans had a paradoxical effect upon both the populace and the Zealots. The people, although they had no knowledge of the Idumaeans' repentance, were encouraged, as if they had been freed of enemies. The Zealots grew haughtier. They acted not as if they had been deserted by allies, but as if they were set free of critics, who were shamed by them and were seeking to turn them away from doing wrong.[55]

New chapters in the reign of terror were written immediately. Gorion or Gurion, son of Joseph, leader during the first phase of the rebellion, a man eminent in rank and family, yet democratic and known for his freedom of speech, was promptly murdered.[56] His frankness, added to his social advantages, was the cause of his destruction.

Niger the Peraean, who had distinguished himself in earlier battles against Cestius and at Ascalon, also did not escape the wrath of the Zealots.[57] Shouting and pointing to his battle scars, this man, whose record of hostility toward Rome was not in doubt, was dragged through the city. When he was brought outside the gates, despairing of salvation, he begged his tormenters at least for a proper burial. He was slain without the promise of a burial, but not before he invoked the vengeance of the Romans upon them.[58]

After Niger's death, Josephus says, the Zealots were relieved of the fear of being removed from power, and there was no section of the populace for whose destruction some justification was not found. The one penalty for charges either of the most serious or inconsequential nature was death, and no one escaped, except because of humble birth or by chance.[59] Insignificance may have been another factor.

If it actually occurred, the escape of the small Christian community from Jerusalem to Pella, to the east of the Jordan, at this time, "commanded by a revelation," may well be an indication of their lack of visibility and prominence.[60] The followers of the Galilaean holy man were not influential enough to be wiped out during the reign of terror.

Josephus's descriptions of *stasis* and its effects on Judaean society, of the Zealots and their role in the events that took place in late 67, of the intervention and murder of the high priests Ananus and Jesus, of the entry into Jerusalem of the Idumaeans, and of the beginning of the reign of terror in Jerusalem all are designed to support his argument that God had decided to destroy Jerusalem and the Temple because of the pollutions committed by Jews. But Josephus's narrative of these horrifying events ignores or obscures facts that help us understand the causes, course, and outcome of the rebellion.

First, the Zealots of 66–67 were connected to the anti-Roman movement that began in 6 CE. Second, the presence of 20,000 Idumaeans in the city meant that there were now 20,000 more mouths to feed in Jerusalem. That total was larger than the number of legionaries that Vespasian brought into the Galilee during the summer of 67. The need to house and feed thousands of Idumaeans must have put an additional strain on the resources of Jerusalem. The majority of Idumaeans eventually decided to leave Jerusalem but not before they further depleted the city's grain stores. They indeed were tarnished by their participation in the reign of terror, but the more significant point was that their presence had advanced neither the cause of freedom nor the strategy to achieve it.

CHAPTER 15

Chaos in the Capitals

THE ROMAN CAMP AND STRATEGY

While terror ruled within the walls of Jerusalem, Vespasian and the Roman army were not idle. After Titus made his way back from Gischala to Caesarea Maritima, Vespasian himself set out from there to Iamnia and Azotus, the ancient Philistine city. These towns were quickly subdued and garrisoned, suggesting that there were rebel Judaeans or at least "unreliables" in these cities. Vespasian then returned to his winter quarters in Caesarea. He brought with him a mass of people who had surrendered (spring 68).[1]

After learning about the strife in Jerusalem, Vespasian's commanders encouraged him to march against the city right away. The consensus was that this was the moment to take advantage of the situation and to strike, before the Jews grew tired or repented of their discord. Vespasian disagreed. If he attacked the city immediately, he said, the attack itself would bring the Jews together. The Jews would then turn their combined force, which was still at its height, against the Romans. If he waited, however, there would be fewer of their enemies. God was a better general than he was. He was delivering the Jews to the Romans without any toil on their part and was granting victory to the Roman generalship without danger.[2]

Vespasian's strategy therefore was *not* to do nothing after conquering the Galilee or to waste time enjoying himself in Caesarea, as some historians have claimed. Rather he decided to be patient and wait: to wait for the Jews in Jerusalem to kill more of each other and for the spring harvest to come, so that it would be easier to gather supplies for the siege of Jerusalem.

Some of the most effective generals in the annals of Roman history had been masters of not engaging Rome's enemies, at least frontally. The strategic hero of Rome's victory over Hannibal during the second Punic War (218–201 BCE) was not the famous Scipio Africanus, as patriotic Roman writers liked to claim, but Quintus Fabius Maximus Verrucosus "Cunctator"—the Delayer— whose strategy of not giving Hannibal the decisive battle he needed to defeat Rome once and for all in Italy eventually forced the invader to depart from the Italian peninsula. For the time being, then, Vespasian took a page from the Delayer's strategic handbook.

The Roman officers, we are told, agreed with Vespasian, though it is far from clear how Josephus knew what the officers had recommended to the Roman commander and what he said in response during the *consilium* or council he held with them. Josephus conceivably could have asked Vespasian about the discussion and the decision later. But whether Josephus made up the exchange or talked to the officers or Vespasian in Rome after the war, events in the late winter and spring of 68 soon proved the wisdom of Vespasian following Fabius's or God's lead. Over the next few months, the different factions in Jerusalem and elsewhere did their best to make Vespasian's task easier and less costly.

WAR AND STRIFE IN JERUSALEM, JUDAEA, AND THE PERAEA

While the Romans were strategizing in Caesarea, large numbers of people in Jerusalem were doing everything possible to escape the city and the Zealots. The guards killed everyone they caught, since it was plausibly assumed that all of those who were trying to flee were on their way over to the Romans or at least just wanted to get out of the city. Safe flight could be purchased, however. The result was that those who tried to escape but were unwilling or unable to pay were labeled as traitors and slaughtered. Heaps of bodies lay unburied along the roads. Perhaps seeing these corpses, many who had intended to flee changed their minds and opted to die within the city walls. The hope of burial within the city made death within the fatherland more tolerable.[3]

The Zealots, we are told, dashed all such hopes. They allowed the burial neither of those who died along the roads nor of those who perished within the city. The penalty for desertion was the same as that for burying a relative: death.

Such is the picture that Josephus presents. After the Cestian disaster Josephus tells his readers that distinguished Jews abandoned Jerusalem like swimmers deserting a sinking ship.[4] In the passage just summarized he gives the impression that there were so many deserters that large lifeboats were needed. What he does not do is to contextualize his description of the desertions, which occurred in the aftermath of the victory of the Zealots over the first rebel government. In fact, as we shall see, the successive waves of desertions from the city here and during the subsequent siege took place at critical junctures during the war and can be explained as reactions to specific events and not necessarily as judgments upon the rebellion's leaders or their ideologies.[5]

Amidst such horrors, an ancient proverb inspired by God about the city and the sanctuary was recalled. The city would be captured and the most holy sanctuary burned to the ground by the dictate of war, the adage went, when civil war invaded the city and native hands first defiled God's sanctuary. The Zealots, according to Josephus, did not disbelieve the prediction. Rather, they gave themselves over as its instrument.[6]

Unsurprisingly, perhaps, Josephus says that the leaders of the revolution began to fight among themselves over issues of authority and power. The Roman historian Tacitus confirms Josephus's account, claiming that at the time there were three generals in the city and three armies.[7] One of the generals that Tacitus had in mind was Josephus's old rival, John of Gischala.

Perhaps aiming at supreme authority, if not outright monarchy, John split off from his colleagues, taking with him a considerable band of followers. Afterward, between John and his rivals there was not yet open conflict. Rather they assumed a defensive posture against each other. The real target of the rivals was the populace of the city itself, as Josephus wanted his readers to believe, which the leaders of the Zealots competed to oppress.[8]

While Jerusalem was wracked by war, tyranny, and factional rivalry, murder and mayhem broke out all over Judaea. After the *sicarii* on Masada learned that the Roman army was resting and that the Jews in Jerusalem were preoccupied by civil war, they undertook greater projects than the raids upon neighboring towns and villages for supplies that they had conducted earlier.[9]

At the time of the Passover feast the dagger-men came down from Masada, marched some 10 miles north, and attacked the toparchy village of Ein Gedi ("Spring of the Kid-Goat"), on the west coast of the Dead Sea, a place famous for its palm trees and balsam.[10] Ein Gedi's proximity and wealth were the magnets that drew the *sicarii* to it.

Those capable of resistance quickly scattered. Seven hundred women and children, however, who were left behind were killed. The houses were then looted and the ripest crops seized before the *sicarii* returned to Masada. Similar raids on the other villages around the fortress were carried out and the whole region was laid waste. This plundering campaign attracted new followers. Fresh recruits joined the dagger-men every day.[11]

Josephus provides little information about what motivated the dagger-men to carry out their raids. His readers are left with the impression that murdering women and children was simply what the *sicarii* did; the nature of their crime against fellow Jews, not their putative Roman enemies, is made even more grave by its timing. It took place during Passover.

The disorder in Jerusalem gave similar bands an opportunity to plunder other parts of Judaea. After ransacking their own villages these small bands fled into the backcountry where they linked up with other groups of robbers. The united bands then proceeded to attack "temples" (*hierois* in Greek), probably meaning synagogues, and cities.[12]

While the robber gangs were roaming around and marauding throughout Judaea, during the first six months of 68 Vespasian and the Roman army were methodically eliminating all pockets of potential resistance before their planned march to Jerusalem. As they did so they encountered no signs of opposition organized by any of the commanders who had been selected by the rebellion's leaders in Jerusalem after the defeat of Cestius in 66, such as Joseph, son of Simon, who was given authority over Jericho, or Manasseh, who was in charge of the Peraea.

Without the knowledge of the locals who favored resistance, in Peritius/Shebat (January 68) the leading men of Gadara in the Peraea had sent an embassy to Vespasian in Caesarea, offering to surrender their city. They did so both because they wanted peace and they were concerned about their property.

As Vespasian made his way first across Samaritis and the River Jordan into the Peraea and then toward Gadara, those who opposed capitulation, seeing the Romans approaching the town, seized and murdered the town's most prominent citizen, a certain Dolesus. For good measure they also mutilated his body. They believed that Dolesus had been responsible for sending out the embassy to Vespasian. That may not have been an unwarranted deduction.

Recognizing that they did not stand a chance of resisting Vespasian, the Gadarans who had killed Dolesus and wanted to continue the struggle against the Romans fled from the city. Those who remained behind voluntarily pulled down the walls of the city, which Vespasian entered without opposition on 4 Dustrus/Adar. A garrison of cavalry and infantry was established in Gadara to protect the residents from those who had fled from the city.[13] Placidus was then sent by Vespasian with 500 cavalry and 3,000 infantry to track down those who had run away from Gadara. Vespasian himself led the rest of the army back to Caesarea.

The fugitives from Gadara took a southwesterly route to the village in the Peraea that Josephus calls Bethennabris (Beth-Nimrin?), about 12 miles to the southwest. There they persuaded or impressed a number of young men to join their ranks. When Placidus and his force appeared, the fugitive army rushed out from behind the walls of the village and attacked the Romans.

The armed fugitives were no match for the Roman cavalry and infantry, who soon drove those who had not been killed immediately back inside the walls of the village. By evening the Romans had broken through the hamlet walls, and a slaughter of the defenseless took place. Those who survived the massacre did their best to stir up further resistance in the countryside. The survivors from Bethennabris and those who joined them from the neighborhood then headed for Jericho. Because of Jericho's large population, they believed that it might provide a safe haven.[14]

Unfortunately for them, Placidus and his cavalry caught up to them before they reached Jericho's fabled walls. Killing all those they encountered, the Romans eventually drove the remaining fugitives to the banks of the Jordan River. The river was apparently uncrossable at the time because of recent rains. With their backs to the river the refugees had no choice but to fight. What followed was not a battle between two trained and armed opponents but rather a wholesale massacre of a mass of armed civilians by a professional army.

Fifteen thousand were killed, and 2,200 were captured. Josephus says that there was no accounting for the number of people who threw themselves into the Jordan. In fact, so many were killed during this battle that not only was the Jordan filled with bodies; eventually masses of corpses drifted down the river into the Dead Sea itself, where the corpses presumably floated on the sea's salty surface. Vast numbers of asses, sheep, camels, and oxen also came into Roman hands.[15] No doubt the Romans used the captured sheep to keep up the non-grain rations of their diet, while the asses, camels, and oxen were conscripted for service as pack animals in the baggage trains of the Roman legions.[16]

Placidus followed up the annihilation of these people with a sweep through the small villages and towns in the southern Peraea. Abila (Tell Abil, south of Bethennabris), Iulias (Betharamphtha/Tell er-Rama), Besimoth (Beth-Jeshimoth?), and all the other local population centers of any significance were attacked, conquered, and garrisoned. Those who sought refuge on the waters of the Dead Sea were also captured after the Romans embarked upon ships. Within a short time all of the Peraea except for the Hasmonean fortress of Machaerus had either surrendered or was conquered.[17] With the exception of that fortress, what would be Vespasian's eastern flank during the impending siege of Jerusalem was now secured.

CUTTING OFF JERUSALEM

During that same winter (from January 68), though it is uncertain precisely when, Vespasian learned of the revolt against the emperor Nero led by C. Iulius Vindex, the governor of Gallia Lugdunensis (north-central France). While the emperor Nero was sending legions from the upper Rhine to confront Vindex, Vespasian made up his mind to prosecute the war in Judaea as aggressively as possible. He did so, Josephus says, because he anticipated that Vindex's revolt would lead to trouble in Rome, and he had concerns for the empire as a whole. The retrospective publication of those concerns in Josephus's text sounds like background material given him to justify Vespasian's later campaign for the position of emperor.[18]

But whatever was on Vespasian's mind early in 68, he took care to secure the villages and towns with garrisons. Decurions were sent to the villages and centurions to the cities. Then, probably in March, he moved the majority of his force from Caesarea southeast to Antipatris. After he restored order there in two days, Vespasian embarked upon a campaign to pacify the places around it.[19]

This pacification campaign in the spring of 68 would bring Vespasian on a semicircular route from the northwest of Jerusalem to the west and then south of the metropolis. The Macedonian Seleucid regent and commander Lysias twice had attacked the Maccabees and Jerusalem following the same route.[20] Vespasian's military objective was to eliminate all pockets of resistance around Jerusalem and also to establish control of all potential supply lines into the city. As they did so the Romans probably anticipated that those who escaped from their operations would gravitate to Jerusalem, thereby swelling its population. A larger population would mean more mouths to feed. That may have been part of Vespasian's plan.

The Roman strategy thus was first to cut off Jerusalem and then to besiege it. Placidus had taken care of the region across the Jordan to the east. Vespasian set out to close the circle to the north and west. Again, there are no indications that any of the generals assigned to organize resistance in the areas along Vespasian's route put up any kind of defense.[21]

After finishing their work in Antipatris, Vespasian and his army set forth the next day, wasting and burning all the nearby places. The toparchy around Thamna (Khirbet Tibne) to the southeast was reduced, and then Vespasian moved on to Lydda and Iamnia. These towns had been subdued earlier. Introduced into them now were large numbers of people who had surrendered elsewhere. Presumably these new settlers were loyal to the Romans. From there Vespasian marched to Emmaus (Imwas, next to Latrun), 18 miles northwest of Jerusalem.[22] After occupying the approaches to the town, a camp was established there, in which the Fifth Legion was left by April 68.[23]

With the rest of his forces Vespasian then advanced to the toparchy of Bethleptepha (Beit Nettif, 12.4 miles southwest of Jerusalem). This place, the neighboring areas, and those bordering on Idumaea were destroyed by fire. Vespasian then captured two towns in the middle of Idumaea itself: Betabris (Beit Guvrin) and Caphartoba. More than 10,000 of the people living there were killed, and over 1,000 became prisoners of war; the rest were expelled from the district. A large force was then stationed there, which conquered and laid waste the mountainous country.[24]

Vespasian then took the rest of his army back to Emmaus and from there, through Samaritis, he passed by Mabartha, later Flavia Neapolis (Shechem/Nablus), on the way to Corea (Tell Mazar) where he set up camp, 2 Daisius/Sivan (May–June 68).[25] The next day Vespasian marched to Jericho, where he was met by Trajan, the commander of the Tenth Legion, with the force he had led out from the Peraea. All of the country beyond the Jordan River had been subdued.[26]

The survivors of the Roman campaign in the Peraea initially fled to Jericho but then deserted the town when it became clear that the Romans were in the vicinity. Vespasian, Trajan, and the Roman army thus found an empty city when they entered it. A garrison comprised of Roman soldiers and auxiliaries was placed in Jericho and also on the hilltop of Adida (Hadid, modern el-Haditha), about three miles east of Lydda. The effect of this was to close the roads that led to Jerusalem both from the east through Jericho and from the west: from Lydda to Emmaus and on to Jerusalem, and from Lydda to Beit-Horon to Jerusalem. It was probably at this time that the community of

Essenes living at Qumran was destroyed, though Josephus does not provide an explicit account of its destruction.[27]

After Jericho and Adida were garrisoned, Vespasian apparently visited the Dead Sea, or the Asphalt Lake as it was called in Greek (*Asphaltitis*). He took the opportunity to investigate the famed buoyancy of its salt waters. To do so he had people who could not swim thrown into the lake with their hands tied behind their backs. All of them floated.

Josephus reports Vespasian's experiment in his description of the topography of the local hill district from Scythopolis (Beth Shean) to the region of Sodom. He says nothing about the implications of the incident for our understanding of Vespasian's character.[28] We might read Josephus's mention of the episode as another indication that Josephus had no desire to whitewash Roman atrocities or Vespasian's character flaws. Josephus, however, does not comment upon or condemn what Vespasian did. It is left up to Josephus's readers to decide whether his lack of any comment is a form of condemnation or simply indicates Josephus's own moral indifference. Either way, the incident reveals that the tax collector's son had a streak of cool cruelty in him. Behind the avuncular mask of Vespasian, created and propagated by the friends of the Flavians, breathed an unpleasant representative of Romulus's seed.

To Gerasa (probably a mistake in Josephus's text for Gezer [Gazara], 4.97 miles southeast of Ramle on the Lydda-to-Jerusalem road) was sent Lucius Annius with cavalry and infantry. After the city was captured, 1,000 young men who had not fled from the city were put to death, and the women and children were made captives. The houses of the residents were first plundered and then burned. Annius then conducted a campaign against the surrounding villages. Whoever was able to flee did so, while those who were unable were slaughtered. The villages themselves were consigned to flames.[29]

With the notable exceptions of Machaerus, Herodeion, and Masada, all potential focal points of resistance surrounding Jerusalem thus were eliminated by lance and fire. Jerusalem was effectively cut off by May 68.[30] Vespasian presumably left the Herodian fortresses unconquered because they were not considered to be a strategic threat at the time when he planned to attack Jerusalem. The people who inhabited the fortresses were not friends of Rome, but neither were they hunkered down behind the walls to engage the Romans. They were there because they wanted to get away from Vespasian and his army, not to confront them. That would do for Vespasian's purposes at the time.

THE DEATH OF NERO

It was after Vespasian had returned to Caesarea by June 68 and was preparing for the assault upon Jerusalem that the news of the emperor Nero's suicide on 9 June reached him. Nero had committed suicide after hearing about revolts by governors in Spain and the commander of the Third Legion in North Africa, following the earlier revolt by Vindex. Assuming that the news was conveyed to Vespasian as quickly as possible, Vespasian could have learned of Nero's death by the end of June.

After he received word of the emperor's death, Vespasian put his plans for the conquest of Jerusalem on hold. He wanted to see what would happen in Rome and who the next emperor would be. Better than anyone else, Vespasian knew that the war against the Jews in the Galilee and Judaea had been Nero's war. It was Nero who had provoked the war by his attempts to get as much money as possible from the Judaeans; it was Nero who had decided to replace Cestius; and it was Nero who had selected him (Vespasian) to be the commander of the war there. Now that the emperor cum artist (artifex) was dead, it was prudent for Vespasian to pause and see what would happen: to make haste slowly.[31] Vespasian would have wanted to receive further instructions for the prosecution of the war from whomever the new emperor might be.

Vespasian eventually found out that the honor of succeeding Nero had fallen upon Servius Sulpicius Galba, a member of a patrician family who had been governor of the province of Tarraconensis (Mediterranean and north-central Spain).[32] As was customary among Roman commanders serving out in the provinces, Vespasian decided to send salutations to Rome's new ruler. He selected his son Titus to bring his greetings to Galba. Titus was to be accompanied by no less a personage than King Agrippa II (November 68).[33]

But while the embassy was still on its way to Rome, having been delayed by winter weather, Galba himself was assassinated in the Roman Forum on 15 January 69. Another former governor, Marcus Salvius Otho, who had been legate of Lusitania (Portugal), was then raised up by the praetorian guards in Rome to supreme power.[34]

At this point, while the original embassy from Vespasian to Galba was perhaps in or near Achaia in Greece, King Agrippa decided to continue on his diplomatic mission to Rome. Titus, however, following a divine impulse according to Josephus, made the fateful decision to return to his father in Caesarea. Divine impulses discounted, perhaps Titus recognized an opportunity in Galba's murder and Otho's subsequent succession. Whatever the explanation, Titus rejoined his father, and together they decided to delay their attack upon Jerusalem until the political situation was clarified.[35]

Nero's death, the succession struggle, and Vespasian's decision to delay his march upon Jerusalem presented the Jews in Jerusalem and elsewhere with a golden opportunity to rethink their war strategy, taking into account the reasons for the Roman successes in the spring and early summer of 68.[36] Instead, they used the unexpected moratorium to continue fighting among themselves.

THE PROSELYTE'S SON

While the Roman war of succession was playing out in Italy, a new front in the civil war of the Jews opened up. After taking part in the earlier attack upon Cestius, Simon, the son of the proselyte Giora from Gerasa, had been expelled from the toparchy of Acrabetene in northern Judaea by the high priest Ananus due to his audacity (*tolme*).[37] Presumably what Josephus meant by this description of Simon was that Ananus could not control Simon. He wasn't alone.

After his expulsion, with the women of his family in tow, by late 66 Simon had made his way to Masada, which was in the hands of those who had seized it at the beginning of the war. Although at first not completely trusted by Masada's rebels and confined to the lower part of Masada (possibly the southern part of the plateau), Simon eventually gained their confidence and then took part in their raids upon neighboring villages described earlier in this chapter.[38]

After the murder of the high priest Ananus in early 68, Simon had set off into the hill country where he succeeded in raising a band of followers by proclaiming freedom for slaves and gifts for the free. His successes against the villages there drew free citizens to his following, and soon Simon had overrun not only the toparchy of Acrabetene. His power extended to the borders of Idumaea. At the village of Nain walls were raised, and henceforth Simon used it as his fortress. In the caves of the valley of Pheretae (perhaps Khirbet Farah, six miles or so northeast of Jerusalem) were stored booty and grain supplies.[39]

To the Zealots in Jerusalem Simon's actions suggested not preparations for war against the Romans but an attack upon them. They therefore sent out an army to confront him. That army was promptly defeated, with heavy casualties.[40] For the moment Simon did not follow up his success with an attack upon the city itself. He did not believe that his forces were strong enough to get through or over Jerusalem's walls. Instead he turned his army, swollen to 20,000 followers, southward in the direction of Idumaea.[41]

The local Idumaean leaders mustered an army of 25,000 soldiers to meet Simon. An all-day battle between the two sides resulted in a bloody draw. After withdrawing to his fortress village of Nain, Simon then set about preparing for a second invasion of Idumaea.[42]

As he was doing so, while encamped in the village of Thekoue (Tekoa), Simon tried to capture Herodeion. He sent a minion of his named Eleazar to the fortress to convince its guard to surrender. But as soon as the guard there understood what Simon's emissary was up to, Eleazar was chased out of the fortress at sword point and died after throwing himself from the ramparts of Herodeion into the valley below.[43] His suicide set an unfortunate precedent.

Although Simon failed to take Herodeion, the attempt did succeed in alarming the Idumaeans. From their camp at the village of Alurus (Halhul?), they decided to send someone out to make an assessment of Simon's army. One of their officers, a man named James, volunteered for the mission. Unfortunately for the Idumaeans, as soon as James met up with Simon's army he made a deal with Simon to betray his own people in exchange for some kind of position of honor in Idumaea.[44]

James went back to the Idumaean army, and the report he gave wildly exaggerated the strength of Simon's army. Based on James's false information, the leaders and the majority of Idumaeans decided to receive Simon without a fight and make him their leader. While the Idumaeans were meeting, James sent a messenger to Simon telling him to come; he would see to it that the Idumaeans were dispersed.

As soon as Simon's army approached the Idumaean camp, James mounted his horse and fled, followed by those he had corrupted. As a result, a terror fell upon the whole multitude, and before it came to a fight the Idumaeans scattered, each man going back to his own home.[45]

After invading Idumaea without having to draw a sword, Simon conquered the small city of Hebron. By local tradition Hebron was the most ancient of cities, older even than Memphis in Egypt.[46] It was associated with both Abraham and Herod the Great, as we have seen, but Simon was not interested in those historical associations. Once he had gathered up a large quantity of booty and grain from Hebron, Simon then embarked upon a campaign of devastation throughout Idumaea. Cities, towns, villages, and even rural homesteads were attacked. Everywhere he went Simon seized provisions for his followers, who had grown to some 40,000, in addition to his troops. What was not taken was trampled down.[47]

None of this was overlooked by the Zealots in Jerusalem. The scale of Simon's successes against the widely feared Idumaeans made the Zealots think twice about attacking him openly. So they resorted to setting up ambushes in the passes. During one of these they had the fortune or, as it turned out, misfortune of capturing Simon's wife and a number of her servants. Simon's womenfolk were quickly brought into Jerusalem.[48]

The Zealots expected Simon to come to Jerusalem and lay down his arms to get his wife back. They obviously had not taken Simon's measure. Simon came to the city. But when he did, rather than negotiate for her release, he proceeded to torture and kill everyone he encountered outside the walls. In some cases he cut the hands off those who were captured and then sent them back inside the city with a message: unless they returned his wife back to him immediately, he would knock down the walls of the city and mete out a similar punishment to every person in the city, regardless of age, guilt, or innocence.[49] That was Simon's idea of how to negotiate.

It was not only the civilians in the city who were terrified by this threat. The Zealots were, too. Simon's wife was sent back to him without further negotiations. Mollified or perhaps simply preoccupied for the moment, Simon took a break from his unrelenting slaughter.[50]

VESPASIAN AND SIMON TO THE FOREFRONT

While Simon was terrorizing everyone he encountered, on the other side of the Mediterranean the Romans were also busy slaughtering each other. The generals of Galba's successor Otho were defeated at Cremona in Cisalpine Gaul on 14 April 69 by the forces of Aulus Vitellius, commander of the Roman army on the lower Rhine. (See map 3.) That defeat led to Otho's suicide and Vitellius's march upon the city of Rome itself with his army.[51]

Vespasian, meanwhile, who would not hear about these events in Italy for at least several weeks and perhaps was frustrated by the lack of direction from a rapidly changing cast of emperors, did not sit still in Caesarea. Having established control over the areas surrounding Jerusalem the year before, Vespasian probably did not want to lose the strategic momentum and psychological advantage that his prior victories had bought him.

Therefore, sometime late in June 69, perhaps around the 23rd, or the 5th of Daisius, a year after his last major operations, Vespasian moved southeastward against the toparchies of Gophna (Jifna, north of Ramallah) and Acrabetta/Acrabatene (some 12 miles north and northeast of Jerusalem). After pacifying these toparchies, the Roman commander then captured the small cities of Bethel (Beitin/Beit-el, southeast of Gophna) and Ephraim (et-Taiyyibe), installing garrisons in both. He then rode up to Jerusalem's walls, killing many whom he came across and taking others prisoner.[52] It would be as close as the future emperor Vespasian would ever get to entering the holy city.[53]

Cerialis, the legate or commander of the Fifth Legion, was then sent on a scorched-earth campaign through upper or northern Idumaea. Caphethra (Hurvat Itri) was burned to the ground and Capharabis surrendered. Hebron, captured earlier by Simon, was taken again, this time by the Romans, who killed young and old alike after they entered the city. The Romans then burned the city to the ground for good measure. The only fortresses still held by Rome's enemies were Herodeion, Machaerus, and Masada. Jerusalem, of course, remained the main Roman strategic objective.[54]

Why didn't Vespasian try to capture Jerusalem then? The short and correct answer is that, even though Vespasian had patiently worked to cut Jerusalem off twice, he had learned from Cestius's example. Besieging and capturing Jerusalem would be an altogether different kind of operation, one that he was not quite prepared for. Perhaps Vespasian also did not think that the infighting among the Jews there had run its course. Most importantly, however, in the back of Vespasian's mind there probably was the nagging thought that it might not be a good idea to get involved in what might turn out to be a protracted siege while the military and political situation in Rome was being sorted out. So, like Fabius, Vespasian delayed.

Simon, meanwhile, reunited with his beloved wife, soon returned to Idumaea and began to drive toward Jerusalem whoever was left alive after the Roman sweep through the country. Following the Romans toward the capital, he recovered his blood lust and, after surrounding Jerusalem's walls yet again, started killing anyone he met outside the walls on their way to work in the countryside. Not without justification Josephus claims that Simon became more an object of fear to the Jerusalemites than even the Romans.[55] The Roman leaders ordered their soldiers to kill Jews for reasons of policy, though ethnic hatred may have been a factor motivating some soldiers. Simon reveled in the bloodshed.

Within the city walls the Zealots acted more harshly than either Simon or the Romans, according to Josephus—though that judgment perhaps tells us more about Josephus's anti-Zealot bias than the real situation. The Galilaeans among the Zealots, who had brought John of Gischala to prominence in Jerusalem, plundered the houses of the rich, murdered men, and violated women. Then, having satiated themselves by these kinds of practices, they supposedly began to dress and make themselves up as women. Josephus tells us that the Zealots imitated not only the ornaments but also the lusts of women and were guilty of unlawful pleasures.[56] Those who fled the city from the Zealots were slain outside the walls by Simon and his men.[57]

Finally, some of John of Gischala's followers had enough. Apparently the sight of the Zealots in pearls was too much for the fierce Idumaeans who had remained in the city. They attacked John, killing many of the Zealots. They drove the remainder into the palace built by Izates's relative Grapte (the royal palace of Queen Helena).[58] The Idumaeans followed the Zealots there and then herded them back into the Temple. Zealots who had been dispersed throughout the city then made their way toward John and his followers in the Temple and massed for a counterattack upon the Idumaeans.[59]

The Idumaeans, meanwhile, met with some of the surviving chief priests and made a fateful decision: with the backing of Jerusalemites who had been dispossessed of their homes and possessions they decided to send the chief priest Matthias to Simon, inviting him into the city as their ally against the Zealots. To this appeal Simon readily consented, entering Jerusalem in Xanthicus/April 69 CE.[60]

Once Simon and his followers were within the city walls, they immediately initiated attacks against the Zealots on the Temple Mount. The Zealots, however, held the higher ground and, having built four towers—the first at the northeast corner, one at the Xystus on the western side, one opposite the lower town, and a fourth above the roof of the priest's chambers—rained rocks and missiles down upon Simon's army from catapults and ballistae. Archers and slingers stationed alongside these machines of war added to the fire.

Simon and his fighters enjoyed a numerical advantage and for that reason were able to hold onto their positions. But as casualties mounted Simon's men began to lose their enthusiasm for the battle.[61] Simon's men were less terrifying and effective than their leader.

Frustrated in his attempt to dislodge John and his Zealots from the Temple, Simon authorized the minting of bronze coins with captions reading "For" or "Of the Redemption of Zion" on the obverse sides and "Year Four" on the reverse. These coins have been interpreted as indicating that Simon saw his mission as messianic in nature. But a more convincing reading of the coins is based upon linking the caption to the dates. The coins come from year 4 of the redemption, which was already underway. These were the coins, in other words, of a Zion that already existed, not some future Zion.[62]

VESPASIAN HAILED AS EMPEROR

While Simon and the Zealots were fighting to a bloody stalemate within Jerusalem, Vespasian, who had returned to Caesarea, learned of Vitellius's entry into the city of Rome and his assumption of the throne. Vespasian was upset about these developments in Rome, but he was deterred from contesting the succession by the distances involved and the season. By the most direct route Rome was more than 1,388 miles away from Caesarea, and to intervene Vespasian would have had to make his way to the capital across the Mediterranean during the winter months when sailing was hazardous. According to fourth-century CE military theorist Vegetius, travel by sea was only safe between mid-March and mid-November.[63]

Vespasian's men did not share their commander's reservations. They believed that Vitellius had been raised to the purple by soldiers who had little experience of war, and they considered Vespasian's claim to the throne to be far superior to that of the new emperor. Contradicting the later, official Flavian account that Vespasian was first hailed as emperor in Alexandria on 1 July 69, Josephus tells us that the soldiers in Caesarea banded together, proclaimed Vespasian emperor, and urged him to save the empire.[64]

At first, we are told, Vespasian demurred. This was a tendentious topos of Roman historiography. Good, patriotic Romans, such as Claudius in 41, were not supposed to want to become the emperor.[65] But Vespasian's officers and the soldiers, with their swords drawn, insisted that he take the job. And thus Vespasian gave in to their proclamation.[66]

Nero had underestimated the tax-collector's son. Vespasian had observed what happened to Roman generals such as Corbulo who aroused Nero's fears. Vespasian's gracelessness back in Corinth in 67 during the emperor's recital may have been intentional, calculated to assuage Nero's anxieties. Vespasian had played the fool and had got the Judaean commission. He did what had to be done in the Galilee and then prepared for the much larger and riskier task of besieging Jerusalem; meanwhile he left Nero's fate to the gods. After the immortals canceled Nero's artistic career permanently Vespasian finally took a risk and reached for the crown. He knew he could count upon the support of his own legionaries, and he thought that he would be backed by the legions of Syria and Egypt; many of the soldiers serving under him were drawn from Syria, and they would be supported by their comrades. So he gave in to his soldiers' demands. As soon as he did, the soldiers clamored to be led against the enemy: not the Jews of Jerusalem but Vitellius in Italy.

Vespasian, who understood imperial logistics and grand strategy better than his men, instead had his eye fixed on Egypt.[67] Egypt supplied one-third of Rome's yearly grain requirements, and ordinarily there were two legions stationed in Alexandria. If Vespasian controlled Egypt, he could starve Rome into submission without unsheathing a sword. But if it came to a fight, with Alexandria's legionaries and his own combat-tested legions at his back, Vespasian would present a very formidable challenge to Vitellius, or anyone else for that matter.[68] Vespasian's characteristic caution and preference for fighting by attacking the "stomach" are again revealed. He may not have had much of an ear for music—or perhaps he did—but he certainly understood logistics and strategy.

Therefore Vespasian wrote to the governor of Egypt, Tiberius Iulius Alexander, asking for his cooperation and help. The governor read Vespasian's letter out loud to his soldiers and demanded that they swear an oath of allegiance to him. The soldiers there readily swore allegiance.[69] Vespasian also went to the trouble of sending an embassy to King Vologaeses of Parthia, in response to which Vologaeses offered to send Vespasian 40,000 cavalry to help out with the war against the Jews.[70] Vespasian did not take the king up on his offer, but after the Roman victory in Jerusalem in 70 Vologaeses did give Titus a gold victory crown at Zeugma.[71]

News of what had happened in Egypt quickly spread, and ominously for Vitellius, the Roman legions in Moesia (roughly Serbia and Bulgaria) and Pannonia (Austria) followed the Alexandrian legions' example. Support for Vespasian was no longer solely an eastern phenomenon. Meanwhile Vespasian, leaving Caesarea for Berytus, was greeted by embassies from Syria and other provinces, who brought him honorary crowns and decrees of congratulation. Gaius Licinius Mucianus, who had replaced Cestius as the legate of Syria by the summer of 67, also came, reporting popular enthusiasm for Vespasian and that oaths of allegiance to him had been taken in every city.[72]

Congratulations or expressions of loyalty were not forthcoming from Judaea. It is more likely that there were sighs of relief. Inevitably Nero's death and the struggle over his replacement would draw Vespasian away from Jerusalem. A respite had been granted.

JOSEPHUS UNSHACKLED

It seems to have been at this time that Josephus won his freedom. Recalling Josephus's prediction that he would become emperor, Vespasian, with his son Titus beside him, brought together his officers and friends, including Mucianus, the governor of Syria, and ordered that Josephus be liberated. Iotapata's losing general had his chains hacked off with an axe.[73] From this point onward Josephus became a kind of unofficial adviser to Vespasian about the war in Judaea. After Titus took over active command of the war, Josephus transitioned from counselor to chief interlocutor with the besieged Jews of Jerusalem on behalf of the soon-to-be new Roman rulers.[74] Josephus's roll of the lots at Iotapata had paid off spectacularly. He might have been tortured to death, executed, or sent off to some amphitheater to fight to the death against a fellow Jew or a lion. Instead, he became an adviser to the son of the emperor-to-be. Agrippa I's reversal of fortune paled in comparison.

VESPASIAN'S ASCENT TO THE THRONE
AND TITUS'S COMMAND

After freeing Josephus, Vespasian made his way to Antioch in Syria. There he decided that the best way to prosecute the war against Vitellius was to send Mucianus with a force of cavalry and infantry to Italy. From the Roman historian Tacitus we know that Mucianus was followed by the Sixth Legion and some 13,000 veterans. Because it was winter, it was decided that Mucianus's army should take the (mainly) overland, though longer, route to Italy, through Cappadocia and Phrygia in Asia Minor.[75]

While Mucianus was en route, Antonius Primus, commander of the Seventh Legion in Pannonia, bordering on the Danube to the north and east—later joined by the Third Legion from Moesia (in the Balkans south of the Danube)—marched toward Rome. Along the way he was met by Vitellius's general Caecina Alienus near Cremona (in northern Italy). After Caecina and his army first went over to Antonius Primus's side, deserting Vitellius's cause, the army changed its mind, chained up Caecina, and decided to fight against Primus and his legions. Outside the walls of Cremona and then within the city, the forces of Primus prevailed, and the whole of the Vitellian army was destroyed (on 24 October 69). Caecina, freed from his bonds, was sent to Vespasian, bringing news of the victory.[76]

In Rome Primus's victory encouraged Vespasian's older brother Sabinus to take a more active role in advancing his brother's interests.[77] It was a fatal mistake.

Gathering up the cohorts of the night brigades in the city on the evening of 18 December 69, Sabinus proceeded to seize the Capitoline hill. (See map 5.) The next day he was joined by many notables, including Vespasian's son, the future emperor Domitian. Unfortunately for Sabinus, Domitian, and their followers, Vitellius's supporters in the city included soldiers from his crack German legions. The Germans quickly counterattacked and, despite fierce resistance, overwhelmed Sabinus's force on the Capitoline, cutting them to pieces. Domitian escaped, disguised as a devotee of the Egyptian goddess Isis.[78] Sabinus was not as fortunate and was captured and executed by Vitellius in front of his palace.[79] Before Sabinus's death, Vitellius's soldiers managed to burn down Rome's greatest temple (19 December), the home of Jupiter Optimus Maximus, after they had plundered its votive offerings.[80] Along with the temple were destroyed 3,000 bronze tablets on which were inscribed decrees of the senate dating back nearly to the city's foundation.[81]

On 20 December, however, Antonius Primus entered the city with his legions. There were battles in three sections of the city. Each ended in the same result: all the Vitellians were killed. Vitellius himself was slain on the Gemonian stairs leading from the Capitoline citadel to the forum. Following the time-honored Roman practice, his body was thrown into the swirling green and often brown waters of the Tiber River.

At least 50,000 were killed amidst these struggles, and the slaughter continued the next day within the city, as Primus's soldiers sought out and indiscriminately massacred supporters of Vitellius. Fortunately for the Roman people, Mucianus arrived in the city that day and put an end to the mayhem. He introduced Domitian to the populace as their ruler until the arrival of his father Vespasian. Within the capital city Vespasian now was acclaimed as emperor.[82]

TITUS BECOMES THE NEW COMMANDER IN CHIEF

Vespasian received the news of what had happened in Rome while in Alexandria, where he had been since the autumn of 69. He immediately planned to take a ship to Rome as soon as the winter was over; yet he did not leave until the summer of 70, as it turned out, arriving in the capital by late September or early October. At the same time he decided to send Titus, accompanied by Josephus, to finish the war in Judaea.[83]

At the time Titus was not quite 30 years old and thus unusually young to be the commander of a major war. Most Roman generals were men in their early forties.[84] Within a week or so Titus marched to Caesarea. Caesarea was to serve as the mustering point and operational base for the army that would be tasked with the conquest of Jerusalem.[85] It was a large port with storage facilities for the supplies that would be needed for the campaign, and by this time it was inhabited by a population that would be more than happy to help out with Jerusalem's siege.[86]

The war of succession in Rome had led to the deaths of tens of thousands of Romans and the destruction of the most important temple in the capital city. Rome, however, had other temples, Jerusalem only one.

CHAPTER 16

"The Son Is Coming"

SPLITTING OF THE REBEL FACTION

While Titus was assembling his army in Caesarea, the rebels within Jerusalem prepared for the Roman attack first by arguing among themselves and then by fighting. The Zealot leader Eleazar, son of Simon, was no longer willing to countenance John of Gischala's alleged crimes and therefore seceded from the Galilaean's faction. Joudes; Simon, the son of Esron; and Ezekias joined Eleazar. Each of these leaders brought his own followers from among the Zealots into the inner court of the Temple. These subfactions positioned themselves above the Temple's sacred gates on the building's façade. John and his followers attacked Eleazar's band from below but to little effect because Eleazar's men, though outnumbered, held the high ground.[1] From their position Eleazar and his followers also had the advantage of controlling the agricultural first fruits that were deposited in the Temple.[2]

Simon, son of Giora, and his followers, who held the Upper City and a large section of the Lower City as well, meanwhile attacked John with renewed vigor. John and his party repelled these attacks from their position above Simon using hand missiles. John also deployed his quick-fire artillery, catapults, and stone-throwers against Eleazar's men, who hurled javelins at them from above. The arrows and stones from John's artillery also indiscriminately wounded or killed Eleazar's fighters and those who had been admitted into the inner Temple to worship, including priests and those there to make sacrifices.[3]

While the missiles, stones, and arrows were whizzing through the air and blood was being shed both inside and outside the sanctuary, the daily sacrifices somehow continued. The area around the Temple, however, was reduced to ashes by fires, and almost all of the city's grain supply was consumed or burned up by John and Simon in their attempts to deprive each other's men of provisions.[4] It doesn't seem to have occurred to anyone that these stores of wheat and barley, which Josephus claimed were enough to feed the city for many years, might be needed later on when the Romans inevitably showed up again. Alternatively, we could understand their actions as simply part of their strategy to prevail in the present struggle.

Those who favored peace with Rome or tried to escape from the city were put to death by the heads of the factions. John meanwhile seized wooden beams that originally had been cut from trees on Mt. Libanus (Lebanon) by King Agrippa II, for the purpose of supporting and elevating the sanctuary, to build defensive towers instead. John had these towers placed against the rear of the Temple's inner court so that he and his men could attack Eleazar and his followers not only from below but also from a position of equal height, opposite the western recess.[5] But before John or any of his men could make full use of the towers the Romans appeared on the horizon.

TITUS'S ARMY

While the rebel factions were fighting in and around the Temple, on Titus's order thousands of Roman legionary soldiers, auxiliaries, and Roman allies were converging on Jerusalem in the spring of 70 from the north, east, and west. The legionaries came from the same legions that Vespasian had used to ravage Judaea (V, X, XV), plus Legio XII Fulminata. Legio XII was the legion that had been ambushed and mauled by the rebels when it retreated from Jerusalem under the command of Cestius.[6]

Because Vespasian had drafted 5,000 soldiers from Legions V, X, and XV to serve with Mucianus during the civil war in Italy, 2,000 handpicked men or one vexillation of 1,000 legionaries each from Legions III Cyrenaica and XXII Deiotariana in Alexandria, as well as 3,000 legionary guards each from Legions IV Scythica and VI Ferrata in Syria, were brought in to make up for the shortfalls to the four legions (V, X, XV, XII).[7] Given the history of relations between the Alexandrian legions and the Jews of Alexandria, the call-up of the Alexandrian legionaries for the campaign had ominous implications for the kind of war that Titus intended to wage against the Jews of Jerusalem.

The four Roman legions mustered for the campaign were supported by 20 cohorts of irregular Syrian infantry (*epikouroi*), eight cavalry wings, and contingents brought by the client kings Agrippa II, Sohaemus of Emesa, and Antiochus of Commagene. A strong force (*valida manus*) of Nabataean Arabs also appeared.[8] Tacitus, who is our source for the royal and Nabataean contributions, does not specify numbers. He also reports that many Romans came from Rome and Italy to take part in the impending operation, though again we are not told how many.[9] Presumably these volunteers were not expecting a difficult operation and thought that there were promotions, decorations, and booty to be gained from taking part in the Judaean war. Their first assumption turned out to be wrong.

At a minimum Titus's legionary army comprised 19,200 Roman legionary soldiers (4 × 4,800), or perhaps as many as 24,000 legionaries, if we accept the figure of 6,000 soldiers per legion.[10] The Syrian auxiliary cohorts added 10,000–20,000 infantrymen to Titus's force, and there would have been at least 4,000 cavalrymen in the eight cavalry wings (*alae*).[11] Neither Josephus nor Tacitus tells us how many men the client kings (Agrippa II, Sohaemus, Antiochus, and Malchus II of Nabataea) brought with them. If they led roughly the same number of soldiers that they contributed to Vespasian's force, the total number of allied infantry and cavalry would have been 11,000 infantry and 4,000 cavalry. At a minimum, therefore, Titus mustered 40,200 infantry and 8,000 cavalrymen for the siege of Jerusalem.[12]

The minimum size of the force Titus assembled (48,200) for the siege was larger than the one Cestius put together for his intervention (29,548) but smaller than Vespasian's (about 60,000). Nevertheless, Titus's siege force was significantly larger than the force Claudius had assembled for the invasion of Britain in 48 CE.[13] Notably, it had fewer auxiliaries (10,000–20,000 compared to 22,360) than Vespasian's army, but more Roman legionaries (at least 19,200 to 14,400). What these comparative totals suggest is that Titus expected Roman citizen infantrymen to bear the brunt of the fighting in capturing Jerusalem. The siege of Jerusalem was to be a Roman legionary operation: it could not be offloaded onto Rome's auxiliaries or allies. Implicitly the makeup of the force indicates that Titus recognized something that some modern historians have not understood: as much as some of the Judaeans' regional neighbors may have hated them, they were not and could not be a strategic threat to Jerusalem and the Jewish rebels.

Only Roman arms were up to the task of penetrating Jerusalem's walls and breaking the rebellion.

If we add up all of the minimum dietary requirements for the legionaries, auxiliary infantry and cavalry, allied contingents, pack animals, and horses, they indicate that Titus would have needed to supply his soldiers with about 119,720–168,400 pounds of food and 96,400–134,000 liquid liters each day, excluding the needs of all military slaves and servants. The pack animals and horses would have required 46,800–66,666 kg of hard fodder, 136,400–193,998 kg of green fodder, and 428,000–606,660 liters of water daily.[14] (See appendix K for the calculations.) Satisfying these supply requirements for the entire army along only one route to Jerusalem would have been very difficult and also strategically dangerous. For that reason Titus chose to advance toward Jerusalem from different directions.

THE ROADS TO JERUSALEM

Titus no doubt planned to converge upon Jerusalem from different directions on the compass to avoid problems of supply and a repeat of the Cestius debacle. Even if the rebels in Jerusalem knew that the Romans were coming, it would be difficult for them to decide which was the most important column to attack. Moreover, as we shall see, Titus apparently saw to it that the columns would arrive at Jerusalem from disparate directions at different times. Titus clearly wanted to make it difficult for his enemies to know how and where to focus resistance.

Titus himself marched out from Caesarea along with Legio XV Apollinaris, commanded by M. Titus Phrygius, and Legio XII Fulminata.[15] The commander of the Twelfth Legion is not named by Josephus.[16] Tiberius Iulius Alexander, the former governor of Judaea (46–48), who had been the first Roman governor to recognize Vespasian as emperor in 69 (while he was prefect of Egypt), accompanied Titus. Unofficially Tiberius was there as an adviser; officially he may have been Titus's chief of staff.[17] Agrippa II and Sohaemus of Emesa, and their contingents, also traveled with the Roman leader.[18] Having been freed from his chains, Josephus too made the trip to Jerusalem and witnessed the subsequent siege of the city. He later claimed that no incident related to it escaped his knowledge.[19]

Sextus Vettulenus Cerialis led Legio V Macedonica southward toward Jerusalem by way of Emmaus. A. Larcius Lepidus Sulpicianus took the long road, bringing Legio X Fretensis to Jerusalem from the west via Jericho.[20] (See map 1.)

The kings' contingents and the auxiliaries led Titus's force as it marched through Samaritis to Gophna, about 13 miles north of Jerusalem. These men were followed by road clearers and camp measurers and the baggage train of the officers. Behind the soldiers who provided security for these outfits came Titus, who was accompanied by picked soldiers and lancers. The legionary cavalry followed. The war machines came along next and, after the engines, the military tribunes and prefects, who also had a picked escort. Trumpeters next preceded the ensigns, who surrounded the eagles (the legionary standards) of the legions. The main body of the legionary infantry from the Twelfth and Fifteenth Legions followed the eagles, marching along in ranks six abreast. The baggage train of the legions marched behind the infantry. That train, which included at least 3,200 pack animals for two legions, must have been several miles long and slow moving.[21] Last came mercenaries, who were followed by a rearguard.[22]

After resting at Gophna for one night, Titus and the column marched for another full day and then camped in the "Valley of Thorns" near the village of Gabath (Gibeah) or the Hill of Saul, the so-called birthplace of Saul, some three miles north of Jerusalem.[23]

Before he brought the legions to the city walls of Jerusalem and encamped there, Titus offered the Jews terms of surrender, according to the third-century CE Roman historian Cassius Dio.[24] Given what had already transpired, Titus probably knew that it was very unlikely that the rebels would come to terms. In addition to the large number of angry, vengeance-seeking Jerusalemites whom Florus had managed to enrage during his governorship in 66, Vespasian's scorched-earth tactics in the Galilee and elsewhere ensured that by the spring of 70 Rome had more than 20,000 hardened enemies in Jerusalem.[25] Most of them probably hated Rome not because Nero had wanted more money from them but because they had lost family members and property to Roman arms and their lives had been turned upside down by the war. Those who had not yet been directly affected by the war probably were cowering in fear of both the rebels and the Romans.

Titus may have made the peace offer to sow discord among the Jews and with an eye on history too. It is impossible to believe that Titus did not anticipate an eventual Roman victory. If the victory were a bloody one, however, Titus probably wanted to be able to claim later that he had given the Jews every opportunity to avoid bloodshed. That would be consistent with his many attempts to get the rebels to give up even after the siege had begun.

TITUS'S RECONNAISSANCE

After Titus's peace offer was left unanswered he took a reconnaissance team of 600 handpicked cavalrymen along the road that led to what is now the Damascus Gate. The purpose of the mission was to assess the city's defenses. As it turned out, the patrol subjected Titus to some of the dangers that often befall those who want to have a look at what is on the "other side of the hill"—what the terrain looks like and how the enemy is deployed.[26]

As long as Titus's cavalry wing moved along the high road directly toward the gate area there was no opposition. But when Titus, accompanied by a small group of followers, split off from the main column and advanced at an oblique angle toward the tower known as Psephinus, at the northwestern corner of the city's outer or third wall, a large number of Jews sallied out from the city through the gate of the Women's Towers, along the same wall to the east, that faced the tombs of the Adiabenians ("Helena's monuments"). (See map 4.) The attackers must have come from among Simon's soldiers since the followers of John of Gischala and Eleazar were settled down in a defensive position within the Temple complex. The Jews broke through the cavalry still advancing along the high road and cut Titus and his companions off from the main scouting force.[27]

Because the land outside the walls was bisected with gardening trenches, cross walls, and fences (in front of Titus) it was impossible for Titus to advance farther. He therefore had no choice but to turn back and try to fight his way through the masses of Jews who had cut him off and so to rejoin the larger cavalry column. Wearing neither a helmet nor a breastplate, Titus was fortunate to make it safely, using his sword to protect himself, as a multitude of arrows whistled by. Two of the cavalrymen who rode with him were not so lucky. One was killed after his horse was speared, and another was dispatched after he dismounted for reasons that are not explained.[28] Neither for the first nor for the last time during the battle of Jerusalem, Titus showed that his personal leadership style involved him fighting either at the frontlines of battle or just behind them, as Roman generals such as Marius and Iulius Caesar had done before him.[29] Officers of modern armies and military historians might deem Titus's reconnaissance mission risky at best, reckless at worst. But Roman officers right up to the top of the command structure were expected to fight alongside their men. The son of the emperor was no exception. That was an essential part of the Roman way of war. Everyone fought.

THE FIRST ROMAN CAMPS

Once Titus was safely back in camp, he was joined that night by the soldiers of the Fifth Legion, who had come from Emmaus. The next day Titus and the Fifth Legion made their way to the high ground of Mt. Scopus, about four-fifths of a mile northeast of Jerusalem's first-century CE urban center. Because of its excellent overview of the city, Mt. Scopus was the time-tested tactical base for attacks upon the city. Deep valleys or hills impeded other approaches to the inner city. Like the Assyrians, Babylonians, Romans (Pompey), and even Jews (Herod in the spring of 37 BCE) before him, Titus began his investment of Jerusalem from the north-northeast. It was the time of the Passover, and the population of the city was greatly enlarged by the number of pilgrims who had made their way to the city.[30] Josephus did not need to spell out for his readers the fateful irony of their being drawn into a city celebrating the liberation of the Jews from Egyptian captivity, now surrounded by the Roman besiegers.

On Mt. Scopus Titus ordered a camp to be built for the Twelfth and Fifteenth Legions. The Fifth Legion was stationed three stadia, or about 1,800 feet, behind their fellow soldiers. The Tenth Legion, which had arrived from Jericho, was ordered to encamp upon the Mount of Olives, to the southeast of Mt. Scopus, about seven-tenths of a mile from the city center.[31] These positions were chosen to give the Romans the advantage of holding high ground on the north and southeast, with an excellent overview of the Temple and blocking a natural escape route to the east.

THE FIRST ATTACK OF THE REBELS

The sudden appearance of the Romans in large numbers, digging in at their camps, concentrated the minds of the rebel factions and shocked them into united action. (See figure 11.) They stopped trying to wipe each other out and made plans to take on the Romans. The first plan was to attack the Romans while they were still constructing their camps. It was executed immediately.[32] Weapons in hand, a large number of Jews raced down into the Valley of the Kidron and then straight up the Mount of Olives to attack the soldiers of the Tenth Legion.

Octavian himself had raised the Tenth Legion, and it had a distinguished service record, including action at the crucial Battle of Actium in 31 BCE. When the Jews attacked, the Romans were still working on the camp in small

FIGURE 11. Jerusalem and the Temple Mount from the Mt. of Olives, where the
Roman Tenth Legion made its camp in 70. David Bivin/BiblePlaces.com.

groups and were without their swords and spears handy. That probably was a
sign of overconfidence but also of negligence, since the Romans were working within open view of their enemies. The legionaries were taken completely
by surprise—perhaps because no Roman would have thought that an attack
up the steep Mount of Olives was likely. It defied tactical wisdom.[33] But it
was also an indication of the Jews' high morale. From day one of the siege of
Jerusalem the Romans learned that they were up against an enemy that was
not going to wait to be attacked.

Many Roman soldiers were struck down before they could arm themselves.
Those who managed to find their weapons and form coherent tactical units
wounded many of their assailants. But reinforcements from within the city overcame the resistance, and the Romans were driven from their half-built camp.
Indeed, the safety of the Tenth Legion itself would have been imperiled at that
point had not Titus, accompanied by handpicked troops, rushed to their aid.[34]

After rebuking those who had run away for their cowardice, Titus rallied the soldiers of the Tenth. He then led his troops on a flanking attack around the Jews. From this we can probably infer that Titus was fighting on horseback. Many were slain and more were wounded before the mass of Jews was driven back downhill into the Kidron Valley. Pushed back to the western side of the valley, the rebel soldiers rallied and counterattacked. The battle then went on back and forth until midday. At some point in the afternoon, concluding that the action had run its course, Titus sent the soldiers of the Tenth Legion back up the Mount of Olives to begin work on their camp again. The reinforcements he brought with him, together with auxiliary cohorts, were deployed to provide force protection for those who worked on the camp.[35] A lesson had been learned but apparently not well enough.

Titus himself underestimated the Jews' desire to get to grips with him and his soldiers. In fact, the Jews had interpreted Titus's withdrawal from the Kidron Valley as flight. So, at the signal of a watchman positioned on the ramparts of the wall, the defenders of Jerusalem launched another attack upon the Romans up on the Mount of Olives.[36]

The soldiers whom Titus had left in a defensive line on the hill turned and fled even before the Jews reached them, leaving Titus in an exposed position, supported only by a few friends. Titus refused to flee in the face of the onslaught. Along with his companions, he aggressively confronted the attackers in front of him, slaying some of them and driving the majority back down the slope. In the face of this deadly response, some of the Jews skirted Titus and his friends, continuing their pursuit of the Romans who had fled their frontline positions up the hill. Titus attacked these men along their flank, trying to check their advance.

The Roman soldiers up on the Mount of Olives, who had begun working on the camp again, saw their fellow soldiers running up from their positions below toward them—an indication that the Roman camp was not being built at the very top of the Mount of Olives. At first they were alarmed and began to scatter. The sight of Titus and a few of his companions standing their ground and fighting with their enemy, however, shamed the legionaries of the Tenth into rallying, and gradually the Romans drove the second wave of attackers back down the hill into the ravine.

Twice within a few hours, by the example of his own courage and calm in the face of fierce attacks, Titus had encouraged the soldiers of the Tenth Legion to save themselves and their unit's reputation. Now, while the Roman commander continued to hold the point position against the Jews on the eastern side of the city, the soldiers of the Tenth Legion returned yet again to building their camp.[37]

From a tactical point of view the first attack of the rebels had failed. They had not prevented the Romans from continuing their work on the camp up on the Mount of Olives. The Romans would have gained confidence from the fact that they had repelled repeated attacks. The Jews, however, had also shown that they were not afraid of the Romans and indeed were a match for them in combat. They had taken casualties. But so had the Romans. Both sides now would have known that the battle for Jerusalem was going to be a bloody fight. Anyone who had come to Jerusalem expecting a walkover and looking for easy decorations and riches must have been brought to his senses. The siege of Jerusalem would not be a repeat of Iapha. The Roman legionaries had training, experience, and discipline on their side. The rebels had none of those attributes. What they did have was courage and the high morale that came from belief in their cause. What they could not agree upon was who should be their leader.

THE STRUGGLE WITHIN THE CITY

As the Romans and Jews took a break from fighting each other on the Mount of Olives, the rebel factions within the city quickly forgot about their common foreign enemy and renewed their internal struggle for supremacy.

On the first night of the Passover festival (14 Xanthicus/Nisan, 70 CE) Eleazar and his followers had opened the gates of the Temple, which they still controlled, permitting citizens to worship within the building during the commemorative celebration of the Jews' liberation and exodus from Egypt.[38] Taking advantage of Eleazar's pious gesture, John managed to insinuate some of his supporters among the worshippers who were admitted into the Temple. These men carried concealed weapons. Once they were safely within the building, John's men threw off their cloaks and revealed themselves to be armed. As soon as they understood what had happened, the Zealots no longer guarded the gates but fled to the safety of the Temple's vaults. In the confusion, as the Zealots deserted their positions on the battlements and John's men consolidated their advantage, many innocent citizens were trampled, beaten, or slain. Some were falsely accused of partisan affiliation and were dispatched, though in reality they were killed for reasons of personal hatred and spite, Josephus claims.[39]

While the innocent were suffering in this way, John offered a truce to the Zealots who had taken refuge within the vaults. The Zealots accepted. The war of three factions within the city thus was reduced to two, and John, now the leader of the consolidated Zealots, held the high ground of the inner Temple court, with all of its stores, against Simon.[40] In his description of this incident Josephus did not need to highlight the incongruity of Jews fighting each other within the Temple during the festival of liberation while just outside the walls of the city Titus and thousands of Roman soldiers were preparing to kill and enslave them.

PREPARING THE GROUND

While John and his men were capturing the inner court of the Temple, Titus and the Roman army were literally preparing the ground for the capture of the city. This was another dimension of the Roman way of waging war, just as crucial to victory as the tactical maneuvers the Roman infantrymen practiced until they became reflexive. For combat on fields of battle inside and outside their empire, Roman legionary soldiers were trained to close aggressively with their enemies in their checkerboard formations, to hurl their *pila* at them from some 30 feet away, to knock them off balance with their shields on contact, and then to kill them with sword thrusts to their vitals. But when the same legionaries besieged those who waited for them behind their walls, as in Jerusalem, the Roman soldiers fought them first with their pickaxes and shovels. If the Roman empire was won by the sword, it was kept by the shovel.

Determined to abandon the Roman position on Mt. Scopus and encamp nearer to the city center, Titus ordered his soldiers to level all the ground between the foot of the hill and the city walls. This must have been an enormous undertaking. Nevertheless, all fences, palisades, and trees on the ground were removed or cut down, presumably by Roman military engineers, who were protected by a handpicked force of infantry and cavalry. All gullies were filled in with dirt, and any protruding rocks were broken up with iron tools. Soon the entire area between the lowest ridges of Mt. Scopus to Herod's Monuments or Tomb was leveled.[41] Nothing was left that could impede the Romans as they maneuvered up to and around the walls and prepared to put their battering rams and artillery into action.

THE FIRST RUSE

As the Romans were smoothing out this ground, some of their soldiers fell for a simple trick. A group of the rebels had come out of the city at the

Women's Towers, located along the northern side of the so-called third or outer wall (the foundations of which had been laid by Agrippa I during the reign of Claudius), as if they had been driven out by those who wanted peace. (See map 4.)[42] Up on the ramparts of the wall their fellow plotters shouted out "Peace!," pleaded for protection, and promised to open the gates to the city. The Jews who supposedly had been forced out of the city pretended to try to force their way back into the city and appealed to be let back in, at the same time making sallies toward the Romans.

Some of the Romans were fooled by this ruse and prepared to take action. Titus was not deceived. Considering that only the day before, when he had invited the defenders of the city to come to terms, he had received no response, he ordered his men to hold their positions.

Despite their commander's order, some of the Roman soldiers who were positioned in front of the camp grabbed their arms and rushed headlong toward the gates and the Jews who were outside them. These Jews initially retreated before the Roman attack. But as soon as the Romans advanced into a position between the towers on either side of the gates, their comrades streamed forth out of the city and attacked the Romans from the rear. The Jews' friends up on the ramparts also hurled stones and missiles down upon the Romans. Many of the attacking Romans were killed, and most were wounded. It was only after a drawn-out battle that the Romans managed to fight off the Jews who had attacked them from behind and to make their way to safety, as far as the memorials of (Queen) Helena, to the north of the third wall.[43]

After this incident Titus threatened the survivors of the ill-advised attack with execution for their lack of discipline and disobedience. He was persuaded not to carry out his threats only by the soldiers' fellow legionaries, who begged for their comrades' lives. They beseeched their commander to forgive the rashness of a few and promised that they would redeem the present mistake by virtuous deeds in the future.[44]

Titus gave in to these entreaties. He probably knew that to execute a large number of his own soldiers before the siege had commenced in earnest would have undermined the soldiers' morale. It also would have handed a second victory to the Jews who had tricked his soldiers. It was better to use the soldiers' guilt to motivate them. As Churchill rightly asserted, in war errors toward the enemy must be lightly judged.[45] So instead of sending the guilty men off to be executed, Titus focused on how best to avenge those who had been killed. The answer was to proceed methodically with preparations for capturing the city.

REDEPLOYING FORWARD

To that end, the job of leveling all the ground up to the walls was completed within four days. Once it was finished, Titus sent handpicked infantry, cavalry, and archers in lines up to the city walls on the northern and western sides. Three lines of infantry led the way, followed by three lines of horsemen, with a single line of archers between the foot soldiers and mounted troops. These lines provided a security screen for the baggage train and the camp followers of the legions, who now advanced to their forward positions.[46] Titus himself encamped about 1,200 feet from the city wall, opposite the Psephinus Tower, at the northwestern corner of the third wall.

Another division of the army dug in opposite the Hippicus Tower. The tower, named after one of Herod's friends, was a quadrangular structure, some 130 feet high to the top of its battlements and about 1,200 feet from the first or old wall.[47] The Tenth Legion remained on the Mount of Olives.[48]

Even as Titus brought his legions closer to Jerusalem's walls, the leaders of the rebellion within the city and their armies reverted to factional infighting. Indeed, from their positions in the Upper City along the third wall and the old city wall, and even in part of the Lower City, Simon and his force of 10,000, commanded by 50 officers, plus 5,000 Idumaeans under 10 officers, showed greater enthusiasm for attacking John's Galilaean army of 6,000, under 20 officers, and the force of 2,400 Zealots led by Eleazar, son of Simon, and Simon, son of Arinus, that held the Temple, the area around it, Ophlas, and the Kidron Valley, than the Romans. If united, the combined factions would have added up to 23,400 fighters, with 8,400 of them in the Temple sanctuary. Any of the city's citizens who disapproved of the factions' activities became a target for all of them.[49]

As civil war raged within Jerusalem's walls, Titus went about his business outside them, looking for the right spot to commence siege operations. He selected a part of the third wall that lay opposite the so-called Tomb of John the high priest (John Hyrcanus I, 135–104 BCE), next to the Towers' Pool, also known as Hezekiah's Pool. (See map 4.) The sepulcher lay somewhere northwest of the present Jaffa Gate. Titus chose that area of the wall to begin the assault because the rampart there was built upon lower ground and the second wall was not connected to it. Titus calculated that breaching the defenses at this point would lead the Romans most directly to the second wall; to the capture of the Antonia, the fortress near the northwest corner of the Temple Mount; and finally to the Temple itself.[50] As it turned out, the most direct route was not an easy route.

After Josephus's friend, the tribune Nicanor, was wounded by an arrow when he got close enough to the city wall to carry on a conversation about peace with some of those on the wall, Titus gave orders for the suburban area outside the wall system to be wasted, for timber to be gathered, and for work to begin on earthworks. Timber (*materia*) for the earthworks was needed, but wood (*lignum*) was also necessary for cooking fires. Scenes of Roman legionaries cutting down trees and carrying them to where the timber would be used for forts and embankments feature prominently in the reliefs of Trajan's Column.[51] Javelin throwers and archers were stationed at intervals between embankments to protect the Roman soldiers after they were divided up into three work teams and began to execute Titus's orders. He also placed "scorpions" (*oxubeleis*), their quick-fire, torsion-powered artillery; catapults; and stone-throwers in front of the embankments to dissuade attackers.[52]

Although John, Eleazar, and their men within the Temple wanted to engage the Roman forces, they hesitated to move from their positions out of greater fear for the nearer enemy, namely Simon. Simon, for his part, had little choice but to respond to the Roman advances. It was primarily against those sections of the city wall that his men held that the Romans were making their rapid progress. Simon therefore brought up his own artillery to the wall. Some of these machines were ones that had been abandoned by Cestius in 66 during his retreat from Jerusalem. Others had come into the rebels' hands when the Roman fortress of Antonia was captured. Unfortunately, however, Simon's men had no training in the use of the Roman artillery. As a result the machines were, if not completely useless, not as useful as they might have been, despite some instruction from deserters.[53] Simon's men thus were reduced to hurling rocks at the Romans from the top of the city wall and shooting arrows at them. Throwing rocks didn't require a technical manual or expert training.

Periodically some of the defenders ran out from within the city and attacked the Romans as they were working. But the Romans, who had vast experience in the effective use of their own artillery, used them not only to stop such attacks but also to render ineffective the attacks from the walls.[54]

The boulders hurled by the Roman stone-throwing artillery weighed as much as a talent apiece, or around 71 pounds, and had an effective range of about 1,200 feet. The impact of these boulders was devastating, both physically and psychologically. The stones could be heard whizzing through the air as they approached their targets and could be seen clearly too, because most either were naturally white or had been painted a whitish color.

To protect themselves, Simon's men developed an early warning system. They stationed men in towers whose job it was to keep their eyes fixed on the Roman artillery and to yell out "the son is coming"—a corruption of the Hebrew for "the stone is coming" (*habben,* the son, corrupted from *ha-eben,* the stone)—whenever they saw one of the stones headed their way. As soon as the men on the wall heard the warning, everyone lay down to let the stone(s) pass by. In response to the Jews' deployment of their early warning system the Romans began to paint the stones black so that they could not be seen by the watchmen. The casualties among the rebels thereafter began to climb again.[55]

THE ATTACK COMMENCES

After the earthworks were completed, Roman military engineers (*tektones*) measured out the distances from the embankments to the wall with lead and a measuring line. The lines were thrown from the embankments, rather than walked out, because the Romans were under fire. Once the engineers were satisfied that the battering rams could reach the wall, the rams were brought up. Artillery was positioned next to the rams so that the defenders of the city could not interfere with the rams. Titus then issued the order to strike.[56]

As soon as the battering rams began to hammer away at the walls, the remaining rival factions, now forced to recognize that they faced a common enemy literally pounding at the door, put aside their internal enmities and once again united against the Romans. Simon allowed the followers of John and Eleazar to come out from the Temple and take up positions along the ramparts of the wall alongside his forces. The followers of John, Eleazar, and Simon fought together side by side as units, though probably not individually, throwing firebrands at the Roman machines and keeping those who were operating the battering rams under constant fire. Bands of attackers also ventured out from the city. These men tore up the hurdles that protected the Roman artillery machines and fell upon the artillerymen (*ballistarii*).

Titus himself was engaged in bringing relief to those who were attacked and seeing to it that cavalry and archers were positioned next to the artillery to provide security. Although one of the rams of the Fifteenth Legion managed to dislodge the corner of a tower during this action, the city wall itself was not breached.[57]

A COUNTERATTACK

A lull in the action then followed. During this hiatus the Romans dispersed from their works and camps, and the Jews within the city looked for an opportunity to attack. Believing wrongly that the Romans had left their positions because they were exhausted and fearful, the Jews rushed out en masse from a hidden gate near the Hippicus Tower, bearing firebrands to burn up the Roman artillery works. As soon as the Jews came near the works, the Roman troops who had been left behind by their comrades mobilized. These soldiers were supported by some from farther away who rushed to their defense. In the ensuing struggle the Jews succeeded in lighting some of the works on fire and would have burned up the lot but for the courage and tenacity of the Alexandrian troops. Their stalwart defense of the artillery gave Titus time to bring up enough cavalry to drive off the attackers.[58]

One of the Jews captured during this action was crucified before the city wall by Titus. Titus intended the crucifixion to be an inducement for the rest of the Jews to surrender.[59] The poor man's death, however, had no effect whatsoever upon the city's defenders. Crucifixions were an all-too-familiar part of the local visual landscape.[60] First-century CE Jews had seen crucifixions before, and they would witness many, many more before the siege was over. Roman cruelty during the siege arguably strengthened rebel resolve, a lesson Titus never fully absorbed. Throughout the war the Romans never appreciated that torturing and maiming Jews did not damage their morale.

Perhaps more damaging to the confidence of the Jews, during the retreat of the attackers back into the city an Arab bowman fighting with the Romans shot and killed the Idumaean leader John right in front of the wall as he was talking to a man he knew from among the ranks. John's death was the cause of grief both to the Idumaeans and the rest of the rebels, we are told, because of his reputation for courage and judgment.[61] The sudden death of an admired leader was more difficult to bear than the sight of a man slowly dying in the Judaean sun.

A ROMAN PANIC AND CAPTURE
OF THE THIRD WALL

On the night after this engagement the Romans experienced a moment of panic. Along each of the embankments Titus had ordered the construction of three towers, approximately 76 feet high with iron casing, from which the Romans could attack the defenders on the ramparts of the city wall from above. That night, one of the Roman towers suddenly collapsed with a tremendous crash. Not knowing what had happened and concluding that they were under attack, the Roman soldiers rushed around to arm themselves. Seeing none of their enemies, they became frightened and began to ask for the nightly password from each other. A near-panic set in until Titus ascertained that the tower's collapse and its terrifying crash were the result of a construction accident. He had this explanation disseminated among the troops.[62]

Despite this setback, the remaining towers proved to give the Romans a decisive advantage. From the towers' platforms the Romans could deploy light artillery, including stone-throwers (*ballistae*), to help clear the rampart walls of defenders. Javelin throwers and archers also could fire away freely at the Jews from the towers, being out of range of any weapon the Jews could bring to bear. Once the defenders of the ramparts had been cleared, the battering rams could be used without fear of interruption or attack. The largest of the rams, known to the Jews as "Victor" for its ability to overcome all obstructions, gradually began to have an effect upon the third, or outer, city wall.[63]

Exhausted by constant combat and sentry duty, the defenders of the wall where Victor had been pounding away decided to retreat from it. They reckoned that defense of the third wall was redundant anyway, given the fact that the city was defended by two more walls. When the Romans therefore climbed up to the breach point that Victor finally made, the defenders retreated back behind the second wall. The Romans who had climbed through the breach and made it up onto the ramparts then scampered down and opened the gates of the third wall to the rest of the army. On the 15th day of the siege (7 Artemisius/Iyyar/April–May), the Romans breached the third or outer wall.[64] The Romans promptly tore down the wall, along with a large part of the northern section of the city that had been enclosed by the wall.[65]

Once within the outer wall of the city, Titus encamped on the spot known as the Camp of the Assyrians. This was the place where Sennacherib's army supposedly had set up their camp during their siege of the city in 622 BCE.[66] The location of the camp is controversial, although a strong case has been made for the valley between the modern streets of Derekh Shkhem or the Nablus Road, and Shivtei Yisra'el, to the northwest of the second wall within the New City.[67] (See map 4.)

CAPTURE OF THE SECOND WALL

Before trying to breach the second wall, Titus apparently offered amnesty to anyone who was willing to surrender.[68] This may have been a humane gesture on Titus's part or an attempt to spare his own men and Rome all of the human and material expenses of the siege. It also could have been done with an eye to future accounts of the campaign. When no one took Titus up on his offer, the Roman attack upon the second wall began immediately. The wall started from the so-called Gennath Gate in the first or old wall and ran first due north, then eastward, and then south to the Antonia Fortress, enclosing about 60 acres of the northern part of the city. The second wall may be dated to the Hasmonean era, though some scholars attribute its construction to Herod.[69] The defenders of the city meanwhile divided up responsibility for defending it. The forces under the command of John fought from the Antonia Fortress, from the northern stoa of the Temple, and from in front of the memorials of Alexander Jannaeus. Simon's men were stationed along the wall next to the tomb of John Hyrcanus, up to the gate through which water was brought to the Hippicus Tower.[70]

Day and night there were running battles between the Romans and the defenders of the city's second wall. Roman soldiers sought to dislodge the Jews from the walls, and groups of Jews came out from the walls and engaged the Romans in hand-to-hand combat. There were feats of great courage on both sides, as soldiers tried to impress their commanders, especially Simon and Titus.[71]

Josephus relates that at one point a cavalry trooper named Longinus from one of the "wings" (alae) charged out from the Roman line on his horse and attacked the Jewish phalanx of infantry, killing two of his enemies. He then disengaged just as quickly as he had appeared and made it back to his own lines unharmed.[72] Normally cavalry soldiers were not able to penetrate lines of infantry because horses will not charge into solid objects or what they perceive to be solid objects, such as lines of infantrymen; it is probable therefore that he managed to break through the line of Jews because at least some of them decided to get out of the way of Longinus and his charging horse.[73]

Such feats may have helped bolster Roman morale and were memorable, but they did not contribute directly to achieving Roman tactical objectives.[74] To breach the second wall Titus needed to bring up a battering ram to hammer away against the strongest tower along the northern wall. As soon as the blows of the ram began to rock the tower, a group of 11 Jews led by a man named Castor, who had been hunkered down beneath the parapet, leapt up and begged for mercy. Titus forbade his archers from firing at Castor and his comrades and asked him what he wanted. Castor replied that he wanted to come down from the tower under Titus's protection. At that point, five of the Jews raised an outcry, saying that they would never be slaves of the Romans but would prefer to die as free men. While this exchange was taking place and Titus was trying to understand the situation, Castor sent word to Simon, telling him to take his time in deliberating upon what measures to take since he apparently could fool Titus for a long time.

Against Titus's orders, an archer eventually shot an arrow at Castor and hit him somewhere around the nose. After pulling the arrow out, Castor complained about what had happened. Titus chastised the archer and tried to enlist Josephus to go to Castor and to offer his hand to him, as a token of guaranteed security.

Suspecting another trick, Josephus declined to go on the mission and tried to persuade his friends not to do so either. Eventually a man called Aeneas (of all names) was found—like Josephus, another deserter—who was willing to undertake the risky mission. As soon as Aeneas approached Castor, who had shouted out for someone to take the silver that he was bringing with him, Castor promptly threw a large rock at him. The rock missed its target but hit and wounded a soldier who accompanied Aeneas.

Realizing that he had been fooled, Titus put the battering ram back into action, and soon the tower was once again on the verge of collapse. As it was coming down Castor and his men set fire to it and then jumped down through the flames into a vault below it.[75]

After the tower collapsed the defenders fled from the ramparts of the wall. Five days after they had captured the first wall, the Romans were in control of at least one section of the second wall. Titus himself made his entry inside the second wall somewhere near the central tower of the north wall accompanied by 1,000 legionaries and handpicked troops.[76]

THE ROMANS' ADVANCE

Titus then made a decision not to expand the breach in the second wall nor to bring his whole force within the area once protected by the second wall. Josephus says he did not follow up on his entry because Titus wanted to spare the city for himself and the Temple for the city itself.[77]

It is more likely, however, that Titus and the assault force held back from a full-scale attack for tactical reasons. After breaching the second wall Titus and his men found themselves in a section of the city where there were wool and blacksmiths' shops and the clothing market. These shops were all set along narrow alleys that slanted down to the rampart walls at oblique angles.[78] From Titus's position it would have been impossible to see where all of the streets or alleys led; he thus wanted to assess this urban terrain before launching any attack. In this district of the city the Jews, who knew the shops and the streets, would have the tactical advantage.[79] Titus must have recognized this immediately and wanted to avoid difficult, street-by-street, house-by-house fighting on unknown turf. We can assume that the cavalrymen and selected troops who were with Titus had little or no training in urban warfare. Moreover, Titus must have had the example in mind of what had happened to Cestius. He did not need to be reminded that Cestius had not fared very well fighting against the Jews within the populated areas of the city at the beginning of the war. His father's experience within the walls of Gamala was another salutary warning.

So Titus offered to let the members of the rebel factions exit from the city freely and promised to restore the property to the civilian population. To the enemy soldiers these offers were interpreted as signs of weakness. They indicated to the rebels that Titus was incapable of capturing the entire city.[80]

After threatening to kill all of the populace who uttered a word about surrender and slaughtering anyone who mentioned peace, the rebels therefore attacked the Roman force that had come through the second wall. As the Jews' numbers grew and they were fighting in streets and from houses they knew, the Roman sentries on the captured wall fled from their positions back to their camp. The rebels then drove the entire Roman force back to the breach point through which it had entered. The Roman force might well have been wiped out but for Titus's intervention once again.

With the help of the tribune Domitius Sabinus, who had played a key role in the siege of Iotapata, the Roman commander positioned archers at the ends of the streets that led to the breach. There, by aiming showers of arrows at their assailants, the archers provided the cover that allowed the Roman soldiers to make their way back out from within the second wall.[81]

When the Romans had been forced out from within the area protected by the second wall, the rebels within the city celebrated their victory. Josephus did what he could in his history to downplay the Roman defeat, suggesting that God had cast a shadow over the rebels' judgment because of their violations of the laws. They were blind to the large number of Romans who were behind those who had been expelled, and they also did not perceive the famine that was creeping up on them.[82] This is the beginning of Josephus's use of the famine's progression in the city to offset stories of Roman setbacks and to hammer home his argument that God was working against the rebels, even when they appeared to be successful.[83] Even without Josephus's help, however, there were solid tactical reasons for the rebels not to prolong their victory celebration.

The fact was that there was still a breach in the wall itself—and the Romans showed no signs of thinking that they had been defeated. Rather they continued their attacks on the hole in the wall incessantly. For three days the defenders repulsed the Romans. But on the fourth day the Romans, led once again by Titus, punched their way through. This time Titus, instead of entering the city and offering terms, paused and tore down the whole of the northern section of the wall. In doing so, Titus made it easier for his men to attack en masse. Then, positioning garrisons of soldiers in the towers of the still-standing southern section of the wall, he began to make plans for the conquest of the final wall.[84]

TITUS AT THE LAST WALL

Having secured his new position, Titus tried to see if he could weaken the resistance of the city's defenders or perhaps save himself from having to assault the third wall by engaging in a bit of psychological warfare. Beneath the eyes of both the rebel soldiers and the civilian population of the city— who could look out over the Roman positions from the old (third) wall and the north side of the Temple—Titus for four days had the cavalry, leading their richly covered horses and doubtlessly the infantry too, parade about in polished silver and gold armor, receiving their pay. During peacetime that pay was doled out in three installments per year, on 1 January, 1 May, and 1 September.[85] The sheer assemblage of troops, the beauty of their armor, and their order were meant to cause dismay among the onlookers.[86]

With some plausibility Josephus claims that the rebels might have been convinced to surrender after seeing this spectacle of Roman wealth and well-being. But they were sure their previous actions had doomed them. They knew that if they gave up their arms they would be killed anyway. Better by far, they concluded, to die in battle.[87]

After four days of Titus's psychological warfare and with no sign that the Jews were prepared to give up, on the fifth day Titus began to have the legions raise two sets of earthworks up against the Antonia Fortress and two more against the Tomb of John.[88] His intention was to break into the Temple by way of the Antonia and into the Upper City via the tomb. Building these embankments was an enormous task, and it would take the Romans 17 days to complete them, on 29 Artemisius, according to Josephus (though that calculation appears to create chronological issues for the events described earlier).[89] While they were hard at work, they were subjected to repeated attacks by the rebels, who continued to fight against each other and the growing hunger within Jerusalem's walls.

CHAPTER 17

"The Job Is Open"

THE ASSAULT ON THE ANTONIA FORTRESS

The intensity of the fighting picked up after the Romans had fought their way to the last of Jerusalem's city walls. When the Romans started to press the siege at the tomb of John and the Antonia Fortress, the rebels responded with a series of attacks upon the workers. The Idumaeans and Simon's troops made sallies against the Romans who were working near the monument of John. The followers of John and the Zealots simultaneously attacked the Romans around the Antonia. During these battles the Jews harassed the Romans by throwing or shooting missiles at the workers, as they had done before when they defended the first two walls. But, having had some time to practice, the rebels also put to more effective use the 300 quick-fire bolt artillery machines and 40 stone-throwers they possessed.[1]

Some historians have argued that Josephus exaggerated the number of bolt- and stone-throwers that the Jews used during this phase of the fighting. The total seems to be too high because the only artillery the Jews could have deployed must have come from the capture of Cestius's machines and those in the Antonia. But making use of whatever number of artillery pieces they possessed, the Jews successfully interrupted the erection of the earthworks.

While the Jews were shelling his workers Titus exhorted the defenders of the city to surrender.[2] These appeals presumably were made in Greek or Latin, the languages Titus knew, rather than in Hebrew or Aramaic. We can infer that Titus did not know either of these related Semitic languages from the fact that when he addressed the defeated Jews later on he used a translator.[3] How many of the rebels would have understood what the Roman commander said in Latin or Greek is unknown.

But we can also deduce that Titus's appeal had no effect whatsoever, because Josephus tells us that after Titus spoke he sent Josephus to address his fellow tribesmen in the "ancestral tongue."[4] By ancestral tongue Josephus may mean Hebrew, which we know was spoken in Judaea to the time of the Mishnah; however, we cannot rule out Aramaic, which was widely spoken throughout the region. In either case, there would have been no reason for Josephus to make his pitch if Titus's exhortation had gained any traction. But it had not. So, like the officers of the Assyrian king Sennacherib, it was Josephus's job to destroy the morale of his own people in the language of Judah.[5] His weapon of choice was an extended history lecture.

JOSEPHUS'S (REVISIONIST) HISTORY LECTURE

Josephus was sent out around the wall, just out of missile range, but still close enough to the defenders on the ramparts to make himself heard. In his later write-up of the speech the historian tells us that he begged his fellow Jews to spare themselves and the people, their country, and the Temple and not to show greater indifference toward them than strangers would. He argued that while the Romans reverenced the Jews' holy things or places, those who had been brought up in them were resolved upon their destruction. Although it was noble to fight for freedom, he said, they should have done so at first. Now the Romans were irresistible. Besides God was on the Roman side. They should repent. The Romans would bear them no malice for the past.[6]

After this initial appeal was received first with derision, then with execrations, and finally by missiles fired in his direction, Josephus took the opportunity to dilate upon the history of the nation of the Jews for the benefit of his listeners—and to demonstrate his tremendous memory. The theme of his oration was that the Jews were making war, not upon the Romans, but against God. Citing examples from Israel's past—the exodus from Egypt, the recovery of the ark from the Philistines, the destruction of Sennacherib's host around Jerusalem, and their restoration from exile by the Persian king Cyrus the Great—Josephus used the past experiences of the *ethnos* to show that if the Jews sat still, they conquered. But if they fought, they were always defeated.

Five examples of the former were cited, four of the latter.[7] The reigns and conquests of King David and Herod the Great were not mentioned in Josephus's revisionist account of the Jews' history. But the essential message was clear enough. They should sit down and surrender.

He went on to elaborate upon the examples of the city's conquest by the Babylonians—comparing himself to the prophet Jeremiah, who had warned King Zedekiah not to give battle against the Babylonians—and by Antiochos IV Epiphanes, who had cut the Jews to pieces in battle and plundered the town, leading to the sanctuary lying desolate for three and one-half years.[8]

Turning to more recent history Josephus went on to blame the Jews themselves for bringing the Roman general Pompey into their country in 63 BCE and for the sack of the city once again during the reign of Antigonus, son of Aristobulus. Pointing out to his listeners how much more impious they were than those who had been defeated in the past, Titus's emissary asked his fellow countrymen how they expected God to be their ally.[9] The point of this reminder about the Jews' experience with the Romans seems to have been that it was civil discord among the Jews themselves that had led to Pompey's profanation of the temple.

If the Romans, including Pompey, Sosius, Vespasian, and Titus, had acted unjustly toward the Jews, certainly God would have seen to their punishment, he averred: whereas, in reality, Pompey and Sosius had taken the city by storm; Vespasian had been elevated to the Roman throne from the war he had waged against them; and for Titus, the waters of Siloam and the springs outside the city, which had all but dried up before, were flowing freely. All of these were signs, Josephus claimed, that God had fled from the holy places and now stood on the side of those against whom the Jews were making war.[10]

Yet salvation was still possible if they would but confess, repent, and lay down their arms. They should have compassion for the city, the Temple, and the countless gifts of nations they were betraying. And if they were not moved by compassion for these, they should at least have pity for their families, their wives, children, and parents, who soon would be the victims of famine or war.

Josephus closed by reminding his listeners that his own mother, wife, and family were involved in these perils. But if they thought he was offering them his advice on their account, they should slay them, taking the blood of his family as the price for their salvation. And he too was prepared to die, if his death would lead to their learning wisdom.[11]

If this long lecture on the history of the Jewish nation was indeed delivered by Josephus to his countrymen from beneath the wall of Jerusalem—

which is highly doubtful, given its great length of more than 1,400 Greek words and its self-justifying content—then, like Titus's speech, it had no effect upon those who had revolted from Roman rule. Perhaps they had a different understanding of their own history. Indeed, they may well have recalled what was written in the book of Deuteronomy by its author(s): that when they went forth against their enemies and saw an army larger than their own, they should not be afraid because the Lord God, who brought them out of Israel, fought with them.[12] From more recent history they also knew that Josephus had a track record of saying that he was prepared to meet death for the sake of his fellow Jews but then having second thoughts about shaking death's hand when formally introduced.

In any case, the "revolutionaries," as Josephus calls them, were not in the least moved by his appeal. Nor did they think it safe to change course. The common people, in contrast, so the historian claims, were motivated to leave the city, though it is hard to believe that Jerusalemites needed a history lecture from Josephus to understand why it was in their interest to get out of the besieged city as quickly as possible. They saw and were experiencing bloodshed and deprivation every day. As the Romans were knocking on the walls of the Antonia it is hardly surprising that the civilian population of the city began to take extraordinary measures to leave the city if it were at all possible.[13] Yet it is no accident that Josephus juxtaposes his history lesson with an account of suffering in the city that he wants his audience to understand as confirming what he told them about the rebels and their cause.

FAMINE AND DEATH IN THE CITY

Indeed, if they were able, people sold their property or whatever other valuables they had for gold coins. Afterward they swallowed the coins, escaped from the city however they could, and then retrieved the coins later when they loosened their bowels. Upon their capture by the Romans outside the city walls, the majority of these people were sent out into the countryside by Titus.[14]

Meanwhile, whoever was suspected of trying to flee the city was killed by the men of John or Simon. On the pretext that they were planning to desert the city, wealthy individuals were also put to death. In reality, Josephus says, the revolutionaries coveted their property.[15]

After grain disappeared from public sight, houses were searched for wheat. If John's or Simon's men found any, the owners of the homes were assaulted for having hidden it. If they found nothing, the people were tortured for having hidden the wheat more successfully. Those who appeared to be well fed were assumed to have food somewhere. The emaciated were ignored because they were believed to have none. Rich people bartered their possessions for wheat, the poor for barley.[16] Of course, eventually both the rich and the poor would have run out of possessions to trade, though it is likely that the poor ran out first.

Some possible confirmation of the population's desperation has been found. In 2013 Israeli archaeologists discovered three cooking pots and a ceramic lamp in one of Jerusalem's cisterns, in the vicinity of a securely dated first-century CE building. The archaeologists speculate that some of the starving residents of the city concealed whatever food they had in these pots and ate it in secret down in the cistern.[17] The inference is that it was too dangerous to eat anything they had while above ground in their homes.

Wives grabbed food from their husbands, children from their fathers, and mothers from their infants. Whenever the revolutionaries saw a house that was closed up, they assumed that its inhabitants were eating. Breaking into such houses, the rebels would confiscate whatever food they could find, beating it out of old men and dragging women by their hair until they gave up what they held in their hands. Neither the old nor the young were spared.

Those who had already managed to swallow what they possessed were horribly tortured. Their orifices were blocked with pulse, and sharpened stakes were driven up through their backsides to make them confess to possessing a loaf of bread or to disclose where a mere handful of barley was hidden. Those who crept out from the city at night to the position of the Roman guards to gather herbs and grass were robbed of what they had gathered when they tried to reenter the city.[18]

Men of wealth and rank were accused of conspiracy or of intending to betray the city to the Romans. After they were brought up before the rebel leaders, they were executed. But the tried-and-true method for getting rid of wealthier men was for informers to be suborned to accuse such men of contemplating desertion. Those who had been plundered by Simon were passed over to John, or the other way around.[19]

At the end of this litany of horrors Josephus claimed that it was impossible to narrate all of the enormities. But just in case his readers had missed the point about those he did relate, he tells his audience that no other city endured such miseries and that since the world began there had been no generation more prolific in crime. In the end they had brought the nation of Hebrews into contempt, so that they would appear to be less impious with respect to foreigners, showing themselves what they were, slaves and scum, the false and abortive product of the nation. They themselves overthrew the polis and forced the unwilling Romans to chalk up such a melancholy victory and all but brought the dilatory fire to the sanctuary.[20] Here and again Josephus wanted to make absolutely clear who was responsible for the suffering of the Hebrews. Thucydidean reserve was not Josephus's rhetorical or personal style.

While those trapped within the city were fighting over whatever scraps of food they could find, Titus and his men were laboring steadily on their earthworks. A cavalry unit was ordered to be on the lookout for those who escaped from the city and made their way into the ravines looking for food. Among them were some of the revolutionaries. But most came from among the poorer citizens of the city. Those who were caught and resisted were beaten, tortured, and crucified by the Romans in front of the walls of the city. Five hundred or more perished daily by such executions.[21]

Josephus tells us that Titus hoped that the spectacle of these crucifixions might persuade those still within the city to surrender. The soldiers, meanwhile, amused themselves by nailing their victims to crosses in different positions. There were so many victims that the Romans ran out of space to put up the crosses and even crosses to nail prisoners to.[22]

So far from being intimidated by this horrible display, the revolutionaries tried to turn it to their advantage. Dragging the relatives of the victims and anyone else who was considering desertion up to the city walls, they forced them to look down upon the gruesome spectacle and to contemplate the fates of those who had sought refuge with the Romans. This tactic indeed dissuaded some from considering desertion. Others, however, instantly fled, preferring crucifixion to starvation.[23] Titus cut the hands off several prisoners and then sent them back to Simon and John. These unfortunate men were instructed to urge the rebel leaders to pause and repent in order to preserve their own lives, their grand city, and the Temple.[24] That atrocity had no effect either.

The Roman commander simultaneously made the rounds of the earthworks, encouraging his workers to complete their tasks. As he was doing so, from the ramparts the Jews insulted Titus and his father, Vespasian. They shouted out that they despised death, preferring it by far to slavery. Nevertheless, they yelled that they would do every harm possible to the Romans while they still breathed. They were unconcerned for their native land, because they were about to die and the universe was a better temple for God than the Temple in Jerusalem. But it would still be saved by the one who lived within it, they asserted, and while they had him as their ally in war, they would scorn all threats unsupported by deeds. For the end of it was with God.[25]

Scholars who have scoured the sources for evidence of what motivated the rebels to fight Rome have often overlooked this passage. At least some of the rebels believed that God was on their side too, regardless of whether they paid for that belief with their lives. It is also worth noting that Josephus, who is often criticized for his bias against the rebels, does not attempt to hide their point of view.

Even with the Romans hammering away at Jerusalem's last wall the Jewish rebels nevertheless were not afraid to die by the sword for the sake of their freedom. And they still had faith that God would intervene for "the redemption of Zion," as bronze coins of different denominations minted in the city during the terrible fourth year of the war proclaimed.[26]

"THE JOB IS OPEN"

As the rebels were making clear to Titus and Josephus that they intended to fight to the death, Antiochus Epiphanes IV, the son of the king of Commagene in Asia Minor, arrived on the scene, bringing with him his bodyguard of "Macedonians" as well as numerous other forces. Although they were not ethnic Macedonians, the bodyguards had been trained and armed in Macedonian military style and were all young men of the same age and height. Upon arrival Antiochus expressed his surprise to Titus that the Romans were hesitating to assault the third wall. Smiling, Titus remarked, "The job is open."[27]

Antiochus and his Macedonian Commagenians made a rush to the wall. Due to his skill and strength, Antiochus himself managed to avoid the missiles the Jews shot at him, meanwhile firing away at the Jews. With few exceptions, however, his young soldiers were not as adept. Almost all of them were overpowered, and with many wounded, they were forced to retreat.[28] Josephus reports that after their defeat the young "Macedonians" reflected that even genuine Macedonians needed Alexander's fortune to conquer.[29] By implication the Commagenians blamed their defeat on their commander's lack of favor with the gods.

THE ROMAN EARTHWORKS DESTROYED

While Antiochus was wasting the lives of his young men at the third wall, the Roman legionaries labored away at the earthworks. The first two were built up by the Fifth Legion against the fortress of Antonia. One of them was raised against the middle of the pool(s) called Struthion, or Sparrow in Greek, at the northwest corner of Antonia, and the second was erected by the Twelfth Legion about 30 feet away.[30] Against the approximately 240 × 140 feet Amygdalon or Towers' (Hezekiah) Pool, the Tenth Legion constructed the third earthwork. About 45 feet away from that, the Fifteenth Legion worked on the embankment at the so-called High Priest's Monument, the Tomb of John Hyrcanus.[31] (See map 4.) Titus's strategy was to attack from a number of different points, thereby preventing the rebels from concentrating their defensive forces.

Even as the legionaries were completing their projects in June 70, the defenders of the city were working furiously to undermine them. John's men had built tunnels underground from the Antonia Fortress to the Roman earthwork. Wooden props supported the earth in these tunnels. When the tunnels were finished, John had a great mass of pitch- and bitumen-smeared timber pushed into the tunnels directly underneath the Roman embankments. The timber was then lit on fire. The resulting conflagration quickly caused the tunnel props to catch fire. When the wooden props were sufficiently weakened or consumed by the fire, the tunnels caved in. The earthworks built above the mines then fell into the smoldering tunnels. Smoke, dust, and fire belched upward from the collapsed works. The Romans could do nothing but watch.[32]

A couple of days later Simon's men attacked the other set of embankments, where the Romans had already brought up battering rams and were hammering away. Three of Simon's charges—a man named Gephthaeus from the village of Garis in the Galilee; Magassarus, a former soldier of the king, probably a defector from Agrippa II's royal army and one of the servants of Mariamme; and Ceagiras, the lame son of Nabataeus from Adiabene—grabbed some torches, rushed forth from the city, and despite being attacked from all sides, succeeded in lighting the battering rams on fire.[33]

Alarmed by the sight of the flames arising from the engines, the Romans rushed down from their camps to put out the fires. From the ramparts the Jews did their best to stop them, and a battle raged alongside the burning battering rams. The fires then spread to the earthworks themselves, and with both the rams and the works on fire, the Romans retreated to their camps. The Jews followed in hot pursuit, and another battle took place along the picket line of Roman sentries who stood guard at the edge of the encampment. Fearing capital punishment if they abandoned their positions, the Roman sentries stood their ground and fought the pursuing Jews until some of those who had fled from the rams turned back to help out their fellow soldiers. The Romans also managed to bring up some "scorpions" (*oxubeleis*), their quick-fire torsion-powered artillery. Positioning these at the camp walls, the Romans kept the Jews, who were now surging out of the city and into the battle, at a safe distance.[34]

It was at this moment of crisis that Titus, who had been off near the Antonia inspecting a new site for yet more earthworks, appeared once again. Leading a handpicked force around the flank of the attackers, Titus and his men gradually drove the Jews back into the city. Titus's flanking attack relieved the immediate pressure on the Roman encampment. But it did not alter the tactical victory achieved by Gephthaeus, Magassarus, Ceagiras, and their friends. Within one hour the earthen constructions that it had taken the Romans almost two weeks to build had been destroyed.[35] God may have been on the Romans' side, as Josephus said. He had also been on Job's side.

A NEW ROMAN STRATEGY

Titus then gathered his officers together and held another council of war (*consilium*). Such a council is depicted on one of the reliefs from the Column of Trajan, showing the emperor Trajan sitting amidst his conversing officers, just after he crossed the Danube River during the first Dacian War.[36] At Titus's council, various options were considered in light of the recent setbacks. Some of his officers recommended an all-out assault on the walls by his entire force. A mass assault had not been tried, they argued, and the Jews would be overcome by their missiles. Others pushed for rebuilding the earthworks. Still another group advised Titus to blockade the city, preventing any supplies from reaching a population that inevitably would run out of food.[37]

Titus considered the various options. He reasoned that it would be difficult to build new earthworks because of the lack of materials. Blockading the city would expose the troops to further, continuous attacks. Titus favored pressing the siege, but he also wanted maximum security. His decision was to build a circumvallation wall around the city that blocked every exit. That was a tactic usually tried at the beginning of an ancient siege.[38] Once all the exits were blocked, Titus hoped that the city's defenders would surrender in despair or because of famine. Meanwhile, he would once again turn his attention to the earthworks. They would not be so easily destroyed by a starving enemy.[39]

The Romans turned to building the wall with great enthusiasm. Beginning at the camp of the Assyrians, where Titus himself was encamped, the wall was constructed down to the new town and then across the Kidron Valley to the Mount of Olives. The Mount was enclosed to the rock called Peristereon or Dovecote, along with the adjacent hill.[40] (See map 4.) Thereafter it was built westward down into the Valley of the Fountain (En-Rogel, south of the foot of the City of David) and then up to the triple-gated tomb of the high priest Ananus (high priest from 6–15 CE and father-in-law of the famous Caiaphas) in the Hinnom Valley.[41] Then, taking in the hill where Pompey had made his camp, the wall turned to the north, leading to the village named the "House of Pulse." After passing that village, it enclosed Herod's memorial and then was connected to the east side of Titus's camp.[42]

The wall was erected in an astonishing three days.[43] The total length of the wall was 23,673 feet or about 5 miles. On its outer side 13 forts were built. These were immediately garrisoned. Sentries patrolled the intervals between the forts at night. From the third-century CE historian Cassius Dio we also learn that Titus discovered, and then had closed off, tunnels that had been dug from beneath the city out to land presumably beyond the Roman lines.[44] Jerusalem was now sealed off from the outside world.

THE FAMINE WORSENS

To the rebel defenders of Jerusalem all uncontested routes of escape from the city were thus cut off. Since no substantial food supplies could be brought into the city, the famine within the walls worsened, and Josephus spares his readers no detail. Children and youths died wherever they collapsed, and the dead were left unburied. Those who were sick did not have the strength to bury their relatives, and those who were strong enough simply could not cope with the numbers of the deceased.[45] Those still of sound mind no doubt remembered the stores of grain that the rebel factions had burned up before the Romans had appeared.

As people were starving to death in the city, Josephus tells us, the "brigands" or *lestai* broke into the houses of the dead and dying and, rifling through their clothing, took whatever of value that they could find, even stripping the bodies of their coverings. At first the dead were buried at public expense because the rebels found the stench from all the corpses to be intolerable. When this was no longer possible the dead were simply thrown over the ramparts of the city wall, down into the ravines beneath the city. Josephus doubtlessly expected his readers to be appalled by the mental image of Jews throwing the bodies of both their loved ones and people they didn't know down into the ravines; what he didn't explain to those who were unfamiliar with Jewish burial customs and the history of Jerusalem was that it was forbidden for the dead to be buried within Jerusalem.[46] So, in fact, under terrible circumstances, while the rebels were getting rid of the dead for the sake of sanitation, what the rebels were also doing was trying to maintain the ritual purity of their city.

Josephus must not have passed on this piece of information to Titus either. For, observing the corpses rotting in the ravines, Titus is said to have raised his hands and called upon God to witness that this was not his work.[47] But of course, it was, as proudly proclaimed by inscriptions put up later in Rome that Titus must have approved. (See chapter 21.)

With supplies of grain coming in from Syria and all the adjoining provinces, he permitted his troops to bring masses of food down beneath the ramparts to display it to the starving inhabitants of the city.[48] At the same time, Titus ordered four new earthworks, much larger than their predecessors, to be built up against Antonia Fortress. Timber for the new mounds had to be hauled from 90 stadia, or more than 10 miles, away.[49]

Although the city was starving into extinction and the Romans were yet again preparing to break into it through the Antonia, the civil discord among the leaders of the revolt did not cease. Simon, whose entry into the city had been facilitated by the high priest Matthias, the son of Boethos, became convinced that the priest was siding with the Romans, perhaps because one of Matthias's sons had fled to them. Matthias was executed in view of the Romans after Simon killed his three other sons before their father's eyes.[50]

After Matthias's murder a priest named Ananias, son of Masbalus; Aristeus, a native of Emmaus and the secretary of the council (*boule*/Sanhedrin?); and 15 other distinguished men were also murdered. Josephus's father was thrown into prison, and an order was issued forbidding people to assemble together. Those who mourned together were also put to death.[51] The presence of the murdered priests and other dignitaries in Jerusalem this late into the siege suggests that they had been supporters of the rebellion. Their murder was a sign that the end was near.

One of Simon's officers, a man named Joudes, who was in charge of one of the towers, having witnessed these executions, hatched a plot with 10 of his men to surrender the ramparts they were guarding to the Romans. The next morning, after dispersing the rest of the men under his command in different directions, at the third hour Joudes shouted out to the Romans from the tower he was guarding. Unfortunately for Joudes and his accomplices, some of the Romans ignored him, while others didn't believe what they heard. Most of the Roman soldiers, however, decided not to respond because they believed they would capture the city shortly and didn't need to take any risks. Given the tricks that the rebels had played upon the Romans in the past, the lack of response was to be expected. As Titus himself began to advance toward the wall with a large force of men, Simon learned of the plot and seized the tower. The conspirators were arrested and executed, and their mutilated bodies were thrown over the ramparts.[52]

At this time Josephus, who continued to make his way around the walls exhorting his countrymen to surrender, no doubt at Titus's behest, was hit in the head by a stone and was knocked to the ground unconscious. Seeing him there, some Jews rushed out of the city to carry off his body. They probably would have succeeded but for a timely intervention by Titus yet again.

Josephus tells us that the rebels prematurely celebrated his death, while the news of his demise demoralized the populace, including his mother. It quickly became apparent to all, however, that Josephus was still alive because, as soon as he recovered from his wound sufficiently, he resumed making his rounds, shouting up to the rebels that he would be revenged upon them for the wound he had suffered. The sight of Josephus still alive animated the populace, we are told, but depressed the rebels.[53]

Even amidst these scenes people still attempted to flee from the city. Some simply jumped down from the city walls. That is hardly as shocking as Josephus wants it to be. The city was now surrounded by a wall, and the people were starving to death. Others rushed out of the city carrying rocks as if they were going to fight the Romans. But in reality they intended to surrender to them.[54]

ROMAN ATROCITIES

Many of those who tried to flee met a horrible end. In some instances, when the starving inhabitants of the city made it into the Roman camp they ate too much, too quickly, and their stomachs burst open, killing them. Those who took nourishment only little by little suffered another, equally hideous fate. One of the people who successfully made it out of the city, a Syrian by birth, was discovered picking gold out of his own excrement: as mentioned, within the city, many of the people who were intending to flee swallowed their money so that it could not be taken from them by rebels who were searching everyone and everywhere for valuables.

When the Syrian's trick was discovered by those in the Roman camp, it was rumored that all of the refugees had swallowed gold, and some of the Syrians and Arabs in the camp proceeded to cut open the bellies of the refugees in search of their gold coins. No less than 2,000 souls perished in this way.[55]

Titus, we are told, was appalled by this atrocious behavior. Summoning the commanders of both the legions and the auxiliary troops, he threatened the foreign troops guilty of these crimes with death if any dared to repeat the crimes, and he ordered the legionaries to search for those suspected of committing the atrocities and to lead them to him.

Nevertheless, the practice seems to have continued. The auxiliary troops rushed out to meet those people who had escaped from the city, killed them, and, if no Romans were looking, cut them open looking for gold. In addition, Josephus himself claims that Roman soldiers too took part in this grisly practice before Titus forbade it. Unsurprisingly, this shameful conduct on the part of Rome's allies and some of its own soldiers led many of the refugees to turn back and flee back into the city.[56]

THE PLUNDERING OF THE TEMPLE

Within the city, when there was no more plunder that could be extracted from the people, according to Josephus, John turned his attention to the Temple. He melted down Temple offerings and then the bowls, trays, and vessels used for public services. These included the bowls for wine that the Roman emperor Augustus and his wife Livia had given to the Temple. John justified his actions by saying that they should not hesitate to use divine things to support God and that those who fought on behalf of the Temple should be supported by it. The sacred wine and oil that traditionally were used to pour over the burnt offerings were also taken from the inner sanctum of the Temple—probably from the Chamber of Oil at the southwest corner of the Court of Women in the Temple complex, where it was usually stored—and distributed to his supporters, who anointed themselves with the oil and drank the wine.[57]

No doubt Josephus expected his Jewish readers to be horrified by the impiety of John and his soldiers helping themselves to the Temple supplies. Roman readers probably would have been puzzled by Josephus's horror. But as Jonathan Price has rightly pointed out, King David himself had consumed consecrated bread, and the Jews who defended the Temple during its siege by Antiochus V also ate Temple food.[58] Moreover, it is not clear from the story Josephus tells about John and his soldiers that they were guilty of eating consecrated food or just food designated for priests alone.[59] Where John was involved, if an action looked like impiety, then it went into Josephus's litany of the rebels' impieties, to be used to justify the defeat of the "tyrants" and the punishment of the impious. Near the end of his account of the war, after stating that John put to death all who proposed just and salutary measures, Josephus claimed that John went further, serving unlawful food at his table.[60] For Josephus that was impiety of a different kind altogether, because it was directed toward God.

While John's men were helping themselves to God's wine cellar, the body count of those who had died from the famine continued to rise. Mannaeus, the son of Lazarus, reported that no less than 115,880 corpses were carried out through the gate that he had been in charge of between early May and mid-July, before he fled to Titus.[61] All of these dead were poor people.

The remainder of the dead were buried by their own relatives. Burial consisted of throwing the corpses out of the city. The total number of the poor whose bodies were thus ejected from the city was calculated by Josephus at 600,000. This rounded-up figure cannot be accurate. Bodies were also piled up into houses.

The price of wheat, meanwhile, skyrocketed. One measure was reported to have sold for one talent, or enough to pay a skilled artisan for 10 years' work under normal circumstances. Later, when no wheat or herbs could be found at all, people searched through the sewers and cow dung for offal and other edible materials.[62]

CHAPTER 18

The More Gentle Minister

THE ROMANS BREACH THE INNER WALL

The Romans completed their new earthworks against the wall around the Antonia in 21 days. For the construction materials they stripped the countryside around Jerusalem of everything they needed, but especially of timber, to a distance of 11 miles from the city.[1] Josephus does not specify in what direction the Romans headed to find the supplies. But on the modern map of Israel the village of Abu Ghosh is 11.7 miles north and west from Jerusalem by car.[2] That gives us some idea of how far out from the city center the Romans needed to go for construction materials. A Roman siege first involved an assault upon the local landscape and vegetation, as Josephus himself recognized and lamented.[3]

Even before the battering rams could be put into position on the new works, on the date of the new moon of the month of Panemus or mid-July 70, John and his men went out and attacked the Romans.[4] The Jews were known for their lightning attacks.[5] Their continued aggressiveness was a sign of their high morale and commitment to their cause despite everything that they had suffered. They were not broken in spirit.

Indeed, as the Romans inched their way closer to the Temple itself the rebels continued to mint half-shekel coins so that people could pay the Temple tax.[6] Remarkably, silver coins minted by the rebels from years 1 right through 4 of the rebellion had a silver content of 98 percent, thus exceeding the precious metal content of the famed Tyrian shekels that had been used to pay the Temple tax since the late second century BCE.[7] The expectation that the Temple tax would be paid was a sign of belief in the future.

The attacks against the new embankments nevertheless were made by small groups of fighters and were intermittent. Moreover, John's men found that the Romans were drawn up in a screen to defend the earthworks and were also using artillery fire to help repel the attackers. In the face of this stalwart defense the Jews were forced to retreat without doing any substantial damage.[8] They had the desire to engage with the Romans but not the numbers to sustain their attacks. Inevitably the constant combat during the siege took its toll. The failure of John and his men indicated that the rebels had lost the initiative in the struggle.

After John and his men retreated, the Romans brought up their siege engines. As they did, the Jews who defended the Antonia greeted them with a barrage of fire and rocks, arrows, and every other kind of missile they had at hand. Despite the fusillade, the Romans got their rams into place and began to pound away against the walls.

Meanwhile, another group of Roman soldiers, crouching beneath their shields, worked away at the foundations with their hands and crowbars. Before nightfall made them suspend their labors, the Romans had removed four stones from the wall's foundation. That evening, as a result of the battering that the wall had absorbed and the collapse of the mine that John had previously dug under it, a section of the wall collapsed.[9]

The effect of the cave-in on the two sides was not what might have been expected. In anticipation of just such a collapse, John and his men had constructed a second wall behind the first. So the crumbling of part of the wall did not cause a panic among the Jews. The realization that there was another wall behind the first one tempered the Romans' euphoria at breaking down part of the first wall. But neither were they utterly despondent.

They understood that the second wall had been built recently and with haste. It therefore could not be as solidly constructed as the Antonia Fortress wall itself. They also knew that their attacks upon the new wall would be made from on top of the fallen debris of the first wall. Therefore they would not have to scale the second wall from ground level. Still, no attack was made upon the new wall until after Titus rallied his troops.[10]

In the speech made to the Roman troops that Josephus reports, Titus claimed that the factional fighting within the city, the famine, the siege, and the spontaneous collapse of the city wall all were signs that God was angry at the rebels. He was giving aid to the Romans, and it was beneath their dignity to betray their divine ally. The Roman commander went on to compare the deaths and fates of the souls of those who died in battle to those of people who died of disease. He argued that if men were doomed to die, as die they must, the sword was the "more gentle" minister of that end than any disease. For that reason it was not noble to deny to the public service what must be surrendered to fate.

At the end of his speech, Titus apparently attempted to convince his soldiers that the new wall would be easy to ascend. If they forced their way up and through, he said, resistance might break down altogether, and he promised that the leader of the successful assault would be given honors to be envied. The survivor of the attack would command those who were presently his equals, whereas blessed reputations for valor would follow those who had fallen.[11]

We cannot know whether Titus delivered such a speech to his troops at the time. We are probably right to suspect that he did not say exactly what Josephus reports, because of the length of the speech and its content.

It is hard to believe that Roman legionaries would have been inspired to close with their hated enemies by a learned disquisition on the fates of their souls. Moreover, in the speech Titus repeats what Josephus himself wrote over and over again in his history: namely, that God had gone over to the Roman side. That may have inspired some Roman soldiers. More uplifting would have been better weaponry and armor, numerical superiority, and more imaginative tactics. We also do not know what Titus's soldiers believed about any possible afterlife, and there is little evidence that Roman soldiers were motivated by appeals to Roman patriotism.[12] The tombstone inscription put up around Emmaus for Publius Oppius . . . cio, a 30-year-old Roman officer (optio) of Legio V Macedonica, who apparently took part in the siege, did not mention that he had died by the more gentle minister.[13]

Soldiers about to go into combat are seldom motivated by appeals to mother (mater), apple pie (malum), or the legionary flag (signum). Some men and women do enlist for reasons of patriotism. But across the centuries soldiers have usually fought for themselves and their comrades. If Titus made a speech to the troops before the next assault, telling them that a sword was the more gentle minister of death, the reaction was probably smirks and discretely rolling eyes. The veterans might have wanted to ask Titus how he knew that dying by the sword was the better way to die. But, as veterans, they would have kept their mouths shut and just got ready to go into battle.

SABINUS THE SYRIAN

Whatever Titus did or did not say at the time, in fact a volunteer to lead an assault upon the wall stepped forward on 3 Panemus. The soldier was a skinny, "dark" Syrian named Sabinus who had been serving in one of the auxiliary cohorts. Before setting off, Sabinus informed Titus that if he failed to carry out his mission—that is, if he were killed—he had sacrificed his life for Titus's sake.[14]

At the sixth hour of the day, or high noon, the Syrian, followed by 11 other volunteers, advanced toward the wall. Why Sabinus and his mates chose to carry out their mission in the white-hot light of Jerusalem's midday summer sun is not known. Perhaps they thought that the Jews would be lying low, trying to stay out of the sun, and that they could surprise them. If so, they were mistaken.

Sabinus and his assault team were greeted by a hail of javelins and arrows aimed at them, with some large boulders rolled down on their heads for good measure. The stones knocked back some of Sabinus's followers. Sabinus himself made it up to the top of the wall and scattered his enemies there. Unfortunately for him, however, at the very moment that he made the defenders of the wall run for their lives, he slipped, stumbled over a rock, and fell down with a crash.[15]

Seeing him on the ground and alone, the Jews regained their courage and attacked from all sides. Although Sabinus managed to wound many of his attackers, he himself was also wounded, and at that point the weight of his protective armor became a deadly disadvantage. Unable to raise his own arm to defend himself Sabinus was overwhelmed and finished off by missiles. Three more of Sabinus's colleagues made it up to the summit, only to be crushed by boulders. The eight other men in the assault team suffered various injuries but eventually made it back to the safety of the Roman lines.[16] Just as promised Sabinus had risked his life on Titus's behalf—and lost. An assault resulting in the death or wounding of all of its team members could not be counted as a success.

IULIANUS

The Roman soldiers were not depressed or deterred by what had happened to Sabinus and his team, however. Rather, they seem to have learned from the failed mission. Two days later, on 5 Panemus, 20 legionary guards of the earthworks, the standard-bearer (*signifier*) of the Fifth Legion, a trumpeter, and two auxiliary cavalrymen set off on another mission, this time at the ninth hour of the night, or 3 A.M.[17] The second group of volunteers presumably had learned that it was not wise to attack in the middle of the day.

Unlike the wide-awake soldiers Sabinus met at noon, the guards whom the second assault team encountered were fast asleep. The somnolent sentries were quickly killed, and the Roman soldiers took possession of the wall. The trumpeter then sounded his horn. That was probably why he was selected for the assault team. At the horn's blast the rest of the defenders of the wall in the area fled, incorrectly assuming that a large number of the Romans had captured the wall. Titus, on the other hand, hearing the sound of the trumpet, immediately understood that his men were inside the wall. After calling his soldiers to arms, he led a force that included his officers and handpicked troops up and through the breach.[18]

The Jews who had been defending the wall retreated into the Temple itself, with the Romans now hot on their heels, some of them through the mine that John had dug to undermine the earthworks. At the entrances to the Temple the followers of John and Simon fought desperately to keep the Romans out of the Temple itself. They knew that if the Romans were able to gain entry into the Temple enclosure, it was the end of their lives, the siege, and the war.[19]

At close quarters, missiles and spears were no longer used. The combat was hand to hand and sword to sword. Romans and Jews looked each other in the eye and fought for their own lives and for those of their friends. There was no space for tactical maneuvers, flight, or pursuit. For those at the front of the battle it was kill or be killed. Those at the back pressed their fellow soldiers forward. The fighting went on, back and forth, stopping and starting, until the seventh hour of day, or 1 P.M. At that time, after 10 hours of on-and-off-again combat, the Romans finally broke off their attack and retreated into the Antonia.[20] In the midst of that retreat, a centurion from a Bithynian auxiliary unit in northern Asia Minor named Iulianus inspired an everlasting (literary) memorial to his courage.

Even as the rest of the Romans were retreating into the Antonia, Iulianus, who apparently had been standing next to Titus himself on the Antonia, suddenly turned around, faced his enemies, and single-handedly drove them back into the inner Temple, slaying everyone he encountered.[21] Yet the gods did not reward his valor. He too tripped and fell, his standard, metal-studded military boot(s) (*caligae*) somehow slipping on the pavement.[22] Roman military boots were not made to give good traction on stone surfaces.[23]

Once Iulianus went down, his enemies surrounded him and hacked him to death, though not quickly, because he was so well protected by his armor.[24] After hours of intense combat Titus and the retreating Romans witnessed the centurion's slow and grisly death from a distance, unable to help. After killing Iulianus the Jews carried off his body, presumably into the Temple compound. Among the Jews that Josephus calls attention to for his valor during this fighting was Judas, the son of Ari. Although Josephus does not tell us how, Judas somehow managed to escape from Jerusalem after this action and ended up fighting the Romans again after the brief siege of Machaerus.[25] The surviving Romans meanwhile were shut up back inside the Antonia.[26]

TITUS'S FINAL APPEALS

At this point Titus ordered the men who were with him to demolish the foundations of the Antonia in preparation for an all-out assault upon the Temple platform. The foundations presumably meant the lower building or glacis, but not the tower that loomed over the Temple; later we find Titus observing the struggle within the Temple from the still-standing tower. He also learned that the daily sacrifice (*olat tamid*) of two one-year-old lambs, the first sacrifice in the morning and the second at sunset, had ceased to be offered to God on 17 Panemus/Tammuz, to the consternation of later sages, either because of a lack of men, as the mistakenly copied text reads or, more likely, of (two) lambs, as edited.[27] Under the circumstances finding enough lambs, along with the traditional wine and meal offerings, to continue the sacrifice would have been more difficult than rounding up a few priests to make the sacrifice. The inability of the rebels to continue to make the sacrifices cannot have helped morale and may even have been taken as an indication that God had abandoned the Temple and the city.[28] That may be right, but it should be noted that even after the sacrifices stopped at least some of the rebels continued to fight.

In any case, Titus instructed Josephus yet again to deliver the same message to John "in the language of the Hebrews," which could be either Hebrew or Aramaic; namely, that if he possessed some evil desire for combat, he should come out with as many men as he should select and fight. But he should not involve the city and the Temple in his own destruction, polluting the holy place and sinning against God. He also granted John leave to fulfill the interrupted sacrifices with such Jews as he might choose.[29] This was the message of Caesar that Josephus, sounding a bit like the field commander of the

Assyrians who appealed to the residents of Jerusalem to surrender during the reign of Sennacherib, delivered in Hebrew or Aramaic not only to John but also to all others within hearing range.

The people, we are told, received the message despondently and in silence. John, on the other hand, cast many invectives and imprecations toward Josephus. After concluding his stream of abuse, he said that he could never fear capture because the city belonged to God.[30]

In reply Josephus called out John for assigning his own sins to the Romans. The Romans, he said, were trying to force him to reestablish the daily sacrifices to God that he had caused to be stopped. He then cited the example of Jeconiah, king of the Jews. When Jeconiah's own behavior had led the Babylonian army against him, rather than surrendering the holy places and seeing the Temple go up in flames, he surrendered himself and his family to the Babylonians and went into captivity.[31]

He reminded John that he (Josephus) was a fellow Jew and that he had no wish to live to become so wretched a war captive as to renounce his own kind or forget their traditions. He then cited an oracle of unknown origins that said that the city would be taken when someone began to slaughter his own countrymen. He asked John if the city and the Temple were not filled up with his corpses. In closing Josephus yet again returned to his explanation for all that had happened. It was God himself, with the Romans, who was bringing fire to purify the Temple and wipe out a city so filled with pollutions.[32]

Not altogether surprisingly, Josephus's speech did not lead John or any of his men to imitate Jeconiah's example. On the contrary, it enflamed their anger against the Romans and their messenger.

The "well-born" in the city had a different attitude, Josephus claims. Some were convinced that they themselves and the city were doomed—perhaps in light of the cessation of the daily sacrifice of lambs to God. But they did nothing out of fear of the guards. Others took action and somehow made their way out of the city. Among them were the chief priests Joseph and Jesus and three sons of the high priest Ishmael, the son of Phiabi; four sons of Matthias; and one son of another Matthias, son of Boethus. They were accompanied by other members of the nobility.[33] Despite what Josephus had stated or implied earlier, their desertions prove beyond doubt that not all of Jerusalem's elites deserted ship at the beginning of the rebellion when the Zealots gained control or even after the Romans broke through Jerusalem's strong walls. In fact, at least some of Jerusalem's most distinguished citizens chose to stay almost until the very end. The war of Jews against Romans was not just a revolt of "foreigners," poor Jews, and non-Jerusalemites.

Titus received the priests and those who fled with them respectfully and sent them northward to the village of Gophna in Judaea so that they would not have to live among the Romans with their theologically objectionable and impure customs. The refugees from the city were told that their property would be returned to them after the war was over.[34] We have no idea whether this promise was fulfilled. In his later works Josephus does not mention land being returned to any priests or their relatives.

When those inside the city could no longer see the prominent deserters outside the wall a rumor spread that the Romans had done away with them. For that reason the desertions stopped for a while. Titus, however, then had the refugees brought back from Gophna, and along with Josephus they made the rounds beneath the ramparts, urging their countrymen to give up or at least to withdraw from the Temple, which, they assured them, the Romans had no desire to destroy.[35]

Their appeals produced results similar to those that Josephus had achieved earlier. After hurling abuse down upon the priests and their sons, the rebels brought their scorpions, catapults, and stone-throwers up above the holy gates and immediately put them to work, leaving the area around the Temple heaped with bodies. Through Josephus, Titus then sent yet another message to John, upbraiding him for polluting the Temple precincts by his actions and guaranteeing that not a single Roman would approach or insult their holy places if they exchanged the place of conflict for somewhere else. Titus, so Josephus reports, told John that he would preserve the Temple for them even if they should not wish it.[36] In hindsight, Josephus's report of Titus's last-ditch effort to persuade the rebels not to continue to fight from within the Temple has to be understood as an attempt to absolve Titus of blame for what followed.

THE FIGHTING RESUMES

After John contemptuously rejected his exhortations, Titus "unwillingly" resumed hostilities. Because of the narrow confines of the space through which the Romans needed to advance, Titus could not bring his entire force into action.[37] Rather, from each legionary century the 30 best soldiers were selected to take part in a new assault. Over each group of 1,000 was appointed a tribune. Sextus Vettulenus Cerialis, the commander of the Fifth

Legion, was then made leader of the assault force. Cerialis was ordered by Titus to attack the guards at about the ninth hour of the night, another 3 A.M. assault.[38]

Titus at first planned to accompany his men on this mission. But his friends dissuaded him, not only because of the danger involved but also because his officers pointed out that he could help more by staying in the Antonia. Under his eyes from there, all the men would try to be good soldiers. To these arguments Titus supposedly acceded.[39] The unstated advantage that Titus gained by staying behind in the Antonia was that he could observe the development of the attack and safely make tactical changes as necessary, such as feeding in reserves if the attack stalled.[40]

THE NIGHT BATTLE

As so often in combat, Titus's assault plan went awry from the start. When Cerialis's force attacked they found the guards not asleep, as they had hoped, but ready for action after snapping to. Right away there was a close encounter, and at the alarm raised by the guards, the few defenders on the spot were quickly joined by a mass of other fighters from within the Temple. The Romans leading the assault characteristically stood their ground in the face of this charge, but in the confined space those in the rear were soon pressing up against their fellow soldiers. In the confusion and hubbub it was impossible for the Roman soldiers to distinguish friends from foes by their voices, and the darkness of the night made it even more difficult to recognize who was who. Soon some of the Romans were simply striking out against anyone they encountered. On the whole, though, the legion's best soldiers maintained their battle order and discipline more effectively than did the rebels. Locking shields together, the Romans moved forward methodically in companies and kept in mind the night's password. The Jews fought in groups, attacking and breaking off their attacks randomly. As a result, many were wounded by their own countrymen.[41]

The sporadic fighting went on in this way until morning light, when it was possible for both sides to withdraw into their own lines, differentiate enemy from friend, use their missiles, and defend themselves in a more orderly way.[42] In the cramped space the two sides then maneuvered forward and backward quickly, with neither side having room to flee or pursue. This style of fighting continued under the eyes of Titus until about the fifth hour of the day (11 A.M.), leaving the adversaries back in possession of the positions

they held when the battle had begun hours before. After eight hours of fighting the Romans and the Jews had fought to a stalemate.[43]

Josephus does not pick out any individual Roman to praise for his bravery during the night battle. Among the rebels he mentions Joudes, son of
Mareotes, and Simon, son of Hosaias, from the faction of Simon; James, son
of Sosas, and Simon, the son of Acatelas, from among the Idumaeans; John's
men Gephthaeus and Alexas; and the Zealot, Simon, son of Ari.[44] Josephus's
precise identification of the Jews who distinguished themselves during this
encounter suggests that he either was an eyewitness to the combat or he at
least learned about it from an unnamed informant among the Jews. It is hard
to believe that any Roman soldier would have been able to identify the Jews
mentioned by Josephus. The fact that Josephus names a Zealot as one of the
Jews who fought courageously lends credibility to his list. Elsewhere Josephus
has almost nothing positive to say about Zealots under any circumstances.

THE ROMAN EARTHWORKS AT THE TEMPLE

Although the Romans had fought the Jews to a draw during the night
battle, from a tactical point of view the operation was another failure. Some
of Rome's best soldiers could not break through into the Temple itself. In
hindsight it is worth noting that in many of the war's firefights the Romans
did not outfight the Jews, certainly individually but also in small groups. The
advantage the Romans had was their ability to sustain coordinated attacks
by well-fed and otherwise well-supported larger groups of troops over time.
Once the Roman she-wolf (*lupa*) had you in her jaws, she just kept chewing.

Thus the Romans focused their efforts on preparing for an all-out assault
upon the Temple. Both sides must have known that the Romans only had to
make one successful attack and the siege would be over.

Working nonstop, the Romans managed to destroy the foundations of the
Antonia in seven days, though again, not its tower. Afterward the legions began to raise up four new earthworks. One of these faced the northwest corner of the inner Temple. A second was raised against the northern exedra
that stood between the two gates. A third was constructed opposite the western stoa of the Temple's outer court. The fourth was put up opposite the
Temple's northern stoa. (See map 4.) To get the timber to build these works,
the Romans were forced to bring in wood from a distance of more than 12
miles away.[45] The prolonged Roman siege was an ecological and environmental disaster for the countryside around the besieged city.

While they were gathering up timber, the Romans were subject to harassing attacks. During one such attack, a group of Jews stole away the unbridled horses of some of the cavalrymen who had left them grazing and unguarded as the Romans gathered wood and fodder.[46] Since horses would have been of little tactical use to the besieged Jews within the narrow streets of Jerusalem, it is likely that the Jews stole the animals for their meat.

Titus had one of the cavalrymen who lost his horse executed. Titus did so to make an example of the offending cavalryman that would send a message about maintaining military discipline.[47] After that, we are told, the cavalrymen and their horses were inseparable.[48]

The Jews initiated other attacks elsewhere. The day after the failed Roman assault upon the Temple, at about the 11th hour of the day (5 P.M.), a group of rebels attacked the Roman guards on the Mount of Olives. The attackers hoped to catch the sentries off duty or perhaps eating their evening meal (*cena*). They were disappointed.

Somehow warned about the attack, the guards and their fellow soldiers from the neighboring forts rallied to the defense of the camp wall and foiled the Jews at the assault point.[49] The failure of the surprise attack contrasts with the striking success the Jews had had against the Romans on the Mount of Olives at the beginning of the siege. Titus had tightened up discipline and preparedness.

During the Roman rally one bold soldier made a name for himself. As the Romans were driving the Jews back down into the ravine from which they had emerged, one of the troopers from the cavalry squadrons named Pedanius galloped down upon the attackers, grabbed one of them by the ankle, and carried him off captive. Pedanius personally presented his young captive to Titus, who expressed admiration for Pedanius's strength and ordered the unfortunate young Jew to be punished.[50] Unit discipline and cohesion were essential elements of the Roman way of war, but there was also room for morale-raising individual feats of arms.

THE BATTLE OF THE STOAS

The defenders of the Temple, recognizing that the building of the new earthworks against the Temple walls was the prelude to their destruction, undertook desperate measures. First, to prevent the Romans from launching attacks from what was left of the Antonia Fortress into the Temple, the rebels set fire to part of the wooden ceiling of the repaired northwest stoa that attached the two buildings.[51] After the fire burned through more than 30 feet of the stoa's roof, they pulled down what remained. A couple of days later, on 24 Panemus, after the Romans set the lower, adjacent stoa on fire and the fire spread some 75 feet, the defenders of the city demolished the rest of the roof and the stoa. The effect of these actions was to cut off any direct connection between the Antonia and the sanctuary.[52]

During these days, a small Jew named Jonathan showed that Jews were just as bold as the Roman auxiliary cavalryman Pedanius. Coming forward opposite the memorial of the high priest John Hyrcanus, Jonathan insulted the Romans, and, like Goliath of Gath, challenged the best of them to a duel.[53] Many of the Roman soldiers looked upon Jonathan with contempt, some with trepidation. Others—again, presumably the veterans—thought that it was wise to avoid a fight with someone who was willing to risk his life for a victory that might bring a glorious death but would not change the outcome of the battle or the war. They may have calculated that, with the battle for the Temple and Jerusalem clearly nearing its conclusion, it would be foolish to take any unnecessary risks. Jonathan was probably crazy; in combat the crazy are best avoided.

Jonathan meanwhile kept up his stream of insults, calling the Romans cowards. Finally a cavalryman named Pudens—ironically, his name meant "bashful" or "modest" in Latin—stepped forward to answer Jonathan's insults, and the two men began to fight each other. For a while Pudens had the upper hand. But at some point he fell—perhaps he too had worn the wrong boots for the pitch—and Jonathan killed him. Standing over Pudens's body with his shield in his left hand and his bloody sword in his right Jonathan jeered at the Romans until a centurion, probably from one of the auxiliary units, named Priscus, meaning "ancient" or "venerable," put an end to Jonathan's celebration with a very well-aimed arrow. Jonathan fell dead on the body of Pudens.[54]

For Josephus the moral of Pudens's *aristeia,* or moment of excellence, was how quickly nemesis could overtake martial success and glory. The triumphant Jonathan died only a few seconds later on the body of the man he had triumphed over. But the incident has more significant implications for our understanding of the adversaries in the war.

First, there were brave men who came from the ranks of ordinary soldiers on both sides. Neither Jonathan nor Pudens seems to have come from a particularly distinguished background nor enjoyed important connections, as far as we know. Second, contrary to the image of the hyperdisciplined Roman soldier in many works on the Roman army, there were Roman soldiers who were willing to step out from their carefully organized lines and fight for reasons other than just tactical advantage. Both Jonathan and Pudens should be understood and classified as natural fighters, the kind of men who, to the embarrassment of many academics and not a few professional soldiers, enjoy combat. Fighting is their métier. Unpalatable as it may seem, there always have been such men, and there always will be.

Shortly after this memorable encounter, a group of Roman soldiers fell victim to yet another well-planned ruse. On 27 Panemus the defenders of the Temple filled up the empty spaces between the beams and the ceiling of the western stoa with flammable material, probably including dried wood, bitumen, and pitch. Then, feigning exhaustion, they retired from their positions. Seeing this, as they were intended to, some of the Roman legionaries climbed up ladders onto the stoa.[55]

As soon as the stoa was crowded with Roman soldiers, the Jews set the whole building on fire. Some of the Romans jumped back down into the city behind them. Others leaped into the middle of their enemies. Those who landed in the city among their friends suffered only fractured bones. Others were not as fortunate. Enveloped by the fire on the stoa, they died where they were, though some chose to die by their own swords rather than to perish in the flames. Josephus tells us that these men died cheerfully at the sight of Titus shouting to them and exhorting others to rescue them.[56] Josephus does not tell his readers how he knew that these poor souls gladly met their fates.

Although none were rescued, some of the Romans did make it back through the fire to the wall of the stoa. There they were attacked and killed to a man by the Jews. The last to fall was a young man named Longus. He fought so bravely that the Jews offered to spare his life if he would give up. His brother Cornelius, who apparently witnessed the whole scene, shouted to him, begging him not to disgrace his reputation or that of Roman arms by surrendering. Unwilling either to do so or to be killed by the Jews, Longus stabbed himself to death with his own sword.[57] The incident is significant because it again underscores the point that Roman discipline was not always automatic or effective. Longus and his fellow soldiers should never have followed the retreating Jews up onto the stoa, falling into their trap. But the episode is revealing for another reason too.

Josephus's story about Longus's suicide provides a positive representation of suicide by a Roman: Josephus's Roman readers were supposed to admire Longus for heeding his brother's admonition and preferring suicide to dishonor. Rather they were supposed to admire the brothers. We need to remember the example of Longus's suicide when we come to the mass murder/suicide of the Jews on Masada and its interpretation.

One of the few Roman survivors of the debacle was a man named Artorius, whose name, somewhat suspiciously, could be translated as the "Weighty Man." Trapped by the flames on top of the stoa, he shouted out to one of his tentmates named Lucius that he would make him heir to all of his property if he came up and caught him when he jumped down from the building. Bravely but unwisely, Lucius came forward and tried to catch his mate. Breaking his fall, Lucius saved Artorius's life but not his own. Artorius's weight and momentum crushed him against the pavement, killing him on the spot.[58] Josephus, unfortunately, does not make clear exactly where Artorius jumped from or landed.[59]

As these brave men died, the fire the Jews had set ended up burning up the stoa all the way to the tower that John had erected over the gates leading out above the Xystus. The rest of it was destroyed by the Jews themselves. One day later the Romans burned the whole of the northern stoa to the point where it met the eastern stoa.[60]

FAMINE AND CANNIBALISM IN THE CITY

As the fight over the stoas raged on, the starving population of the city was driven to desperate acts. People began to eat belts, shoes, and even the leather from shields. Tufts of dried-up grass were eaten, and small quantities of stalks sold for the equivalent of four days' wages.[61]

Notoriously, Josephus also reports the story of a wealthy woman named Maria—in Josephus's Greek, probably Mariam in Hebrew or Aramaic—the daughter of Eleazar, who had fled to Jerusalem from the village of Beth-ezuba in the Peraea among a multitude. After the rebels had taken Maria's property and food, she slew her own son, roasted him, and ate half of him—thereby fulfilling a curse predicted after it previously had been fulfilled during the Babylonian siege of Judah.[62] When Maria finished eating part of her own child, she then stored what remained. After the rebels returned to her house they threatened to kill her unless she produced what she had cooked. Bringing out what was left of her son, Maria urged them to eat as she had eaten and not to be weaker than a woman or to have more compassion than a mother. The rebels passed on her offer. They left her home shaking, we are told.[63]

The incident was understood throughout the city as an abomination, or *mysos* in Greek, Josephus tells us, and there was a zeal for death among the starving population and a blessing for those who had died already, before they heard of or witnessed such evils.[64]

News of the cannibalism was reported quickly to the Romans and made its way to Titus. The Roman commander supposedly proclaimed himself innocent of this matter before God. He had offered the Jews peace, self-rule, and forgiveness for all prior offenses, he asserted, while they preferred discord to agreement, war to peace, starvation to plenitude and prosperity, and having set fire to the Temple that he and the Roman army were trying to save, they deserved such food. He vowed, however, to conceal this horror of infant-eating beneath the ruin of the fatherland itself and not to leave upon the face of the earth, for the sun to see, a city in which mothers were nourished in such a way.[65]

There may well have been a rich woman named Maria or Mariam from the Peraea who went to Jerusalem and resorted to eating part of her own child after the rebels took her property and her food. But this act was not historically unprecedented among the Greeks, the "barbarians," or even the Jews, as Josephus wrongly claimed.[66] The Greek Potidaeans resorted to cannibalism during the Athenian siege of their city in 432–430 BCE, as Josephus, an avid reader of Thucydides, must have known.[67] The Alexandrian historian Appian reports that during the siege of Numantia in Spain by the Roman general Scipio Aemilianus in 134–133 BCE, the besieged Numantines boiled and ate first those who had died of natural causes and then started killing and eating their weaker comrades.[68] When the Syrian king Ben-hadad besieged Samaria, women there reportedly agreed to eat each other's sons.[69] During the Babylonian siege of Solomon's Temple in 587–586 BCE, women supposedly boiled and ate their own children.[70]

Cannibalism among the besieged was a historical reality regardless of ethnicity in antiquity. But it was also a Graeco-Roman literary topos, created under the influence of prior literary models, and then disseminated to produce reactions among those who read about it, and to shape what readers thought about larger issues. As Price has pointed out, Josephus cannot possibly have witnessed the scene he describes in such horrifying detail.[71] What was the intended reaction to the story Josephus told about Maria and Titus's reaction to her cannibalism, and what was the point of emphasizing it to the point of misleading readers about its historically singular nature?

Josephus's account of Maria's cannibalism may well have been intended to encourage sympathy for Jews who suffered during the siege of Jerusalem;

Josephus thought that the responsibility for that suffering lay with the Jewish "tyrants."[72] But described as it is, where it is—just before his account of the destruction of the Temple and the massacre that took place while it was being destroyed—the story of Maria's cannibalism more importantly is used to distract Josephus's Roman readers from focusing on Titus's responsibility for letting his soldiers destroy God's Temple and a large part of the city. Jews who read Josephus's report of the episode and knew their own book well would undoubtedly have been reminded that God himself had threatened that if the Jews defied him he would punish them seven times for their sins and that they would eat their sons and daughters.[73] Maria's cannibalism in other words fulfilled a biblical prophecy.

Josephus wanted his horrified readers to understand that humanity, not inhumanity, forced his unwilling Roman patron and friend Titus to destroy the Temple that God himself had ordered to be built for him and the holy city. Those who had sunk to the subhuman level of eating their own children (*teknophagia* in Greek) had to be eliminated. They had become like animals, killing and eating each other. Killing such subhumans was not a crime but, in fact, was God's will, as Josephus so often reminded his readers.

THE ROMANS SET FIRE TO THE TEMPLE GATES

After siege engines had been used against the wall for six days and the Romans had failed to undermine the foundations of the northern gate, on 8 Lous Titus ordered that battering rams be brought up to a position opposite the western exedra of the Temple's outer court. Against these walls, however, even the battering rams failed.[74]

The Romans then threw ladders up against the surviving porticoes on the north. Some of the Romans who climbed up the ladders were knocked off and fell headlong to the ground. Others were slain by the Jews as they tried to step off the ladders. The Jews tilted some of the ladders sideways and sent them crashing to the ground with the Roman soldiers still holding onto them. Josephus singles out Eleazar, Simon's nephew, for his conspicuous bravery during the engagement. The attempt to scale the wall with ladders was a complete failure. Recognizing that their efforts were fruitless, Titus gave an order for the gates to be set on fire.[75]

Remarkably, even as the Romans were preparing to burn their way into the Temple compound, deserters continued to come over to the Roman side, including Ananus of Emmaus, one of Simon's chief officers, and Archelaus, the son of Magaddatus. Titus believed they deserved to be executed because they only surrendered out of necessity, when their city was in flames, but he spared them anyway.[76] Their desertions signify that even those closest to Simon thought that further resistance was pointless. Simon obviously did not agree.

Josephus does not specify exactly which of the gates Titus ordered to be burned. But it is likely that the ones he had in mind were the four gates on each of the northern and southern sides of the Temple complex and the one (a double gate) on the east; that gate led into and out from the Women's Court, the farthest space into the Temple itself that women were allowed to enter, as described earlier by Josephus and mentioned later in a rabbinic source.[77] These are likely to be the gates meant because we know that they, though made of wood, were covered with silver, and Josephus tells his readers that after the Romans set fire to the gates, the silver of the gates melted quickly, spreading the fire to the wood.[78]

Since silver melts at more than 1,700 degrees Fahrenheit, it follows that the fire set by the Romans on these doors must have been extremely hot. Wood, by comparison, burns at around 450 degrees. Controlling fires of such heat would have been very difficult at best, even if the Romans had wished to do so. The flames thus quickly spread from the woodwork to the stoas in the Women's Court. The Jews inside were powerless to stop the fire that burned throughout the day and into the night.[79]

The next day Titus gave an order for the fire to be put out and for a roadway to be made up the 12 (to 14) semicircular steps to "the gates" to clear the way for the impending final assault by the legions.[80] It was on these steps that the Levites sang the 15 Psalms of Ascent, probably as they made their way to visit the Temple during the three major festivals.[81] The "gates" Josephus specifies must be the Gate of Nicanor, the triple gate with its two central doors of Corinthian bronze, which served as the main point of entry up to the Court of Israelites, though only for the ritually pure.[82] (See map 4 inset.)

Titus then called for another council.[83] This would turn out be one of the most famous and controversial meetings in the tragically intertwined histories of the Romans and the Jews.

In attendance were Tiberius Iulius Alexander, the prefect of all forces; Sextus Cerialis, commander of the Fifth Legion; Larcius Lepidus, commander of the Tenth Legion; Titus Phrygius, commander of the Fifteenth Legion; Fronto Haterius, commander of the two legions from Alexandria; and Marcus Antonius Iulianus, procurator of Judaea. The rest of the procurators and military tribunes were also present. The main subject for discussion was what to do about the Temple.[84]

Some argued in favor of its destruction because, as long as it was standing, they said that it would be a focal point of rebellion. Others were of the opinion that if the Jews left it and did not store weapons there, it should be saved. But if they chose to use it as a base to make war it should be burned. We are not told who among the attendees favored which alternative.

Titus stated, according to Josephus, that even if the Jews did mount it (the Temple) and use it to fight from he would not take vengeance upon objects without a soul instead of men, nor would he burn down such a great work. Burning the Temple down would only cause harm to the Romans, even as it would be an ornament of their rule as long as it survived. Fronto, Tiberius Iulius Alexander, and Cerialis supported Titus's position, and the matter was settled by Titus who, as the commander, following Roman practice, always made the final decision after considering the opinions expressed. The Temple was to be spared, according to Josephus's report about the meeting.[85]

Josephus's description of what happened at the meeting and the decision not to destroy the Temple confirms what he told his readers near the beginning of the *War*. It was the tyrants of the Jews who brought down upon the Temple the unwilling hands of the Romans and the fire. Titus had been anxious to save the city and the Temple, and the burning of the Temple had been done against his wishes.[86] Josephus makes the same points several more times in book 6 of the *War* where the destruction of the Temple is described.[87]

Because the Temple was burned by the Romans very soon after this meeting, some historians have argued that Josephus must not have told the truth about what happened at the *consilium* and about Titus's intentions with respect to the Temple. Josephus's Roman patrons Titus and Vespasian were among the readers of his work, and Titus would not have wanted to have his name go down in history as the man responsible for destroying one of the greatest monuments in the ancient world.[88]

The third-century historian Cassius Dio reports that after the defenders of the Temple unintentionally burned down the barrier around the Temple precinct, so that the Temple was opened to the Romans, the soldiers nevertheless held back because of their superstition, but Titus urged them on, and the defenders continued to fight (within the Temple) until a part of it was set on fire.[89] The implication is that Titus either didn't care if the Romans destroyed the Temple or actually wanted to destroy it. Later Christian historians were less ambiguous.

The Christian historian and hagiographer Sulpicius Severus, whose Latin *Chronica,* written in 401, was supposedly based upon a lost passage from book 5 of Tacitus's *Histories,* claimed that Titus explicitly intended for the Temple to be destroyed without delay, so that the religion of the Jews and the Christians should be more completely eradicated.[90] Working independently, Orosius, who also drew upon the lost section of Tacitus's histories, made the same claim around 418 in his *Histories against the Pagans.*[91] Orosius in fact asserted that Titus burned the Temple after it was captured and he had had a chance to think about it and admire the Temple first. He decided to do it because the (Christian) church was spreading all over the world, and so it was the will of God that the useless Temple be destroyed.[92]

For Sulpicius the destruction of the Temple and the subsequent captivity of the Judaeans were proof to the world of their having been punished for laying impious hands on Christ.[93] The German scholar Jacob Bernays argued for the basic credibility of Sulpicius's version of how and why the Temple was destroyed in a monograph about Sulpicius's *Chronica* published in 1861, and many prominent classical historians have accepted Bernays's conclusions, if not all of his arguments.[94]

A close reading of Sulpicius's account of Titus authorizing the destruction of the Temple (2.30.6–8) reveals, however, that it is based upon a tendentious rewriting of Josephus's version of the fateful meeting Titus held with his officers before the destruction of the Temple, and not upon a lost passage of Tacitus.[95] Furthermore, later in his account of the burning of the Temple, Josephus makes clear that it was against Titus's orders that Roman soldiers started or accelerated the fire that led to its destruction.

As we shall see, the Roman commander did what he could to stop the fire, if we follow Josephus's narrative. But his soldiers disobeyed his orders. It is precisely the unflattering implications of this version of the events about Titus's military leadership that lend credibility to Josephus' account of how the Temple was destroyed.[96] Who bears ultimate responsibility for what happened is a separate question, addressed in the next chapter.

On the next day, beginning around 8 A.M., the defenders of the Temple, at this point the surviving Zealots and Galilaeans, made a series of sallies out through the eastern gate, attacking the Roman guards. These attacks were repulsed by 11 A.M., after Titus had handpicked cavalry brought up to assist the guards.[97]

With the fighting halted for the time being Titus withdrew inside the Antonia to his *poste de commandement opérationnel* (battle command post).

From this position he would have the advantage of being able to see the action as it developed and to make tactical adjustments. His intention seems to have been to launch a final assault the next day. But as soon as he had set up his observation post somewhere from within the fortress a new attack was launched.[98]

A fight had broken out between the guards of the Temple and the Roman troops who were attempting to put out the fire in the inner court. The Romans got the upper hand in this struggle and followed the Temple guards to the Temple itself. At that point, on the 10th day of the month of Lous, an unnamed Roman soldier, acting upon some kind of demonic impulse (*daimonio horme*), grabbed one of the firebrands, and climbing up on one of his fellow's shoulders, the soldier then threw the brand through one of the golden windows into the northern storerooms that surrounded the inner sanctum or court of the Temple.[99] The word Josephus used to characterize the soldier's impulse was the same one he used to describe the change of wind at Gamala that had led to its destruction: demonic or divine.

A flame shot up immediately.[100]

CHAPTER 19

Woe to the Jerusalemites

THE DESTRUCTION OF THE TEMPLE

As the fire raced toward the holiest space in Jerusalem, Titus was taking a nap. Roused from his slumber and followed by his general officers and the galvanized mass of legionaries, Titus armed himself with a bow and arrows and rushed to the Temple. After arriving there Titus reportedly killed 12 of the city's defenders with 12 arrows.[1] At some point, when he presumably had run out of arrows, Josephus claims that Titus shouted to his men and signaled with his right hand that the fire was to be put out.[2]

Caught up in the chaos most of the Roman soldiers neither heard Titus nor saw his hand signal. Some of the soldiers who did hear him pretended not to have and shouted to their comrades up ahead to throw their burning brands into the fire too. The rebels were no longer capable of defending themselves, and there was butchery and flight all around. Most of those slain at the time were unarmed civilians. Bodies began to pile up around the unhewn fieldstone altar and the Temple court (*azarah*) in front of the Temple building itself.[3] Streams of blood flowed down the steps of the Temple, carrying the bodies of the slain downward from above.[4] This may be a piece of Josephan purple prose; but under the circumstances the blood of those killed by the Romans may well have stained the 12 steps up to the porch (*ulam*) of the inner sanctum.

356

Titus and his general officers somehow made their way through the porch, beneath the golden vine that hung over the doorway, into the Temple itself and looked at the holy place of the sanctuary and the things in it.[5] This probably means that they entered the area known as the *heikhal* (literally, temple), where the gold Table of Shewbread, the seven-branched menorah that God had ordered Moses to make, and the incense altar were or had been kept.[6] Since the daily service had been stopped on 17 Panemus/Tammuz three weeks before, however, it is likely that Titus did not see the Table or the menorah in place. It is hard to believe that the rebels or whoever was in control of the space had simply left such valuable items where they had been used, knowing that the Romans were likely to break into the holy place.[7]

After passing through the *heikhal* Titus entered the inner chamber, *debir* in Hebrew, or Holy of Holies (*hagiou de hagion*) as it is called in Josephus's Greek.[8] There was no statue or representation of a god or goddess in the space, as Titus would have expected to see in the inner room of a Greek or Roman Temple. Rather, as Josephus wrote, in this space there stood nothing whatever, unapproachable, inviolable, invisible to all.[9] What this difficult sentence probably means is that Josephus understood the *debir* to be the space where God was present but could not be approached, touched, or seen.

The only object to be seen in the inner chamber was the Foundation Rock, or *Even ha-Shetiyah* in Hebrew. The Rock was the place where, in a rectangular-shaped depression, the Ark of the Covenant, with the Deuteronomy Scroll, stood in Solomon's Temple, and from which the world had been created according to talmudic sages.[10] (See figure 12.) There, every year on Yom Kippur, the high priest offered incense on a fire before God and sprinkled the blood of a sacrificed bull.[11]

Finding nothing worth looting in what would become one of the most theologically contested spaces in the world, Titus came back out and once again ordered the fire to be extinguished. A centurion named Liberalius was told to club anyone who disobeyed Titus's order. But nothing could check the Roman soldiers. There were too many of them, and battle madness, their hatred of the Jews, and their desire for plunder overpowered their famous military discipline.[12]

That discipline had been tested and then broken by the siege itself. While there was plenty of water to be found within the walls of Jerusalem, outside of those walls, and therefore throughout the siege, the Romans had suffered from a lack of water; what water there was had to be borne to Jerusalem from at least four miles away. Jewish soldiers, who made their way out of the city

FIGURE 12. The Temple Mount from the south. Beneath the Dome of the Rock
was the Foundation Rock, where the world had been created according to
talmudic sources. William Schlegel/BiblePlaces.com.

by its underground tunnels, also attacked the Roman water carriers.[13] Despite
these attacks somewhere between 96,400 and 134,000 liquid liters had to be
found and then transported to the Roman legionaries, auxiliaries, and allies
every day. That cannot have been an easy task in the middle of Jerusalem's
summer heat. Unlike the Jerusalemites, the Romans had plenty of food. But
fodder for their animals and the timber for their cooking fires and for building the earthworks also had to be obtained and then transported into the city
from many miles away, in fact from farther away than the water.

The resistance by the rebels had been unexpectedly resilient and determined, at times contemptuous, even fanatical in Roman eyes. For most of
the siege the weather must have been unbearably hot for the soldiers wearing
their body armor. By the time Titus's soldiers broke into the inner sanctum
of the Temple, their hatred for the Jews must have overcome all the restraints
that military discipline required of them.[14] *Tohar HaNeshek*, or purity of arms,
the ethical doctrine of distinguishing between combatants and noncomba-

tants in battle, was completely forgotten. The Romans were no longer capable of treating their enemies like human beings. They wanted to take their suffering out on anyone or anything they found. They were done listening to their officers, done holding back. They just wanted to kill.

The inner court itself was set ablaze by someone who thrust a firebrand into the hinges of one of the gates. There was nothing now that could save the Holy of Holies from the conflagration.[15] The fire had spread too widely, and it was simply too hot. The *debir* was destroyed in a raging inferno. In fact, stone uncovered in excavations along the western and southern walls of the Temple Mount that belonged to the upper walls and colonnades burned at temperatures that reached 1,472 degrees Fahrenheit.[16]

According to Josephus's calculation, since its rebuilding by Haggai, the Temple had stood for 639 years and 45 days before it was burned down during the second year of Vespasian's reign, on 10 Lous/Av (July–August), the same day on which the former Temple had been burned down by the king of the Babylonians (i.e., the Temple of Solomon destroyed by Nebuchadnezzar).[17] The same date is given in the book of Jeremiah, though in the second book of Kings a date three days earlier is specified (7 Lous/Av), and rabbinic writers dated the destruction of both temples to 9 Lous/Av.[18] All of the sources agree, however, that within a very short period of time the Romans destroyed a building and a sanctuary that had taken the Jews decades to restore and make into one of the most beautiful structures on earth, starting during the reign of Herod in 23–22 BCE.

If Josephus is telling the truth, it had not been Titus's intention to burn down the Temple. As Josephus related the story of how it was destroyed, he was careful to point out to his readers that Titus repeatedly expressed his desire to save the Temple and tried to have the fire that destroyed it put out. Titus no doubt nodded his head in approval as he read Josephus's account of how the Temple was incinerated.

Yet the destruction of the Temple took place on Titus's watch, and as commander of the Roman soldiers who set the Temple on fire, he bore ultimate responsibility for its destruction. Titus had at least four months to consider what he would do with the Temple before he held the *consilium* about its fate that Josephus reports, just as Alexander the Great had four months to think about what he would do with the Persian royal palaces at Persepolis before he let his soldiers burn them in April of 330 BCE.[19] Titus's inability to restrain his soldiers does not absolve him of responsibility for what happened. His soldiers' rage and indiscipline after months of frustrating fighting under difficult conditions were foreseeable. It has not been sufficiently emphasized that, however chaotic the situation was after the unnamed soldier threw his brand into the inner sanctuary, that did not prevent Titus from looting the Temple of its treasures before the building burned down, as we know he did from the display of those treasures in Titus's triumph a year later, and as is implied on their depiction on his triumphal arch in Rome.[20] Titus evidently had time to rob the Temple but not to save it.

A stronger and more effective commander would have issued stricter rules of engagement to his soldiers and seen to their enforcement. But Titus did not. That failure should have resulted in his removal from his position by his superior. Instead his superior—his father Vespasian—and the Roman Senate decided that Titus merited a triumph, and the desecration of the Temple became one of the ideological cornerstones of the Flavian dynasty's propaganda.

With the whole Temple now ablaze, a massacre ensued. The Romans cut down everyone they encountered, regardless of age, rank, or holiness. It made no difference whether they resisted or asked for mercy. The noise that rose up from the scene was deafening. The roar of the fire's flames was mixed up with the screams and groans of those being slaughtered. The war cries of the Roman legionaries as they swept forward were answered by the howls of the rebels, who now were fighting against both the flames and the sword. There were also the shrieks of the civilians who, having been cut off above, met their fates when they tried to flee and ran straight into the arms of their enemies. From below the Temple in the city there was lamentation and wailing when people saw the Temple on fire and began to understand what was transpiring above them. The sounds of this hideous symphony of death, destruction, and grief echoed northeastward all the way into the Peraean hills.[21]

Yet the human suffering was even more awful than the uproar. The Temple hill was a mass of flames. The rivers of blood flowed more copiously than the flames of the fire, and the numbers of the dead far exceeded those of their slayers. Soldiers climbed over heaps of bodies in pursuit of those who were fleeing.

The crowd of "brigands" somehow managed to make their way through the Romans and escaped into the city below. To do so they must have gone through the Temple's outer court and from there found their way down into the Upper City, which had not yet been occupied by the Romans.[22] Josephus provides no details about how they managed to pass through the lines of the rampaging Roman soldiers. But perhaps since the Romans were preoccupied with slaughter and plunder there simply were no lines.

Some of the priests ripped up spikes from the sanctuary and threw them at the Romans but to no effect. Most retreated to a wall and awaited their fates. Two of the priests—Meirus, son of Belgas, and Josephus, son of Dalaeus—chose to leap into the flames of the burning Temple.[23] The historian Josephus does not suggest that their suicides were sacrilegious.

With the Temple on fire the Romans then put the surrounding buildings to the torch. These included what remained of the porticoes and gates, except those on the eastern and southern sides. They burned the treasury store-houses and their contents, including the money that the rich had deposited there before the outbreak of the war, the sacred garments of the priests, and other valuables.[24] The compulsion to destroy overcame even greed.

Around 6,000 or so Jews took refuge on the outer (eastern) stoa of the Temple. Among them were poor women and children. Some may have been family members of the Temple's last defenders and the priests. When the Roman soldiers subsequently set fire to that stoa from below, all of them perished, either by jumping away out of the flames or into the fiery inferno itself.[25]

A VOICE AGAINST THE TEMPLE

They owed their annihilation, according to Josephus, to one of the many unnamed false prophets at work in the city at the time. He had proclaimed to the people that God ordered them to go up to the court of the Temple and to receive there the tokens of their salvation. Alas, the prophetic laments of another man, a certain Jesus, son of Ananias, who had appeared during the governorship of Albinus, proved to be totally reliable.[26]

At the feast of the Tabernacles in 62 this Jesus had suddenly appeared in the city and, taking up a position in the Temple, uttered the same prophecy over and over: "A voice from the east, a voice from the west, a voice from the four winds; a voice against Jerusalem and the Temple, a voice against the bridegroom and the bride, a voice against the whole people."[27]

Eventually Jesus was arrested by some of the leading citizens who were irritated by his ill-omened refrain. Even though they had him beaten, Jesus neither defended himself nor changed his prophetic tune. Concluding that Jesus was operating under some kind of divine impulse, the magistrates brought him before the Roman procurator Albinus. After asking Jesus who he was, where he came from, and why he kept repeating the same words, Albinus had Jesus scourged to the bone. In response Jesus neither explained himself nor begged for mercy. Rather he answered every lash with the same words: "Woe to the Jerusalemites." Persuaded that Jesus was some kind of maniac, Albinus let him go. Thereafter, for years, up until the outbreak of the war, and most loudly at festivals, Jesus repeated the words, "Woe to the Jerusalemites," to all men, whether they cudgeled him or offered him food.

When the war came, although the meaning of his revelation had become clear, Jesus continued on his prophetic mission. One day, however, after he mounted the city wall and shouted out, "Woe yet again to the city and to the people and to the Temple and woe to me as well," a ballista ball fired from a Roman stone-thrower struck and killed him just after he uttered the last word.[28] As he predicted, Jesus himself became a victim of his own prophecy.[29]

THE PROFANATION OF THE TEMPLE

With the Temple still in flames, the Roman soldiers brought their military standards into the middle of the Temple court, opposite the eastern gate. There they made sacrifices to the standards (*signa*).[30] What this probably means is that they sacrificed in front of whatever images were engraved on their standards. Beneath the legionary eagle on such standards typically there was a head or bust of the reigning Roman emperor, with whom the standards were closely associated.[31] In this case that would have been Vespasian. During the governorship of Pontius Pilate, it will be recalled, his introduction of military standards into Jerusalem had caused a massive protest.[32]

After these sacrifices the soldiers hailed Titus as imperator or commander with acclamations. Before the Temple was completely consumed, the Romans then sought out whatever valuables had survived the conflagration. Subsequently, we are told, the plunder that the Roman soldiers gathered up was so vast that the gold standard in Syria soon depreciated by half.[33]

THE FATES OF THE SURVIVORS

For several days the priests who had not fled during the final Roman assault held out on the wall of the sanctuary. On the fifth day, however, having not eaten since the Temple was captured and burned, the priests came down and were brought to Titus by guards. There they pleaded for their lives. Titus denied their request, telling them that the one thing for which he might have spared their lives—the Temple—was now gone and that it was fitting for them as priests to expire with the Temple. They were led away to be executed.[34]

The followers of John and Simon, who had fled from the Temple into the city but still were enclosed within the wall, then invited Titus to a conference. Hoping at least to spare the city from destruction, we are told, Titus consented. The Roman commander took up a position on the bridge, over what is known today as Wilson's Arch, on the west of the outer court of the Temple. With their followers behind them, John and Simon stood opposite Titus. After directing his troops to hold their tempers and their fire Titus addressed the rebels and their leaders through an interpreter.[35] We know that the Romans deployed military interpreters to communicate with the peoples of their provinces.[36] It is possible that Josephus himself was the one who interpreted Titus's speech to the Jews. The theme of his speech, as reported by Josephus, was Roman humanity and Jewish ingratitude.

Since the time of Pompey's conquest the Jews had never ceased to rebel, he said. Yet the Romans had allowed them to occupy their own lands and to live under their own kings. The Romans had let them exact tribute for their God and collect offerings, which the Jews then used to make preparations for war against the Romans. Vespasian had come to their country not to make war upon them after the Cestius incident but to warn them. He had ravaged the Galilee and the surrounding countryside to give them time to repent. And when Vespasian and Titus were called away to Egypt to deal with Rome's internal problems, the Jews had used the opportunity to prepare for hostilities. They had sent embassies to their friends across the Euphrates inciting revolt, and when Titus had come back to the city, he had urged them to pause and gave pledges of security to deserters. He had brought his siege engines up to the city walls reluctantly and had restrained his soldiers.

He had offered the Jews free and safe passage away from the Temple or an opportunity for battle elsewhere, but they had chosen to fight there and had set fire to the Temple themselves. And after all of this they had invited him to a conference? After they had lost their Temple? Yet they still stood at arms and did not even pretend to be suppliants. Their people had been killed, the Temple no longer existed, their city was at his mercy, and their lives were in his hands. Did they consider it to be glorious bravery to die in the last ditch? Yet Titus stated that he would not emulate their mad frenzy. If they threw down their arms and surrendered, he would grant them their lives, like a lenient master of a house who punished the incorrigible but saved the rest for himself.[37]

A VOICE AGAINST JERUSALEM

The speech must have pleased Titus's and Josephus's Roman friends when they read it in Josephus's work, years after the destruction of Jerusalem, filled as it reportedly was with tendentious assertions, such as the claim that Vespasian came to Judaea to "warn" the Jews. What Vespasian and his soldiers had done at Iotapata, in the stadium of Tiberias, where the unarmed prisoners from Tarichaeae were cut down, and to the infants at Gamala went beyond warnings.

In any case, however, the response of the rebels to Titus's (or Josephus's) paean of self-justification was that they had vowed never to accept a pledge from Titus. They asked leave, however, to pass through the Romans' fortified line with their wives and children. They intended to retire to the desert and to leave the city to Titus.[38] Josephus does not make clear what they meant by the "desert." They could have meant the Judaean desert or perhaps one of the Herodian fortresses that had not yet been captured by the Romans, such as Masada.

Angry that the Jews seemed to be offering proposals to him as if they were the victors, Titus ordered it proclaimed that they should neither be allowed to leave nor to hope for terms any longer. He would pardon none. They should fight with all their power, he said, and save themselves because from then on what he did would be governed by the law of war. He then turned the city over to the soldiers to burn and sack.[39]

First there was a one-day hiatus. On the next day the soldiers set fire to the archive, the Akra (the fortress), the council chamber where the Sanhedrin met, and the area to the south of the Temple called the Ophel/Ophlas or the upper part of the spur of the Lower City.[40] (See map 4.) Imprints of shop arches burned into the southern wall of the Temple Mount at the southeast corner are visible to this day; the imprints imply that Roman soldiers deliberately set fires within shops whose back walls were formed by the mount's southern wall.[41]

The fire spread all the way down to the palace of Queen Helena of Adiabene in the Lower City, among the Adiabenian palaces. Streets and houses were also set alight. While the fire raged, the sons and brothers of Izates, king of Adiabene, sought a pledge of security from Titus. Though infuriated, presumably because the Adiabenians asked for protection only after the Temple had been taken and destroyed, Titus nevertheless granted their request. Later, the king's relatives were brought in chains to Rome as hostages.[42]

The rebels meanwhile had fled to Herod's Palace in the Upper City. Herod's Palace and the (as yet undiscovered) palace of the Hasmoneans were situated on the city's western hill. It was there that Jerusalem's wealthy lived. The rebels killed everyone who had previously taken refuge within the 50-foot walls of Herod's Palace, to the number of 8,400. As so often, these numbers in Josephus must be greatly inflated. They then looted all the money they found. Two Roman soldiers were also captured.[43]

The first, an infantryman, was slain on the spot and his body dragged around the city. The rebels bound and blindfolded the second soldier, a cavalryman, either a legionary or auxiliary *eques*. He was taken to a place where the rebels intended to behead him in view of the Romans. But when they reached the spot and an officer named Ardalas drew his sword to cut off his head, the prisoner made a run for it and escaped to the Romans.

The standard Roman military penalty for someone who allowed himself to be captured alive by an enemy was execution. But Titus, we are told, could not bear to have the punishment carried out. Instead, the soldier was deprived of his arms and kicked out of his legion, the equivalent of a modern dishonorable discharge (*missio ignominiosa*).[44] The lesser punishment Titus inflicted arguably helped reinforce the system of rewards and punishments by which Roman commanders maintained discipline.[45]

The next day the Romans set the entire Lower City on fire right up to the Siloam Pool. While the city burned the Romans apparently also searched for valuables. Nothing was found. Before they had retreated to the Upper City the rebels had gathered up anything of value.[46]

Even as the Lower City was burning, Josephus continued to make entreaties to his fellow countrymen. These pleas were ignored or ridiculed, just as all previous ones had been. The rebels, on the contrary, though driven to the Upper City, used their energies to lie in wait for anyone who tried to escape. Those who were caught were killed and their bodies were thrown to the dogs. Yet people still tried to get away.[47]

The rebel leaders and their followers placed their last hopes on the underground passages of the city. They retreated into these tunnels, where they thought the Romans would not search for them. After the Romans departed from the city they intended to climb back up and escape. Anyone else who fled from the fires above ground into these passages they robbed and killed. If the victims were carrying food it was confiscated and eaten. Fights broke out among the rebels over the spoils.[48]

The Romans, who presumably were unaware of the rebels' escape into the tunnels, made preparations for an assault upon the Upper City. This required building yet more earthworks—the fifth and final set. Their construction represented a considerable challenge. All the timber in the surrounding area already had been used to build the earlier works. The Romans nevertheless once again set to work. Although Josephus does not provide any information, it must have been the case that the Romans gathered up the necessary wood from much farther afield, more than 12 miles from the city.

The four legions were given the job of constructing the earthworks against the wall on the western side of the Upper City, opposite the royal Palace of Herod. The auxiliaries were tasked with the construction of those to the east.[49] The point of building these embankments was to give the Romans the advantage of attacking the Upper City from high ground.

While the Romans were scrounging around for building materials, the leaders of the remaining Idumaeans met in secret and decided to surrender, if that were still possible. Five delegates were sent to Titus. Despite the tardiness of the Idumaeans' appeal, Titus accepted their request because he hoped that their surrender would persuade the leaders of the Jews to give up too.

When the five delegates got back into the Upper City, however, Simon discovered their plan to surrender, just as the Idumaeans were getting ready to depart. The five delegates were executed at once, and the other leaders of the Idumaeans were arrested and imprisoned, including James, the son of Sosas. He had been among those who had brought the Idumaeans to Jerusalem. The rest of the Idumaeans were watched, though not carefully enough, as it transpired.

Although many were slain by Simon's men as they tried to escape, large numbers of the Idumaeans deserted to the Romans. Those who were citizens were allowed to remain with their Roman captors and then go where they wished. But the rest, with the women and children, were sold into slavery. There were nearly 40,000 citizens; Josephus does not enumerate the number of the enslaved.[50]

It was at this time, too, that the priest Jesus, son of Thebuthi, who was given a pledge of safety by Titus, and the Temple treasurer, Phineas, who was captured, delivered over to the Romans some of the Temple's treasures. From the sanctuary wall Jesus gave up two lampstands similar to the ones inside the Temple, along with massive golden tables, drinking bowls and plates, veils, the garments of the high priests studded with precious stones, and many other items used during public worship.

Phineas surrendered the coats and belts worn by the priests, the purple and scarlet kept for repairs to the Temple's veil, and a massive amount of cinnamon, cassia, and other spices. While the Temple was still standing, the spices had been mixed together every day and used in sacrifices to God. He also gave up sacred decorations and many other things by which he bought his pardon from Titus.[51] Some of this booty may have been carried along through the streets of Rome in Titus's triumph a year later. We know that treasures from the Temple were subsequently stored in Rome's Temple of Peace.

After 18 days of labor, the Romans completed their new earthworks and promptly brought up their siege engines on 7 Gorpiaeus/Elul (August–September). Some of the rebels fled immediately to what remained of the Akra. Others headed for the underground tunnels. Those who stayed to fight at the walls were quickly overpowered. When a section of the wall was broken down, the western wall was breached. As the Romans began searching for them, the rebel leaders were seized with panic and came down from the Hippicus, Phasael, and Mariamme Towers in which they had holed up. From there they fled into the canyon below the Siloam Pool. After they regained their composure, they made their way down into the underground tunnels as well.[52]

Suddenly triumphant after so much fighting, the Romans then placed their standards upon the towers of the Upper City. The anticlimactic planting of the imperial *signa* was the prelude to a massacre. Coursing through the alleys of the Upper City, the Romans killed with their swords anyone they encountered. The houses in which some took refuge were burned to the ground. In some cases, when they entered houses looking for loot, the Romans found whole families already dead, all of the family members having starved to death. Soon the alleyways were also filled with the corpses of those the Romans killed. The indiscriminate slaughter ceased toward the evening when darkness fell.[53] Night, not orders, put a halt to the killing.

As darkness spread over the city the fires gained new life. By the morning the whole city of Jerusalem was engulfed in flames.[54] It was perhaps in this conflagration that the young woman in her mid-twenties, whose forearm was discovered by archaeologists in 1970 in the so-called Burnt House, lost her life, when the mansion she was in, located in the eastern part of the Upper City, collapsed on top of her.[55] (See map 4.)

A stone weight with a personal inscription in Aramaic found in the Burnt House, reading "Of Bar Kathros" or "Of the son of Kathros," has been cited to argue that the house was at least in part some kind of factory or workshop, in which was used a stone scale produced or authorized by the Kathros family, one of the families of priests perhaps associated with the family of the high priest Caiaphas.[56] Some scholars have argued that the weight was utilized to weigh the tithes that priests received; more recently, others have plausibly claimed that the purpose of the stone weight was to measure commodities that were being produced in the house. In that case, the famous "Burnt House" may be better understood as a kind of factory, and not necessarily a home of the Bar Kathros family.[57]

When Titus entered the city he was said to have been amazed at the strength of the towers that the rebel leaders had abandoned in a panic. Later, after the population of the city had been systematically slaughtered, Titus razed the city walls except for the section that enclosed Jerusalem on the west. The western wall of the city was left intact to help protect the garrison that the Romans left behind. Josephus also says that Titus left the Phasael, Hippicus, and Mariamme Towers standing as a kind of memorial to his fortune, the character of the city, and the strength of the city's defenses. Subsequently Titus ordered the rest of the city and the Temple to be razed to the ground.[58]

Almost 2,000 years later some of the huge stones that fell down from the Temple Mount walls still lie on the pavement of the street that runs alongside the so-called Western Wall (in fact, the Herodian-era retaining wall).[59] These stones were probably among those pulled down by the Romans during their systematic destruction of the Temple and the city. Ironically, these stones, which few people notice, let alone pause to contemplate—and not the Western Wall—are the remains most directly connected to the architecture of the Temple itself and to the Temple's destruction by the Romans.

After freeing the prisoners who had been held by the rebel leaders, Titus ordered his men to kill only those they met who were armed and who resisted. The rest were to be taken prisoner. The troops nevertheless killed the old and weak, again ignoring their commander's explicit directions. Those who were younger and were in reasonable condition were herded into the area on the Temple Mount that had been the Court of Women. One of Titus's freedmen was appointed as their prison warden, and the commander's friend Fronto was put in charge of deciding the fate of each prisoner individually.[60]

All of those who were deemed to be seditious or brigands were executed. The tallest and handsomest of the young men were spared, so that they could march in the triumphal procession of Titus in Rome. Out of all the rest, those over the age of 17 were sent in chains to work in Egypt. Vast numbers of others were distributed to the Roman provinces to die by the sword or to be killed by wild animals in theaters (*damnatio ad bestias*). Prisoners under the age of 17 were sold into slavery.[61]

As Fronto was making up his mind about the fates of the prisoners, 11,000 of them died of starvation. Josephus tells us that some of these unfortunates were denied food by the Romans. But others refused it. In any case there was not enough food for such a multitude.[62]

In his autobiography, Josephus later claimed to have rescued his own brother and 50 friends from among the prisoners by petitioning Titus. After receiving permission, he also entered the Temple area where the women and children were and, recognizing about 190 friends and acquaintances among the prisoners, had them liberated. Finally, upon seeing three men he knew in Tekoa who were among those being crucified, he was granted leave to have them taken down. Two of the men subsequently died, but the third survived.[63]

The total number of prisoners captured throughout the war was reckoned by Josephus to be 97,000. Because the Romans kept track of the number of slaves who were sold in the aftermath of their wars, many historians have considered this figure to be plausible.[64] Josephus also claims that during the siege 1,100,000 perished, most of them Jews who had come into Jerusalem from outside to celebrate Passover and got stuck in the city. At least some of them seemingly died from some unspecified pestilence that Josephus claims was the result of the overcrowding in the city at festival time.[65] Few historians have been able to bring themselves to accept such a large number of casualties in a city of some 450 acres.[66] The numbers no doubt were inflated by Josephus to flatter his Roman patrons. A city the size of Jerusalem (about 1 square mile at its core) could have accommodated a population of perhaps 50,000. It seems reasonable to conclude that tens of thousands (20,000–30,000?), not hundreds of thousands or even more than a million people, died during the siege of Jerusalem, even if the population of the city was swollen by the numbers who had come into the city to celebrate the Passover.[67]

Of those who survived it is sobering and poignant to recognize that we know very little about what happened to the tens of thousands of Jews who were enslaved when Jerusalem fell. One of the few exceptions is the case of a young woman named Claudia Aster. On her funerary epitaph from Puteoli in Italy we learn that she was a captive from Jerusalem who lived for 25 years and that her grave was tended to by Tiberius Claudius Masculus, a freedman of the emperor.[68] Claudia Aster, whose Hebrew name would have been Esther, it seems, had been one of the fortunate few to survive the annihilation of Jerusalem. She had been bought by a freedman of the emperor, probably married him after receiving her freedom, and was provided with a grave and some record that she had existed.

THE SEARCH FOR THE LEADERS

After the Romans had slaughtered or enslaved the majority of the Jews that they encountered within the city, they made a search for those who had hidden in the underground tunnels. Ripping up the ground they soon found them too. Anyone discovered alive was killed immediately. But the Romans also found a great many who were already dead. They had killed each other or starved to death. There were more than 2,000 of such corpses. Despite the stench from all the dead bodies, some of the Romans, motivated by greed, went on searching through the tunnels and found many valuable objects. They also came upon many of the rebel leaders' prisoners, who were brought up out of the depths.[69] The remains of just such an underground mine or drainage tunnel, running out from beneath the west side of the Temple Mount southward toward the Siloam Pool, were uncovered by archaeologists in 2007.[70]

John also emerged from the underground warren alive. Perhaps on 2 September John asked for the pledge of security from the Romans that he had turned down many times during the siege. John eventually was sentenced to "life in chains."[71] His exact fate is unknown, though some historians suspect that he was brought to Rome, marched in Titus's and Vespasian's triumph, and was executed there.

After the capture of John the Romans set fire to the outlying sections of the city and tore down what was left of the city walls. According to the later church historian Eusebius, Vespasian himself ordered that a search be made for all who were of the house of David, so that there might be left no one of the royal family among the Jews.[72] In the end Vespasian had not come to warn the Jews; he had come to end their independence and their sacrificial cult in perpetuity.

Not for the first time in its long history Jerusalem, "the most illustrious of the cities of the east," was destroyed, this time by the Romans, probably by the end of August 70.[73] Thus was the end of the siege of the Jerusalemites.

PART FOUR

Jupiter Capitolinus and the God of Israel

CHAPTER 20

The Tragedies of Triumph

AWARDS, SACRIFICES, MONUMENTS, AND PUBLIC DISPLAYS

After the resistance in Jerusalem had been eradicated, Titus decided to leave a garrison in what remained of the city. The assignment was given to the Tenth Legion, supported by some cavalry squadrons and infantry cohorts. Henceforth the camp of the Tenth Legion was established on the (then) southwestern hill of the city, near what is now the Jaffa Gate. Command of the Tenth was assigned to Sextus Vettulenus Cerialis, who became the first legate (*legatus Augusti pro praetore*) of the province of Judaea.[1] A fiscal procurator of the province was also based in Caesarea Maritima.[2] Herod's old palace to the north of the theater in Caesarea was renovated into a mansion for the new legate.[3]

Some Jews still lived in the city and the surrounding countryside after Jerusalem was garrisoned. But their numbers were small, and lands that once belonged to the population and the royal family became the property of the emperor and were worked by people as quasi-tenants (*coloni* in Latin).[4] The Roman writer Pliny the Elder calls the toparchy of the countryside Orine.[5] That name probably relates to the hilly topography of the area, but we do not know for certain how or why the Romans chose the name for the toparchy.

One of the beneficiaries of the redistribution of land in Judaea was none other than Josephus. Titus gave Josephus land, probably from what had been royal estates in the Jezreel Plain, because a Roman garrison had been quartered on the land he held in or around Jerusalem.[6] Vespasian subsequently gave Josephus a large tract of land in Judaea.[7] That land was later exempted from taxes by Domitian.[8] Josephus presumably enjoyed the benefits of these imperial gifts in absentia. For after the conclusion of the war, taking with him sacred books by Titus's permission, Josephus went to Rome, where he resided in the house that Vespasian had lived in before he became emperor.[9] There the ex-commander of the two Galilees received Roman citizenship and a pension and wrote his account of the war, first in his own language—probably meaning Aramaic—which was sent to "the barbarians in the interior."[10] Among the "barbarians," he tells us, were the Parthians, Babylonians, the most remote Arabian tribes, Jews who lived on the eastern side of the Euphrates, and the Adiabenians.[11] He subsequently "translated" that Aramaic account into Greek.[12] How closely Josephus's Greek version of the war followed its Aramaic predecessor is a matter of unresolvable scholarly debate, since nothing of the Aramaic text survives.

There were land-tenure and demographic changes outside the occupied capital too. Some 800 military veterans were settled at the site of Ammaous (probably Moza), and after 70 Roman legionary soldiers such as the senior centurion of Legio X Fretensis, Tiberius Claudius Italicus, made their home in Caesarea Maritima, constituted as a colony of Roman citizens (*colonia civium Romanorum*) by Vespasian at an uncertain date.[13] On coins and inscriptions, Herod's dream city, where Vespasian was first proclaimed emperor by his soldiers, was afterward entitled *Colonia Prima Flavia Augusta Caesariensis,* or alternatively *Caesarea.*[14] Augustus and Dea Roma, Mithras, Tyche, Isis, and Serapis, in association with Kore, Demeter, Asklepios, Hygieia, Apollo, possibly Hekate and Dionysos, and probably other Graeco-Roman deities too, such as Ephesian Artemis, were worshiped in the Roman colony. The Latin language was used in Caesarea and in the region around it in public inscriptions for officials up to the early fourth century CE, such as in the honorary inscription for the pontifex, public magistrate, and orator Marcus Flavius Agrippa, inscribed on a statue base in the theater of Maiumas (Kefar Shuni), 3.7 miles northeast of Caesarea.[15]

Before the war was even over, then, Romans were transforming Judaea into a militarized zone, where Roman citizens, many of them ex-soldiers, planted roots and spread their culture.[16] Just as the conquests of Alexander the Great in 332 BCE and his successors introduced into the region large numbers of people who had few, if any, personal or cultural connections to the peoples, languages, and cultures of the Middle and Near East, so too did the Roman victory in Jerusalem in 70.

As the ethnic and cultural landscape of Judaea was being altered, Titus held an awards ceremony in Jerusalem. Standing on a tribunal in the center of his former camp, he praised his soldiers for their obedience, courage, and actions. By these, he said, they had increased the power of their fatherland and shown to all men that neither the multitude of their enemies, nor the strength of their country, nor the great size of their cities, nor the unreasoning recklessness and beast-like savagery of their enemies could confound the courage of the Romans, no matter how often their enemies might have discovered an ally in fortune. He told his men that it was glorious to have brought such a long war to a conclusion.[17]

Then, echoing a line from the Athenian historian Thucydides, Titus (or Josephus) said that they could not have prayed for a happier conclusion when they began the war.[18] But what was a more glorious and splendid testimonial to them, he claimed, was that those whom they had elected to be the governors and leaders of the Romans' rule (primarily Vespasian) and sent to the fatherland were being saluted universally. Their rulings were being obeyed, and they, their electors, were being regarded thankfully. Finally, he told the soldiers that he admired them all, but that upon those who had distinguished themselves in the fighting he would immediately bestow gifts and honors.[19]

Those who had performed brilliant deeds during the war had their names read out, and golden crowns were placed upon their heads by the Roman commander. Such crowns were ordinarily bestowed upon Roman soldiers who had climbed over the walls of an enemy's city (*corona muralis*) or made it across the ramparts of a foe's camp (*corona vallaris*). Soldiers also received golden neck chains (torques), small golden spears, and Roman standards made of silver.[20] They were given promotions, as well as silver and gold and vestments from the spoils. Among those honored by Titus and Vespasian for extraordinary service during the Judaean war was Gaius Velius Rufus, chief centurion of Legio XII Fulminata, who was decorated with a rampart crown, necklaces, ornaments, and armbands.[21] We don't know what Velius did to merit all of these awards.

Titus then descended from his tribunal and, after making many blessings for the whole army amidst many acclamations, turned to sacrifices for the victories. A large number of oxen were brought up to the altars, and after they were sacrificed, the meat was distributed to the troops for a feast.[22] The sacrifice confirms that Titus's logistical supply system was nowhere near collapse, despite the demands and length of Jerusalem's siege.[23] In any case the Romans still had plenty of oxen around. Superior supply had contributed at least as much to the Roman victory in Jerusalem as fighting prowess.

For three days Titus himself joined in the celebratory dining with his officers. Afterward the soldiers were sent off to their new assignments. The Tenth Legion settled down into its guard duty in Jerusalem rather than returning to its previous encampment on the Euphrates. The Twelfth Legion, which had been commanded by Cestius at the beginning of the war and previously had been stationed at Raphaneae in Upper Syria, was posted to the region known as Melitene, along the Euphrates. Notwithstanding the feats of Gaius Velius Rufus, the Twelfth apparently had done nothing to reestablish its martial reputation during the war, and some historians have speculated that Josephus never mentioned the name of its new commander after the Cestius disaster because that man may have been living in Rome when Josephus produced his account(s) of the war there. Josephus may not have wished to make enemies in his adopted city. In any case, the redeployment of the Twelfth to the Euphrates was no reward. Titus took the Fifth and Fifteenth Legions with him first to Caesarea Maritima in the autumn of 70, where the spoils from the war were taken as well, and then eventually they were all brought to Egypt.[24]

Before leaving Caesarea, Titus made a trip northward to Caesarea Philippi. He took along some of the prisoners from the war. At Caesarea Philippi, Titus had put on all kinds of spectacles. Some of the prisoners were thrown to wild animals, while others were forced to fight each other in mass gladiatorial combats. These Roman-style spectacles became distinctive features of the region's urban scene after the Roman victory in 70.[25] It was also while Titus was in Caesarea Philippi that he learned of the capture of Simon, son of Giora, who up to that time had eluded the Roman soldiers in Jerusalem.[26]

In the final hours before the fall of Jerusalem Simon and a group of his closest friends, along with some stonecutters, had climbed down into one of the secret underground passages of the city, bringing enough food to survive for many days.[27] Their plan was to make their way as far as the existing passageways extended and then, when they found the ends, to have the stonecutters hack their way through to an escape route, presumably outside the Roman lines. Unfortunately for them, however, the work of the stonecutters went very slowly, and they began to run out of food. Undaunted, Simon decided to dress himself up in white tunics covered by a purple mantle and then to pop up out of the ground where the Temple had once stood.[28]

Those who witnessed his emergence were duly stunned at the apparition and at first kept a safe and silent distance. Having overcome their fear, however, they asked Simon who he was. Simon refused to answer but demanded to see the Roman general.

Terentius Rufus, who had been left in command of the Roman force in Jerusalem for the time being, was soon brought to the scene. The local commander was not impressed by Simon's chthonic epiphany. He clapped Simon in chains and sent a message to Titus in Caesarea Philippi informing him of how Simon had been captured. The rest of Jerusalem's subterranean passages were then more thoroughly searched. A large number of rebels were discovered and no doubt put in irons like Simon. Wearing his, Simon was sent along to Titus when he returned from Caesarea Philippi to Caesarea Maritima.[29]

Back in Maritima, Titus celebrated his brother Domitian's eighteenth birthday on 24 October. For the festivities no less than 2,500 Jews from the war were sent to die, either in the Herodian hippodrome/stadium or in the theater, fighting beasts or each other with swords. Some also were burned to death. After Titus had moved on to Berytus, which was the site of a Roman colony at the time, more captives still perished, to provide entertainment during the celebration of Vespasian's birthday on 17 November.[30] Herod the Great could never have imagined that so many of the descendants of his subjects would meet gruesome deaths in the sport and entertainment venues that he had provided for cities throughout the region.

THE JEWS OF SYRIA

Further misfortunes overwhelmed the Jews of Syrian Antioch around the same time. Although Antiochus Epiphanes (r. 175–164 BCE) had captured Jerusalem and erected a desecrating sacrilege (i.e., a statue) on the altar of burnt offering in the Temple, his Seleucid successors had adopted a far more humane and tolerant policy toward the large numbers of Jews who lived within Syria.[31] To the Jews of Antioch had been returned all brass votive objects taken from Jerusalem during its sack by Antiochus, and they were granted citizen rights equal to those of the Greek citizens of the city by Seleucus I Nicator, the former commander of Alexander the Great's elite infantry and founder of the Seleucid dynasty in Syria.[32] Many Greeks living in Antioch were said to be attracted to the religious ceremonies of the Jews.[33]

The situation changed when the war in the Galilee broke out. After Vespasian's arrival in Syria at the beginning of the war, at a time when there was widespread hostility toward the Jews, a Jew named Antiochus, who was the son of the chief magistrate of the Jews of Antioch, for some reason took it upon himself to enter the theater and denounce his own father and the other Jews of the city. He accused them of plotting to burn down Antioch one night. He furthermore produced some Jews from outside the city who supposedly were conspirators in the plot.[34] What Antiochus's motive was we don't know.

Having heard these accusations, the infuriated Antiochenes made a rush after the Jews of the city. Incited by Antiochus they tried to force the Jews to sacrifice according to Greek practices. A few did so. Those who resisted were massacred. After gaining the support of some of the troops of the Roman general, Antiochus then instituted a kind of reign of terror over his fellow Jews, including abolishing their right to rest on the Sabbath. Soon enough, Jews in other cities were being persecuted in the same way.[35]

After a fire broke out that burned down the four-sided market, the archive building, the magistrates' office, and the basilicas of Antioch, Antiochus seized the opportunity to accuse the Jews of setting the conflagration. Already primed to believe the worst about them, the Antiochenes once more began to vent their fury upon the Jews.[36]

It was only with difficulty that the acting governor of Syria, Gnaeus Collega, was able to restrain the mob and buy some time to put the evidence about what had happened before Caesar himself.[37] In the end, Collega's investigation revealed that the fire had been set by a group of debtors, who believed that if they destroyed the marketplace and the public record office their money troubles would be over. Not one Jew was found to have been involved.[38]

Although the Jews of Antioch were exonerated of the crime of starting the fire in Antioch, Antiochus's hate-mongering succeeded in creating an atmosphere of animosity toward the Jews who lived throughout Syria. And thus, when Titus made his way from Berytus to the Syrian cities and again put on expensive displays of more Jewish prisoners fighting to the death in the cities, we can reasonably surmise that these ghastly spectacles were well attended and enthusiastically celebrated.[39]

Attempting to take advantage of the situation, the people of Antioch petitioned Titus to expel the Jews from their city altogether. But Titus refused their request.[40] After making a trip to Zeugma, where he received a gold crown of congratulation from the Parthian king Vologaeses for his victory over the Jews, Titus returned to Antioch, where the town council and assembly once more asked him to throw the Jews out of the city. In response Titus informed the Antiochenes that it was not possible to do so because the country of the Jews had been destroyed and no other place would receive them. There was nowhere to expel them to.[41]

The frustrated Antiochenes then sent another petition to Titus. This time they asked him at least to revoke the Jews' civic privileges. This too was denied.[42] Perhaps Titus understood that if the Jews of Antioch had their local privileges abolished, this would set a precedent for other cities, and the result ultimately would be even more friction between Jews and non-Jews in the cities of Syria, more public disorder, and more appeals made to him and his father. Eventually there also would be more of the kind of ethnic violence that had helped precipitate the war in the first place. Whatever his motive, Titus clearly disappointed the Antiochenes before he left the city on his way back to Jerusalem. This, at least, is how Josephus wants us to understand the story.

But the details of the coupled stories he tells about relations between the Jews and non-Jews in the city tend to obscure the more significant point that whatever tensions and issues there were between the two groups by the beginning of the war, they did not cease when the fighting in Jerusalem was over. Judaism was not destroyed along with the Temple. But the lives of many Jews in the regional diaspora became far less secure after 70.[43]

In Jerusalem, meanwhile, Josephus says that Titus felt great sorrow about the destruction of the city and heaped curses upon the authors of the revolt who had brought its punishment upon so glorious and great a city. As we shall see, however, that was not how Titus's attitude toward what he had done in Judaea was later advertised in Rome.

THE TRIUMPH IN ROME

During Titus's last days in Jerusalem, the Romans continued to dig through the city's ruins looking for valuables, assisted by prisoners who revealed to them where the most precious articles had been buried during the siege.[44] Afterward Titus marched through the desert to Alexandria in Egypt.

Once he reached Alexander's greatest civic foundation, he sent the Fifth Legion back to its station in the province of Moesia (Oescus in the lower Danube) and the Fifteenth to Pannonia (Carnuntum in Lower Austria). Seven hundred of the war captives, plus the rebel leaders Simon and John, were then transported by ship to Italy to march in the inevitable triumph through the streets of Rome.[45] Titus himself followed, accompanied by Josephus.[46] The sons and some other relatives of the king of Adiabene were also brought along as hostages to prevent the Adiabenians from aiding the Jews again in the future.[47]

Even before Judaea had been subdued and Vespasian got to Rome, the Senate had conferred upon him the right to extend the *pomerium* or ritual boundary of the city, within which auspices to determine the will of the gods could be taken.[48] Such a right was usually awarded only after a major military victory. The third-century CE historian Cassius Dio says that after news of Jerusalem's capture reached Rome, the Senate also authorized the construction of several triumphal arches to commemorate the victory.[49] At least some of these have not survived, though the famous Arch of Titus, which was dedicated about 10 years later, may have been included in the original plan for the series of arches. (For the Arch of Titus, see the later discussion in this chapter.)

Upon Titus's arrival in Rome, he was greeted by his father Vespasian and his brother Domitian, and the city extended to Titus a reception equal to the one that it had given to his father upon his return, but with the added luster that Domitian was there to greet his brother.[50] A panel from the Palazzo della Cancelleria in Rome apparently depicts a kind of synthesis of the receptions given to both Vespasian and Titus. On Frieze B of the panel personifications of the Senate and the Roman people greet them.[51] Probably after some consultation with Vespasian it was soon decided to celebrate one triumph in common, rather than the separate triumphs for Vespasian and Titus originally decreed by the Senate.[52]

The night before the triumph was to take place the whole army marched out in its companies and divisions under its officers near the gates of the Temple of Isis in the Campus Martius, where Vespasian, Domitian, and Titus were spending the night. (See map 5 for what follows.) The Flavians may have chosen to pass the night in the temple of the Egyptian deity because of Vespasian's and Titus's connections to Egypt and the cult of Isis. Vespasian, it will be recalled, supposedly had been acclaimed emperor first by the legions stationed in Egypt and was initiated into the cult of Serapis (which was often associated with Isis), and Titus had hired the Alexandrian Tiberius Iulius Alexander as his chief of staff for the war against the Jews.[53] Domitian also had eluded Vitellius's forces during the fighting in Rome in 69 by dressing up as a follower of Isis.[54] If so, the choice of where to spend the night before the triumphal procession indicates that, contrary to modern theories, Vespasian and Titus did not intentionally avoid all potential reminders of their triumph over their Roman rivals in 69 during the triumphal spectacle.

On the morning of the triumph during the summer of 71 the entire city of Rome turned out to watch.[55] One historian has estimated that a crowd of 300,000 or more might have assembled to witness the triumphal procession through the city.[56] At the break of day Vespasian and Titus emerged from the temple wearing laurel crowns, dressed in traditional purple robes. Vespasian and Titus walked to the Porticus of Octavia, which had been built by the emperor Augustus for his sister, where they were awaited by the senators, the chief magistrates, and the members of the equestrian order. In front of the stoas a tribunal had been put up, with chairs of ivory (*sellae curules*) placed upon it. From the time of the early Republic, Roman magistrates with *imperium* (the power of command) and certain priests had sat upon such chairs.[57] Vespasian and Titus mounted the platform and took their seats. Father and son were unarmed, wearing silk robes, and now crowned with bays.

As soon as Vespasian and Titus were seated, the troops began to shout out acclamations. After acknowledging the soldiers' plaudits, Vespasian motioned for silence. After the troops quieted down Vespasian veiled most of his head with his mantle, following standard Roman practice. As Jews did, Romans sacrificed with their heads covered. The emperor then made the traditional prayers. Presumably these were prayers of thanksgiving to the gods for the victory in the war. Titus followed suit. When the prayers were completed, Vespasian dismissed the troops to a breakfast that was furnished for them. He and Titus then withdrew to the so-called *Porta Triumphalis* or Triumphal Gate, located somewhere between the capitol and the Tiber River. There they ate, and then, after putting on triumphal robes and sacrificing to the gods whose statues were next to the gate, they sent the procession on its way, driving off through the theaters, so that the view for the crowds would be easier.[58] It is possible that, by "theaters" in the plural, what Josephus meant were the still mostly intact theater of Marcellus and the Circus Maximus, which could be understood as a kind of theater or space where spectators were entertained.[59]

The triumphal procession exhibited the greatness of the Romans' hegemony, the story of the war, and its captives. First, there was a mass of silver, gold, and ivory carried along, not as if borne in a procession, as Josephus reports, but as if it flowed like a river. There were also tapestries, some of them dyed purple. Others were embroidered in Babylonian style, with portraits on them. There were transparent gems to be seen, set in gold crowns, and some in other fashions that were so numerous that they belied the idea of their rarity. Images of the gods, of enormous size and made of the finest materials, were also carried along. Next came many different kinds of animals, suitably ornamented. Their handlers wore garments of purple woven together with gold.[60] The ornaments worn by the rest of those who marched in the procession were of amazing richness, and even the captives wore beautiful garments. Among them presumably were the 700 young Jews who had been brought to Rome by Titus, the Adiabenians perhaps, and the rebel leaders.[61]

More impressive still were the moving scaffolds of the procession. Many of them were three or four stories high, and the frames of all were made of gold and crafted ivory. Tapestries of interwoven gold enfolded many of them. Separate parts of these scaffolds told the story of the war. On one, a once prosperous country was shown in ruins. On another, phalanxes of the enemy were being destroyed. Here there were people in flight; there, others were being led into captivity. Walls of great height were destroyed by siege engines, and strong fortresses were overcome. Strongly defended cities were overwhelmed, and an army was shown surging within the rampart walls. A whole area was seen to be awash with blood, and the hands of supplicants were seen raised up, imploring for mercy, unable to offer resistance. Fire enveloped temples, and the roofs of houses were pulled down upon the heads of their owners. Rivers were running, not over a sown land, providing drinking water to men or beasts, but through a countryside in flames. On each of the scaffolds was depicted the general of the captured city in the posture in which he was captured. It is at least possible that Josephus, who had led the defense of Iotapata, was one of the captive generals so depicted. A number of ships came behind the scaffolds, perhaps representing the ones that had taken part in the naval battle on the Sea of Galilee.[62]

The spoils from the war were carried along in massive heaps. Of these, those taken from the Temple in Jerusalem were most conspicuous. There was a golden table weighing many talents and also a golden lampstand (menorah), with its seven branches. It was presumably on the table carried in the procession that the so-called bread of the presence (Shewbread) was set every week for God in the Temple.[63] The lampstand was perhaps one of the ones that was used within the Tabernacle and was symbolic of the honor Jews associated with the number seven.[64] Seven was the number of the days of the week, and the Sabbath was on the seventh day; elsewhere Josephus explained the seven branches of the menorah in terms of planetary symbolism, since there were five wandering planets or stars, in addition to the sun and the moon.[65] Following the table and the lampstand in the triumphal procession was the law of the Jews.[66] Next there were a great many men carrying gold

FIGURE 13. The *carcer*, or prison, on the northeastern slope of the Capitoline
Hill in Rome where Simon bar Giora perhaps was executed in 71 at the end
of the triumph of Vespasian and Titus. G. Rogers.

and ivory images of Victory. Behind these drove Vespasian first, followed by
Titus, with Domitian riding beside them, magnificently adorned, on a horse
worthy of admiration.[67]

Simon bar Giora may have marched in front of Vespasian. On the reverse
side of a gold coin (*aureus*) minted at Lugdunum in Gaul in 71, at any rate, a
bearded figure identified by some scholars as Simon is shown, with his hands
tied behind his back, marching in front of Vespasian in his chariot.[68]

The procession ended at the Temple of Jupiter Capitolinus on the Capitoline Hill in Rome. There the participants waited for the news of the execution of Simon, the leader of the revolt. A rope had been put over his head,
and as he was led along in the procession he was scourged by those who led
him. He was taken to the *carcer,* an underground detention cell that was
carved down into the rock on the northeastern slope of the Capitoline Hill,
where, by Roman law, those condemned to death for wrongdoing were executed by strangulation.[69] (See figure 13.)

Simon bar Giora is the only individual specifically named by the sources
as having been executed in connection with the triumph.[70] His ritualized

punishment was perhaps an indication that he was considered to be the most dangerous of Rome's enemies during the war. After it was announced that there was an end to Simon, the people shouted with joy.[71]

The end of Simon's story took place a long way away from his birthplace, whether it was in the Decapolis, Gezer, or somewhere else. If Simon's father was indeed a convert to Judaism, the irony that a first-generation Jew was the foreign general executed by the Romans at the climax of Vespasian's and Titus's triumphal celebration was perhaps lost on everyone but the victim himself. Neither a social revolutionary nor a messianic figure, Simon bar Giora was essentially a local warlord who paid the ghastly ritual price for Cestius's humiliation and the war of the Jews against Romans because someone had to, for the sake of Roman pride and vengeance. Or it may just be that we alone see it as ironic that the son of a convert from outside Jerusalem became the symbol of and scapegoat for the revolt of the Jews from Rome.

Sacrifices were then made, together with the customary prayers. If triumphal precedent was observed, these sacrifices took place just outside the recently destroyed Temple of Jupiter Optimus Maximus on the Capitoline. After making the sacrifices, the conquering commanders went into the palace. They entertained some at a feast, while for others sumptuous preparations had been made for feasting in their own homes.[72]

Some scholars have argued that the Flavian triumph as described by Josephus was an exercise in deception and misdirection, a kind of Potemkin triumph. According to this theory, the war fought by the Flavians against the Jews was not a foreign war against a rebellious people, and the real fighting done by the Flavians and their supporters had been against other Romans during the Roman civil war of 68–69. Vespasian had no convincing claim to a triumph, because all he had accomplished was to capture Iotapata and to face some "unpleasantness" in the eastern Galilee and the Golan. These scholars argue that during the triumph Vespasian and Titus attempted to associate the Judaean War with Egypt and a larger eastern settlement and that the spoils displayed in the triumphal procession were mostly props gathered up to suggest the east. They were not riches taken from the Jews of Judaea itself.

They further claim that the representations of the war on the multistoried scaffolds, with scenes of the countryside being ravaged, enemy phalanxes being routed, walls being wrecked by machines and fortresses being captured, and rivers flowing through a land in flames on every side, bore no resemblance to the actual fighting during the war, as described by Josephus. From this it follows that Josephus's description of the triumph is intentionally ironic at the very least. The Flavians' display of the golden table, the lampstand, and the law of the Jews taken from the inner sanctuary of the Temple as the main plunder from the war was pathetic. Finally, Simon's selection as the enemy villain to be executed at the end of the spectacle underscored the make-believe nature of the triumph.[73]

The arguments adduced to support the theory that the Flavian triumph was a sham beg a number of questions. Is it true that the main action in 68–69 was against Romans and there was very little fighting during the war in the Galilee and Judaea? The Flavians did fight against their rivals for the throne of Rome in 68–69. But Vespasian and Titus and three Roman legions (XV, V, X), plus handpicked men from other legions (III, XXI, IV, and VI) and auxiliary cohorts and cavalry, from 67–70 fought non-Romans at Gabara, Iotapata, Iapha, Mt. Gerizim, Joppa, Tiberias, Tarichaeae, Gamala, Itaburion, Iamnia, Azotus, Bethennabris, Abila, Iulias, Besimoth, Betabris and Caphartoba on the border of Idumaea, and in Jerusalem. It is wrong that there was no war of Romans against rebellious Jews during these years. Moreover, Josephus's own credibility as a writer among his Roman sponsors and friends depended upon his readers accepting that his descriptions of the fighting at sites such as Iotapata, Gamala, and Jerusalem were largely accurate—and often harrowing. Josephus's terrible description of Roman soldiers throwing infants off the cliff at Gamala is not a scene that leaves readers wondering whether its author is trying to impress them by ironic undermining of his own account of it.

Vespasian was the commander-in-chief of the Roman forces operating in the Galilee in 67 and 68 up to Nero's death, and if Josephus is right, there was sustained resistance to Vespasian at Gamala and Iotapata in particular. If Josephus is not right about that resistance or the intensity of the fighting that took place during those sieges, then we have no idea what really happened there. Ballista stones and arrowheads found at battle sites do not speak for themselves and cannot tell us how the battles at Iotapata and Gamala developed and were concluded. What we think we know about what happened during those battles over days and weeks can only be based upon historical narratives—which means Josephus's narrative(s). Of course, those narratives are literary creations, constructed to support the ideas of its author about how the war came about and why the Romans won. But to take one example out of hundreds of possibilities, we would know very little or nothing about the tactical measures and countermeasures that the Jews and the Romans used during the siege of Iotapata without Josephus's detailed descriptions of them.

There is numismatic evidence that Vespasian tried to associate his regime with the Egyptian goddess Isis, but none of the props or spoils that were carried in the triumphal procession came from Egypt or represented it, and no one alive in 71 would have witnessed a triumph in which Egyptian artifacts had been used to lay claim to a larger eastern settlement. That some of the props displayed in the procession were locally produced does not mean that the triumph itself was seen as some kind of fake.

A Roman triumph was by definition a performance, a live, moving spectacle, a representation of deeds as the Greek historian Polybius put it, and a local one at that.[74] It was not a work of history composed to be read and critiqued word by word, line by line, by scholars. Nor was it a documentary film, with experts on hand to correct the director's inaccuracies, mistakes, or exaggerations. Moreover, there is no evidence whatsoever that spectators who came to watch a triumphal procession expected to see an exact, accurate, scene-by-scene, chronological representation of what had happened during a war.

It is also not easy to identify to whom the triumph of the Flavians as described by Josephus would have been seen as a fraud or an exercise in misdirection, distracting people from thinking about the Flavians' triumph over their Roman foes during the recent civil wars. If Josephus witnessed the triumph, as is, of course, almost certain, it is hard to believe that he would have been thinking that the Flavians were pulling the wool over the spectators' eyes as he watched 700 of his fellow Jews being paraded through the streets of Rome. It is also unlikely that he would have thought it was farcical when he saw Romans carrying the golden table, the lampstand, and the laws of the Jews through the streets of Rome in triumph. Would Josephus and at least some of the approximately 40,000 Jews who lived in Rome at the time and witnessed the triumph have considered the display of these sacred objects stolen from their now-destroyed Temple "pathetic"?[75]

No doubt there was plenty of pathos evoked during the triumph of Vespasian and Titus in 71. But most of it must have been felt by Jews who witnessed the terrible procession and saw some of the oldest and holiest relics of their people being carried by their Roman conquerors through the streets of the adopted city. That was a sight worth lamenting over.

As for the rest of Rome's population, we should ask whether the hundreds of thousands who witnessed Vespasian, Titus, and Domitian riding through the streets of Rome really would have been thinking about Vitellius, Otho, and Galba at the time or about specific past triumphs, for that matter. Most of the spectators surely were not Roman historians, and there is no explicit evidence that the Flavians planned their triumph with earlier triumphs in mind. Our knowledge of the route of the Flavian procession, for instance, is based largely upon Josephus's somewhat imprecise account. Nor do we know what "informed" Romans were thinking.[76] No source names such people. The only people whose reactions to the Flavian triumph in 71 we know of are Josephus and Vespasian himself, who is reported to have said that it served him right for being such a fool as to wish for a triumph in his old age, as if it were owed to his ancestors or had been among his ambitions.[77] As far as we know, Josephus had not attended any previous triumph, and the comment attributed to Vespasian hardly implies that he was thinking about the triumphs of Rome's prior *triumphatores,* such as Caesar or Augustus.

Most of the spectators were probably more focused on what they saw moving past them, right in front of their eyes. They were not there to quibble over footnotes to history or to compare the Flavian triumph to ones they had never witnessed, such as Pompey's triumph for his eastern victories in 61 BCE or Octavian's in 29 BCE. They were there to celebrate Rome's triumph over the recalcitrant Jews and to enjoy the festivities. That their idea of enjoying the triumph included celebrating the strangling of the defeated foreign general may strike many of us as horrifying. But that does not mean that the triumph itself was, or was seen as, some kind of sham. Alas, the subjugation and suffering of the Jews shown in the procession and Simon's murder at the end of the "triumph" were all too real.

The population of Rome expected and demanded military victory, and Vespasian and Titus gave them what they wanted: the moving spectacle of a violent military victory over a defeated and humiliated people. In Caesarea Philippi, Caesarea Maritima, Berytus, the cities of Syria, and especially in Rome, the suffering of Jews sold and bought imperial legitimacy for a dynasty that had simultaneously fought and won a bloody civil war. The more realistic the spectacle of the Jews' suffering, the more convincing was the victors' claim to imperial authority—and the less people probably focused upon the Flavians' victory over their fellow Romans. That was the point.

MONUMENTS, INSCRIPTIONS, AND MONETIZING VICTORY

The victors' message of victory and deserved authority began with a building program that commenced even before Vespasian had returned to Rome. The initiative was particularly important for a first-generation Roman senator who came from a relatively humble background. The overall message of the program was peace, associated especially with the reign of Augustus, after Nero's controversial rule, the civil wars that followed his suicide, and the victory in the Judaean War.[78] Evaded was the fact that it had been Nero who had appointed Vespasian to be the commander of the war that gave the tax collector's son the opportunity to reach for the imperial throne.

While Vespasian was still in Alexandria in the winter of 69, waiting to make a safe journey back across the Mediterranean to Rome, he assigned the work of rebuilding the capitol, including the Temple of Jupiter Capitolinus, which had burned down during the civil war, to Lucius Vestinius, though the architect in charge may have been the famous Rabirius. The Corinthian columns and capitals of the reconstructed temple were made from Pentelic marble, probably taken from the Temple of Olympian Zeus in Athens.[79] Almost a century earlier Octavian also had restored the Capitolium and the theater of Pompey, claiming to have done so at great expense and without having his own name put on the altar.[80]

When he finally made it back to Rome by October 70, Vespasian was promoted as the first to take part in the clearing of the Capitoline site, supposedly carrying some of the debris away on his neck (i.e., probably a stone of some kind in a basket on his neck).[81] The Temple of Jupiter was to be rebuilt, unlike the Temple of the defeated Jews. Vespasian's and Titus's triumph in 71 ended at the still unfinished Temple of Jupiter Capitolinus. The reconstruction was finished in 75.[82] Jupiter had defeated the god of the Jews—or so the Flavians' program of urban reconstruction asserted.

After the triumph was celebrated, Vespasian decided to build a Temple of Peace.[83] It was built to the southeast of the Forum Augustum, on the other side of the Via Argiletum and, subsequently, the Forum Transitorium, constructed by Domitian in the late 80s. The project was dedicated during the sixth year of Vespasian's reign, probably in the summer of 75.[84]

The structure had the shape of an almost square forum, about 150 by 140 meters, with porticoes on all four sides. There were six sequences of four oblong boxes in the middle of the square. It is possible that statuary was displayed for public viewing on these boxes or stands.[85] In any case we know that the temple was decorated with masterworks of painting and sculpture, some of them relocated from the sitting rooms of Nero's *Domus Aurea* or Golden House, including works by Greek artistic masters such as Pheidias, Polykleitos, and Leochares.

The relocation of these art masterpieces made it possible for ordinary Romans to see them; they no longer belonged to the private collection of Nero but to the Roman people. Within the building were also stored vessels of gold taken from the Jerusalem Temple, and other treasures including the Table of the Shewbread and the seven-branched menorah from the *heikhal,* or sanctuary chamber of the Temple, versions or specimens of which were also depicted on the Arch of Titus.[86] The display of the relocated Greek art from the *Domus Aurea* and the treasures looted from the Jerusalem Temple or from where they had been hidden in Jerusalem neatly symbolized the Flavians' attempt to disassociate their regime from Nero at the same time that it reminded viewers of the triumph over the Jews. Nero's fall and the defeat of the Jews made possible the *Pax Flaviana.* Vespasian's Temple of Peace signified a Roman kind of peace; a peace that followed victory in a war.

At least some of the priceless objects from the Temple of the Jews remained in Rome for nearly four centuries until they were taken to North Africa by Gaiseric after the Vandals sacked Rome in 455, and were then brought to Constantinople and Justinian by the general Belisarius in 534.[87] The Byzantine historian Procopius claims that, seeing the ornaments of the Jews that Titus had brought to Rome after the capture of Jerusalem among Belisarius's war booty, a Jew persuaded Justinian to send the treasures of the Jews back to Jerusalem, where they were deposited in the sanctuaries of the Christians.[88] According to one theory the menorah from the Temple of Peace remained in Jerusalem until the city was captured by the Sassanians in 614. What happened to it afterward is unknown. Another one of the lampstands looted by the Romans in 70, perhaps the menorah depicted on the Arch of Titus, might have been taken to Constantinople in 330, where it remained until the imperial palace of the New Rome was conquered by the Franks and Venetians in 1204.[89]

The copy of the Torah from the Temple and the purple hangings from the sanctuary meanwhile were kept in the imperial palaces on the Palatine Hill.[90] We do not know what became of them. But from the mid–first century CE until the mid–fifth century the artifacts of the destroyed Temple of the Jews were on display in the center of Rome to remind everyone of the Jews' defeat and the loss of their national shrine.

Vespasian probably began work on the amphitheater in Rome (the *Amphitheatrum* mentioned by the poet Martial and biographer Suetonius) shortly after his and Titus's triumph. The 50,000-seat "Colosseum," as it has been known colloquially since the medieval period because of the colossal statue of the sun god Sol installed nearby, opened during the reign of Titus in 80 CE, with 100 consecutive days of games and spectacles. Many of these took place in the amphitheater, and construction continued into the reign of Domitian "to the shields," or to the highest level of the façade.[91]

Bronze coins from the reigns of Titus and Domitian, a second-century CE funerary relief from the tomb of the Haterii in Rome, and architectural remains, especially a travertine block in front of an engaged column, indicate that the central entrances to the Colosseum, along its long and short directional axes, were elaborated in the form of triumphal arches, above which there were mounted triumphal, four-horse chariots (*quadrigae*) driven by the Roman emperor. These triumphal arch/entrances were intended to serve as visual reminders of the building's connection to the victory over the Jews and the Flavian triumph in 71.[92] A less imposing but far more historically significant indicator of the amphitheater's relationship to the outcome of the Judaean War was rediscovered in the mid-1990s.

After carefully examining nail holes that had once fastened a number of gold-plated bronze letters to a lintel stone, the Hungarian-born classical scholar Geza Alföldy was able to read a Flavian-era inscription that subsequently had been covered over by a fifth-century inscription. The earlier inscription perhaps was inscribed on the lintel stone over the amphitheater's southern exit, though Alföldy surmised that copies of the inscription had been put up over all of the Colosseum's main exits and there possibly was a larger version of the inscription above the podium in the center of the structure as well. (See figures 14 and 15.) Alföldy read the surviving example of the inscription as stating that the (new?) amphitheater had been paid for "from the spoils" of the war ([ex] *manubi*[i]*s*).[93]

The dedicator of the original inscription was Vespasian; Titus later had the *T* from his own *praenomen* (personal name) added to the inscription before the Colosseum was opened up to the public in 80. What this inscription probably means is that spoils from the war were used to help subsidize the cost of building the amphitheater. Nowhere does the restored inscription say that the amphitheater was built solely from the war's booty, as some scholars have tried to make the inscription say. Nevertheless, the inscription is of the upmost importance for recognizing that Vespasian and Titus wanted the millions of people who visited the amphitheater to be reminded of the connection between its construction and their victory in the war against the Jews.

The famous Arch "of" Titus, situated atop the Velian hill along the Via Sacra at the southeast entrance of the Roman Forum (*Forum Romanum*), prob-

FIGURE 14. The Colosseum inscription claiming that the amphitheater had been built from the spoils of the war. The nail holes that fastened the gold-plated bronze letters of the original inscription to the lintel are visible at the bottom of the stone. G. Rogers.

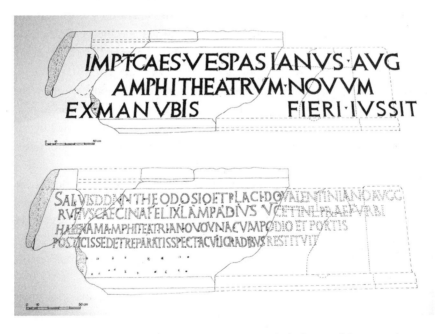

FIGURE 15. The Colosseum "spoils" inscription with the letters of the original, Flavian-era inscription restored beneath the writing of the later, fifth-century CE inscription. G. Rogers.

ably was planned as a triumphal arch, dedicated "to" Titus ("*Divo Tito Divi Vespasiani f(ilio)*") by the Senate and Roman people. Construction may have begun as early as 70, even if it was later finished by Domitian, though it may have been fully elaborated as a commemorative arch in memory of Titus by Domitian only after Titus's death in 81.[94]

Inside the single, approximately 2.5-meter-wide archway or bay of the monument are frieze panels. The panel on the southern side shows Titus and Roman soldiers, preceded by a bound captive, about to pass through a decorated arch, following their victory over the Jews. The bound captive must be a representative of a captured Jew from the Judaean War. The Romans carry spoils taken from the Temple in Jerusalem, including an oblong, hexagonal or octagonal two-board table of Shewbread (unfortunately damaged), with cups or receptacles of different sizes and volumes standing on it, perhaps to be used for offerings or libations; two (perhaps) silver trumpets of the Roman tuba-type, again of unequal sizes; and a specimen or example of the gold candelabrum.[95] (See figure 16.)

At least some of the objects shown (the offering table, a menorah, trumpets) are representations of the real physical objects that were carried in Vespasian's and Titus's triumph in 71 and that were later displayed in the Temple of Peace. Because there were multiple examples of each of these objects in the Temple itself it is impossible to say that the individual objects depicted on the relief correspond to specific objects that once belonged to the Temple. Surely, however, those who saw the relief panel in the ancient world were intended to believe that they were looking at real objects—booty—from the Temple. The understanding of millions of tourists who still stop and look at the relief is probably very much the same. The menorah being carried by the triumphant Roman soldiers is the single most evocative visual symbol in existence of Rome's victory over the Jews in the war.

On the northern interior panel Titus is shown driving a four-horse, triumphal chariot that is led by the goddess Roma, the personification of the city, and Roman lictors. Alongside Titus are the deities Honos, Virtus, and Victoria, the last of whom is placing a laurel wreath crown on Titus's head. Personifications of the Roman Senate and the Roman people escort the chariot.

Less famous, but perhaps more revealing about the Flavians' use of the war to exaggerate—or lie about—their martial success in Judaea, was the triple-bay arch, dedicated by the Senate and the people of Rome to Titus by early 81 CE on the (curved) hemicycle of the Circus Maximus's southeast side

FIGURE 16. The panel on the southern side of the Arch of Titus in Rome showing Roman soldiers carrying the spoils from the Jerusalem Temple. G. Rogers.

(which replaced the arch of Lucius Stertinius from 186 BCE, destroyed by Nero in 68). (See map 5 and figure 17.)

Sculptural fragments from the Circus Maximus Arch seem to relate scenes from the war in Judaea.[96] Its dedicatory inscription reads,

> The Senate and People of Rome to Imp(erator) Titus Caesar Vespasianus, son of the Deified Vespasianus, pontifex maximus, with *tribunicia potestas* for the tenth time, (hailed as) Imp(erator) for the seventeenth time, consul for the eighth time, their princeps, because on the instructions and advice of his father, and under his auspices, he subdued the race of the Jews, and destroyed the city of Jerusalem, which by all generals, kings, or races previous to himself had either been attacked in vain or not even attempted at all.[97]

The last three claims were false: Titus himself had not subdued the race of the Jews by the time the arch and its inscription were put up, as we shall see; he had not destroyed Jerusalem, at least according to Josephus; and

FIGURE 17. View from the southeastern side of the Circus Maximus in Rome.
On this side was located the triple-bay arch dedicated by the Senate and the
Roman people to Titus in 81, honoring him for subduing the race of the Jews and
destroying Jerusalem. G. Rogers.

Jerusalem had been captured at least five times before Titus had done so in
70, as Josephus informs his readers.[98] Nevertheless, based upon the
150,000–250,000 seating capacity of the Circus Maximus, millions of spectators must have seen this inscription and been reminded of Titus's victory
over the Jews from 81 CE. The arch and presumably the inscription on it
were still standing into the ninth century CE, when the now-lost inscription
was copied.[99]

Most significantly, the inscription, though making false claims about the
facts, in a general way nevertheless contradicts Josephus's apologetic account,
in which Titus struggled to prevent the destruction of Jerusalem, including
its Temple. The inscription unapologetically, if falsely, celebrated Titus's destruction of Jerusalem. The authorizers of the inscription apparently did not
buy Josephus's attempt to relieve Titus of responsibility for the destruction of
the holy city.

Coins depicting Judaea's subjugation were minted by 70 at the latest, and
coins advertising the victory, modeled on Augustan-era coins advertising his

victory over Egypt in 30 BCE, with the Latin inscription "Judaea Capta," or Judaea Captured, inscribed on their reverse sides, were minted into the reign of Domitian and circulated throughout the empire.[100] At least some of those coins may have been used to pay the two-denarii tax that Vespasian imposed on all Jews throughout the Roman empire for the fund called the *fiscus iudaicus,* which, in effect, replaced the half-shekel tax that all free male Jews paid yearly as an offering to their God.[101] The new Roman fund was tapped to rebuild the Temple of Jupiter Capitolinus that had been burned down during the fighting in Rome in 69.[102]

Even though the rebuilt Roman temple was consecrated by 21 June 70, after sacrifices were made and the site was purified, the tax on Jews would be collected until the assassination of Domitian on 18 September 96 CE.[103] The temple consecrated in 70 burned down again in 80, and its replacement was then completed during Domitian's reign. Presumably the taxes collected after 80 helped finance construction of the replacement temple.[104]

After Domitian's murder, his successor Nerva apparently canceled the tax, giving Jews in Rome and throughout the empire a respite from the punitive collection. The tax, however, was apparently reinstated by the new emperor, Trajan, just after Nerva's death on 27 January 98 CE and then was paid by Jews into the third century CE.[105] Trajan's father, it will be recalled, had served under Vespasian during the war as commander of Legio X Fretensis.

Agrippa II, Rome's loyal ally throughout the war, also had coins minted with images of Nike or Victory on them, the final proof of whose side he had been on, though, of course, none had been needed since the outbreak of the war.[106] His reward was a secure home in Rome and the award of the rank of a praetor.[107] Agrippa went on to have coins minted honoring Vespasian and Titus after both passed away (86–87).[108] It was no accident at all that Agrippa II retained his kingdom until his death in 100. Very early on Agrippa II had identified the stronger horse in the conflict, and he rode it to his end.

Soon after destruction of the Temple and of a large part of Jerusalem, Judaea's capture became one of the primary justifications for the rule of the Flavians, whose founder could not claim descent from an aristocratic—let alone, a Iulio-Claudian—background.[109] The Flavian dynasty built its authority to rule Rome on the rubble of the Temple and the capture of Judaea. The monuments they rebuilt, built, or had dedicated to them at key locations in

FIGURE 18. View of the Roman Forum from the Capitoline Hill, with the Flavian
Amphitheater rising up in the background to the upper left, and the Arch of
Titus in the middle ground to the right. G. Rogers.

the center of Rome were reminders of their victory for millions of people in
Rome over the centuries.

The rebuilding of the Capitoline Temple of Jupiter to the west of the Roman Forum, begun shortly after the flames in Jerusalem had been extinguished, paid tribute to Jupiter's victory over the God of the Jews. The
Temple of Peace, begun after the Flavian triumph in 71, associated the new
dynasty with Augustus (and his program of restoration and peace after an
earlier round of Roman civil wars) and the war against the Jews. The Flavian
Amphitheater was begun at the same time. Countless people must have seen
the inscriptions declaring that the building had been built from the spoils of
the war. Millions must have passed through the Arch of Titus before the bay
was chained off, observing Titus in his chariot, Roman soldiers hoisting the
treasures from the Temple of the Jews, and a bound Jew being led captive in
front of Titus.

As they entered the Roman Forum from the east through the single bay
of the Arch of Titus, visitors would have a framed view of the forum and,
rising above it, the rebuilt Capitoline Temple of Jupiter. That view encour-

aged people to link the Arch of Titus and the Flavian dynasty with Jupiter and his temple on the Capitoline. From the direction of the Capitoline, the Flavian Amphitheater, built from the spoils of the war, rose up in the background beyond the Arch of Titus. (See figure 18.) South of the Arch of Titus, on the other side of the Palatine Hill, from 81 into the ninth century CE, tens of millions of spectators must have seen the inscription on the Circus Maximus Arch in which it was falsely claimed that Titus had subdued the Jews and captured Jerusalem for the first time.

But even as the Temple of Peace and the other monuments glorifying the Flavians' unapologetic triumph over the Jews were being built or planned, the war of Jews against Romans continued. Not all of the Jews knew that they had been subdued.

CHAPTER 21

Masada

THE CAPTURE OF HERODEION

Even before Vespasian dedicated his new Temple of Peace in Rome, there was more fighting in Judaea. Sextus Lucilius Bassus, who had replaced Sextus Vettulenus Cerialis as legate of Judaea in 71 or 72, captured the fortress of Herodeion, where Herod the Great was interred, less than eight miles southeast of Jerusalem, without any great effort, as far as we can tell from Josephus.[1]

The march to Herodeion could have been made in half a day. When Bassus entered the royal palaces of Upper Herodeion, he must have learned that while rebels occupied the site during the war they had turned the large dining room (*triclinium*) in the western half of the palaces into a synagogue. They also may have been responsible for vandalizing the rose-colored stone sarcophagus in which Herod the Great probably had been laid to rest.[2] If they were responsible, it probably was done because of Herod's well-known friendly relations with the Romans.

THE SIEGE OF MACHAERUS

Bassus then turned his attention to the formidable fortress of Machaerus, some 4.5 miles east of the Dead Sea near its northern end. It was built on a

FIGURE 19. View of the fortress of Machaerus from the east.
Todd Bolen/BiblePlaces.com.

high, rocky elevation some 2,300 feet above sea level on the south bank of
Wadi Zarqa Ma'in, with deep ravines on the northeast and southwest sides.[3]
(See figure 19.) Machaerus, as we have seen, had been seized by Jews from its
garrison in around 66 at the beginning of the revolt.[4]

The first fortress on the hill apparently had been built during the reign of
the Hasmonean ruler Alexander Jannaeus (104–78 BCE). It was destroyed by
the Roman general Gabinius in 57 BCE during his war with Aristobulus.[5]
Subsequently, Herod the Great had enclosed a larger area with walls and towers and founded a town there, on the approximately 1.6-acre site of the northeastern slope. Above the town, on the summit of the ridge, he then had another
wall with three rectangular towers put up. Each was 90 feet high.[6] In the center of the upper fortress there was a great palace, and Herod had cisterns
constructed to provide the inhabitants of the site with a supply of fresh drinking water. The cisterns were connected to an aqueduct. The fortress was also
well stocked with a large quantity of darts and war engines.[7] No doubt Herod
originally conceived of Machaerus as another potential bolt-hole he could flee
to if some of his family members or the people of Jerusalem ejected him from
Jerusalem.

From the Romans' point of view Machaerus could not be ignored indefinitely. The fortress was located at a strategic point to the east of the Dead Sea. Occupied by enemies it threatened the Roman province to the west; in Roman hands it would be a bulwark against potentially hostile forces to the east. After the fall of Jerusalem it was still a magnet for refugees or resisters to Roman influence and rule. Indeed, what happened to those who had holed up in Machaerus after it was taken by Bassus shows that he was not just interested in capturing the fortress. He intended to wipe out all resistance and resisters in the region.

Bassus's original plan of attack apparently was to fill up the ravine on the southeast side of the fortress because its approach was easier than on the other sides, to build up an embankment there, and then to launch his assault on the town.[8] While Bassus and his men set about their work, the defenders of the bastion, who seemed to understand his plan, apparently decided to make their stand from within the walls of Herod's fortifications on the summit. Non-Jews living on Machaerus were forced to stay down in the lower city, where they would absorb the brunt of the initial Roman assault.[9]

Bassus, realizing in turn that in the end he would have to deal with the defenders at the summit, began work on a second embankment. The remains of this project have been found along the northwestern ridge of the site. The point of building this second embankment was to bring the Romans up to a position on a level with the defenders on the summit, starting from the higher (2,133 feet) ground on the northwest. Beneath and around the entire site Bassus and his men also surrounded Machaerus with a rectangular circumvallation wall to prevent anyone from escaping.[10] Into the wall were incorporated a number of fixed camps, from which the Romans might keep an eye out for potential escapees.[11]

While Bassus and his men were laboring on the earthworks, just as Jews in Jerusalem and elsewhere earlier in the war had done, the defenders of the fortress did what they could to impede the Roman efforts. Harassing sallies were made against those working on the mound. During these many Jews and Romans died.[12] The Roman siege of Machaerus might then have proceeded in much the same way that the siege and ultimate capture of Jerusalem had occurred but for a shocking incident.

Eleazar of Machaerus

Fighting on behalf of the Jews was a young man named Eleazar, who had made himself conspicuous by his martial skills and leadership during the attacks upon the Roman workmen. His example apparently encouraged others to take part in the raids more enthusiastically, and he also was the last to withdraw from the fighting, covering the retreat of his fellow Jews.

After one of these skirmishes, Eleazar foolishly loitered outside the gates of the fortress, talking with those on the walls. A certain soldier of the Roman camp named Rufus saw a chance to take advantage of the situation and took it. He ran out suddenly, picked up Eleazar, armor and all, and carried him back to the Roman camp.

Bassus ordered Eleazar to be stripped and brought to a spot where everyone in the fortress could see him. There he was savagely whipped in full view of the horrified onlookers in the fortress. Bassus then gave an order for a cross to be brought up. Thinking that Eleazar was about to be crucified in front of their eyes, the inhabitants of Machaerus let forth piercing shrieks.

At that point Eleazar shouted out to his comrades not to disregard him, now that he was going to suffer a miserable death, and urged them to save themselves by surrendering to Roman power and fortune. Those within the citadel were moved by Eleazar's plea, and his appeals were backed by others who interceded on his behalf; it seems that Eleazar came from a large and wealthy family. A delegation was sent out to Bassus to discuss terms of surrender. The Jews asked for Eleazar to be spared and for safe leave from Machaerus. To these terms Bassus agreed.[13] From Bassus's point of view Eleazar's capture and the capitulation of the Jews were a godsend. He could achieve his objective of neutralizing Machaerus as a threat without having to pursue a tiresome siege. There was only one problem: what to do about the non-Jewish residents of the city.

The End of Resistance at Machaerus

The non-Jews who had been pushed down into the lower city learned that the agreement made with Bassus apparently applied only to the Jews. They therefore planned to escape from the fortress in secret that very night. No sooner had the gates of the city been opened that evening to allow for their escape from the city than those Jews who had made the agreement with Bassus informed the Romans of the plan. The bravest of the escapees managed to fight their way through the Romans. Those still trapped in the lower town were not as fortunate.

Seventeen hundred men were slain, and the women and children were captured and subsequently sold into slavery. Josephus never explains why the non-Jews did not try to surrender or why the Romans killed all of the men. Perhaps the Romans simply weren't interested in showing any mercy. Bassus nevertheless honored the pact he had made with the Jews who held the upper citadel. They were allowed to leave the fortress.[14]

Subsequently, however, Bassus and his troops became aware that a group of Jews, who somehow had managed to flee from Jerusalem during the Roman siege and had made their way to Machaerus, apparently were among those who had been allowed to leave the fortress. After escaping from Machaerus these Jews had gathered within a wooded area, called Iardes by Josephus.[15] Since Iardes is a Hebrew cognate for Jordan, what the text probably means is that these people had presumably fled to the relative safety of a place concealed by some kind of grove of trees that had grown up along the valley of the Jordan River. The area has not been identified, but it must have been somewhere along the river, to the south of Machaerus.

Advancing to the grove after surrounding the refugees with cavalry to block off all avenues of escape, Bassus and his infantrymen cut down the trees that afforded the Jews some cover. Deprived suddenly of the trees' protective screen, the Jews decided upon an attack.

Unfortunately for them, they were no match for the professional Roman soldiers, including those of the Tenth Legion who had taken part in the brief siege. In the fighting, 12 Roman soldiers were killed, and a few more were wounded. Three thousand Jews, on the other hand, were slain, including their leader Judas, the son of Ari, who had been one of the Zealot leaders of the revolt in Jerusalem and was one of the few Jews who apparently escaped from the city through an underground passage. There were no male survivors of the battle.[16] It was not just Machaerus that the Romans wanted. It was the destruction of all potential resisters, no matter where they were.

Judas's participation in the defense of Machaerus indicates that the resistance of Jews to Rome did not end with the destruction of the Temple. The war of Jews against Rome was not over in 70 CE either for Jews or Romans, even as the Romans set about drastically changing the pattern of land tenure in Judaea.

It was about this time that Vespasian ordered Bassus and the procurator Laberius Maximus to sell land belonging to Jews that he (the emperor) had not taken as his own private property. It is probable that the sale of the lands applied to zones where the rebellion had been focused.[17]

Sometime after these orders were given to Bassus and his procurator, Bassus suddenly died, of unknown causes, in 72 or 73.[18] His replacement as governor was L. Flavius Silva Nonius Bassus. Flavius Silva had been military tribune of Legio IIII Scythica in Syria around 64 under Ummidius Quadratus or Domitius Corbulo, quaestor, tribune of the plebs, and legate of the Legio XXI Rapax.[19] Silva's prior military service indicates that he was already familiar with the region and its conflicts.

Finding the rest of Judaea subdued, Silva, along with the soldiers of the Roman Tenth Legion who had been involved in the sieges of Gamala and Jerusalem, supported by somewhere between 3,000 to 8,000 auxiliary troops, turned their attention to the fortress of Masada.[20] Captured first by rebels at the beginning of the revolt, it would be the last of the Herodian fortresses to fall.

THE FORTRESS OF MASADA

The fortress refuge of Masada had been built up during the Hasmonean period on top of the mesa that rises up to a height of some 1,180 feet above the western shore of the Dead Sea.[21] The mesa's diamond-shaped plateau measures around 1,900 feet from its northern tip to its southern end and just over 650 feet from west to east at its broadest point. (See figure 20.) On all four sides there are cliffs leading down into deep ravines. There are several ascent paths up to the summit, but only two are viable for most people, especially during the hot summer months: one up from the Dead Sea side on the east; and the second from the west.[22]

In antiquity the path up the eastern side was called the Snake (*ophis* in Greek), because of its narrow, winding, and semi-circuitous route up to the crest. On the western side of the mesa a natural rock spur rose up gradually from the valley floor to a height only about 50 feet short of the 290-foot-high summit on that side. The natural spur was called *Leuke,* or White, for the color of the stone spur.[23]

The summit of Masada forms a rhombic-shaped plain or plateau comprising some 20 acres of land rather than a precipice. The plateau rises up from its lowest point at the south to its peak on the north. It was upon this plain that the high priest Jonathan, the brother of the more famous Judas Maccabaeus, supposedly built the first fortress and named the site Masada, though some scholars argue that it was Alexander Jannaeus (r. 103–76 BCE) who began fortifying the site.[24]

From about 37 BCE Herod the Great significantly enlarged and expanded the fortress and also added residential palaces.[25] A quick sketch of Herod's building program helps us understand the living situation of the inhabitants

FIGURE 20. Aerial view of Masada from the south. Todd Bolen/BiblePlaces.com.

of Masada at the time of the Roman siege in 73 or 74 and the character of the community.

In the middle years of the second decade BCE Herod had constructed a casement wall of local white stone that encircled the entire summit for almost a mile (4,250 feet), except in the north where the terrace palace was situated; the wall was built apparently after the rest of the buildings on the site were completed. It was 18 feet high and 12 feet wide; its outer wall was 4.6 feet thick. Above the wall, at intervals of about 131 feet, were erected 27 rectangular towers. These were connected to at least 70 apartments that ran along the interior course of the wall. In these apartments lived the approximately 800 soldiers whom Herod installed as a guard on Masada.[26]

During the mid-30s BCE Herod had built a palace on the western slope of the mount.[27] The palace had a wall and four towers at the corners, each of them 90 feet high. Within the palace were apartments, stoas, and baths built around an inner courtyard. Above the buildings of the palace there was another story in which staff or other servants could have found accommodation. The western palace probably served as Herod's residence when he stayed at Masada, and it was here that Herod would have conducted business.[28] Its plan seems to have been based upon a similar palace at Jericho.

Access from the palace to the summit was by a sunken road that could not be seen by those outside. In addition, Herod had raised a great tower at the narrowest point up to the summit on the western side, making access on that side at least as difficult as the route up the Snake Path on the east.

Another palace was erected on the north side of the mesa during the mid-20s BCE. The northern palace was intentionally segregated from the rest of the summit by a large wall made of stone covered with white plaster. The entrance to the upper terrace of the palace was through a courtyard and guardhouse on the eastern side of the wall.

The various rooms of this palace were built up and supported on three terraces, one above another, that were constructed down the cliff on the northern edge of Masada. The rooms on the highest terrace apparently comprised living quarters for Herod and his family members. These rooms were decorated with frescoes and had mosaic floors. After about 15 BCE the mosaic floors of the bathhouse and the upper terrace of the northern palace were replaced by floors of inlaid stone plaques (*opus sectile*). The *triclinium* (dining room) of the upper terrace had "Second Style" Roman wall paintings.[29] A colonnade encircled the round reception hall (*tholos*) on the middle terrace, and the rectangular lowest terrace had a colonnaded central hall that was probably used for receiving guests and holding banquets.[30] The Corinthian column capitals from the buildings of the terraces still retain their floral and geometric designs, indicating that Herod chose to show respect for Jewish religious sensitivities and artistic traditions; that is, none have forbidden images on them. Below the eastern side of the lowest terrace there was a small bathhouse.[31]

A much larger bathhouse was built to the south of the stone wall that separated the northern palace from the rest of the summit. In keeping with Roman architectural precedents the bathhouse had a dressing room (*apodyterium*), a room of moderate heat (*tepidarium*), a cold-water bath room (*frigidarium*), and a hot-water bath room (*caldarium*).[32] The bathhouse clearly was intended to be used by Herod, his family, and guests.

To the east and south of the northern palace's large bathhouse there were food storage rooms. In these rooms were ceramic jars that once held enough grain to feed the inhabitants of Masada for years. Some of that grain probably was produced from Masada's rich soil, most of it on the southern area of the summit.[33] In addition to grain, we know from inscriptions on jars recovered at the site that when Herod and his friends stayed at the site they subsisted on a diet that included dried figs, berries, olives, fish, dough, meat, and herbs.[34]

Herod being Herod however, the king did not live by bread alone up on Masada. By 19 BCE he paid for the importation of Philonian wine from the estate of Lucius Laenius, near Brundisium in Apulia.[35] Wine from the estate of Tiberius was also imported, as well as high-end Massic wine from Monte Massico in Campania, (white) Amineum, (sweet white) Caecubum from Latium, and Tarantinum (from Trentum in Apulia).[36] Masada's Herodian wine cellar was well stocked; his tastes seemed to have inclined toward Italian whites.

Herod also had expensive and possibly kosher fish sauces, including garum, made from fish fermented in salt, muria, and allec imported to the fortress from Spain.[37] These fish sauces were very popular among wealthy, sophisticated Romans. Their importation from across the Mediterranean to Masada must have cost a fortune. In fact, the excavators of Masada found some 1,500 jars of various sizes that were used to store both basic food items and the imported delicacies, including the fish condiments.[38] Although some of these stores had been put there at least a century before, when the *sicarii* captured Masada at the beginning of the war in 66 many of these provisions were still edible because of the arid climate of the region.[39]

Water was gathered on Masada from two sources. Floodwaters from dammed collection pools on the adjoining wadis or dry riverbeds, now named Nahal Masada and Nahal Ben-Yair, were channeled into two rows of cisterns (four in the lower row, eight in the higher) on the northwestern slope of Masada by two aqueducts. The cisterns could hold up to one million gallons of water. In addition, rainwater filled cisterns cut out of the rock by Herod after Antigonus's unsuccessful siege of his women and other family members up on Masada.[40]

In fact, archaeologists have identified at least 14 large cisterns at the site, as well as many other smaller collection pools. By one estimate, each of the large cisterns could provide enough drinking water for 1,000 people for a year.[41] Masada's abundant supplies of food and water collection systems meant that those who held Masada could not be starved into submission. Nor would they die of thirst.

At the time of the occupation of Masada by the *sicarii* and others, pools for ritual purification (*miqva'ot*) were also built into one of the rooms inside the Herodian wall on the southeast side of the fortress and in another room used for administration in the northern palace.[42] Other ritual baths have been tentatively identified within a bathhouse in the western palace complex and in a quarry to the south of the complex.[43]

As many as 21 ritual baths have been discovered.[44] Two-thirds of these seem to have built between 66 and 74, though scholars continue to debate the dates and function of some of the pools. Certainly, some were ritual baths. But others may have been pools for bathing or washing.[45] The significance of the discovery of these baths on Masada, built and used by the *sicarii* and the rest of the inhabitants of the site, suggests that at least some and perhaps most of Masada's residents attempted to observe purification laws. Those laws required Jews to immerse themselves in baths of what qualified as undrawn water (i.e., baths filled by rain, streams, lakes, and the like) before coming into the presence of Israel's God.[46] The large number of stone vessel "mugs" found on Masada (31 complete and 110 fragments), which perhaps were used for ritual handwashing, provide additional evidence for an attempt to observe purity laws.[47]

There were enough arms for 10,000 men on Masada and great quantities of unworked iron, brass, and lead.[48] Herod had deposited all of the food provisions and weapons on Masada in case he needed to flee from his own people or from Cleopatra VII. Cleopatra, as we have seen, repeatedly urged Mark Antony to depose Herod and give his throne to her. Despite his many alleged crimes, however, Herod's own subjects never rose up effectively against him, and Antony resisted at least one of Cleopatra's wishes.

In 66 Menahem and his friends had raided Herod's armory up on Masada, looking for weapons to fight against the Roman auxiliary garrison in Jerusalem.[49] After Eleazar and the *sicarii* seized it by some kind of tactical surprise attack, Masada became the refuge of the dagger-men and the last serious tactical challenge of the war for the Romans.[50] The rebel leader Eleazar was the grandson of Judas the Galilaean, who had persuaded many Jews not to enroll in the census carried out under Quirinius.

Once the *sicarii* took control of Herod's fortress they set about converting the Herodian buildings to their own uses. Palaces, bathhouses, and fortifications were reconstructed into living spaces for the 967 or so men, woman, and children who apparently were with Eleazar at the end of the Roman siege.[51]

It is worth noting that coin finds from the site indicate that people made their way to Masada throughout the duration of the war (years 1 through 5, beginning in 66), though the largest influx seems to have come during years 2 through 4, before the Flavian assault on Jerusalem began.[52] Based upon the distribution of coin finds and other small objects, such as 384 spindle whorls for making cloth, some archaeologists have argued that there were different kinds of groups living on Masada in the years from 66 to the end of the Roman siege.[53] Among these were families, single male refugees, and perhaps the members of an ascetic community. Some may have come to Masada from the Essene community of Qumran.[54]

The mesa is called Masada on a papyrus documenting a bill of divorce (*get*) discovered at Wadi Murabba'at, to the south of Qumran, dated to the first day of Marheshvan in year 6 at Masada.[55] The bill of divorce provided legal proof that a certain Joseph, who lived up on Masada, divorced his wife Mariam, who also was residing in Masada. Year 6 of the revolt would be 71, and the dating formula indicates that whoever drew up the document considered that the revolt had continued after the Temple's destruction in 70. The papyrus's find-spot furthermore suggests that at least some individuals who spent time on Masada left it before the Roman siege.

From an inscription in Aramaic on an ostracon found in one of the casement rooms of Masada (L1237), some scholars conclude that Aqavia, the son of the high priest Ananias and the brother of Eleazar, who was instrumental in bringing about the cessation of daily sacrifices for the Roman emperor in 66, was one of the inhabitants of Masada, though we do not know when he got to Masada or whether he perished there.[56] Aqavia used his own name and that of his father to testify to the quality and *kashrut* (fitness for consumption) of whatever were the contents of the jar from which the pot sherd came. If Aqavia was one of the occupants of Masada during the siege, that would be another indication of the connections between the earlier phases of the revolt, culminating in the siege and destruction of the Temple in Jerusalem, and the occupation and siege of Masada.

Most of the families on Masada apparently lived in small rooms that the rebels constructed either within the casement wall that was built for nearly a mile around the entire perimeter, except for the area of the northern palace, or were attached to it along its inner face. The rooms uncovered thus far could have housed somewhere between 500 and 600 people.[57] The large number of ovens and stoves found within these rooms underscores one of the primary concerns of their inhabitants: baking and cooking food.[58] The conversion of one room within the western casement wall into a tannery and of a reception room of Herod's western palace into a factory for making arrowheads reflects other priorities: making leather, perhaps for clothing or sandals, and manufacturing arms.[59]

The discovery of a large number of loom weights concentrated in a group of casement wall rooms suggests that weaving clothes was another ongoing activity. Women would have woven the clothes worn by Masada's inhabitants and probably repaired them too.[60] If Herod's Masada had the architectural profile and resources of an exclusive royal resort, when the *sicarii* occupied Masada the fortress resembled and had the utilitarian atmosphere of a refugee camp in which men and women labored away to provide the necessities of life.

The wartime occupants also built a small synagogue in a casement of the fortification wall on the northwest side of the Masada. The meeting room could accommodate around 250 people. The synagogue's entrance faced east. The Israeli general and archaeologist Yigael Yadin, who conducted the most extensive excavations on the summit of Masada, believed that the synagogue was built during the reign of Herod, though some later scholars have argued that it was only converted into a synagogue at the time of the revolt.[61]

Although the meeting room seems to have evolved out of a previous structure, during the time of the revolt it included a room at its rear that functioned as a repository for a collection of sacred texts. Later on such a space in a synagogue would be called a *genizah* (Hebrew for archive or repository). Underneath the floor of the Masada *genizah,* in two pits that must have been deliberately dug, archaeologists discovered fragments of Hebrew literary texts including ones from the books of Genesis, Leviticus, Deuteronomy, Ezekiel, and Psalms.[62] There were also remains of nonbiblical works, including the Songs of the Sabbath Sacrifice and the Joshua Apocryphon.[63] A fragment of the book of Jubilees was found among the debris in the casement tower where the tannery was located.[64]

A large number (951) of nonliterary texts have also been recovered. The majority consist of just a few letters on ostraca; others give individual names or lists of names. Some of the inscriptions on jars designate priestly shares. Others entitled their owners to food supplies. Some texts provide examples of writing exercises, and there are papyri and ostraca with Greek or Latin writing on them.[65]

Because fragments or copies of the same nonbiblical texts were found among the Dead Sea Scrolls in Qumran, some scholars have argued that the presence of the texts on Masada at the time suggests that members of the Essene sect had made their way to the fortress before the Roman destruction of Qumran in 68.[66] Others argue that it cannot be assumed that such works were circulated only among Essenes.[67] Inferring that only members of specific sectarian groupings kept and read certain texts makes unsupportable assumptions about ancient reading habits.

If the *sicarii* are considered to be sectarians, however, we know from Josephus that there were "sectarians" living on Masada from 66 to 73–74. There may have been others who belonged to some of the groupings that Josephus described as schools or philosophies. We also know from the numismatic and papyrological evidence that people came to and left Masada during the war years. It is not unreasonable to assume therefore that the inhabitants of Masada had information about the war's events, including the destruction of the Temple and Jerusalem's capture. At least some of the inhabitants were literate readers of the Hebrew Bible, as well as other texts, and efforts were made to observe purity laws. The sum total of evidence clearly indicates that those who occupied Masada during the early 70s comprised a changing and disparate community of men, women, and children who were determined to live away from and outside Rome's aggressive militarization of Judaea. What they were not was an army. And yet, despite that fact, when they were attacked by one of the most formidable legions in the Roman army, at least some of the inhabitants of Masada chose to resist.

THE ROMAN ARMY AT MASADA

Flavius Silva and his army of about 8,000 Roman legionaries and auxiliaries made their way to Masada by the end of winter in 74.[68] As soon as the Romans arrived they built a circumvallation wall around the perimeter of the mesa. As at Jerusalem, the purpose of this wall was to prevent anyone from escaping from the enclosed area; its remains are visible to the eye from the summit to this day. No contravallation wall for defense against any relief force apparently was deemed to be necessary.

The finished circumvallation wall was some 4,500 meters or 3.6 kilometers (2.23 miles) long, 1.6 meters wide, and 3 meters (10 to 12 feet) high. Eight garrisons or siege camps, labeled A through H by archaeologists, were also constructed to block any escape from the fortress and to house troops during the siege. The two largest camps, F on the western side and B on the eastern side, probably accommodated the men of the Tenth Legion, whose numbers have been estimated at anywhere between 3,500 and 5,000 soldiers, though there is no explicit evidence for their numbers or the number of auxiliaries with them.[69] The other camps, some of them integrated into the wall system (Camps E and A) and some outside it (C), were smaller and probably were where the

FIGURE 21. Outlines of walls of Roman legionary Camp F on the western
side of Masada. G. Rogers.

auxiliary units encamped. Camp F lay northwest of Masada, outside the siege
wall. (See figure 21.)

It was probably from Camp F that the Roman commander Flavius Silva
oversaw construction of the ramp and earthworks up the western side of
Masada that the Romans built to bring themselves into a position to capture the fortress. Excavations carried out in 1995 at this camp revealed that
the square-shaped Roman camp was surrounded by a wall of stones 10 to 12
feet high. The area within the camp was divided up by lower stone walls
that served as bases for tents, probably made from leather panels that were
stitched together.[70]

These tent units, called *contubernia* in Latin, would have provided cramped
living and sleeping quarters for a *contubernium* of eight Roman legionary soldiers.[71] The eight-man squads were the core organizational units of the Roman army. The eight tentmates barracked, cooked, and ate together and fought
side by side.[72] The sleeping units excavated by archaeologists in 1995 at the
Masada fortresses of the Romans only had enough room for about four

soldiers; from this it can be inferred that half of each squad rested while the other half was on active duty.

In the middle of the camp, at the intersection of the camp's crossing roads, the excavators also identified the *praetorium,* or commander's abode. This is where Flavius Silva himself would have had his personal quarters.[73] Among the finds at this location were imported glassware from Italy and Nabataean bowls.[74] Roman commanders during this period lived more luxuriously in the field than their soldiers and dined like aristocrats, reclining on couches.[75]

Next to the commander's residence was the tribunal, or speaker's platform, from which Silva would have mustered and addressed the soldiers. Nearby there was also a large *triclinium* for the officers. The camp headquarters (*principia*) were situated just inside the enclosure wall of the camp.[76] In most Roman legionary camps the commander's house and the granary were adjacent to the headquarters.

Because the wall and camps of the Romans at Masada were miles away from any adequate food or water source, supplies had to be brought for the Roman soldiers, their slaves, and pack animals from great distances.[77] Pack animals would have been needed to bring food or water from Ein Gedi along the coastal road, about 11 miles away, and then up and over the narrow, twisting path that was outside the Roman circumvallation wall to the northeast. But heavier supplies presumably were conveyed to Silva's army along the easier, though longer, interior route from Hebron, some 21 miles away by the most direct route; it was still longer when other roads were taken.[78] The Romans certainly used Jews as water carriers.[79] Roman soldiers and military slaves may also have had to serve as water carriers (*aquatores* in Latin, *hudreumenoi* in Greek).[80] Camp B was located outside the circumvallation wall to the southeast, and it was probably to this camp that supplies carried by boats on the Dead Sea were brought.

Historians have estimated that the Roman army of about 8,000 soldiers that besieged Masada would have required around 16 tons of food and 26,000 liters of water per day to keep it fed and hydrated in the arid climate of the locale.[81] (See appendix L for my estimates.) Those estimates are lower than the ones for the armies of Cestius, Vespasian, and Titus, all of whom had much larger armies serving under them. But we should also take into account the difficulties of resupplying an army at Masada versus one in the Galilee or even around Jerusalem. Feeding and hydrating a besieging army at Masada would have been a logistical challenge.[82]

The grain ration of the Roman soldiers, if it was to be consumed as bread, still needed to be baked. Evidence of cooking hearths has been found at the Romans camps at Masada.[83] The Roman soldiers probably slept on the stone benches found in some of their quarters, but may also have reclined on them while they ate.[84]

A receipt for medical supplies found during the exploration of the site shows that the Romans had set up some kind of medical facility, presumably for those who had problems coping with the environment or the defenders of Masada.[85]

Having surrounded the site with a wall and camps that prevented escape and also secured his own supply lines, Silva began siege operations that Josephus described in detail, though there is no evidence that he was present.

THE ROMAN STRATEGY

The narrow path up the Snake was untenable for a mass military assault force. Therefore, there was only one feasible way up to the summit of Masada for Silva and the Roman soldiers, the natural white-rock spur on the western side of the mesa, the *Leuke*. (See figure 22.) Josephus reported that the rock spur was 300 cubits or about 200 feet below the elevation of Masada.[86] As noted previously Herod had had a tower built at the narrowest point of the path up the spur, some 1,500 feet away from the crest.[87] It was no doubt at the beginning of the spur's incline that Silva ordered his soldiers to build an embankment that in essence would complete the upper stretch of the natural stone ramp up to the top of Masada.[88]

Working enthusiastically, and with many hands involved, Silva's men raised up an earthwork that reached a height of 200 cubits (about 133 feet).[89] If Silva's soldiers followed standard Roman engineering techniques, the embankment would have been constructed of wooden framing enclosing sand and gravel fill. To provide a more secure base for war engines, a 50 cubits (75 feet) high and broad platform, made of large, closely fitted stones, was then constructed on top of the embankment.[90] This work must have taken a month or so.[91] The embankment and the platform together would have reached a height within about 42 feet of Masada's summit on its western side.[92]

Silva also had built a massive siege tower 90 feet high. It was encased in iron to provide protection against attacks. From the tower the Roman soldiers fired missiles from many quick-fire machines and stone-throwers.[93] If the Romans used 30 artillery pieces against Masada's defenders, they could

FIGURE 22. View looking down the *Leuke* from the western side of Masada. G. Rogers.

have hit positions every 10 feet along the approximately 330-feet-long north-western wall above the Roman ramp at intervals of five minutes.[94] Unbroken ballista stones recovered from the site on average weigh somewhere between 1.3 and 7 pounds, though a few boulders weighing between 30 and 50 pounds also were shot at the defenders.[95] Continuous barrages of these stones quickly cleared Masada's wall of defenders and forced the Jews to keep their heads down.[96]

After this suppressing hail of stones had done its job, Silva brought up a great battering ram. Although it was not an easy job, the battering ram, working ceaselessly, breached the wall, reducing it to rubble.[97]

The Romans soon discovered that the rebels had taken the precaution of constructing a second defensive wall, just as their fellow Jews had done in the case of the third or inner wall of Jerusalem. The second wall at Masada was probably constructed within the casement wall. It was formed of two parallel walls of wooden beams laid out lengthwise and joined at their ends a wall's distance apart from each other. The wooden beams were likely removed from the roofs of other buildings on the summit.[98] Connected at right angles to the lengthwise beams were shorter beams. In the space between the longer planks there was dirt fill.[99]

Such a construction, while perhaps less formidable visually than a traditional, fixed stone wall, provided a better defense because it could absorb the battering from a ram more easily.[100] Essentially, the dirt fill absorbed the force of the blows from the ram. Taking a page from the Roman military engineering handbook, in effect the rebels had thrown up their own wooden-encased embankment against the Roman battering ram.

The weakness of such a wall, with its wooden frame, was its susceptibility to fire. Silva soon recognized this and ordered his men to throw burning torches at it. The wall quickly was alight, and great flames blazed up into the air. As the flames shot up, a north wind at first blew the fire into the faces of the Romans and for a short period of time endangered the Roman siege engines. But then the wind, as if "out of demonic forethought" (*ek daimoniou pronoias*), reversed and blew the fire in the other direction, to the south against the wood of the wall, which caught fire completely. The Romans understood that the destruction of the second wall had removed the last obstacle between themselves and their enemies. They therefore joyfully returned to their camps, ready to launch what they thought would be the final assault the next day. Josephus, as at both Gamala and the burning of the Temple, saw God's provision in the change of wind direction at Masada that led to the destruction of the Jews' last line of defense.[101]

Josephus's description of how the Romans labored to build the ramp on the *Leuke* up to a point where they could attack the defenders of Masada from their giant siege tower gives his readers a vivid picture of the Romans' technical mastery of siege warfare. It is a scene that builds up the drama of his narrative as it becomes clear that, as soon as the Romans complete the earthwork and bring up their artillery and ram, the end is near for the Jews of Masada.

Some archaeologists have argued, however, that Josephus's story of the Romans' need to build such a ramp and mount a siege tower atop a massive stone cube is belied by the physical facts and the archaeological remains at the site.[102] The central problem in his account is that the natural spur he describes the Romans extending by their artificial ramp reaches almost 80 percent of the way from the floor of the valley up to the summit, or about 42 feet below the summit on that side. At most, what the Romans needed to do, according to this theory, was to straighten out and widen the natural stone spur up toward the summit so that soldiers and artillery could make their way up it. After doing this the Romans only had to smooth off the ground at the top so that machines could be put into action from a level surface. The multistory siege tower of the Romans then would have given them a platform to clear the defenders from their defensive wall.

Further studies have even questioned whether Silva had to build up a ramp to widen access up the spur. These authors claim that there is no evidence for such a widening or for a high stone platform on top of the present spur.[103] The minimalist scholarly view of what happened is that the ramp itself was not completed, no giant tower was ever raised, and no battering ram was used against Masada's walls.

Taken together, these studies imply that the siege operation at Masada was not much of an engineering feat. A barrage of stones was fired at the defenders, as we know from all of the ballista stones found inside Masada's walls. But there was no repeat of the kind of technically challenging and prolonged siege operation that took place in Jerusalem. It seems to have been rather easy for the Romans to breach Masada's defenses. The famous siege of Masada, in other words, was a military non-event, an easy victory.

The doubts raised about Josephus's description of the Romans' siegecraft at Masada have been challenged in turn. There is, in fact, evidence for the construction of the ramp, built of artificial, man-made fill consisting of packed stone, rubble, and earth, held in place by tamarisk and date-palm timber bracing midway up (or down) the spur. Near the bottom of the spur some of the tops of the timber used to construct the framing can still be seen.[104] At the top of the ramp, the remains of the artificial fill only measure one meter wide, though the base beneath it is 5.5 meters wide. Erosion over time could plausibly explain why the fill has disintegrated, and 5.5 meters is probably enough room for a siege tower that housed a battering ram and possibly other artillery.[105] At least part of Josephus's description of the siege ramp therefore is not inconsistent with remains visible almost 2,000 years later.[106]

Moreover, precisely at the point in the casement wall opposite where the siege tower was supposed to have been brought up, there is a large breach in the defensive wall. No other convincing explanation for the existence of the breach at that point has been argued. The logical conclusion is that it was at that point that the Roman ram broke down the Herodian-era wall.[107] Concentrations of the surviving ballista and arrowheads are also clustered along the northwest side of the mountain. It is highly likely that these stones and arrows were shot at the defenders of Masada by the Romans as covering or suppressive fire while the battering ram was doing its work.[108]

As elsewhere in his descriptions of topography and man-made machines to overcome it, Josephus may well have exaggerated some of the engineering difficulties the Romans faced at Masada. We need to remember that Josephus was not present at the siege, and furthermore, there is no evidence that Josephus ever visited Masada. But there is a difference between exaggeration and outright fabrication.

If Josephus had invented the story of the siege, surely one or many of the thousands of Roman soldiers involved in the operation would have challenged his account at some point. Indeed, Josephus's rather precise figures for the size of the earthworks and the platform on top of it suggest eyewitness Roman sources for the measurements.[109] Only the Roman soldiers who built the embankment and the siege tower or the officers who directed the operation would have known such details.

There is no evidence that anyone in antiquity questioned the essential outline of Josephus's story of the Roman siege of Masada and how it was done, and the archaeological evidence uncovered and interpreted thus far does not decisively contradict his literary account. Very little remains of the half-mile-long mole that Alexander the Great had built out from the city of old Tyre on the mainland to the island city of Tyre during his siege of Tyre in 332 BCE. Yet no one suggests that the Alexander sources such as Diodorus Siculus made up the story of the mole.[110] In any case, however, the reason why historians care whether the Romans built an embankment up to the summit of Masada such as the one Josephus describes is not because we want to know whether Josephus accurately reported every detail about construction of the embankment or the siege tower platform at Masada down to the last cubit. Rather it is because of what Josephus tells us about what happened after the Romans breached the walls of the summit and it became clear that the Romans would capture Masada.

THE SPEECHES OF ELEAZAR

Eleazar, the leader of the *sicarii,* must have recognized the significance of the second wall's breach. Flight was impossible. There were no more means of mortal deliverance, and no more brave deeds could save his people. At most he had some 300 fighting men under his command, calculating that at least half the people on Masada were women and children and that some of the men on the mesa would have been too old, too young, or too ill to fight effectively.[111] We know that the inhabitants of Masada did make weapons for themselves, and some may have been combat veterans. But there is no evidence that they had any sort of military organization. The residents of Masada in 73 or 74 were mostly civilians who were there to get away from the Romans, not to fight them. Eleazar also would have known what the Romans would do to their women and children if—when—the Romans were victorious the next day. The women would have been raped and killed or enslaved, the children also enslaved or killed. That was not speculation: it was how the Romans had treated women, children, and even infants elsewhere during the war, for instance during the final fighting at Gamala. It is not implausible to surmise that Eleazar and others on Masada knew about such atrocities from those who had made their way to the fortress during the war. Knowing all of this, Josephus writes that Eleazar gathered up the bravest of his followers and made a speech to them that is quoted in full:

> Long since, my brave men, we determined neither to serve the Romans nor any other save God, for he alone is man's true and just master; and now the time is come which bids us verify that resolution by deeds. At this crisis let us not disgrace ourselves; we who in the past refused to submit even to slavery involving no danger, let us not now, along with slavery, deliberately accept the irreparable punishments awaiting us if we are to be taken alive by the Romans. For as we were the first of all to revolt, so we are the last to fight against them. Moreover, I believe that it is God who has granted us this favor, that we have it in our power to die well and in freedom—a privilege denied to others who have met unexpected defeat. Our fate in the morning is certain capture, but there is still the choice of a noble death with our dearest. For our enemies, passionately though they pray to take us alive, can no more prevent this than we can now hope to defeat them in battle. Maybe, indeed, we ought from the very first—when, having chosen to assert our freedom, we invariably experienced such hard treatment from one another, and still harder from our foes—we ought to have read God's purpose and to have recognized that the nation of Jews, once dear to him, had been doomed to destruction. For had he continued to be gracious, or but moderately incensed, he would never have overlooked such wholesale destruction or have abandoned his most holy city to be burnt and razed to the ground by our enemies. But did we hope that we alone of all the tribes of Jews would survive and preserve our freedom, as persons guiltless toward God and without a hand in crime—we who had even been the instructors of the rest? See,

now, how he exposes the vanity of our expectations, by visiting us with such dire distress as exceeds all that we could anticipate. For not even the impregnable nature of this fortress has availed us salvation; no, though ample provisions are ours, piles of arms, and an abundance of every other thing needed, yet we have been deprived, manifestly by God himself, of all hope of salvation. For it was not of their own accord that those flames which were driving against the enemy turned back upon the wall constructed by us; no, all this shows anger at the many wrongs which we madly dared to inflict upon our countrymen. Let us not pay to our bitterest foes the Romans the penalty for those crimes but to God, by the act of our own hands. It will be more tolerable than the other. Let our wives die not dishonored, our children unacquainted with slavery; and, when they are gone, let us give a generous service to each other, preserving our freedom as a noble winding-sheet. But first let us destroy our money and the fortress by fire; for the Romans, I know clearly, will be grieved to lose at once our bodies and the profits. Let us spare only our provisions; for they will testify, when we are dead, that it was not want which defeated us, but that, in keeping with our initial resolve, we chose death over slavery.[112]

Because of the outcome of the siege—the deaths of all but a few of Masada's inhabitants—we can never be sure whether what Josephus reports Eleazar to have said is what the rebel leader really spoke to those who ultimately bore responsibility for taking the lives of their fellow Jews. There is no evidence that Josephus ever interviewed any of the few Jewish survivors of the siege.[113]

Moreover, the thrust of what Josephus claims were Eleazar's arguments about why Jerusalem was burned and razed, and why it was necessary for the rebels to kill their own flesh and blood, is consistent with what Josephus himself wrote elsewhere about the causes of the Jews' misfortune. It was God's will because of the sins of the Jews, specifically the Jewish tyrants, though the *sicarii* are blamed as well. The fault, from Josephus's point of view, lay with Jews themselves; the Romans were just God's instrument to punish Jews for their impiety. Josephus's Roman patrons and friends ultimately were not to blame for the destruction of the Temple or of the Jews in Jerusalem, Masada, and elsewhere.

In the first speech attributed to Eleazar, Josephus reports that Eleazar had come to the conclusion that the *sicarii* had only themselves to blame for their own plight. God was punishing them for the crimes they committed against their own countrymen.[114]

Josephus then reports a second, much longer speech of Eleazar. (See appendix N for a full translation.) It was supposedly given because the first speech had only managed to convince some of his listeners. Others, who were filled with compassion for their children and families and were not happy about the prospect of their own deaths, by their whimpers and tears were in danger of dissuading those who were ready for death from carrying out Eleazar's plan.[115]

The themes of the second speech were freedom as the result of death, the immortality of the soul, the willingness of the Indians to endure life before releasing their souls from their bodies, and that it was God's will that they die. The Jews should not blame themselves nor give credit to the Romans for the outcome of the war, Eleazar supposedly said; a more powerful cause gave the Romans a semblance of victory. Citing the examples of the massacred Jews of Caesarea, Scythopolis, Damascus, and the rest of Syria and in Egypt, Eleazar reportedly asked what Roman weapon had slain them.

As for those who took up arms against Rome on their own soil, they lacked nothing to inspire confidence in their success but were destroyed anyway, the lucky in battle, the unlucky in the arena or enslaved. Founded by God, Jerusalem had been swept away. Without hope of avenging themselves upon their enemies, the right course of action was to have pity on themselves, their children, and women and to hasten to die. Better to die together than to see their wives led off to violence, their children enslaved. This end was God's sending. Since the Romans' desire was their capture, they should make haste to leave them amazed at their death and admiring their courage.[116]

Eleazar would have expanded upon his elegy for the rebels and freedom, but his listeners cut him off, overcome with a desire to get on with the deed.[117]

Did Eleazar make the second speech that Josephus reports?[118] We should accept the veracity of Josephus's version of Eleazar's second speech with more than a pinch of salt. The Greek text of the speech is almost seven pages long, or 195 lines in the Loeb edition (depending upon some textual issues). It is hard to imagine that any of the survivors, if they heard the speech, could have remembered it well enough to relate what Eleazar said in such detail to anyone, including Josephus. As far as we know, none of the Jewish survivors of what happened on Masada were Homeric rhapsodes, able to remember and repeat passages of a speech that they only could have heard once. In addition, some of the themes and topics of the speech, such as the sections on the immortality of the soul, sleep, conversing with God, and the self-immolation of

Indians, are much more plausibly to be understood as products of Josephus's research while he was in Rome, laboring away in his study with access to Greek and Latin philosophical and ethnographic texts. The motifs of God decreeing the destruction of the Jewish people for their error(s) and the exculpation of the Romans are also consistent with Josephus's often repeated judgments about who was responsible for the war and its outcome that are found throughout his works.[119]

In fact, the second speech of Eleazar reads more plausibly as an indictment of his fellow Jews by Josephus and as an apologia for his own conduct during the war. In his second speech Eleazar confirmed what Josephus had been telling everyone since his surrender at Iotapata: God was on the side of the Romans and indeed was actively helping them in battle. At Gamala and Masada, God had turned the tide of battle at key points.

At the same time, Josephus's Roman readers might not have been pleased by everything they read in the speech. Eleazar's justification for the Jews' decision to kill each other and themselves probably should be read against the background of prior examples during the war where individuals chose self-destruction over surrender.

The speech implied that if the Romans took the Jews on Masada alive their treatment of them would have been far from humane. That idea would not have flattered Josephus's Roman friends when they read it. And Eleazar once again makes the point that the Romans are really instruments of God. Moreover, if the *sicarii* and their families follow Eleazar's advice and kill each other they will achieve a kind of victory; when the Romans find their bodies, they will admire their courage. As we have seen, in some circumstances during the fighting in Jerusalem, it was morally defensible, even for Roman soldiers such as Longus (see chapter 19), to commit suicide rather than to be captured or killed. Self-destruction in the face of dishonor is not necessarily an indefensible or ignoble choice, even in the case of individuals whose prior actions Josephus deplored and blamed for the war and its tragic consequences.[120] This is the interpretation of what happened on top of Masada that Josephus wanted his readers to accept—because, as Josephus makes us see, that is what happened—or did it?

Because we can never know whether Eleazar spoke the words Josephus puts into his mouth and that were presumably reported to the Romans by one of the survivors, the only way we can plausibly reconstruct what Eleazar and the other Jews thought is from the evidence for their actions. That evidence derives not only from the texts of Josephus but also from archaeology.

THE END OF RESISTANCE AT MASADA

After listening to Eleazar's speech, Josephus says that the rebels kissed their loved ones goodbye and slew their wives and children. Afterward they set all their provisions on fire and then drew lots to decide who would kill the rest. Ten men were selected. The rest of the men lay down next to their wives and children and exposed their throats to the winners of the lottery. After the 10 had killed their comrades there was a second drawing of lots. The winner dispatched the other nine, set the palaces on fire, and then drove his sword through his own body, falling dead next to his family.[121]

Thus only one Jew broke the Jewish prohibition against suicide, except when done to avoid committing murder, adultery, and idolatry. Josephus tells us that all of the men, women, and children who died had done so in the belief that they had left not a living soul from among them to fall into the hands of the Romans.[122] He then concludes his account of what happened to the Jews on Masada by informing his readers that this *pathos* or tragedy occurred on 15 Xanthicus, or about 11 April, probably in 74.[123] What he did not choose to spell out was that the Macedonian calendar date of 15 Xanthicus was 15 Nisan, the first day of Passover on the Hebrew calendar. Josephus probably assumed that his Jewish readers would understand and feel the tragic irony. One scholar who has studied the evidence for the logistics of the siege has estimated that it lasted for about seven weeks.[124] That would imply that the siege began around the end of February.

To add to the sense of tragic irony Josephus makes clear that those who had defied the Romans on Masada were deluded in their belief that none of them would ever fall into Roman hands. An old woman and another woman, a relative of Eleazar, along with five children, did in fact survive the death lotteries. These women and children had hidden themselves in one of the cisterns on the site while the rest of the rebels were carrying out the executions.[125]

Having no idea what was happening on top of Masada, by daybreak the Romans were preparing for the final assault upon the rock fortress. In full armor they advanced over gangways that bridged the distance from the earthworks to Masada's walls. Along the walls, however, they encountered no opposition. Only flames and silence greeted them. At a loss, the Romans shouted out, calling forth to any who were within. There was no response until the two women emerged from their hiding place. They reported to the Romans both what had been said by Eleazar and how the deed itself had been done.[126] Josephus does not inform his readers how the women could have heard what

Eleazar said and then managed to slip away with the children and hide in the cistern or how they communicated with the Romans, unless they knew Latin or Greek. The most plausible explanation must be that there were Hebrew or Aramaic speakers or interpreters in Silva's army or attached to it to whom the women related their story. The interpreters then translated the tale into Latin or Greek for the Romans.

At first the Romans did not believe what they were told. But soon the story of the survivors was confirmed. After clearing a path through the flames in the palaces, the Romans found the mass of the slain, perhaps in the western palace built by Herod, rather than the private residence of the northern palace.[127] But did that resistance conclude with a mass suicide/murder as Josephus describes it?

More than 1,900 years after the fall of Masada, Yigael Yadin reported that he had found a group of 12 ostraca in a room to the west of the large bathhouse in the northern palace complex of Masada. On these were inscribed names, all of them written in Hebrew. One of the inscribed names was ben Yair.[128] That inscribed ostracon is now displayed as the very last object in the permanent exhibition of the Masada Museum.

Yadin argued that the ostraca were the lots used by the Jews to decide which 10 men would kill their fellow defenders of Masada as the Romans were preparing their final assault; the ostracon with the name ben Yair on it belonged to none other than Eleazar, son of Yair, the leader of the resistance to the Romans.[129]

Yadin's argument about the names on the pottery sherds and their connection to Josephus's story of the mass murder/suicide has been the subject of ongoing discussion and debate.[130] Some scholars have pointed out that names of other individuals and lists of names have been found on other pottery fragments on the site. Therefore we really do not know whether the inscribed ostraca Yadin discovered belonged to men who Josephus says were allotted the responsibility to slay their fellow Jews or perhaps were inscribed with their names for some other purposes, such as receiving distributions of food. Others have reminded us that Josephus specified that 10 men were allotted to kill everyone else first, not 11 or 12.[131]

Some critics have also argued that Yadin accepted and sought to prove the story of the mass suicide essentially to create a myth of heroic resistance for the sake of modern Israeli nationalist ideology.[132] Other scholars have questioned whether there was a mass suicide at all. Archaeologists have never found the bones of a large number of people either on top of Masada or nearby. To date the skeletons of three individuals have been found on the lowest terrace of the northern palace of Masada, and the skeletal remains of another 5 to 25 people have been discovered in a cistern on the southeastern side of the mountain.[133]

A huge pile of chalky dirt and artifacts heaped up against the outside of the plaster-coated stone wall that separated the rooms of Herod's northern palace from the rest of the summit to the south has, however, been uncovered. According to one theory, that pile constitutes the remains of a siege ramp that the Romans built to besiege rebels who had taken refuge within the inner rooms of Herod's northern palace and who fought there to the death.[134] In that case, at least some rebels on Masada opted out of the suicide pact described by Josephus or perhaps never were part of it.

None of these criticisms or theories, however, decisively disproves the essential story Josephus tells about the mass murder/suicide on Masada. The lack of mass skeletal remains at Masada can be explained plausibly, and comparative data are relevant too. Rather than leaving the corpses of the dead Jews to rot where they were, the Romans very likely burned the bodies of the dead *sicarii* and the others together en masse. Since the Romans intended to occupy Masada they would not have wanted to leave a mass of rotting corpses heaped up on the site. That would have been an invitation to putrefaction and disease.

Burning the bodies would have destroyed all of the organic materials and perhaps most of the bones too, if the fire were hot enough. What was not burned up would have been buried in some kind of pit. Over time the remains of the bones probably disintegrated in the pit. None of the bones of those who were massacred by Alexander the Great and the Macedonians at the conclusion of the sieges of Tyre or Gaza in 332 BCE have ever been found; the climate at Gaza would have been similar to that of Masada. Yet no one doubts that thousands (or hundreds anyway, taking into account the exaggerations of sources) died in both places, just as all the Graeco-Roman sources report.

If Eleazar and the other leaders had been captured in the spring of 74, they undoubtedly would have been publicly executed in some amphitheater in Syria or brought to Rome for execution. That is exactly what Josephus tells us that Titus did with thousands of the survivors of the siege of Jerusalem. Given his antipathy toward the *sicarii*, Josephus surely would have described their executions. But he did not, either in the *War* or the *Antiquities,* after he had years to correct or rethink his account of the siege. Finally, the existence of what could be evidence for a second Roman siege ramp and the fighting that went on, presumably after the mass murder/suicide that Josephus describes, does not disprove his basic story. First, the date of the remains is controversial, and second, Josephus himself makes clear that there were survivors of the pact in any case: two women and five children. Perhaps there were other people who opted out of the lottery or simply hid before it took place.

The use of Masada as a modern, nationalist myth should not be used tendentiously against the ancient evidence of Josephus's text or the archaeological evidence for what happened.[135] If what happened on Masada has been cited to support nationalist objectives in Israel, the responsibility for that lies with those who have done so, not Flavius Josephus or mute material remains that cannot have an agenda. Only ancient evidence to the contrary can refute the story Josephus tells about the mass murder/suicide at Masada.

We have every reason to analyze and question the accuracy of the speeches that Josephus attributes to Eleazar as he urged his fellow rebels to kill first their wives and children and then each other. What we know is that, in the form in which we have them, those speeches were composed by Flavius Josephus after the event, to be read by Greek and Roman readers, for whom suicide in the face of the despotic power of emperors such as Nero was understood at the time not as a violation of the law but as a noble reaction to tyranny.[136] It is also worth pointing out that, as we have seen, in Josephus's text there are examples where Roman soldiers are reported to have committed suicide rather than to be captured; Josephus does not criticize their actions, but instead presents their choices as heroic.[137] We should not assume that Josephus or his Roman readers would have seen the Jews' murder/suicide on Masada as unheroic. One of the most poignant reliefs on the Column of Trajan shows the last surviving Dacians in a besieged city drinking poison rather than submitting to capture, enslavement, and worse.[138] The relief was produced by Romans, not Dacians.

Highly embellished as they are, and bearing traces of ethnographic and philosophical research, the speeches that Josephus wrote for Eleazar nevertheless only make sense in light of the outcome Josephus describes on top of Masada. They are pointless if the Jews on top of Masada did not kill each other before the Romans arrived on the summit of the plateau but instead surrendered; that fact would have been immediately apparent to the large number of prominent Romans and others with whom Josephus says he shared his text. The essential question about the siege and capture of Masada by Silva and the Romans is not whether the Romans had to build a large ramp up the *Leuke* and a great siege tower or whether Eleazar ben Yair said exactly what Josephus reports. It is whether Jews on top of Masada in 74 first resisted Silva and his soldiers and then took their own lives or submitted to execution by their fellow Jews rather than surrender to the Romans. The rest isn't just commentary; but it is what really matters.

Until we find evidence that irrefutably disproves Josephus's account of the siege of Masada and the story of the mass suicide atop Masada in the spring of 74, Josephus's story is the one for which we possess the most convincing evidence. The breach in the defensive wall on top of Masada is the most compelling evidence that the Romans found it necessary to break through the wall to capture the summit of Masada; the existence of that breach only makes sense if the Romans were forced to overcome resistance by at least some of the inhabitants of Masada. The discovery of an inscription or a papyrus that contradicts Josephus's account of the mass murder/suicide on Masada would cause us to question rightly what really happened. But that has not happened yet. The burden of proof is upon those who want to disprove what Josephus wrote about the end of rebels on Masada. If Josephus is right about the mass suicide of Masada's defenders in 73 or 74, what is the significance of their actions?

Josephus calls the inhabitants of Masada bandits (*lestai*). But they were bandits to Josephus because they had chosen to live outside of and away from authorities that he supported, such as the high priests and the priestly elites of Jerusalem and, after his surrender at Iotapata, the Romans.[139]

To call the inhabitants of Masada in 73–74 "bandits" is therefore to adopt the terminology of the imperial and, by 74, the colonial power in Judaea, even if the camp on Masada included a mix of families, *sicarii,* and solitary individuals. At least some of the Jews who had made their way there since 66 had gone to Masada to avoid the Romans, not to fight them. Those who wanted to fight the Romans, like Simon bar Giora, came and then left.

But the presence of Eleazar and the *sicarii* on Masada inextricably linked Masada in 74 to the outbreak of the revolt, the course of the war, and the events of 70, even if they had lived there for eight years. They were not bandits. They were rebels. And Eleazar ben Yair was one of the revolution's leaders.

Over the years since 66 at least some of Masada's refugees took part in raids that resulted in the deaths of other Jews. When the Romans finally showed up in 74 they did not find the siege of Masada to be as great a challenge as the siege of Jerusalem, apart from the logistical issue of supply. Nor did the inhabitants of Masada put up the kind of prolonged resistance that occurred at Iotapata, Gamala, or Jerusalem.[140] They simply could not, because the active defenders of Masada numbered very few individuals who could offer any sort of armed resistance to a legion of Rome's finest soldiers. Recognizing that they could not prevail in battle and perhaps knowing of the fates of those who had been taken captive by the Romans in Jerusalem, Eleazar and the Jews of Masada chose to deny the Romans the satisfaction of killing them on the spot or watching them die in the arenas of their cities.

Eleazar ben Yair and the Jews on Masada remained true to their cause, to themselves, and to their God. As far as we can know most plausibly they chose death over submission, slavery, or worse. Even Josephus could not find a way to disguise their courage, and it is very likely that he did not wish to do so. Writing under the gaze of his Roman patrons Josephus repeatedly assured them that his God had decided to favor them. Josephus saw the actions of the *sicarii* as sinful, misguided, and disastrous for the Jewish people. But his account of who they were and what they did acknowledges the Jews' courage and commitment to their cause—even of the misguided and sacrilegious dagger-men. In the very first sentence of the first speech that Josephus attributed to Eleazar at Masada, Josephus reiterated the idea that had led Judas the Galilaean to urge revolt from Rome in 6 CE: Eleazar and his men had long since determined neither to serve the Romans nor any other except God.[141] In doing so, Josephus—no unqualified admirer of Eleazar and the dagger-men—drew a straight, unbroken line between Eleazar and Judas. The resistance of the *sicarii* at Masada may have been unwise, counterproductive, or even futile from Josephus's point of view.[142] But they died without compromising their beliefs.

The Romans at Masada remained true to their gods and practices as well, ceasing military operations only after all pockets of resistance were completely eradicated. As is always the case in situations of imperialism and domination, fear was the most effective force multiplier: the Romans controlled their enormous empire more by the fear of force rather than by force itself. Leaving a pocket of potential resistance or a camp of "bandits" up on a mesa within or on the border of a Roman province indefinitely would have undermined the psychological advantage Rome needed to maintain control over its imperium. Crucial to the maintenance of that advantage was the threat of irresistible force. To be credible, however, threats of force at least occasionally need to be followed up on.

The Romans' conquest of Masada was a testament to their commitment to complete victory in the interests of maintaining a monopoly on force within their empire. The mass suicide of the Jews atop Masada was their testament not to allow themselves to be conquered. Sinners they may have been in Josephus's eyes. But they died free, with no master other than their God.

THE RESISTANCE IN EGYPT

Josephus presented the fall of Masada as the last battle of the war of Jews against Romans.[143] Afterward Flavius Silva left a garrison at Masada and returned to his headquarters in Caesarea.[144] Following his return to Rome in 81 he held the still prestigious, ancient position of consul *ordinarius* (the consul at the beginning of the year), along with Asinius Pollio Verrucosus, though the hero of Masada was not given an officially awarded ovation for his triumph. Vespasian and Titus may not have wished to share any glory with the ex-legate of Judaea. Or they may have thought that a governorship marked by a victory over enemies who slew each other did not merit the highest military honor that could be awarded to non-members of the imperial family. Scaffolds moving through the streets of Rome showing large numbers of Jews killing their wives and children probably would not have inspired feelings of superiority and triumph among Rome's populace. The war of Jews against Romans was over. Except it wasn't.

Despite their unparalleled efforts over eight years, the Romans had not wiped out all resistance. The Flavians' war against Jews may have ended in 70. Vespasian became the Roman emperor, and he and Titus got their triumph. But the rebellion of Jews against Rome was not finished, even after Masada fell.

During the fighting in Judaea, a group of Jews had made their way to Alexandria in Egypt. There they inspired some of the Jews living in Egypt to assert their freedom, to look upon the Romans as no stronger than themselves, and to believe God alone was their master, Josephus reports. That phrase openly echoed Judas the Galilaean's call to arms against the Romans in 6 CE, as Josephus must have recognized and intended, and the dagger-men's use of that rallying cry in Egypt linked them to the resistance of Jews to Rome since 6, despite what had happened in 70. When certain prominent Jews in Egypt opposed them, the rebels murdered them, according to Josephus, and then pressed on with their revolutionary incitements. The war of Jews against other Jews continued too.

The leaders of the local elders' council of Jews then held a general meeting of the Jews. At the meeting the elders argued that the *sicarii* were the source of their troubles and that they were trying to involve others in evils that were their due. They advised their fellow Jews to steer clear of the misfortunes the *sicarii* would bring to them and instead to deliver them over to the Romans. Six hundred of the *sicarii* were seized on the spot.

Some who managed to flee into Egypt and Thebes were later brought back and delivered over to the Romans. These *sicarii* were subjected to every form of torture to make them acknowledge Caesar as their master. Not one of them, including their children, could be induced to do so.[145]

The Roman governor, a man named Lupus whose full Roman name is not known, reported what had been going on in Alexandria to Vespasian. Fearing another revolt, Vespasian ordered the destruction of the Jewish temple in the district called Onias, which was situated in Leontopolis in Egypt.[146]

The temple had been built by Onias IV, who was the son or, less likely, the nephew of Onias III, the high priest that Menelaus arranged to have murdered in 170 BCE.[147] Onias IV had fled from Jerusalem after the Seleucid king Demetrius I Soter (r. 162–150 BCE) had thrown his support behind the Hellenizing high priest Alcimus. Onias IV had proposed to the Ptolemaic king Ptolemy VI Philometor, Antiochus's enemy, that he would make the nation of Jews his war ally if Ptolemy would grant him permission to build a temple somewhere in Egypt to worship God after the custom of Onias's ancestors. Ptolemy then granted Onias a piece of land about 22 miles from Memphis, in the district of Heliopolis, both for the temple and a military colony. There Onias built a fortress and a temple, not architecturally similar to the great Temple in Jerusalem sacked by Antiochus but decorated with comparable offerings, complete with a golden lamp suspended from a golden chain. The Ptolemaic king also gave Onias a large tract of land, the revenues from which were used to support the priests of his temple and their sacrifices to God by Onias and his successors, known as the Oniads.[148]

Lupus, having heard back from Vespasian, made his way to Onias's temple. There he stripped the temple of some of its valuables and then closed it. After Lupus's death, his successor Paulinus also came to the temple, and he took the rest of its treasures. He then closed the gates to the sanctuary and barred all access to it. Josephus tells us that the temple had been open for 343 years before it was shut.[149] With the closing of the temple in Egypt came the conclusion of the sacrificial cult dedicated to the worship of the God of Abraham and Moses.

It can be plausibly argued that by that action Vespasian signaled that he wanted the sacrificial cult of the Jews to be ended.[150] If that is true it means that the Flavians' war against the Jews was fought not just to quell an insurrection by some Jews and to provide a justification for their usurpation of power in Rome. They wished to triumph over and eradicate a competitive sacrificial cult.

UNREST IN LIBYA

Unrest also spread to nearby Libya. There, a weaver named Jonathan, either a *sicarius* himself or inspired by them, gathered a group of followers and led them out into the desert, promising them manifestations of signs and phantoms.

Informed of Jonathan's activities by some of the Jews in Cyrene, Catullus—designated by Josephus as the *hegemon* of the *Pentapolis* (Five Polis) region of Libya, but in reality the proconsul of Crete and Cyrene—mobilized a force of cavalry and infantry and led them out into the desert against Jonathan and his adherents.[151] The majority of these Jews, who were unarmed, were slain. A few were made prisoner, apparently including Jonathan, who attempted to convince the governor that the wealthiest Jews had put him up to what he had done.

Catullus, wanting to be able to claim that he too had fought and presumably won a war against the Jews, exaggerated the importance of the affair. He induced Jonathan to accuse the Alexandrian Jew Alexander and his wife Berenice, with whom he (Catullus) had quarreled, of having been behind the movement. Alexander and Berenice and 3,000 other wealthy Jews then were put to death. Their property was confiscated and given over to the revenue accounts or treasury of the emperor.[152]

After achieving this local "success," Catullus induced Jonathan and some others to accuse a number of reputable Jews in Alexandria and Rome itself of sedition. Josephus was among the Jews in Rome accused of providing weapons and money to Jonathan. But Catullus and his cat's paw Jonathan had overplayed their hand. When Catullus came to Rome, bringing Jonathan and his associates with him, wearing their chains, the case was heard by Vespasian himself. Vespasian investigated the facts but was also influenced by a direct appeal by Josephus's friend and patron Titus. Jonathan, not Josephus, was found guilty and was first tortured and then burned alive.[153]

Catullus escaped Vespasian's judgment but not that of a higher power, or so Josephus claims. For soon the ex-governor was beset by an incurable disease that not only racked his body but also unbalanced his mind. Terrors plagued him, and he saw the ghosts of his victims at his side. He leapt from his bed as if being tortured and burned with fire. His disease rapidly grew worse, and then his bowels became ulcerated and fell out, demonstrating, Josephus reports with great satisfaction, how God amply punishes the wicked.[154]

PART FIVE

God's Plan

CHAPTER 22

The Causes of the War(s)

CONTINGENT WARS OF CHOICES

King Herod the Great was not a strict observer of the Ten Commandments, let alone the 613 *mitzvot* of the Torah. Yet, for most of his long reign he kept the peace between Jews and Romans, Jews and non-Jews, and among Jews in his kingdom. By the late 60s CE, however, at least 23,400 Jews were fighting a war against Romans, the Romans' regional allies, Greeks, Syrians, and each other. How and why did that happen?

Since the late 1970s historians have cited connections between theological and socioeconomic factors that led to the war, a breakdown in relations between Jerusalem's ruling elite and Roman governors, the incompetence of Judaea's ruling class, and the almost accidental nature of the war's onset.[1] Most recently, in a major work of scholarship about the war Steven Mason offered a regional thesis about the war's origins:

> I shall propose rather that the beginnings of the war had little to do with long-term antagonism. The great power favored Jerusalem as regional broker of its imperium, and Judean leaders turned habitually to Rome for support, nearly always with success. Judea's real, and finally existential threats, were local. When Rome proved an unreliable protector of its interests, late in Nero's reign, Judeans predictably resorted

to armed self-help—against their neighbours. Because Rome demanded a monopoly on armed force, and Judea's most virulent enemies were protected as auxiliary forces of the empire, when the Roman legate in Syria finally intervened, he had no choice but to act against those Judeans who had taken up arms. Even still, his pacification measures were narrowly limited. But it is not possible to control the outcome of armed interventions, and one thing led to another.[2]

Josephus, who repeatedly tells his readers why he thinks the Temple was destroyed and the Jews lost the war, has far less to say about the war's cause(s), at least systematically. There is no extended explanation in any of his writings to support a hypothesis about the war's cause, as there was in Thucydides's famous history of the Peloponnesian War.[3] In the absence of a systematic analysis of the factors that led to the outbreak of the war in Josephus or other sources, the best we can do is to point to the choices or decisions of Jews, Romans, and others that led not just to a dispute, a spasm of violence, or a riot but rather to mass violence over time—in other words, a war.

All of their choices or decisions might not have been made at all, could have gone the other way, or could have been reversed. Some seemed not to be related to the conflict or had unintended consequences. The central point, however, is that the war was a contingent historical event that resulted from an accumulation and combination of human decisions made over time. The war did not have to happen; in fact, it probably never would have happened but for a small number of crucial choices made by individuals. These choices led to a situation where war became not only thinkable for enough people to start a war, but desirable.[4]

Once that situation obtained it did not take some large-scale event for the war to begin. On the contrary, as so often in the history of human conflict, a small-scale, almost trivial incident led to the start of the war.[5] The incident set in motion a series of actions and reactions involving ever-greater numbers of people such that a critical mass was reached and the war began. While there were individuals and groups that wanted to stop the fighting, there were too many others who did not.

It is a self-comforting piety for many to opine that wars are started by people who really do not want to fight. Sometimes people are dragged into wars, and often people do not wish to fight, even as the war is raging. But at other times large numbers of people do wish to fight. In the case of the war of Jews and Romans (and others), at least some of the Jews fought because they wanted to be free from rule by Romans. Romans fought because they wanted to continue to rule. Jews and non-Jews fought because many of them did not like each other and non-Jews were helping the Romans. Jews fought Jews because they disagreed about the theological warrant or wisdom of fighting the Romans and their allies. The war of Jews against Romans and others was a Sadducean war of free choice.[6]

THE END OF THE HERODIAN COMPROMISE

War between the Jews of Judaea and Romans must have seemed unlikely, if not impossible, in 4 BCE. Early on Herod had identified Rome as the power he should hitch his fortune to, and for the better part of a half-century his choice paid off for him and for the majority of Jews of his kingdom. Herod never seriously wavered in his loyalty to Rome, and as a result Rome's rulers supported him. Everyone knew that Rome—that is, Augustus—had Herod's back. Conflict, let alone war, with the Romans was highly unlikely. Whatever ethnic, cultural, or religious tensions there were between Jews and non-Jews within Herod's realm or around it in the region, Herod relieved those by sticking to his general principle of avoiding offending Jews on their turf and giving non-Jews what they wanted or, at least, what distracted them on theirs. Among Jews and within Judaism Herod knew enough not to provoke resistance by claiming to be what he was not, unlike the Hasmoneans who made themselves both high priests and kings.[7] Herod was a king crowned by the Romans. But he was not a priest or a high priest. He did not try to usurp the theological authority of the high priest, the Temple administration, or the priesthood, and he tried to avoid conflict with adherents of the Josephan schools of philosophy. His authority and power were based upon his friendship with Rome and his command of his army. Despite his later reputation for personal extravagance and cruelty, for Herod, like Augustus, real power was what mattered and it was enough.

Herod's death removed the constraints upon all of the suppressed conflicts and tensions. Even before his position as ethnarch was confirmed by Augustus, Herod's son Archelaus had trouble managing his own people and resorted to armed violence to put down unrest and quell attempts to revisit the issue of the execution of the sophists Judas and Matthias.

While Augustus was trying to decide what to do with Herod's kingdom the overzealous procurator Sabinus nearly caused a full-scale rebellion by his attempts to get hold of the royal treasury in Jerusalem. A war of Jews against

Romans in 4 BCE was only avoided by the quick and strong action of Varus,
the governor of Syria. But before Varus managed to snuff out the incipient
revolt there were attacks against the rich, the Romans, and the royalists.

In Rome meanwhile Augustus clearly saw the danger of political instability, based upon the animosities of Herod's family members and subjects,
in the strategically important region. It was the reason why he split up Herod's
kingdom after his death. Dividing up Herod's kingdom was an Augustan
compliment to his client and friend Herod but a political mistake. Bestowing pieces of Herod's territory upon multiple rulers meant that each one of
them had to deal with the same problems Herod had dealt with alone. In
effect, Augustus multiplied the number of places where the conflicts had to
be managed by a greater number of surrogates. But there was no Herod to
put in charge of any one of them. That was a prescription for more trouble,
not less.

Some of Herod's immediate successors did better than others. His main
heir, Archelaus, the tetrarch in Judaea, tried to disassociate himself from his
father but displayed a familial flexibility toward Levite law that scandalized
some and then managed to offend both Jews and Samaritans to such a degree that Augustus sent him packing to Gaul. In hindsight, Augustus probably regretted that he had not started sending out prefects to Judaea in 4 BCE.

TIERED AUTHORITY

At that point (6 CE) Judaea became a kind of composite state, with tiers
of authority that were not always clearly defined and differentiated. The result was confusion and conflict, and not only among modern scholars trying
to figure out Judaea's administrative status. Locally there was the Temple administration, the high priest and his advisers, all of the other priests, and the
sectarian groupings with their different interpretations of the law. We talk and
write about first century CE Judaism, but of course we should be thinking
first in terms of Judaisms.

Above the diverse representatives of Judaisms sat a Roman prefect who
had local auxiliary troops at his disposal and capital jurisdiction. Up in Antioch the Roman legate of Syria meanwhile commanded four Roman legions
that could be marched down into Judaea to resolve disputes. The Syrian legate answered to the emperor in Rome, who was advised by his council and
whose power ultimately depended upon the legions, as Tacitus told his readers explicitly. Communications among all of these authorities took time

because of the distances between all of them. At times those distances worked to the advantage of the Judaeans, sometimes to their disadvantage.

The choices and decisions of all the individuals within these different structures made for radical policy changes, sometimes rapidly. None of the fault lines within Judaean society and the wider region disappeared as a result of Augustus's decision to send out a prefect in 6 CE. Now, however, it was up to the prefect and the soldiers who served under him to resolve disputes that Herod had taken care of for decades. Inevitably there were those who did not like his decisions. It was not for nothing that the Romans had hesitated to put Judaea under a prefect, preferring to rule through a client king or an ethnarch. Once that was done, instead of the high priest or the king being the object—or target—of scrutiny by the people, it was now the Roman governor.

The arrival of the first prefect Coponius and of Quirinius as governor of Syria immediately caused a conflict because Quirinius had been instructed to carry out a property assessment. Most Jews dutifully declared the value of their property. But Judas the Galilaean and the Pharisee Zaddok led a popular resistance movement, the goal of which was independence, based upon a literal reading of scripture. For them, unlike Herod, it was not possible to be both a Jew and a Roman—or a Roman slave. The movement they inspired failed, but its theologically justified liberation ideology did not go away. From the very beginning of Judaea being placed under the jurisdiction of a prefect, there was resistance.

Having got off on the wrong foot Coponius had to deal with the problem of some Samaritans scattering human bones in the Temple sanctuary to cause its pollution. In the aftermath of that incident it is likely that the position of the Temple captain was created, along with the guards who served under him. Eleazar the Temple captain played a key role in halting sacrifices on behalf of the emperor and Rome in 66, an action that signified a breach in relations between Judaea and Rome. Eleazar never would have been in a position to influence events so decisively in 66 but for the creation of a position in the aftermath of an incident that had nothing to do with opposition to Rome. The Samaritans weren't interested in causing trouble for Rome; the object of their hostility was their related or co-religionists.

During the prefecture of Pontius Pilate several of the prefect's actions provoked reactions and made Rome unpopular with different groups in Judaea. In addition to alienating the followers of Jesus for the next 2,000 years, Pilate's introduction of shields into Herod's palace and then military standards into Jerusalem (if these were separate incidents) led to massive protests. His use of Temple funds to build an aqueduct for the city caused a riot that led to the deaths of many Jews. It was perhaps not a coincidence that during Pilate's governorship a series of charismatic teacher/prophets appeared, some of whose followers, including both Jews and Samaritans, were killed by Pilate's soldiers. In a small country such incidents cannot have created positive attitudes toward Rome or its government.

Yet not all interactions were problematic. Vitellius, the governor of Syria, went out of his way to secure Jewish control of the high priest's vestments and got all taxes on agricultural products remitted for Jerusalemites, at least temporarily. Such interventions must have won Vitellius, if not Rome, friends. Positive memories, however, could be quickly erased. After Tiberius's death in 37 CE his successor Gaius, for reasons that are not completely clear, decided that he wanted to have a statue of himself installed somewhere within the Temple. Only the stalling tactics of Publius Petronius, the governor of Syria, and the pleas of Agrippa I prevented that from happening and a war from breaking out between Jews and Romans in 39–40.

After Gaius's assassination in 41, Agrippa I's appointment by Claudius as ruler over Herod's former kingdom, minus its Greek cities, represented a reversion to the arrangement that Augustus had authorized for Herod. Agrippa's rule was perhaps the best, last chance for a local leader to try to address, resolve, or keep a lid on some of the tensions that persisted within Judaea. Agrippa's subsidization of the offering costs of the Nazirites, for instance, was an attempt to address inequalities of wealth within the priestly courses. At the same time Agrippa seems not to have been very tolerant of different interpretations of the law, to judge by his execution of the apostle James. So there were ongoing theological and social conflicts among Jews.

The attempted introduction of a statue of the emperor into a synagogue at Dor was no doubt a deliberate provocation, meant to challenge Agrippa's authority. Agrippa's relations with Marsus, the Roman governor of Syria, were also tense, and Marsus clearly was suspicious of Agrippa. His suspicions and the actions that he and Claudius took to trim Agrippa's sails by forcing him to cease building the north defensive wall in Jerusalem and breaking up his meeting with other regional client kings cannot have sent a positive signal to Agrippa's subjects about their king.

Agrippa's death and the imperial response to the reaction of the Caesareans and Sebastenians to it was an inflection point on the road to the war that broke out in 66, as Josephus rightly observed. Claudius's decision not to remove the Caesarean and Sebastenian soldiers who had insulted Agrippa and his family after the king's death was a mistake because it sent out a deeply destabilizing message. To the soldiers Claudius's reversal of his prior decision to send the offending soldiers to Pontus conveyed the message that they could insult and mock the very Jewish king they were supposed to serve; to Jews the message was that Romans could not be trusted to enforce discipline among their soldiers, even in the case of their own hand-selected king. Leaving the Caesarean and the Sebastenian soldiers where they were also meant that the memory of Claudius's decision would be passed down into the next generation. We can't trace a straight line of evidence for hostility toward Jews by the Sebastenians and Caesarians between 44 and 66, but the evidence of open hostility is there at both dates.

After Agrippa's death Claudius decided to send out procurators to govern Judaea, under the watchful eye of the legate of Syria. Some did their best to keep the peace, but the actions of others expanded the numbers of the anti-Roman resistance, increased conflict between Jews and Syrians or Greeks inside Judaea and the region, and further polarized Jews. The procurator Fadus sided with the Philadelphians in their dispute with Peraean Jews over the village of Zia, and his executions of the brigand Tholomaeus and the "magician" Theudas were meant to help establish security in the countryside. But brigands and charismatic leaders were a problem throughout the period from 44 to 66, and it is hard to disentangle criminality from resistance or reactions to a desperate situation.

Fadus also managed to undermine the authority of the priestly hierarchy in Jerusalem by attempting to have the high priest's tunic and robe stored in the fortress of Antonia. Claudius gave supervision of the garments to King Herod of Chalcis, but the incident was a sign of mistrust between the emperor's man on the ground and influential priests in Jerusalem. That was not the way to gain the support of local elites, through whom the Romans generally preferred to rule. The famine during the governorship of Tiberius Iulius Alexander cannot have improved the general atmosphere in Judaea, and it is notable that Queen Helena of Adiabene was remembered as the figure who did the most to help the people get through that difficult period—not the Roman governor. It was during this time that James (or Jacob) and Simon, the sons of Judas the Galilaean who advocated rebellion in 6 CE, were executed. Although the sources are not explicit, it is hard to resist at least broaching the hypothesis that, following in the footsteps of their father, they were involved in some kind of resistance to Roman rule.

Cumanus's governorship (48–52 CE) was marked by tensions between soldiers and civilians in Jerusalem, leading to a riot in which thousands were trampled to death; by the robbery of Caesar's slave Stephanus; and by a confrontation between Galilaeans and Samaritans over the route the Galilaeans took to Jerusalem during the festivals. Cumanus's unwillingness to act quickly after the murder of Jews cannot have inspired confidence in his administration. His successor Felix also tried to address the issue of brigandage in the countryside. But his use of the dagger-men to advance his agenda set a disastrous precedent.

Josephus later claimed that it was because of the actions of the dagger-men who murdered people in the Temple that God decided to purge the city by fire and enslave the Jews. But God had help. The Roman government was complicit in unleashing the dagger-men, and it is hardly an accident that during Felix's tenure as procurator ever-larger groups of people were willing to follow prophets or false prophets out into the desert. In Caesarea, meanwhile, Jews and Greeks escalated their dispute over who should have what rights in the city. By the end of Felix's governorship in 60 some of the battle lines of the coming war were clearly visible.

Nero's cancellation of the equal citizen rights of the Jews of Caesarea and his award of rule over the city to the Greeks during Festus's procuratorship intensified the conflict between Jews and Greeks and Syrians in that city and virtually guaranteed that the struggle would reach a point of mass violence. In the countryside Festus also had to deal with bands of "brigands." The *sicarii* meanwhile carried on their campaign against their enemies both in Jerusalem and in the villages. The conflict between King Agrippa II and some of the most influential men in Jerusalem over the wall in the Temple that blocked his view shows that even at the highest levels of Judaean society there was strife. Nero's intervention on behalf of those who wanted the wall left in place also shows, however, that he was not ineluctably hostile to the men who made decisions about the Temple and its structures.

Festus's successor Albinus (62–64) also had strained relations with the high priest Ananus over the execution of James, the brother of Jesus, and alienated Jews at every level by his burdensome taxes. Albinus's imaginative, but unscrupulous, methods of raising the money that Nero apparently demanded led to systemic corruption, as people paid bribes to get relatives out of jail or to secure immunity. The leaders in Jerusalem formed gangs for the sake of self-protection, and at least some of the *sicarii* seem to have subsidized their resistance movement through a criminal kidnapping enterprise. The sudden unemployment of 18,000 men who had been working on projects associated with the Temple complex cannot have helped the economic circumstances of many Jerusalemites.

Very soon after he succeeded Albinus as governor, Gessius Florus became a silent partner of the brigands that his predecessors had tried to contain. After Nero awarded the Syrian Caesareans rule over Caesarea, Florus made clear that he had no intention of protecting the Jews of Caesarea legally or otherwise. As so often in the outbreak of wars, the war of Jews against Romans, against their non-Jewish neighbors, and against each other began with a trivial incident, a non-Jewish Caesarean provocatively making a sacrifice next to a synagogue in Caesarea. Florus refused to intervene to put an end to the violence in Caesarea and then withdrew 17 talents from the Temple treasury in Jerusalem. The point of no return was reached when Florus let his soldiers twice massacre large numbers of unarmed Jews in and around Jerusalem. After so much blood had been shed the arguments of those who cautioned restraint and self-interest were no longer persuasive.

There had been conflicts among Jews about the interpretation of the law, religious versus secular authority, and other issues for centuries before the Romans became a presence in the eastern Mediterranean. Jews had been in conflict with non-Jews over land and resources in the region for even longer. The imposition of Roman rule over Jews in Judaea created another layer of authority within which all of those conflicts and tensions would be negotiated and resolved or not.

After Herod's death the Romans never found another Herod who could be both a loyal client of whoever was in charge in Rome and an effective king of Jews and non-Jews. It was for that reason that his kingdom was broken up, and a Roman governor was eventually sent out to Judaea. That decision was always likely to lead to the appointment of governors whose loyalties were first and last to the emperor—and when conflicts between Jews and non-Jews arose under their jurisdiction, if they or the emperors came down on the side of the non-Jews, unhappiness with Roman rule and with non-Jews was bound to increase among Jews.

While some governors seem to have gone out of their way to understand their Jewish subjects and their laws and traditions, others did not. A decisive turning point was reached when Claudius decided to let the Sebastenians and the Caesareans stay on to serve as the primary police force and paramilitary in Judaea after they insulted Agrippa I and his family. That decision sent the message that the Romans had chosen the side of the ethnic enemies of the

Jews. Twenty years later the policies of Nero and the actions of Florus in particular helped push a much larger number of Jews over into the camp of those who saw no alternative but active resistance to the Romans. The war of Jews against Romans in 66 was a war against a specific emperor, his chosen governors, and their actions and policies. Just as there were Jews with very different attitudes toward Romans and Rome in 66, there were different Romans, with different ideas about how to govern the Jews.

We cannot ask the tens of thousands of Jews who took up arms against Rome in 66 at what point and why "the light hand" of Roman rule was no longer light enough for them.[8] What we know is that, from the time that the first prefect was sent out to Judaea, there were Jews who felt that serving both God and Caesar was impossible. Sixty years later, after the grandson of the man who led the resistance in 6 CE convinced enough of his fellow Jews to declare their independence from Rome by halting sacrifices for Caesar and Rome, Jewish rebels minted coins that marked the years of Zion's freedom or redemption since they rebelled from Rome.

Josephus also tells his readers, after describing the destruction of the Temple, that what had incited the rebels to revolt was an ambiguous oracle found in their sacred books predicting that someone from their country would become the ruler of the world. The rebels understood this to mean someone of their own country, presumably a Jew; but, according to Josephus, the oracle really predicted the sovereignty of Vespasian, who was proclaimed emperor in Judaea.[9]

Josephus does not identify for his readers who it was that was persuaded to revolt based upon the oracle. But the oracle itself was about worldly rule (*hegemonia*), not some messianic promise, let alone salvation after death. The Jews who took on and fought the ancient Mediterranean world's superpower were fighting for the freedom of Zion, here and now, not there and then. Their freedom and redemption began when Eleazar refused to make sacrifices for Rome or the emperor. He and his followers were only willing to serve one master, and that master was not the Roman emperor. Confirmation of this can be found in some passages in Josephus that many historians—who have a tendency to pass over the actual evidence of the fighting that took place during the war—have ignored or underappreciated.

In his description of the fighting between Jews and Romans at the second wall during the siege of Jerusalem in 70, Josephus reports that a group of five Jews yelled down to the Roman soldiers that they would never be slaves to the Romans but preferred to die as free men.[10] After Titus and the Romans breached that wall, during the fighting around the first wall, as Titus was making his way around, beneath the ramparts, more Jews hurled abuse at Titus and Vespasian, adding that they despised death, preferring it by far to slavery.[11] Josephus, our prime and indispensable source for the war, may very well have heard what these Jews yelled at the Romans. He certainly was present.

The Romans fought in 66 because they wanted to hold on to their hard-won imperium, particularly over an area that occupied the north–south land route between Syria and Egypt and trade routes from the Mediterranean coast eastward to the Arabian plateau. It is simply not true that the Romans had got hold of their imperial territory without bloodshed; and they were willing to shed more blood to keep hold of it. The Carthaginians and the Gauls would have been surprised to learn that they had merely been intimidated into submission.

Cestius's defeat had to be avenged. Nero could not afford to be seen either internally or externally as soft on insurrection within the empire. That was especially true for an artist-emperor. But he also needed money.

The Jews had a Temple with a rich treasury. Both Nero and Vespasian wanted to access those riches. As the war developed, the Roman war of revenge and self-interest turned into a kind of religious war, the objective of which was to eradicate the sacrificial cult of Judaism—though not necessarily all of the practices and traditions of all Jews—precisely because the Temple cult had been, and could be, the magnet for organized resistance to Rome. It was the Temple, and the sacrifices made there to the God of the Jews, that brought Jews from all over the Roman empire to Jerusalem and united them into a people (an *ethnos* in Greek) who could revolt effectively from Rome. Judaism without a Temple was not a potential problem for Rome—or so Vespasian thought.

In the short term Vespasian and his sons got what they wanted out of the war: a justification for the foundation of their dynasty; a revenue stream to help put Rome back on its economic feet and to build monuments in Rome to remind people of why the Flavians deserved to be their rulers; and the elimination of the Temple-based sacrificial cult of the Jews that Vespasian understood as a competitive threat to Rome's rule in the Near East. In fact, over the long run, Vespasian's and Titus's triumph ended in Rome's defeat because the Flavians misconstrued the real challenge to their imperium.

Wars of Jews against Rome, their neighbors, and among themselves could have broken out in 4 BCE or 39 CE. The war that began in 66 was the result of human decisions. It was not inevitable. Nor was its course and outcome.

CHAPTER 23

The Course and Outcome of the War

Near the beginning of the *War,* Josephus provides a brief statement about the course of the war of Jews against Rome and its outcome:

That domestic strife brought it down, and that the tyrants of the Jews drew both the unwilling hands of the Romans and the fire upon the temple, Titus Caesar, the one who destroyed it, is witness. Toward the people, kept under guard by the rebels, he showed pity throughout the entire war; and often willingly deferred the capture of the city, and gave opportunity for a change of mind on the part of those responsible through protracting the siege. Now in case anyone should criticize us for what we say, accusing the tyrants and their bandit bloc, or for groaning over the misfortunes of our native place, let him grant indulgence for compassion that is contrary to the law of history. For of all those ruled by the Romans it was the lot of our city to reach the greatest fortune and to fall to the depth of misfortunes. In my opinion indeed, the misfortunes of all since the beginning fall short in comparison to those of the Jews, and since the cause was not any other tribe, it was impossible to overcome grief.[1]

Thus Josephus blamed what happened during the war and its outcome—the destruction of the Temple and much of Jerusalem—upon the tyrants of the Jews; that is, Eleazar, John, and Simon. Later, in book 4 of the *War,* in the context of his encomia for the high priests Ananus and Jesus, Josephus wrote that God had condemned the city to destruction and desired to purge the sanctuary by fire for its pollutions.[2] At the beginning of book 5 of the same work, after describing how the missiles fired by the different rebel factions had killed those who had come to the Temple to sacrifice, Josephus claimed that the Romans had come to Jerusalem to purge the city's internal pollutions with fire.[3] A similar idea is repeated in book 5 in Josephus's account of the speech he made to his own countrymen beneath Jerusalem's third wall. There he asserted that the Deity had fled from the holy places and taken his stand on the side of those with whom the rebels were at war.[4] In book 6 he comes back to the idea that the destruction of the Temple was a divine punishment for the Jews' sins.[5] By their sins, they had started a war against God. God had let his own house be destroyed rather than countenance the sins of his people.

Later in life, Josephus wrote in the *Antiquities* that it was because of the impiety of the assassins, who murdered people such as the high priest Jonathan during the governorship of Felix, that God turned away from Jerusalem, deemed the Temple an unclean dwelling place for himself, brought in the Romans to purify the city by fire, and inflicted slavery upon the Jews. All of these misfortunes were God's punishment of Jews.[6] Earlier Josephus had identified those who assassinated Jonathan as *sicarii*.[7]

Essential to Josephus's conception of the course of the war and its terrible consequences is the idea that it was the impiety or sins of Jews that led to the punishments.[8] God was not responsible for that impiety; Jews themselves were. Their choices led to divine punishment.[9]

This conception of what caused the war and its outcome is consistent with what scholars have called the "Tun-Ergehen-Zusammenhang," or action-consequence paradigm between God and the Hebrews/Israelites/Jews. The paradigm of Jews being punished for lack of faith or immoral behavior often included the active participation of non-Jews in the relationship.[10]

There are numerous passages in the Hebrew Bible that interpret the historical experience of Jews in the way Josephus presents it in the *War*. This idea that if Israel was faithful to Yahweh and to the covenant then all would be well, but if it departed from them, disaster would follow, is found in the books of Exodus, Deuteronomy especially, and elsewhere.[11] In Isaiah the prophet memorably prophesied, supposedly before the Assyrian capture of Israel around 740 BCE, that Assyria was the rod of Yahweh's anger and the staff of his fury and that Yahweh sent him (Assyria) against a godless nation.[12]

In the case of the revolt of 66 the overall sin for Josephus, however, was not godlessness. Rather, it was the civil discord among the Jews themselves, resulting in the shedding of blood within the Temple and other crimes that he identified as the main reason why the rebels had to be punished by God through the Romans.[13]

Thus in 66 the Romans, like the Assyrians before them, were only the instrument by which God inflicted upon the Jews their deserved punishments. The Jews were free to be obedient or to be sinful and to reap the consequences. When Jews fought among themselves and shed each other's blood they incurred God's righteous wrath and suffered deserved punishment. But the Romans—unlike the Jews—did not really have independent historical agency in the working out of God's master plan or providence.[14]

The advantage of subscribing to Josephus's explanation for what happened is that it provides for a sense of historical control, albeit at a terrible cost. In Josephus's presentation of the war and its outcome the theological system worked. The impious were punished for their sins by God's tool, the unwilling Romans. But Josephus was writing from the point of view of a survivor whose family and educational background were connected to the priestly hierarchy in Jerusalem and whose strategy for winning the war had been disastrously wrong. He was also writing in the company of the victors, who not only were reading over his shoulder but also, quite literally, vetted and endorsed his version of events.[15]

STRATEGY, TACTICS, AND LOGISTICS OF THE REBELS

It is easier to escape Josephus's history than his theology. Some of the hillsides of the site of Iotapata might be called cliff-like. But Iotapata is not surrounded by sheer cliffs. The Jews undoubtedly suffered tens of thousands of casualties during the war. But there cannot have been 1.1 million Judaeans killed during the revolt. There are many contradictions in Josephus's works. They have been systematically cataloged by Jonathan Price.[16] Josephus's idea that Jews or the "tyrants" sinned in 66 and therefore brought catastrophe down upon the Jewish people, however, has stuck, both among believers and non-believers, with fateful consequences.

Josephus attributed the Jews' defeat to their God.[17] In fact, as we have seen, Josephus represented God as taking an active role at key moments during the siege of Gamala, the destruction of the Temple, and the capture of Masada to drive home his point that while this was a war of Jews against Rome, against non-Jews, and each other, it was finally a war of some Jews against God—and there was only ever going to be one victor in that war.

In one sense, Josephus was right. Some Jews were at least in part responsible for their defeat. But not because of God or their own impiety. Rather, although as far back as the creation of the book of Deuteronomy, explicit rules for waging war—perhaps the world's first written rules of engagement—had been set out for Jews, those who revolted in 66 lost because throughout the different phases of the war their leaders, including Josephus, never formulated and executed a strategy, tactics, and logistics in light of an assessment of who their enemy was, how their enemy was likely to fight, and how the war against such an enemy could be won.[18] Without such an analysis that was subsequently put into action, the immense bravery and sacrifices of tens of thousands of Jews during the war were wasted.[19] The course of the war and its outcome, in other words, were also contingent events, based upon human choices that turned out to be mistaken and led to failure.

Part of the reason for this failure was that, as far as we know, almost all the military leaders of the rebellion had no formal military training or experience before they were appointed to their leadership positions or assumed them.[20] They were selected or self-selected for those positions by virtue of their family backgrounds, wealth, and religious or cultic expertise. Social status and knowledge of scripture and cultic practices are not necessarily the best preparation for developing the skills or leadership qualities a general needs to lead armies and put men into positions to fight and win wars.

Despite what many, though not quite all, scholars have assumed or written about the Roman army, no army is invincible.[21] The Romans themselves knew that better than many of their modern admirers. Rome's march to domination of the Mediterranean world was interrupted by a series of disastrous military defeats, from Cannae in 216 BCE to the Teutoburg Forest in 9 CE. Every war can be lost. And every war can be won or at least not lost, which is not the same thing, as Churchill, who spent a good part of his very long life fighting, directing, or reflecting upon wars, observed. A stalemate is better than a checkmate.[22]

After their initial victory over Cestius in 66 and the distribution of leadership positions to the various regional commanders, the rebel Jews conceded the strategic initiative to the Romans even before the first real battle was fought. From the Galilee in 67 to Masada in 73 or 74, Jews chose to fight a defensive war from behind the walls of their fortified villages, towns, cities,

and hilltops. Part of the reason for this undoubtedly was that the vast majority of Jews at the time lived in such towns and villages. But the villages and
cities in the Galilee and Judaea were not built for the sake of defending their
inhabitants, especially against skilled, professional besiegers.[23] Rather they
grew up organically where they did to give their inhabitants access to the land
they farmed to feed themselves and to afford them some protection from local threats. The sieges that the rebels drew the Romans into were enormously
expensive for the Romans, but they had the resources and logistical systems
to pay that cost. Making the fortified population centers of the Galilee and
Judaea into the central battlegrounds of the war in 66 was a strategic mistake.

Josephus and the Jews fought Rome's kind of war in the Galilee and Judaea with the likely, though of course not inevitable, outcome in almost every
case. Moreover, even after the lessons of following their strategic approach
became unmistakably clear from what transpired in the Galilee in 67, instead
of changing their strategy, the rebels simply pulled back and chose to fight
from behind the walls of the largest and best fortified city, Jerusalem—with
the exact same outcome. What happened in Jerusalem was what had happened before at Iotapata and Gamala. The only difference was the scale of
the fortifications, the difficulty of the siege, and the immensity of its disastrous conclusion.

This was the case despite the fact that there was a hiatus in the Judaean
War after the death of Nero in early June of 68. During the pause from fighting that the Roman civil war afforded the rebels, their leaders had an opportunity to reassess the way they were fighting the war. Yet they never changed
their strategy or absorbed the hard lessons of their previous defeats. Rather,
after the Romans temporarily ceased military operations the Jews spent the
time fighting each other. That much Josephus got right, though his literary
focus on the internal infighting, to support his argument about the role that
stasis played in the Jewish defeat, has obscured the more important strategic
lesson.

Other than from the speech of Agrippa II at the very beginning of the
revolt, we get no sense that fighting a different kind of war—as opposed to
not fighting at all—was ever considered by those who were in charge of pros-
ecuting the war. Indeed, in Agrippa's famous speech, one key point that the
king apparently passed over was the need for leadership and strategic thinking. Agrippa offered the Jews in his audience at the Xystus a simple choice
between capitulation or destruction. That was not strategic thinking or leadership, at least if victory was the goal.

Some might argue that it was inevitable that the rebels would end up fighting from behind Jerusalem's walls and then from within the walls of the Temple Mount itself. There is something to that argument. The Temple after all was the focal point of the national sacrificial cult. Yet if the rebellion was undertaken so that Jews should have no master other than God, it is hard to see how bringing four enemy legions to the walled cultic center of Zion was a wise strategy for achieving the goal of freeing themselves from Roman rule— and it was from Roman rule that the rebels were attempting to free themselves, not from their neighbors.

None of Judaea's close regional neighbors posed an existential threat to Jerusalem in 66. The Jews of Judaea may have been hated by many of their neighbors, but none of them was capable of besieging and destroying Jerusalem. Most of Judaea's closest neighbors were ruled by Rome and had been defeated by Herod or other Jewish armies in the past, sometimes repeatedly. The other heavyweight strategic power in the neighborhood, Parthia, had every reason to look on the troubles Rome had with the Jews of Jerusalem with silent approbation.

The rebels lost because they had no military strategy—a purposeful use of violence for a political end—likely to achieve their strategic objective of gaining freedom based upon a disinterested and accurate assessment of who their enemy was and what the enemy's likely course of action would be.[24] There apparently was no strategic thinking founded upon the plausible hypothesis that, after the rout of Cestius, the Romans would put together a large army of legions, auxiliary units, and allies; invade the Galilee and Judaea from Ptolemais; and besiege those Jews who retreated behind the walls of their towns and cities. The time to counter the Roman strategy was not when the Romans were at Jerusalem's walls but when they were establishing their strategic bases. Fighting far from Rome with their regional allies by their sides, the Romans were dependent upon those allies and the resources they could provide to make possible their attacks upon the Jews. The most effective way to fight the Romans in 66–67 would have been to attack their long supply lines: the leaders of the revolt needed an aggressive, forward strategy. By the time Titus and the Romans got to the walls of Jerusalem it was too late.

The tactics of the rebels were also repetitious and predictable, if Josephus's accounts of the war's battles are credible. When besieged in their villages and towns the rebels adopted various countermeasures, attacking those who were working on the ramps and earthworks and those who operated the war machines. In these attacks groups of Jews and individual Jews often outfought the Romans in close encounters.[25] Josephus's descriptions of these individual duels, with Jews often prevailing, incidentally support the case that his intention was not to flatter his Roman readers. But the Jews did not have the numbers or organization to sustain their attacks. Despite their bravery and clever countermeasures, the rebels were never able to break the sieges. Walls, no matter how thick or high, in the end are not adequate protection against a determined opponent, even if those living behind such walls have an adequate water supply, as did the defenders of Jerusalem.[26]

Historians love to cite examples of sieges that were unsuccessful, such as the Athenian siege of Syracuse in 414 BCE during the Peloponnesian War or Napoleon's investment of Acre (Akko) in 1799, conveniently forgetting that, in the case of Acre, it had been successfully besieged before, most notably in July 1191 during the Third Crusade.[27]

Virtually every great walled city in antiquity was captured and sacked at one time or another before 66 CE. Troy, Athens (repeatedly), and even Rome were successfully besieged. The most famous story in the history of Graeco-Roman civilization is the *fall* of Troy, not its successful resistance to the 10-year siege by the Achaeans. Nor was this solely a Graeco-Roman rule in antiquity, as literate Jews would have known from their own history. After they had fled from Egypt, the Israelites themselves had taken all 60 high-walled, gated, and barred cities of Argob, the kingdom of Og in Bashan; when they crossed over into the promised land, they also supposedly brought down Jericho's wall with one blast of the rams' trumpets and a great shout.[28]

In fact, as Josephus himself noted, Jerusalem had been captured five times before Titus and the Romans took the city in 70, despite all the wall building of its leaders and people.[29] Then, as now, walls do not protect men, as the first-century BCE Greek geographer Strabo of Amaseia observed.[30] Instead, they trap them. Brave soldiers fighting from behind fixed fortifications almost always lose, as historical examples from Masada to the Alamo to Dien Bien Phu teach us.

The least visible, though perhaps decisive, failure of the rebels, however, was logistical. In each theater of the war the rebels simply resupplied themselves as best as they could without outside help. The idea in the Galilee at the beginning of the war was that at least some of the soldiers would be used to gather grain in the countryside while their fellow soldiers would remain in the towns and cities, protecting them from behind the city walls. It does not seem to have occurred to Josephus or the other rebel leaders that the Romans would take or devastate the countryside itself, thereby depriving them of the grain the Jews had intended to gather.

The rebels did nothing to try to prevent Vespasian from cutting them off from access to supplies from outside Jerusalem, and in Jerusalem the rebels John and Simon deliberately destroyed the city's grain supplies.[31] The logistical failure is all the more striking given the fact that, although we do not know the details, it is obvious that Josephus, who wrote extensively about Herod, his army, and his expenditures, knew very well that some sort of organized commissariat was essential to success in warfare.[32] During Herod's war against Antigonus in the Galilee, Herod had placed his brother Pheroras in charge of the commissariat, as Josephus noted.[33]

The smuggling of some food into Jerusalem during the siege in 70 could never make up for what was lost when the Jews lost access to the countryside around Jerusalem. The Romans, in contrast, were able to rely upon supplies brought along secured supply lines that stretched northward into Syria and the adjacent provinces.[34] Along those lines huge amounts of food were conveyed to the Roman armies that fought the Jews. (See appendix M for the combined totals from Cestius's brief campaign in 66, Vespasian's northern campaign in 67, Titus's siege of Jerusalem in 70, and Silva's siege of Masada.) Water was an issue for the Romans but never caused them to alter their strategy.[35]

As far as the narrative of Josephus reveals, there also was no intelligence gathering about the Roman enemy and the deployment of Roman troops, let alone an attempt to think empathetically about how the Romans thought about warfare, as opposed to the organization of their legions, which Josephus proudly claimed to have copied. This failure is hard to understand because there were examples of such operations and attempts described in the Hebrew Bible, and Josephus himself knew about Herod's "secret service" and internal security service. Herod himself is reported by Josephus to have dressed up in disguise and mingled with crowds of people to find out information about his own rule.[36] In 66 the rebels apparently did little or no intelligence gathering, and there was no attempt to enter into the minds of the Romans to understand the connections between their culture and their way of making war.

ROMAN STRATEGY, TACTICS, AND LOGISTICS

After Cestius's defeat the Romans put together a task force that was large enough to besiege and then capture all of the main population centers in the north and then Judaea. In all such cases the Romans established strategic bases of provision, sometimes drawing upon resources from hundreds of miles away, then advanced to operational and, finally, tactical bases. Once they established tactical bases the Romans cordoned off all such towns, cities, and fortresses with walls and lines of infantry and cavalry and then besieged them using exactly the same tactics in each case. They built ramps and earthworks and then brought up war machines, including battering rams, to the fortifications. They used catapults to clear the walls of defenders and battering rams to break through the walls. At immense logistical cost, the Romans did exactly what anyone in Jerusalem should have known they finally would do: come to Jerusalem in force and find a way to break into the city or starve it into submission.

After the capture of Jerusalem Titus should have handed out decorations to his army's engineers and mules. They were the ones who provided the margin of victory. Mules, as much as or more than men, were responsible for the Roman victory over the rebels.

From the beginning of the war the Romans followed their historical military doctrine of aggressively confronting their enemies with force as quickly as possible.[37] The Romans had strategic scale on their side, and it was predictable that they would use it. The rebels got a reprieve from the Romans following this doctrine only because of the death of Nero and the ensuing Roman civil war.

Individually, the rebels against Rome from 66 to 74 fought as bravely as human beings have fought in history. Indeed, individual Jews or small groups of them repeatedly routed Roman units during the war from the time of Cestius's disastrous intervention almost to the destruction of the Temple in 70.[38] The Jewish rebels did not run away, as so many of Rome's enemies had in the past, when the legionaries hurled their *pila* at their enemies and charged.

But great courage and boldness alone are not enough to produce victory and win freedom against a well-trained, well-led professional army following a clear strategy, backed up by adequate logistics, and applying practiced and adaptive tactics.[39] Vespasian, Titus, and the Roman legionaries under their command were not fundamentally interested in gaining the hearts and subduing the minds of their adversaries. What they wanted was fear, respect, and victory. The Roman idea of a population-centric military campaign was one in which the population surrendered or was annihilated.

Individual heroism makes for great literature but not necessarily military victory. In fact, the rebels may have had too many heroes and not enough real leaders, or even one leader who could conceptualize and enact a strategy for winning the war or set up an effective command-and-control structure to wage war, as Moses had done for the Israelites.[40]

LEADERSHIP

In 66 the rebels needed a David, a Judas Maccabaeus, or a Herod to lead them—someone who understood the tactical utility of adaptability, dispersal, mobility, and surprise as instruments of a broader strategy. Herod, for instance, had not hesitated to abandon Jerusalem in 40 BCE at the approach of the Parthians. In doing so he lived to fight another day, and in the end he prevailed. Instead, among other generals, the rebels in 66 had Josephus, a thoughtful and learned young man, living during troubled times for his people, and later a writer of immense importance for historians of the period—but not a strategic thinker or planner for war.

The only indication that Josephus ever thought strategically about the war was the request he sent to Jerusalem from the Galilee either to send him more battle-ready troops or to authorize him to surrender. His attempt to create a duplicate Roman army in the Galilee in only a few weeks, if it really happened, should have set off alarm bells in Jerusalem. Josephus could write brilliantly about Herod, but he could not out-Herod Herod in the way that really mattered in 66: not on the retrospective fields of historiographic combat, but on real battlefields, where Herod, when he was even younger than Josephus, fighting against formidable armies, rarely lost.[41]

The Romans, in contrast, had Vespasian and Titus. No doubt Josephus's narratives of the war were constructed to flatter the Romans who spared his life after the siege of Iotapata and gave him a safe and secure retirement in Rome. But reading between the lines of Josephus's flattering portraits of Vespasian and his son Titus we can also see why they were more effective commanders than their counterparts among the Jews, even if Titus was a relatively inexperienced commander who got the job of taking Jerusalem essentially because his father was Vespasian.

Following classic Roman models of generalship and leadership, both Vespasian and Titus planned their campaigns carefully; directed operations from behind the lines, near the front and at the front as tactical situations required; personally fought in battles; and encouraged or punished their troops to maintain discipline and morale. In other words, they displayed the *virtus,* or courage, that was expected historically of Rome's generals.[42] It was the example of their courage that literally encouraged the men who served under them.

In sum, the rebels lost the war not because of their impiety or lack of morale—the willingness to fight and die for their cause. According to their own lights, pious they were, and Josephus provides numerous examples of individual Jews or groups of Jews who were willing to engage with their enemies and fight to the end. If anything, Josephus's narrative reveals that the morale of Jews remained remarkably high throughout the war, no matter how many of their men were wounded, tortured, or killed or their women and children violated or enslaved. But in this case devotion to their cause of freedom was not enough. They were defeated due to a far greater sin, in warfare at least: inflexible, fractured leadership with no conception of how to fight and win a war against an enemy whose tactics, logistics, and strategy should have been studied, understood, and countered. War is indeed a violent teacher, and those who ignore its lessons usually suffer the consequences.

There was no Judas Maccabaeus or Herod there in 66 to show the Jews the way to victory or at least survival and to lead them to it. Judas Maccabaeus was an able and charismatic leader. Herod was undoubtedly brutal and possibly deranged by the end of his life. But he was also a winner in both peace and war, and in warfare second-place finishers win no prizes.

In contrast, the Romans were ably, if cautiously, led first by Vespasian and then by his son Titus. If Vespasian had been killed at Iotapata, instead of merely being wounded, the outcome of the war might have been very different. But he was not, and the Romans went on to win the war. Most modern scholars have assumed or argued that this outcome was inevitable, no matter what strategy the rebels followed. In war, however, nothing is written.

COULD THE REBELS HAVE WON?

Influenced consciously or unconsciously by Josephus's theological interpretation of the war, most scholars and students of history have regarded the defeat of the Jews who revolted against Rome in 66, if not as divinely preordained, then certainly as militarily inevitable. Judaea was a small province of the Roman empire without a trained and experienced standing army of its own. The only contemporary, battle-tested local troops in the area were the soldiers who served in the auxiliary cohorts of the region. Most of them were non-Jews and were hostile to the Jews, as Josephus makes clear. Rome was the most powerful empire the ancient world had ever seen, and the Roman emperors could put into the field against any foe tens of thousands of professional soldiers, led by officers with decades of leadership experience.

The Romans indeed had "supériorité de nombres, supériorité d'armes, supériorité de méthodes."[43] The only way the Jews could have won was by a miracle.[44]

The idea that the revolt was doomed to fail the moment it began is arguable, especially if we assume that the rebels planned to fight the way they did: directed by a divided leadership and fighting from behind the walls of villages, towns, and cities by courageous but militarily unskilled and inexperienced civilians.

But what if the revolt was not fought the way it was? What if, instead of engaging in defensive battles against the large, concentrated forces of the Roman legions and their allies, the rebels avoided static confrontations?

A Strategy of Dispersal

The revolutionaries in 66 could have followed the example of David. When Saul was trying to get rid of him David fled to the strongholds of the wilderness, in the hill country of the wilderness of Ziph (Khirbet Zif) and then Ein Gedi.[45] Along the escarpment facing the Dead Sea to its east there were thousands of caves in which rebels could have hidden and used as bases. Or, to take an example from their more recent history, they could have imitated Matthias and his sons. After they had slain the Seleucid king Antiochus Epiphanes's garrison commander Bacchides (or Apelles) and his soldiers in Modein, they promptly fled into the wilderness or the hills, where they launched a guerilla-style or partisan war against the Seleucid army and its collaborators.

The Maccabees helped their countrymen achieve the greatest degree of political and religious freedom that Jews would experience between the fourth century BCE and 1948, because they did not care about property, did not fight from behind walls, and were willing to do whatever it took to win their freedom, including fleeing into the wilderness and fighting on the Sabbath—even though doing so violated the spirit, if not the letter, of a biblical prohibition. Could a Maccabean-style guerilla campaign in 66 have produced better results against Rome's powerful legions? Could they have caused the Romans to flee before the Jews "seven ways"?[46]

When wars are lost it is easy to claim that the losers chose the wrong strategy. In the case of the failed revolt of 66, however, it is at least worth asking whether a different strategy had a chance of leading to a different result. Could a campaign of strategic dispersal have produced a better result than what was achieved? Could it have led to freedom or a tolerable degree of freedom?

Every historical situation is different. Differences in topography, sizes of forces, leadership, and many other factors make it hard to generalize across cultures and time periods. But strategies of dispersal or insurgencies have usually required a set of conditions to be present for such campaigns to have a chance of success: among those conditions have been a sympathetic civilian population; support from outside the main theater of war; effective leadership; and the will to win.[47]

Although there were people in the villages and towns of the Galilee and Judaea who favored accommodation with Rome, many people were hostile to the Romans. The proof of this is that there was sustained resistance to the Roman legions by those Jews who fought from behind the walls of Iotapata, Gamala, Jerusalem, Masada, and elsewhere.

During insurgency-counterinsurgency wars it is rare for the civilian population to be unified in their support for either the dominant power or the insurgents. That certainly was the case in 66. But Josephus's texts indicate that there were tens of thousands of Jews who were hostile to Rome at the time; those who hated Rome could have helped the insurgents by providing them with shelter, food, and intelligence during a prolonged campaign, as the helpful harlot Rahab did when she hid the two spies sent out by Joshua to view the land, before he led the people of Israel into the promised land.[48]

The Judaean wilderness along the western side of the Dead Sea might have provided a base of operations for a well-organized and mobile resistance movement. The logistical costs of fighting such a war for the Romans would have been high because of the lack of water in the area and the need to carry supplies by pack animals or wagons.[49]

Such a strategy was tried, beginning in 132 CE, during the Bar Kokhba revolt. Fighting a classic guerilla-style war against the Romans, the rebels managed to inflict devastating defeats upon them.[50] Unfortunately for them, the disastrous consequences of the defeat during the earlier revolt made it more difficult for the rebels of the second revolt to find support from the civilian population and to sustain their efforts.

The Adiabenian Option

Insurgents might also have made use of their proximity to the kingdom of Parthia or one of the 18 or so semi-independent client states over which the Parthians exercised some control. Parthia, which shared a border with the Roman province of Syria, was one of the few strategic threats to the Romans in the Near East and had been in conflict with Rome almost since the Ar-sacid dynasty established its rule by 100 BCE. Some historians have opined that the Parthian "option" was not a viable one for the rebels. But Josephus, Cassius Dio, and the Romans themselves beg to differ.

Josephus suggests that at least some of the rebels considered the possibil-ity of involving Parthians or those living in Parthian territories in their war. Before the Roman army reached the walls of Jerusalem, the rebels were hop-ing that their fellow countrymen from across the Euphrates would join in the rebellion; after the destruction of the Temple, Titus was said to have claimed that embassies were sent to the friends of the revolutionaries beyond the Eu-phrates.[51] Those embassies were probably sent in late 69 or even 70, suggest-ing that they were dispatched as a kind of hail Mary pass with the Romans closing in on Jerusalem. As far as we know the embassies did not lead to any help being sent, though the third-century CE historian Cassius Dio reports that during the siege the rebels were assisted by many of their countrymen from the region and also their coreligionists from within the Roman empire and from across the Euphrates.[52] We do not know how many Jews from across the Euphrates came to Jerusalem, but it is not true that securing assistance from areas that were under Parthian control was some kind of fantasy.

The rebels had to have been aware that tensions and at times open hos-tilities between Parthia and Rome dated back to the time of the Roman general Lucullus (69 BCE); these conflicts included Surena's famous defeat of Crassus and his army in 53 BCE at Carrhae (Harran) and the capture of their military standards, as well as the defeat of another Roman army led by Antony's generals and the loss of their standards too in 36 BCE. In fact, dur-ing the late first century BCE, from their capital of Ctesiphon on the Tigris River (about 21 miles south of present-day Baghdad), Parthian satraps and members of their royal family had intervened for the sake of their own inter-ests in Judaea.[53]

Augustus managed to achieve a diplomatic *modus vivendi* with the Par-thians after recovering the military standards lost by three Roman armies from the Parthian king Phraates in 20 BCE.[54] The recovery of the standards, how-ever, did not alter the reality that Rome and the Parthians had their own in-terests in the region and that at times those interests conflicted or could be played upon. At his treason trial, Herod's son Alexander alleged that his father was considering switching loyalties from Augustus to the Parthian king; such a claim could only be effective (even rhetorically) if it was something that Ro-mans realistically feared.[55]

Tensions between Rome and Parthia did not end with Augustus's death. A few decades later, early in the reign of Nero, Rome and Parthia came into armed conflict over Armenia, which bordered on both Cappadocia and the Roman province of Syria, and specifically the issue of who should be its ruler. The story is worth briefly reviewing because it reminds us that, not that long before the revolt of 66 broke out, relations between Rome and Parthia were far from cordial.

After the Parthian king Vologaeses I put his own brother Tiridates on the throne in Armenia, the Romans intervened and replaced Vologaeses's brother with Tigranes, the great-grandson of Herod the Great.[56] For reasons unknown Tigranes proceeded to attack the Parthian client kingdom of Adiabene, ruled by Monobazos II. Vologaeses and Monobazos responded by trying to knock Tigranes off his Armenian throne. A Roman relief army led by Caesennius Paetus was defeated by Vologaeses. With the experienced Roman general Corbulo advancing toward him with four legions, Vologaeses made peace with Rome. His brother Tiridates was allowed to become king of Armenia, but only after acknowledging that Nero had granted the kingdom to him as a gift.[57]

This episode shows that Vologaeses did not fancy a full-scale confrontation with Rome just at the time that the revolt of Jews in Judaea was breaking out, and it is doubtful that Vologaeses would have wanted to irritate Nero by supporting rebels in Jerusalem either overtly or even covertly. Vologaeses, after all, had essentially got what he wanted—his brother Tiridates on the throne of Armenia and a Roman army taught a sharp lesson.[58] A full-scale Parthian attack upon Syria in 66 was not going to happen.

But support of the rebels by one of Parthia's client kings, particularly Monobazos II of Adiabene, located in what is now Iraqi Kurdistan, was not implausible after his experiences with Rome's choice for king of Armenia, the great-grandson of Herod. Monobazos and his family, who had begun to observe Jewish law since 20 CE, had reasons to be sympathetic to the rebels and in 66, at least, might have provided the Jewish fighters with sanctuary and financial support to help keep the Romans preoccupied, off-balance, and away from their kingdom and interests.

Foreign sanctuaries or safe zones have always been crucial to the success or failure of insurgencies, especially during those periods when rebels have been hard-pressed by their enemies.[59] And indeed, although Josephus provides no details, the surrender of members of the Adiabenian royal house in Jerusalem after the destruction of the Temple in 70 proves that there was support for the revolt from within the family; it also incidentally disproves the assertion of Agrippa II at the beginning of the war that Jews could look for no help from that direction.[60]

After Jerusalem was captured by the Romans, we know that at least some of the Adiabenians who surrendered were transported to Rome by Titus.[61] There they were held as hostages to ensure the loyalty of those left behind. Taking the Adiabenians hostage would have made no sense unless their support for those who rebelled was understood to be a realistic possibility. The Adiabenian, if not Parthian, option for the rebels in 66 was real, though the client kingdom of Adiabene could never be a strategic threat to Rome.

That it might have been in the interest of these neighbors to the east of Judaea to help the rebels during their revolt is indicated by the fact that, in between the first and second revolts in Judaea (66–132), the Parthians themselves would be the objects of a major Roman invasion led by the emperor Trajan. The Parthians had good strategic reasons for supporting people who wanted to fight the Romans, if only to distract or unsettle them. If the Romans responded to that Parthian support by directing their armies and resources toward Parthia that would have directly benefited the rebels in Judaea.

Different Leaders and Different Strategies

Among the Jews who took up arms against Rome in 66 there were some leaders capable of inspiring the kind of loyalty, discipline, and sacrifice that are necessary to carry out a successful guerilla war. John of Gischala, Simon bar Giora, the Idumaean generals, and Eleazar ben Yair all inspired their followers to risk their lives for the sake of their cause(s). Whether any of them would have made effective commanders of unconventional forces we cannot know, although we have seen that Simon bar Giora was a successful raider around Masada and Idumaea before he was invited into Jerusalem, and Eleazar ben Yair's actions before the siege of Masada suggest that he too was capable of leading raids.

What we do know is that historically such leaders had emerged in Judaea from among the people, including Judas Maccabaeus, his sons, and Eleazar's ancestor Judas. There were models of successful military leadership in the history of the Jews that could have been imitated, even if the leadership of a successful war of dispersal usually emerges from the war itself. It is worth remembering that John of Gischala and Simon, who arguably were the most effective leaders during the revolt, came from outside Jerusalem.

Was there a road to victory if Jews had fought such a war against Rome
in 66? Could an indirect, unconventional war have produced better results
than a conventional war did? Perhaps not, though there are plenty of indications in Josephus's accounts of the war that the Jews excelled at bold, hit-
and-run tactics and were not as successful in direct, large-scale confrontations.

In any case the Romans surely would have adjusted their own strategy and
tactics to an insurgency. Rome needed to maintain its monopoly of force
within its empire precisely because its power depended upon it. As previously
noted, in 66 there were roughly 150,000 legionary infantrymen spread out over
an empire of at least 2 million square miles; that is .075 citizen soldiers per
square mile. However, it is worth remembering that the legions were not
distributed evenly over the empire; four of them, or 15 percent of the total,
were stationed in nearby Syria.[62] To keep their grip on their empire the Romans needed to destroy internal opposition, no matter the tactical and logistical challenges.

In fact, tactical flexibility was one of the Roman army's hallmarks.[63] The
organization, discipline, and logistical practices of the Roman army made it
possible for the Romans to fight different kinds of wars against different kinds
of enemies. In response to a Judaean insurgency, the Romans would have
made use of Jewish collaborators who knew the topography of the region, as
they did fighting the conventional campaign they waged. The Romans would
have tried to destroy the food supplies of the insurgents and would have detained suspected insurgents and their sympathizers.[64] They would not have
hesitated to destroy towns or villages that were thought to have given aid and
comfort to the rebels, though this response might also have stiffened resistance and created new enemies. The Romans, in other words, would have done
what those who have fought counterinsurgency campaigns have done historically, and they may have been successful, as well-led and well-executed
counterinsurgency campaigns usually have been throughout history. Most
insurgencies do not succeed.

But a hit-and-run campaign of harassment and withdrawal fought by Jews
over a long period of time might have made successive Roman emperors
carefully consider the costs of maintaining Judaea as a province over the long
run, rather than as a client kingdom, for instance. The Hasmoneans had driven
out the much closer Seleucids; why not the Romans? Judaea, it always should
be remembered, was removed from the jurisdiction of prefects in 41, only to
be given over to the supervision of procurators in 44 after the death of King
Agrippa I. So there was precedent for granting Judaea and its leadership greater

autonomy under a local ruler. That autonomy existed, of course, within the strong gravitational pull of Rome's regional domination. Such autonomy may not have been enough for men who wanted no other master than God.

Yet relative autonomy, with the Temple still standing, might have been taken as a victory—and in war what matters is victory. The reason why we understand the war of Jews against Rome from 66 to 74 and its outcome the way we do is that the only detailed account of its causes, course, and "inevitable" outcome was written and rewritten by a participant in, and then historian of, the war, who was at least in part responsible for producing its tragic result.

Why does it matter what caused a war that ended almost 2,000 years ago, what determined its course, and what its outcome was?

CHAPTER 24

In the Beginning Were the Words

Many scholars have downplayed the scale and significance of the revolt of Jews against Romans (66–74 CE).

The war of Jews against Romans was not small, short, or insignificant.

The war was not small, however we choose to measure its scale. The war involved the largest concentration of Roman and allied forces during the early Roman empire, the longest siege of a city in all of imperial history, and astronomical human and material resources. The cost of winning the war is now incalculable.

But it clearly took a massive effort for the Romans to defeat all of the Jewish rebels. The fighting lasted for eight or nine years (66 to 74–75), and there were tens of thousands of Jewish, Roman, and other casualties and even more people enslaved as a result of the war.

A new Roman dynasty of rulers seized power in the middle of the war and legitimized its claim to rule the Roman empire on the basis of its victory over the Jews in the war. As soon as the new dynasty established itself in Rome it had built a number of monuments in the capital to remind people of this victory. One of those, the Flavian Amphitheater or Colosseum, is visited by more than four million people every year. The Colosseum is the metonym of the eternal city: Rome is the Colosseum; the Colosseum is Rome. Rome's metonym was built from spoils of the war of Jews against Romans.

Even before the fighting was over the Romans radically changed the organization of their rule in the Near East. After nearly 150 years of hesitant Roman engagement in the Near East, what had been an administrative bridgehead became an integrated military and provincial system. This change had immense historical repercussions. It was within or on the borders of the Romans' reorganized Near Eastern empire that the religions of the book (rabbinic Judaism, Christianity, and Islam) evolved or were born in relation to Graeco-Roman civilization and its religious practices, at times peacefully, though often not, and spread out over the world.

Neither the Jews nor Judaism were destroyed by the war's outcome. Remarkably, Judaism was reinterpreted and revivified after the war, at least partially in response to the war's course and conclusion, including the destruction of the Temple. A third Temple was not built on the ruins of the Second Temple destroyed in 70 by the Romans under Titus's command, and the sacrificial cult centered on the Temple in Jerusalem was intentionally eradicated by the Romans. In the aftermath of the Jews' defeat, Jews, Christians, polytheists, and Muslims all offered theological interpretations of the significance of the war and the Temple's destruction, just as Jews had done after the destruction of Solomon's Temple.[1] Those interpretations continue to be debated vigorously, and the question of who should speak for what constitutes correct observation of the law of Moses after the destruction of the Temple has as many answers today as it did during the late first century CE. Some, probably the majority of Jews alive now, follow the Herodian model of observation and engagement with non-Jews and their traditions and cultures, if not his treatment of family members and Jews who challenged his authority. Herodians argue that it is possible to be both a Jew and a Roman, both legally and culturally. Others reject the Herodian model, arguing with Judas the Galilaean that it is not possible to have Caesar as a master after God. There is only one king of Israel.

Many unforgivable crimes have been perpetrated against Jews over the centuries since 70. Moreover, to speak the truth—which is the fundamental job of historians—as the great Oxford Roman historian Sir Fergus Millar rightly said, hatred of Jews just for being Jews continues. Nevertheless, the existence of the debate about the origins, course, and outcome of the failed revolt of 66 is a sign of survival and, ultimately, victory.

The Romans won the war, and most of the wars since, but Jews have won the peace. The long, difficult road many Jews have walked since 70 has often been a *Via Dolorosa*. But it has indeed led back to the promised land.

The Roman generals Pompey and Titus perhaps did not find what they expected when they fought their way into the Holy of Holies. Used to bowing down before richly adorned statues of deities, and probably hoping to see something extraordinary that would explain why so many Jews were willing to die rather than break the law of Moses, they instead found nothing. But they were looking only with their eyes. They could never comprehend the idea of a space set aside for the presence of a divinity of such power, majesty, and singularity that no man-made representation could do him justice. Titus destroyed the house of that presence and thereby thought he conquered the God of Israel. His father and the Roman Senate gave him a triumph for his efforts.

What Titus, Vespasian, and Domitian failed to understand was that the divine presence lived on in something that was much harder to destroy: a book that ancient Jews believed had been written by God himself or at least had been divinely inspired.

The unnamed Roman soldier who tore in half the scroll copy of the law of Moses during the governorship of Cumanus understood better the nature of the book's challenge to Rome's rule than did the residents of the Palatine. Unlike the Temple, the book was transportable and could be reproduced infinitely, by word of mouth and in writing. It was not susceptible to sieges. Because the book survived there was and still is a voice and a plan: there is a purpose; history has a meaning; and God still acts in it. Forgiveness and redemption are still possible.

Josephus understood himself to be the prophet of Vespasian's ascent to the Roman throne and God's punishment of Jews for the impiety of the tyrants. But Josephus the prophet was allowed to see only one of the early scenes in God's grand drama. He could not explore or know what was in the depths of the sea.[2] The destruction of Herod's Temple by the Flavians was the terrible precondition for a return to God's presence and mastery through his words and the continued interpretation of them.

Vespasian and the Romans destroyed God's sacrificial cult and thought they had defeated the God of Israel. But the emperors were wrong. They had ensured God's victory. Justin Martyr, Origen, and Eusebius argued that the destruction of the Temple was the proof by history that God had ended his covenant with the Jews; it was rather the sign that God's bond with his people did not require a Temple. The Christian apologists got wrong both the significance of the Temple's destruction and the "irrevocable" nature of God's rejection of his people. Mosaic law was not destroyed along with the Temple, and the covenant was not abrogated.

The rabbis of the Babylonian Talmud disagreed with the Christian apologists. The destruction of the Jerusalem Temple validated the covenant. Other sages rejected the Deuteronomic theodicy of sin and divine punishment altogether, absolving Israel of blame or arguing that God suffered along with his people. Still together, God and Israel consoled each other.[3] God had not forgotten Jerusalem's fall or the travails of his chosen people.

After the Temple was gone Jews were turned to God's words. Almost two thousand years later, 4.1 billion Jews, Christians, and Muslims still read and try to live by the commandments (*mitzvot*) of Israel's God. They constitute a majority of the world's population. Ethical monotheism rules over the dry land. In the beginning, and until now, was the word of God.

On Thursday, 16 January 2020, I was walking along the walls of the Old City of Jerusalem near the Beit Shalom Archaeological Gardens. I happened to come across a group of young Israeli soldiers who were sitting together on the grass near the wall.

To judge by their light-green berets they belonged to a Nahal Brigade. The soldiers looked young, like high school seniors: thin; trim; thoughtful. A woman was reading to them in Hebrew from a book. I asked someone else who was watching what was going on. He told me that the woman was quoting some passages from the Torah about obeying the law. The young soldiers, he said, were taking their military oaths to sacrifice their lives if necessary for the freedom of Israel. (See figure 23.)

FIGURE 23. Young soldiers of the Israeli Defense Forces beneath the walls of the Old City of Jerusalem. G. Rogers.

Contexts and Contentions

Sources for the War

Our main source for the history of the war of Jews against Romans is Flavius Josephus, born Yosef ben-Mattityahu in 37 CE, during the first year of the reign of the emperor Gaius, or Caligula.[1] He was descended from the first and most prestigious of the 24 courses (*mishmarot*) or clans of priests (Jehoiarib) on his father's side and, on his mother's side, from Asamonaeus (*Hashmon*), from whom many high priests and kings of the *ethnos* or nation of the Jews descended.[2] Josephus claimed to be a priest, of priestly descent, an interpreter of dreams, and skillful at understanding the words spoken ambiguously by God.[3] The context in which he asserted that last claim was the passage in his account of the war where Josephus explains his justification for surrendering to the Romans after the capture of Iotapata in 67. As a priest Josephus may well have done service at the Temple when the shift of his clan of priests came around, as it would have at least twice per year.[4]

Josephus and his brother Matthias, or Mattathias, were brought up and educated in Jerusalem, apparently first by their parents, since no teachers are mentioned, and by the age of 14 Josephus already had a reputation for a great memory and understanding. He tells readers of his so-called *Life* that the chief priests of the city and its leading men used to come to him constantly for exact information about legal points. Clearly Josephus wanted his readers to understand that he had been a precocious student.

At about the age of 16 he decided to make an inquiry into the different sects or philosophies of the nation, including the Pharisees, the Sadducees, and the Essenes, as a quest to find the best philosophy of Judaism. Eventually he passed through the courses of all three, and he also lived in the wilderness for three years as the disciple of a certain Bannus, a hermit who wore only what was provided for by trees, ate only what grew in nature, and purified himself with cold water, day and night. After his time with Bannus, Josephus returned to Jerusalem and, at the age of 19, began to live his life according to the rule of the Pharisees, whom he compared to the Stoics, though he does not say that he became a member of that philosophical school or sect.[5]

In 64 CE, Josephus traveled to Rome for the first time, accompanying some priests sent there by the Roman governor Felix to defend themselves before the emperor Nero against some unspecified charge. Although shipwrecked somewhere in the Adriatic along the way, Josephus eventually reached Puteoli, and while he was in Italy, he formed a friendship with an actor named Aliturus who was a Jew and a favorite of Nero. Aliturus introduced Josephus to Nero's wife Poppaea, and through her intervention Josephus managed to get the priests acquitted and also received great gifts from the empress.[6]

When he returned to his homeland, Josephus says that he found the beginnings of many revolutionary movements and enthusiasm for revolt against the Romans. Josephus claims that he attempted to dissuade the revolutionaries from their purpose but to no avail; their madness (*mania*) was too much for him.[7]

Fearing that his attempt to discourage his countrymen from revolting would be construed as siding with the enemy, Josephus tells us that he sought asylum within the inner court of the Temple. When Menahem and the chiefs of the so-called brigands had been killed, Josephus came out from the Temple and opened up communications with the chief priests and the leading Pharisees. Powerless to check the revolutionaries, he states, he and his companions professed to agree with their views but suggested that they should not make any move, and leave their enemies alone if they advanced, so that they could claim that they only had taken up arms after they had been attacked. This strategy was suggested to give Cestius, the governor of Syria, time to come (to Jerusalem) with a large army and put an end to the revolution.[8] However, according to his own, earlier account of the war, Josephus was given command of the two Galilees and Gamala at the beginning of the general revolt.[9] Josephus scraped together an army, fortified some of the Galilee's most important towns, and then personally led the resistance to the Roman siege of Iotapata.

After the Romans, commanded by the future emperor Vespasian, breached Iotapata's walls, Josephus hid in an underground cavern with some survivors of the Roman assault (Tammuz 67 CE). As the Romans closed in, Josephus entered into a suicide pact with his fellow Jews, only to go back on it after all but one other member of the pact had died. Following his surrender to Vespasian, Josephus saved his own life by prophesying that Vespasian would become emperor.[10] At some later point Vespasian gave him permission to marry a woman who had been taken captive at Caesarea.[11] After he was freed by Vespasian, following Vespasian's acclamation as emperor by the legions in Alexandria on 1 July 69, Josephus then spent most of the rest of the war trying to convince his fellow Jews to give up.[12] While he was doing so he witnessed the burning of the Temple and the sack of Jerusalem.

After the fall of his native country, Josephus asked Titus for the freedom of some of his countrymen, including his brother and 50 friends; he also requested a gift of the sacred books. He tells us that he liberated all 190 or so friends and acquaintances that he recognized when he entered the Temple after its capture. In addition, he convinced Titus to release three of his friends whom he saw being crucified on his way back from Tekoa. Two of them subsequently died, but the third one survived.[13]

Josephus accompanied Titus back to Rome, sailing from Alexandria, and perhaps witnessed the joint Flavian triumph of Titus and Vespasian in Rome.[14] He lived at least at first in the unidentified house on the Quirinal Hill in Region VI of Rome that Vespasian had occupied before he became emperor, and received Roman citizenship, signified by the adoption of Vespasian's *nomen* Flavius, and a pension.[15] Although many accusations of disloyalty were brought against T(itus) Flavius Josephus, none of the accusations ultimately were convincing to Vespasian, who gave Josephus a large plot of land in Judaea, in addition to the one given to him by Titus.[16] He had married for a second time when he was with Vespasian in Alexandria in December of 69. By his second wife, whom he later divorced, he had three children. One of those children, Hyrcanus, survived until the time that Josephus wrote his autobiography. Josephus subsequently (by 77 CE anyway) married a Jewess from a notable Cretan family, who gave birth to two sons, Justus the Elder (b. 77) and Simonides Agrippa (b. 79).[17] The children of his Jewish wives would not have inherited Josephus's Roman citizenship.

After Vespasian's death Titus continued to heap honors upon Josephus, including exempting his property in Judaea from taxation.[18] Eusebius reports that there was a statue of Josephus in Rome.[19] All of the benefits that were given to Josephus after he reached Rome probably do not mean that he was somehow an intimate of the *boni viri et locupletes,* or the great and the good; on the other hand, he was alive and materially comfortable.[20] He learned Greek well enough to write books in that difficult language that are read and puzzled over to this day, but his understanding of the course and outcome of the war he fought in and became the main source for can only be understood within a Jewish theological framework. He must have picked up at least some Latin, though his knowledge of Latin literature is referred to only once, in a single citation of Livy.[21]

After making his way to Rome, Josephus composed a number of works providing information about the war. There is no explicit evidence that any-one other than Josephus actually composed any of the works. The first of these, usually called *The Jewish War,* a title the work did not have, was prob-ably completed, in its Greek-language version, with the linguistic and per-haps literary help of some unnamed people, by the early summer of 79, though some scholars have argued for dates of completion during the reigns of Titus, Domitian, or later still, based on the favor shown to Titus and Domitian in books 6 and 7 of the work.[22] Its division into seven books was apparently Josephus's own choice.[23] An earlier, though not precisely dated, work on the war in Josephus's ancestral language of Aramaic (probably) was sent across the Euphrates to the Parthians, the Babylonians, the most remote Arabian tribes, and the Adiabenians, in what is now Iraqi Kurdistan.[24] Ini-tially at least, that lost Aramaic version of what happened during the war may have been the most important source of information that peoples living east of the Euphrates River, including Babylonian Jews, had for the conflict; potentially, because it is far from clear that even the literate among the peoples that Josephus names as recipients would have been able to read the western Aramaic dialect in which it is most reasonable to assume Josephus wrote his Aramaic *War.* Most of the peoples Josephus names instead spoke and read a quite different eastern Aramaic dialect.[25]

In his later autobiography Josephus asserted that King Agrippa II wrote 62 letters to Josephus verifying the accuracy of his Greek-language work, and he quotes two letters from Agrippa that imply that Josephus had sent drafts of the *War's* books to the king for review.[26] In the same work it is also im-plied that Josephus himself read Titus's commentaries (*hupomnemata*) about the siege of Jerusalem and those of Vespasian about warfare in the Decapolis.[27] After the *War* was completed, Josephus provided copies of it first to Vespasian and Titus; other copies were given or sold (though the latter may be a textual mistake) to Agrippa and others, such as Iulius Archelaus, the grandson of Herod's associate Alexas, and to many other Romans who had participated in the war.[28]

Included among these may have been some of the commanders who attended the meeting Titus held during the late summer of 70 at which the fate of the Temple was debated: among the participants were the prefect of the forces, Tiberius Iulius Alexander; Sextus Vettulenus Cerialis, the legate of Legio V Macedonica; Larcius Lepidus, legate of Legio X Fretensis; M. Titus Phrygius, legate of Legio XV Apollonaris; and Titus's *praefectus castrorum*, Fronto Haterius.[29] Of course, as with modern works of history, it does not follow that those who have read a book and praised it before its wider distribution approved of all of its arguments or interpretation of the war. What we do know is that, according to Josephus, the purpose of his work was to console those who had been defeated by the Romans and to deter others who might be tempted to revolt.[30]

During the reign of Titus's brother Domitian (81–96 CE) Josephus wrote his massive (20 books, 60,000 lines) *Archaeologica* (in Greek), or *Antiquities* as the title is often translated in English, completed between September of 93 and September of 94—first for a Greek-reading audience in Rome itself; then what is often called his *Life,* though Josephus does not call it that, in the same year, as a kind of continuation of, or supplement to, the *Antiquities,* though really focused upon the period from December of 66 CE to mid-May of 67, for the sake of defending his reputation against accusations made by Justus of Tiberias, including the charge that he had initially fomented revolution; and then his last literary work, *On the Antiquity of the Jews* or *Against Apion,* by 95 or 96, before the death of Domitian, a refutation of Greek and Roman misconceptions about Jews and Judaism, and a polemic against Greek writers who propagated such misconceptions.[31]

Josephus's later works seem to have been written under the patronage of a certain Epaphroditus, probably a freedman, who encouraged Josephus to write them and to whom the last two books were dedicated.[32] Thus far historians have been unable to convincingly identify who Josephus's patron Epaphroditus was.[33] Debates about the identity of Josephus's patron unfortunately have usually, but not always, obscured a far more important point about Josephus and his later writings.

Given the hostility of the Flavian regime, especially during the later years of Domitian's reign, to Jewish religion and Jews, as expressed in the monuments celebrating the destruction of the Temple and the punitive tax imposed only upon Jews in the Roman empire, it took some courage for Josephus to compose and disseminate works that explained and justified the history, customs, and religion of his people to a Greek-reading audience. What is heretofore unexplained is how Josephus managed to maintain the favor of Domitian—who was the most rigorous collector of the punitive, empire-wide two-denarii tax upon Jews and during whose reign people were condemned for adopting Judaism—at the same time that Josephus was writing the works (*Antiquities, Life, Against Apion*) in which he proudly defends the history and religion of the Jews.[34] One possibility has to be that Domitian simply never managed to make his way through Josephus's later works.

Whether he relied upon sources such as Nicolaus of Damascus for what happened before and during the early stages of the war, as we know he did, the testimony of deserters, as he later claimed, or his own memory of what he saw, Josephus's works are historically indispensable for what happened in Judaea and elsewhere in the region between 66 and 74.[35] The *War* in particular is our only extant, continuous narrative source for the details of how the war was fought. Without the *War*, no coherent narrative of the revolt is possible. To choose one example out of hundreds that could be cited, either Josephus is right about how John of Gischala tricked Titus and the Romans and escaped from Gischala to Jerusalem in November of 67, or we have no idea how that happened.

Because of the role Josephus played in the revolt and its aftermath, what Josephus tells us about the causes of the war and the reasons why the Romans won, however, cannot be accepted at face value. Moreover, there are discrepancies between his accounts of events in the *War* and in his *Life* that some scholars have argued result from the pressures to which he was progressively subjected while living in Rome over a 30-year period, not to mention in response to critiques of his earlier work.[36] Others, however, have played down these discrepancies.[37]

Josephus's actions and writings have led many readers to conclude that he was fundamentally on the side of the Romans or the Jews, that he was a coward, and that he was a traitor to the Jews.[38] However, none of these starkly stated conclusions is completely convincing, as this book shows. Even though Titus signed the books of his work and ordered them to be published, Josephus's *War of Jews against the Romans* was not simply a work of flattery of Vespasian, Titus, the Roman army, and Rome itself.[39] Vespasian is shown to be a competent and thorough commander but also duplicitous and cruel. Titus is often represented as courageous in battle, sensitive, and merciful, but also occasionally naïve and gullible. Roman soldiers are usually disciplined and brave but also sadistic and foolish in Josephus's history. Rome itself is no bringer of peace or prosperity. Neither the *War* nor the *Antiquities* were "official" histories; though influenced by the works of Thucydides, Polybius, and Iulius Caesar, Josephus's writings were the works of an individual with a complicated, unique point of view about what happened and why.

Josephus's Rome is an instrument of God used to punish the Jews for their sins, just as Jews had been punished in the past for their transgressions.[40] Josephus's fellow Jews are praised for their courage but also criticized in unsparing terms. All of these representations of the participants in the war and their actions, including those of Josephus himself, are best understood in the overall context and framework of Josephus's account of the war itself. Of course, that account, or accounts, since Josephus gives information relevant to understanding the war throughout his writings, are products of Josephus's values and philosophy of history. Rhetoric and the concerns of rhetorical education shaped those in turn, but so did theology or a theological understanding of history, as we shall see.

At one time other contemporary, primary literary sources for the war existed. From Josephus's later writings we know that both Vespasian and Titus kept notebooks, or what were probably called *commentarii* in Latin, about the war, including events in the Decapolis, to the east of the Jordan River, after Vespasian's invasion of the Galilee.[41] Titus's notebook apparently covered the siege of Jerusalem. But these notebooks have not survived, and the information Josephus gives about their contents is minimal. Other near-contemporary or later literary sources, including Tacitus, Suetonius, and Cassius Dio, provide some important details and information about events and characters involved in the war.[42] The Jewish Alexandrian philosopher Philo is an important source for Jewish life in the Egyptian diaspora and for relations between Jews and Rome during the first century CE.[43] But none of these authors wrote full narratives about the war; in general, as far as we know, very little narrative history was written about the reigns of the Flavian emperors when the war was still ongoing or when Josephus was living and writing his works in Rome, because it was "too difficult, too dangerous, and perhaps simply unfashionable."[44] Rabbinic literature, written long after the events of the war, occasionally includes interesting details about people, events, or aspects of the conflict. But the historicity of the details has to be accepted with caution since the writers tended to make use of the details to support interpretations of scripture. Some of the details are consistent with data from contemporary sources, but others are not, cannot be verified or falsified, and do not necessarily advance our understanding of the revolt.[45] It is interesting to learn, for instance, that Ananias, the son of Nedebaeus, had a reputation as a glutton.[46] But his apparent gluttony does not help us understand his opposition to the revolutionary leader Menahem.

Inscriptions, coins, papyri, and archaeological evidence allow us to supplement and check the information Josephus provides. The ongoing publication of the inscriptions from the region since 2010 (*Corpus Inscriptionum Iudaeae/Palaestinae*) makes possible new insights into the causes, course, and outcome of the war. But in a fundamental sense, the war of Jews against Rome that we can know about in detail is Josephus's war, and that is both a blessing and a challenge. Without Josephus we would know that there was a war of Jews against Rome during the first century CE. But we would know far less about its alleged causes and course, and therefore no real history or interpretation of the war would be possible. The destruction of the Temple of the Jews by the Romans in 70 is one of the turning points of history; it is only because of the works of Flavius Josephus that we can argue about how and why that happened, and therefore how we should understand its significance.

Chronology: From the Herodian Model to the Arch of Titus in the Circus Maximus

What follows is a basic chronology of events that are central to the causes, course, and outcome of the war of Jews against Romans, using the now standard abbreviations of BCE for dates before the Common Era and CE for the Common Era. More precise dates that derive from our sources are provided within the chapters and notes of this book. Josephus, for instance, often gives readers the day and month that an event took place using the names of the aligned lunar months of the Macedonian or Hebrew calendars or both. Within this book I have tried to give readers a sense of how those lunar calendar days and months correspond to the Roman Julian (solar) calendar. Sometimes, however, it is only possible to give a date within a range of days within a month. Where there are chronological problems that affect key points of the narrative they are usually discussed in notes.

73 BCE: Birth of Herod (the Great)

63 BCE: Pompey's reorganization of eastern Roman provinces; Hasmonean kingdom becomes subordinate to province of Syria; birth of Octavian

47 BCE: Antipater, father of Herod, made Roman citizen and procurator; Herod made governor of Galilee

46 BCE: Sextus Caesar appoints Herod governor of Coele-Syria

44 BCE: Iulius Caesar assassinated

41 BCE:	Herod and brother Phasael made tetrarchs
40 BCE:	Herod appointed king of Judaea, Galilee, and Peraea by Roman Senate
37–early 36 BCE:	Herod and Sosius besiege and capture Jerusalem; Herod's kingship effectively begins
35 BCE:	Aristobulus III drowned in Jericho
31 BCE:	Battle of Actium, victory of Octavian over Antony
30 BCE:	Octavian confirms Herod as king of Judaea
29 BCE:	Mariamme I executed
27 BCE:	Sebaste (in Samaria) founded
23/22–15/14 BCE:	Construction of new Temple Mount in Jerusalem
22–10 BCE:	Caesarea Maritima constructed
15 BCE:	Agrippa visits Judaea
7 BCE:	Alexander and Aristobulus strangled in Sebaste
4 BCE:	Destruction of golden eagle over Temple Great Gate; death of Herod; Archelaus made ethnarch of Judaea, Samaria, and Idumaea
6 CE:	Archelaus deposed and exiled by Augustus; Judaea put under jurisdiction of Roman prefect
41 CE:	Agrippa I made king
44 CE:	Death of Agrippa I; Judaea put under jurisdiction of procurator
61 CE:	Nero gives the Syrians rule over Caesarea
July 64 CE:	Great fire in Rome
April 66 CE:	Cestius Gallus, governor of Syria, visits Jerusalem during Passover
May 66 CE:	Fighting among Jews, Greeks, and Syrians breaks out over access to synagogue in Caesarea; Florus takes 17 talents from Temple treasury; massacres in Jerusalem and outside it
Late June 66 CE:	Report of Neapolitanus to Cestius
Early summer, 66 CE:	Speech of Agrippa II to Jews recommending obedience to Rome and Florus; Agrippa stoned out of Jerusalem
Mid–late summer 66 CE:	Gifts and sacrifices from foreigners at Temple halted
16 August 66 CE:	Murder of high priest Ananias and Ezekias; murder of Menahem, a few days after murder of Ananias and Ezekias
19 August 66 CE:	Cestius leaves Antioch with army

About 23 August 66 CE:	Massacre of Roman auxiliary garrison in Jerusalem; afterward massacre of the Jews of Caesarea; ethnic warfare spreads throughout the region
Mid-October 66 CE:	End of Cestius's intervention in Jerusalem
Autumn 66 CE:	Generals to conduct war are appointed in Jerusalem; Josephus becomes general for the Galilees and Gamala; Josephus and John of Gischala vie for leadership in the north
Winter 67 CE:	Vespasian appointed with special command for Judaea
Mid-April 67 CE:	Vespasian and his army in Ptolemais
May–June 67 CE:	Siege of Iotapata; fall of Iotapata, 1 Panemus/Tammuz/30 June–1 July 67 (after about a 38- to 47-day siege); Josephus surrenders
Early September 67 CE:	Tarichaeae pacified
19–20 October 67 CE:	Fall of Gamala, 23 Huperberetaeus
Winter 67–68 CE:	Idumaeans enter Jerusalem
Late 67–early 68 CE:	Vindex Revolt in Gallia Lugdunensis
Spring 68 CE:	Vespasian captures and garrisons Azotus and Iamnia
9 June 68 CE:	Suicide of Nero
June 68 CE:	Destruction of the Essene community at Qumran
Xanthicus/April 69 CE:	Simon enters Jerusalem
14 April 69 CE:	Defeat of Otho's forces at Cremona
1 July 69 CE:	Legions in Alexandria acclaim Vespasian as emperor
Before Passover 70 CE:	Beginning of Roman siege of Jerusalem
17 Panemus/Tammuz 70 CE:	Daily Temple sacrifices stop
End of August 70 CE (10 Lous/Av):	Temple burns down
70 CE:	Work on Arch of Titus on Velia begins; finished during reign of Domitian
June 71 CE:	Triumph of Vespasian and Titus in Rome
Mid-April 74 CE:	Murder/suicide of inhabitants of Masada
Summer 75 CE:	Temple of Peace dedicated in Rome
80 CE:	Opening of the Flavian Amphitheater in Rome
Early 81 CE:	Arch in Circus Maximus dedicated to Titus

The Costs of Munificence

Where did Herod get the money to pay for his munificence outside and inside his kingdom? How much did it cost to be an international public benefactor—indeed, a benefactor of lasting historical significance? How much did eternal philanthropic fame cost? How did Herod's projects affect the economy of his kingdom?[1]

First, Herod came from money. His Idumaean father Antipater was said to have possessed a large fortune.[2] We don't know how large that fortune was or how much of it was passed down to Herod. (Herod did have brothers.) But by 40 BCE we know that Herod was worth at least 300 talents, in coined silver, since that was the amount that he was able to raise to ransom his brother Phasael, who had been captured by the Parthians and turned over to Herod's rival Antigonus. Phasael committed suicide before Herod could make the payment.[3]

By the end of his life Herod was worth much more. In his will, in addition to other gifts to members of his family, Herod left 15 million silver coins to Augustus and his wife.[4] So Herod's personal fortune was roughly eight times larger in 4 BCE than it had been when he started out.[5] Part of that fortune probably came from the wealth of the enemies he had defeated after he became king, including their lands.[6] Tenants who worked on what became royal lands no doubt paid what was in effect a tribute to Herod.[7] After he captured Jerusalem Herod confiscated the military equipment of the wealthy, as well as silver and gold, and he used some of it to give gifts to Antony and his friends.[8] Later, after the execution of Hyrcanus II in 30 BCE, Herod took possession of his fortune, which amounted to at least 300 talents.[9] Herod seems to have owned estates outside his kingdom, and he no doubt derived income from them.[10] Herod was also reported to have received lavish "contributions" (or bribes), although these are not quantified, and he may have profited from his appointment by Augustus to the position of procurator of Syria in 20 BCE.[11]

Josephus claimed that Herod personally paid for the Temple's reconstruction, though we know that at least some other individuals made contributions to the project.[12] Where did Herod get the money to pay for the rest of his benefactions and his other expenses? There seem to have been both extraordinary and ordinary revenue streams.

We know that Herod received money from the Jericho palm and balsam tree plantations that he rented for 200 talents per year from Cleopatra, from his exploitation of the copper mines on Cyprus, and from tax-farming operations in Syria, Asia Minor, and Nabataea.[13] He was accused of pillaging gold ornaments from David's Tomb in Jerusalem and was planning to open the coffins of Solomon and David but supposedly stopped when two of his bodyguards were incinerated by a flame.[14]

Most scholars, however, have interpreted the Josephan report about the tomb robbery as a flagrant smear.[15] David's tomb had already been looted by ruler and high priest John Hyrcanus I (r. 135–134 to 104 BCE) a century before, and Herod was not short of cash near the end of his life, to judge by the money he left to Augustus and other family members.[16] It is much more likely that at some time between about 10 and 5 BCE Herod, in an attempt to connect himself and his monarchy to that of David, undertook a renovation of the great king's tomb that Josephus then turned into a story about impiety. In any case, these extraordinary windfalls cannot have subsidized all of the projects described earlier. The funds used for Herod's benefactions must have been financed through the regular collection of taxes.

These taxes included a poll (head) tax, a levy on salt, the so-called wreath tax (*aurum coronarium*), a toll on traders and businessmen, a house tax instituted by Herod, and customs duties.[17] The tolls and duties, usually classified as indirect taxes and collected by Herod, were probably his greatest revenue producers.[18] According to Josephus, Herod collected annually some 12 million drachmas from levies in his territories.[19]

The rebuilding of the Temple encouraged pilgrimage to Jerusalem at the time of the major festivals. Both the inhabitants of the city and the pilgrims

benefited from waters brought to the pool of Hezekiah by the aqueduct Herod
had built, which brought water into the city from "Solomon's Pools" near
Bethlehem.[20] The money the pilgrims spent on travel, sacrifices, and living
expenses stimulated the economy on a regular basis. The accumulated wealth
of the Temple and the yearly collection of the half-shekel (approximately 2
Roman denarii) Temple tax, normatively collected from all nonpriestly Jewish males over 20 years old, contributed somewhere between 500,000 and 1
million shekels to the Temple treasury every year.[21] The biblically mandated
Temple tax—paid in person when people came to one of the three great festivals, by messengers, or through community-wide deliveries in silver Tyrian
shekels and other local currencies—was used to purchase animals for sacrifice and for other sacrificial purposes; it also funded road repairs, the operation and maintenance of ritual baths, and the repair of aqueducts, roads, walls,
and towers.[22]

The collection of both the half-shekel tax and the agricultural first fruits
no doubt increased the wealth of the priests in Jerusalem but also was essential to what we would call the infrastructure of Jerusalem and its economy.
But the business created by a larger pilgrimage economy did not just benefit
Jerusalem and its priests. Recent studies have shown that Herod's Jerusalem
became a center for the production of stone vessels, ossuaries, oil lamps, and
other household items that were sold and used outside Judaea.[23]

The monies Herod collected—from about 3,000,000 to 4,500,000
denarii—paid the wages of his soldiers: about 3,000–5,000 soldiers during
the war against Antigonus from 39–37 BCE, 25,000 during the war against
the Nabataeans in 32, and around 18,000 at Herod's death. The wages for
Herod's army might have comprised 60 to 90 percent of Herod's budget—if
such a modern concept can be used.[24]

Tax revenues also must have helped subsidize Herod's foreign and domestic building projects, his administration, the public games and festivals he
sponsored, and gifts he made to his patrons and friends.[25] It has been estimated that more than 10,000 laborers were required for the work on the
Temple Mount alone.[26] Another historian has argued that at least 50,000
workers worked on Herod's building projects during his reign.[27] These workers cannot have labored for free.

One regular expense that Herod did not have was paying tribute to Rome.
As a friend and client king of Rome, Herod and, by extension, his subjects
were free from having to pay tribute to Rome, at least from the time that Octavian confirmed his kingship in 30 BCE.[28] The most important effect of

this for the questions raised in this book must be that, whatever the tax burden was for Judaeans during Herod's reign, it could not be understood as a burden imposed upon them by Rome.

Herod did, however, have some extraordinary expenses. Following a drought that led to a famine and plague outbreak in 25–24 BCE Herod had the gold and silver ornaments of his own palace melted down and made into coins to buy Egyptian grain for his people and for Syrians as well. Winter clothing was provided for those who needed it, and the next year he sent 50,000 men into the fields to help with the harvest and supported them financially while they were working.[29] A few years later, perhaps in 20 BCE, Herod lowered taxes on the subjects in his kingdom by one-third. In 14 BCE, after returning from a trip to Pontus and his intervention on behalf of the Jews of Ionia, taxes were lowered by Herod again, this time by one-quarter, to relieve the burdens placed upon his subjects.[30]

Herod used his own wealth and that of his subjects to pay the soldiers who provided security for his kingdom and to make benefactions to cities and peoples both outside and inside Judaea. Some of the costs can be quantified fairly precisely; others, such as the rebuilding of the Temple, cannot. Although the taxes Herod collected no doubt placed financial burdens upon his subjects, at least part of the pain imposed was offset by the creation of the construction and other types of jobs needed to execute all of these projects.[31]

The Jews of Judaea had paid taxes under the Persians, Alexander the Great's Macedonian successors, and the Hasmoneans too.[32] One modern study of the coins minted during Herod's reign has suggested that Herod's building projects stimulated the economy in the short term and had significant long-lasting positive effects by encouraging pilgrimage (to Jerusalem) and trade.[33] Archaeological surveys of the Galilee and Samaritis indicate increased settlement and a rising tide of economic activity and population, usually a sign of increased prosperity.[34]

The Herodian Dynasty

Ruler	Dates	Area(s)
Herod (the Great)	40 BCE	King of Jews
		War 1.282; *Antiquities* 14.389; Appian, *Civil Wars* 5.75, who includes Idumaea and Samaritis; Strabo, *Geography* 16.2.46
	30 BCE	Kingship confirmed by Octavian
		War 1.392; *Antiquities* 15.195
		Cities added
		War 1.396; *Antiquities* 15.217
	24–23 BCE	Batanaea, Trachonitis, Auranitis added
		War 1.398; *Antiquities* 15.343
	20 BCE	Gaulanitis, Hulata, Panias added by Augustus
		Antiquities 15.360
Pheroras Younger brother of Herod	20 BCE	Tetrarch of Peraea
		War 1.483; *Antiquities* 15.362

Ruler	Dates	Area(s)
Herod Archelaus Son of Herod and Malthace	4 BCE–6 CE	Tetrarch Judaea, Idumaea, Samaritis Caesarea, Sebaste, Joppa Jerusalem *War* 2.93; 96–97; *Antiquities* 17.317, 17.319–20
	6 CE	exiled *War* 2.111; *Antiquities* 17.344
Herod Antipater (Antipas) Son of Herod and Malthace	4 BCE–39 CE	Tetrarch of Peraea, Galilee *War* 2.95; *Antiquities* 17.318
Herod Philip Son of Herod and Cleopatra	4 BCE–34 CE	Tetrarch of Batanaea, Trachonitis Zenodorus's territory (Ituraea) *War* 2.95; *Antiquities* 17.319
Agrippa I Son of Aristobulus IV and Berenice	37 CE–44 CE	King
	37 CE	Tetrarchy of Philip, tetrarchy of Lysanias
	39 CE	Tetrarchy of Herod Antipas (Galilee, Peraea)
	41 CE–44 CE	Herod's kingdom (Judaea, Samaritis) Trachonitis, Auranitis Abila, Anti-Lebanon *War* 2.181; *Antiquities* 18.237 *War* 2.183; *Antiquities* 18.252 *War* 2.215; *Antiquities* 19.275
Herod of Chalcis Son of Aristobulus IV and Berenice	41 CE–48 CE	King of Chalcis Authority over Temple, vessels and selection of high priests *War* 2.217; *Antiquities* 20.15

Ruler	Dates	Area(s)
Agrippa II	50 CE–53 CE	King of Chalcis
Son of Agrippa I		Authority over Temple and
and Cypros		selection of high priests
	53 CE	Tetrarchy of Philip
		(Gaulanitis, Batanaea, Trachonitis, Auranitis)
		Tetrarchy of Lysanias
		Tetrarchy of Varus
	54 CE	Tiberias, Tarichaeae
		Iulias, 14 villages
Ruled as king		Tetrarchy of Lysanias,
		territory of Varus (Mt. Lebanon)
	54 CE–92/93 CE	Abila, Iulias (Peraea),
		Tarichaeae, Tiberias (Galilee)
	?	Gamala, Sogane in Gaulanitis
		Seleucia, allotted
	?	Arcea, northern Lebanon
	67 CE	Mt. Libanus to Lake Tiberias
		(north to south)
		Arpha (east of Trachonitis)
		to Iulias (Bethsaida)
		(east to west)
		full extent of kingdom
		War 2.223; *Antiquities* 20.104
		War 2.247; *Antiquities* 20.138
		War 2.252; *Antiquities* 20.159
		War 4.2
		War 7.97
		War 3.57–58

High Priests from Herod the Great to 68 CE

(Josephus, *Antiquities* abbreviated as *Ant.*)

Name	Dates	Source
Hananel Babylonian Jew; appointed by Herod; deposed; reappointed	37–35 BCE	*Ant.* 15.22, 15.34, 15.39–41, 15.56
Aristobulus III 17-year-old son of Alexandra; appointed by Herod; murdered on Herod's order	35 BCE	*War* 1.437 *Ant.* 15.23, 15.31–41, 15.51–56, 15.64, 20.247–48
Hananel Reappointed by Herod	35–30? BCE	*Ant.* 15.56
Joshua/Jesus Son of Phiabi, Egyptian family, from Leontopolis?; deposed by Herod so he could appoint Simon	30?–24/22 BCE	*Ant.* 15.322

Name	Dates	Source

Simon
  Son of Boethus;
  Alexandrian;
  appointed and deposed by Herod;
  Herod married Simon's daughter,
  Mariamme (II);
  son is Herod II
	c. 24/22–25 BCE	*Ant.* 15.320, 15.322,
		17.78, 18.109, 18.136

Matthias
  Son of Theophilus;
  Jerusalemite;
  appointed and deposed by Herod
  after intercourse dream on night
  before day of fast (Yom Kippur)
	5–4 BCE	*Ant.* 17.78, 17.164–67

Joseph, son of Ellemus Jerusalemite	One day one hour, 4 BCE	*Ant.* 17.166–67 *Yoma* 1.4

Joazar
  son of Boethus;
  brother of Mariamme II;
  appointed by Herod; deposed by
  Archelaus
	4 BCE	*Ant.* 17.164, 17.339

Eleazar
  Son of Boethus;
  appointed by Archelaus
	4 BCE	*Ant.* 17.339

Joshua/Jesus
  Son of Seë;
  appointed by Archelaus
	4 BCE–?	*Ant.* 17.341

Joazar
  Son of Boethus;
  urged compliance with Roman
  census in 6 CE;
  deposed by Quirinius
	6 CE (or earlier)	*Ant.* 18.3, 18.26

Ananus
  Son of Seth;
  appointed by Quirinius;
  deposed by Gratus;
  five sons become high priests
  (Eleazar, Jonathan, Theophilus,
  Matthias, Ananus)
	6–15 CE	*Ant.* 18.26, 18.34,
		18.95, 19.297, 19.313,
		20.197–98

Name	Dates	Source
Ishmael Son of Phiabi; appointed and deposed by Valerius Gratus	15–16? CE	*Ant.* 18.34
Eleazar Son of Ananus; appointed and deposed by Valerius Gratus	16–17? CE	*Ant.* 18.34
Simon Son of Camith; appointed and deposed by Valerius Gratus	17–18 CE	*Ant.* 18.34
Joseph Caiaphas Son-in-law of Ananus; appointed by Valerius Gratus; deposed by Vitellius	18–36 to 37 CE	*Ant.* 18.35, 18.95
Jonathan Son of Ananus; appointed and deposed by Vitellius	36 or 37 CE	*Ant.* 18.95, 18.123
Theophilus Son of Ananus; appointed by Vitellius; deposed by Agrippa I	37–41 CE	*Ant.* 18.123, 19.297
Simon Cantheras Son of Boethus; appointed and deposed by Agrippa I	41–42 CE	*Ant.* 19.297–98, 313
Matthias Son of Ananus; appointed and deposed by Agrippa I	42–43? CE	*Ant.* 19.316, 19.342
Elionaeus Son or brother of Simon Cantheras; appointed by Agrippa I; deposed by Herod of Chalcis	43?–45 CE	*Ant.* 19.342, 20.16
Joseph Son of Camei; appointed and removed by Herod of Chalcis	45–48 CE	*Ant.* 20.16, 20.103

Name	Dates	Source
Ananias	48–59 CE	*Ant.* 20.103, 20.131
Son of Nedebaeus;		*War* 2.243,
appointed by Herod of Chalcis;		2.426, 2.429, 2.441
sent to Rome by Quadratus; father of Eleazar the Temple captain; house burnt;		
murdered by "brigands"		
Ishmael	59–61 CE	*Ant.* 20.179, 20.194–95
Son of Phiabi;		*War* 6.114
appointed by Agrippa II; went on delegation to Nero in Rome; deposed by Agrippa II		
Joseph Kabi	61–62 CE	*Ant.* 20.196–97
Son of Simon;		
appointed and deposed by Agrippa II		
Ananus	62 CE	*Ant.* 20.197–203
Son of Ananus;	(3 months)	*War* 4.314–18
appointed and deposed by Agrippa II; put James, brother of Jesus, and others on trial;		
murdered by Idumaeans		
Jesus	62–63? CE	*Ant.* 20.203, 20.213
Son of Damnaeus;		
appointed and deposed by Agrippa II		
Jesus	63–64 CE	*Ant.* 20.213, 20.223
Son of Gamaliel;		
appointed and deposed by Agrippa II		
Matthias	64–66? CE	*Ant.* 20.223
Son of Theophilus;		
appointed by Agrippa II; deposed by rebels?		
Phannias	68? CE	*War* 4.155–57
Son of Samuel;		*Ant.* 20.227
appointed by lot		

APPENDIX F

Tiers of Authority from Rome to Judaea

ROMAN EMPERORS FROM 6 TO 96 CE

Emperor	Reign
Augustus (Imperator Caesar Augustus)	27 BCE–14 CE
Tiberius (Tiberius Caesar Augustus)	14–37 CE
Gaius (Caius Caesar Augustus Germanicus)	37–41 CE
Claudius (Tiberius Claudius Caesar Augustus Germanicus)	41–54 CE
Nero (Imperator Nero Claudius Caesar Augustus Germanicus)	54–68 CE
Galba (Servius Sulpicius Galba Imperator Caesar Augustus)	68–69 CE
Otho (Imperator Marcus Salvius Otho Caesar Augustus)	69 CE
Vitellius (Aulus Vitellius Augustus Germanicus Imperator)	69 CE
Vespasian (Imperator Caesar Augustus Vespasianus Augustus)	69–79 CE
Titus (Imperator Titus Caesar Vespasianus Augustus)	79–81 CE
Domitian (Imperator Caesar Domitianus Augustus)	81–96 CE

ADMINISTRATION OF SYRIA FROM THE DEATH OF HEROD UNTIL THE END OF THE GREAT REVOLT

Governor	Title	Dates	Source
Publius Quinctilius Varus	Legatus	7/6 BCE–4 CE	*War* 1.20; *Ant.* 17.250–52, 17.286–99
? (Lucius Calpurnius Piso)	Legatus	4–1 BCE	Tacitus, *Annals* 6.10
Gaius Iulius Caesar Vipsanianus	Legatus	1 BCE–4 CE	Cassius Dio 55.10.18
Lucius Volusius Saturninus	Legatus	4–5 CE	Syme (1989) pp. 101, 338
Publius Sulpicius Quirinius	Legatus	6–12 CE	*Ant.* 18.1
Quintus Caecilius Metellus Creticus Silanus	Legatus	12–17 CE	Tacitus, *Annals* 2.4, 2.43
Gnaeus Calpurnius Piso	Legatus	17–19 CE	Tacitus, *Annals* 2.43
Gnaeus Sentius Saturninus	Legatus	19–21 CE	Tacitus, *Annals* 2.74; *Ant.* 14.229 CIL 6703
Lucius Aelius Lamia	Legatus	22–32 CE	Tacitus, *Annals* 6.27.2
Lucius Pomponius Flaccus	Legatus	c. 32–35 CE	*Ant.* 18.150–54; Tacitus, *Annals* 6.27
Lucius Vitellius Veteris	Legatus	35–38 CE	*Ant.* 18.88–95
Publius Petronius	Legatus	39–42 CE	*War* 2.185–203; *Ant.* 18.261–309
C. Vibius Marsus	Legatus	42–45 CE	*Ant.* 19.316
Cassius Longinus	Legatus	45–50 CE	*Ant.* 20.1
Gaius Ummidius Durmius Quadratus	Legatus	50–60 CE	*War* 2.239, 2.241–44; *Ant.* 20.125–30 Tacitus, *Annals* 12.48.1–2
Gnaeus Domitius Corbulo	Legatus	60–63 CE	Tacitus, *Annals* 14.26
Gaius Cestius Gallus	Legatus	63–67 CE	Tacitus, *Annals* 15.25.3
Gaius Licinius Mucianus	Legatus	67–69 CE	*War* 4.32, 4.495, 4.605, 4.621, 4.624, 4.632, 4.654. 5.43; *Ant.* 12.120
Lucius Caesennius Paetus	Legatus	70–72 CE	*War* 7.59, 7.220, 7.225, 7.230, 7.238
Aulus Marius Celsus	Legatus	72–73 CE	Syme (1981) pp. 133–34 Eck (1982) p. 291
Marcus Ulpius Traianus	Legatus	73–78 CE	Eck (1982) p. 293

ADMINISTRATION OF JUDAEA FROM 6 CE UNTIL THE END OF THE GREAT REVOLT

Governor	Title	Dates	Source
Coponius	Prefect	6–9 CE	*War* 2.117; *Ant.* 18.2
Marcus Ambivulus	Prefect	9–12 CE	*Ant.* 18.31
Annius Rufus	Prefect	12–15 CE	*Ant.* 18.32
Valerius Gratus	Prefect	15–26 CE	*Ant.* 18.33
Pontius Pilatus	Prefect	26–36 CE	*War* 2.169-77; *Ant.* 18.55–64, 18.85–89
Marcellus?	Prefect?	36–37? CE	*Ant.* 18.89
Marullus?	Hipparch?	37–41? CE	*Ant.* 18.237
Agrippa I	King	41–44 CE	*War* 2.181; *Ant.* 18.237
Cuspius Fadus	Procurator	44–46 CE	*War* 2.220; *Ant.* 19.363
Tiberius Iulius Alexander	Prefect?	46–48 CE	*War* 2.220, 2.223
Ventidius Cumanus	Procurator	48–52 CE	*War* 2.223; *Ant.* 20. 103
Marcus Antonius Felix	Procurator	52–60 CE	*War* 2.247, 2.252–53; *Ant.* 20.137
Porcius Festus	Procurator	60–62 CE	*War* 2.271; *Ant.* 20.182
Lucceius Albinus	Procurator	62–64 CE	*War* 2.272; *Ant.* 20.197, 20.200
Gessius Florus	Procurator	64–67 CE	*Ant.* 20.215
Marcus Antonius Iulianus	Procurator	67–70 CE	*War* 6.238
Sextus Vettulenus Cerialis	Legate	70–71 CE	*War* 7.163
Lucilius Bassus	Legate	71–72 CE	*War* 7.163
Lucius Flavius Silva	Legate	72–81 CE	*War* 7.252

The Roman Legion around 4 BCE

The legion of the early Roman empire was theoretically divided up into 10 cohorts (*cohortes*) of 480 men each; each cohort was made up of six centuries (*centuriae*) of 80 soldiers, or 60 centuries per legion overall. The 60 centuries were further split up into 10 squads of 8 soldiers, called *contubernia*.[1] The members of the *contubernia* were tentmates and fought together in line. All of these soldiers were Roman citizens. Most seem to have enlisted between the ages of 18 and 23, and about half made it to discharge after 25 years of service.[2]

The commander of each legion was the legate (*legatus*). Legates were men of senatorial status and were personal appointees of the emperors, usually after serving as praetors in Rome. The average length of command was three years.[3] Serving directly under the legate were six tribunes. The highest-ranking tribune was usually a young man in his early twenties, of senatorial status, who was preparing for a career in the imperial administration (*tribunus laticlavius*). The other five tribunes were of equestrian status (*tribuni angusticlavii*).[4] By the time of Nero the positions of the tribunes were regularized into a kind of sequence of appointments, starting from the *praefectus cohortis* (prefect of a cohort of auxiliary soldiers), then *tribunus militum,* and then *praefectus equitum.* The point of such a system was to give these officers command experience. Most of the tribunes were appointed when they were in their late twenties or thirties.[5] Each legion also included an equestrian prefect of the camp (*praefectus castrorum*), who essentially served as the quartermaster for the legion with overall responsibility for administration of the legion's logistics.[6] The majority of the legions' senior officers were men whose main qualification for commanding soldiers was their socioeconomic status in Roman society.

Beneath these officers in the command structure of the legion were the 59 centurions of each legion.[7] Centurions of different ranks commanded each of the six centuries of 80 men that comprised a cohort. The senior centurion of the whole cohort held the title of *pilus prior*.[8] Centurions could be appointed to that rank by the emperor, but most seem to have worked their way up to their positions. In the hierarchy of officers within the legion the centurions occupied a middle rank.[9] Beneath the centurions served subordinate officers (*principales*), including the *optio*, who was second in command of the century to the centurion, a *signifier*, who bore the century's standard (*signum*), and a *tesserarius*, who was in charge of the watch. Both the *optiones* and the standard-bearers earned double pay, while the *tesserarius* was paid one and half times the standard.[10]

Alongside the Roman citizen infantry of each legion served 120 cavalrymen (*equites legionis*). These cavalrymen were probably first trained as infantrymen and then appointed to their legionary cavalry units, which were commanded by centurions.[11]

The Roman Province of Judaea, 6 CE?

For the conversion of Archelaus's ethnarchy to a Roman province in 6 CE, see *War* 2.117 and *Antiquities* 17.342–44. In *Antiquities* 17.355, however, Josephus says that the land of Archelaus (*Archelaou choras*) was added to Syria (*hupotelous prosnemetheises te Suron*) and that Quirinius, a man of consular rank, was sent by Augustus to take a census of property in Syria and to sell the estate of Archelaus. Then, in *Antiquities* 18.2, Josephus writes that Quirinius was sent to Syria as governor, and Coponius was sent along with him to rule over the Jews with full authority (*hegesomenos Ioudaion te epi pasin exousia*). Based upon these seemingly contradictory statements in Josephus, Mason (2016) pp. 239–45, has argued that Judaea was not made a province in 6 CE but rather was part of the province of Syria. Using the famous Pilate inscription from Caesarea as one piece of evidence, Eck too has argued that the prefect of Judaea was not the governor of an independent province of Judaea but was subordinate to the governor of Syria. These scholars may be correct.

What has not been explained, perhaps, is how Coponius could have been given full authority within his jurisdiction and not be independent of the governor in Syria, at least judicially. In 17 CE (11 years after the new arrangement was made), according to one informed observer from the Roman side—the historian Tacitus—Syria and Judaea (note the plural) appealed to Tiberius to have taxes lessened: "et provinciae Syria atque Iudaea fessae oneribus deminutionem tributi orabant" (*Annals* 2.42). Tacitus's statement implies that at that time Syria and Judaea were separate provinces, at least with respect to taxation. In fact, a detailed review of interactions between and among Roman governors, and then with local authorities from the death of Herod to the outbreak of the revolt in 66, reveals that beneath the surface of administrative titles and categories neat and clear lines of authority between Syria and Judaea are a mirage.

After Herod's death, Sabinus, the procurator of Syria (*Surias epitropos*), apparently thought that he had the authority to do an assessment of Herod's estate, before he was stopped (initially) by the legate of Syria, Quinctilius Varus. But after Varus left Caesarea for Antioch, Sabinus persisted, going up to Jerusalem and taking possession of the royal palaces (*War* 2.16–19; *Antiquities* 17.221–23). These actions took place after Herod's death but before Judaea became part of the ethnarchy of Archelaus (along with Idumaea and Samaritis) by Augustus's decision. While he was ethnarch Archelaus deposed the high priest Joazar, replacing him with his brother Eleazar (*War* 2.7; *Antiquities* 17.207–9, 17.339; Eleazar was soon replaced by the high priest Jesus, 17.341). It was Joazar who persuaded Jews to declare the value of their property during the census conducted by Quirinius, the legate of Syria, and Coponius, the prefect (*Antiquities* 18.1–3). Valerius Gratus appointed no less than four high priests during his prefecture from 15 to 26 CE (*Antiquities* 18.33–35). There is no sign of the involvement of the Syrian legate. During Pilate's governorship, probably from 26 to 36 CE, he used money from the offering fund of the Temple to subsidize the building of an aqueduct for Jerusalem (*War* 2.175–77; *Antiquities* 18.60–62). If he consulted any of the high priests or priests there is no record of those consultations. The execution of Jesus is perhaps the most famous example of the capital jurisdiction of a Roman prefect; however the "trial" of Jesus is represented in the Gospels, without Pilate's assent the crucifixion of Jesus never would have happened.

While Pilate was prefect, Vitellius, the legate of Syria, visited Jerusalem during Passover and, at least for the duration of the festival, remitted all taxes in agricultural produce and helped the Jews get the sacred robe of the high priest placed under the authority of Jews (*Antiquities* 15.403–5, 18.90–95). The inference, therefore, is that previously it had not been. Vitellius was also responsible for deposing Caiaphas as high priest and replacing him with Jonathan (*Antiquities* 15.403–5, 18.90–95). In 39 Petronius, then the legate of Syria, was ordered by Gaius to install a statue of him as Zeus in the Temple in Jerusalem. The governor was instructed to use force if necessary (*War* 2.184–85; *Antiquities* 18.261; *Embassy to Gaius* 185–89). The (temporary) governor of

Judaea at the time, possibly Marullus, apparently was not consulted. The high priest is not named among the prominent Jews who led the resistance to the plan. After Gaius's death on 24 January of 41 the emperor Claudius confirmed the rule of Agrippa I over his grandfather Herod's kingdom (comprising Judaea and Samaritis), to which were added Trachonitis, Aurantis, Abila, the tetrarchy of Lysanias, and the Anti-Lebanon (*War* 2.204–17; *Antiquities* 19.236–75).

After Agrippa I was made king he nevertheless sought the aid of Petronius, the governor of Syria, to deal with the problem of some young men who had set up a statue of Claudius in the synagogue of Dor (*Antiquities* 19.300–311). The incident took place when Agrippa supposedly was the king of an independent kingdom, outside Roman provincial jurisdiction altogether. During Agrippa's reign, Petronius's replacement, Vibius Marsus, intervened to prevent the king from building the new north defensive wall of Jerusalem (*War* 2.218–19, 5.147–55; *Antiquities* 19.326–27) and broke up a meeting between Agrippa and the other regional kings at Tiberias (*Antiquities* 19.338–42).

Tacitus claims that after the death of Agrippa I Judaea and Ituraea were added to the province of Syria; however, Josephus, who grew up in Judaea, reports that Claudius again reduced the kingdoms (*basileias*) he (Agrippa) had ruled over to a province (*eparchian*) and sent out a governor (*epitropon*; *Annals* 12.23.1; *War* 2.220; *Antiquities* 19.363). The governors of the province thenceforth were designated as procurators. Supervision of the Temple and the right to appoint high priests were given over to Herod of Chalcis (*Antiquities* 20.15–16, 20.103).

Lines of authority during the period of the procurators (44–66) are no more clear. Fadus obviously thought it was within his authority to execute or exile Jews who lived within the Peraea and Idumaea, as well as "magicians" (*Antiquities* 20.3–4, 5, 20.97–99); he also attempted to seize control of the high priest's tunic and robe (*Antiquities* 20.6–8). Herod of Chalcis meanwhile received authority over the Temple and its holy vessels and the choice of high priests (*Antiquities* 20.15–16, 20.103). Tiberius Iulius Alexander had the sons of Judas the Galilaean executed, on his own authority (*Antiquities* 20.102). After the death of Herod of Chalcis, Agrippa II was given supervision of the Temple and the right to appoint high priests (*War* 2.223; *Antiquities* 20.104). During the procuratorship of Ventidius Cumanus, by his order, Rome's auxiliary soldiers killed 30,000 during the Passover festival (*War* 2.225–27; *Antiquities* 20.108–12). He also punished villagers who did not intervene during the robbery of Caesar's slave Stephanus and had executed a soldier who ripped up a copy of the laws (*War* 2.228–31; *Antiquities* 20.113–17).

Cumanus also punished Jews who had attacked Samaritans in retaliation for their attacks upon Galilaeans traveling to Jerusalem for a festival (*War* 2.232–38; *Antiquities* 20.118–24). But Ummidius Quadratus, the legate of Syria, intervened after an appeal from the Samaritans. Quadratus punished both the Samaritans and the Jews who had been involved (*War* 2.241; *Antiquities* 20.129). After prominent Jews and Samaritans were sent to Rome, Claudius himself heard the cases of both sides and had executed three of the Samaritans. Cumanus was exiled and a tribune was executed (*War* 2.245–46; *Antiquities* 20.134–36).

Felix conducted campaigns against "bandits" in Judaea (*War* 2.253; *Antiquities* 20.160–61) and against the followers of anti-Roman "false prophets" (*War* 2.263; *Antiquities* 20.171–72). He also set soldiers under his command upon Jews in Caesarea after one of their running street battles with non-Jewish Caesareans (*War* 2.266–70; *Antiquities* 20.173–78). While Festus was procurator Nero gave rule over Caesarea to the non-Jews (*Antiquities* 20.183; *War* 2.284). He also intervened to settle a dispute between King Agrippa II and some of the Temple authorities over a wall that blocked Agrippa's view of the Temple from his palace. Nero ultimately ruled in favor of those who were behind the building of the wall (*Antiquities* 20.189–96). Before Festus's successor arrived (62 CE) the high priest had James, the brother of Jesus, executed (*Antiquities* 20.197–200). For some crimes, therefore, some high priests thought that they had capital authority.

Josephus represents Florus thinking that his main job as governor was to extract money from the Jews by all means necessary, including violence. Nero's decision to award the non-Jews of Caesarea rule over the city meanwhile emboldened non-Jews and incited interethnic violence there. Florus's refusal to intervene and then the massacre of Jews who protested his withdrawals from the Temple treasury led to a breakdown of all law and order.

There is also the evidence of Judaea's status provided by coinage. Neither the silver nor the bronze coins minted by the various groups in and around Jerusalem during the years of the revolt (silver coins from years 1–5, bronze from years 2–4 only) name the state in revolt as Judaea. Instead, in the legends on the obverse sides of the silver coins are engraved "Shekel" or "Half-Shekel of Israel." On the bronze reverse sides are engraved "Freedom of Zion" in year 3 and "For the Redemption of Zion" in year 4. Some have argued that these legends support the case that there was no independent province named Judaea in 66. But the coins were minted by Jews who were rebels against Rome, and Judaea was the Roman/Latin name for the province. Naming the coins

"Shekel" or "Half-Shekel of Israel" or "Freedom of Zion" in Paleo-Hebrew letters was precisely a rejection of the Roman name for the state of the Jews and an assertion of an older, independent identity of the ethnos. After the war was over the Flavian emperors had coins minted with the famous inscription "Judaea Capta." The coins were not inscribed "Syria Capta." Finally, as we know, Josephus circulated drafts of the *War* among prominent Romans, including Titus himself. Did Titus simply not know that Judaea was not a province from 6 to 44 CE? Did he forget to point out that fact to Josephus before the *War* was more widely circulated?

Beneath the surface of Josephus's confused account of whether Judaea was a "province" from 6 to 41 and, again, from 44 to 66 lie complicated and changing data about what jurisdiction actually meant with respect to the control of finances, security, the administration of justice, the appointment of high priests, and authority over Temple property for Roman and local officials. The closer we look at the evidence, the more quickly clear lines of authority and jurisdiction dissolve. Syrian legates, Syrian procurators, and Judaean prefects, kings, and procurators all were involved with the finances of Judaea and the administration of justice. High priests were appointed and deposed by ethnarchs, Syrian legates, procurators, the king of Judaea, the king of Chalcis, and King Agrippa II. Ethnarchs, legates, governors of Judaea, and kings supervised Temple property and the high priests' wardrobe at different times. Above all of these officials sat Roman emperors who reviewed and made decisions about relations among those officials. There was no fixed administration of Judaea from 4 BCE to 66 CE.

For works accepting Josephus's original statement that Judaea became a province in 6 CE, see Mommsen (1887) 2: 200–203; Stevenson (1939) p. 46; Schürer I (2014) pp. 330–35; Levick (1999) p. 71; Sicker (2001) pp. 115–20; Schäfer (2003b) pp. 105–9; and Grabbe (2010) p. 25. For the views of those who argue that Judaea was part of Syria until Vespasian's arrival, see Brunt (1983) pp. 55–56; Ghiretti (1985) pp. 751–66; Franke (1996) pp. 236–37; Eck (2003) p. 98; (2007) pp. 1–54, 108; Sartre (2005) pp. 93, 103–4, 127; Bernett (2007) pp. 188–89; Labbé (2012); and Mason (2016) pp. 240–45.

Cestius's Army, Summer 66 CE

The following figures do not include the requirements of the many troops from the towns (*ton poleon epikouroi*) who joined Cestius before he made his way into the Galilee, as Josephus tells us they did at *War* 2.502; however, he does not tell us how many of these troops there were. Also not included are statistics for military slaves and free servants. There must have been a substantial number of slaves and servants, but again Josephus provides no numbers.

DAILY SUPPLY REQUIREMENTS

Soldiers (Low Unit Total Estimate)

	Food (pounds)	Liquids (liters)
Legionaries	30,780	21,600
10,800 × 2.85 pounds of food and 2.0 liquid liters		
(assumes 4,800-soldier legion)		
Auxiliaries	7,500	6,000
(infantry)		
3,000 × 2.5 pounds of food and 2.0 liquid liters		
(assumes 500-infantry soldier cohort)		

	Food (pounds)	Liquids (liters)
Auxiliaries	5,000	4,000
(cavalry)		
2,000 × 2.5 pounds of food and 2.0 liquid liters		
(assumes 500-cavalryman *ala*)		
Allies	27,334	27,334
13,667 × 2.0 pounds of food and 2.0 liquid liters		
Totals		
29,467	70,614	58,934

Lowest number of legionaries, auxiliaries, and allied soldiers (excludes requirements of military slaves and troop contributions from Syrian towns)

DAILY SUPPLY REQUIREMENTS

Soldiers (High Unit Total Estimate)

	Food (pounds)	Liquids (liters)
Legionaries	34,200	24,000
12,000 × 2.85 pounds of food and 2.0 liquid liters		
(assumes 6,000 soldiers per legion)		
Auxiliaries	15,000	12,000
(infantry)		
6,000 × 2.5 pounds of food and 2.0 liquid liters		
(assumes 1,000-soldier infantry cohort)		
Auxiliaries	10,000	8,000
(cavalry)		
4,000 × 2.5 pounds of food and 2.0 liquid liters		
(assumes 1,000-cavalryman *ala*)		
Allies	27,334	27,334
13,667 × 2.0 pounds of food and 2.0 liquid liters		
Totals		
35,667	86,534	71,334

Highest number of legionaries, auxiliaries, and allied soldiers (excludes requirements of military slaves and troop contributions from Syrian towns)

Animals (Lowest Totals)

	Hard Fodder (kg)	Green Fodder (kg)	Water (liters)
Pack animals	7,200	21,600	72,000
legionaries, 1 per 3 legionaries			
3,600 animals for 10,800 legionaries			
Pack animals	2,000	6,000	20,000
auxiliaries, 1 per 3 auxiliary infantrymen			
1,000 animals for 3,000 auxiliary infantry			
Pack animals	2,000	6,000	20,000
auxiliary cavalry			
1,000 animals for 2,000 auxiliary cavalrymen			
Horses	5,000	14,000	40,000
auxiliary cavalry			
2,000 horses for 2,000 auxiliary cavalrymen[1]			
Pack animals	5,778	17,334	57,780
allied infantry			
2,889 animals for 8,667 infantry			
Pack animals	5,000	15,000	50,000
allied mounted troops			
2,500 animals for 5,000 mounted troops			
Allied horses	12,500	35,000	100,000
5,000 horses for 5,000 cavalrymen			
Totals	39,478	114,934	359,780

Animals (Highest)

	Hard Fodder (kg)	Green Fodder (kg)	Water (liters)
Pack animals	8,000	24,000	80,000
legionaries, 1 per 3 legionaries			
4,000 animals for 12,000 legionaries			
Pack animals	4,000	12,000	40,000
auxiliaries, 1 per 3 auxiliary infantrymen			
2,000 animals for 6,000 auxiliary infantry			
Pack animals	4,000	12,000	
auxiliary cavalry			40,000
2,000 animals for 4,000 auxiliary cavalrymen			
Horses	10,000	28,000	80,000
auxiliary cavalry			
4,000 horses for 4,000 auxiliary cavalrymen			
Pack animals	5,778	17,334	57,780
allied infantry			
2,889 animals for 8,667 infantry			
Pack animals	5,000	15,000	50,000
allied mounted troops			
2,500 animals for 5,000 mounted troops			
Allied horses	12,500	35,000	100,000
5,000 horses for 5,000 cavalrymen			
Totals	49,278	143,334	447,780

OVERALL TOTALS

Size of Cestius's Army and Supply Train (Lowest Totals)

29,467 soldiers
10,989 pack animals
7,000 horses
or

Size of Cestius' Army and Supply Train (Highest Totals)

35,667 soldiers
13,389 pack animals
9,000 horses

Daily Food Requirements for 29,467 Soldiers, 10,989 Pack Animals, and 7,000 Horses

SOLDIERS

70,614 pounds of food, 58,934 liquid liters for the army excluding needs of military slaves and Syrian irregulars

ANIMALS

39,478 kg of hard fodder, 114,934 kg of green fodder, 359,780 liters of water

Daily Food Requirements for 35,667 Soldiers, 13,389 Pack Animals, and 9,000 Horses

SOLDIERS

86,534 pounds of food and 71,334 liquid liters for the army excluding needs of military slaves and Syrian irregulars

ANIMALS

49,278 kg of hard fodder, 143,334 kg of green fodder, and 447,780 liquid liters

---

Cestius's legionaries needed to ingest about 3,000 calories from 2.85 pounds of food per day and to drink at least two liters of water or other liquids.[2] For the 4,800–6,000 men of Legio XII Fulminata and the 6,000 men of the other Syrian vexillations, that would add up to 30,780–34,200 pounds of food and 21,600–24,000 liquid liters that had to be carried or found and distributed daily.

For the sake of argument let us assume that the food rations of the auxiliaries were a little less generous—2.5 pounds per day—though still two liquid liters were required. The 5,000–10,000 auxiliary infantry cohorts and cavalry wings thus would require 12,500–25,000 pounds of food and 10,000–20,000 liquid liters daily. The allied kings Antiochus IV of Commagene, Agrippa II, and Sohaemus of Emesa might have provided less food—perhaps two pounds per man. But the same amount of liquids would be necessary. Altogether the allied kings would still need to find 27,334 pounds of food and 27,334 liquid liters daily for their approximately 13,667 men.[3]

Every day Cestius's army needed to have somewhere between 70,614 and 86,534 pounds of food and 58,934–71,334 liquid liters available. These totals do not include what was needed to feed and hydrate the military slaves and free, nonmilitary personnel who provided logistical support for Cestius's army. By one estimate there must have been around 1,200 military slaves per each 4,800-man legion (a one-to-four ratio).[4] That would make a minimum of 2,700 slaves for a legionary army of 10,800. The auxiliary cohorts also relied upon military slaves for support, perhaps 120 per each auxiliary infantry cohort; that would add up to at least 720 for the six infantry cohorts assembled at Antioch in 66. We do not have contemporary information about the number of servants for the auxiliary cavalry, but they must have had them. There also must have been slaves or servants who served the troops of the allied kings (*calones* and *lixae*), but we have no idea how many. The point is that the military slaves would also have to eat and drink.

The animals themselves had to have their needs taken care of, too. The horses of Cestius's cavalrymen and the donkeys, mules, and oxen that carried the legions' supplies needed hard and dry fodder (or pasturage) and water daily. By one estimate every horse of the cavalrymen would have required 2.5 kg of hard fodder, 7 kg of dry or green fodder, and 20 liters of water per day. Every mule required 2 kg of hard fodder, 6 kg of dry fodder, and also 20 liters of water.[5] Excluded from these estimates are feed for horses of legionary cavalrymen.

If one pack animal was needed for every three legionary soldiers it would mean that 3,600–4,000 animals would have been needed to carry the equipment of Cestius's 10,800–12,000 legionaries. For the 3,600–4,000 pack animals of 10,800–12,000 legionaries, 7,200–8,000 kg of hard fodder, 21,600–24,000 kg of green fodder, and 72,000–80,0000 liters of water would have to be supplied daily.

The 1,000–2,000 pack animals for the 3,000–6,000 auxiliary infantry would require 2,000–4,000 kg of hard fodder, 6,000–12,000 kg of green fodder, and 20,000–40,000 liters of water. For the 1,000–2,000 pack animals of the 2,000–4,000 auxiliary cavalrymen, 2,000–4,000 kg of hard fodder, 6,000–12,000 kg of green fodder, and 20,000–24,000 liters of water were necessary The 2,000–4,000 horses of the auxiliary cavalry needed 5,000–10,000 kg of hard fodder, 14,000–28,000 kg of green fodder, and 40,000–80,000 liters of water daily.

For the 2,889 pack animals of the 8,667 allied infantry, 5,778 kg of hard fodder, 17,334 kg of green fodder, and 57,780 liters of water were necessary. The 2,500 pack animals of the 5,000 allied cavalrymen might have required 5,000 kg of hard fodder, 15,000 kg of green fodder, and 50,000 liters of water. And the 5,000 horses of the 5,000 allied cavalry needed 12,500 kg of hard fodder, 35,000 kg of green fodder, and 100,000 liters of water.

Vespasian's Army at Ptolemais, Spring 67 CE

DAILY SUPPLY REQUIREMENTS

Soldiers (Low Unit Total Estimate)

	Food (pounds)	Liquids (liters)
Legionaries	41,040	28,800
14,400 × 2.85 pounds of food and 2.0 liquid liters		
Cohorts	48,400	38,720
19,360 × 2.5 pounds of food and 2.0 liquid liters		
(10 cohorts of 1,000, 13 cohorts of 600, plus 120 cavalrymen per cohort of 600)		
Cavalry	7,500	6,000
3,000 × 2.5 pounds of food and 2.0 liquid liters		
(one squadron from Caesarea, five from Syria)		
Allies	30,000	30,000
15,000 × 2.0 pounds of food and 2.0 liquid liters		
Military slaves	7,200	7,200
low total		
3,600 for 14,400 legionaries		
3,600 slaves × 2.0 pounds of food and 2.0 liquid liters		

	Food (pounds)	Liquids (liters)
Military slaves	9,680	9,680
4,840 for 19,360 auxiliary cohorts		
4,840 slaves × 2.0 pounds of food and 2.0 liquid liters		
Military slaves	1,500	1,500
750 for 3,000 auxiliary cavalry		
750 slaves × 2.0 pounds of food plus 2.0 liquid liters		
Lowest number of legionaries, auxiliaries, and allied soldiers		
51,760		
Totals	126,940	103,520
(excludes requirements of military slaves)		

DAILY SUPPLY REQUIREMENTS

Soldiers (High Unit Total Estimate)

	Food (pounds)	Liquids (liters)
Legionaries	51,300	36,000
18,000 × 2.85 pounds of food and 2.0 liquid liters		
Cohorts	48,400	38,720
19,360 × 2.5 pounds of food and 2.0 liquid liters		
(10 cohorts of 1,000, 13 cohorts of 600, plus 120 cavalrymen per cohort of 600)		
Cavalry	15,000	12,000
6,000 × 2.5 pounds of food and 2.0 liquid liters		
(one squadron from Caesarea, five from Syria)		
Allies	30,000	30,000
15,000 × 2.0 pounds of food and 2.0 liquid liters		
Military slaves	9,000	9,000
4,500 for 18,000 legionaries		
4,500 slaves × 2.0 pounds of food and 2.0 liquid liters		
(one slave per legionary)		
Military slaves	9,680	9,680
4,840 for 19,360 auxiliary cohorts		
4,840 slaves × 2.0 pounds of food and 2.0 liquid liters		

	Food (pounds)	Liquids (liters)
Military slaves	3,000	3,000
1,500 for 6,000 auxiliary cavalry		
1,500 slaves × 2.0 pounds of food plus 2.0 liquid liters		
Highest number of legionaries, auxiliaries, and allied soldiers		
58,360		
Totals	144,700	116,720
(excludes requirements of military slaves)		

Animals (Lowest Totals)

	Hard Fodder (kg)	Green Fodder (kg)	Water (liters)
Pack animals	9,600	28,800	96,000
4,800 for 14,400 legionaries			
Pack animals	11,866	35,598	118,660
5,933 for 17,800 infantry auxiliaries			
Pack animals	1,560	4,680	15,600
780 for 1,560 cavalry auxiliaries			
Pack animals	3,000	9,000	30,000
1,500 for 3,000 cavalrymen from Caesarea and Syria			
Pack animals	7,334	22,002	73,340
3,667 for 11,000 allied infantry			
Pack animals	4,000	12,000	40,000
2,000 for 4,000 allied cavalry			
Horses	3,900	10,920	31,200
1,560 for 1,560 cavalrymen of cohorts			
Horses	7,500	21,000	60,000
3,000 for 3,000 auxiliary cavalry from Caesarea and Syria			
Horses	10,000	28,000	80,000
4,000 for 4,000 allied cavalry			
Totals	58,760	172,000	544,800

Animals (Highest Totals)

	Hard Fodder (kg)	Green Fodder (kg)	Water (liters)
Pack animals 6,000 for 18,000 legionaries	12,000	36,000	120,000
Pack animals 5,933 for 17,800 infantry auxiliaries	11,866	35,598	118,660
Pack animals 780 for 1,560 cavalry auxiliaries	1,560	4,680	15,600
Pack animals 3,000 for 6,000 cavalrymen from Caesarea and Syria	6,000	18,000	60,000
Pack animals 3,667 for 11,000 allied infantry	7,334	22,002	73,340
Pack animals 2,000 for 4,000 allied cavalry	4,000	12,000	40,000
Horses 1,560 for 1,560 cavalrymen of cohorts	3,900	10,920	31,200
Horses 6,000 for 6,000 auxiliary cavalry from Caesarea and Syria	13,800	42,000	120,000
Horses 4,000 for 4000 allied cavalry	10,000	28,000	80,000
Totals	70,460	209,200	658,800

TOTALS

Low Unit Estimates

51,760 soldiers
9,190 military slaves, excluding slaves and servants of allies
18,680 pack animals
8,560 horses

TOTALS

High Unit Estimates

58,360 soldiers
10,840 military slaves excluding slaves and servants of allies
21,380 pack animals
11,560 horses

DAILY FOOD AND LIQUID REQUIREMENTS

Low Estimate

SOLDIERS

126,940 pounds of food and 103,520 liquid liters, excluding needs of military slaves

DAILY FOOD AND LIQUID REQUIREMENTS

High Estimate

SOLDIERS

144,700 pounds of food and 116,720 liquid liters, excluding needs of military slaves

DAILY FOOD AND LIQUID REQUIREMENTS

Low Estimate

ANIMALS

58,760 kg of dry fodder
172,000 kg of green fodder
544,800 liquid liters for animals

DAILY FOOD AND LIQUID REQUIREMENTS

High Estimate

ANIMALS

70,460 kg of dry fodder
209,200 kg green fodder
658,800 liquid liters for animals

Vespasian's 14,400–18,000 legionaries would have required 41,040–51,300 pounds of food per day (2.85 pounds per man), plus 28,800–36,000 liquid liters (2 liquid liters daily). His 23 auxiliary cohorts (of 19,360 men) would have needed at least 48,400 pounds of food daily (calculated at 2.5 pounds per day per man) and 38,720 liters of water or other liquids. The 3,000–6,000 cavalrymen from Caesarea and Syria would have needed between 7,500 and 15,000 pounds of food daily and 6,000 to 12,000 liquid liters. The allied kings would have needed to provide 30,000 pounds of food and 30,000 liquid liters (at 2 pounds and 2 liquid liters per man). Altogether the soldiers of Vespasian's army needed between 126,940 and 144,700 pounds of food per day and 103,520–116,720 liquid liters. Some estimates are given for the numbers of military slaves and servants who might have been used for the legions and auxiliary cohorts and their food and water requirements as well. We do not know how many slaves accompanied the royal armies; therefore the food and water requirements of the slaves were not added to the totals.

The supplies and equipment of the 51,760–58,360 legionaries, auxiliaries, and allies that they could not carry would have to have been transported by pack animals. If one pack animal was needed to carry the equipment of every three infantrymen and one for every two cavalrymen, then Vespasian needed between 18,680 and 21,380 pack animals, each of which required 2 kg of hard fodder, 6 kg of green fodder, and 20 liters of water per day. The horses of the 8,560 to 11,560 cavalrymen would each have required 2.5 kg of hard fodder, 7 kg of dry or green fodder, and 20 liters of water per day. That works out to somewhere between 58,760 and 70,460 kg of hard fodder, 172,000 and 209,200 kg of green fodder, and 544,800 and 658,800 liquid liters needed daily. These estimates exclude provisions needed for extra pack animals and horses that unquestionably would have accompanied the army to replace animals that became sick or died.

Titus's Army, Spring 70 CE

DAILY SUPPLY REQUIREMENTS

Soldiers (Low Unit Totals)

	Food (pounds)	Liquids (liters)
Legionaries	54,720	38,400
19,200 × 2.85 pounds of food and 2.0 liquid liters		
assumes 4,800-soldier legion		
Auxiliaries	25,000	20,000
(irregular infantry)		
10,000 × 2.5 pounds of food and 2.0 liters of water		
assumes 500-soldier cohort		
Cavalry	10,000	8,000
4,000 × 2.5 pounds of food and 2.0 liters of water		
assumes 500-cavalryman *ala*		
Allies	30,000	30,000
15,000 × 2.0 pounds of food and 2.0 liters of water		
Totals (low unit)	119,720	96,400
(excluding military slaves and free servants)		
Military slaves	9,600	9,600
(low unit number)		
4,800 × 2.0 pounds of food and 2.0 liters of water		

Soldiers (High Unit Totals)

	Food (pounds)	Liquids (liters)
Legionaries	68,400	48,000
24,000 × 2.85 pounds of food and 2.0 liquid liters		
assumes 6,000-soldier legion		
Auxiliaries	50,000	40,000
(infantry)		
20,000 × 2.5 pounds of food and 2.0 liters of water		
assumes 1,000-soldier cohort		
Cavalry	20,000	16,000
8,000 × 2.5 pounds of food		
assumes 1,000-cavalryman *ala*		
Allies	30,000	30,000
15,000 × 2.0 pounds of food and 2.0 liters of water		
Totals (high unit)	168,400	134,000
(excluding military slaves and free servants)		
Military slaves		
(high unit number)	12,000	12,000
6,000 × 2.0 pounds of food and 2.0 liters of water		

Animals (Low Numbers)

	Hard Fodder (kg)	Green Fodder (kg)	Water (liters)
Pack animals	12,800	38,400	128,000
legions			
6,400 for 19,200 legionaries			
Pack animals	6,666	19,998	66,660
auxiliaries			
3,333 for 10,000 auxiliaries			
Horses	10,000	28,000	80,000
cavalry			
4,000 horses for 4,000 cavalrymen			

	Hard Fodder (kg)	Green Fodder (kg)	Water (liters)
Pack animals allies 3,667 for 11,000 allied infantrymen	7,334	22,002	73,340
Horses 4,000 horses for 4,000 allied cavalrymen	10,000	28,000	80,000
Totals (low unit)	46,800	136,400	428,000

Animals (High Numbers)

	Hard Fodder (kg)	Green Fodder (kg)	Water (liters)
Pack animals legion 8,000 for 24,000 legionaries	16,000	48,000	160,000
Pack animals auxiliaries 6,666 for 20,000 auxiliaries	13,332	39,996	133,320
Horses cavalry 8,000 horses for 8,000 cavalrymen	20,000	56,000	160,000
Pack animals allies 3,667 for 11,000 allied infantrymen	7,334	22,002	73,340
Horses 4,000 horses for 4,000 allied cavalrymen	10,000	28,000	80,000
Totals (high unit)	66,666	193,998	606,660

TOTAL NUMBER OF SOLDIERS AND ANIMALS

48,200 (40,200 infantrymen, 8,000 cavalry)—67,000 (55,000 infantrymen, 12,000 cavalry) soldiers

13,400–18,333 pack animals

8,000–12,000 horses

For the Army

119,720 pounds of food and 96,400 liquid liters, excluding needs of military slaves and free servants daily (low estimate)
168,400 pounds of food and 134,000 liquid liters, excluding needs of military slaves and free servants daily (high estimate)

For the Animals

46,800 kg (dry fodder), 136,400 kg (green fodder), 428,000 liquid liters (low estimate)
66,666 kg (dry fodder), 193,998 kg (green fodder), 606,660 liquid liters (high estimate)

DURATION OF SIEGE, MID-APRIL TO END OF AUGUST (?), 70 CE: FOUR MONTHS

Total Requirements for Army, Low and High Estimates

14,366,200 pounds of food, 11,568,000 liters (low estimate)
20,208,000 pounds of food, 16,080,000 liters (high estimate)
Excludes totals for marches to Jerusalem and return

Total Requirements for Animals, Low and High Estimates

5,616,000 kg (dry fodder), 16,368,000 kg (green fodder), 51,360,000 liters
7,999,920 kg (dry fodder), 23,279,760 kg (green fodder), 72,799,200 liters
Excludes totals for marches to Jerusalem and return

To feed and hydrate Titus's 19,200–24,000 legionaries daily would have required between 54,720 and 68,400 pounds of food and 38,400 to 48,000 liquid liters.[1] The estimated 4,800–6,000 military slaves who served a legionary army of 19,200–24,000 would also have to be fed and supplied with liquids, as would the estimated 6,400–8,000 pack animals for the legions alone.[2] If we calculate the requirements of the slaves at a base level of two pounds of food per slave and two liters per day, that would add up to 9,600–12,000 pounds of food and 9,600–12,000 liquid liters.

For the legions' 6,400–8,000 pack animals, 12,800–16,000 kg of hard fodder, 38,400–48,000 kg of green fodder, and 128,000–160,000 liters of water would have to be carried or found.[3] Excluded from these estimates are feed for legionary horses because Josephus does not mention any of the legionaries bringing mounts to the campaign.

The 10,000–20,000 irregular auxiliary infantrymen needed 25,000–50,000 pounds of food daily and 20,000–40,000 liquid liters; the 4,000–8,000 cavalrymen needed 10,000–20,000 pounds of food and 8,000–16,000 liquid liters daily.[4] The 10,000–20,000 infantry auxiliaries would have needed around 3,333–6,666 pack animals to help carry their food and equipment. Those pack animals required 6,666–13,332 kg of dry fodder, 19,998–39,996 kg of green fodder, and 66,660–133,320 liters of water per day.[5]

The horses of the 4,000 to 8,000 auxiliary cavalry needed 10,000–20,000 kg of dry fodder, 28,000–56,000 kg of green fodder, and 80,000–160,000 liters of water daily.[6]

The combined 15,000-man contingent of the allied kings might have needed at least 30,000 pounds of food and 30,000 liquid liters daily for the soldiers and 10,000 kg of dry fodder, 28,000 kg of green fodder, and 80,000 liters of water per day for its 4,000 horses.[7] If the allied contingents also used pack animals to carry their equipment at a ratio of one pack animal for every three soldiers, then they would have required 3,667 animals. Those animals would have needed 7,334 pounds of hard fodder, 22,002 pounds of green fodder, and 73,340 liters of water.

If we add up all of these minimum requirements, they indicate that, excluding what was needed for military slaves and servants, Titus would have needed to supply his army with 119,720–168,400 pounds of food every day and 96,400–138,000 liquid liters. The pack animals and horses would have needed an estimated 46,800–66,666 kg of hard fodder, 136,400–193,998 kg of green fodder, and 428,000–606,660 liters of water daily.

During a four-month siege from April until August of 70 CE Titus's soldiers would have required between 14,366,200 and 20,208,00 pounds of food and 11,568,000 and 16,080,000 liters of water. The animals needed between 5,616,000 and 7,999,920 kg of hard fodder, 16,368,000 and 23,279,760 kg of green fodder, and 51,360,000 and 72,799,200 liters of water.

Silva's Army at Masada, Spring 74 CE

DAILY SUPPLY REQUIREMENTS

Soldiers (Low Unit Total Estimate)

	Food (pounds)	Liquids (liters)
Legionaries	13,680	9,600
4,800 × 2.85 pounds of food and 2.0 liquid liters		
Auxiliaries	8,000	6,400
3,200 × 2.5 pounds of food and 2.0 liquid liters		
Military slaves	4,000	4,000
2,000 × 2.0 pounds of food and 2.0 liquid liters		
Porters	6,000	6,000
3,000 × 2.0 pounds of food and 2.0 liquid liters		

LOW TOTALS FOR SOLDIERS ONLY

21,680 pounds of food for 4,800 legionaries and 3,200 auxiliaries daily
16,000 liquid liters for 4,800 legionaries and 3,200 auxiliaries daily

Soldiers (High Unit Total Estimate)

Legionaries   17,100   12,000
6,000 × 2.85 pounds and 2.0 liquid liters
Auxiliaries   8,000   6,400
3,200 × 2.5 pounds of food and 2.0 liquid liters
Military slaves   4,000   4,000
2,000 × 2.0 pounds of food and 2.0 liquid liters
Porters   6,000   6,000
3,000 × 2.0 pounds of food and 2.0 liquid liters

HIGH TOTALS FOR SOLDIERS ONLY

25,100 pounds of food for 6,000 legionaries and 3,200 auxiliaries daily
18,400 liquid liters for 6,000 legionaries and 3,200 auxiliaries daily

Animals (Lowest Totals)

	Hard fodder (kg)	**Green fodder (kg)**	**Water (liters)**
Pack animals 1,600 for 4,800 legionaries	3,200	9,600	32,000
Pack animals 1,067 for 3,200 auxiliaries	2,134	6,402	21,340

LOW TOTALS FOR ANIMALS

	5,334	16,002	53,340

Animals (Highest Totals)

Pack animals 2,000 for 6,000 legionaries	4,000	12,000	40,000
Pack animals 1,067 for 3,200 auxiliary soldiers	2,134	6,402	21,340

HIGH TOTALS FOR ANIMALS

	6,134	18,402	61,340

SEVEN-WEEK SIEGE TOTALS

1,062,320 pounds of food for 4,800 legionaries and 3,200 auxiliaries

1,229,900 pounds of food for 6,000 legionaries and 3,200 auxiliaries

784,000 liquid liters for 4,800 legionaries and 3,200 auxiliaries

901,600 liquid liters for 6,000 legionaries and 3,200 auxiliaries

261,366 kg of hard fodder, 784,098 kg of green fodder, and 2,613,660 liquid liters for 2,667 pack animals

300,556 kg of hard fodder, 901,698 kg of green fodder, and 3,005,660 liquid liters for 3,067 pack animals

Four Campaigns

I. CESTIUS'S THREE-WEEK NON-SIEGE OF JERUSALEM, LATE SUMMER 66 CE

From Lydda to Jerusalem and Back to Antipatris, September–October 66 CE (3 Weeks, around 15 Tishri/Huperberetaeus–8 Cheshvan/Dius)

LOW ESTIMATE OF TROOP STRENGTH

29,467 legionaries, auxiliaries, and allied soldiers (excluding military slaves and Syrian troop contributions)

LOW ESTIMATE OF DAILY FOOD AND LIQUID REQUIREMENTS FOR SOLDIERS

70,614 pounds of food and 58,934 liquid liters

LOW ESTIMATE OF FOOD AND LIQUID REQUIREMENTS FOR SOLDIERS OVER 21 DAYS

1,482,894 pounds of food and 1,237,614 liquid liters

LOW ESTIMATE OF ANIMALS

10,989 pack animals and 7,000 horses

LOW ESTIMATE OF DAILY FOOD AND LIQUID REQUIREMENTS
FOR ANIMALS

39,478 kg of hard fodder, 114,934 kg of green fodder, 359,780 liters of water

LOW ESTIMATE OF ANIMAL FOOD AND LIQUID
REQUIREMENTS FOR 10 DAYS

394,780 kg hard fodder, 1,149,340 kg of green fodder, 3,597,800 liters of water for animals over 10 days (assuming that Simon captured half the animals during his initial attack and more were lost during Cestius's retreat from Jerusalem)

II. VESPASIAN'S CAMPAIGNS IN THE NORTH, 67 CE

From Ptolemais to Gamala, March–Mid-October 67
(about 7 Months or 210 Days)

LOW ESTIMATE OF TROOP STRENGTH

51,760 legionaries, auxiliaries, and allied soldiers (excluding military slaves and Syrian troop contributions)

LOW ESTIMATE OF DAILY FOOD AND LIQUID REQUIREMENTS
FOR SOLDIERS

126,940 pounds of food and 103,520 liquid liters

LOW ESTIMATE OF FOOD AND LIQUID REQUIREMENTS
FOR SOLDIERS FOR 210 DAYS

26,657,400 pounds of food and 21,739,200 liters

LOW ESTIMATE OF ANIMALS

18,680 pack animals and 8,560 horses

LOW ESTIMATE OF DAILY FOOD AND LIQUID REQUIREMENTS
FOR ANIMALS

58,760 kg of dry fodder, 172,000 kg of green fodder, 544,800 liquid liters

LOW ESTIMATE OF ANIMAL FOOD AND LIQUID REQUIREMENTS
FOR 210 DAYS

12,339,600 kg (dry fodder), 36,120,000 kg (green fodder), 114,408,000 liquid liters

III. TITUS'S SIEGE OF JERUSALEM, APRIL–AUGUST 70

Mid-April to End of August (?), 70
(about Four Months or 120 Days)

LOW ESTIMATE OF TROOP STRENGTH

48,200 soldiers (40,200 infantrymen, 8,000 cavalry)

LOW ESTIMATE OF DAILY FOOD AND LIQUID REQUIREMENTS
FOR SOLDIERS

119,720 pounds of food and 96,400 liquid liters

LOW ESTIMATE OF FOOD AND LIQUID REQUIREMENTS
FOR SOLDIERS OVER 120 DAYS

14,366,200 pounds of food and 11,568,000 liters (excludes totals for marches
to Jerusalem and return)

LOW ESTIMATE OF ANIMALS

13,400 pack animals and 8,000 horses

LOW ESTIMATE OF DAILY FOOD AND LIQUID REQUIREMENTS
FOR ANIMALS

46,800 kg (dry fodder), 136,400 kg (green fodder), 428,000 liquid liters

LOW ESTIMATE OF FOOD AND LIQUID REQUIREMENTS
FOR ANIMALS OVER 120 DAYS

5,616,000 kg (dry fodder), 16,368, 000 kg (green fodder), 51,360,000 liters

IV. FLAVIUS SILVA'S SIEGE OF MASADA

Spring/Summer of 73 or 74 CE (Seven Weeks or 49 Days?)

LOW ESTIMATE OF TROOP STRENGTH

8,000 soldiers (4,800 legionaries, 3,200 auxiliaries)

LOW ESTIMATE OF DAILY FOOD AND LIQUID REQUIREMENTS
FOR SOLDIERS

21,680 pounds of food and 16,000 liquid liters

LOW ESTIMATE OF FOOD AND LIQUID REQUIREMENTS
FOR SOLDIERS FOR 49 DAYS

1,062,320 pounds of food and 784,000 liquid liters

LOW ESTIMATE OF ANIMALS

2,667 pack animals

LOW ESTIMATE OF DAILY FOOD AND LIQUID REQUIREMENTS
FOR ANIMALS

5,334 kg of hard fodder, 16,002 kg of green fodder, 53,340 liquid liters

LOW ESTIMATE OF FOOD AND LIQUID REQUIREMENTS
FOR ANIMALS OVER 49 DAYS

261,366 kg of hard fodder, 784,098 kg of green fodder, 2,613,660 liquid liters

FOUR CAMPAIGNS

Soldiers	Food (pounds)	Liquid Liters
Cestius	1,482,894	1,237,614
Three weeks in 66 CE		
(lowest estimate)		
Vespasian	26,657,400	21,739,200
Seven months in 67		
(lowest estimate)		
Titus	14,366,200	11,568,000
Seven weeks in 70		
(lowest estimate)		
Silva	1,062,320	784,000
49 days, 73 or 74		
(lowest estimate)		
Totals	43,568,814	35,328,814

Animals	Hard Fodder (kg)	Green Fodder (kg)	Liquid Liters
Cestius 　Three weeks in 66 　(lowest estimate)	394,780	1,149,340	3,597,800
Vespasian 　Seven months in 67 　(lowest estimate)	12,339,600	36,120,000	114,408,000
Titus 　Seven weeks in 70 CE 　(lowest estimate)	5,616,000	16,368, 000	51,360,000
Silva 　49 days in 73 or 74	261,366	784,098	2,613,660
Totals	18,611,746	54,421,438	171,979,460

These four campaigns represented the decisive actions of the war of Jews against Romans. In operational terms the campaigns were spread out over about 400 days. To supply the soldiers who participated in these campaigns the Romans required at least 43,568,814 pounds of food and 35,328,814 liquid liters or 9,332,885 gallons. The animals required 18,611,746 kg of hard fodder, 54,421,438 kg of green fodder, and 171,979,460 liquid liters or 45,432,167 gallons.

During the four campaigns described in this table, the soldiers of Cestius, Vespasian, Titus, and Silva consumed a minimum of 43,568,814 pounds of food. According to the National Hot Dog and Sausage Council, fans at all the Major League baseball games played (2,430) in 2018 ate 19,000,000 hot dogs. Each ballpark frank weighs about 1.6 ounces; 19 million ballpark franks weigh 30,400,000 ounces or 1,900,000 pounds. The total weight of the food consumed by Roman soldiers during these four campaigns, 43,568,814 pounds, divided by 1,900,000 equals 22.9. Therefore, during the four campaigns the Roman and allied soldiers consumed the equivalent weight of hot dogs that fans at all Major League Baseball games would consume for nearly 23 seasons, assuming the same number of games played and roughly the same attendance.

By some estimates 60% of the Roman military diet was grain-based, mainly wheat: 60% of 43,568,814 pounds is 26,141,288.4 pounds. Using modern farming techniques one acre of land can produce about 37 bushels or 2,200 pounds of wheat. To produce 26,141,288.4 pounds of grain using modern techniques therefore would require about 11,882 acres of land. If ancient techniques were half as effective it would follow that to produce 26,141,288 pounds of grain would have required about 23,764 acres. There are 640 acres in a square mile. To produce the grain necessary to supply 60% of the food needed by the armies of Cestius, Vespasian, Titus, and Silva during the four campaigns described here would have required the total grain production of 37 square miles. To keep the soldiers who took part in these campaigns hydrated would have required enough liquid to fill up 14 Olympic-sized (660,253-gallon) swimming pools. The animals would have needed 68 Olympic-sized pools.

The Second Speech of Eleazar ben Yair

Deeply, indeed, was I deceived thinking that I should have brave men as associates in our struggles on behalf of freedom—men determined to live well or to die. But you, it seems, were no better than the common herd in virtue or in courage, you who are afraid even of that death that will deliver you from the greatest ills, when in such a cause you ought neither to hesitate an instant nor wait for counsel. For from of old, since the dawn of intelligence, we have been continually taught by those precepts, ancestral and divine—confirmed by the deeds and noble spirit of our forefathers—that life, not death, is misfortune for men. For it is death which gives freedom to the souls and permits them to depart to their own pure abodes, there to be free from all calamity; but so long as a soul is imprisoned in a mortal body and tainted with all of its miseries, it is, in truth, dead, for association with what is mortal does not befit that which is divine. True, the soul possesses great capacity, even while imprisoned in the body; for it makes the latter its organ of perception, invisibly swaying it and directing it onward in its actions beyond the range of mortal nature. But it is not until, freed from the weight that drags it down to the earth, and clings about it, the soul is restored to its proper sphere, that it enjoys a blessed energy and a power untrammeled on every side, remaining, like God himself, invisible to human eyes. For even while in the body it is withdrawn from view, unperceived it comes and unseen departs, itself of a nature one and incorruptible, but a cause of change to the body. For whatever the soul has touched lives and flourishes, whatever it abandons withers and dies; so abundant is her wealth of immortality.

Let sleep furnish you with a most convincing indicator of what I say— sleep, in which the soul, undistracted by the body, while enjoying in perfect independence the most delightful repose, holds converse with God by right of kinship, ranges the universe and foretells many things that are to come. Why then should we fear death who welcome the repose of sleep? And is it not surely foolish, while pursuing freedom in this life, to grudge ourselves that which is eternal?

We ought, indeed, blest with our home training to afford others an example of readiness to die; if, however, we really need an assurance in this matter from other nations, let us look at those Indians who profess the practice of philosophy. Brave men that they are, they reluctantly endure the period of life, as some necessary service due to nature, but hasten to release their souls from their bodies; and though no calamity impels or drives them from the scene, from sheer longing for the immortal state they announce to their comrades that they are about to leave. Nor is there any who would hinder them: no, all congratulate them and each gives them commissions to his loved ones; so certain and absolutely sincere is their belief in the intercourse which souls hold with one another. Then, after listening to these behests, they commit their bodies to the fire, that so the soul may be parted from the body in the utmost purity, and expire amidst hymns of praise. Indeed, their dearest ones escort them to their death more readily than do the rest of mankind their fellow-citizens when starting on a very long journey; for themselves they weep, but them they count happy as now regaining immortal rank. Are we not, then, ashamed of being more mean-spirited than Indians, and of bringing, by our lack of daring, shameful reproach upon our fatherland's traditions, which are the envy of mankind?

Yet, even had we from the first been schooled in the opposite doctrine and taught that man's highest blessing is life and that death is a misfortune, still the crisis is one that calls upon us to bear it with a brave heart, since it is by God's will and of necessity that we are to die. For long since, so it seems, God passed this decree against the whole Jewish nation in common, that we must quit this life if we would not use it aright. Do not attach the blame to yourselves, nor credit to the Romans, that this war with them has been the ruin of all of us; for the intervention of some more powerful cause has afforded them the semblance of victory.

What Roman weapons, I ask, slew the Jews of Caesarea? No, they had not even contemplated revolt from Rome, but were engaged in keeping their

Sabbath festival, when the Caesarean mob rushed upon them and massacred them, unresisting, with their wives and children, without even the slightest respect for the Romans, who regarded as enemies only us who had revolted. But I shall be told that the Caesareans had a standing quarrel with the Jews living with them and seized the opportunity to satisfy their ancient hatred. What then shall we say of the Jews in Scythopolis, who had the audacity to wage war on us in the cause of the Greeks, but refused to unite with us, their kinsmen, in resisting the Romans? Much benefit, to be sure, did they reap from their goodwill and loyalty to the men of Scythopolis! Ruthlessly butchered by them, they and all their families—that was the payment that they received for their alliance; the fate from which they saved their neighbors at our hands, that they endured, as though they had themselves desired to inflict it. Time would fail me now to name each instance individually; for, as you know, there is not a city in Syria that has not slain the Jews living among them, though more hostile to us than to the Romans. Thus, the people of Damascus, though unable even to invent a plausible pretext, deluged their city with the foulest slaughter, butchering eighteen thousand Jews, with their wives and families. As for Egypt, we are told that the number of those who there perished in tortures perhaps exceeded sixty thousand.

Those Jews, maybe, perished as they did, because they were on alien soil, where they found themselves no match for their enemies. But consider all those who in their own territory embarked on war against the Romans: what did they lack of all that could inspire them with hopes of assured success? Arms, ramparts, fortresses very near impregnable, a spirit undaunted by risks to be run in the cause of freedom—these encouraged all to revolt. Yet these availed but for a brief time, and after buoying us up with hopes proved the beginning of greater disasters. For all were taken, all succumbed to the enemy, as though furnished for his more glorious triumph, and not for the protection of those who provided them. Those men who fell in battle may be fitly congratulated, for they died defending, not betraying, freedom; but the multitudes in Roman hands who would not pity? Who would not rush to his death before he shared their fate? Of them some have perished on the rack or tortured by fire and scourge; others, half-devoured by wild beasts, have been preserved alive to provide them with a second repast, after affording entertainment and sport for their foes. But most miserable of all must be reckoned those still alive, who have often prayed for death and are denied the favor.

And where now is that great city, the mother-city of the whole nation of Jews, entrenched behind all those lines of ramparts, screened by all those forts and massive towers, that could scarce contain her munitions of war, and held all those myriads of armed defenders? What has become of her that was believed to have God for her founder? Uprooted from her base she has been swept away, and the sole memorial of her remaining is that of the slain still quartered in her ruins! Unfortunate old men sit beside the ashes of the shrine and a few women, reserved by the enemy for basest outrage.

Which of us, taking these things to heart, could bear to behold the sun, even could he live secure from peril? Who such a foe to his fatherland, so unmanly, so fond of life, as not to regret that he is still alive today? No, I wish we had all been dead long before we saw that holy city razed by an enemy's hands, that sacred sanctuary so profanely uprooted! Not seeing that we have been beguiled by a not ignoble hope, that we might by chance find means of avenging her of her foes, and now that hope has vanished and left us alone in our distress, let us hasten to die honorably; let us have pity on ourselves, our children and our wives, while it is still in our power to find pity from ourselves. For we were born for death, we and those we have begotten: and this even the fortunate cannot escape. But outrage and servitude and the sight of our wives being led to shame with their children—these are no necessary evils imposed by nature on humanity, but befall, through their own cowardice, those who, having the chance of forestalling them by death, refuse to take it. But we, priding ourselves on our courage, revolted from the Romans, and now at the last, when they offered us our lives, we refused the offer. Who then can fail to foresee their wrath if they take us alive? Wretched will be the young whose vigorous frames can sustain many tortures, wretched the more advanced in years whose age is incapable of bearing such calamities. Is a man to see his wife led off to violence, to hear the voice of a child crying "Father!" when his own hands are bound? No, while those hands are free and grasp the sword, let them render an honorable service. Un-enslaved by the enemy let us quit this life together! This our laws enjoin, this our wives and children beg of us. The need for this is of God's sending, the reverse of this is the Romans' desire, and their fear is lest a single one of us should die before capture. Haste we then to leave them, instead of their hoped-for enjoyment at securing us, amazement at our death and admiration of our courage.

Key Topographical Sites in the Regions of the War, Jerusalem, and Rome

Abila:	Tell Abil in Jordan; town of Decapolis south of Bethennabris in the Peraea; also known as Seleucia; captured and garrisoned by Placidus early in 68 CE
Abila/Abela:	Souq Wadi Barada in Syria, town about 12 miles northwest of Damascus, part of tetrarchy of Lysanias given to Agrippa I as gift by Gaius/Caligula, confirmed by Claudius
Acchabaron:	Caves in the Upper Galilee; one of the sites that Josephus fortified in 66 CE; probably should be identified with caves along the cliffs south of Akhbara
Acco/Ptolemais:	City on the northern coast of Israel between Caesarea and Tyre; renamed Ptolemais; staging point for Cestius's and Vespasian's campaigns to the south
Achaia:	Region in western Greece where Nero was on an artistic tour when Cestius's intervention in Jerusalem failed in 66 CE
Acrabetta/Acrabatene:	District/toparchy on Judaea's frontier with Samaritis to the north, some 12 miles north-northeast of Jerusalem; put under the command of John, son of Ananias, in 66 CE; overrun by Simon in early 68; invaded by Vespasian in June 69
Adiabene:	Client kingdom of Parthian empire; clustered around area of Arbela (modern Irbil) in Iraqi Kurdistan; rulers converted to Judaism in first century CE
Adida:	Hadid; el-Haditha; about three miles east of Lydda; garrisoned by Vespasian

Agrippias: Khirbet Teda in Gaza; Greek coastal town named Anthedon, just to the northwest of Gaza; renamed Agrippias by Herod the Great in 12 BCE in honor of Augustus's friend Agrippa after it was added to Herod's kingdom; laid waste by Jews at the beginning of the revolt

Alexandreion: Qarn (Horn) el-Sartaba, West Bank; Hasmonean hill fortress in Samaritis, overlooking Jordan valley; occupied by the soldiers of Herod's rival Antigonus; after being abandoned, it was refortified for Herod by Pheroras; Alexander and Aristobulus were buried there after their execution in 7 BCE

Alexandria: City in Nile Delta founded by Alexander the Great; site of clashes between Greeks and Jews living there throughout first century CE

Alurus: Halhul; village to the east of Beth Zur; camp of the Idumaeans during their struggle against Simon bar Giora

Anthedon: Khirbet Teda in Gaza; Greek coastal town just to the northwest of Gaza; renamed Agrippias by Herod the Great in 12 BCE in honor of Augustus's friend Agrippa after it was added to Herod's kingdom; laid waste by the Jews at the beginning of the revolt

Antioch: Greek city founded along eastern side of Orontes River in Syria; seat of the Roman governors of Syria during the first century CE; Herod the Great had its main street paved in marble

Antipatris: Aphek/Apheq; town on plain of Sharon rebuilt by Herod about 9 BCE on road from Caesarea to Jerusalem in honor of his father Antipater

Apamea: Qalaat al-Madiq; Hellenistic-era city on the right bank of the Orontes; when the Jewish revolt broke out, its inhabitants spared the Jews who lived in their midst

Apheku: Aphek Turris, tower near Antipatris; some Jews fled there as Cestius's army approached in 66

Archelaïs: Khirbet el-Beiyudat; village on road from Jericho (about 7.5 miles north) to Scythopolis built by Herod the Great's son Archelaus; Salome left it in her will to Livia, and Agrippa I built a road station there

Asamon: Atzmon; hill village on a mountain about 1,730 feet above sea level, to the south of Iotapata and across the valley from Sepphoris; taken by Caesennius Gallus after rebels had fled there

Ascalon: Tel Ashkelon; modern Ashkelon in Israel; coastal town; Herod the Great had baths, fountains, and colonnades built for it; palace there given to Salome by Caesar Augustus in 4 BCE; unsuccessfully attacked by the rebels after the defeat of Cestius in 66

Asphaltitis: "Asphalt"; Greek name for the Dead Sea

Athens: Capital city of Attica in Greece; Herod made offerings and was honored there

Auranitis: Jebel Druze; biblical Hauran; region south of Damascus, southeast of Batanaea; not included in the original kingdom given to Herod by the Romans in 40 BCE but gifted to him at the end of 27 BCE; initially given to Philip by Caesar Augustus in 4 BCE; then given to Agrippa I by Claudius

Azotus: Tel Ashdod/Isdud in Israel; ancient Philistine,
                                  subsequently Hellenized city, just (3.1 miles)
                                  inland but with associated harbor; given to
                                  Herod's sister Salome in his will; confirmed by
                                  Caesar Augustus; garrisoned by Vespasian
                                  during the revolt in the spring of 68

Balanaea: Baniyas; Syrian coastal city; Herod cut its taxes

Batanaea: Biblical Bashan ("Smooth Plain"); region
                                  northeast of the Jordan River; east of Gaulanitis
                                  and west of Trachonitis (Al-Lega); not included
                                  in the original kingdom given to Herod by the
                                  Romans in 40 BCE but gifted to him at the end
                                  of 27 BCE; included in the tetrarchy of Herod
                                  the Great's son Philip; at Bathyra in Batanaea
                                  there was a Herodian military colony

Bathyra: As-Sanamyn?; on border between Batanaea and
                                  Trachonitis; site of Herodian-era Babylonian
                                  military colony

Beit-Horon, Lower: Beit Ur al-Tachta, village northwest of Jerusalem
                                  where Cestius was ambushed at the beginning of
                                  the revolt in 66

Beit-Horon, Upper: Beit Ur al-Fawqa, village northwest of Jerusalem
                                  (two miles to the east of Lower Beit-Horon),
                                  through which Cestius passed on his way to and
                                  from Jerusalem in the autumn of 66

Bersabe: Beer-Sheva in the Galilee; village at the northern
                                  point of the Lower Galilee; fortified by Josephus
                                  in 66

Berytus (Berytos):   Beirut in Lebanon; Herod the Great had halls,
                                  porticoes, temples, and marketplaces built
                                  for it; included a colony of Roman legionaries
                                  established by Augustus in 15 BCE; given a
                                  theater and statues by Agrippa II; contributed
                                  troops to Varus's punitive expedition

Besara: Beit Shearim; village in the southwestern hills of
                                  the Lower Galilee; focal point of literary activities
                                  of Rabbi Judah ha-Nasi around 200 CE

Betabris: Beit Guvrin; village in the middle of Idumaea;
                                  captured by Vespasian

Betharamphtha (Betharamatha): Tell er-Rama in Jordan; town in Peraea along road
                                  from Jericho to Philadelphia; site of royal palaces
                                  built by Herod; renamed Livias/Iulias; walled by
                                  Herod Antipas; palaces burned by Peraean rebels
                                  at time of the Pentecost revolt in 4 BCE

Bethel:	Beitin; village 12 Roman miles north of Jerusalem; captured by Vespasian in the early summer of 69
Bethennabris/Bethnamaris:	Tell Nimrin; village in the Peraea about 12 miles southwest of Gadara; attacked and captured by Placidus in the spring of 68
Bethleptepha:	Beit Nettif; village 12.4 miles southwest of Jerusalem in Judaea; destroyed by Vespasian in the spring of 68
Bethsaida/Iulias:	El-Araj (probably) or et-Tell (less likely); fishing village of the Gaulanitis, situated at the northeast corner of the Sea of Galilee; renamed Iulia/Iulias after Augustus's wife Livia/Iulia by Herod Philip
Byblos:	Phoenician city, conquered by Alexander the Great; Herod the Great built a city wall for Byblos
Caesarea Maritima:	Harbor city on the Mediterranean coast; seat of the Roman governor during the first century CE; originally a Phoenician town; built up from Straton's Tower by Herod the Great from about 22 to 10 or 9 BCE
Caesarea Philippi:	Paneion/Panias/Banias in the Gaulanitis at the foot of Mt. Hermon; near the source of Jordan River where Herod the Great had temple of Augustus built; city (as opposed to the sanctuary) built up by Philip the Tetrarch; enlarged and renamed Neronias Irenopolis by Agrippa II in 61
Callirrhoe:	Ain ez-Zara in Jordan: location of hot springs visited by Herod seeking a cure for his disease(s) in 4 BCE
Canatha:	Qanawat; polis in Auranitis, part of Decapolis, near Canatha at S'ia; Herod patronized the Temple of Ba'al Shamim there
Capharabis:	Village in Upper Idumaea; surrendered to Cerialis
Caphareccho:	Kefar Ata; village in the Galilee; fortified by Josephus in 66
Caphethra:	Village in Upper Idumaea; burned by Cerialis
Cappadocia:	Region in what is now southeastern Turkey; became a militarized Roman province in 17
Chabulon:	Kabul; village in the foothills of the west Galilee near Ptolemais; attacked by Cestius in the summer of 66 and burned
Chalcis:	Kingdom in the central Beqaa Valley of Lebanon, ruled over by Herod II, grandson of Herod the Great, until his death in 48

Chios: Greek island in the northern Aegean; Herod had a stoa built there and paid off a loan from Augustus

Cilicia: Coastal region of Asia Minor; Herod relieved taxes of towns there

Commagene: Kingdom in southern Anatolia (Turkey), centered on its capital of Samosata on the Upper Euphrates; integrated into the Roman province of Syria around 17 but became dependent client kingdom in 38 under Antiochus IV, who supplied troops for the Roman interventions in the Galilee and Judaea led by Cestius, Vespasian, and Titus

Cos: Greek island in the Dodecanese chain; Herod the Great endowed a gymnasiarchy there

Ctesiphon: Capital of the Parthian empire; on the Tigris River about 21 miles south of modern Baghdad

Cypros: Tell el-'Aqaba; fortress overlooking Jericho and the Wadi Qelt; rebuilt by Herod in two stages (around 34 and 28 BCE) as a memorial to his Nabataean princess mother

Cyrrhus: Town 60 miles northeast of Antioch (Syria) on the River Afrin; winter quarters of Legio X Fretensis

Dabaritta: Deburiah/Daburiyya in the Lower Galilee, at the base of Mt. Tabor to the west; about 5 miles east of Nazareth; town of young men who robbed Ptolemy, Agrippa II's overseer

Damascus: Dimashq; city in southwestern Syria for which Herod the Great had a gymnasium and theater built; site of pogrom of Jews after Cestius's defeat in 66

Decapolis: Administrative association of 10 cities (at times) located (mainly) in the area to the east of the Rift Valley between Syria, Iturea, Nabataea, and Judaea

Docus/Dok: Jebel Qarantal: Hasmonean fortress overlooking (modern) Jericho; occupied by Antigonus during Herod's struggle to take over his kingdom; Herod improved the water system there

Dora/Dor: Coastal town about 19 miles south of Haifa with a Hippodamian plan; young Dorians profaned the synagogue of Dor by introducing a statue of Claudius into it

Drusion: Tower/lighthouse named for Augustus's stepson Drusus, built at end of Caesarea's southern breakwater by Herod

Ein Gedi: Tell Goren; some 10 miles north of Masada along the west coast of the Dead Sea; raided by the *sicarii* of Masada

Elis: District in southern Greece; Eleans responsible for the celebration of the Olympic games; Herod endowed celebrations

Emesa: Homs in modern Syria; Arab state on the Orontes River; King Sohaemus of Emesa contributed troops to the Roman interventions in the Galilee and Judaea led by Cestius, Vespasian, and Titus

Emmaus/later Nicopolis: 'Imwas, near where Roman *centuria* attacked during Pentecost revolt; in 68 Vespasian marched to Emmaus from Caesarea; Legio V marched from Emmaus to Jerusalem in 70

Ephraim: Et-Tayyibe; village east of Gophna captured by Vespasian in the early summer of 69

Esebonitis/Hesbonitis: Hesbon; district in the Peraea around Esebon, rebuilt by Herod the Great around 25 BCE; site of a Herodian military colony

Falacrina: Hometown of Vespasian in Sabine hills of Italy

Gaba: Sha'ar ha-'Amaqim; town in the southwestern Galilee where handpicked cavalry from Herod's army were settled

Gabaon/Gibeon: al-Jib; hill town 6 miles north-northwest of Jerusalem where Cestius camped on the way to Jerusalem and during his retreat

Gabara: Arabah; village or town in the Lower Galilee, six miles north of Iotapata, destroyed by Vespasian and the Romans in the spring of 67

Gadara: Um Qeis; polis of Decapolis, at the northern boundary of the Peraea; given to Herod in late 27 BCE; attacked by Vespasian and Placidus in February of 68

Galilee: Josephus tells his readers that the Galilee, divided up into Upper and Lower Galilee, was enveloped by Phoenicia and Syria (*War* 3.35); in more detail the region was bounded by the Carmel Mountain range at its southeastern point down to the north face of Mt. Gilboa at its southwestern endpoint; Ptolemais and its territory defined its western border; on the east, the Jordan River and the Sea of Galilee divided the Galilee from Gaulanitis and the region of the Decapolis; to the north the territory of the Galilee lay south of the ladder of Tyre to the area around Lake Huleh

Gamala: Gamala in Aramaic; Gamla in Hebrew; fortified town in the territory of Agrippa II in the Gaulanitis (Golan); 7.5 miles northeast of the Sea of Galilee's northernmost point; besieged and captured by Vespasian during the autumn of 67

Garis: Village about 2.5 miles to the east of Sepphoris in the Galilee; abandoned at the approach of Vespasian's army in 67, before the capture of Gabara and Iotapata

Gaulanitis: Region to the east of the Sea of Galilee and the Jordan
                           River from Hippos/Hippus at its southwest point, up north
                           to the slopes of Mt. Hermon, with its eastern and southern
                           boundaries defined by the Yarmuk River and its tributaries;
                           included in the tetrarchy of Herod the Great's son Philip;
                           the rebel stronghold of Gamala in the Gaulanitis was
                           captured and destroyed by Vespasian and his army in the
                           autumn of 67

Gaza: Tell Harube; free city along the via Maris; Philistine and
                           Ptolemaic cultural influences; ceded to Herod by Augustus
                           in 30 BCE; annexed to Syria after Herod's death by Augustus;
                           attacked by Jews in 66 after the massacre in Caesarea

Gema/Ginae: Modern Jenin; village at the top of the plain of Esdraelon/
                           Jezreel

Gennesar, Lake: Name Josephus uses for the Sea of Galilee; Hebrew, Kinneret

Gerasa: Jerash in Jordan; in the Decapolis east of the Jordan River;
                           probable hometown of revolutionary leader Simon

Gerizim, Mt: Jebel a-Tur (overlooking modern Nablus); site of the
                           Samaritan fortress and temple and the Hellenistic city;
                           captured and the temple there razed by John Hyrcanus I;
                           its inhabitants were massacred by Cerialis in 67

Gezer: Gazara; 4.97 miles southeast of Ramle; possible hometown
                           of the rebel Simon; captured by Lucius Annius during the
                           revolt in the spring of 68

Gibeah: Gabath Saul; supposed birthplace of King Saul; village some
                           three to four miles north of Jerusalem; Titus encamped
                           near it on his way to Jerusalem in the spring of 70

Gilead: Yegar-Sahadutha (Aramaic); mountainous area east of the
                           Jordan

Gischala: Gush Halav; largest town in the Upper Galilee, home of
                           John, besieged by Titus

Gophna: Jifna; village to the north of Ramallah; put under command
                           of John, son of Ananias, in 66; Titus camped at Gophna
                           for one night on his way to Jerusalem; place to which
                           several high priests, the sons of high priests. and other
                           notables were sent after fleeing from Jerusalem during the
                           latter stages of the siege of the city in the summer of 70

Hammath: Location of hot springs and community a few miles to the
                           south of Tiberias on the western coast of the Sea of Galilee

Hebron/Kiriath Arba: Haram el-Khalil; site in Idumaea about 19 miles south of
                           Jerusalem, where, during the 30s BCE, Herod had a
                           building built above the caves of Machpelah, which
                           Abraham had purchased as a burial ground; captured by
                           Simon during the revolt; Cerialis later destroyed the town

Herodeion: Possibly Khirbet es-Samra; northeast of the mouth of the Jordan River; fortress on frontier of Arabia

Herodeion/Herodia/Herodium: Jebel Fureidis; toparchy and fortress/palace about 7.5 miles south of Jerusalem where Herod the Great built a fortress-palace and was also buried; destroyed by the Romans in 71

Heshbon: Tell Hesban; town referred to as Esbous, Esebonitis/Essebonitis/Hesbonitis; across the Jordan in the Peraea; conquered by Hyrcanus I in 128 BCE; Herod settled veterans there

Hippos/Hippus: Susita (Aramaic)/Qal'at al-Hisn (Arabic); small town in the Decapolis on the eastern side of the Sea of Galilee; given to Herod at the end of 27 BCE; a massacre of Jews took place there after the destruction of the Jews of Scythopolis

Hyrcania: Khirbet el-Mird; Hasmonean fortress built on a hill above the Buqei'a Valley to the southwest of Qumran, near the Wadi Kidron and the Mar Saba monastery; razed by Gabinius; refortified by Herod; after his execution by his father Herod the Great, Antipater was buried there

Iamnia: Yavneh; given to Herod's sister Salome by Caesar Augustus in 4 BCE; where the Roman tribune Neapolitanus met Agrippa II in 66; captured and garrisoned by Vespasian in the spring of 68; where re-formulation(s) of Judaism took place after the failure of the revolt

Iapha: Yaphia; village southwest of Nazareth in the Lower Galilee; some 9.3 miles south of Iotapata, where Josephus lived; Josephus fortified the village in 66; it was captured by the Romans under M. Ulpius Traianus and Titus in the spring of 67

Iardes: Wooded area along Jordan River where Bassus and his soldiers massacred survivors of the siege of Machaerus

Idumaea: Region of rolling hills bordering on Judaea some 10 miles to the south of Jerusalem (and to the east along the middle section of the Dead Sea shore), including Marissa (destroyed by the Parthians), Adora, Hebron, Engedi, and Masada; today the northern Negev desert; homeland of Herod's family

Ionia: Region of western Asia Minor; Herod provided "liberality" to all districts

Iotapata: Yodefat; fortified town in the Galilee 5.6 miles north (and west) of
                    Sepphoris; besieged and captured by Vespasian in around 47 days
                    in 67; Josephus surrendered to Vespasian here

Itaburion: Mt. Tabor in the Lower Galilee; fortified by Josephus in 66; while
                    Vespasian was besieging Gamala, the tribune Placidus captured
                    Itaburion

Ituraea: Mainly mountainous region of southern Syria spread over the
                    southern part of the Anti-Lebanon Mountains; its main cities were
                    Chalcis, Abila, and Heliopolis (in Baalbek); Herod seems to have
                    had jurisdiction over Ituraea from about 47 to 37 BCE (when
                    Antony forced Herod to cede Ituraea to Cleopatra); after Herod's
                    death parts of it were included in the territory given to the tetrarch
                    Herod Philip; Agrippa II's deputy Noarus came from the nobility
                    of Ituraea

Iulias: *See* Bethsaida/Iulias

Iulias: Betharamtha; village in the Peraea south of Abila; captured and
                    garrisoned by Placidus early in 68

Jamnith: Khirbet Yamnit; Jamnith was one of the villages Josephus claimed
                    to have fortified after his appointment to the generalship of the
                    Galilees and Gamala in 66

Jericho: Tell es-Sultan; desert oasis city in the Jordan Valley northwest of
                    the north shore of the Dead Sea; built up by Herod the Great with
                    three palaces; royal palace(s) upgraded by Archelaus before his
                    banishment in 6

Joppa: Yafo in Israel; coastal port city used by Jerusalemites; conquered by
                    Simon the Hasmonean, giving the dynasty a vital Mediterranean
                    port; made subject to Archelaus after Herod's death; captured by
                    Cestius; put under the command of John the Essene in 66; taken
                    by Vespasian in 67

Judaea: Small (about 50 miles, north to south, by 20 miles, west to east)
                    region with the royal capital of Jerusalem at its center; bounded to
                    the north by the territory of Samaritis; to the south by Idumaea;
                    to the west by the Shephelah (lowland limestone hills, with scrub
                    and woods), and farther east by coastal Philistia; and to the east
                    and southeast by the Dead Sea; densely populated according to
                    Josephus, though belied by the settlement record

Kedasa: Qedesh; Tyrian village six miles northeast of Gischala, where Titus
                    encamped as John of Gischala escaped

Lacedaemon: Sparta in the Peloponnesus; Herod made offerings there

Ladder of Tyre: Promontory of el Musheirifeh or en-Naqurah, 12 miles north of
                    Acre/Acco/Ptolemais

Laodicea: Latakya; coastal city in northern Syria; Herod the Great had an
                    aqueduct built for it; winter quarters of Legio VI Ferrata

Leontopolis: City northeast of Memphis, at the southern end of the Nile Delta where a temple was built by Onias IV during the reign of Ptolemy VI Philometor for the worship of Yahweh and sacrifices to him were made; Vespasian had the temple destroyed in 73 or 74

Lugdunum: City in Gaul (modern Lyon) to which Herod Antipas was exiled

Lycia: Region of southern Asia Minor; Herod provided gifts

Lydda/Diospolis: Lod, 9.3 miles southeast of Tel Aviv; captured and burned by Cestius around 11–15 Tishri of 66

Mabartha: Flavia Neapolis/Shechem/Nablus; Vespasian passed Mabartha in the late spring of 68

Machaerus: Jebel al-Mishnaqa in Jordan, near village of Mukawer; fortress refuge 4.5 miles east of the Dead Sea in the ancient Peraea, on the border with Nabataea; originally a Hasmonean fortress built by Alexander Jannaeus around 90 BCE; after its destruction by the Roman Gabinius in 57 BCE it was rebuilt by Herod the Great after around 30 BCE; after being demolished in 36 CE by Aretas IV of Nabataea it was then rebuilt by the Romans; captured again by the Romans (Legio X Fretensis) in 71

Magdala/Migdal: *See* Tarichaeae/Magdala

Mamre: Ramet el-Khalil; site in Idumaea some 2.5 miles north of Hebron; Herod had it enclosed with a sanctuary wall during the 30s BCE

Marisa/Maresha: Tell Sandahannah in the Judaean Shephelah (lowlands); in western Idumaea (during the Hellenistic Period), about 25 miles southwest of Jerusalem; conquered by the Hasmoneans by 108–107 BCE; many different ethnic groups lived there; possibly the hometown of Herod's family

Masada: Mesa, overlooking the Dead Sea from the west; fortresses built there by Hasmoneans; greatly expanded by Herod; where Roman siege took place in 73 or 74 and 967 Jews slew each other rather than surrender to the Romans

Melitene: Region along Euphrates (near modern Malatya in eastern Turkey); Legio XII Fulminata sent there after the destruction of Jerusalem in 70

Mero: Maruss (Arabic) in the Upper Galilee; one of the places fortified by Josephus in 66

Modein: Tel al-Ras; ancient village located at the northeastern edge of the Low Shephelah about 15 miles from Jerusalem; where Matthias, the leader of the resistance movement in 166 BCE, lived with his four sons

Moesia: Roman province in Balkans south of the Danube River; Legio V sent back there (Oescus) after the destruction of Jerusalem in 70

Nabataea: Kingdom to the east of Judaea, with changing areas of occupation
                     during the third and second centuries BCE; expanded up north
                     to Damascus by the 30s BCE; ruled by Aretas IV in 4 BCE;
                     homeland of Herod's mother Cypros; in Josephus Nabataea is
                     usually interchangeable with Arabia

Narbata: Town/toparchy, some six to seven miles southeast of Caesarea;
                     many Jews moved there from Caesarea because of persecution in 66

Neara: Village a few miles north of Jericho; Archelaus redirected its water
                     source

Nicopolis: "Victory" city in Epirus, on the west coast of Greece; Herod
                     endowed public buildings there

Oresa: Khirbet Khoreisa; town south of Hebron captured by Herod after
                     he rescued his family from Masada (after his return from Rome in
                     39 BCE)

Paneas/Banias: *See* Caesarea Philippi

Pannonia: Roman province south and west of the Danube, with Noricum
                     and Upper Italy to its west and Dalmatia and (Upper) Moseia
                     to its south; Legio XV was sent there after the destruction of
                     Jerusalem in 70

Parthia: Region/kingdom of northeastern Iran; from the early second
                     century BCE, base of the Arsacid dynasty that conquered most of
                     Iran and came into contact and conflict with the Romans along the
                     Euphrates from the time of Pompey and Crassus

Pella: Fahil; on the northern boundary of the Peraea; one of the cities in
                     the Decapolis; sacked by the Jews in retaliation for the Syrian
                     massacre of Jews in Caesarea

Pentapolis: "Five-polis" or association of five cities in Libya; western portion of
                     Cyrenaica

Peraea: Region east of the Jordan River Valley from Machaerus north
                     to Pella (but not including it) and Gadara (not mentioned by
                     Josephus); west from Philadelphia (though also not in it) to the
                     Jordan River; its lands were bounded by Moab to the south and
                     Arabia, Heshbonitis (Hesbon), Philadelphia, and Gerasa to the
                     east, according to Josephus; Herod had his brother Pheroras made
                     tetrarch of the region by Augustus's permission; Pheroras ruled
                     over the Pereaea until 5 BCE

Pergamon: City in Mysia in western Asia Minor; Herod made offerings there

Phasaelis: Fasayli; town 8.7 miles northeast of Jericho, perhaps founded by
                     Herod the Great in honor of his older brother; included in the
                     toparchy of Salome in Herod's will; confirmed by Caesar Augustus

Phaselis: Greek coastal city in Lycia; Herod provided Phaselis with tax relief

Philadelphia: Amman in Jordan, polis of the Decapolis to the east of the Jordan
                     River; became focus of dispute with local Jews over village of Zia
                     in 44 CE, attacked by Jews in 66 after the massacre at Caesarea

Pontus: Roman province on the southern coast of the Black Sea

Ptolemais: Akko/Acre; Herod the Great had a gymnasium built for it; served as the mustering point for the invasions of the Galilee and Judaea by Cestius, Vespasian, and Titus

Qumran: Settlement by northwestern shore of the Dead Sea, about eight miles south of Jericho; destroyed by the Romans in 68; where the Dead Sea Scrolls were found in 11 caves nearby in 1946–47

Rabbath-Ammon: Amman in Jordan

Raphaneae: Home of the Twelfth legion before the war of 66–74; located on the road south of Apamea in Syria

Rhodes: Largest island in Dodecanese chain; Herod the Great subsidized shipbuilding there and rebuilt the Pythian Temple

Ruma: Galilaean village; home of Netiras and Philip, who fought the Romans at Iotapata

Saba: Village in the Galilee; hometown of Eleazar, who fought at Iotapata

Samaria/Sebaste: Capital city of the northern kingdom of Israel; main site of Samaritis; rebuilt by Herod the Great as Sebaste in 27 BCE, with temple dedicated to Roma and Augustus; inhabited by a nearby veteran colony

Samaritis: Region described by Josephus (along with Judaea) between the Galilee to the north and Judaea to the south; its northern border ran roughly along the line of the Mt. Carmel range (to the northwest) to the southwest with a focal point at Ginae (Jenin), where its eastern border was formed by the Jordan River; its southern border was an uncertain boundary that began a few miles north of Jerusalem; to the west its border followed the line of the hill country southward

Samos: Island just off the coast of western Asia Minor; Herod made gifts to the Samians

Samosata: Samsat; capital of Commagene, on the west bank of the Euphrates; 180 miles northeast of Antioch; non-winter camp of Legio VI Ferrata

Sappho/Sampho: Saffa (?); fortified village in Samaritis

Scythopolis: Biblical Beth Shean (House of Shan); between Nahal Asi and Nahal Harod, south of the Sea of Galilee; largest town in the Decapolis during the first century CE; site of massacre of Jews in 66

Sebastos: Greek word for emperor; name of the harbor of Caesarea

Selame: Salameh; village in Galilee between Beer-Sheva and Iotapata fortified by Josephus in 66

Seleucia: Seluqiyeh (?); village in the Gaulanitis fortified by Josephus in 66

Sennabris/Philoteria: Beth Yerah/Khirbet el-Karak (ruin of the fortress); on the southern shore of the Sea of Galilee; site of one of Vespasian's camps

Seph: Safad (?)/Tzefat; site in Lower Galilee fortified by Josephus in 66

Sepphoris: Tzippori; fortified by Herod Antipas and renamed Autocratoris; largest town in the Lower Galilee in 66 and became bastion of loyalty to Rome

Sidon: Saïda; Phoenician city; Herod the Great had a theater built for it

Sigoph: Village in the Galilee fortified by Josephus in 66

Soganaea: Yehudiyye in the Lower Golan or Sujen or Siyar es-Sujen in the Upper Golan; village fortified by Josephus in 66

Soganai: Village in Lower Galillee, fortified by Josephus in 66

Solyma: Unidentified village in the east part of the Gaulanitis; revolted against Agrippa II

Straton's Tower: Founded during the period of Persian rule; rebuilt and renamed Caesarea by Herod the Great

Tabor, Mt.: Itaburion; mountain in the Galilee, 1,840 feet above sea level; captured by Placidus

Tarichaeae/Magdala: Migdal; walled village about 3.4 miles north of Tiberias along the northwestern shore of the Sea of Galilee; where Josephus faced down the followers of John of Gischala and Jesus, son of Sapphias, in the hippodrome; pacified by Vespasian in 67

Thamna: Khirbet Tibne; toparchy put under command of John the Essene in 66

Thekoa: Tekoa; village about 5 miles south of Bethlehem

Thella: Khirbet Tleil; village on the southern shore (in antiquity) of Lake Semechonitis (modern Huleh in Arabic) that marked the northern boundary of the Upper Galilee

Threx: Hasmonean fortress overlooking Jericho; part of chain of fortresses built for security against Nabataeans and cities of Decapolis

Tiberias: Polis on the coast of the Sea of Galilee between Mt. Berenice (west) and the sea (east); founded by Herod Antipas by 20–21 CE; included Greek-style institutions and buildings; in 67 there were three factions in the city; surrendered to Vespasian in 67 without a fight

Tirithana: Village in Samaritis at the foot of Mt. Gerizim

Trachonitis: Rough stone region (modern Al-Leja); south and east of Damascus; not included in the original kingdom given to Herod by the Romans in 40 BCE but gifted to him at the end of 27 BCE; included in the tetrarchy of Herod's son Philip; after his death became part of the province of Syria

Tripolis:	Tripoli; northern Phoenician and Greek city where Herod the Great had a gymnasium built
Tyre:	Sur; Phoenician coastal city; Herod the Great had halls, porticoes, temples, and marketplaces built for it
Tyros:	Araq el-Emir in Transjordan; home/fortress of the Tobiads built by Hyrcanus
Vienna:	Vienne; city in Gaul to which Archelaus was exiled by Augustus in 6 CE
Xaloth:	Iksal (Arabic); village in the Jezreel Plain of Lower Galilee
Zeugma/Seleucia:	Belkis; Commagenian town on the west bank of the middle Euphrates, some 120 miles northeast of Antioch, Syria; base of Legio IIII Scythica
Zia:	Village in the Peraea 15 miles west of Philadelphia; became involved in boundary dispute with Jews of Peraea

JERUSALEM TOPOGRAPHY

Adiabenian Palaces:	Palaces of the rulers of Adiabene, who converted to Judaism and moved to Jerusalem; located to the south of the Temple Mount in the Lower City; at the Givati site in the City of David
Agrippeion:	Wing of Herod the Great's palace in Jerusalem; named in honor of Agrippa
Akra:	"High Point"; Seleucid-era fortress built on the southeast corner of the Temple Mount during the reign of Antiochos IV Epiphanes; razed by Simon in 141 BCE; sections of the wall and one tower from the fortress have been found under the Givati parking lot south of the city walls (near the Dung Gate) and the Temple Mount
Amygdalon pool:	Towers'/Hezekiah pool, against which the Roman Tenth legion built an embankment in 70
Ananus Tomb:	Tomb of high priest Ananus; in the southern end of the Hinnom Valley
Antonia:	Fortress connected to Temple by porticoes; on the northwestern corner of the Temple Mount; built by Herod the Great on top of a previous Hasmonean-era fortress; named for his Roman patron Antony; remains today are (probably) under the Ummariya School
Barclay's Gate:	One of the gates in the western section of the temenos wall built by Herod giving access to the Temple Mount
Basilica:	"Royal Stoa"; colonnaded building built by Herod on the south side of the Temple Mount; its 162 columns had gilded capitals
Bezetha:	Suburb of the New City of Jerusalem; to the north-northwest of the Temple; enclosed by the so-called third wall built by Herod Agrippa I; Cestius led his army into the New City on 30 Huperberetaeus and set fire to Bezetha

"Burnt House":	House in the eastern part of the Upper City associated with priestly Kathros family; destroyed in the fighting in Jerusalem during the Roman siege or by the Romans in its aftermath
Caesarion:	Wing of Herod the Great's palace in Jerusalem; named in honor of Caesar (Augustus)
Caiaphas's Palace:	Palace south of the palace of Herod in the Upper City
Camp of the Assyrians:	Military camp where Sennacherib's army supposedly had set up camp during their siege of the city in 622 BCE; probably located in the valley between the modern streets Shivtei Yisra'el and Derekh Shkhem (the Nablus Road), to the north of the second wall within the New City; where Titus encamped after breaching the third wall
Chamber of Sanhedrin:	*Lishkath ha-Gazith* in the Mishnah; probably located beside and to the east of the Xystus in the direction of the Temple Mount but outside the Upper City; set afire by the Romans after the destruction of the Temple
Court of Nations:	Court of the Temple in Jerusalem; probably located where the Dome of the Rock is today
David's Tomb:	Controversially said to be located in the Upper City on Mt. Zion
Essene Gate:	Gate at southwestern corner of the Lower City
First Wall:	Wall built during the Hasmonean period (second half of the second century BCE); enclosed the Upper City of Jerusalem on the western hill of the city
Gennath Gate:	Gate in the First Wall; at the Gennath (Garden) Gate the Second Wall began that enclosed Jerusalem's northern section, connecting up to the Antonia Fortress; now in the Jewish Quarter of the city
Gihon Spring:	Spring outside the city wall, providing water to the Siloam Pool (fountain or reservoir) at the southeastern corner of the Lower City or City of David (essentially Jerusalem's southeastern hill)
Hasmonean Palace:	In the northeastern section of the Upper City, west of the Temple Mount and the Bridge or Wilson's Arch
Herod's Monuments:	Structures that originally were intended to serve as burial places for Herod and his relatives; they probably were located outside the first wall, adjacent to the Serpent's Pool
Herod's Palace(s):	Built between 29 to 28 and 23 BCE; located to the east of Jerusalem's western wall in the Upper City (under today's Armenian Garden); inside the Third Wall; covering about 11 acres
Hezekiah's Pool:	Towers' Pool; next to the Tomb of John Hyrcanus; Titus began his siege of Jerusalem's walls here along the Third Wall in the spring of 70

Hinnom Valley:	Valley beginning at today's Jaffa Gate; intersects with the Kidron and Tyropoeon Valleys at the southern end of the City of David
Hippicus:	One of three towers built by Herod the Great as part of the citadel that guarded his palace to the south; located at the northwestern corner of the First Wall; named after Herod's friend who had fallen in battle
Hippodrome:	Also called an amphitheater by Josephus; possibly located in the Lower City; some scholars think it was located farther south of the city
Huldah Gates:	Double gates, two main entrance and exit gates on the southern side of the Temple Mount
Huldah's Tomb:	Tomb of the prophetess Huldah; probably located south of Huldah's Gates in the Lower City
Kidron Valley:	Ravine running north-south between the Temple Mount and the Mount of Olives
Lower City:	Spur or hill of the old City of David southwest of the Temple Mount, where the Akra, council chamber, Ophel/Ophlas, and palace of Queen Helena were located
Mariamme:	One of three towers built by Herod the Great as part of the citadel that guarded his palace to the south; located at the northwestern corner of the First Wall; named after his Hasmonean wife
Mount of Olives:	Hill to the east of Jerusalem's center, across the Kidron Valley, where the Roman Tenth Legion encamped in 70 at the beginning of the siege of Jerusalem
Mount Scopus:	Hill 0.87 miles to the north-northeast of the city center of Jerusalem; where Cestius originally pitched his camp in 66; in 70 CE Titus initially had a camp for the Twelfth and Fifteenth Legions there
Nicanor Gate:	Triple gate with doors made of Corinthian bronze; provided access to the inner temple area from the Court of Women to the east
Ophlas (in Greek):	Opel (Hebrew); hill south of the Temple Mount, southeast of the Huldah Gates, and northeast of the city of David, rebuilt during the fifth century BCE; where Menahem was killed by Eleazar's men in August of 66; held by John and his men in spring of 70; set ablaze by the Romans after the destruction of the Temple
Palace of Queen Helena:	Palace located on the southeastern hill of Jerusalem in the Lower City (in the center of the Acra/Akra); probably beneath the modern Givati parking lot, outside of the Dung Gate; supposedly built by "Grapte"; the fire the Romans set after the destruction of the Temple reached the palace

Peristereon:	"Dovecote"; rock on the western slope of the southern section of the Mount of Olives; incorporated into circumvallation wall built by Titus in Jerusalem
Phasael Tower:	Tallest of three towers built by Herod the Great as part of the citadel that guarded his palace to the south; at the northwestern corner of the First Wall; named after Herod's older brother
Pool of Israel:	Birket Isra'in (Arabic); now in the Valley of St. Anne; pool or reservoir adjacent to the northeastern side of the Temple Mount
Psephinus Tower:	Tower at northwestern corner of Third or Outer Wall
Robinson's Arch:	Arch above stairway (and gate) at southwestern corner of Temple Mount; named after Edward Robinson who discovered the arch in 1839
Royal Stoa:	*See* Basilica; two-story building built on south side of enlarged Herodian Temple Mount
Second Wall:	Built by Alexander Jannaeus or more likely Herod, enclosing an area of more than 60 acres north of the First Wall
Serpent's Pool:	Birket es Sultan (Barquq); Sultan's Pool; reservoir to the west of Mt. Zion in the upper part of the Hinnom Valley, outside the first wall
Sheep Pools:	Also known as Pools of Bethesda (House of Mercy); located near Lions' Gate today; reservoirs north of the Temple Mount, alongside Sheep Market
Siloam Pool:	Pool (reservoir) within the city wall at the southeast corner of the city
Struthion Pools:	"Sparrow" (Greek) pools around the northwest corner of Antonia
Temple Mount	*Har ha-bayit;* esplanade on which stood the so-called Second Temple, consecrated by 516 BCE; enlarged by Herod after about 23 BCE to roughly twice the size of its predecessor; locus of fighting during the Roman siege in the summer of 70
Theater:	Perhaps located south and west of the Temple Mount in the Upper City
Third Wall:	Construction started by King Agrippa I; enclosed Bezetha Quarter or the Upper City; finished as the revolt broke out in 66
Timber Market:	Outside today's Damascus Gate; in the Upper City
Tomb of Hyrcanus:	Tomb of John Hyrcanus I (135 to 105–104 BCE); adjacent to the Towers' Pool or Hezekiah's Pool; Titus began his siege of Jerusalem's walls here along the Third Wall in the spring of 70
Tomb of Jannaeus:	Tomb of Alexander Jannaeus; within the Third Wall in the Upper City, north of the Temple Mount

Tomb of Kings:	Tomb of Queen Helena and Izates, north of Jerusalem's third wall, opposite the gate from the Women's Towers
Towers' Pool:	Hezekiah's Pool; next to the tomb of John Hyrcanus; Titus began his siege of Jerusalem's walls along the Third Wall here in the spring of 70
Tyropoeon Valley:	"Valley of the Cheese-Makers" in Greek; Central Valley today; valley west of the City of David dividing what is called the "Old City" today from the Damascus Gate southward, intersecting with the Kidron Valley at the southern end of the City of David
Upper Agora:	Market to the east of Herod's palace in the Upper City
Upper City:	Built on ridge of western hill at the end of the first Temple period; resettled during the second century BCE; essentially where Jerusalem's Jewish Quarter is today; many (but not all) of Jerusalem's wealthy families lived in this area during the first century CE
Western ("Wailing") Wall:	Temenos wall on the western side of the expanded Temple Mount organized by Herod
Wilson's Arch:	Easternmost arch integrated into the western wall of the Temple mount at connection point of the bridge that connected the Temple to the Xystus
Women's Towers:	Gate near the Psephinus Tower at northwestern corner of the third wall
Xystus:	Long colonnade or portico, with open exercise and meeting area adjacent; east of the Hasmonean Palace; later used as an assembly place
Zion:	Originally the name of the southeast hill of Jerusalem; alternately called the City of David

ROMAN TOPOGRAPHY

Amphitheater:	Amphitheatrum (Colosseum), built on the site of the great lake in the atrium of Nero's Domus Aurea (Golden House) during reign of Vespasian, though dedicated by Titus
Arch of Titus:	Arch in the Roman Forum, along the Via Sacra; completed during reign of Domitian
Capitoline:	Hill in Rome between the Roman Forum and the Campus Martius; where Temple of Jupiter Optimus Maximus is located; temple burned down by Vitellius's soldiers 19 December 69 CE
Mamertine prison:	Located at the northeast end of the Roman Forum; where Simon bar Giora was executed at the end of the triumph of Vespasian and Titus in the summer of 71

Palatine Hill: Location of the Temple of Apollo in Rome; where Caesar Augustus listened to arguments about what to do with Herod's kingdom in 4 BCE

Porta Triumphalis: Location uncertain but perhaps east of the Porta Flumentana near the Capitoline; through which the triumphal procession of Vespasian and Titus entered the city of Rome in the summer of 71

Porticus of Octavia: Porticus built by Augustus in honor of his sister Octavia Minor, enclosing temples of Jupiter Stator and Juno Regina; where Vespasian and Titus received senators, chief magistrates, and equestrians on the morning of their triumph

Temple of Isis: Located in the Campus Martius; where Vespasian, Titus, and Domitian spent the night before Vespasian's and Titus's triumph during the summer of 71

Temple of Jupiter Capitolinus: Located on Capitoline Hill; the second version of the temple was burned down during fighting in Rome on 19 December 69 CE; it was here that the triumphal procession of Vespasian and Titus ended in the summer of 71

Temple of Peace: Located southeast of the Forum Romanum between the Via Sacra and the Carinae; completed during the sixth year of Vespasian's reign; within it were stored the Table of Shewbread and the seven-branched candlestick from the Jerusalem Temple

Abbreviations

AE	L'Année épigraphique
AJN	American Journal of Numismatics
AJP	American Journal of Philology
AS	Ancient Society
BA	Biblical Archaeologist
BAIAS	Bulletin of the Anglo-Israel Archaeological Society
BAR	Biblical Archaeology Review
BASOR	Bulletin of the American Schools of Oriental Research
CHJ	Cambridge History of Judaism
CIIP	Corpus Inscriptionum Iudaeae/Palaestinae
CIL	Corpus Inscriptionum Latinarum
CPJ	Corpus Papyrorum Judaicarum
CQ	Classical Quarterly
CRAI	Comptes rendus de l'Académie des inscriptions et belles lettres
CW	The Classical World
EI	Eretz-Israel
FGrH	Die Fragmente der Griechischen Historiker
GCS	Griechischen Christlichen Schriftsteller der ersten Jahrhunderte
GLAJJ	Greek and Latin Authors on Jews and Judaism
GRBS	Greek, Roman, and Byzantine Studies
HSCP	Harvard Studies in Classical Philology
HTR	Harvard Theological Review

HUCA	Hebrew Union College Annual
IEJ	Israel Exploration Journal
IG	Inscriptiones graecae
IJNA	International Journal of Nautical Archaeology
ILS	Inscriptiones Latinae Selectae
INJ	Israel Numismatic Journal
INR	Israel Numismatic Research
JAJ	Journal of Ancient Judaism
JBL	Journal of Biblical Literature
JJS	Journal of Jewish Studies
JNES	Journal of Near Eastern Studies
JQR	Jewish Quarterly Review
JRA	Journal of Roman Archaeology
JRS	Journal of Roman Studies
JSJ	Journal for the Study of Judaism in the Persian, Hellenistic, and Roman Period
NEA	Near Eastern Archaeology
NEAEHL	The New Encyclopedia of Archaeological Excavations in the Holy Land
NovT	Novum Testamentum
NTS	New Testament Studies
OEANE	Oxford Encyclopedia of Archaeology in the Near East
OGIS	Orientis graeci inscriptiones selectae
OLZ	Orientalistische Literaturzeitung
PEQ	Palestine Exploration Quarterly
RB	Revue Biblique
REG	Revue des Études Grecques
REJ	Revue des Études Juives
RM	Rheinisches Museum für Philologie
SCI	Scripta Classica Israelica
Transeu	Transeuphratène
UF	Ugarit-Forschungen
ZDPV	Zeitschrift des Deutschen Palästina-Vereins
ZPE	Zeitschrift für Papyrologie und Epigraphik

Notes

INTRODUCTION: A SMALL AND INSIGNIFICANT WAR?

1. Josephus, *The War of Jews against Romans* (hereafter *War*) Book 2.289. Book and chapter references to Josephus's *War* and his other writings, including the *Antiquities, Life,* and *Against Apion,* hereafter refer to the English translations of those works by Thackeray, Marcus, and Feldman. Full bibliographic citations to translations by these authors can be found in the references.
2. *War* 2.285; for the location of a synagogue there that might be the one referred to in Josephus's text, see Patrich (2007) p. 109; Krause (2017) generally for the representation of synagogues by Josephus. It is tempting to associate the synagogue that Josephus mentions with "the Synagogue site" in Govaars, Spiro, and White (2009), located in "Field O" of the Caesarea Maritima excavations on the coast to the north of the Crusader Castle. The uncertainties about the dating of published materials from that site, however, warrant caution. Here and throughout this work I translate *Ioudaioi* in Josephus's texts as "Jews" because in the vast majority of cases where Josephus uses the term to describe a person or people in his accounts of the war, the person or persons are Jews, even if they are Roman citizens, such as Josephus himself. Judaea may be a place, a kingdom that includes non-Jews in it, and Josephus may have moved from conceiving of *Iudaioi* as the people of a territory to people with a religious affiliation, but a *Iudaios* is a Jew in most references in Josephus's works. For discussion, see D. Schwartz (2005) pp. 68–78, (2007b) pp. 3–27, (2014); Mason (2007) pp. 457–512; Esler (2009) pp. 73–91.
3. *War* 2.285–86.
4. *War* 2.286–88.
5. *War* 2.289–90. ,
6. *War* 2.291–92.
7. *War* 2.293–95.
8. *War* 2.296–308.

9. Or *har ha-bayit,* the mountain of the house, as the pre-Herodian temenos was called in Hebrew. For the argument that technically only the 500 square cubit pre-Herodian sanctuary was called the "mountain of the house," see Ritmeyer (2006) p. 339.

10. *War* 2.309–32.

11. *War* 2.333–41.

12. *War* 2.342–401.

13. *War* 2.405–7.

14. *War* 2.408–10.

15. Philo, *Embassy to Gaius* 157.

16. D. Schwartz (2009a) p. 393.

17. For background information about Josephus as a source for the war, see appendix A, "Sources for the War."

18. See Lapin (2017c) p. 245, (2017a) pp. 414–15; he gives a population for Jerusalem of 33,000.

19. *War* 6.420.

20. For the population estimate, see Lapin (2017a) p. 415.

21. See Millar (2005) pp. 101–28 for an overview.

22. See Mason (1991) pp. 125–28 for the argument that the Greek word *hairesis* should be translated as the school founded by Judas the Galilaean in 6 CE rather than as the sect; and Klawans (2012) p. 9, arguing that where there are multiple schools of thought, the term "sectarianism" is useful. For a summary of the views of those who argue that the Essenes and the Sadducees disappeared or were unable to respond to the crisis, as well as the counterarguments, see Klawans (2012) pp. 201–6.

23. *War* 2.154–58; Klawans (2012) p. 34.

24. See Goodman (1994b) pp. 347–56; Herr (2009) pp. 211–36; Klawans (2012) pp. 17–18, 215–22.

25. For the number of 4,000 Essenes, see *Antiquities* 18.20.

26. For a similar conclusion about the theological argument, see Klawans (2012) p. 215, although Klawans rightly points out that we have no definite idea how and why the Essenes and Sadducees disappeared.

27. See generally Cohn (2012) and Gregerman (2016) pp. 137–213 on rabbinic views from the midrash Lamentations Rabbah.

28. For doubts about the historicity of the story, which is found in rabbinic accounts, see Bavli Gittin 56a–b; Lamentations Rabati 1.5.31; Abot de Rabbi Nathan, Version A ("The Fathers According to Rabbi Nathan") chapter 4; and Abot de Rabbi Nathan, Version B, chapter 6, but not in Josephus; see Price (1992) pp. 264–70. As Price rightly points out, while the story of Johanan's escape from Jerusalem fits the circumstances of what Josephus reports about the state of the city (in early 69) and could be used to support the case that Johanan left the city by June of 69, in the rabbinic sources there are just too many historical impossibilities—in particular, the meeting between Johanan and Vespasian—for the second half of the story to be accepted. Most importantly, the sages unfortunately substituted Vespasian for Titus as the besieger of Jerusalem: Vespasian rode up to the city walls of Jerusalem but did not take part in the siege (*War* 4.551). Since they never met, Johanan cannot have told Vespasian that he would become emperor and then received Iamnia as the site for his academy.

29. Rajak (2002) p. 128 n. 65, p. 188; Cohn (2012).

30. Vermes (2014) p. 35 dates the loss of independence from the time when the Roman general Pompey entered the Holy of Holies in the Temple in 63 BCE until 1948.

31. Mason (2016) pp. 14, 508, 511.

32. Mason (2016) p. 43.

33. Tacitus, *Annals* 4.5.1 reports 25 legions during the reign of Tiberius. For the 28 legions during the early empire, see Keppie (1998) pp. 142–43, 190, 205–13. Included in Keppie's list of attested first-century CE legions are I Germanica; II Augusta; III Augusta; III Cyrenaica; III Gallica; IIII Macedonica (disbanded in 69 CE but re-formed as IIII Flavia Felix); IIII Scyth-

ica; V Alaudae; V Macedonica; VI Ferrata; VI Victrix; VII Claudia; VIII Augusta; IX Hispana; X Fretensis; X Gemina; XI Claudia; XII Fulminata; XIII Gemina; XIV Gemina; XV Apollonaris; XVI Gallica; XVII (destroyed with Varus in 9 CE); XVIII (destroyed with Varus in 9 CE); XIX (destroyed with Varus in 9 CE); XX Valeria Victrix; XXI Rapax; XXII Deotariana; XV Primigenia (raised by Gaius in 39 CE); XXII Primigenia (raised by Gaius); I Italica (raised by Nero in 66 or 67); II Adiutrix (raised during civil war in 69). Depending on the date you choose to mark the total, you could argue for 28 legions at the beginning of the great revolt or 29 by the time of Jerusalem's siege. On the total number of legionaries during the period, see the estimates of Hopkins (1978) p. 33 for 156,000 citizen soldiers out of a citizen population of 1,800,000 in 23 BCE; Rankov (2007) p. 71, giving a figure on paper of approximately 160,000 in the middle of the second century CE, including 28 legions, the praetorian and urban cohorts, and the *equites singulares Augusti;* and Bang (2013) p. 419, giving a "realistic strength" of 110,000 to 123,200 and a "notional strength" of 137,500 to 154,000. For the size of the empire, see Bang (2013) p. 427.

34. Numbers 20.8–12, reflecting one of the priestly editorial traditions. In Deuteronomy 1.36 and 3.26, God is angry with Moses on account of the actions of the people. In both cases there is guilt, whether personal or collective.

35. In Deutcronomy 34 Moses, in good health, seems to die for no other reason than that he had reached the 120-year life span allotted to humans by God in Genesis 6.3. The connection between the ordinance in Genesis and Moses's good health was noted by Josephus in *Antiquities* 1.152, 3.85, 4.176–93. Schmid (2007) p. 250 attributes this explanatory *inclusio* about ordinances to a Pentateuchal redactor.

36. For example, see *War* 4.323; *Antiquities* 20.165–66. For the composition of Josephus's *War* and the *Antiquities,* see appendix A.

37. Ezra 4.23

38. Baruch 2.1–12.

39. B. Shabbat 119b; Yom 9b. For a summary of different rabbinic views, see Gafni (2007) p. 306; Gregerman (2016) pp. 144–45.

40. Lamentations Rabbah 5.1; Gregerman (2016) pp. 191–94.

41. Gregerman (2016) p. 225. Schumer (2017a) argues convincingly that the rabbis remembered and memorialized the destruction of the Temple in their writings not only to establish their authority but also for their own sets of memorial purposes. Most importantly, Schumer argues persuasively that these literary commemorations have to be understood in context and that they changed over time.

42. Justin Martyr, *Dialogue with Trypho* 16, 72, 135; Origen, *Against Celsus* 4.32, 4.73, 5.31, 8.69, 2.8; Eusebius, *Proof of the Gospel* 8.2, 399d–400a; 6.18, 285a; 9.3, 425b; 6.23, 303a; 10.6, 486a; 1.6, 18b–c; Gregerman (2016) pp. 27–28, 45–47, 56, 69–71, 73, 76–78, 83; 88–89, 110, 111–19, 122, 131, 135.

43. For example, Gregorios Nazianzenos, *Oration* 5.3–4; Gregerman (2016) pp. 230–31.

44. See Pipes (2001) pp. 49–66 for a survey.

45. *Jerusalem Post,* 27 October 2015, "Grand Mufti: There Was Never a Jewish Temple on Temple Mount." In the article the mufti is quoted as saying in 2010, "There never was a Temple in any period, nor was there, at any time, any place of worship for the Jews or others at the Aksa Mosque site."

46. Nusseibeh (2009) p. 372, arguing that the sanctity of the location of the Haram Al-Sharif must have preceded Muhammad's visit to it.

47. Although most scholars do not disagree that its destruction was a cataclysmic event, one that represented a turning point in the periodization of the historical experience of Jews, see Schremer (2008) pp. 183–99, (2010); Klawans (2010) pp. 278–309, (2012) pp. 180–81; Tuval (2012) pp. 181–239; S. Schwartz (2014) pp. 85–89.

48. For a still valuable, though partial, catalog of such revolts, see Dyson (1971).

49. Tacitus, *Annals* 1.3, 2.88; Cassius Dio 57.18.1; Matyszak (2004) pp. 164–77; Murdoch (2006).

50. Tacitus, *Annals* 14.29–39; Matyszak (2004) pp. 178–90.

51. Tacitus, *Histories* 4.12–37.

52. For discussion of the effects and their interpretations, see Herr (2009) pp. 211–36. D. Schwartz (2012) pp. 1–19 argues that Judaism itself was shattered by the events of 70 and 135 CE. For another view, see Klawans (2012) pp. 180–209.

53. On the scale of the operation, see Millar (2005) pp. 101–2.

54. Notably since the 1960s by the adherents of the Temple Mount Faithful, led initially by the secularist Gershon Salomon and, since the 1980s, by the supporters of the Temple Institute, founded by Rabbi Yisrael Ariel.

55. See Haggai 1.1–8; for Zerubbabel's descent, see 1 Chronicles 3.19; for the completion of the Temple in the sixth year of the rule of Darius I, see Ezra 6.15.

56. See Inbari (2009) for an excellent overview of the different groups that wish to build a third temple; Persico (2014); see also Klawans (2012) pp. 198–200 (with bibliography in the notes) on the controversy over whether the destruction of the Temple made atonement impossible.

57. Staff, *Times of Israel*, 1 August 2017.

58. Persico (2014).

59. For the practice and location of the trumpeter, see *War* 4.582; for the inscription (sign) in Hebrew reading "to the place of trumpeting for" on the parapet stone from the roof at the southwest corner of the Temple Mount, confirming the tradition mentioned by Josephus, see *CIIP Vol. I, Part 1* (2010) no. 5 pp. 49–50; Richardson and Fisher (2018) p. 302 for exegesis.

60. Approximately 2.3 billion Christians, 1.8 billion Muslims, and 14.7 million Jews at the end of 2018, according to the statistics of the Central Bureau of Statistics of Israel; see https://www.timesofisrael.com/number-of-jews-worldwide-nears-1925s-level/.

61. See Gregerman (2016) p. 1 n. 2 for biblical references to how the destruction of the First Temple conditioned responses to the destruction of the Second Temple. Eusebius is the author most closely associated with the idea that the Jews' alleged execution of Jesus was the worst sin of all and therefore merited the greatest punishment; see *Proof of the Gospel* 9.1, 419b. For Eusebius, the sin was so great that it led to the irrevocable abridgment of the covenant; 10.6, 486a.

62. Gregerman (2016) p. 196.

CHAPTER 1. HEROD AGONISTES

1. The characterization of Herod as Herod the Horrible is taken from Vermes (2014) p. xi, who states that Herod was "heroic and horrible." The vast majority of scholars accept the spring of 4 BCE as the season and year in which Herod's reign and life ended. For evidence supporting Josephus's dating of his death shortly before Passover (in the spring of 4 BCE), see Kushnir-Stein (1995a) pp. 73–86, (2007) pp. 55–56; Kokkinos (1998) pp. 372–73, argues for 5 BCE; and more recently, for an attempt to re-date Herod's reign and death date (which has not yet convinced most scholars), see Steinmann (2009) pp. 1–29. For the idea that there would be a judgment of the dead, with punishments for the wicked, see Daniel 12.2.

2. *War* 1.656–57; *Antiquities* 17.168–70. Both of Josephus's accounts of Herod's illness and subsequent death seem to be based on the firsthand account of Nicolaus of Damascus. On the medical cause(s) of Herod's death, see the insightful article by Kokkinos (2002b) pp. 28–35, 62, supporting a diagnosis of heart and kidney failure; and (2007a) p. 280. Richardson and Fisher (2018) p. 41, attribute it to chronic kidney disease and Fournier's gangrene.

3. 1 Maccabees 1.21–23; Rajak (2002) p. 98 n. 31.

4. For a list of key sites in the region of the war, in Jerusalem, and in Rome, see appendix O.

5. *War* 1.657–58.

6. *War* 1.187; *Antiquities* 14.127; Richardson and Fisher (2018) p. 95 for a succinct narrative of Antipater's actions at the time. Justin, *Dialogue with Trypho*, reports that Ashkelon was An-

tipater's birthplace. See Kokkinos (1998) pp. 128–36 for a brilliant argument about Antipater's origins, his dynasty, and the coinage of Ashkelon.

7. *War* 1.187–92; *Antiquities* 14.127–36.

8. *War* 1.194; *Antiquities* 14.137; Grabbe (2010) p. 21. Richardson and Fisher (2018) pp. 96–98 persuasively show how Josephus's account of Antipater's action is shaped to downplay Hyrcanus's role. For Josephus Hyrcanus is really a figurehead; Antipater is the real power. One important source for this presentation is probably Nicolaus of Damascus.

9. *War* 1.199, 203; *Antiquities* 14.158, where Josephus writes that Herod was 15 years old at the time of his appointment as *strategos,* or general, which is inconsistent with his statement in *Antiquities* 17.148 that Herod was around 70 when he died in 4 BCE; Marshak (2015) p. 75. For the boundaries of the Galilee according to Josephus, see *War* 3.35–42 and appendix O on topography, "Galilee."

10. *War* 1.204–5; *Antiquities* 14.159–60.

11. *War* 1.210–11; *Antiquities* 14.165.

12. *War* 1.212–13; *Antiquities* 14.167–80. For doubts about Samaritis's inclusion in Herod's territory because it was under Hyrcanus's control, see Marshak (2015) p. 77 n. 2.

13. Strabo, *Geography* 16.2.21, includes the much larger area of Palestine, Idumaea, and Judaea; Richardson and Fisher (2018) p. 102 have a more limited area.

14. *War* 1.242–44; *Antiquities* 14.326; Shatzman (1991) p. 148; Udoh (2006) p. 109, suggesting 41–40 BCE; Grabbe (2010) p. 22; Richardson and Fisher (2018) p. 111.

15. *War* 1.248, 258; *Antiquities* 14.331.

16. *War* 1.249–64; *Antiquities* 14.340–53.

17. *War* 1.265–67; *Antiquities* 14.354–62.

18. *War* 15.267, 274–79; *Antiquities* 14.370–80.

19. *War* 1.282–85; *Antiquities* 14.381–89; Appian, *Civil Wars* 5.75, who includes Idumaea and Samaritis; Strabo, *Geography* 16.2.46, Judaea. Rocca (2008) p. 22 correctly points out that Herod's Latin title would have been *Rex Iudaeorum,* though in Josephus it is given as *Basileus* in Greek.

20. *War* 1. 286–357; *Antiquities* 14.390–491; for the (contested) date of Jerusalem's capture, see Richardson (1996) p. 160 n. 31; Richardson and Fisher (2018) pp. 124–26, explaining that the dating uncertainty revolves around questions about when the famine and sabbatical year mentioned by Josephus in *Antiquities* 14.475 took place; Josephus dates the end of the siege to the consulships of Marcus Agrippa and Caninius Gallus, in the 158th Olympiad, in the third month of the fast, 27 years after Pompey's capture of Jerusalem; that would seem to date the end of the siege to mid-37, but detailed chronological studies argue that the siege ended sometime in 36; see Mahieu (2012) pp. 60–99; for the hypothesis that Gaulanitis was part of Herod's kingdom from the start, see Hartal (2003) p. 249; about the dating, see Ariel and Fontanille (2012) p. 96,

21. *War* 1.358; *Antiquities* 15.2,15.6. According to Josephus, after Herod took Jerusalem, he converted all the valuables he had into money, which was then sent to Antony and his staff.

22. *War* 1.437; *Antiquities* 15.39–41, 15.50–61.

23. *War* 1.273, 1.433–34; *Antiquities* 14.365–67, 15.11–22, 15.161–82. The first version of Hyrcanus's undoing in the *Antiquities* (15.161–73) was supposedly based upon Herod's *Memoirs,* as Josephus tells his readers (15.174), although we have no way of checking that since the *Memoirs* no longer exist.

24. Despite Antony sending Alexas of Laodicea to Herod to persuade him to remain loyal; Plutarch, *Life of Antony* 72.2.

25. *War* 1.386–93; *Antiquities* 15.161–63, 15.183–98, 15.343; Grabbe (2010) p. 23.

26. *War* 1.393; *Antiquities* 15.195–96, 15.199–200.

27. *War* 1.396–97; *Antiquities* 15.217.

28. The so-called Type 5 coins; see Ariel and Fontanille (2012) pp. 177–80 for the arguments linking the coin type to Octavian's confirmation of Herod's rule and to Herod's need for money to reorganize his military and pay for reconstruction projects after an earthquake in 31 BCE; see p. 113 for the iconographic associations of the coins.

29. *War* 1.441–44; *Antiquities* 15.68–70, 15.85–87, 16.184–87 for Josephus's claim that the death of Mariamme was an example of Herod's cruelty and that the charge of sexual misconduct against her was false; 16.202–39. See Richardson and Fisher (2018) pp. 140–44 for an admirable attempt to sort out the contradictory and confusing versions of the story recounted in *War* and *Antiquities*. The kernel of truth behind the stories seems to be that when Herod went off to Rhodes in 30 BCE he left Mariamme in the care of two stewards named Joseph and Soëmus; when he returned Salome and Alexandra accused Mariamme of adultery with Soëmus, who had revealed to Mariamme that Herod had ordered her execution if he did not return from his interview with Octavian. Finally, it was Soëmus and Mariamme who were executed.

30. *Antiquities* 15.247–51.

31. *Antiquities* 15.253–66; Marshak (2012) pp. 125–29; Richardson and Fisher (2018) p. 145. Costobar had attempted to set up a breakaway state allied to and supported by Egypt.

32. *War* 1.535–37; see *Antiquities* 16.356 for Herod's consultation of the emperor, probably necessary because (according to Josephus, *Antiquities* 15.342–43) the boys had been educated in the house of "Pollio" (possibly Gaius Asinius Pollio) and of Augustus himself; in any case they spent five years in Rome before Herod summoned them home in 17 BCE; *War* 1.551; *Antiquities* 16.184–87, where Josephus denies that the boys were guilty of treachery; 16.394.

33. Matthew 2.1–18; Richardson and Fisher (2018) pp. 390–91.

34. *War* 1.578; *Antiquities* 17.41–51, 17.58. The tetrarchy of Peraea apparently had been granted to Pheroras by Augustus as a favor to Herod, at the end of the emperor's visit to Judaea in 20 BCE; see *War* 1.483; *Antiquities* 15.362. For the passages in Josephus about the fine imposed upon the Pharisees for their refusal to swear an oath of loyalty and the exile of Pheroras and his wife, see Mason (1991) pp. 260–80; Richardson (1996) pp. 237–38, 254–58; Richardson and Fisher (2018) pp. 189, 344; Klawans (2012) p. 142.

35. *War* 1.241, 1.432, 1.590–91; *Antiquities* 14.300, 17.68; for indirect dowries, see Richardson and Fisher (2018) p. 367.

36. *War* 1.622–28; *Antiquities* 17.94–98.

37. *War* 1.647.

38. *War* 1.648–55; *Antiquities* 17.149–67; Gruen (2009) pp. 15–16; Baumgarten (2011) pp. 7–21; Klawans (2012) p. 167. In the version of the story written up later in the *Antiquities* Matthias, who had instigated the incident, was burned alive with some of his followers, but the fate of Judas is not specified. Note that Josephus does not identify the two sophists as members of any of the "philosophies" or schools (Pharisees, Sadducees, Essenes, Fourth Philosophy) that he describes in *War* or *Antiquities*. Many scholars have understood the two men as Pharisees. The fact, however, that the sophists supposedly urged the young men to hack down the eagle and not fear death for their action because the souls of those who died for their country were immortal suggests that the sophists' theology configures most closely with what Josephus tells us about the beliefs of the Essenes. For those beliefs about the immortality of the souls, see Klawans (2012) pp. 111–15, 117 n. 78.

39. *War* 1.416; Richardson (1996) p. 17 argues for the gate now above Wilson's Arch; see also p. 213; Richardson and Fisher (2018) pp. 40–41 persuasively arguing that the gate above Wilson's Arch is most likely because it was along the route to the Temple from the Upper City, where wealthy people more tolerant of Herod's Hellenism lived, and it was also along the route from Herod's palace near the modern Jaffa Gate to enter the Temple.

40. Ariel and Fontanille (2012) pp. 56–57, 63, Table 8; coin no. 66 in Meshorer (2001) p. 183.

41. Deuteronomy 32.11. God is likened to an eagle in Moses's song; in Ezekiel 1.10, the faces of the visions he saw had the faces of eagles on the back; see also Ezekiel 17.7; Fuks (2002) pp. 241–42; Ariel and Fontanille (2012) pp. 56, 73, 79, for the eagle on Herod's undated Type 16 coins, pointing out that the eagle on Tyrian shekels was associated with Melkart and the single cornucopia/eagle type was the second most common type of undated provenanced coins; see Marshak (2015) pp. 286–87 for discussion of representations of figures on Herodian-era coins and those of his successors; for a recent theory arguing that the eagle was an eastern symbol and had nothing to do with Roman iconography, see Rocca (2018) pp. 477–508; as Richardson and Fisher (2018) pp. 315–16 point out, this is the only coin (type) of Herod's on which there is a living being shown; the image therefore might have caused offense to at least some of Herod's Jewish subjects, but its offensiveness might have been mitigated if the eagle image was seen and understood as a polyvalent reference to the golden eagle on the Temple (which could be read as a scripturally warranted reference to God's power) or as a kind of variant of the eagle on Tyrian shekels, with which the Jews paid the Temple tax, without much fuss being raised.

42. Macrobius, *Saturnalia* 2.4.11. The judgment is wittier in Greek than Latin, since in Greek (which Augustus knew) pig is *hus* and son *huios*. Augustus, apparently, was fond of puns.

43. *Antiquities* 14.377–78; *War* 1.280–81 on his lack of money.

44. *War* 1.424.

45. *War* 1.422; Hall (2004) pp. 46–49 for Berytus. A fragmentary Latin inscription, *CRAI* (1927) pp. 243–44, also refers to a temple that Herod had built, which Queen Berenice and King Agrippa (Herod's great-grandchildren) then had completely rebuilt; see Richardson and Fisher (2018) p. 297 for the inscription. Unfortunately, the inscription does not identify the temple. At some point the *colonia* of Berytus also acquired an amphitheater, which we know from the fact that prisoners from the war of the Jews against Rome were made to fight wild beasts or each other in it; *War* 7.39–40.

46. *War* 1.425; *Antiquities* 16.148; Will (1997) pp. 99–113; Roller (1998) pp. 214–16.

47. *Antiquities* 16.18–19, 16.26; Roller (1998) pp. 49, 100, 121, 127, 220, 223–24; Marshak (2015) p. 236–37 n. 6.

48. *War* 1.423.

49. See Jacobson (1993–94) pp. 31–34 for discussion of the inscription.

50. *War* 1.425; for the gifts to the Samians, see Roller (1998) p. 235; for Pergamon, see Roller (1998) p. 231.

51. For a full discussion of the initiatives on behalf of these diaspora Jews, see Richardson and Fisher (2018) pp. 172–75.

52. *Antiquities* 16.27–57.

53. *Antiquities* 16.58–65.

54. *Antiquities* 16.167–70.

55. *Antiquities* 16.26.

56. *War* 1.428; Roller (1998) pp. 127–28, (2007) p. 319.

57. *War* 1.425; *Antiquities* 16.23–24; Roller (1998) pp. 236–37; for the Athenian honorary inscriptions for Herod, see *OGIS* 414 (*IG* 2.2.3440), an inscription of a statue base from east of the Parthenon, where the temple dedicated to Roma and Augustus was located, and thus raising the possibility that Herod was honored with the statue (that stood on the base) and the inscription for providing some kind of support for the Roman temple; 427 (*IG* 2.2.3441), an inscription found on the Acropolis of Athens, west of the Erechtheion, in the second line of which the people honor Herod "the pious (*eusebes*) King and friend of the Emperor" who can only be Augustus, because of his moral excellence and beneficence; Roller (1998) pp. 219–20; Richardson and Fisher (2018) pp. 295–96. The third inscription, *SEG* 12 (1955) 150, comes from the agora of Athens, and what survives of it repeats verbatim the dedication of the

previous inscription found near the Erechtheion, but crucially it is missing the name of Herod; Merritt (1952) p. 370; Richardson and Fisher (2018) p. 296.

58. For the Nicopolis benefaction(s), see *War* 1.425; *Antiquities* 16.147; Netzer (1987) pp. 121–28; Rocca (2008) pp. 46–47.

59. *War* 1.426–47; *Antiquities* 16.149; Richardson (1996) p. xix; Richardson and Fisher (2018), dating his presidency to the time of a fourth visit to Rome in 8 BCE; Roller (1998) pp. 74, 230–31; Bernett (2007) pp. 117–26, 352–53; Marshak (2015) p. 235 n. 4.

60. Genesis 13.18, 18.1–15; *War* 4.530–33; *Antiquities* 1.237 for Sarah buried there; 1.256 for Abraham buried there; *War* 4.554–5 for Hebron burned down by Cerialis during the Jewish revolt; Jacobson (1981) pp. 73–80; Miller (1985).

61. Richardson (1996) pp. 60–61; Richardson and Fisher (2018) p. 247.

62. *Antiquities* 13.417, possessions of Alexandra at Hyrcania (76–67 BCE); Strabo, *Geography* 16.2.40, Pompey destroys Hyrcania (63 BCE); *War* 1.161, Hyrcania fortified by Alexander, son of Aristobulus; *War* 1.167–68 and *Antiquities* 14.89, Hyrcania surrendered by Alexander to Gabinius, demolished by Gabinius (57 BCE); *War* 1.364, Hyrcania captured by Herod (33–32 BCE); *Antiquities* 15.366, Herod has disaffected executed at Hyrcania (20 BCE); *Antiquities* 16.13, Herod entertains Agrippa at Hyrcania; *War* 1.664 and *Antiquities* 17.187, Antipater buried at Hyrcania (4 BCE); *War* 1.407, 1.417 and *Antiquities* 16.143, Herod builds walls and accommodations of Cypros (30s BCE); *War* 2.484, Cypros captured by Judaean rebels and demolished during early years of revolt; 1 Maccabees 16.11–16, Docus, called Dok, where Simon Maccabaeus and his two sons were murdered; *War* 1.54–56 and *Antiquities* 13.230–35, Ptolemy withdraws to Docus (Dagon); Strabo, *Geography*, 16.2.40, Pompey destroys fortresses in passes to Jericho, possibly including Docus (63 BCE); *Antiquities* 13.417, possessions of Alexandra in Alexandreion; *War* 1.134 and *Antiquities* 14.49, Aristobulus takes refuge in Alexandreion during war against Pompey and is commanded to come down; Strabo, *Geography* 16.2.40, Pompey destroys Alexandreion (63 BCE); *War* 1.161 and *Antiquities* 14.83, Alexandreion fortified by Alexander against Gabinius, Roman governor of Syria; *War* 1.163–68 and *Antiquities* 14.86, 89, Gabinius captures and demolishes Alexandreion; *War* 1.171 and *Antiquities* 14.92, Aristobulus retakes Alexandreion and attempts to refortify it; *War* 1.308 and *Antiquities* 14.419, Pheroras refortifies Alexandreion by Herod's order (39–38 BCE); *Antiquities* 15.185, Herod puts Mariamme in Alexandreion before meeting Octavian on Rhodes; *Antiquities* 16.13, Herod entertains Agrippa at Alexandreion; *War* 1.528, letter of Alexander to governor of Alexandreion requesting admission to the fortress and use of arms there once he and his brother Aristobulus succeed in killing Herod; *Antiquities* 16.317, governor of Alexandreion arrested and accused of having promised to receive Alexander and Aristobulus into the garrison and to supply them with the king's money stored there; *War* 1.551, Alexander and Aristobulus buried at Alexandreion after their execution in 7 BCE. For discussion of Herod's early fortifications, see Richardson (1996) pp. 179–80, 192, 198–99; Richardson and Fisher (2018) pp. 236–37, 243–49; Rocca (2008) pp. 153–90. See Rozenberg (2017) p. 174, on the wall paintings in the bathhouses of Cypros; Marshak (2015) p. 117 n. 7.

63. For the combined functions of these sites, see Netzer (2017b) pp. 162–65. Early on in Herod's reign the king perhaps thought of these fortresses in strategic terms; yet the work done at them shows that almost all of them became multifunctional, with most of the investment being made in structures that essentially catered to comfort and entertainment.

64. For Moses encamping on the plain over Jericho, the prosperous city of palm trees and producer of balsam, *Antiquities* 4.100; Moses arrives at Abaris overlooking Jericho, *Antiquities* 4.325; Joshua sends scouts to Jericho, and Israelites camp 10 stades from Jericho after crossing the Jordan, *Antiquities* 5.20; Jericho and Canaanites conquered by Joshua and the Israelites after six days of trumpeting around the walls; everyone killed except Rahab and her family, *Antiquities* 5.27–32; Herod builds new buildings at Jericho between the fortress of Cypros

and the former palaces, *War* 1.402; Netzer (2017a) pp. 100–117 on the excavations of the palaces at Jericho; Richardson and Fisher (2018) pp. 255–56 on the second palace, the effect of which was to create a kind of artificial oasis surrounding its pools; 274–75 on the third palace; Japp (2000) p. 121, arguing that the first palace was not Herodian but the villa of a rich Judaean; Gleason (2014) pp. 76–97.

65. *War* 1.407.

66. *War* 1.407, 1.659 (called a hippodrome); *Antiquities* 17.175, 17.193; Roller (1998) pp. 171–74; Wilson and Tzaferis (2007) p. 132; Netzer (2009) pp. 174–75; Patrich (2009b) pp. 201–4.

67. Patrich (2009b) p. 193; Weiss (2017) p. 230.

68. *War* 2.59 and *Antiquities* 17.277, royal palace burned by insurgents in 4 BCE; *War* 2.168 and *Antiquities* 18.27, built into a city by Herod Antipas; *War* 4.438, Iulias attacked by Placidus; *Antiquities* 20.159, Iulias in the Peraea given to Agrippa.

69. *War* 1.418, 2.98, given to Herod's sister Salome after Herod's death; *War* 2.167, at her death she bequeathed Phasaelis's palm groves to Augustus's wife Iulia; *Antiquities* 16.144–45; Pliny, *Natural History* 13.4.44, on the dates around Jericho, including Phasaelis, Livias, and Archelaïs.

70. Vörös (2012) pp. 30–41, 68, (2013) pp. 153, 155, (2017) pp. 30–39, 60.

71. *War* 1.419; for Herodeion as a toparchy, see *War* 3.54–55 and Pliny, *Natural History* 5.14; for the dating, see Kokkinos (1998) pp. 221–22; Netzer, Porat, Kalman, and Chachy-Laureys (2017a) p. 133; Richardson and Fisher (2018) p. 238; Magness (2019a) pp. 87–89.

72. *War* 1.263–65; *Antiquities* 14.352–60, 15.323, where Josephus reports that after his wedding (with Mariamme II) was concluded, Herod built (the) fortress in the area where he had defeated the Jews after being expelled from the realm when Antigonus was in charge.

73. *War* 1.420.

74. Rozenberg (2017) p. 187.

75. Weiss (2017) p. 235.

76. Rozenberg (2017) pp. 179–89.

77. Rozenberg (2017) p. 217.

78. *CIIP Vol. IV, Part 2* (2018) no. 3329 pp. 767–68; Ecker (2012) pp. 15–20.

79. *Antiquities* 16.13, Herod entertains Agrippa at Herodeion; Richardson and Fisher (2018) pp. 262–64, 278–81.

80. Netzer et al. (2017a) p. 140.

81. *War* 1.421; Netzer et al. (2017a) pp. 141–47; Richardson and Fisher (2018) pp. 264–65.

82. *War* 1.673; *Antiquities* 17.199.

83. Samaria (later Sebaste) supposedly was founded during the reign of Omri, the king of Israel at some time between 876 and 869 BCE, and was destroyed by John Hyrcanus, though partially repopulated by the Roman governor of Syria, Aulus Gabinius.

   See further Samaria besieged by Aristobulus and Antigonus, sons of John Hyrcanus; Sebaste founded by Herod, *War* 1.64 and *Antiquities* 13.275; Sebaste named for Augustus, *War* 1.118; Samaria repopulated by Gabinius, *War* 1.166; foundation of the city by Herod, *War* 1.403; Herod suffers illness in Samaria (Sebaste) after the execution of Mariamme, *Antiquities* 15.246; Agrippa entertained in Sebaste, *Antiquities* 16.13; Alexander and Aristobulus strangled there, *War* 1.551 and *Antiquities* 16.394; Sebaste given to Archelaus, *War* 2.97 and *Antiquities* 17.320; Sebaste celebrates death of Agrippa I, *Antiquities* 19.356–61; Sebaste criticized by Fadus, cavalry cohort from Sebaste ordered to Pontus, *Antiquities* 19.364–65; most of those in military service under the Romans from Caesarea and Sebaste, *Antiquities* 20.176; Florus leaves Ceasarea for Sebaste, *War* 2.288; Jews appeal to Florus in Sebaste, *War* 2.292; Sebaste burned by the rebels, *War* 2.460; *Antiquities* 15.296; Reisner, Fisher, and Lyon (1924); Crowfoot, Kenyon, and Sukenik (1942); Lichtenberger (1999) pp. 209–12; (2009) p. 46; Mahieu (2008) pp. 183–96; Ariel (2009) p. 121; Marshak (2015) pp. 149–50; Richardson and Fisher (2018) pp. 251–54; Magness (2019a) pp. 85–86.

84. Marshak (2015) p. 15.
85. See Ariel and Fontanille (2012) pp. 134, 164 for numismatic evidence related to the temple's foundation; Marshak (2015) pp. 209–11, for general discussion. Marshak seems to imply that Augustus was worshipped as a god in the temple but does not cite the evidence for that conclusion.
86. For discussions of the temple's plan, see Barag (1993b) pp. 3–18; Netzer (2009) p. 176.
87. Magness (2001) pp. 157–77.
88. *War* 1.403; *Antiquities* 15.292–93, 15.296–98; Roller (1998) pp. 209–12; Netzer (2007) pp. 71–74; Patrich (2009b) pp. 199–201; Weiss (2017) p. 231; Richardson and Fisher (2018) p. 254.
89. *War* 1.403; *Antiquities* 15.292–93, 15.296–98; Shatzman (1991) pp. 180, 191; Marshak (2015) pp. 182, 272 on the ethnic composition of Samaria and Sebaste; Richardson and Fisher (2018) p. 254.
90. *War* 3.36; *Antiquities* 15.294 for Gaba; *Antiquities* 17.23–28 for Bathyra; *Antiquities* 15.294 for Heshbon; *War* 2.55 for Idumaea.
91. Shatzman (1991) p. 181.
92. *War* 1.304 and *Antiquities* 14.414. It is possible, though not certain, that the mansion or combination of mansions excavated on the acropolis of Sepphoris are or represent an expansion of the Herodian palace; see Iamim (2016) pp. 96–113.
93. *War* 2.56; *Antiquities* 17.271.
94. *War* 1.404–6, in which Josephus very clearly states that the *naos* of white marble dedicated to him (Augustus) there was near the sources of the Jordan and the name of the place (*topos*) was Paneion; in *Antiquities* 15.363–64, however, Josephus says that Herod erected to him (again Augustus) a most beautiful *naos* of white stone near (*plesion*) the place called Paneion. For proposed sites, see Ma'oz (1996) pp. 1–5, in front of the cave of Pan at Panias; Netzer (2008) p. 219, about 328 feet west of the cave; Bernett (2007) pp. 127–28, 130–46, arguing for the structure to the west of the caves in Banias or Panias in agreement with Netzer; and also Overman, Olive, and Nelson (2007) pp. 177–96, arguing for Khirbet Omrit; Nelson (2015), temple built by Philip; Richardson and Fisher (2018) pp. 273–74, arguing that no definitive judgment can be made yet.
95. For the coins showing the Herodian Augusteum, see Meshorer (2001) pp. 85–90, coin 96 from 1–2 CE; coins 97, 97a, 97b, 98, and 98b from 8–9 CE; coins 99 and 99a from 12–13 CE; 100 and 100a probably from 14 CE; 101, 101a, 101b, 101c, and 101d from 15–16 CE; 102, 102a, and 103 from 26–27 CE; 104 and 105 from 29–30 CE; 106 from 30–31 CE; and 109 from 33–34 CE; see also Wilson and Tzaferis (2007) pp. 137, 141; Jacobson (2007b) p. 149 for the temple order.
96. *OGIS* 415; Millar (1993) pp. 395–96; Richardson and Fisher (2018) pp. 294–95, arguing that since the building of the temple can be dated to the 30s BCE, so too might the inscription and Herod's benefaction.
97. *War* 1.417; *Antiquities* 16.142–43. For Aphek-Antipatris, see Kochavi (1989); Netzer (2007) pp. 83–84. For a construction date toward the end of Herod's reign based in part upon the low number of Herodian coin types found there, see Ariel and Fontanille (2012) p. 161.
98. *War* 1.87, 416; *Antiquities* 13.357; for the annexation, see *War* 1.396; *Antiquities* 15.217; and for Anthedon generally, see *CIIP Vol. III* (2014) pp. 381–87.
99. *War* 1.422, 2.98 and *Antiquities* 17.321, for the palace at Ascalon given to Salome; by around 65 CE Ascalon had a Greek-style boule and demos (assembly), as we know from its honorary decree for the centurion Aulus Instuleius Tenax; see *CIIP Vol. III* (2014) pp. 272–73 no. 2335, and an honorary decree by the same bodies for Tiberius Iulius Miccio, *CIIP Vol. III* (2014) pp. 274–75, no. 2336. See Hall (2004) pp. 46–49 for Berytus. At some point the *colonia* of Berytus also acquired an amphitheater, which we know from the fact that prisoners from the war of Jews against Rome were made to fight wild beasts or each other in it; *War* 7.39–40.

100. *War* 1.408–15; *Antiquities* 15.293, 15.331; for Straton's Tower, see Raban (1992) pp. 7–22; for the mid-first-century BCE walls of Straton's Tower, see Hilliard (1992) pp. 42–48; for Straton's Tower as a Ptolemaic foundation, see Stieglitz (1996) pp. 593–608; for Demetrias, see Kushnir-Stein (1995c) pp. 9–14; for the grid system of Caesarea, see Netzer (2007) pp. 77–78; see Patrich (2007) p. 101 for the "white stone" as the result of applying a thick layer of white lime plaster to the city's structures; see Marshak (2015) pp. 151–53, 272 on the ethnic mix in Caesarea; for the inclusive construction dates, see Ariel and Fontanille (2012) p. 182; Netzer (2017a) p. 96; Richardson and Fisher (2018) pp. 265–73.

101. For the construction date of the harbor, see *Antiquities* 16.13, reporting that the harbor had been completed by the time of Agrippa's visit to Caesarea in 15 BCE. Altogether the total area of the Caesarea harbor seems to have been around 100,000,000 square feet, or slightly more than 13 times as large as the Piraeus harbor of Athens; see Marshak (2015) p. 219 for the comparison.

102. *War* 1.411–12; *Antiquities* 15.334–36; Holum, Hohlfelder, Bull, and Raban (1988) pp. 90–105.

103. For the harbor construction and use of Roman concrete, see Hohlfelder (1999) pp. 154–63; Hohlfelder, Brandon, and Oleson (2007) pp. 409–15; Brandon (2015) pp. 45–62; Marshak (2015) p. 220; Richardson and Fisher (2018) pp. 265–66.

104. *War* 1.413–14; *Antiquities* 15.339; Holum et al. (1988) pp. 88–89, 113, 142; Holum (1999) pp. 12–34, (2004) pp. 184–99; Netzer (2007) p. 79; Burrell (2009) p. 222; Marshak (2015) p. 212.

105. In literary sources synagogues in Caesarea are referred to by Josephus (as we have seen earlier), in rabbinic sources after the first revolt, and by John Malalas during the sixth century CE, but thus far material evidence supporting the claims of the literary sources have been found only to the north of the Crusader fortress of Caesarea in an area excavated by Avi-Yonah in 1956 and 1962. None of the inscriptions from the area published in *CIIP* thus far certainly antedate 70 CE.

106. *Antiquities* 15.331, 341; Gleason, Burrell, Netzer, Taylor, and Williams (1998) pp. 23–52; Patrich (2007) p. 110; Burrell (2009) pp. 223–24; Richardson and Fisher (2018) pp. 271–72.

107. *War* 1.415; *Antiquities* 15.341, 16.136–41; Gleason et al. (1998) p. 32 for the "amphitheater"/hippodrome; Porath (2013), (2015); Weiss (2013) p. 230; for the theater as one of the venues for the festival, see Patrich (2007) pp. 113–16, (2009b) pp. 187, 193–97, 204–8; Ariel and Fontanille (2012) pp. 27, 185; see Weiss (2017) p. 227 for its architecture and Richardson and Fisher (2018) p. 238 for the dating.

108. Netzer (2006) p. 102; Magness (2019a) p. 84. During the reign of Hadrian a new aqueduct was built for the city; multiple inscriptions in *CIIP Vol. II* (2011) refer to its building by units of Roman legions, including X Fretensis (1200, 1203, 1205, 1206, 1207, 1208); XXII Deiotariana (1201); II Traiana (1202); and VI Ferrata (1204, 1209).

109. Coin Type 15, Ariel and Fontanille (2012) pp. 111, 113–15, 181–82.

110. For recent comprehensive accounts of Herod's projects in Jerusalem, see Roller (1998) pp. 174–82; Levine (2002) 187–254, 313–50; Netzer (2008) 119–78; Richardson and Fisher (2018) pp. 236–41 (in chronological list of building projects), 249, 276–78.

111. *War* 1.401; *Antiquities* 15.292; Ritmeyer (2006) pp. 123–31, 201, 216–19, 334–37, arguing that after Pompey destroyed the fortress named Baris at the northwestern corner of the square, Hasmonean Temple Mount in 63 BCE, Herod rebuilt the Baris Towers early in his reign after his defeat of Antigonus (after 37) and named the newly rebuilt fortress Antonia, in honor of his patron Antony. However, after the Battle of Actium in 31 BCE and Antony's death in 30, when Herod began his rebuilding of the Temple Mount (beginning around 23 BCE), he built a second fortress in a different location at the northwest corner of the new mount that was also called Antonia; Netzer (2007) pp. 74–75; Marshak (2015) pp. 106–8.

112. *War* 5.238–45.

113. *War* 5.244.

114. For descriptions of the enlargement of the Temple Mount and the (rebuilt) Second Temple, see *War* 5.184–226; *Antiquities* 15.391–425; and in the mid-second-century CE Mishnaic tractate, Middot (Measurements) 2.1–5.4. For Josephus's claim that Herod rebuilt the Temple at his own expense, see *Antiquities* 15.380. For some kind of donation to the pavement of the Temple complex by Paris or Sparis, the son of Akeson, see *CIIP Vol. I, Part 1* (2010) no. 3 pp. 46–47. There is an immense modern bibliography about the project. Among the most influential contributions are B. Mazar (1975); Jacobson (1980) pp. 33–40, (1999a) pp. 42–53, 62–64, (1999b) pp. 54–63, 74, (1999c) pp. 67–76, (2002a) pp. 19–27, 60–61; Jacobson and Gibson (1995) pp. 162–70; Ben-Dov (1986) pp. 40–49; Ritmeyer and Ritmeyer (1989) pp. 23–24, 26–27, 29, 32, 35–37, 40, 42; Bahat (1995) pp. 31–47, (1999a) pp. 38–58, (2009) pp. 235–45; Roller (1998) pp. 176–78; Lichtenberger (1999) pp. 131–42; Japp (2000) pp. 126–30; Netzer (2006) pp. 137–78; Marshak (2015) pp. 312–34.

115. *War* 5.201, and see 5.205 for Alexander's gift; see chapter 19 of this book for the "Gate of Nicanor."

116. *Antiquities* 15.382–87 for Herod's speech. It may be that the source for the speech as it appears in *Antiquities* is Nicolaus of Damascus, who is used extensively by Josephus in this later work.

117. *Antiquities* 15.386–87.

118. Marshak (2015) p. 313 n. 1 is surely correct that Herod was promoting himself and his monarchy, not advancing messianic claims, by rebuilding the Temple.

119. *Antiquities* 15.388–90 for assembling the materials and organizing the workforce.

120. *War* 1.401; *Antiquities* 15.380, 400 for the leveling of the ground on the summit; Netzer (2006) pp. 87–88; Jacobson (2007b) pp. 157–58; Rocca (2008) p. 300. The earlier date for the beginning of the project is crucially supported by a fragmentary inscription documenting some kind of donation to the pavement of the Temple complex by Paris or Sparis, perhaps a Jew living in Rhodes, by 21–20 or 18–17 BCE; see *CIIP Vol. I, Part 1* (2010) no. 3 pp. 46–47, which also implies that Herod did not pay for the entire project. A fragmentary first-century CE Aramaic inscription from area XV south of the Temple Mount may also provide further evidence of some kind of donation made to the project by the son of Mattiya; see *CIIP Vol. I, Part 1* (2010) no. 4 p. 48. For the project beginning with the eradication of the foundations, see *Antiquities* 15.391.

121. Marshak (2015) p. 318.

122. Netzer (2006) pp. 161–62; Marshak (2015) p. 319 n. 5.

123. Middot (Measurements) 2.1 gives the area of the first (Solomonic) Temple Mount as 500 square cubits (or about 861 feet); it would therefore be that area that Herod doubled. For the platform's square shape, see *Antiquities* 15.399. For modern estimates of the Herodian platform's surface area, see Bahat (1999a) p. 43, (2009) pp. 238–40; Ritmeyer (2006) p. 143, who claims it is 35–36 acres; Marshak (2015) p. 316.

124. The base of the Giza pyramid covers an area of about 13.3 acres.

125. Jacobson (2007b) p. 146; for the acreage of the White House plot, see http://www .whitehousemuseum.org/grounds.htm.

126. *War* 5.190–92; for the Herodian practice, see Fischer and Stein (1994).

127. *Antiquities* 15.402.

128. For the Greek practice, see Marshak (2015) p. 327.

129. For example, Mark 11.15–17; Matthew 21.12–15; Luke 19.45–46; John 2.13–16. On the stoas, see Bahat (2009) p. 242.

130. *Antiquities* 15.411–16.

131. *Antiquities* 15.416.

132. For hypotheses about the architecture, size, and function of the Royal Stoa, see Ritmeyer and Ritmeyer (1989) pp. 23–24, 26–27, 29, 32, 35–37, 40, 42; Lalor (1997) p. 104; Roller (1998)

p. 177; Lichtenberger (1999) pp. 133–34; Japp (2000) p. 129; Ritmeyer (2006) pp. 90–94; Netzer (2009) pp. 165–71, 177; Marshak (2015) pp. 324–25 no. 10; see Peleg-Barkat (2017) for the fundamental architectural study and interpretation.

133. It is implied in a later talmudic tractate, b. Baba Bathra 3b, that work on the *naos* went on for three years. Unfortunately, neither this later source nor Josephus provides the exact details of the work.

134. For the work on the courts and porticoes, see *Antiquities* 15.420; for the work on the Temple for 18 months, see 15.421; on the work being completed during the governorship of Albinus, see *Antiquities* 20.219. Part of the problem in assessing the work done on the Temple itself during Herod's reign is that there is no scholarly consensus about the exact size and architectural features of the Second Temple that was built as a result of the decree of Cyrus II according to Ezra 6.3–4. For descriptions of the Second Temple before the Herodian renovation, see Josephus, *Against Apion* 1.198–99; the problematic *Letter of Aristeas* 83–104; and *The Wisdom of Ben Sira (Sirach)* 50.1–2.

135. Richardson and Fisher (2018) pp. 335–37. Given the general scholarly presentation of Herod's relationships with women it is surprising that more has not been made of the significance of this choice by Herod, even if a religious body of some kind had to sanction it.

136. John 2.18–20.

137. *CIIP Vol. I, Part I* (2010) no. 54 pp. 97–98; Naveh (1970) pp. 33–37; Richardson and Fisher (2018) p. 304.

138. *Antiquities* 20.219. Afterward, according to Josephus (*Antiquities* 20.222), Agrippa II supposedly put some of these workers back on the payroll, employing them to pave the city in white stone.

139. *War* 1.401.

140. *Antiquities* 15.421–23.

141. Philo, *Embassy to Gaius* 317 for the sheep and bull sacrifices.

142. Lapin (2017a) p. 420.

143. *War* 2.197, 409; *Against Apion* 2.77; Philo, *Embassy to Gaius* 157, 317. Scholars are divided on the issue of who paid for the sacrifice(s): among recent contributors to the debate, Barclay (2013) p. 210 n. 268 and Rives (2014) p. 123 argue that the Romans paid for the sacrifices; Lapin (2017a) p. 421 n. 20 claims that the Temple administration did, arguing that Josephus was a later and local source.

144. *War* 2.280; later, at 6.425 Josephus estimated the number at 2.7 million. Historians have been unable to accept such totals. Some scholars would estimate that somewhere between 125,000 and several hundred thousand people came into the city at Passover; for their estimates, see Jeremias (1969) pp. 77–84, 125,000; Sanders (1992) pp. 127–28, 350,000–500,000; Levine (2002) p. 251, 125,000–300,00. Lapin (2017a) p. 424 estimates a total of 62,000 for all three festivals. For Jerusalem and the Temple as a pilgrim site, see Bahat and Rubenstein (1990) pp. 40–53; S. Schwartz (2001a) pp. 68–69; Strange (2003) pp. 109–10; Rocca (2008) p. 235.

145. *War* 1.401–2; Bava Batra 4a; Klawans (2012) p. 197.

146. Jacobson (2007b) p. 158.

147. Babylonian Talmud, Sukkah 51b, quoted in D. Schwartz (2007a) p. 47; Jacobson (2007b) pp. 151–52 argues that polished limestone was used instead of white marble (which Herod did not use on his other projects) and that gold plating only appeared on the eastern side.

148. Babylonian Talmud, Bava Batra 4a.

149. Netzer (2001) p. 125 dates the construction of the main palace in Jerusalem's Upper City to the period between 25–20 BCE, (2017a) pp. 90–91; Richardson and Fisher (2018) pp. 237, 249 date it to about 23 BCE. For the Upper City, see *War* 2.246.

150. *War* 1.402, 5.176–83; *Antiquities* 15.318; for the inclusive dates, see *Antiquities* 15.292, 15.318. The palace was located in the area where the modern Armenian Gardens are today, but no

substantial remains of the building have survived, at least above ground level. For relatively recent excavations in the area of the palace and to its south, see Sivan and Solar (1994) pp. 168–76; Broshi and Gibson (1994) pp. 147–55.

151. *War* 5.166; *Antiquities* 16.144; often, though not universally, identified with the Tower of David (podium) in the citadel near the Jaffa Gate; see Kokkinos (2007a) p. 285; Marshak (2015) p. 257 n. 25.

152. For Hippicus, about whom nothing is known except that he died valiantly in war, see *War* 5.162.

153. For the towers and the citadel, see *War* 2.439; 5.134, 144, 147, esp. 161, 163–65, 284; 7.1.

154. *War* 2.329, 440.

155. *Antiquities* 15.268–71.

156. *Antiquities* 15.272, 15.275, 15.279–91; Fuks (2002) p. 239; Patrich (2002) pp. 231–39, (2009b) pp. 185–86, 190–92; Bernett (2007) pp. 56–57; Gruen (2009) p. 15; Marshak (2015) pp. 203, 298; see Richardson and Fisher (2018) p. 147, suggesting that the offending decorations were in an amphitheater, not a theater.

157. *Antiquities* 15.268–71, 15.273–74; the hippodrome in Jerusalem is also mentioned at *War* 2.44; *Antiquities* 17.255; for ideas about the location, see Lämmer (1973) pp. 190–94; Bernett (2007) pp. 54, 56; Weiss (2017) p. 226; Richardson and Fisher (2018) p. 249 suggest south or southwest of the city, somewhere on an open plain.

158. *Antiquities* 15.272, 15.328–30; Fuks (2002) p. 240. Japp (2007) p. 244, surveying both public and private decorative art during Herod's reign, concludes that Herod observed the Second Commandment in the parts of his kingdom where the majority of the inhabitants were Jews.

159. Klawans (2012) pp. 165–68.

160. As suggested by Kokkinos (1998) p. 95 n. 39. Idumaea was the Greek word for Edom, known from the Hebrew Bible—for example, in Genesis 25.30, where Esau is known as Edom because he was starving. For the argument for more peaceful, voluntary "conversion," see Kasher (1988) pp. 46–78. For Cypros's origins, see *War* 1.181, where Josephus reports that she came from a distinguished family of Arabia, though in *Antiquities* 1.121 he says that she came from an Arab family in Idumaea. The way scholars usually resolve this confusion is to hypothesize that Arabian and Nabataean are one and the same in the *War* and *Antiquities*; see Richardson (1996) pp. 62–63.

161. *Antiquities* 14.403; Richardson (1996) pp. 52–53, rejecting all the reasons why some may have considered that Herod was not a Jew; Richardson and Fisher (2018) pp. 60–61. See Eckhardt (2012a) pp. 91–115 on the meaning and significance of the put-down. The point of such a slur was not that it was true; it was thrown out to be personally and politically damaging, regardless of whether anyone believed it or not.

162. Richardson (1996) p. 42; Richardson and Fisher (2018) p. 369; Ariel and Fontanille (2012) p. 10.

163. Genesis 25.19–26; for the Idumaeans and Jewish practices, see Kasher (1988) pp. 44–77.

164. *Antiquities* 13.257–58; though in Strabo, *Geography* 16.2.34, the Idumaeans began to share customs with the Judaeans because they had been pushed off their land by the Nabataeans.

165. Marshak (2015) p. 71 also sees and recognizes the implications for Herod. Zadok was the leading priest during the time of David.

166. Such as Herod's first appointee, the Babylonian Jew Hananel; for Herod's preference for diaspora Jews to fulfill the office, see Goodman (1987) pp. 41–42, 111–12, 118–20; S. Schwartz (2001a) pp. 68, 73–74; Richardson (2004) pp. 293–94; Richardson and Fisher (2018) p. 128, 333–34; Marshak (2015) pp. 306–9.

167. *Antiquities* 15.368–70, 17.42–51; for the number of Pharisees, see *Antiquities* 17.42.

168. For the laments, see Tosefta Menahot (Meal Offerings) 13.21; Babylonian Talmud Pesahim 57a; VanderKam (2004) pp. 394–490, 493; Keddie (2019) pp. 87–88.

169. Cicero, *In Defense of Flaccus* 28, 67; 1 Maccabees 1.20–24; 2 Maccabees 5.15–16 (composed sometime between 124 and 63 BCE); *War* 1.152–53; *Antiquities* 14.72–73, in which Pompey and not a few of his men entered the Holy of Holies but, out of piety, did not touch the golden table, the libation vessels, the spices, and the treasury; Cassius Dio 37.16.1–4; *Antiquities* 14.105–9 on Crassus stealing 2,000 talents and all the gold from the Temple.

170. As Josephus states in *Antiquities* 15.420; he was involved with the building of the porticoes and the outer courts, and it is implied that he did enter them.

171. Exodus 20.12.

172. *Antiquities* 16.6, 16.90–130; *War* 1.452–56; Kokkinos (1998) pp. 182 n. 22, 367–75; Netzer (2007) p. 87, (2009) p. 172.

173. For discussion, see Marshak (2015) pp. 191–93, 290–91.

174. Suetonius, *Augustus* 28.3; Cassius Dio 56.30.3.

175. For ashlar and plaster used on the temple of Augustus and Rome in Caesarea, see Patrich (2007) p. 107.

176. Kasher and Witztum (2007) pp. 116–18 on Herod's complex.

177. *Antiquities* 16.141.

178. See the insightful analysis of Rajak (2007) pp. 23–34, for the ways in which Josephus presents Herod the Roman and Herod the Jewish king in the *War* and *Antiquities*. For a sensitive and nuanced analysis of the ways in which Herod achieved this (Herod the Roman *and* Jewish king), citing evidence for Herodian marriages, the incorporation of ritual baths into Roman bathhouses in Herod's Judaean palaces, and how Herod's inclination toward Rome (as reflected in speeches) served the religious interests of Jews, see Regev (2010) pp. 197–222; more recently on Herod's foundations outside of Jerusalem, see Marshak (2015) pp. 209–17, 272–75, 284–311.

179. Geiger (2009) pp. 165–67; Vermes (2014) p. 100.

180. S. Schwartz (2013) p. 185 is a notable exception.

181. *War* 1.319, 326 (*tous ta herodou phronountas*), 358; *Antiquities* 14.436, 14.450, 15.1; Richardson and Fisher (2018) 347–48.

182. For Herod's dyed hair, see *War* 1.490; *Antiquities* 16.233; for Glaphyra's taunts, see *War* 1.476–77; on Herod's marriage strategies, see Hanson (1989) pp. 142–51; Richardson and Fisher (2018) pp. 370–71.

183. For the inscription, see Kokkinos (2007a) pp. 280–81.

184. Schürer I (2014) p. 311, "Herod's Judaism was, by all accounts, very superficial."; Smallwood (1981) p. 82; Jacobson (1988) p. 392, (2001) pp. 100–104; Mendels (1992) p. 212; Fuks (2002) pp. 238–45; Richardson (2006) pp. 30–32; Landau (2006) pp. 117, 165; Kasher and Witztum (2007) pp. 187–90; 410–17; Regev (2010) pp. 197–222; Vermes (2014) p. xi; Marshak (2015) pp. 285–94.

185. *Antiquities* 15.267.

186. *Antiquities* 18.130, 18.133, 18.136.

187. *Antiquities* 16.1–4.

188. Exodus 22.1–2.

189. See Marshak (2015) p. 300 for a similar conclusion.

190. Lucan, *Pharsalia* 10.138; *Antiquities* 15.96–103 for Cleopatra making advances to Herod; yet Herod, persuaded by his friends, understood that if he succumbed he risked a breach with his patron Mark Antony. For the stone weight on which Herod is called pious and a friend of Caesar, see *CIIP Vol. I, Part 1* (2010) no. 666 pp. 660–61; on a lead weight from Ashdod, Herod is pious and a friend of Caesar; see *CIIP Vol. III* (2014) no. 2300 pp. 210–11.

191. Following the hypothesis of Meshorer, who argued that the dated coins from Samaria had pagan symbols and the undated Jerusalem coins had Jewish symbols; for a critique of this division, see Ariel and Fontanille (2012) p. 102. They argue that Herod's dated (a few years

after his ascension) and undated coins (from the summer of 37 and later; p. 159) were both minted in Jerusalem and that the minters avoided images that would offend Jewish sensibilities, sometimes by ambiguity; Richardson and Fisher (2018) pp. 317–19 accept most of the conclusions based upon the research of Ariel and Fontanille, though make the point that if we look at both inscriptions and coins, what comes across is a noticeable self-restraint in Herod's self-representation. What we might then go on to think about is how and why that can help us adjust or modify the picture we get from Josephus, who hardly represents self-restraint as Herod's defining characteristic.

192. Van Henten (2001) pp. 116–45; Marshak (2015) pp. 66–67 on the building activities of Simon in 143 BCE and then the Hellenic-style honors and self-representation.

193. *War* 1.659–60; *Antiquities* 17.173–79.

194. *War* 1.661–64; *Antiquities* 17.182–87.

195. *War* 1.664; *Antiquities* 17.187. The unexcavated Hasmonean fortress built on a hill above the Buqei'a Valley to the southwest of Qumran; see Netzer (2001) p. 75.

196. *War* 1.664; *Antiquities* 17.188–89; for Herod's marriage to Malthace, probably around 28 BCE, see *War* 1.562; *Antiquities* 17.20; Kokkinos (1998) p. 225; Pummer (2009) pp. 212–16, concluding that Malthace, despite her Greek name, was a Samaritan; for Herod's seven wills, see Richardson and Fisher (2018) pp. 362–65.

197. Richardson (1996) p. 18; Kushnir-Stein (1995a) pp. 73–86; Mahieu (2012) pp. 235–87, 289–358, arguing for 1 BCE; Richardson and Fisher (2018) pp. 42–43.

198. *War* 1.665–67; *Antiquities* 17.190, 17.193–95; for Alexas, see Kokkinos (1998) pp. 185–86; see Weiss (2017) p. 225, who argues plausibly that the "hippodrome" and the "amphitheater" Josephus mentions at Jericho are really two parts or buildings of a single multipurpose structure: today what we would call a sports complex.

199. *War* 1.668; *Antiquities* 17.189. Note that under Herod 3,000 Idumaeans had been sent to Trachonitis to try to control the raiding by brigands there; *Antiquities* 16.285, 16.292; see Shatzman (1991) p. 173 for the transfer. Salome's 500,000 silver coins were probably drachma and equivalent to 50 talents in weight, rather than the slightly heavier Roman denarii; see Shatzman (1991) p. 197.

200. *War* 1.669–70; *Antiquities* 17.190, 17.194–95.

201. *War* 1.670–71; *Antiquities* 17.196–97.

202. Galatians from Gaul; see Rocca (2009) p. 145 and n. 51.

203. *War* 1.672–73; *Antiquities* 17.198–99. Possibly these first few units named in the *War* account comprised Herod's royal guard of 2,000; see Shatzman (1991) pp. 184–85; Porat, Chachy, and Kalman (2015) pp. 519–34.

204. *War* 1.673; *Antiquities* 17.199.

205. See the brilliant article by Magness (2019b) p. 273.

206. Foerster (2017) p. 276.

207. Magness (2012) p. 236 for the Absalom Tomb, (2019b) pp. 266–67, 269–70 for the Augustan, Alexandrian, and Olympian inspirations.

208. Netzer (2011) pp. 37–48, 70. There have been attempts to argue that Herod must have been buried elsewhere at Herodeion and that he was not interred in the ornately decorated, reddish-colored sarcophagus that Netzer and his team discovered there in early April 2007; arguments can be made for Herod's interment within the base of the site's (Upper Herodeion's) circular east tower: for alternative interpretations and questions, see Roller (2007) pp. 164–68, esp. 167, on the burial site; Jacobson (2007a) pp. 147–48; Patrich and Arubas (2013) pp. 287–300; Foerster (2017) pp. 266–77; Shanks (2014) pp. 40–48; Richardson and Fisher (2018) pp. 278–81. The argument against the reddish sarcophagus seems to be that it is not "royal" enough for Herod. This begs the question of how we might know what Herod or those who buried him thought was appropriately "royal." As Richardson points out, the mau-

soleum is the only one ever discovered at Herodeion, where we know that Herod was buried; the red sarcophagus and the other two found in the mausoleum date to the right period; and no alternative identification has been posed. In addition, the red sarcophagus's destruction is an argument in favor of it belonging to Herod: the most persuasive hypothesis about the deliberate shattering of the sarcophagus is that it was done by rebels who held Herodeion during the war. Breaking into a sarcophagus looking for loot would cause damage; smashing it into pieces indicates animus. We can surmise that none of the rebels would have been admirers of Herod, the "friend" of Rome, as Herod is referred to in two inscriptions; see Meshorer (1970) pp. 97–8; Kushnir-Stein (1995b) pp. 81–84.

209. 1 Maccabees 9.73.

CHAPTER 2. THE LITTLE REVOLT OF 4 BCE

1. A significant indicator of the continuity between the reigns of Herod and Archelaus is that Archelaus seems to have had minted about the same number of coins per year as his father; see Ariel and Fontanille (2012) p. 157. One reason for this might have been economic self-interest; it is also possible that Archelaus, like Herod, understood that coins could be used to promote policies and positive perceptions of his rule, especially within the central part of his kingdom, where his minted coins seem to have circulated most widely.

2. *War* 2.1; *Antiquities* 17.200.

3. *War* 2.1–3; *Antiquities* 17.200–203; for the process and eventual settlement, see Labbé (2012) pp. 67–87.

4. *War* 2.4; *Antiquities* 17.204–5.

5. *War* 2.5–7; *Antiquities* 17.206–7.

6. *War* 2.8–9; *Antiquities* 17.210–12.

7. See Lapin (2017a) p. 424 for the estimate of the number of pilgrims for all three major festivals (about 62,000) and the city's population.

8. Pilgrims might have expended about 374,000 denarii per year during the celebration of the three major festivals, with 250,000 denarii of that in Jerusalem; see Lapin (2017a) p. 439.

9. See the later discussion for the unit sizes.

10. *War* 2.10–12; *Antiquities* 17.213–16.

11. This probably means cavalry that were brought from Caesarea, where we know that at least later several *alae,* or wings, were based.

12. *War* 2.12–13; *Antiquities* 17.217–18.

13. For the biblical requirement that people attend the three festivals each year (in principle), see Deuteronomy 16.16; the potential for conflict was, of course, connected to the large number of people who traveled to Jerusalem to make sacrifices (and pay the half-shekel tax) and who expanded its population at the time. Because Sukkot was celebrated after farmers had finished plowing and sowing, according to one interpretation of the evidence it was the festival when the greatest number of pilgrims came to Jerusalem; see Meshorer (2001) p. 125.

14. Memorialized according to Meshorer (2001) p. 79; coins 70, 71, and 72 had galleys and galley prows on them.

15. *War* 2.14–15; *Antiquities* 17.219–20.

16. *War* 2.16–19; *Antiquities* 17.221–23.

17. Richardson and Fisher (2018) p. 364.

18. *War* 2.20–24; *Antiquities* 17.224–28.

19. Perhaps Augustus wanted to give young Gaius a taste of what it was like to deal with the subjects of Roman imperium should he ever ascend to the throne in Rome; Gaius, however, was spared the experience due to his death in Lycia in 4 CE.

20. *War* 2.25; *Antiquities* 17.229.

21. *War* 2.26–32; *Antiquities* 17.230–40.

22. *War* 2.33–36; *Antiquities* 17.240–47.

23. Fragment 136 in Jacoby (1926); for a short review of Nicolaus's career and the ways in which it resembled and prefigured Josephus's career in Rome, see Bowersock (2005) p. 57.

24. *War* 2.37–38; *Antiquities* 17.248–49.

25. *War* 2.39–40; *Antiquities* 17.250–1. This story could be an awkward flashback to what Josephus told his readers about the sequence of events at *War* 2.16–19 and *Antiquities* 17.221–23, where he has Varus returning to Antioch directly from Caesarea, skipping his detour to Jerusalem; more likely, it refers to a trip by Varus from Antioch to Jerusalem with his legions after he returned to Antioch. In either case it is not a paradigm of clarity.

26. Roth (1994) pp. 346–62; Goldsworthy (1996) p. 13; Keppie (1998) p. 173; Roth (2012) p. 21. Note that estimates of the size of Roman legions after the mid–first century CE vary, first because, as Keppie points out, the precise total is nowhere reliably attested, and second, during the reign of Nero (according to some scholars) or Vespasian or Domitian, the size of the first cohort of a legion was increased to 960 so that the standard size of a legion became 5,280 men. Later on, in *War* 3.67–69, Josephus does seem to refer to the Roman legion's size as around 6,000. But he seems to be basing his totals on a paper strength total of 100-man centuries and infantry cohorts of 600. In the absence of specific totals in Josephus's works for the size of legions during specific actions in this book, I adopt the nominal standard size of 4,800 men per legion. If the Roman legions that fought under Cestius, Vespasian, Titus, and Flavius Silva in the Galilee, Judaea, and at Masada during the revolt from 66 to 74 were larger than that, those numbers will strengthen the case made here for the investment in men and treasure that Rome made in the war effort. Larger legions (Keppie's estimate is 5,000–6,000) meant more soldiers who needed to be paid, supplied, and supported logistically. For an overview and more detail on the organization of the Roman legion at the time, see appendix G, "The Roman Legion around 4 BCE."

27. Lapin (2017a) p. 414.

28. Exodus 23.16, 34.22; Leviticus 23.9–21; Deuteronomy 26.1–11. The date when the festival was celebrated changed because its starting time was mandated to be calculated by counting seven weeks from the date when the barley *omer* (sheaf) was waved. It was on the day after that (i.e., 50 days) that an offering of new grain was to be made to God; see Leviticus 23.15–16. The problem is that no clear date is set out for the waving of the barley *omer*. On the festival's associations with the covenant in biblical texts, see VanderKam (2001) p. 206.

29. VanderKam (2001) p. 206; Magness (2019a) p. 97.

30. Levine (2002) pp. 340–43; Reich (2014) pp. 298–305, estimating 30,000; Lapin (2017c) p. 244.

31. *War* 42.41–44; *Antiquities* 17.252–55; for a possible reference to the site of the Herodian hippodrome "in the plain" (though requiring an emendation of Josephus's text), see *Antiquities* 15.268, where the large amphitheater mentioned might be the hippodrome.

32. *War* 2.45–48; *Antiquities* 17.256–60. For the flat roofs of the porticoes, see Jacobson (2007b) p. 166.

33. *War* 2.49–50; *Antiquities* 17.261–64. In the latter passage Sabinus took the 400 talents for himself, apart from what the soldiers stole.

34. See Shatzman (1991) pp. 185–86 for the bulk of the royal army being Jews and the Sebastenians as "foreign, pagan soldiers"; p. 194 for the estimate of the size of Rufus's cavalry unit. For speculation on the Roman ethnicity of Gratus and Rufus, largely based upon their Latin names, see Marshak (2015) p. 187.

35. *War* 2.51–54; *Antiquities* 17.265–68.

36. Schäfer (2003b) p. 101.

37. *War* 2.55, 75–77; *Antiquities* 17.269–70, 17.297. It is possible, though not certain, that the 2,000 veterans had been given land in Idumaea, making them into a kind of force that could be called up to provide security against the neighboring Nabataeans.

38. *War* 2.56; *Antiquities* 17.271–72.
39. The royal archers from Trachonitis were probably recruited from the 3,000 Idumaeans that Herod had settled in Trachonitis; see *Antiquities* 16.285; Shatzman (1991) p. 274.
40. *War* 2.57–59; *Antiquities* 17.273–77; Tacitus, *Histories* 5.9.1.
41. For Emmaus as Nicopolis, see *CIIP Vol. 4, Part 1* (2018) pp. 441–49; Fisher, Isaac, and Roll (1996) pp. 151–59.
42. *War* 2.60–65; *Antiquities* 17.278–84; Roth (2012) p. 283, citing the incident as an example of the Roman army unsuccessfully providing security for supply transport.
43. *War* 2.66–67; *Antiquities* 17.286. Berytus included a Roman colony of ex-legionaries established by Augustus in 15 BCE.
44. Saddington (1982), (2009) p. 304; Goldsworthy (1996) pp. 18–21, 68; Keppie (1998) pp. 182–86; Southern (2007) pp. 120–24.
45. Keppie (1998) p. 185.
46. *War* 2.68; *Antiquities* 17.287–89. The famous Khazneh (treasury, in Arabic) in Petra may be Aretas's tomb.
47. *War* 2.69–71; *Antiquities* 17.289–91.
48. From their Latin names we might deduce that these two commanders were Roman citizens, though to be certain we would need their full Roman names (*tria nomina*).
49. *War* 2.72–75; *Antiquities* 17.292–95.
50. Goodman (2007c) pp. 381–82.
51. *War* 2.76–79; *Antiquities* 17.295–99; for the veterans and the episode, see Shatzman (1991) p. 182.
52. For the "War of Varus," see the second-century CE *Seder Olam Rabbah* (Great Order of the World) 30.
53. *War* 2.80; *Antiquities* 17.299–300.
54. *War* 2.81–83; *Antiquities* 17.301–3.
55. *War* 2.84–91; *Antiquities* 17.304–14.
56. *War* 2.92; *Antiquities* 17.315–16.
57. The position of ethnarch was later symbolized on coins minted during Archelaus's reign by the appearance of a helmet; see Meshorer (2001) p. 79–80, coin 73.
58. *War* 2.93, 2.96–97; *Antiquities* 17.317, 17.319–20; Grabbe (2010) p. 25; Sharon (2010) pp. 472–93. Sharon convincingly argues that the title of ethnarch during the Hasmonean period originally meant the ruler over a people; in Josephus's account of the ethnarchy granted to Archelaus by Augustus, the ethnarchy is, however, defined explicitly in geographical terms. It could be argued that when Josephus uses the term "ethnarch" to describe Archelaus's title what he meant was ruler over the people in the areas that he lists.
59. *War* 2.95; *Antiquities* 17.319. Augustus had added these bandit-ridden areas to Herod's territory; *War* 1.398.
60. Nicolaus of Damascus, *FGrH* 90 F 136; Strabo, *Geography* 16.2.46 (765); *War* 2.94–95; *Antiquities* 17.318–19; Luke 3.1; Sartre (2005) p. 94; Wilson and Tzaferis (2007) p. 131.
61. Sartre (2005) p. 94.
62. The totals would be about 850 talents according to *War* 2.93–98 and 1,050 talents based upon the reported totals in *Antiquities* 17.318–21.
63. Azotus here probably means the inland site of Tel Ashdod, about 3.1 miles from the sea, rather than coastal Ashdod-Yam to the northwest. In *Antiquities* 13.395 Josephus refers to the city implying that it is on the coast, but elsewhere, at 14.75–76 and *War* 1.156, he refers to it as an inland city.
64. *War* 2.98; *Antiquities* 17.189, 17.321.
65. On toparchies in the region and their persistence into the Herodian period and the period of the revolt, see Isaac (1998) pp. 165–68; Rocca (2008) pp. 200–203; Choi (2013) 127–30; Keddie (2019) pp. 25–32.

66. *War* 2.98–100; *Antiquities* 17.321–23.

67. That was so, despite Herod's ill-advised campaign against Nabataea in 12 BCE that earned him a rebuke from Augustus, *Antiquities* 16.271–99. The point is that, after the rebuke and the intervention of Nicolaus of Damascus on Herod's behalf, Augustus considered giving Herod rule over Arabia. That was an expression of confidence in Herod's loyalty.

68. For a different conclusion, see Goodman (2007c) pp. 382, 384.

CHAPTER 3. FROM ETHNARCHY TO PROVINCE

1. *War* 2.7; *Antiquities* 17.207–9, 17.339. Eleazar was soon replaced by the high priest Jesus, 17.341.

2. *Antiquities* 17.340; Hizmi (2008) pp. 48–59, 78; *CIIP Vol. IV, Part 1* (2018a) p. 41.

3. Alexander had been executed in 7 BCE; see chapter 2. After Alexander's death, Glaphyra then married the Mauretanian king Juba, but the marriage was dissolved.

4. *War* 2.115; *Antiquities* 17.340–41; Leviticus 18.16, 20.21.

5. *War* 2.116; *Antiquities* 17.349–53.

6. The stories about the fates of Glaphyra and Archelaus inspired Josephus to compose a passage about divine providence and the immortality of the soul; see *Antiquities* 17.354.

7. *War* 2.111–13; *Antiquities* 17.342–44, 17.355, 18.1; Cassius Dio 55.27.6. What this may mean is that the emperor took over the lands in order to put them up for auction by Quirinius, the legate of Syria; if so, that would encourage private land ownership, something Herod himself had done through his land grants.

8. As is implied at *Antiquities* 18.31, since it was not included in the original, Augustan distribution.

9. *War* 2.117; *Antiquities* 18.1. For the controversies about the creation of the Roman province of Judaea in 6 CE, see appendix H, "The Roman Province of Judaea, 6 CE?"

10. Rocca (2009) pp. 10–22; Mason (2016) pp. 258–59. Note that Josephus does not say explicitly that the auxiliaries in 6 CE were Samarians or Samaritans when Coponius was appointed.

11. *Antiquities* 19.365.

12. *War* 2.234–36 (the festival); *Antiquities* 20.118–22 (a festival).

13. *Antiquities* 20.176.

14. *War* 3.66; for the numbers in the different auxiliary units, see Roth (2012) pp. 336–37.

15. *War* 2.236.

16. *Antiquities* 18.1; cf. *War* 2.117 for Coponius being sent out.

17. Luke 2.1–5; cf. Acts 5.37; Sartre (2005) pp. 94–96.

18. *CIL* 3.6687 = *ILS* 2683; Boffo (1994) pp. 185–89, 200.

19. *Antiquities* 18.2.

20. Keddie (2019) pp. 122–28.

21. *Antiquities* 18.1–3; Grabbe (2010) p. 25.

22. Millar (1993) p. 47; Keddie (2019) pp. 130–33, offering informed estimates for the rates based upon evidence from Egypt and making allowances for differential rates for different kinds of property. The problem in assessing whether the Roman rates were high or low goes beyond the issue of a lack of evidence for 6 CE, however; we also do not know the tax rates under Archelaus or Herod. Therefore, we cannot say whether the rates imposed in 6 CE represented an increase, a decrease, or a continuation of rates that people were used to.

23. *War* 2.118, with a slightly different formulation of the same expression at 2.433; *Antiquities* 18.4.

24. *War* 2.56, 118; *Antiquities* 14.158–59, 17.271–72, 18.2–10, 18.73.

25. *War* 7.253.

26. *War* 7.253–58. Mason (2016) pp. 254–57 argues that the description of the dagger-men here in the *War* refers to the period of the later revolt. But the phrase *tote gar* directly follows the

sentence that reads, "He was a descendant of the Judas who, as we have said before, induced multitudes of Jews to refuse to enroll themselves, when Quirinius was sent as censor into Judaea." The phrase "at that time" therefore refers explicitly to Judas's time period (6 CE).

27. *Antiquities* 18.6–10.

28. Luke 2.1–2, for the census; Acts 5.37.

29. *War* 2.433, 7.253.

30. *War* 7.253.

31. Mason (2016) p. 249.

32. *War* 2.118 "*Romaiois.*"

33. As Mason (2016) p. 249 asserts.

34. Deuteronomy 17.15–16, 33.5, in which God is the king in Jeshurun; Joshua 23.16; 1 Samuel 8.7, 12.12; *Against Apion* 2.164–66. Although Josephus does not mention it in his brief gloss on the revolt, he must have known that even King David supposedly had endured divine retribution for conducting a census of Judah and Israel: see 2 Samuel 24.1–15.

35. Goodman (2007c) pp. 200–201.

36. God as king is repeated many times in the Hebrew Bible; see, e.g., Exodus 15.18; Judges 8.22–23; 1 Samuel 12.12; 1 Chronicles 16.31; Psalms 10.16, 47.8, 93.1, 96.10, 97.1, 99.1; Isaiah 24.23, 33.22.

37. *Antiquities* 14.41.

38. For such censuses, see Exodus 30.12, 38.26; Numbers 1.2, 4.2, 4.22. Note that these are censuses ordered by God or by Israelites—not foreigners.

39. Exodus 3.13.

40. For example, Exodus 34.14; Deuteronomy 4.39, 5.7–8, 6.13–14, 7.4, 8.19–20, 11.16, 13.2–4, 13.6–11, 13.12–18, 17.2–7.

41. Isaiah 44.6–8; Satlow (2014) pp. 60–61.

42. A point seen by Klawans (2012) p. 164.

43. Joshua 23.14–16.

44. See Deuteronomy 17.14–20 for the idea of accepting a king, but only one that God has chosen.

45. Mason (2016) p. 253.

46. For the (contested) origins of the Samaritans as descendants of the colonists who had been sent to occupy the land of Israel by Shalmanezer V or Sargon II and then intermarried with Jews there, see 2 Kings 17.24–41; Dušek (2012) pp. 74–81; Vermes (2014) p. 6.

47. Nehemiah 2.10.

48. Archaeological evidence, however, shows conclusively that the building of the original Samaritan Temple on Mt. Gerizim should be dated to the reign of Sanballat I, at least a century before Alexander's arrival in the region; see Bull (1968) pp. 58–72; Magen (2007) pp. 157–211.

49. For the story about Alexander's correspondence with the high priest Jaddus and Sanballat III and the conflicts between the peoples, see *Antiquities* 11.317–47; Pummer (2009) pp. 222–25.

50. *Antiquities* 18.29–30. Because the text of Josephus is corrupt in part here and he provides no evidence about who were the Samaritans who allegedly perpetrated this act, some scholars argue that this incident (minimally) should not be used as evidence for further hostility between Jews and Samaritans during the first century CE; see Pummer (2009) pp. 222–30.

51. For the guards, see *War* 6.294. On the issue of the temple captain, note also that Simon, the enemy of the high priest Onias III, is also called a captain of the Temple in 2 Maccabees 3. Whether this is the same position as the first-century CE office is uncertain. In the gospel of Luke, narrating the arrest of Jesus, there is a reference to the chief priests and "officers" (*strategois* and *strategous*) of the Temple, which should mean that in addition to the Temple captain there were other Temple military officers; see Luke 22.4, 22.52.

52. *Antiquities* 18.31.

53. *War* 2.167; *Antiquities* 18.31. The case of Marcus Ambivulus or Ambibulus is a good example of why Josephus's writings are invaluable; apart from some coins minted during his prefecture (e.g., Hendin (1987) pp. 83–84, nos. 101–3; Meshorer (2001) pp. 168, 256, nos. 313–15) we have no other evidence for Ambivulus's prefecture or even his existence.

54. *Antiquities* 18.32. Rufus apparently is referred to in what may be a second-century CE copy of a first-century inscription (*SEG* 8.98) from Sebaste, possibly in a pairing with Valerius Gratus, Rufus's successor as prefect of Judaea; Rufus and Gratus are specified by Josephus (*War* 2.52; *Antiquities* 17.266) to have commanded the Sebastenians at the time that Sabinus was besieged in Jerusalem after Herod the Great died; see Vardaman (1998b) pp. 191–202 and Kokkinos (2012) p. 107, for the textual emendation of the inscription and the arguments.

55. *Annals* 1.6–13.

56. *War* 2.167–68.

57. For Sepphoris's fortification and renaming by Herod Antipas, see *Antiquities* 18.27; for its burning by Gaius during Varus's campaign, see *War* 2.68; *Antiquities* 17.289. For Herod Antipas's building or walling of Betharamphtha (sometimes spelled Beth Haramtha) and renaming the town Iulias, see *War* 2.168; *Antiquities* 18.27. For the destruction of the palaces of "Betharamatha" by Peraean rebels in 4 BCE, see *War* 2.59.

58. Meyers (2002) pp. 118–19; Schumer (2017b) pp. 90–111 argues for a population of somewhere between 2,500 and 5,000.

59. Rutgers (1998) pp. 179–95.

60. *Antiquities* 18.27; the word *proschema* that Josephus uses to describe Sepphoris is sometimes translated as "ornament" but has strong defensive connotations. The difference in translation has implications for what kind of place we understand Sepphoris to have been before and after the revolt of 66. Translating the word as "ornament" would imply that Sepphoris was a kind of fully decked-out Graeco-Roman city before 66; scholars, however, are now arguing that Sepphoris's urban development into a kind of recognizable Graeco-Roman polis, both architecturally and institutionally, belongs to the period after 66. See Weiss (2007) pp. 385–414, esp. 403–4, 408.

61. For Antipas's coins dating from year 24 of Antipas' reign or 20–21 CE, see Kushnir-Stein (2007) p. 56. Meshorer (2001) p. 81, coins nos. 75–78, dates the inauguration of Tiberias to 19–20 CE because the earliest coins minted in Tiberias during the Roman era date to year 24 of Antipas's reign, which began in 4 BCE. The year 24 coins have the name of the city Tiberias within a wreath on one side and a reed, a symbol of Kinneret, on the other.

62. *War* 2.168; *Antiquities* 18.36–38; for Antipas's coins dating from year 24, which equals 20–21 CE, see Kushnir-Stein (2007) p. 56.

63. Reed (2000) p. 82.

64. Reed (2000) p. 217; Sartre (2005) p. 98.

65. For the council, see *Life* 169, 284, 300, 313, 381; for the chief magistrate, *Life* 134, 271, 294; for the 10 overseers, *Life* 69, 168, 296; for the demos, *War* 2.619; for the market supervisor, *Antiquities* 18.149.

66. For the character of the foundation, see Jensen (2010) pp. 135–48; Richardson and Fisher (2018) p. 384.

67. *War* 2.168, Tiberias built by Herod in the Galilee; 2.619, stadium in Tiberias located on a hill but near the water; 3.539, stadium; *Life* 85, hot baths; 92, stadium; 277, prayer house or synagogue; 293, prayer house; 331, stadium. The identifications of the stadium and palace are controversial. Accepting that the remains of a wall north of the city on the seashore are part of the stadium are Hartal (2002) pp. 22–24 and Weiss (2007) pp. 390–91. Bonnie (2017) doubts that the ashlar wall belongs to a stadium and argues for a less developed structure away from the seashore. Keddie (2019) concludes that archaeological traces of the stadium have not been found. For Antipas's palace, see Hirschfeld and Galor (2007); Jensen (2010)

pp. 141–44; Keddie (2019) pp. 56–57, pointing out that the remains of the excavated building identified with Antipas's palace at the site, including its *opus sectile* floor and the bases of its painted and molded plaster pillars, make it a candidate for the identification, but it also could just be a mansion that belonged to a wealthy elite.

68. Meyers and Chancey (2012) p. 119; Weiss (2014) pp. 58, 68.
69. *Life* 64–66.
70. Schäfer (2003b) p. 103; Chancey (2005) pp. 221–29.
71. For Paneas/Caesarea Philippi, see Mark 8.27; Matthew 16.13; *War* 2.168; *Antiquities* 18.28; Wilson (2004); Wilson and Tzaferis (2007) pp. 131–32; for Bethsaida/Julias, *Antiquities* 18.28; Arav and Freund (1995), (1999), (2004), (2009); Shroder, Jol, and Reeder (2009) pp. 293–309, arguing against El-Araj as Bethsaida; Arav (2011) pp. 92–100; Notley (2007) pp. 220–30, arguing that Et-Tell cannot be Bethsaida, because Josephus and others situate Bethsaida on the lake, whereas Et-Tell is about 1.8 miles north of the lake and higher than 23 feet above sea level; Meshorer (2001) p. 88, coin no. 106; Sartre (2005) p. 97, argues that Iulias was named after Augustus's daughter Iulia, though she was banished to the island of Pandateria in 2 BCE, and it seems doubtful that he would rename the town after Augustus's disgraced daughter; for a brief overview, see Savage (2011).
72. For example, Meshorer (2001) p. 86, coins no. 95, 95a, and 96; Schäfer (2003b) p. 102; Meyers and Chancey (2012) p. 123; Marshak (2015) pp. 15–16; Richardson and Fisher (2018) p. 393.
73. Meshorer (2001) p. 90.
74. *Antiquities* 18.33–35; see appendix E, "High Priests from Herod the Great to 68 CE," with sources noted. The high priest Ananus, in fact, had five sons who at one time or another became high priests: Eleazar, Jonathan, Theophilus, Matthias, and Ananus. It is possible that Caiaphas's tomb and ossuary plus inscription should be identified with the ossuary of Joseph Qyf'; see *CIIP Vol. I, Part I* (2010) no. 461 pp. 48–85, though the Aramaic inscriptions of the ossuary do not mention the high priesthood at all. For Caiaphas, his family, and the archaeological remains, see VanderKam (2004) pp. 426–36; Evans (2006) pp. 323–40; Hachlili (2005) pp. 264–68; Keddie (2019) pp. 232–33.
75. For the famous Pilate inscription, discovered in Caesarea in 1961 (now Israel Museum Inv. No. IAA 1961–529), see Frova (1961) pp. 419–34; Vardaman (1962) pp. 70–71; Lehmann and Holum (1999) pp. 67–70; Alföldy (2002) pp. 85–108; *CIIP Vol. II* (2011) no. 1277 pp. 228–30.
76. *CIIP Vol. II* (2011) no. 1277 pp. 229.
77. To confuse our understanding of Pilate's official office, Tacitus, *Annals* 15.44.3, refers to Jesus's sentence being carried out *per procuratorem Pontium Pilatum*. For the date of Jesus's crucifixion, see Sartre (2005) p. 114 n. 151. Pilate, of course, has been the focus of a great deal of scholarship; for some influential recent studies, see Alföldy (1999) pp. 85–108; H. Bond (1998); Jaroés (2002); Taylor (2006b) pp. 555–82; Demandt (2012).
78. *Antiquities* 18.63–64.
79. Smallwood (1970) p. 24.
80. *Embassy to Gaius* 299.
81. *Embassy to Gaius* 300.
82. *Embassy to Gaius* 301–3.
83. *Embassy to Gaius* 304.
84. For such a reconstruction of the inscription (which was probably in Latin, just as was the famous Pilate inscription from the lighthouse in Caesarea), see the splendid entry of W. Eck for *CIIP Vol. I, Part I* (2010) no. 14 p. 61. Eck suggests a possible reconstruction of the inscription with standard word abbreviations, as follows: "Ti(berio) Caesari divi Aug(usti) f(ilio) divi Iuli nep(oti) Augusto Pontius Pilatus, praefectus Iudaeae." See also Eck (2007) p. 59 n. 8.
85. *War* 2.169.

86. *Antiquities* 18.55.
87. *War* 2.170–74; *Antiquities* 18.56–59; for Pilate and the imperial cult, see Taylor (2006b) pp. 555–82.
88. For the coins, see Meshorer (2001) pp. 170–72. See Taylor (2006b); Bernett (2007) pp. 199–204; Kokkinos (2012) pp. 85–112 for arguments that the coins were part of an attempt to promote the imperial cult and would have been offensive to religious sensibilities; and Mason (2016) p. 266 for arguments against; more generally for the introduction of the imperial cult into the region, see Kropp (2009) pp. 99–150.
89. Keddie (2019) pp. 165–68.
90. *War* 2.175–77; *Antiquities* 18.60–62; on the aqueduct, see Patrich (1982) pp. 25–39.
91. *Antiquities* 18.85–87 for the episode in 36; *War* 1.63; *Antiquities* 13.255–56 for Hyrcanus I's defeat of the Samaritans and the destruction of their temple; Megillath Ta'anith (21 Kislev); Magen (2007) pp. 158–60, 183; Blenkinsopp (2007) p. 386; Pummer (2009) pp. 230–42; Mason (2016) p. 233.
92. After the time of Jesus in Samaritis a man named Dositheos announced that he was the messiah that Moses had predicted would come: Origen, *Against Celsus* 1.57, 7.11.
93. Deuteronomy 18.15, 18; 2 Maccabees 2.4–8; Eupolemus in Eusebius, *Preparation for the Gospel* 9.39.5; Pummer (2009) pp. 236–38 for analysis.
94. *Antiquities* 18.87.
95. Whether the *boule* of the Samaritans that Josephus mentions here was a council similar to those of poleis with the institutional structures of Greek cities, such as Tiberias, is uncertain.
96. *Antiquities* 18.88–89.
97. *Antiquities* 18.89, 237. It is uncertain whether Vitellius had the authority to appoint a procurator, even on an interim basis. Marullus is specifically designated as a cavalry commander (*hipparchen*) by Josephus.
98. Richardson and Fisher (2018) p. 397.
99. On Pilate and different aspects of his governorship, among many studies, see most recently Alföldy (1999) pp. 85–118; Taylor (2006b) pp. 555–82.
100. *Antiquities* 15.403–5, 18.90–95. It is in the earlier version of the story that Josephus reports that Vitellius agreed to write to Tiberias about where the vestments should be kept; given the ramifications of the decision, that seems to be the more plausible sequence of action.
101. VanderKam (2001) p. 180.
102. Exodus 39.1.
103. Matthew 14.1-12; Mark 6.17–28.
104. *Antiquities* 18.109–15; for the episode, see Richardson and Fisher (2018) p. 395.
105. *Antiquities* 15.403–5, 18.90–95; for the complicated chronological issues, see VanderKam (2004) pp. 431–35.
106. *Antiquities* 18.125.

CHAPTER 4. THE OWL AND THE GOLDEN CHAIN

1. *War* 1.551; *Antiquities* 16.394; for a full account of Agrippa's life, see D. Schwartz (1990).
2. *Antiquities* 18.143.
3. *Antiquities* 18.145–47.
4. For *agoranomoi* and their responsibilities in Greek cities, see Bresson (2016) pp. 246–49; in Judaea, see Rosenfeld and Menirav (2005) pp. 19–20.
5. *Antiquities* 18.148–50.
6. *Antiquities* 18.151–55.
7. For Anthedon given to Herod by Augustus, see *Antiquities* 15.217. The existence of a procurator for Iamnia proves that after the death of Augustus's wife Livia, to whom it had been given after the death of Herod's sister Salome, Iamnia was a patrimonial, imperial posses-

sion. Serving under Capito appears to have been Iulius Mellon, procurator of the palm groves near Iamnia; see *CIIP Vol. III* (2014) no. 2268 p. 166, a funeral inscription in Latin for Mellon's wife Iulia Grata.

8. *Antiquities* 18.155–58.
9. *Antiquities* 18.159–60.
10. *Antiquities* 18.161–64
11. *Antiquities* 18.164–65.
12. *Antiquities* 18.166–67. On the unresolved debate about whether the text should be reedited to mean that the man was a Samaritan or just a Samarian, see Pummer (2009) pp. 268–70.
13. *Antiquities* 18.168–94 for the fuller version of the story; *War* 2.179–80, reporting that Agrippa's prayer was made at a dinner party. See D. Schwartz (1990) pp. 45–53 for Agrippa's early career and the argument that Agrippa was put in chains by Tiberius not for the prayer but because of his inability to pay back the loan he had taken from the imperial treasury.
14. *Antiquities* 18.195–200.
15. *Antiquities* 18.201. Josephus does not reveal whether Agrippa helped the German gain his freedom.
16. Gambetti (2009) pp. 154–56 argues that it was Gaius who made the request that the Senate give Agrippa the honor so that Agrippa, as Gaius's agent, could deliver to Flaccus his reappointment *mandata;* however, the evidence for this is at best circumstantial.
17. *War* 2.181; *Antiquities* 18.237; Philo, *Against Flaccus* 6 (40); Grabbe (2010) p. 26.
18. *War* 2.181–83 ("cis Spanian" or Spain; possibly meaning Saint Bertrand de Comminges, now in the Pyrenees, where Pompey had founded a Roman military colony in 72 BCE); *Antiquities* 18.238–55 (Lugdunum); Schäfer (2003b) p. 104; Kushnir-Stein (2007) p. 56, who follows the "current view" that Antipas was dismissed as early as the summer of 39 BCE, but also gives an alternative time for his dismissal—between mid-September of 39 and the spring of 40, while Gaius was in Gaul.
19. *War* 2.184; *Antiquities* 18.256.
20. Philo, *Against Flaccus* 26.
21. For the connections between the two cases, see Sly (2000) pp. 249–65.
22. Gambetti (2009) pp. 151–58 for a narrative of these events.
23. Philo, *Against Flaccus* 34, 36–39; for Isidorus's possible involvement, see Gambetti (2009) pp. 159–62.
24. Philo, *Against Flaccus* 103; Gambetti (2009) pp. 164–65.
25. Exodus 20.4; Philo, *Against Flaccus* 41–42; Giambetti (2009) pp. 18, 167–72.
26. *Against Flaccus* 47–52.
27. *Against Flaccus* 54; Gambetti (2009) pp. 172–76 for the translation of the passage and its implications.
28. *Against Flaccus* 55; *Embassy to Gaius* 124, 128.
29. *Against Flaccus* 56, 122; *Embassy to Gaius* 127–28 for descriptions of the area to which they were legally confined.
30. Philo, *Embassy to Gaius* 133–35.
31. Philo, *Against Flaccus* 62–72; *Embassy to Gaius* 127–32.
32. Philo, *Against Flaccus* 80–85.
33. For the *iustitium,* see Cassius Dio 59.11.5; for Gaius's declaration of the mourning period, see Philo, *Against Flaccus* 56; and for an interpretation of Flaccus's arrest, see Gambetti (2009) pp. 192–93.
34. Philo, *Embassy to Gaius* 370; Josephus, *Antiquities* 18.259.
35. Philo, *Embassy to Gaius* 349.
36. *Antiquities* 18.259.
37. *Antiquities* 18.259; Philo, *Embassy to Gaius* 370.
38. Pliny, *Natural History* Preface 25.
39. For a translation and commentary on the refutation, see Barclay (2013).

40. *Antiquities* 18.257–58.
41. Gambetti (2009) p. 216.
42. *Embassy to Gaius* 353, 357.
43. *Embassy to Gaius* 358–67.
44. *Antiquities* 18.260; Philo, *Embassy to Gaius* 368–73; Tacitus, *Histories* 5.9.1, claiming that Gaius ordered the Jews to set up a statue of him in the Temple.
45. A less positive interpretation of Petronius's actions at this time is presented by Philo, *Embassy to Gaius* 210–17, 245.
46. For example, Leviticus 26.1.
47. *War* 2.184–85; *Antiquities* 18.261; *Embassy to Gaius* 185–89; Grabbe (2010) p. 26.
48. *Embassy to Gaius* 199–203.
49. Andrade (2010) pp. 364–65.
50. For the four legions based in Syria—III Gallica, VI Ferrata, X Fretensis on the middle Euphrates frontier and XII Fulminata at Raphaneae—during (and after) the reign of Tiberius, see Tacitus, *Annals* 4.5. In addition to the paper strength of these 19,200 legionary soldiers under the command of the governor, there would have been around 32 cohorts or 16,000 auxiliary soldiers available to be deployed. These auxiliary cohorts of about 500 were usually locally recruited.
51. Philo, *Embassy to Gaius* 207; *War* 2.186–87; *Antiquities* 18.262.
52. *War* 2.192–93; *Antiquities* 18.263–69.
53. *War* 2.195–201; *Antiquities* 18.270–72.
54. *Antiquities* 18.273–74.
55. *War* 2.201–2; *Antiquities* 18.276–83.
56. *Antiquities* 18.284–88.
57. Philo, *Embassy to Gaius* 276–329, supposedly preserving the letter Agrippa wrote to the emperor trying to persuade him to desist; D. Schwartz (1990) pp. 77–89; *Antiquities* 18.289–301.
58. *War* 2.203; *Antiquities* 18.289–302.
59. *War* 2.203; *Antiquities* 18.305–9, 19.17–114; Suetonius, *Caligula* 58.1–3.
60. *Antiquities* 19.21; Suetonius, *Caligula* 56.2.
61. *War* 2.204–17; *Antiquities* 19.236–75.
62. Meshorer (2001) pp. 100–101, coin no. 124 on the obverse of which Agrippa I and his brother Herod of Chalcis raise their hands with wreaths toward the central figure, Claudius. On the reverse in Greek was an inscription reading, "A vow and treaty of friendship and alliance between the great king Agrippa and Augustus Caesar and the people of Rome."
63. Millar (1993) p. 59.
64. Cassius Dio 60.8.2–3; Goodman (2007c) p. 84.
65. *Antiquities* 19.278–85. For discussion of the authenticity of the letter to Syria, see Gambetti (2009) pp. 234–38.
66. *Antiquities* 19.286–91; for the episode, see Harker (2008) pp. 9–24; Gambetti (2009).
67. For extended analysis, see Gambetti (2009) pp. 230–38.
68. *Papyrus Oxyrhychus* XLII 3021 column iii lines 55–56.
69. *Papyrus Londinensis* VI 1912.
70. Lines 73–78.
71. Lines 84–88.
72. Lines 89–98.
73. Gambetti (2009) pp. 222–23.
74. Gambetti (2009) pp. 223–27.
75. The case for the edict cited by Josephus being an outright forgery is not persuasive; there are too many similarities between the contents of the letter Claudius sent to the Alexandrians

and the edict Josephus references. In addition, there surely would have been a record of Claudius's letter in Rome, against which Josephus's text could have been checked by the Roman readers he mentions had previewed his work—assuming that any of them were diligent enough to track the text down. That is not an impossible assumption. We know that at least some of the people who received copies of Josephus's *War* were based in Rome.

76. Acts 18.2; Suetonius, *Life of Claudius* 25; Cassius Dio 60.6.6–7; Richardson and Fisher (2018) p. 401.

77. *Antiquities* 19.293-94.

78. For the Nazirites, see Judges 13.5–7; Numbers 6.1–21; *CIIP Vol. I, Part 1* (2010) no. 70 pp. 114–15 for the approximately first-century BCE to first-century CE Hebrew and Aramaic inscription on the ossuary of Hananiya, son of Yehonatan, the Nazirite (*hnzr*); Chepey (2005) for a survey; Goodman (2007c) p. 301.

79. Ritmeyer (2006) p. 353.

80. Numbers 6.20.

81. *Nazir* 19b.

82. For his reputation for piety, see Schäfer (2003b) p. 112.

83. In Mark 3.17 James is nicknamed *Boanerges* or Son of Thunder, an allusion to his temper perhaps but also his forcefulness.

84. Acts of the Apostles 12.1–19.

85. *Antiquities* 19.294–96.

86. Theophilus the high priest from 37–41 (referred to in *Antiquities* 18.123–24 and 19.297) is also attested as the father of Yehohanan and grandfather of Yehohana in the ossuary (now in the Hecht Museum), Aramaic/Hebrew inscription, *CIIP Vol. I, Part 1* (2010) no. 534 p. 550; see also VanderKam (2004) pp. 440–43.

87. *Antiquities* 19.297–99, 19.317–26.

88. *Antiquities* 19.300–311. For Dor's location and the shifting boundary between Judaea and Syria in the area during the Roman imperial period, see *CIIP Vol. II* (2011) pp. 831–36.

89. Millar (1993) pp. 60–61.

90. Millar (2006) pp. 139–63.

91. *Antiquities* 19.297. Simon, son of Boethos, surnamed Cantheras, known from an inscription on an ossuary; *CIIP Vol. I, Part 1* (2010) no. 76 pp. 119–20.

92. *Antiquities* 19.312–16.

93. *War* 2.218–19, 5.147–59 and *Antiquities* 19.326–27; D. Schwartz (1990) pp. 140–44.

94. For Agrippa's coins with his title of friend of the emperor (since 40–41) and other such inscriptions and images of the Roman emperors and their family members, see Burnett (1987) pp. 25–38; Meshorer (2001) pp. 95, coin 119; 99, coin 122 (pointing out that the title occurs on coins of Agrippa I only during the reign of Claudius and never during the rule of Gaius); and Kushnir-Stein (2007) pp. 57–58.

95. *Antiquities* 19.328, 335–37.

96. Patrich (2008) pp. 1673–80 for the hippodrome or stadium in Caesarea; Hizmi (2008) pp. 48–59, 78 for the road station in Archelaïs (Khirbet el-Beiyudat).

97. *Antiquities* 19.352.

98. *Antiquities* 19.338–42; D. Schwartz (1990) pp. 137–40.

99. *Antiquities* 19.343; probably games in celebration of Claudius's safe return from the invasion of Britain (the *hyper soterias*) in the spring of 44 CE.

100. *War* 2.219; *Antiquities* 19.344–51. This is the version of the story Josephus gives. The author of Acts 12.20–23 gives an alternative version in which Agrippa was struck down by an angel of God because he did not honor God. The dying king was beset by the obligatory worms.

101. *Antiquities* 19.356–59.

CHAPTER 5. PROCURATORS, PROPHETS, AND DAGGER-MEN

1. *Antiquities* 19.360–62.
2. *Annals* 12.23.1: "Ituraeique et Iudaei defunctis regibus Sohaemo atque Agrippa provinciae Syriae additi."
3. *Histories* 2.78.4: "Haud dubia destinatione discessere Mucianus Antiochiam, Vespasianus Caesaream: illa Syriae, hoc Iudaeae caput est."
4. *War* 2.220; *Antiquities* 19.363; Grabbe (2010) p. 26.
5. *Antiquities* 19.363.
6. *Antiquities* 20.15–16, 20.103.
7. *Antiquities* 20.1.
8. Note that Roman plans in 26 CE to send Thracian auxiliaries away from the areas from which they had been recruited provoked a similar reaction; see Tacitus, *Annals* 4.46.1.
9. *Antiquities* 19.366; Saddington (1982) p. 50.
10. Mason (2016) p. 270 n. 251 suggests that Josephus invented or inflated Claudius's plan to remove the offending soldiers, supporting his suggestion by asking whether the better part of a legion could be withdrawn from the Euphrates (to be sent south), to be placed under the command of an equestrian procurator, with legionary cohorts rotating in and out of Jerusalem; he also asks how Josephus could know what Claudius had planned or said to his advisers. These are important questions to ask, but of course the emperor could order units of any kind to be transferred to any place he wanted. As far as a source for Claudius's plan is concerned, there is no direct evidence for it other than the report in *Antiquities*. One personal source for the story, however, might have been Agrippa II, who seems to have been in Rome at the time and of course knew Josephus well, at least later. In any case, it is not clear why the story should be suspect just because it occurs only in *Antiquities*.
11. *Antiquities* 19.366.
12. *Antiquities* 19.366.
13. *Antiquities* 20.2; for the location of the village, see Eusebius, *Onomasticon* 94.3; and for the episode, Millar (1993) p. 64.
14. *Antiquities* 20.3–4.
15. Millar (1993) p. 64.
16. *Antiquities* 20.5.
17. Who the "chief priests" Josephus mentions here and elsewhere are and how they are different from other priests supposedly descended from the sons of Aaron (the lineage of the priests as a whole) are unknown. It may be that the chief priests Josephus refers to were priestly members of the families of high priests; see VanderKam (2001) pp. 181–82.
18. *Antiquities* 20.6–8. God himself had supposedly ordered the making of the sacred priestly garments to be worn by Aaron and his sons; see Exodus 28.1–43, 39.1–31.
19. *Antiquities* 20.9–10.
20. Suetonius, *Claudius* 42.2.
21. *Antiquities* 20.9–14.
22. *Antiquities* 20.15–16.
23. Millar (1993) p. 63.
24. Acts 5.36; *Antiquities* 20.97–99; Schäfer (2003b) p. 114.
25. For the office, see Thomas (1982).
26. *War* 2.220; *Antiquities* 18.259, 20.100; for Tiberius Iulius Alexander as governor, see Turner (1954) pp. 54–64; Burr (1955); Schäfer (2003b) pp. 114–15; Goodman (2007c) pp. 151–52.
27. Rajak (2005) p. 86.
28. *Antiquities* 5.147 for King Izates.
29. *Antiquities* 20.17.

30. *Antiquities* 20.19.
31. Rogers (2004) p. 255.
32. *Antiquities* 20.22, 32.
33. *Antiquities* 20.34–35.
34. *Antiquities* 20.38–46.
35. *Antiquities* 20.49–50.
36. Noted in Acts 11.27–30; *Antiquities* 20.51–52, 20.53, 20.101, 3.320 for the Claudian context.
37. Yoma 3.10.
38. Numbers 5.11–31.
39. *War* 6.356.
40. *War* 5.253; Ben-Ami and Tchekhanovets (2011) pp. 231–39; Ben-Ami (2013b) pp. 22–31; Notley and Garcia (2014) pp. 28–40, 62, 64; for doubts about the identification, see Keddie (2019) p. 235, based upon the "austerity" of the architecture and material culture of the complex.
41. *Antiquities* 20.54–91.
42. *Antiquities* 20.91.
43. *Antiquities* 20.94. For the sarcophagi from the tomb, including that of Queen Zaddan, with its inscription in Syriac and Hebrew letters, see Foerster (1998) pp. 295–98.
44. Pausanias, *Description of Greece* 8.16.4–5. For the sarcophagus with an inscription "Sadan the Queen (line 1 in Seleucid Aramaic), Sada the Queen (line 2 in Jewish script)," which some scholars believe to belong to Helena, see *CIIP Vol. I, Part 1* (2010) no. 123 pp. 165–66, with an extensive bibliography on the text, though there is no consensus about the attribution; in addition, the bones of the woman in the sarcophagus are those of a young woman, not an older woman, as Helena was when she died. Keddie (2019) p. 235 n. 213 argues briefly that the sarcophagus of Helena was in chamber G of the tomb, the lid from which is in the Louvre. The "Tombeau des Rois" in east Jerusalem, which nevertheless falls under the jurisdiction of the government of France, was reopened to the public in 2019, though not without controversy, since some Jews consider the site to be an active burial ground for Jews in which they should be allowed to pray.
45. *Antiquities* 20.102; for the date, see Sartre (2005) p. 115.
46. Mason (2016) pp. 253, 271.
47. *Antiquities* 20.103.
48. Acts 23.1–2, 24.1.
49. Pesachim 57a.
50. *War* 2.429, 2.441.
51. *War* 2.223; *Antiquities* 20.104, 20.224–51 on the office and list of high priests; Millar (1993) p. 63; Goodman (2007c) pp. 8, 363.
52. Tacitus, *Annals* 12.54.1; *War* 2.223–24; *Antiquities* 20.105–8.
53. *War* 2.225–27; *Antiquities* 20.108–12; Eusebius, *Ecclesiastical History* 2.19.1 (30,000); Schäfer (2003b) p. 115.
54. *War* 2.228–29.
55. *Antiquities* 20.113–14.
56. *War* 2.229–31; *Antiquities* 20.115–17; Schäfer (2003b) p. 115; S. Schwartz (2014) pp. 1–3 for a thoughtful reflection on why the tearing up of a scroll should have such serious consequences.
57. Goodman (2007c) p. 387.
58. Represented as a dispute between the Samaritans and the Galilaeans in Tacitus's confused, summary account, *Annals* 12.54.
59. *War* 2.232–33; *Antiquities* 20.118–19; Tacitus, *Annals* 12.54 for a nonspecific account of the warfare between Galilaeans and Samaritans during Cumanus's governorship; for the episode, see Millar (1993) pp. 64–65, who emphasizes how what happened suggests how difficult it was to maintain order among the densely populated and well-armed villages of the

region; see also Schäfer (2003b) p. 115; Pummer (2009) pp. 251–62 for the most recent detailed analysis of the incident, arguing that the expanded version in the *Antiquities* is intended to shift responsibility for what happened onto the Samaritans.

60. *War* 2.234–35; *Antiquities* 20.120–1, downplaying the devastation of the massacre.

61. *War* 2.236–38; *Antiquities* 20.122–24.

62. *War* 2.239–40; *Antiquities* 20.125–27; for the representatives of the Samaritans and the Jews, see Pummer (2009) p. 253.

63. *War* 2.241; *Antiquities* 20.129.

64. *War* 2.242; *Antiquities* 20.130.

65. *War* 2.243–44; *Antiquities* 20.131–33.

66. *War* 2.245–46; *Antiquities* 20.134–36.

67. Mason (2016) p. 272.

68. Pummer (2009) pp. 261.

69. Isaac (1992) pp. 322–23; Millar (1993) p. 65; Isaac (1998) pp. 93–94.

70. *War* 2.247; *Antiquities* 20.137; Suetonius, *Claudius* 28; *Acts* 24.24.

71. *War* 2.247, 223; *Antiquities* 20.138; Millar (1993) p. 63. Chalcis seems to have been placed under the jurisdiction of the legate of Syria.

72. *War* 2.252; *Antiquities* 20.158–59; Millar (1993) p. 66.

73. *War* 2.253; *Antiquities* 20.160–1; Schäfer (2003b) p. 115; Sartre (2005) p. 115.

74. *War* 2.254.

75. *Antiquities* 20.163. Doras is a name known from the Hebrew/Aramaic inscription on an ossuary now in Beth Shemesh, *CIIP Vol. I, Part 1* (2010) no. 495 p. 516.

76. *War* 2.255–56; *Antiquities* 20.164.

77. *War* 2.257; *Antiquities* 20.165.

78. *Antiquities* 20.166.

79. *War* 2.258–62; *Antiquities* 20.167–70; *Acts* 21.38. The discrepancy between the numbers of the Egyptian's followers in *War* and in Acts illustrates why we should be cautious about Josephus's numbers in general. The problem, however, is that we have no objective way of assessing the accuracy of either total. All we can do with certainty is to conclude that both sources cannot be correct.

80. *War* 2.263; *Antiquities* 20.171–72.

81. Goodman (2007c) p. 390.

82. *War* 2.264–65; *Antiquities* 20.172.

83. Goodman (2007c) p. 390.

84. For example, *War* 7.259–61.

85. For the ethnic makeup of Caesarea's population at the time, see *War* 3.409–10. In *War* 2.266 what the Jews wanted was precedence; in *Antiquities* 20.173 the issue was equality of civic rights, or *isopoliteia*. See Andrade (2010) pp. 366–68 for the conflict.

86. *War* 2.266–70; *Antiquities* 20.173–78.

87. *Antiquities* 20.179–81; Schäfer (2003b) p. 116.

88. Deuteronomy 14.22–28.

89. Leviticus 27.30–32.

90. Numbers 18.21–28.

91. Keddie (2019) p. 179.

CHAPTER 6. THE FUSE

1. *Antiquities* 20.182.

2. Josephus is not clear or consistent in his identification of the different ethnic groups in Caesarea and elsewhere; in *War* 2.284, for instance, he identifies the petitioners to Nero about

civic rights in Caesarea as Greeks (*Hellenes*) but refers to them in *Antiquities* 20.173 as Syrians. The apparent contradiction can possibly be resolved by assuming that the latter qualify as Hellenes because they are Greek speaking, though their native language might have been Aramaic and their ethnic background or cultural identification was Syrian or Near Eastern. Josephus's use of the word "Syrian" is complicated by the fact that, after Pompey's conquests in the region in 63 BCE, Syria, and therefore Syrians, could refer not exclusively to individuals' linguistic, ethnic, or cultural characteristics but also to a collective regional "ethnicity." For that reason ethnic Hellenes living in the region could also be identified as Syrians. So there are Syrian Greeks and Greek Syrians. What they were not, however, were Jews.

3. For Nero's phihellenism, see Griffin (1984) pp. 208–20.

4. *Antiquities* 20.183; *War* 2.284, putting the receipt of the decision later and out of context.

5. *War* 2.284; *Antiquities* 20.184.

6. *War* 2.271; *Antiquities* 20.165, 20.185–87.

7. *Antiquities* 20.188.

8. For the palace of the Hasmoneans, which was located on the Xystus and was connected to the Temple by a bridge, see *War* 2.344. The gate into the Temple Mount connected to that bridge is the one above Wilson's Arch today.

9. *Antiquities* 20.189–96.

10. For the controversies about the date of the patriarchate, see S. Schwartz (2014) pp. 118–22; for different points of view about the existence of a formally constituted group of judges or advisers versus a group that was called together by kings, high priests, or, later, patriarchs on an ad hoc basis, see Goodblatt (1994) pp. 77–130; Sanders (1985) pp. 472–90, (1992) pp. 472–90; Goodman (1987) pp. 113–16; McLaren (1991) 213–17; VanderKam (2001) pp. 184–85; Sharon (2012) pp. 423–32; Marshak (2015) p. 79.

11. *Antiquities* 20.197–200. Eusebius, *Ecclesiastical History* 2.23.2–3 cites Clement who reported that James was thrown from the Temple pinnacle and when he apparently survived was beaten to death with a club.

12. Eusebius, *Ecclesiastical History* 2.23.18.

13. *Antiquities* 20.201–3; Magness (2012) pp. 248–50.

14. *Antiquities* 20.204.

15. *War* 2.272–76; *Antiquities* 20.215.

16. For the grain dole (*plebs frumentaria*), see Garnsey (1988) p. 236.

17. For the expenditures, see Duncan-Jones (1994) p. 45; Wolters (2000–2001) p. 580.

18. Tacitus, *Annals* 15.18.1–3.

19. *War* 2.272–76.

20. *Antiquities* 20.205–7, 181.

21. Keddie (2019) p. 188.

22. *Antiquities* 20.208–10.

23. Meshorer (2001) pp. 105–6, coins 129–32.

24. *Antiquities* 20.211–12.

25. *Antiquities* 20.213.

26. *Antiquities* 20.214.

27. *Antiquities* 20.215.

28. *Antiquities* 20.219–22.

29. *Antiquities* 20.223.

30. *Annals* 5.10.

31. For the fire, its effects, and the costs of rebuilding, see the main ancient sources (Tacitus, *Annals* 15.38.1–45.1–2; Suetonius, *Life of Nero* 38.1–3; Cassius Dio 62.16.1–18.5); and Walsh (2019) pp. 73–95; 65 for the duration of the fire; 65–72 on the extent of the damage and the sources' shaping of the information about the destruction.

32. Champlin (2003) p. 318 n. 9.

33. Dio 62.18.5; Morgan (2006) p. 48.
34. Walsh (2019) p. 76.
35. *Natural History* 17.5; Suetonius, *Nero* 38.1; Cassius Dio 62.16.1. For a clear, balanced, and readable account of the question of Nero's guilt, see Champlin (2003) pp. 178–85; Walsh (2019) pp. 78–85 for a lively discussion.
36. For both individuals and communities being squeezed for cash, see Tacitus, *Annals* 15.45.1 (Italy, the provinces, the federate communities, and free states); Suetonius, *Nero* 38.3 (bankrupting the provinces and individuals); Cassius Dio 62.18.5.
37. See Eck (2011) pp. 45–68 for an overview of Josephus's representation of the actions of the Roman governors.
38. For the changing views of Nero among scholars and more widely, see Griffin (2013) pp. 467–80.
39. April of the Julian calendar, Nisan/Xanthicus according to the Hebrew/Macedonian lunar month equivalents used by Josephus. Josephus based the figures of 3 million in Jerusalem at this time and an equally impossible figure of 2.7 million in *War* 6.425 upon the number of sacrifices that took place during the Passover festival. Those figures may have been generated for Cestius (to pass along to Nero) by Jews who wanted to emphasize the importance of their ethnos. For Cestius's appointment, see Tacitus, *Annals* 15.25.3.
40. *War* 2.277–83; *Antiquities* 20.252–58; Millar (1993) p. 69.
41. *War* 2.284–85; *Antiquities* 20.257.
42. For modern accounts of the background and incident, see Levine (1974) pp. 381–97; Kasher (1990) pp. 245–68; Andrade (2010) pp. 342–70.
43. Keddie (2019) p. 142.
44. *War* 2.285–88.
45. *War* 2.289.
46. The question of how and why the sacrifice of some birds was intended as an insult (as Josephus makes clear it was) has puzzled historians. Some have pointed to the Pentateuch for an explanation. In the Pentateuch a sacrifice of birds is specified for recovered lepers; according to Alexandrian Greek anti-Jewish propaganda attributed to Manetho and Lysimachus by Josephus, Jews originally were lepers who were kicked out of Egypt (*Against Apion* I.229, I.279–87, I.304). Thus the sacrifice in Caesarea was meant to be a reminder of the Jews' origins as an unclean and contagious community. If such propaganda lay behind the incident in 66, however, Josephus does not mention it. A simpler explanation may suffice. Any sacrifice of any kind by a polytheist to or for any deity or deities next to a synagogue would have been understood by Jews by this time as a deliberate challenge to their belief in the existence of one god to whom sacrifices had to be made at one place, the Jerusalem Temple. It was, as Josephus put it in *War* 2.289, an outrage to the Jews' laws and a desecration of the spot (289). For bird sacrifice in Graeco-Roman culture, see the review article of Villing (2017).
47. Villing (2017) p. 98.
48. *War* 2.290.
49. Because of his Latin name it is possible, though not certain, that Iucundus was a Roman.
50. *War* 2.291–92.
51. Considered a "trivial" tax to punish the Jews for wrangling with Florus over Caesarea by Sartre (2005) p. 118. But 17 talents were equivalent to more than 100,000 drachmas, and the point was that it was simply taken from the Temple treasury.
52. Lapin (2017a) p. 441 n. 71.
53. Mason (2016) pp. 315–18.
54. *War* 2.293–95. See Schäfer (2003b) p. 117 for the attempt to take over the treasury as the spark that lit off the revolt.
55. *War* 2.296.

56. *War* 2.297–300.
57. *War* 2.301–4.
58. The Upper Agora, *War* 2.305, 2.315; the Timber Market, 2.530; the Wool Market, 5.331; and the Lower Market, in the Tyropoeon Valley, Keddie (2019) p. 149.
59. *War* 2.305–8.
60. Since the time of the emperor Augustus (31 BCE–14 CE) the minimum level of wealth for members of the order was 100,000 denarii; see Jones (1964) pp. 7–8.
61. Agrippa II seems to have been born in 28; Berenice in 29.
62. For Berenice's (ultimately unhappy) relationship with Titus, see Suetonius, *Life of Titus* 7.1–2; Cassius Dio 66.15.3–4.
63. *War* 2.309–14.
64. *War* 2.315–19.
65. *War* 2.320.
66. *War* 2.321–24.
67. *War* 2.325–27.
68. *War* 2.328–29.
69. *War* 2.330–31.
70. *War* 2.331–32.

CHAPTER 7. THE REGIONAL CLEANSING

1. *War* 2.333–34.
2. Hopkins (1966) p. 263; Duncan-Jones (1990) p. 103.
3. Mason (2016) p. 321. See *CIL* 6.33950 for his first consulate in 35 CE under Tiberius; a second, undated one under Gaius; and his third consulate by 42 under Claudius, *AE* (1982) 199. For his appointment as *legatus* of Syria in 63, see Tacitus, *Annals* 15.25.3.
4. *War* 2.280.
5. Suetonius, *Augustus* 25.4.
6. *War* 2.334–35.
7. *War* 2.335.
8. *War* 2.336–38.
9. *War* 2.338–39.
10. *War* 2.339–40; for the Siloam Pool, see *War* 5.140, 5.505, 6.363; John 9.7, where Jesus sent the blind man to wash his eyes; for the Gihon Spring, which provided the waters for the pool, see Reich and Shukron (1998) pp. 136–37, (1999) pp. 77–78; Magness (2012) pp. 37–44 on the area, (2019a) p. 70.
11. *War* 5.193, 6.124; *Antiquities* 15.417; Middot 2.3, 2 feet, 10 inches high. The balustrade did not need to be extended to the north because there was no northern gate giving access to the inner courts; see Ritmeyer (2006) p. 347.
12. For the *Soreg*, see Middot 2.3; for the warning inscription, see *CIIP Vol. I, Part 1* (2010) no. 2 pp. 42–45 with extensive notes.
13. See Richardson and Fisher (2018) pp. 301–2 for acute observations.
14. *War* 2.341.
15. *War* 2.342.
16. Rajak (2002) p. 117.
17. *War* 2.343–44. For the Xystus, see 1 Maccabees 1.14-15 and 2 Maccabees 4.12–14; *War* 2.344, 4.581, 5.144, 6.191, 6.325, 6.377.
18. *War* 2.345–401.
19. *War* 2.402–4.

20. *War* 2.405.

21. *War* 2.406. Josephus does not tell his readers that a process had been put in place whereby Florus would be replaced.

22. *War* 2.407.

23. *War* 3.443–44.

24. For Agrippa visiting Cestius in Antioch, see *War* 2.481; for Berytus (Beirut), see *Life* 49.

25. On the influence of rhetoric on speeches in Josephus's works, see Price (2008) pp. 6–24; Mason (2008) pp. 265–68; (2016) pp. 73–80.

26. *War* 2.390.

27. For God being on the side of the Romans, see *War* 5.412; *Antiquities* 20.165–66; and for discussion of the speech, see Friedländer (1873); Domaszewski (1892) pp. 207–18; Schürer, Vol. 1 (2014) p. 486 n. 4; Goodman (2007c) pp. 63–65.

28. As Josephus himself informs us, among the readers of his final authorized version of the war were "the Emperors" (Vespasian, Titus); "many others" who had taken part in the war, such as King Agrippa and certain of his relatives; a large number of his compatriots who were versed in Greek learning, including Archelaus, husband of Agrippa's sister Mariamme; and Herod (which one, we are not sure), to whom Josephus sold copies of his volumes. See *Life* 361–63 and *Against Apion* 1.50–51.

29. *War* 2.408. The Greek word *lathra* could mean some sort of tactical trick or perhaps an attack that was not detected. Could they have made their way up Masada along an unguarded path, or were there too few guards stationed on Masada to keep watch over all the possible attack routes?

30. *War* 2.409.

31. *War* 2.409–10.

32. *War* 2.409.

33. Rajak (2002) p. 117; Mason (2016) p. 276.

34. For example, *War* 2.197; *Against Apion* 2.76–77 on homage and sacrifices in honor of the emperors and Roman people; Philo, *Embassy to Gaius* 157, on the daily perpetual sacrifices subsidized by Caesar Augustus; 317, for whole burnt offerings (two sheep and a bull) offered up every day to God, financed by Augustus's own revenues. Hundreds of years before, during the fifth century BCE, the Jews had interceded with Yahweh on behalf of their Persian rulers; see Ezra 6.10.

35. Rajak (2002) p. 117.

36. Goldstein and Fontanille (2006) pp. 8–32.

37. Genesis 32.28, 35.10, 49.2–28.

38. 2 Samuel 5.7; 1 Kings 8.1; 2 Kings 19.21.

39. Goldstein and Fontanille (2006) p. 26.

40. Kanael (1953) p. 20.

41. Kadman (1960) pp. 84–87.

42. Meshorer (2001) pp. 127–28.

43. Rappaport (2007) pp. 105–6, 109–11, 114.

44. Mason (2016) pp. 478–79.

45. Tacitus, *Annals* 15.45.1–2, makes clear that Italy, Asia, and Achaia also were squeezed for contributions.

46. For the Gate and the doors, see *War* 5.201; Middoth 1.4, 2.3, 2.6; Yoma 2.3–4. In Yoma 38a Nicanor went to Alexandria to bring the doors for the eastern gate of the Temple. But on the way a storm threatened to sink the ship he was on and drown him. The passengers on the ship threw one of the heavy doors overboard to lighten the ship but the storm continued. As they prepared to throw the second door into the sea, Nicanor held onto the door and told them to throw him overboard with it. After that the storm subsided. When they got to Acco they found the first door under the ship. But some also said that a sea creature had swal-

lowed the first door and spewed it up on the land. For the first century BCE to the first century CE ossuary and inscription (probably) for the sons of Nicanor on Mt. Scopus, see Kloner and Zissu (2007) pp. 179–81; *CIIP Vol. I, Part 1* (2010) no. 98 pp. 140–41.

47. *War* 2.411–16.

48. Ezra 6.9, 7.11–24; *Letter of Aristeas* 33, 42, 51–82; *Antiquities* 12.138–44; 2 Maccabees 3.3.

49. Ezra 7.23.

50. *War* 2.417.

51. *War* 2.418–19.

52. Note that Josephus's unsparing representation of Florus's motivation is further proof that the *War* was not written to exculpate all Romans for the outbreak of the war.

53. *War* 2.420–21; Philip's rank is given at 2.556. Bathyra in Batanaea was the site of a Herodian military colony, originally led by a Babylonian Jew; see *Antiquities* 17.23–28. Some of the early colonists were kinsmen of the Jew and therefore presumably Jews, but there also were 500 cavalrymen, whose ethnic identities are not known. The original military colony and village were freed from taxation, but the Romans imposed a tribute upon the later inhabitants of the town.

54. Mason (2016) p. 307.

55. *War* 2.422, counting backward seven days from the beginning of the feast of wood carrying that began on 14–15 Av according to Josephus's reckoning; Mason (2016) p. 304.

56. For the publication of the results of the excavations in this area conducted since 1969, including those of the so-called Burnt House, see Avigad (1983), (1989a); Geva (2000), (2003), (2006), (2010a), (2014b), (2017).

57. Avigad (1983) pp. 129–31; J. Schwartz (2010) pp. 308–19.

58. For some examples, see *CIIP Vol. III* (2014) no. 2274–78 pp. 172–77 from the Miriam House of Kibbutz Palmachim.

59. *War* 2.422–24.

60. *War* 2.425–27; for the date, see Mishnah Taanith 4.8; in Bava Batra 121b 15 Av (or Ab) was the day when they stopped cutting wood for the arrangement of the wood on the altar, because wood cut from then on would not dry properly and would be unfit for use in the Temple.

61. Nehemiah 10.34 Lapin (2017a) pp. 442–44 for the enormous quantities of wood needed to keep the sacrificial fires going.

62. For the calculations, see Lapin (2017a) pp. 442–43.

63. *War* 2.426.

64. Ananias's palace has been identified, with the approximately 600-square-meter palatial mansion located on the eastern hill of the Upper City, just opposite from the southwestern corner of the Herodian Temple Mount.

65. The archive building was probably located on the hill between the Hasmonean palace and the Xystus, as can be inferred from *War* 2.344.

66. *War* 2.427.

67. Keddie (2019) pp. 102–3.

68. *War* 2.428–29.

69. *War* 2.430.

70. On the ethnic origins of the auxiliaries, see *War* 2.268.

71. *War* 2.431–32.

72. *War* 2.433–34.

73. On the rebels' weaponry, see Price (1992) pp. 121–22.

74. *War* 2.408.

75. *War* 2.434-40.

76. *War* 2.444. Mason (2016) pp. 444–50 makes a strong case that when Josephus uses the Greek word *zelotes* or one of its cognates to describe the followers of Menahem, Eleazar, and John in the *War* he is using the Greek term (translating an unknown Hebrew word) either sarcastically or

ironically to distinguish the people it is applied to from other individuals in Israel's history such as Phineas or Matthias, whose devotion to the law and actions made them worthy of emulation. If that is correct it would help to solve the apparent contradiction between Josephus's use of the term "zealots" here to describe Menahem's supporters and then Josephus calling the occupiers of Masada led by Menahem's relative Eleazar Ben Yair *sicarii*. The issue is further confused by Yadin calling the people on top of Masada in 73–74 CE zealots.

77. For the Ophlas, see *War* 5.145. The Ophlas (Hebrew, *Ophel*) was located just to the south of the Temple Mount's eastern corner; essentially it comprised the area between the Temple Mount and the city of David.

78. *War* 2.447, 7.297.

79. *War* 2.449–56.

80. *War* 2.456.

81. *War* 2.457. If the Jews of Caesarea were a minority in the city, as is likely, they were a sizable minority.

82. *War* 2.457.

83. *Antiquities* 13.395–97 for Josephus's list of the cities in Syria, Idumaea, and Phoenicia held by the Jews just before Jannaeus's death. For the histories and archaeological remains of Pella and Scythopolis, see Smith and Day (1989); Mazar (2006).

84. See Seigne (2002) pp. 6–22; Hoffman (2002) pp. 109–12; Mason (2016) p. 276.

85. In his *Life* 42, Josephus claims that Justus of Tiberias was responsible for burning the villages belonging to Hippos and Gadara; for Hippos's urban development, see Segal and Eisenberg (2007) pp. 86–107.

86. Philo, *Embassy to Gaius* 30.205. Note, however, that Josephus, *Antiquities* 14.190–216, cites a decree of Gaius Caesar ordering that Hyrcanus's children rule over the Jewish nation and that the high priest and ethnarch should be the protector of those Jews who were unjustly treated. The decree was to be engraved in Greek and Latin letters on a bronze tablet, to be set up in the capitol and at Sidon, Tyre, and Ascalon. For Ascalon's history and culture, see the marvelous introductory essay in *CIIP Vol. III* (2014) pp. 237–52.

87. *War* 2.458–60. For Gaza in general and as a trade center, see the comprehensive introduction in *CIIP Vol. III* (2014) pp. 409–29; see p. 418 for doubts about whether Gaza or Anthedon was actually razed.

88. *War* 2.461–65.

89. Deuteronomy 28.23.

90. Bavli Megillah 3b; Gregerman (2016) p. 201.

91. *War* 2.466–76; Goodman (2007c) pp. 164–65; Klawans (2012) p. 131, arguing that Simon's death is not presented as a heroic martyrdom in Josephus because Simon had spilled the blood of his fellow Jews; for the episode as a kind of anticipation of the murder/suicide at Masada, see Mason (2016) p. 99.

92. *War* 2.477–78.

93. *Life* 43–44.

94. *War* 2.479–80.

95. After the small kingdom in Lebanon to which he was heir was included in the territory given to Agrippa II.

96. *War* 2.481–83; *Life* 52–61 gives a different version of what happened. In the *Life*, the Syrian Caesareans led Varus (Noarus) to believe that he would replace Agrippa II after the Romans put him to death. Subsequently, Varus united with the people of Trachonitis in an attack upon the Jews of Ecbatana (the one in the region, not Ecbatana in Media). Varus sent 12 Jews from Caesarea to the Jews of Ecbatana to tell them that he had heard that they were going to attack Agrippa. Varus told them to send 70 of their leading men to him to prove that the report was false. When they did, Varus's royal troops killed the envoys and 69 of the Jews from

Ecbatana; one got away, reported what had happened to his fellow Jews, and the Jews of Ecbatana escaped to Gamala.

97. *War* 2.484–86.

98. *War* 2.490–93.

99. *War* 2.494.

100. The Delta Section of the city (the fourth, starting with alpha) has been convincingly located on the western side of the city, near the artificial harbor of Kibotos, by Gambetti (2009) pp. 34–35.

101. *War* 2.495–97; later on, in the speech attributed to Eleazar ben Yair on Masada at book 7.367, the casualty figure is 60,000.

102. *War* 2.498.

103. I owe this insight into the history of warfare to Col. Ralph Peters.

CHAPTER 8. THE CLADES CESTIANA (CESTIAN DISASTER)

1. *War* 2.481 for Agrippa's trip to see Cestius.

2. One check that we have upon whether this actually happened, and indeed for Agrippa's actions before and during the war generally, is Josephus's testimony in his *Life* 362 that he presented his history to Agrippa and certain of his relatives immediately after it was written up. Josephus surely would have known in advance that if he did not tell the truth about Agrippa's actions in 66 then Agrippa and others would have known. Agrippa knew what had happened to him and knew what he told Cestius.

3. *War* 2.406, 409.

4. *War* 2.421 for the dispatch of the cavalry.

5. *War* 2.426.

6. *War* 2.499. In Josephus's narrative of the *War* it is directly after his description of the inter-ethnic violence between Greeks and Jews in Alexandria (2.487–98) that he reports that Cestius decided to act. From this presentation readers might get the impression that Cestius intervened in the Galilee and Judaea during the summer of 66 because of the events that had happened, not only Agrippa's expulsion from Jerusalem, the rejection of gifts or sacrifices from foreigners by the Temple servants, and the defeat and evacuation of Agrippa's cavalry from the Upper City of Jerusalem (2.426); but also the murders of Ananias, Ezekias, and Menahem (2.428–48); the massacre of the Roman garrison (2.449–56); the massacre of Caesarea's Jews and reprisals in the Syrian villages and neighboring cities (2.457–65); the slaughter of the Jews of Scythopolis (466–76); the fates of Jews in Syria (2.477–80); the murder of the 80 Jews in Agrippa's kingdom and the capture of Cypros and Machaerus (2.481–86); and finally the ethnic strife in Alexandria. But Cestius could not have planned for his campaign in the south; gathered up Legio XII from its base at Raphaneae to the south of Antioch and the other Syrian vexillations from their bases, X Fretensis at Cyrrhus, 60 miles away in northern Syria near the Marsyas (Afrin) River, IIII Scythica near Zeugma, 120 miles away on the middle Euphrates, and VI Ferrata at Apamea on the Orontes River or Laodicea on the coast, both more than 50 miles away; then conducted operations in the Galilee, and made it to Lydda by around 15 Tishri (as Josephus reports at 2.515), after hearing about all of these developments, unless he had begun planning in early Av/Lous or mid-July 66. Just to summon a vexillation from Zeugma (if one of the legions was stationed there) and have it join Cestius in Antioch would have taken about 12 days. The minimum amount of time Cestius would have needed to plan the operation, communicate with the legions, assemble his army, and conduct all of the operations described would have been a month. The significance of this chronological review is that it indicates that Cestius did not assemble his force in response to

the widespread warfare in Syria and Egypt that Josephus describes in *War* 2.441–98. Rather it was the news of Agrippa's failure to stamp out the conflict in Jerusalem and the situation there that led Cestius to act. It was Agrippa who turned Cestius's ear. The chronology also helps us understand the kind of force Cestius put together and what its goals were.

7. *War* 2.500; for Raphaneae as the base of XII Fulminata, see *War* 7.18.

8. Caesar, *Commentaries on the Gallic War* 1.10; Tacitus, *Annals* 15.15.1–16.1; Cassius Dio 62.21.1–4; Keppie (1998) pp. 82, 209–10 for a succinct history of the legion.

9. Since we know from Tacitus's brief survey of the disposition of Roman legions from the time of Augustus in *Annals* 4.5 that there were four legions stationed in Syria.

10. *War* 2.500. The bases of IIII Scythica, VI Ferrata, and X Fretensis at the time are not entirely certain. Zeugma was probably the base of IIII Scythica, some 120 miles northeast of Antioch. It would have taken at least two weeks for a messenger to get out to Zeugma and for the vexillation to make it to Antioch. Tacitus, *Annals* 2.57.2, names Cyrrhus as the winter quarters of X Fretensis. Cyrrhus was about 60 miles, or a rapid three-day march, northeast of Antioch. To send a messenger to Cyrrhus with orders for Legio X Fretensis to march and for the vexillation to reach Antioch would have taken at least a week. At *Annals* 2.79.2 Tacitus implies that the winter quarters of Legio VI Ferrata were near Laodicea, though its nonwinter quarters seem to have been at Samosata, 180 miles northeast of Antioch.

11. Mason (2016) p. 310 gives the higher troop strengths for the legion at the time, either 5,400 or 6,000. Josephus frustratingly does not give an exact figure.

12. *War* 2.500.

13. Saddington (1982) p. 102, giving the low and high numbers of 500 and 1,000; Goldsworthy (1996) pp. 21–24, including tables 2 and 3, giving totals for the different kinds of cohorts and *alae*; Keppie (1998) pp. 182–83; Roth (2012) p. 337; Mason (2016) p. 141.

14. Pseudo-Hyginus, *On the Building of Camps* 16; Arrian, *Essay on Tactics* 18; Keppie (1998) pp. 182–84, noting that by this time a hierarchical sequence of command for the auxiliary officers had been established, from *praefectus cohortis* to *tribunus militum* to *praefectus alae*; Goldsworthy (2000) p. 214; Roth (2012) pp. 335–36.

15. Goldsworthy (1996) p. 21 for these points about the numbers of active service soldiers; see also Scheidel (1996) p. 121.

16. Unfortunately, Josephus does not specify what less (*elattous*) than 2,000 cavalry means here. For the sake of argument I propose that the number should be around 1,667; if Agrippa provided 1,667 cavalrymen, that would bring the allied cavalry contribution up to about 5,000 (Antiochus bringing 2,000 cavalry and Sohaemus 1,333). On issues of communications and timing, assuming that Cestius sent out a request to Antiochus for troops from Antioch, it would have taken that request at least nine days to reach Samosata, the Commagenian capital, 180 miles northeast of Antioch on the Upper Euphrates, and at least another nine days for the Commagenian contingent to march to Antioch. Time must also have been needed for Antiochus to muster his force.

17. Mason (2016) p. 311 suggests that Sohaemus's contingent may have met up with Cestius's task force in Tripolis as it made its way south. That would make sense logistically since Emesa was much closer to Tripolis to the west than to Antioch to the north, but Josephus does not provide details about the linkup.

18. Roth (2012) p. 114.

19. Roth (2012) pp. 9–13, 42–43, 67, 119, 330, where Roth notes that his estimate of the Roman ration is smaller and lighter in weight than that of other scholars. The adoption of Roth's estimates strengthens the argument made here. If the ration was larger and heavier, that would mean that Roman soldiers and their pack animals had to carry more weight and find more food on campaign than is estimated here. For estimates of annual civilian, urban grain consumption at about 250 kg or 551 lbs. of wheat per year, see Jongman (2013) pp. 592–618, 599.

20. Roth (2012) p. 18.
21. *War* 3.95.
22. For the seasonal planting of wheat and the other food that would have been ripening during the summer in 66, see Roth (2012) pp. 137, 139.
23. Roth (2012) p. 122.
24. Coarelli (2000) p. 107 Plate 63 (XLII–XLIII/LXI–LXII).
25. *War* 2.546.
26. Roth (2012) pp. 61–67, 198.
27. Roth (2012) p. 128.
28. See appendix I, "Cestius's Army."
29. See appendix I, "Cestius's Army."
30. Roth (2012) p. 237.
31. Roth (2012) pp. 117–55.
32. The health hazards associated with "waste" pits used by the U.S. Army in Afghanistan are now being recognized; see https://www.cbsnews.com/news/burn-pit-military-lung-disease-thousands-of-veterans-fear-burn-pits-exposed-them-to-lethal-disease-2019-08-17/.
33. Goldsworthy (1996) pp. 293–94.
34. Probably along the military road that Claudius had ordered to be built. I thank Ben Isaac for pointing out the sequence to me.
35. *War* 1.290; *Antiquities* 14.394.
36. Isaac (1992) pp. 322–23.
37. See chapter 7; see Mason (2016) p. 330 for the chronology.
38. *War* 2.502.
39. *War* 2.503; Marshak (2015) p. 10.
40. *War* 2.503–4.
41. *War* 2.505–6.
42. At least later converted into a Roman military road, as is known from a series of military milestones; see Lehmann and Holum (2000) nos. 100–107.
43. The town seems to have had a Greek-style council (*boule*) since the time of the reign of Claudius, when it and the *demos* (citizen assembly) erected a statue for the senator and legate Lucius Popillius Balbus; see *CIIP Vol. III* (2014) no. 2173 pp. 34–35.
44. *War* 2.507–9.
45. *War* 2.509; for Narbata's location relative to Caesarea, see also 2.291.
46. *War* 2.510.
47. *Life* 31.
48. For the Roman propensity for flanking attacks, see Goldsworthy (1996) p. 142.
49. *War* 2.511–12.
50. *War* 2.513; see Dar and Applebaum (1973) pp. 91–99 for the road.
51. See *War* 3.124 for the Roman norm of marching six abreast, but also 2.173 for a formation of three abreast and 5.131 for seven abreast; and Mason (2016) p. 291, for the spacing and estimates of the column lengths.
52. Depending upon the formations of the non-Roman soldiers and how the animals were led; see Mason (2016) p. 292.
53. *War* 2.515. Apparently, unlike the inhabitants of Lydda, they were not going to attend the festival of the Tabernacles.
54. Deuteronomy 16.13–15; John 7.2–8.59 for Jesus's teaching in the Temple and on the Mount of Olives during the festival.
55. Of course, if individuals or families procrastinated and only planned to show up for the last day of the festival, in theory they could have left two or three days before the last day of the festival, on 22 or 23 Tishri; thus, on the 19th or 20th. In that case Cestius could have arrived at the deserted town on 18 or 19 Tishri.

56. *War* 2.516. Josephus does not tell us who the 50 people were.

57. Har-El (1981) pp. 8–19; for the road and Cestius's route along the road, see Fischer, Isaac, and Roll (1996) pp. 12–14.

58. For traces of steps cut by the engineers, see Mason (2016) p. 291, citing the engraving of Wilson from 1881.

59. *War* 2.516.

60. 2 Samuel 2.13.

61. Confusingly, Josephus gives the distance from Gabaon to Jerusalem as 50 stades in *War* 2.517 and 40 stades in *Antiquities* 7.283. Apparently they moved closer together as Josephus aged.

62. From Caesarea to Antipatris, three days; Antipatris to Lydda, one day; Lydda to Gabaon, one day.

63. *War* 2.521.

64. *War* 2.517.

65. Suetonius, *Vespasian* 4.5; Goldsworthy (1996) p. 203. If Josephus is right this should mean that the Jews attacked on 22 or 23 Tishri, a week after the festival began.

66. This numerical precision lends some credibility to Josephus's totals; they also could have been checked by Josephus's Roman readers.

67. *War* 2.518–20. Silas might be an Aramaic name but also could be a transliteration of a Latin name, either Silva or Silanus. That raises the possibility that Silas might have had experience as a Roman auxiliary soldier.

68. *War* 2.521.

69. Aramaic *giora* or Hebrew *ger* means foreigner. For the arguments about the significance of Simon's patronymic, see Mason (2016) pp. 457–58.

70. *War* 4.486–89; 4.503; Fuks (1985–88) pp. 106–19; Fischer, Isaac, and Roll (1996) pp. 162–63; Mason (2016) pp. 458–59; especially *CIIP Vol. IV, Part 1* (2018) pp. 187–229 for a priceless introductory essay and inscriptions from Gezer.

71. On the evidence for Jewish proselytes during the period, see Cohen (1999a) pp. 140–74.

72. *War* 2.522.

73. For analyses of the confrontation and issues with Josephus's description of it, see Bar-Kochva (1976) pp. 13–21; Gichon (1981) pp. 39–62; Mason (2016) pp. 290–306.

74. *War* 2.517–18.

75. *War* 2.521.

76. Goldsworthy (1996) p. 293, table 5.

77. Harmand (1967) p. 132 n. 240; Goldsworthy (1996) p. 112.

78. Gichon (1981) pp. 39, 53.

79. Bar-Kochva (1976) p. 18.

80. *War* 2.516.

81. For the *taxeis,* see *War* 2.518.

82. *War* 2.522.

83. *War* 2.523–26.

84. *War* 2.527–28.

85. *War* 2.528–30.

86. *War* 2.531–32.

87. *War* 2.283.

88. Before, Cestius had been to Jerusalem as a kind of honored guest; when he came in 66 he was an enemy general.

89. *War* 2.533–34.

90. *War* 2.534–37; Ritmeyer (2006) p. 123.

91. Coarelli (2000) p. 124, Plate 80 (L–LI/LXX–LXXI).

92. *War* 2.538–39.

93. On the March 1 starting date of most Roman campaigns, see Roth (2012) p. 279.

94. The Pool of Israel, or *Birket Isra'in* in Arabic, was built with walls extending from the east wall of the Temple Mount and a wall on the north, sloping down toward the west, as well.

95. Sadler and Serdiville (2016) p. 116.

96. *War* 2.540–42.

97. *War* 2.542–44.

98. *War* 2.545–46.

99. *War* 2.547-50. Some historians have assumed that it was lower Beit-Horon that Cestius reached, but Josephus does not specify this; from his description of the topography during the ambush it is more likely that the Romans were attacked during their ascent into upper Beit-Horon. For the arguments about where the attacks took place, see Bar-Kochva (1976) p. 19; Gichon (1981) pp. 57–59; Mason (2016) pp. 299–301.

100. *War* 2.531.

101. The inclusion of battering rams (*helepoleis*) among the captured equipment might suggest that Cestius went to Jerusalem prepared for a siege, but Josephus never says that Cestius deployed them when he was in Jerusalem. And Roman legions routinely brought battering rams and catapults (*oxubeleis*) with them on campaigns.

102. *War* 5.267 for Simon using some of Cestius's artillery; 5.359 for the totals.

103. *War* 2.564–65.

104. Though Simon and his men are credited with carrying off many of Cestius's baggage mules after Cestius was attacked on the way to Jerusalem; see *War* 2.521.

105. *War* 2.555.

106. Mason (2016) pp. 282.

107. Velleius Paterculus, *Roman History* 2.117–20; Tacitus, *Annals* 1.3, 1.10, 1.43, 1.55–71, 2.7, 2.41, 2.45; Suetonius, *Augustus* 23.2.

108. Later on, during the fighting in Jerusalem, the rebels are said in *War* 5.357–59 to have had in their possession 300 quick-fire bolt artillery and 40 stone-throwers.

109. Goldsworthy (1996) p. 88.

CHAPTER 9. JOHN OF GISCHALA

1. Costobar and Saul were probably the grandsons of Herod's governor of Idumaea and Gaza, the husband of Herod's sister Salome. Both Philip's father, Iacimus, and his grandfather Zamaris had been governor of the veteran colony/village of Bathyra.

2. *War* 2.556–58. In his *Life* 407–9, Josephus confusingly writes that Philip was dispatched to Nero but never spoke to him because of the disturbances and the civil war.

3. The large number is inferred in part from the reference to synagogues in the city in Acts 9.2.

4. *War* 2.560.

5. *War* 2.561; later on, at 7.368, in the famous speech attributed to Eleazar on Masada, Josephus gives the number slain as 18,000.

6. *War* 2.562.

7. See perhaps the locus classicus of the antithetical topos in Herodotus, *Histories* 8.111.3, describing the famous incident when the Athenians led by Themistocles went to the island of Andros to get money from the Andrians, bringing their two mighty gods, Persuasion and Necessity, and the Andrians replied that they could not pay the Athenians because they had two gods on their side, Poverty and Helplessness; for the antithesis of persuasion versus force in Josephus, see *Antiquities* 4.17.

8. *War* 2.562–63.

9. That is true even if, as Cestius was preparing to intervene in the south, Ananus attempted to negotiate with the Romans. In Josephus's works Ananus comes across as a kind of moderate patriot who prepared for the worst-case scenario of a Roman siege while trying to find a

political solution. When the negotiations did not bear fruit and the war outside Jerusalem intensified, Ananus and the other moderates were probably pushed into a less flexible position. For the involvement of "Revolutionary High Priests," see Price (1992) pp. 40–42.

10. Proving that not all Essenes spent the war in Qumran. John was later killed during the rebels' attack upon Ascalon; see *War* 3.9–19. Not all Essenes were pacifists.

11. *War* 2.566–68; *Life* 28–29.

12. *War* 2.562–65; Horsley (2002) p. 89.

13. Niger's name, "Black" in Latin, indicates that he may have been a Roman citizen, though he might also have been a non–Roman citizen auxiliary soldier.

14. Price (1992) p. 53.

15. *Life* 29.

16. *War* 2.572–84.

17. *War* 3.9–12.

18. *War* 3.13–21.

19. *War* 2.569–71; *Life* 29, 79; for discussion of Justus and the *Life* as a response to Justus's critique, see Rajak (1973) pp. 345–68; Mason (1991) pp. 316–24; Rodgers (2006) pp. 169–92.

20. *War* 2.572–74; *Life* 156, 187–88, claiming to have fortified Sepphoris and with a list of cities in the Lower Galilee that is textually corrupt, adding Komus and Papha. Tarichaeae, Tiberias, and Gamala were situated within the territory of Agrippa. No contemporary wall has yet been found at Tarichaeae. Note that Josephus claims to have fortified Soganaea in the Gaulanitis at *War* 2.574 and the village of the Soganai in Lower Galilee, *Life* 188.

21. *War* 2.574; *Life* 188 versus 30 where the Sepphoreans were pro-Roman. Thus, the contradictory assertions at least beg the question: who were the walls built to defend against, Romans or rebels?

22. *War* 2.575; also called the son of Leios at 2.585.

23. *Life* 189.

24. *War* 2.575–76.

25. *War* 2.577.

26. *War* 2.577–82.

27. The 60,000 infantrymen cited here (5.583) were presumably the young men who had undergone the training Josephus talks about at 5.578–79; they were from the 100,000 men who had been recruited (5.576). In *Life* 77 Josephus claimed to have recruited more mercenaries from among the brigands when he was at Gischala. He also names a few individual recruits, such as Eleazar, the son of Sameas, from the village of Saab in the Galilee, and Netir and Philip from the village of Ruma in the Galilee, who fought at Iotapata; see *War* 3.229, 233.

28. Another problem is that most historians estimate the total number of the inhabitants of Palestine to have been somewhere between 750,000 and 1,000,000. Josephus's Grand Army of the Galilee therefore is imagined to comprise almost 10% of the population. For discussion and population estimates, see Broshi (2001) pp. 86–120; Lapin (2017c) pp. 241–53.

29. *War* 2.584.

30. *War* 2.585–89.

31. For John of Gischala, Josephus's rivalry with him, and his role in the revolt, see Rappaport (1982), (2013).

32. *War* 2.590; *Life* 70–73; Rappaport (2013) pp. 76–77.

33. Mishnah, *m. A. Zar.* 2.6; Goodman (2007c) p. 277.

34. *War* 2.591–92; *Life* 74–76. In the *Life* version of the story Josephus lets slip that he gave John permission to send the olive oil to Caesarea because he was afraid of being stoned by the mob if he did not. Josephus, in other words, did have advance knowledge of John's scheme. For analysis, see Rappaport (2013) p. 76.

35. *War* 2.593–94.

36. *War* 2.595; *Life* 126–27.
37. *War* 5.596; *Life* 127.
38. For the excavations at Tarichaeae (Magdala), see De Luca (2009) pp. 343–562, 571–72; Leibner (2009) pp. 214–40; Aviam (2013); De Luca and Lena (2015a) pp. 113–63, (2015b) pp. 280–342. The grid layout of streets and public baths adjacent to a public square in the northern part of Tarichaeae suggests the cultural influence of Graeco-Roman urban planning and values. But the town's large synagogue also indicates that its population included at least some well-off Jews, who expressed their piety through regular prayer and study. For a succinct overview of the Magdala synagogue, see Aviam (2018) pp. 127–33; for the Magdala stone and its functional interpretations, see Hachlili (2013) p. 41; De Luca and Lena (2015b) p. 317; Fine (2017) pp. 27–38; Aviam (platform for reading the Torah) and Bauckham (representation of Temple, collection table for first fruits) (2018) pp. 135–59.
39. *War* 2.597; *Life* 128.
40. *Life* 131.
41. *War* 2.598; *Life* 129.
42. *War* 2.599; *Life* 132–35, 138. No remnants of the hippodrome have been discovered yet.
43. *War* 2.600; *Life* 136.
44. *War* 2.601–2; *Life* 138.
45. *War* 2.605–7; *Life* 141–44.
46. *War* 2.608–9; *Life* 143–44.
47. *War* 2.610; *Life* 144–45.
48. *War* 2.611–12; *Life* 146–47.
49. *War* 612–13.
50. *Life* 147–48.
51. *War* 2.614–15.
52. *War* 2.615–16; *Life* 84–89.
53. For the stadium, see Patrich (2009b) p. 208; for the population estimate, see Aviam and Richardson (2001) p. 196.
54. *War* 2.616–19; *Life* 90–96.
55. *War* 2.620–21; *Life* 97–100.
56. *War* 2.623–25; *Life* 100, 368–72.
57. The only mention of John's brother Simon in Josephus's writings comes in the *Life* 190, 195–96. He does not appear in the *War*, and we do not know if he subsequently was in Jerusalem with John during the siege.
58. On the constitution and government of the "First Regime," see Price (1992) pp. 63–67.
59. Though Jonathan's participation is cut out of the account in the *War*, perhaps because of his prominence and friendship with Josephus. His participation in the recall embassy thus may have been too damaging to include in the earlier version of the story.
60. *Life* 200.
61. *War* 2.626–28; *Life* 189–202. Josephus's account of the whole episode continues on in much greater detail until chapter 332.
62. *Life* 205–9.
63. *War* 2.629–31; in his *Life* 309–11, Josephus attributes his success to the people in Jerusalem who had risen up against Ananus, Simon, and their friends.
64. *War* 2.632–33; *Life* 155–58.
65. *War* 2.634–37; *Life* 159–67.
66. *War* 2.638–41; *Life* 168–69.
67. Schäfer (2003b) pp. 123–24.
68. *War* 2.642–44; *Life* 170–73.
69. *War* 2.645–46.

70. *War* 2.218–19, 5.147–59; *Antiquities* 19.326–27.

71. *War* 2.649.

72. Mason (2016) p. 110 claims that in Josephus's portrait Ananus represents elite values rather than pro- or anti-Roman ideology. But Josephus had made clear earlier that Ananus had taken part in preparations for war against Rome. At the time of his appointment he had worked to raise the city walls. In the context, that action could only be in preparation for a Roman siege. Ananus cannot have feared a siege by any of Judaea's regional competitors, unless as allies of the Romans.

73. *War* 2.647–50.

74. *War* 2.652–54, 4.503–8.

CHAPTER 10. COMETH THE HOUR

1. *War* 3.1.

2. *War* 3.1.

3. *War* 3.3–5; Suetonius, *Life of Vespasian* 2.1. Though he apparently was planning a new campaign against the Jews after his defeat, as we know from his promise to the people of Sepphoris that he would return to protect them from anti-Roman Galilaeans and Josephus (referred to in Josephus's *Life* 373 –74, 394–97), Cestius could not have led the campaign in any case because he seems to have died in the winter or spring of 67. See Tacitus, *Histories* 5.10. Cestius's replacement as legate in Syria, Mucianus, arrived there by the summer of 67; see *War* 4.32.

4. Suetonius, *Life of Vespasian* 2.1; Levick (1999) pp. xxi, 4.

5. Suetonius, *Vespasian* 1.2.

6. Suetonius, *Vespasian* 2.3–4.2; *War* 3.4–5.

7. Suetonius, *Vespasian* 4.2–3.

8. Suetonius, *Vespasian* 4.3.

9. See Goldsworthy (1996) p. 122 on the Romans' lack of a military college.

10. Suetonius, *Vespasian* 4.4; cf. Tacitus, *Annals* 16.5.3.

11. Cassius Dio 63.17.6.

12. For the best recent, short account of Corbulo's career, see Goldsworthy (2016) pp. 297–327.

13. Suetonius, *Vespasian* 4.5.

14. *War* 3.8.

15. Keppie (1998) p. 210.

16. Suetonius, *Life of Titus* 1.1–4.1.

17. *War* 3.8, 29.

18. *War* 3.29.

19. Hosler (2018) pp. 16, 176.

20. *War* 3.30.

21. *War* 3.30–34; *Life* 347, 373, 394, which confusingly imply that two requests for a garrison were made to Cestius, first after his intervention and then again before Vespasian came. One possible way to resolve this confusion would be to hypothesize that the first request was not fulfilled, whereas the second one was. Whatever the case, it is likely that the force sent was relatively small. Otherwise it is hard to understand why such a large force would be sent in the spring of 67.

22. *War* 3.31–33, 59; *Life* 394; for the range of estimates of the size of Sepphoris during the first century, see Reed (2000) pp. 78–79; Mason (2016) pp. 361–62 hypothesizes that the tribune Placidus, who was sent to Ptolemais by Cestius Gallus in *Life* 213–15, is the same man who commanded the new garrison under Vespasian.

23. Goldsworthy (1996) p. 27.

24. Meshorer (2001) pp. 104–5, coins 127–28; cf. Meyers (2002) pp. 110–20 for Sepphoris as a "City of Peace."

25. War 3.64–65. For the population estimate, see Reed (2000) p. 80; for the tearing down of the fortress, see Meyers and Chancey (2012) p. 144.

26. War 3.64–67. As with my calculation for the size of Cestius's army I give estimates from the lower calculation of historians for the number of legionaries per legion, 4,800, to the upper, maximum total of 6,000. If one of the higher numbers, such as 5,400 or 6,000 men per legion, is correct, it strengthens the case I make for the scale and expense of the war.

27. War 3.66; Suetonius, Life of Vespasian 4.6 gives totals of two legions, eight alae, and 10 cohorts added to the forces in Judaea but does not mention the legion brought by Titus. Josephus's unit totals are set out in greater detail and are followed here; Saddington (1982) pp. 102–3 also follows his totals.

28. War 3.68.

29. War 3.69; Saddington (1982) p. 103 estimates somewhere between 56,000 and 59,000.

30. War 3.69.

31. See appendix J, "Vespasian's Army."

32. See appendix J, "Vespasian's Army," for the totals.

33. Goldsworthy (1996) p. 37.

34. Goodman (2007c) pp. 405–6.

35. War 3.43, 2.576, 2.583–84.

36. The empire comprised approximately 1.5 million square miles during the first century CE; see Bang (2013) p. 427.

37. Tacitus, Annals 4.5.1.

38. War 3.59–63.

39. War 3.111–14.

40. Goldsworthy (1996) pp. 184–86.

41. For the relief, see Coarelli (2000) p. 49 plate 5 (VI–VII/IV–V).

42. War 3.115–26; Goldsworthy (1996) p. 107.

43. Notably, Josephus does not provide evidence that Cestius took care to include screening elements of auxiliary cavalry either at the front or rear of his column as he was making his way through the defiles of Beit-Horon.

44. Roth (2012) pp. 11–12. Note that in my estimations of the legionary cohort unit numbers here and elsewhere, I base my estimates on ranges of soldiers per cohort and legion. Those ranges do not take into account the possibility that the first cohort of each legion was a double cohort, as some scholars think was the case at the time of the revolt. I do not base my estimates on that possibility because nowhere in any of Josephus's writings about the Roman legions that took part in the war does he state explicitly that any of the first cohorts were double in number.

45. For a brief overview of the basic weaponry, see Keppie (1998) p. 173.

46. Bishop and Coulston (1993) pp. 81–82; Goldsworthy (1996) pp. 210–11.

47. Goldsworthy (1996) pp. 213–16.

48. Goldsworthy (1996) p. 221.

49. Goldsworthy (1996) p. 216.

50. War 3.95; Goldsworthy (1996) pp. 183, 197–201.

51. Bishop and Coulston (1993); Goldsworthy (1996) pp. 17, 216–18.

52. Goldsworthy (1996) p. 17.

53. Antiquities 14.204, 14.225–40; on the conscription of Jews into military service on Sardinia in 19 CE, see Tacitus, Annals 2.85; Suetonius, Tiberius 36; Antiquities 18.81–84.

54. Keppie (1998) pp. 180–81.

55. Goldsworthy (2000) p. 28.

56. War 3.129; Life 395, 412.

57. *War* 3.130–1.
58. *War* 3.138–39. Josephus's attitude at this time is represented by Mason (2016) pp. 109–10 as exemplifying his concern with honor and the people's well-being; "In this presentation, we notice, either fighting on (with adequate troops) or immediate surrender would be an equally acceptable moral choice. Irrational and immoral behavior would be to sustain the conflict without a viable force and watch the nation destroyed for no purpose." But Josephus led the defense of Iotapata *after* sending his letter to Jerusalem and indeed witnessed the destruction of the Temple and much of Jerusalem in 70.
59. Mason (2016) pp. 109–10.
60. Described by Josephus in his *Life* 123 as one of the three greatest cities (*poleis . . . megistai*) in the Galilee (along with Tiberias and Sepphoris); Aviam and Richardson (2001) p. 177.
61. *War* 3.132–4; *Life* 123.
62. Coarelli (2000) p. 73 Plate 29 (XXII/XXXI).
63. *War* 3.141.
64. *War* 3.158, "*plen oligou pasa kremnos.*"
65. *War* 3.158–60.
66. Aviam (2008) pp. 2076–77.
67. Aviam (2008) p. 2077. On 15 July 2017 I inspected the north-northwestern side of the hill of Iotapata with a former combat engineer, and experienced veteran, of one of the Israeli Defense Forces' elite infantry brigades. We both observed that while ascending the 100 or so yards up the hill on the northwestern side would have been a relatively easy task for a disciplined assault team, after that the gradient of the hill becomes far more acute, and it would have been difficult for soldiers to make the ascent up to the city walls, especially under fire. We returned to the site together on Tuesday 14 January 2019, armed with an inclinometer, and confirmed that the gradient, while variable up the northwestern side, in places measured at least a 9% incline. In addition, it is about 180 feet from the base of the remains of the casement wall down to the first level ground (about 36 feet below the modern Roman "spears" monument). An assault team making its way up the northwestern hill might therefore have been under fire for almost two-thirds the length of an American football field. Iotapata does not have cliffs on all sides as Josephus wrote, but the ascent up the northwestern side of Iotapata under fire would not have been a Sunday stroll.
68. *Epitome of Military Science* 3.13.
69. *War* 3.142.
70. *Life* 234.
71. Roth (2012) p. 217.
72. *War* 3.141–44.

CHAPTER 11. "I GO, NOT AS A TRAITOR, BUT AS YOUR SERVANT"

1. *War* 3.141–288, 3.316–408.
2. *War* 3.145–49.
3. For the roles played by archers and slingers in the opening phases of battles, see Goldsworthy (1996) pp. 183–90.
4. *War* 3.150–57.
5. For such *consilia*, see Goldsworthy (1996) pp. 131–33.
6. *War* 3.161–62; Aviam (2004b) pp. 110–22.
7. *War* 3.162–64. A hurdle is a light fence constructed out of interwoven materials such as wooden stakes and branches that gives protection to artillery and personnel.
8. *War* 3.95.

9. *War* 3.165.

10. *War* 3.166–68. Vegetius, *Epitome of Military Science* 2.25 gives the number of carriage ballistas per legion as 55. But he is writing during the late fourth century CE.

11. *War* 3.169–70.

12. *War* 3.171–77.

13. *War* 3.178–80.

14. *War* 3.181–85.

15. *War* 3.186–89.

16. *War* 3.190–92.

17. *War* 3.193–200.

18. *War* 3.201–6.

19. *War* 3.207–12.

20. *War* 3.213–21.

21. *War* 3.222–26.

22. *War* 3. 3.226–28.

23. The name Natira is found in a first-century BCE to first-century CE inscription on an ossuary among those found in the Alkeldama Caves of the Kidron Valley; see *CIIP Vol. I, Part 1* (2010) no. 306 pp. 329–30, noting that the name is also found among the Nabataeans.

24. For the history of Legio X Fretensis's deployments, see Goldsworthy (2003) p. 51; Dando-Collins (2010) pp. 152–60.

25. *War* 3.229–34.

26. For the *architecti,* see Southern (2007) p. 104.

27. *War* 3.235–39; for the knee wound, see Suetonius, *Life of Vespasian* 4.6.

28. *War* 3.240–48.

29. Goldsworthy (1996) p. 190.

30. *War* 3.251–52.

31. *War* 3.253–57.

32. For the use of noise to intimidate in battle, see Goldsworthy (1996) pp. 195–97.

33. *War* 3.258–64.

34. *War* 3.265–70.

35. *War* 3.271–82.

36. *War* 3.282.

37. *War* 3.283–88.

38. *War* 3.289.

39. *War* 3.289–97.

40. *War* 3.298–305.

41. Bourgel (2016) pp. 505–23.

42. *War* 3.307–8.

43. *Antiquities* 18.85–89; *War* 2.245.

44. *War* 3.313–14.

45. *War* 3.307–15. An alternative version of what happened may be preserved in a cast from an inscription now in the École Biblique in Jerusalem. The inscription purportedly reveals that it was Trajan who attacked the Samaritans in the spring, possibly during the feast of Shavuot, and killed 10,000 of them. Strugnell (1967) argued for the inscription's authenticity; for a review of doubts about it, see Pummer (2009) pp. 266–68.

46. It is possible that some of these men were descendants of the veterans whom Herod had settled in Samaria; see *Antiquities* 15.296.

47. *War* 3.316–28.

48. *War* 3.329–39.

49. Aviam (2004b) p. 119. Josephus therefore must have exaggerated the casualty figures to intensify his readers' sense of pathos about the city's destruction.

50. *War* 3.338.
51. Unfortunately, the inclusive dates that Josephus relates within his description of the siege add up not to 47 days, but perhaps to 38 or 42 at most, if we include the time it took for the Romans to prepare the road to Iotapata from Gabara. See Mason (2016) p. 364 n. 89 for the dating difficulties from the time Josephus left Tiberias on 21 Artemisius and Iotapata's fall on 1 Panemus/Tammuz.
52. *War* 3.111–14; Mason (2016) p. 369.
53. Mason (2016) p. 377.
54. *War* 3.141.
55. Based upon multiplying the daily supply requirements of Vespasian's task force by seven weeks. Note that these figures do not include the requirements for military slaves, free servants, and the troops from the villages who joined Vespasian. Thus, 126,940 pounds of food daily for 51,760 legionaries, auxiliaries, and allies multiplied by 49 days equals 5,966,180 pounds; 103,520 liters of liquid for 51,760 legionaries, auxiliaries, and allies multiplied by 49 days equals 4,865,440 liters of water; 58,760 kg of dry fodder daily, 172,000 kg of green fodder, and 544,806 liters of liquid daily for 18,680 pack animals and 8,560 horses multiplied by 49 days equals 2,761,720 kg of dry fodder, 8,084,000 kg of green fodder, and 25,605,882 liquid liters.
56. For sleeping with fathers as a euphemism for dying, see Deuteronomy 31.16.
57. *War* 3.340–42.
58. *War* 3.343–44.
59. We cannot be sure of Nicanor's background; possibly he was a tribune of an auxiliary cohort and close to Agrippa II. For his friendship with Titus, see *War* 5.261.
60. *War* 3.344–49.
61. *War* 3.350–54.
62. *War* 3.355–60.
63. 1 Samuel 31.4.
64. *War* 3.361–82. For an analysis of the speech and comparisons between it and the speeches attributed to Eleazar ben Yair on Masada, see Ladouceur (1980) pp. 245–60; Gray (1993) pp. 44–52; Elledge (2006) pp. 67–69; Kelley (2004) pp. 271–73; Weitzman (2004) pp. 230–45; Klawans (2012) pp. 118–19.
65. *War* 3.383–86.
66. All kinds of theories have been advanced about how Josephus might have manipulated the lottery to ensure that he at least would have been among the last to choose a lot and that when that happened he would be able to use his considerable powers of persuasion to convince the last survivor(s) not to complete the lottery. But the text does not tell us how the lottery was conducted. For potential (though unprovable) manipulation of the lottery, see Herstein and Kaplansky (1974) pp. 121–28.
67. *War* 3.387–91; see Weitzman (2004) pp. 230–45, arguing for a reading of the story as a way to enlist the Roman ethos of a noble death without alienating imperial rulers suspicious of suicide as a challenge to their authority.
68. *War* 3.439.
69. *War* 3.352; Rajak (2002) p. 18.
70. Rajak (2002) p. 170; *War* 3.407, for Jewish prisoners from Iotapata confirming to Vespasian Josephus's prophecy that Iotapata would fall in 47 days.
71. *War* 3.392–99.
72. *War* 3.400–402; Suetonius, *Life of Vespasian* 5.6.
73. *War* 3.403–8.
74. The probability of "dogs," as the Romans called rolling double ones with two, six-sided dice, is 2.78%. After what had occurred at Iotapata Josephus perhaps would have taken those odds.
75. *Against Apion* 1.49.

CHAPTER 12. VESPASIAN THE WAR CRIMINAL

1. Millar (1993) pp. 73, 84–85. As Millar points out, it was no accident that after the war was over Caesarea was honored with the status of a Roman colony and received the name Colonia Prima Flavia Augusta Caesarea.

2. *War* 3.409–13; between July 69 and the beginning of 70 the Romans built a road linking Caesarea and Scythopolis by way of Legio (Caparcotna) and on to Pella and Gerasa; we know this from a milestone found in a field several hundred meters from the western edge of Afula in the Jezreel Valley; see Isaac and Roll (1976) pp. 9–14; (1982).

3. *War* 1.156, 166; *Antiquities* 13.280 for the betrayal of Scythopolis.

4. *War* 3.414–18.

5. *War* 3.419–31.

6. *War* 3.432–37.

7. *War* 3.438–42.

8. Agrippa had renamed Caesarea as Neronias-Irenopolis in 61; after Nero's suicide and the damnation of his memory by the Roman senate (*damnatio memoriae*), the new name was dropped.

9. Polybius 16.18.2; *War* 1.404–6; *Antiquities* 15.360; Berlin (1999) pp. 27–45 for the excavations and analysis of the ceramics; Wilson and Tzaferis (2007) p. 131.

10. *War* 3.514; *Antiquities* 20.211; Wilson and Tzaferis (2007) p 135.

11. *Life* 61.

12. *War* 3.443–44.

13. *War* 2.252; *Antiquities* 20.159.

14. *War* 3.445

15. *War* 2.252; *Antiquities* 20.159.

16. Josephus's description of Justus's actions and motives is colored by Justus's later criticism of Josephus's actions; see Rajak (1973) for Justus's career and writings. For his part, Justus's criticisms of Josephus must have been influenced by Josephus's imprisonment of Justus and his father during the troubles in the Galilee, *Life* 175.

17. *Life* 33–39.

18. *War* 3.446.

19. We are not sure why Josephus chose to use the Republican-era office title of decurion for this officer.

20. *War* 3.447–52; for Jesus as the head of the bandits, 3.450; as chief magistrate, 2.599, and *Life* 134, 278, 294, 300.

21. *War* 3.453–55.

22. *War* 3.456–57.

23. *Life* 354; Josephus claims that there were 2,000 Tiberians in Jerusalem during the siege.

24. *War* 3.458–61.

25. *War* 3.462–66. For the excavations there, revealing the town to have had a large synagogue and at least four ritual baths, see Aviam (2013) pp. 205–20, (2018) pp. 127–33; Zapata-Meza and Sanz-Rincón (2017) pp. 37–42.

26. *War* 3.467–70.

27. *War* 3.471–84.

28. For the speeches made by Roman generals before battles as reported in sources, see Goldsworthy (1996) pp. 145–48. In this case it was not impossible for Titus to have made a speech that could have been heard by 600 cavalrymen. But its contents cannot be corroborated from sources other than Josephus.

29. *War* 3.485–86.

30. Goldsworthy (1996) p. 166.

31. *War* 3.487–91.

32. *War* 3.492–93.
33. *War* 3.494–502.
34. *War* 3.503–5.
35. *War* 3.522–31.
36. Even if this is Josephus's retrospective view, the logic behind that view depends upon the idea that there was deep-seated opposition to Rome in the area.
37. *War* 3.532–38.
38. *War* 3.539–40.
39. *War* 5.536.
40. *Life of Vespasian* 15.1.
41. *War* 3.541.
42. *War* 3.542; *Life* 142.

CHAPTER 13. THE CAMEL'S HUMP

1. *War* 4.1–2.
2. Syon (1992–1993) pp. 34–55.
3. Meshorer (2001), coin 217, pp. 130–31. For the rabbinic term *prutah* (s.), *prutot* (pl.) for bronze coins, see Hendin (2009) p. 106.
4. Genesis 15.13–18; Mishnah tractate Menahot 10.4 for the context of the first-fruit grain offering; and Meshorer (2001) p. 117 for the interpretation.
5. Mershorer (2001) pp. 117–18, 131.
6. Farhi (2006) pp. 72–74; Arbel (2014) pp. 233–38 for another alternative.
7. Syon (2014a) pp. 143–44; Goodman (2007c) pp. 14–15.
8. Gutmann (1981) pp. 30–34.
9. *War* 4.8.
10. *War* 2.574, 4.5–9; *Arakhin.* 9.6; Syon (2008) pp. 53–65; Syon and Yavor (2008) 1739–42; Magness (2012) p. 292.
11. *War* 1.105.
12. *War* 4.2.
13. *War* 4.10; *Life* 114.
14. *Life* 179–84. For the complicated story, the details of which leave many questions unanswered, see Mason (2016) pp. 380–81.
15. *Life* 185, 187.
16. *War* 4.83.
17. *War* 4.11.
18. *War* 4.13.
19. *War* 4.14–16.
20. *War* 4.17; Syon (2008) pp. 58–59; Holley (2014) pp. 35–55.
21. *War* 4.18–19. Josephus's characterization of their mood might seem to be contradicted by his earlier statement that there was a spring within the city walls (4.8). The contradiction might be resolved by hypothesizing that the spring was not sufficient for what they thought might be a prolonged siege. On the leaders, note that Chares was a Greek name but was used by some Jews, as we know from an inscription of ossuary 10 found in cave 2, chamber B, of the Akeldama caves of the Kidron Valley, *CIIP Vol. I, Part 1* (2010) no. 290 pp. 312–13.
22. *War* 4.19. To confuse matters, in his autobiography (*Life* 177–78, 186) he identifies Chares and Joseph (Jesus), allegedly the brother-in-law of Justus of Tiberius, as supporters of King Agrippa! The contradictory presentation of Chares's and Jesus's attitude can possibly be

explained by imagining that the two leaders, like other individuals during the war, such as the high priest Ananus, in fact were ambivalent the whole time about relations with Rome, and Josephus chose to interpret their actions differently in *War* and then 20 years later in his autobiography.

23. For the arrowheads, see Magness (2014) pp. 21–33.
24. *War* 4.20.
25. *War* 4.21.
26. *War* 4.22–23.
27. *War* 4.24–25.
28. *War* 4.26–30.
29. *War* 4.31–36.
30. *War* 4.39–48.
31. *War* 4.49–51.
32. *War* 4.52–53.
33. *War* 2.573, 4.54–56; *Life* 188.
34. *War* 4.57–59.
35. *War* 4.60–61.
36. *War* 4.62–64.
37. *War* 4.64–66.
38. *War* 4.67–68.
39. *War* 4.69.
40. *War* 4.70–72.
41. *War* 4.73–75.
42. *War* 4.76. Josephus's description of this providential wind is in keeping with his theme of God helping the Romans in the war.
43. *War* 4.76–77.
44. *War* 4.78–79.
45. Lamentations Rabbah 137b; Gregerman (2016) pp. 166–69.
46. *War* 4.63; 83; for the Julian date, see Mason (2016) p. 378.
47. *War* 4.87–91.
48. *War* 4.84–87; Tarichaeae fell on 8 Gorpiaeus, according to *War* 3.542.
49. *War* 4.92; see Rappaport (2013) pp. 93–96 for the episode, arguing that the size of the force sent by Vespasian indicates that John was not seen as anti-Roman.
50. See Rappaport (1982) pp. 479–93 on John and his representation in Josephus.
51. *War* 4.98–102.
52. *War* 4.103–4.
53. On the border with Lebanon. Kedasa apparently served as a camp for the generals of the Seleucid king Demetrius II Nicator during his war against Jonathan Maccabaeus; *Antiquities* 13.154.
54. *War* 4.105.
55. *Life* 43–44.
56. *War* 4.106–11; Rappaport (2013) p. 98 suggests that Josephus invented the story of the escape. But no explanation of why John and his followers went directly to Jerusalem—the epicenter of the revolt—is offered.
57. *War* 4.112–14.
58. *War* 4.115.
59. *War* 4.116–20.
60. Mason (2016) p. 403.

CHAPTER 14. "NOW YOU HAVE OUR VOTE"

1. *War* 4.121–23.
2. *War* 4.124–27.
3. *War* 4.128.
4. *War* 4.128–33.
5. Thucydides 3.69–85.
6. *War* 4.133–36.
7. *War* 4.135–46.
8. *War* 4.153–55.
9. Midrash Rabbah Leviticus 26.9; Tanhuma 48a; Yalkut 1.63.1.
10. *War* 4.155.
11. *War* 4.156–57.
12. 2 Maccabees 4.23–24; *Antiquities* 12.239, wrongly identifying Menelaus as the brother of Onias III and Jason; VanderKam (2004) pp. 192, 200, 203–4; Atkinson (2016) p. 24.
13. For example, Ananus appointed by Quirinius, *Antiquities* 18.26; Jonathan, son of Ananus by Vitellius; Ishmael, son of Phiabi by Valerius Gratus; Simon by Agrippa I, 19.297; Jesus, son of Gamaliel by Agrippa II.
14. Schäfer (2003b) p. 125; Klawans (2012) p. 19.
15. *Antiquities* 14.203 for the tithes to be paid to the high priest Hyrcanus and his sons.
16. *War* 4.158–61; *Life* 189–98, 309 for the story of the attempted replacement of Josephus.
17. Numbers 25.6–15; Graetz (1949) p. 234; Hengel (1989) pp. 380–404.
18. 1 Maccabees 2.24–27.
19. Mason (2016) pp. 449.
20. *War* 2.433–44.
21. *War* 2.562–65.
22. *War* 4.162–92.
23. *War* 4.193–203.
24. Leviticus 16.29–31; Goodman (2007c) p. 169.
25. *War* 4.204–7.
26. *War* 4.208–9.
27. *War* 4.210–15.
28. *War* 4.216–25; for Eleazar, son of Simon, earlier, see *War* 2.564–65.
29. For Josephus's representation of the Idumaeans, see Applebaum (2009) pp. 1–22.
30. *Antiquities* 13.257–58.
31. *War* 4.226–29.
32. For a short summary of the political history of Idumaea from 600 BCE into the Hasmonean period, see Lemaire (2006) pp. 418–19.
33. *Antiquities* 16.285.
34. *War* 2.55.
35. *War* 4.233–35.
36. *War* 4.236.
37. *War* 4.238–69.
38. *War* 4.270–82.
39. *War* 4.283.
40. *War* 4.286–87.
41. *War* 4.288–89.
42. *War* 4.290–305.
43. *War* 4.305–13.
44. *War* 4.314–17.

45. In Ananus's case, notwithstanding a more negative assessment of the high priest in *Antiquities* 20.199–203, where the story of James's execution might be a later Christian interpolation.
46. *War* 4.318–25.
47. *War* 4.326–29.
48. *War* 4.330–33.
49. Mason (2016) p. 410.
50. *War* 4.334–39.
51. *War* 4.340–44.
52. *War* 4.345–52.
53. For example, *War* 4.566–70, where "all" the Idumaeans break from John and attack him and his faction.
54. Possibly Gerasa (Jerash) in Jordan, though other places bearing the same (or a similar) name in Judaea itself have been suggested; for the arguments, see Mason (2016) p. 458. Later, at *War* 5.249 Josephus has 10 Idumaean leaders and 5,000 soldiers fighting with Simon. This almost certainly is an exaggeration.
55. *War* 4.353–55.
56. *War* 4.358.
57. *War* 2.520, 3.11–28.
58. *War* 4.359–62.
59. *War* 4.363–65.
60. Eusebius, *Ecclesiastical History* 3.5.2–3; Epiphanius, *Against Heresies* 29.7; *On Measures and Weights* 15 (warned by an angel of God). See Koester (1989) pp. 89–106 for a discussion of the creation of the tradition.

CHAPTER 15. CHAOS IN THE CAPITALS

1. *War* 4.130; Mason (2016) p. 406.
2. *War* 4.366–76.
3. *War* 4.377–80.
4. *War* 2.556.
5. Price (1992) pp. 258–60.
6. *War* 4.381–88
7. Tacitus, *Histories* 5.12.
8. *War* 4.389–97.
9. *War* 4.399–401.
10. *Antiquities* 9.7; Pliny, *Natural History* 5.73.
11. *War* 4.402–5.
12. *War* 4.407–9.
13. *War* 4.413–18.
14. *War* 4.419–32.
15. *War* 4.433–37.
16. Roth (2012) p. 30.
17. *War* 4.438–39.
18. See Price (1992) p. 218 on the problematic chronology.
19. *War* 4.440–43.
20. 1 Maccabees 4.26–28, 6.28–31; 2 Maccabees 11.4, 5–6, 13.1–2; *Antiquities* 12.313, 12.366–68, for the campaigns in the 160s BCE.
21. *War* 2.566–68; *Life* 28–29. John the Essene was killed at Ascalon just after the defeat of Cestius, but we have no record that Jesus and Eleazar did anything in Idumaea or that John defended Gophna or Acrabatene.

22. Lamentations Rabbah 1.52; for Emmaus/Imwas, see Fischer, Isaac, and Roll (1996) pp. 151–59.

23. *War* 4.443–45.

24. *War* 4.445–48.

25. For Tell Mazar, see De Groot (1993) pp. 989–91.

26. *War* 4.449–50. As Mason points out (2016) p. 413, there are problems of chronology with Josephus's account of these operations, since Josephus has Vespasian camped at Emmaus on 2 Daisius (or late May) of 68 at *War* 4.449, then taking Jericho and Adida (4.486–90), and then setting out from Caesarea on 5 Daisius (4.550), after Josephus's long excursus on the topography and climate of Jericho (4.451–85). If the events described after 4.550 do not belong to 69 CE, then the most plausible solution is to argue that, because Josephus was interweaving accounts of Vespasian's campaigns, the Jericho excursus, events in Rome including the death of Nero, and civil war in Judaea and Rome, he compressed his chronology, and the initial operations against the villages around Caesarea should be dated earlier in the spring of 68.

27. *War* 4.451; for Adida, see Fischer, Isaac, and Roll (1996) pp. 173–76.

28. *War* 4.476–77.

29. *War* 4.486–89.

30. *War* 4.490.

31. Suetonius, *Nero* 49.1.

32. *War* 4.498; Tacitus, *Histories* 1.10, 2.1–4.

33. *War* 4.498.

34. Suetonius, *Galba* 19, 20.2; *Otho* 6; Wellesley (1975) pp. 26–27; Morgan (2006) p. 70.

35. *War* 4.500–502.

36. The idea that the rebels might not have understood the potential implications of Nero's death for the war is belied by the fact that the Romans did not follow up their successes of early 68 with an immediate assault upon the capital. More than a year would pass before Jerusalem was besieged.

37. *War* 2.521, 2.652–53, 4.503–4.

38. *War* 4.505.

39. *War* 4.506–13.

40. *War* 4.514.

41. *War* 4.515.

42. *War* 4.516–17.

43. *War* 4.518–19.

44. *War* 4.520–23.

45. *War* 4.524–28.

46. Where the so-called Tomb of the Patriarchs (built by Herod the Great) was located. For Hebron's history and excavations there, see *NEAEHL* II (1993) pp. 606–9; *OEANE* III (1997) pp. 13–14; *CIIP Vol. IV, Part 2* (2018) pp. 1305–11.

47. *War* 4.529–37.

48. *War* 4.538–39.

49. *War* 4.540–43.

50. *War* 4.544.

51. For the complicated maneuvering and then first battle of Cremona, see Tacitus, *Histories* 2.11.1–45.1; Cassius Dio 63–64.10.3.

52. *War* 4.545–51. For the excavations at Beitin, see Dever *OEANE* I (1997) pp. 300–301.

53. It is possible that it was during this brief campaign in 69 that Roman soldiers under Vespasian's command killed the seven young women (ages 17–25) and one male child whose bones were found in 2013 in a cave at Khirbet el-Maqatir (nine miles north of Jerusalem). For the identification and dating of the deaths of the individuals and their controversial reburial at

the settlement of Ofra on the West Bank, see *Times of Israel,* "A 2,000-Year-Old Murder Leads to an Illicit Burial in the Heart of the West Bank," 12 September 2017.

54. *War* 4.552–55.

55. *War* 4.556–58.

56. Josephus's description of John and his men "becoming" women may be part of a Josephan thematic cluster intended to demonstrate the masculine valor of Jews (but not John), as Mason (2016) p. 106 argues. But what if John's men did act in the way Josephus describes? Just because actions are used to develop literary themes does not mean they did not happen.

57. *War* 4.558–65.

58. Tentatively identified by D. Ben-Ami underneath the Givati parking lot outside the Dung Gate.

59. *War* 4.566–70.

60. *War* 4.572–77 for the date.

61. *War* 4.577–84.

62. For discussion of Simon's coins and their interpretation, see Rajak (2002) p. 142; Rappaport (2007) pp. 103–16.

63. *War* 4.585–91; Vegetius, *Epitome* 4.40.

64. Suetonius, *Life of Vespasian* 6.3; Tacitus, *Histories* 2.79, gives the official sequence that Vespasian was acclaimed emperor first by Tiberius Iulius Alexander and then the army in Egypt on 1 July; Suetonius dates Vespasian's acclamation by the army in Judaea to 11 July. For discussion of the Alexandrian acclamation, see Montevecchi (1981) pp. 155–70. In *War* 4.601–4, Josephus claims that Vespasian was first acclaimed by the army in Caesarea though he does not give the exact date.

65. Cassius Dio 60.1.3.

66. *War* 4.592–604; For the official, Flavian version of the chronology of the proclamation, see Tacitus, *Histories* 2.79; Suetonius, *Life of Vespasian* 6.3; discussion in Firpo (2009) pp. 42–45.

67. Suetonius, *Life of Vespasian* 7.1.

68. *War* 4.605–6.

69. More detail about the Alexandrian acclamation comes from *P. Fouad* 8 (republished in Sherk (1988) no. 81, in which Vespasian is acclaimed as divine, savior, a benefactor, and son of Ammon.

70. Tacitus, *Histories* 2.82, 4.51.

71. *War* 7.105.

72. *War* 4.32, 4.616–20.

73. *War* 4.622–29.

74. As we know from his later assertions in *Against Apion* 1.48–49, 1.55.

75. *War* 4.630–32; Tacitus, *Histories* 2.83.

76. *War* 4.633–44; Tacitus, *Histories* 3.33–34.

77. *War* 4.645; Tacitus, *Histories* 3.64–65, 3.70.

78. Suetonius, *Domitian* 1.2; Tacitus, *Histories* 3.74.

79. *War* 4.646–49; Tacitus, *Histories* 3.74.

80. *War* 4.649; Tacitus, *Histories* 3.71–72; Suetonius, *Life of Vitellius* 15.3; Cassius Dio 64.17.

81. Suetonius, *Life of Vespasian* 8.5.

82. *War* 4.650–55; Tacitus, *Histories* 3.79–4.3.

83. *War* 4.656–58.

84. Goldsworthy (1996) p. 122.

85. *War* 4.659–63.

86. Millar (1993) pp. 73, 84–85; Roth (2012) p. 175.

CHAPTER 16. "THE SON IS COMING"

1. *War* 5.1–10.
2. *War* 5.21.
3. *War* 5.11–18.
4. *War* 5.21–26; Tacitus, *Histories* 5.12.3 seems to put this event earlier but does not provide a precise context. This incident is also described in the Talmud, b. Gittin 56a, as the result of the rabbis appealing to the Zealots to let them make peace with the Romans; the Zealots denied their request and then burned up all the wheat and barley. That may have been how and why the wheat and barley were burned, but it was also in the interests of the author(s) to claim to have tried to make peace with the Romans given the outcome of the war.
5. *War* 5.27–38.
6. *War* 5.40–41.
7. *War* 5.43–44.
8. Tacitus, *Histories* 5.1.2–3; Millar (2005) p. 101, arguing that it was Rabel of Nabataea who supplied the Arab contingent.
9. Tacitus, *Histories* 5.1.3.
10. It should be emphasized that I am deliberately using the minimum numbers for the paper strength of Roman legions and auxiliary units at the time; Saddington (1982) p. 131 argues for the high total of 6,000 legionaries per legion and thus 24,000 Roman legionaries in Titus's army in 70. If the totals should be higher, such as 5,400 or 6,000 infantrymen per legion, then not only the troop strength estimates but also the logistical needs of the soldiers, their servants, and their pack animals need to be adjusted. Increasing the estimates strengthens my argument about the scale of the Roman investment in the war.
11. Saddington (1982) p. 131. There might have been 1,000 soldiers in each cohort, thus producing a total of 20,000 auxiliary infantrymen, though the size of each cohort might have been 500, too. Unfortunately, neither Josephus nor any other source gives precise figures.
12. Though the totals may be significantly higher if we assume higher unit estimates; for the details and the estimates, see appendix K, "Titus's Army."
13. Millar (2005) p. 101.
14. See appendix K, "Titus's Army." The totals given here exclude estimates for the military slaves and servants because, apart from some evidence for the number of such people who served the Roman legionaries, we have no reliable evidence for the number of slaves attached to auxiliary units of the Roman army, let alone for allied contingents. The margins for error therefore are very large and would distort my estimates for the logistical requirements, especially with respect to the food and liquid needs of the army.
15. For Phrygius as commander of the Fifteenth Legion, see *War* 6.237. Price (1992) pp. 127, 226 suggests that Titus set out from Caesarea on about 8 Xanthicus/Nisan/March–April and that may be right, but Josephus does not give a specific date.
16. It is possible that Josephus did not name the Twelfth Legion's leader because he did not want to embarrass someone who was not seen as a successful commander; an alternative explanation could be that the man had influential friends in Rome whom Josephus did not want to offend.
17. *War* 5.45–46, 6.237, where Tiberius is called eparch of all the forces.
18. *War* 5.47.
19. *Against Apion* 1.48–49. This statement obviously cannot have been completely accurate. As we shall see, Josephus often reports what was going on inside Jerusalem during the siege, which he could only have learned about later. Even his knowledge of what was happening within the Roman camps must have been partial and imperfect. For what Josephus could not and did not observe personally, there is no definite proof or written sources other than the *Com-*

mentarii of Vespasian and Titus. Of course, it does not follow that even Josephus's reports of what he personally observed can be assumed to be truthful or impartial. For the rest, the most plausible conclusion is that his reconstructions are based upon his general knowledge and perhaps contemporary oral sources.

20. *War* 5.42. For the commanders of these legions, see *War* 6.237.
21. For the numbers, see Goldsworthy (1996) p. 290.
22. *War* 5.47–50.
23. *War* 5.51; for "Gibeah of Saul," see 1 Samuel 11.4.
24. Cassius Dio 65–66.4.1.
25. See the later discussion of the numbers of the different rebel factions.
26. Goldsworthy (1996) pp. 125–31.
27. *War* 5.54–56. For the Psephinus (Psephinos) Tower, see 5.159–60.
28. *War* 5.57–65.
29. For Roman generals fighting at the front or just behind it, from which position they could rally troops, see Goldsworthy (1996) pp. 156–63.
30. *War* 5.99.
31. *War* 5.67–70.
32. *War* 5.71–75.
33. Josephus does not tell us exactly where on the Mount of Olives the Roman camp was located. His description of the Romans being taken by surprise when the Jews attacked, however, suggests that they were not digging in at the summit of the hill, which was approximately 800 meters high. If they were, they surely would have had time to arm themselves as the Jews advanced uphill.
34. *War* 5.76–81.
35. *War* 5.82–84.
36. The attack must have come from the direction of the so-called first or old wall, since it was the one that was opposite the Kidron Valley.
37. *War* 5.85–97.
38. *War* 5.99.
39. Tacitus, *Histories* 5.12, has Eleazar killed at this time, but in his account Josephus has the two leaders and their men fighting together.
40. *War* 5.98–105; noted also by Tacitus, *Histories* 5.12.4; for festivals in Josephus's works, see Colautti (2002) and Siggelkow-Berner (2011).
41. *War* 5.106–8, cf. 5.507. The "monuments of Herod" apparently comprised some kind of round structure intended by Herod before 31 BCE to serve as a burial place for his relatives and perhaps also as his tomb, before he changed his mind and had Herodeion constructed. It was probably located outside the first wall, northwest of the Damascus Gate. See Netzer (1983) pp. 52, 55, 59, (2007) p. 75.
42. *War* 5.152–53.
43. *War* 5.109–19.
44. *War* 5.120–27.
45. Churchill (2000) p. 377.
46. These divisions must include Legions V, XII, and XV. For Josephus's descriptions of the way the Romans organized their ranks during the war, see Goldsworthy (1996) p. 180. Ordinarily a shallower rank of infantry indicated more confidence in a century or unit. Here Titus seems to have prioritized security and mobile coverage.
47. *War* 5.163–65. The first wall began at the southeast corner of the Temple Mount and was built up on the ridge above the Kidron Valley, passed two towers, and then after passing the Siloam Pool turned westward along the southern slopes of the Western Hills of the city, past the Essene Gate, then northward to Herod's palace, and from there back eastward where it

intersected with the second wall near the Gennath (Garden) Gate, and then farther west to the western portico of the Temple Mount. Built during the period of the first Temple according to *War* 5.143, parts of it were repaired by the Hasmoneans, as we know from 1 Maccabees 12.37.

48. *War* 5.128–35.

49. *War* 5.248–57. The unit totals of the rebel factions are rounded up, and the numbers of their officers are schematic enough to arouse suspicion about the accuracy of Josephus's report. But we do not know that he is wrong about the overall totals. No other source provides a corrective. Simply dismissing the totals because they seem to be high (according to what evidence?) is not a persuasive historical methodology.

50. *War* 5.258–60. The second wall began at the Gennath Gate and followed a northward course and probably made a westward turn just before where the Damascus Gate is located today; from there the wall continued on to a juncture point at which it turned south and connected to the Antonia Fortress.

51. For example, Coarelli (2000) p. 57 Plate 13 (XIII/XII/XIV); p. 58 Plate 14 (XIII/XIV–XVI).

52. *War* 5.261–63.

53. Cassius Dio 65.5.4 also mentions deserters from the Roman side to the Jews during the war.

54. *War* 5.266–69.

55. *War* 5.270–74.

56. *War* 5.275–76.

57. *War* 5.277–83.

58. *War* 5.284–87.

59. *War* 5.289.

60. See Samuelsson (2011).

61. *War* 5.290; this incident also reveals that not all the Idumaeans left Jerusalem after becoming disillusioned with the Zealots, as Josephus reported earlier, *War* 4.345–53.

62. *War* 5.291–95.

63. *War* 5.296–98.

64. This dating, however, creates problems for Josephus's later dating of the commencement of the siege. At *War* 5.567, Josephus claims that Titus encamped before Jerusalem's walls on 14 Xanthicus/Nisan, which would mean that the siege began during the celebration of Passover. Counting backward 15 days from 7 Artemisius, however, would imply that the siege began on 23 Nisan, or after Passover. The point of the earlier dating would seem to be to show how the beginning of the siege, which would end with the destruction of Jerusalem, coincided—ironically—with the celebration of the festival of liberation.

65. *War* 5.299–302.

66. 2 Kings 19.35; 2 Chronicles 32.21; Isaiah 37.36; *War* 5.303, 5.504.

67. Dąbrowa (2015) p. 28.

68. Dio 65–66.3.5.

69. *War* 5.146 for the wall's course; Meyers and Chancey (2012) p. 38 for its construction date.

70. *War* 5.303–4.

71. *War* 5.305–11.

72. *War* 5.312–14.

73. Goldsworthy (1996) p. 231.

74. Goldsworthy (1996) p. 280.

75. *War* 5.317–30.

76. *War* 5.331.

77. *War* 5.332–34.

78. *War* 5.331–33.

79. The tactical problem of orientation for the Roman soldiers will be instantly relatable to anyone who has spent any time at all in the souk of any modern Middle Eastern city.

80. *War* 5.335.
81. *War* 5.336–41.
82. *War* 5.342–43.
83. Price (1992) pp. 274–75.
84. *War* 5.342–47.
85. Southern (2007) p. 109.
86. *War* 5.348–53.
87. *War* 5.354–55.
88. *War* 5.356.
89. *War* 5.466. Price (1992) pp. 227–28 argues that the figure of 17 days for completion of the earthworks must be wrong. The works were completed, as Josephus says, at 5.466 on 29 Artemisius, after 7, not 17, days of work, which therefore must have begun on 23 Artemisius. It would follow that the payment of the army took place from 19–22 Artemisius.

CHAPTER 17. "THE JOB IS OPEN"

1. *War* 5.357–59.
2. *War* 5.360.
3. *War* 6.327.
4. *War* 5.361.
5. 2 Chronicles 32.18.
6. *War* 5.363–74.
7. *War* 5.375–90.
8. *War* 5.391–94.
9. *War* 5.395–403.
10. *War* 5.403–13.
11. *War* 5.404–19.
12. Deuteronomy 20.1–2.
13. See Price (1992) pp. 135–38 for a fine, sensitive exploration of the complex motivations of those who deserted the city at the time.
14. *War* 5.420–23.
15. *War* 5.424.
16. *War* 5.425–28.
17. Gannon (2013).
18. *War* 5.429–38.
19. *War* 5.439–41.
20. *War* 5.442–44
21. *War* 5.446–50.
22. *War* 5.450–51.
23. *War* 5.452–54.
24. *War* 4.455–56.
25. *War* 5.456–59.
26. Meshorer (2001) pp. 127–31, coins no. 211, 213, 214.
27. *War* 5.460–63, "*koinos ho ponos.*"
28. *War* 5.463–65.
29. *War* 5.465.
30. The Struthion Pool was the catchment pool for the waters brought by aqueduct from the northern part of the Tyropoeon Valley and served as the main water supply source for the Antonia Fortress.
31. *War* 5.466–68.

32. *War* 5.469–72.
33. *War* 5.473–76.
34. *War* 5.477–85.
35. *War* 5.486–90.
36. Coarelli (2000) p. 51 Plate 7 (VIII–IX/V–VI).
37. *War* 5.491–94.
38. Titus's resort to building the wall at this point may be seen as a kind of tactical concession; it was probably what he should have done as soon as he arrived. As we shall see, Flavius Silva had such a wall built as soon as he arrived at Masada in 73 or 74.
39. *War* 5.495–501.
40. For the topography, see Ussishkin (1974) pp. 70–72.
41. Possibly the triple-gated tomb in the so-called Akeldama (Aramaic) or Field of Blood, mentioned in Matthew 27.7, where the field is bought with the blood money returned to the Temple authorities, and Acts 1.18–19, where Judas bought a field with the money, to the south of the monastery of St. Onuphrius. For Ananus, see VanderKam (2004) pp. 420–24.
42. *War* 5.502–7. For the "Herod Monuments" (*mnemeion*), see *War* 5.108.
43. *War* 5.508–11.
44. Cassius Dio 65–66.4.5.
45. *War* 5.512–14.
46. Price (1992) p. 159.
47. *War* 5.515–19.
48. *War* 5.520; this is one of the few references in Josephus's account of the war to the Roman supply system during the siege. The adjoining provinces here should mean Cilicia and Commagene, considered to be part of the province of Syria; Cappadocia, Galatia, Pamphylia, and perhaps even Egypt.
49. *War* 5.522–23.
50. *War* 5.527–31.
51. *War* 5.532–33.
52. *War* 5.534–40.
53. *War* 5.541–47.
54. *War* 5.548.
55. *War* 5.548–52.
56. *War* 5.553-61.
57. *War* 5.562–66; Ritmeyer (2006) p. 354.
58. 1 Samuel 21.7; 1 Maccabees 6.53; Price (1992) pp. 151–52.
59. Price (1992) p. 153.
60. *War* 7.263–63.
61. Here, the precision of the figure and Josephus's citation of his source provide some evidence against the general conclusion that Josephus simply rounded up figures.
62. *War* 5.567–72.

CHAPTER 18. THE MORE GENTLE MINISTER

1. *War* 6.5.
2. Along Routes 50 and 1.
3. *War* 6.6–8.
4. *War* 6.15.
5. *War* 6.17–18; Goldsworthy (1996) p. 194.
6. For example, Meshorer (2001) p. 130, coin no. 216.
7. Mason (2016) p. 474, quoting the unpublished papers of Deutsch.

8. *War* 6.16–22.

9. *War* 6.23–28.

10. *War* 6.29–32.

11. *War* 6.33–53.

12. Mason (2016) p. 428; see Goldsworthy (1996) pp. 250–51, arguing that based upon this speech it is impossible to know whether the beliefs described in it were common, but that begs the question of whether the speech as written up was actually delivered.

13. *CIIP Vol. IV, Part 1* (2018) no. 3094 pp. 468–69. The inscription does not say that he died during the siege of Jerusalem, but that has to be a strong possibility, given the fact that he died at 30 years old and was buried at Emmaus, where we know Legio V Macedonica was stationed (*War* 4.445), only 18 miles away from Jerusalem. For the tombstones of other members of the legion from Emmaus, see nos. 3095, 3096, 3097.

14. *War* 6.54–57.

15. *War* 6.58–64.

16. *War* 6.65–67.

17. *War* 6.68.

18. *War* 6.69–70.

19. *War* 6.71-73.

20. *War* 6.74–80.

21. *War* 6.81–83.

22. *War* 6.84–85.

23. The hobnails of Roman military boots were made according to a standard, empire-wide pattern and specification; see Van Driel-Murray (1985) p. 54; Roth (2012) p. 21 n. 94.

24. *War* 6.86–90.

25. *War* 7.215.

26. *War* 6.91. Josephus gives a list of the Jews from the various factions who had distinguished themselves during the fighting (6.92): from John's army, Alexas and Gyphthaeus; from Simon's, Malachias, Judas, son of Merton, with James, the son of Sosas, one of the Idumaean generals; and from the Zealots, Simon and Judas.

27. *War* 6.93–95; for the required sacrifices, see Exodus 29.38–42; Numbers 28.3–8; m. Taanith 4.6.

28. Price (1992) p. 166.

29. *War* 6.95.

30. *War* 6.98–99.

31. 2 Kings 24.15; *War* 6.99–104.

32. *War* 6.107–10.

33. *War* 6.113–14. Price (1992) pp. 166–67 argues that Josephus has made a mistake here. According to his understanding, the three sons of Matthias, the son of Boethus, deserted at this time; the fourth son had already come out, and this fourth son was the son of the other Matthias whom Josephus mentions. That may be correct, but Josephus does not specifically identify either Matthias as the son of Boethus in the passage.

34. *War* 6.115.

35. *War* 6.116–20.

36. *War* 6.121–28.

37. Ritmeyer (2006) p. 340 argues that the narrow space was between the square Temple Mount and the Herodian porticoes.

38. *War* 6.129–31.

39. *War* 6.132–35.

40. For the advantages of Roman commanders staying behind the lines of battle in towns, see Goldsworthy (1996) pp. 153–54.

41. *War* 6.136–40.

42. For lulls during combat, see Goldsworthy (1996) pp. 224–25.
43. *War* 6.141–47.
44. *War* 6.148.
45. *War* 6.149–51.
46. *War* 6.153.
47. For such punishments, see Southern (2007) pp. 146–48.
48. *War* 6.154–56.
49. *War* 6.157–60.
50. *War* 6.161–63.
51. The stoas had been repaired at the urging of Agrippa II after being destroyed by the rebels at the very beginning of the war to prevent Florus from gaining access to the Temple; see *War* 2.330–31, 2.405.
52. *War* 6.164–68; Cassius Dio 65.6.1.
53. 1 Samuel 17.8–10.
54. *War* 6.169–76.
55. *War* 6.177–79.
56. *War* 6.180–84.
57. *War* 6.185–87.
58. *War* 6.188–89.
59. See Mason (2016) p. 432 for speculation about where the incident took place; two possibilities are from the colonnade roof to the Tyropoeon Valley (about 100 feet below), or perhaps Lucius was on the Temple platform, or only 40 feet below Artorius.
60. *War* 6.190–92.
61. *War* 6.193–200.
62. Deuteronomy 28.53–57. During the siege of Samaria by Ben-Hadad of Aram, two women also had cooked and eaten the son of the first woman; see 2 Kings 6.28–29.
63. *War* 6.201–12.
64. *War* 6.212–13.
65. *War* 6.214–9.
66. *War* 6.199.
67. Thucydides, *History of the Peloponnesian War* 2.70.1.
68. Appian, *Roman History* 15.96.
69. 2 Kings 6.24–29.
70. Lamentations 4.10.
71. Price (1992) p. 155.
72. Chapman (2007a) pp. 419–26.
73. Leviticus 26.15–33.
74. *War* 6.220–21.
75. *War* 6.221–28.
76. *War* 6.229–30.
77. Middot 2.6; Ritmeyer (2006) p. 340.
78. For the gates, see Josephus's description of them at *War* 5.197–206 and their burning in 70, *War* 6.232.
79. *War* 6.232–35.
80. *War* 6.236; Middot 2.3 has 12 steps; Josephus, *War* 5.195 has 14 steps.
81. Psalms 120–34.
82. *War* 5.201; *Antiquities* 15.418. For discussion of the connections between Nicanor and the Gate, see Roussel (1924) pp. 79–92; J. Schwartz (1991) pp. 245–83.
83. *War* 6.236.
84. *War* 6.237–38.

85. *War* 6.239–43.
86. *War* 1.10, 1.27–28.
87. *War* 6.128, 6.216, 6.236, 6.240, 6.256.
88. For Josephus's readers, see *Life* 361–67; *Against Apion* 1.51.
89. Cassius Dio 66.6.2–3.
90. *Chronica* 2.30, 6–7; followed and expanded upon by Bernays (1861); accepted by Barnes (1977), (2005) among others.
91. For discussion, see Barnes (1977) pp. 224–31.
92. *Histories against the Pagans* 7.9.5–6.
93. *Chronica* 2.30.8.
94. Bernays (1861); Barnes (1977) pp. 224–31, (2005) pp. 129–44; Rives (2005) pp. 145–66.
95. As Rajak pointed out in the original, 1983 edition of her seminal work on Josephus (p. 208); followed and elaborated upon by Mason (2016) pp. 494–98.
96. Beck (1862) pp. 27–40; Rajak (2002) pp. 207–11; Leoni (2007) pp. 39–51; Mason (2016) pp. 487–502, for full discussion.
97. *War* 6.244–48.
98. *War* 6.249–51.
99. *War* 6.252.
100. *War* 6.252–53.

CHAPTER 19. WOE TO THE JERUSALEMITES

1. Suetonius, *Life of Titus* 5.2.
2. *War* 6.254–56.
3. For the unfinished altar, see Exodus 20.25; for its dimensions, see Middot 3.1.
4. *War* 6.257–59.
5. *War* 6.260, *tou naou to hagion kai ta en auto*.
6. Exodus 25.23–40 for the Table of Shewbread and the menorah; for its position in the western half of the holy place, see Yarden (1991) p. 43, quoting rabbinic sources; 1 Chronicles 28.18 and 2 Chronicles 2.4 for the incense altar in the First Temple; Ritmeyer (2006) pp. 388–90 for a description of the *heikhal*.
7. Yarden (1991) p. 30.
8. *War* 5.219.
9. *War* 5.219.
10. Ritmeyer (2006) pp. 242, 265–77 for the location of the Holy of Holies above "the Rock" that is the summit point of Mt. Moriah and the position of the ark during the First Temple period; Jacobson (2007b) p. 152; for the significance of the Foundation Rock to Judaism, see Yoma 54b.
11. Leviticus 16.12–14.
12. *War* 6.261–63.
13. Cassius Dio 65.4.5; in Timochares's *Life of Antiochus,* quoted by Eusebius, *Preparation for the Gospel* 9.35.1, it was claimed that the area around the city was waterless for 40 furlongs or stadia, or about 4.5 miles. That is probably incorrect, but some of the water that the Romans had access to outside the city was undrinkable, and the water from the city's two aqueducts that they no doubt accessed might not have been sufficient for such a large army, especially in midsummer. For Jerusalem's abundant sources of water, see Price (1992) pp. 248–50.
14. *War* 6.263.
15. *War* 6.265.
16. Shimron and Peleg-Barkat (2010) pp. 56–62.
17. *War* 6.250, 268–70.

18. Jeremiah 52.12; 2 Kings 25.8; m. Taanith 4.6.

19. Rogers (2004) pp. 126–27.

20. Though Rives (2005) p. 148 has seen the significance of this.

21. *War* 6.271–74.

22. *War* 6.277.

23. *War* 6.278–80.

24. *War* 6.275–82.

25. *War* 6.283–84.

26. *War* 6.285, 300.

27. *War* 6.301.

28. *War* 6.302–9. See Klawans (2012) p. 193, who insightfully notes that Jesus's prophecy included the idea that destruction to Jerusalem would come again.

29. For the episode, see Klawans (2012) p. 193.

30. *War* 6.316.

31. B. Campbell (1994) pp. 131–33, citing multiple inscriptions and literary sources for the religious associations of the standards.

32. *War* 2.169 and book 3.

33. *War* 6.317.

34. *War* 6.321–22.

35. *War* 6.323–27.

36. Southern (2007) p. 228.

37. *War* 6.328–50.

38. *War* 6.351.

39. *War* 6.352–53.

40. Ritmeyer (2006) pp. 201, 207–11 locates the Seleucid-era Akra Fortress to the south of the square, pre-Herodian Temple Mount.

41. Ritmeyer (2006) p. 100.

42. *War* 6.354–57.

43. *War* 6.358–59.

44. *War* 6.359–62.

45. For the system, see the remarks of Goldsworthy (1996) p. 167.

46. *War* 6.363.

47. *War* 6.365–69.

48. *War* 6.370–73.

49. *War* 6.374–77.

50. *War* 6.378–86.

51. *War* 6.387–91; for discussion of which sacred treasures these were, see Yarden (1991) p. 30.

52. *War* 6.392–402.

53. *War* 6.403–7.

54. *War* 6.407–8.

55. Avigad (1983) p. 125; Arensburg (2010) pp. 288–89; Geva (2010b) pp. 67–68.

56. *CIIP Vol. I, Part 1* (2010) no. 674 pp. 666–67. Because of the extensive infighting among the different groups of rebels in the area of the Upper City during the Roman siege (e.g., *War* 2.426–29) it is also possible that the house was burned before the final Roman conquest of the Temple; see Geva (2010b) pp. 66–69.

57. For the tithing hypothesis, see Reich (2009) p. 181; for the argument that the weight was used to weigh products, possibly by a market supervisor who was a member of the Bar Kathros family, see Geva (2010c) p. 178; Keddie (2019) pp. 144–49 for discussion.

58. *War* 6.409–13, 7.1–4. Of the towers, the remains of only the lower part of one still stands; it is known today as David's Tower and is located just to the right inside the Jaffe Gate. The

remains have been identified with either the Phasael Tower or (more likely) the Hippicus Tower. See Geva (1981) pp. 57–65.

59. Geva (2010b) p. 68.
60. *War* 6.414–16.
61. *War* 6.417–18.
62. *War* 6.419.
63. *Life* 419–21.
64. S. Schwartz (2014) p. 83.
65. *War* 6.421.
66. See the remarks of McGing (2002) pp. 95–97.
67. *War* 6.420-21. Note that Tacitus, *Histories* 5.13, citing an unnamed source, says that 600,000 were besieged in the city. For the numbers, see Broshi (1977b) pp. 65–74, estimating the population of Jerusalem at 80,000 at the time of the destruction; see Geva (2014a) pp. 144–48 for lower numbers.
68. *CIL* 10.1971.
69. *War* 6.429–32.
70. Reich and Shukron (2011) pp. 241–55.
71. *War* 6.433–34.
72. *History of the Church* 3.12.
73. *War* 6.433–42; Pliny, *Natural History* 5.70, "Hierosolyma, longe clarissima urbium orientis"; Goodman (2007c) p. 443.

CHAPTER 20. THE TRAGEDIES OF TRIUMPH

1. *War* 7.5, 7.17, 7.163. The presence of soldiers from Legio X Fretensis who were stationed in Jerusalem after 70 CE is verified by a number of inscriptions found in the city; see *CIIP Vol. I, Part 2* (2012) nos. 717, 721, 722–27, pp. 16–17, 22–24, 25–30. For Cerialis's career, see Eck (1970) pp. 92–93; after Cerialis completed his tenure as legate of Judaea he subsequently became suffect consul in Rome, curator of public works, governor of Moesia (74–78), and proconsul of Africa (83–84); Magness (2002b) pp. 189–212.
2. For Vespasian sending a letter to the procurator Laberius Maximus ordering that all land of Jews should be disposed of (in reality, sold), see *War* 7.216; Cotton and Eck (2005b) pp. 23–44.
3. *CIIP Vol. II* (2011) no. 1282 pp. 238–39. I thank Ben Isaac for clarifying this for me.
4. *War* 7.216; Schäfer (1995) p. 131. Other sources suggest that some private ownership continued.
5. *Natural History* 5.70; Cotton and Ecker (2019) p. 682.
6. *Life* 422, 425, 429, 422.
7. *Life* 425.
8. *Life* 429.
9. *Life* 418, 423.
10. *War* 1.3.
11. *War* 1.6.
12. *War* 1.3.
13. *War* 7.217. For the funerary monument and inscription for Claudius Italicus, see *CIIP Vol. II* (2011) no. 1350 pp. 309–10; for the *primipili* Valerius Martialis about 165 CE and Iulius Agrippa also in Caesarea, see nos. 1228 pp. 160–62, 185–86, 1248 in the same volume. On the date of Caesarea becoming a Roman colony, see Pliny, *Natural History* book 5, chap. 14, "Idumaea, Palaestina, and Samaria"; Patrich (2009a) pp. 135–56.

14. For example, Kadman (1957) p. 46 corpus nos. 20–21 for the coins; for the epigraphic evidence, see *CIIP Vol. II* (2011) no. 1228 pp. 160–62; no. 1368 pp. 325–27; no. 1736 pp. 617–18, where the name of the colony is incised on twin lead weights in Latin; no. 2095 lines 2–3, pp. 810–12.

15. Gersht (1996) pp. 305–24 for representations of the deities in Caesarea; Painter (2000) pp. 2005–25; Eck (2009) pp. 13–42 on Latin's use; *CIIP Vol. II* (2011) no. 2095 pp. 810–12 for the Agrippa inscription.

16. Goodman (2007c) pp. 438–39.

17. *War* 7.6–7.

18. Thucydides 3.82.3.

19. *War* 7.8–12.

20. For such awards and decorations (*dona*), see generally Maxfield (1981); Southern (2007) pp. 150–52.

21. For Rufus's honorary inscription, see B. Campbell (1994) no. 94 p. 53.

22. *War* 7.16.

23. Roth (2012) p. 31.

24. *War* 7.5, 7.17–20, 7.117; Mason (2016) p. 419.

25. Millar (1993) p. 78.

26. *War* 7.23–25.

27. Josephus does not specify the location of the passageway into which Simon escaped; one possibility has to be one of the tunnels underneath the Temple Mount platform. On the complex of cisterns, chambers, and conduits, see Price (1992) pp. 286–90 for an older but still valuable overview of the area around and underneath the Temple Mount; for a slightly more recent overview, see Gibson and Jacobson (1996).

28. Edwards (2001) p. 155. It has been suggested that Simon was trying to avoid detection by wearing an outfit that resembled the *paludamentum* worn by Roman military officers. That might have been Simon's strategy, but that assumes that people would not have been at least somewhat curious why a Roman officer suddenly rose up out of the earth.

29. *War* 7.26–36.

30. *War* 7.37–40.

31. 1 Maccabees 54a.

32. *War* 7.44; *Antiquities* 12.119; *Against Apion* 2.39.

33. *War* 7.41–45.

34. *War* 7.46–47; for the episode, see Rajak (2005) p. 94.

35. *War* 7.47–53.

36. *War* 7.54–57.

37. For Collega, see Eck (1982) pp. 287–89.

38. *War* 7.58–62.

39. *War* 7.96.

40. *War* 7.103–4.

41. *War* 7.104–9.

42. *War* 7.110–11.

43. Rajak (2005) p. 95.

44. *War* 7.112–15.

45. *War* 7.117–18.

46. *Life* 422.

47. *War* 6.357.

48. *CIL* 6.930.

49. For the arches, see Cassius Dio 65–66.7.2 epitome.

50. *War* 7.119.

51. Toynbee (1957).
52. *War* 7.121.
53. *War* 4.617, 5.46; Curran (2007) pp. 86–88.
54. Suetonius, *Domitian* 1.2.
55. *War* 7.116–22; for modern accounts and interpretations of the triumph, see Weber (1921) pp. 282–83; Künzl (1988) pp. 14–15; Itgenshorst (2005) pp. 26–27; Beard (2007) pp. 93–96, 99–101, 119, 145, 151–53; Mason (2016) pp. 19–33.
56. Künzl (1988) p. 72.
57. Livy, 2.31.3, 1.20.2.
58. *War* 7.123–31.
59. For this as a possibility, see Millar (2005) p. 105. The alternatives would be the theaters of Pompey and Balbus, but that would require the procession to reverse direction and cross the pomerium. That seems to be an unlikely route.
60. As Josephus has written, these were manifestations of Rome's hegemony; the fact that they were not specifically "Judaean" does not mean that their inclusion in the procession was an attempt to deceive people about the kinds of spoils that emanated from the war.
61. *War* 7.132–38.
62. *War* 7.139–47.
63. Yarden (1991) p. 71, with discussion and references to the practice described in 1 Samuel 21 and elsewhere.
64. Yarden (1991) pp. 30–31, 43, 68, who reviews the literary sources and shows convincingly that there were three similar but not identical specimens of the menorah and the table used in the Herodian Temple. For a comprehensive history of the seven-branched menorah, see Fine (2016).
65. *War* 5.217; Yarden (1991) p. 44.
66. It is possible that the "laws" were some of the sacred volumes that Josephus himself was allowed by Titus to take from the Temple after its destruction, as he tells his readers in his *Life* 418.
67. *War* 7.148–52.
68. Deutsch (2010) pp. 51–53.
69. Now in the basement of the museum beneath the Church of San Giuseppe dei Falegnami; Beard (2007) pp. 128–29.
70. Cassius Dio 66.6.7.
71. *War* 7.153–55.
72. *War* 7.155–57.
73. Mason (2016) pp. 18–33.
74. Polybius 6.15.8.
75. For the estimate of the number of Jews in Rome, see Bowersock (2005) p. 54.
76. Mason (2016) p. 17.
77. Suetonius, *Life of Vespasian* 12.1.
78. For a synthesizing account, see Darwall-Smith (1996). Whether Vespasian and his sons appreciated that it was Nero, whose architectural footprint they were trying to erase, who had provoked the Judaean War that gave them the opportunity to seize power, we do not know.
79. Plutarch, *Life of Publicola* 15.4.
80. *Res Gestae* 4.20.
81. Tacitus, *Histories* 4.53.1; Suetonius, *Life of Vespasian* 8.5.
82. Elkins (2019) p. 15.
83. Suetonius, *Life of Vespasian* 9.1; Darwall-Smith (1996) pp. 55–68.
84. Cassius Dio 66.15.1; Stamper (2005) p. 156; Tucci (2017).
85. Millar (2005) pp. 110–11.

86. *War* 7.148–49, 159–61; Cassius Dio 65–66.7.2; Yarden (1991) p. 56; Panzram (2002) pp. 173–78; Stamper (2005) pp. 156, 169.

87. Though not, apparently, the Table of the Shewbread, which apparently was taken from Rome by Alaric in 410 and subsequently was brought to Spain by the Visigoths after being hidden from Theoderic; see Yarden (1991) p. 84.

88. Theophanes, *Chronographia* 199; Procopius, *The Vandal War* 4.9.5–9.

89. Yarden (1991) p. 65.

90. *War* 7.162.

91. Martial, *On the Spectacles* 1.7, 2.5; Suetonius, *Life of Vespasian* 9.1; *Life of Titus* 7.3; for the games, Cassius Dio 66.25. For general works on the amphitheater, see Coarelli and Gabucci (2001); Hopkins and Beard (2005); Welch (2007); and, most recently, the short and lively Elkins (2019) pp. 29–31 on the building history. For the "Colossus," see Bergmann (1994).

92. For the coins, the Haterii relief (Musei Vaticani-Museo Gregoriano Profano, inv. 9997), and the architectural elements, see Elkins (2019) pp. 26–27.

93. Alföldy (1995), pp. 195–226 for the inscription, *CIL* 6.40454a = *AE* 1995, 111b, over the lintel; Feldman (2001) pp. 21–30, 60; Millar (2005) pp. 117–19; Hopkins and Beard (2005) pp. 32–34; Mason (2016) p. 35.

94. For the dedicatory inscription and date, see *CIL* 6.945 = *ILS* 265; P. Davies (2004) p. 19, for its dedication; Stamper (2005) p. 168, noting that the arch's construction date is not firmly established. If it is a triumphal arch, it probably was begun shortly after 70 and was completed or rededicated by Domitian in 81. But if it is a commemorative arch, it would have been built after Titus's death, therefore between 82 and 90. For the architecture and sculpture, see the standard work by Pfanner (1983); Kleiner (1992) pp. 183–91; and Stamper (2005) p. 168.

95. For the most detailed examination and discussion of the individual artifacts on the Arch relief, see Yarden (1991) pp. 71–102.

96. Parisi Presicce (2008) pp. 345–54; Buonfiglio, Pergola, and Zanzi (2016) pp. 288–90.

97. *CIL* 6.944 = *ILS* 264:

> Senatus Populusq(ue) Romanus Imp(eratori) Tito Caesari divi Vespasiani f(ilio) Vespasian[o] Augusto, pontif(ici) max(imo), trib(unicia) pot(estate) X, imp(eratori) XVII, [c]o(n)s(uli) VIII, p(atri) p(atriae), principi suo, quod praeceptis patr[is] consiliisq(ue) et auspiciis gentem Iudaeorum domuit et urbem Hierusolymam omnibus ante se ducibus, regibus, gentibus aut frustra petitam aut omnino intemptatam delevit.

98. *War* 6.435–37.

99. See Pliny, *Natural History* 36.102 for the 250,000 estimate; Millar (2005) pp. 119–20 for modern guesses. For Josephus's list of the five times Jerusalem had been conquered before 70, see *War* 6.435–37.

100. Meshorer (2001) pp. 185–93.

101. See Exodus 30.11–16.

102. *War* 4.649, 7.218 on the tax; Tacitus, *Histories* 3.71–73, on the destruction in 69; Cassius Dio 65–66.7.2.

103. For the reconsecration, see Tacitus, *Histories* 4.53. For Domitian's rigorous collection of the tax, see Suetonius, *Domitian* 12.2.

104. See Stamper (2005) pp. 151–56 for the replacement temple.

105. On Nerva, the cancellation of the two-drachmas tax, and its reinstitution under Trajan, see Goodman (2007b) pp. 81–89, (2007c) pp. 446–52.

106. Meshorer (2001) p. 106, coin no. 134, apparently minted in Tiberias.

107. Cassius Dio 65.15.4.

108. Meshorer (2001) p. 112.

109. Levick (2009) p. 15.

CHAPTER 21. MASADA

1. *War* 7.163; for Bassus and his career, see Eck (1999a). Bassus may be referred to as a legate with praetorian rank of the province Syria Palaestina on the now-lost fragment of an inscription on a column seen in Caesarea in 1924; see *CIIP Vol. II* (2011) no. 1237(a) pp. 171–72.

2. We do not know who destroyed the sarcophagus. For discussion of the sarcophagi in the mausoleum at Herodeion, see Foerster (2017) pp. 266–77.

3. For the location, topography, and excavations, see Vörös (2010) pp. 349–61, (2012) 30–41, 68, (2013), (2015a) pp. 52–61, (2015b), (2017) 30–39, 60.

4. *War* 2.485–86.

5. *War* 1.168, 7.171.

6. *War* 7.172–73.

7. *War* 7.174–77.

8. *War* 7.190.

9. *War* 7.190–92.

10. The shorter sides of the wall were built on the ridges on the opposing sides of Machaerus.

11. Mason (2016) p. 522.

12. *War* 7.193.

13. *War* 7.196–206.

14. *War* 7.206–209.

15. Josephus does not tell his readers why Bassus should have decided to hunt down and kill Jews with whom he made a pact to leave Machaerus safely.

16. *War* 7.210–15; for Judas, who had distinguished himself during the fighting over the Antonia in Jerusalem, see *War* 6.92

17. Rajak (2002) p. 174.

18. Eck (1999a) pp. 109–20.

19. For Silva's career, see *AE* 1969/70 nos. 183a and 183b; Eck (1969) pp. 282–89, (1970) pp. 93–111; McDermott (1973) pp. 335–51.

20. *War* 7.252. Josephus does not provide exact numbers for the strength of the Tenth Legion at Masada or for the auxiliary soldiers. For that reason, archaeologists and historians have tried to estimate their numbers based upon the number of Roman camps built around the base of Masada (eight) and the size of the sleeping quarters for the eight-man units (*contubernia*) within the camps. For various estimates, see Yadin (1966) p. 223 (a total of 15,000 soldiers); Ben-Tor (2009) pp. 237–40; G. Davies (2011) p. 81 n. 15 (estimating closer to 8,000).

21. The Hasmonean building activity is based upon statements in *War* 1.237, 4.399, 7.285 (mentioning Jonathan, brother of Judas Maccabaeus); *Antiquities* 14.296, which presupposes the existence of fortresses earlier than Herodian construction. Thus far, however, Josephus's statements have not been confirmed by the identification of Hasmonean-era dated buildings. For the ship's shape of the mesa, see Jacobson (2006) pp. 99–117.

22. There is a steep ascent route on the southern side of Masada and several paths up the north side too. See Ben-Tor (2009) pp. 23–27.

23. *War* 7.305.

24. *War* 7.285; though most scholars do not agree that the first structures built on Masada were Hasmonean; see Marshak (2015) p. 120; Magness (2019a) p. 113 on the debate about whether Josephus meant that it was Jonathan Maccabaeus or Alexander Jannaeus who first built up fortifications on Masada.

25. Netzer (1991a) p. xv argues that there were three phases to the Herodian construction program on Masada. The first, from about 37 to 30 BCE; the second, from 30 to 20; and the third, from about 20 to 4 BCE.

26. *War* 1.267.

27. Probably on the side of the mesa where his father Antipater had had constructed the core of what became the western palace; see Netzer (2017a) p. 83.
28. Yadin (1966) pp. 117–34.
29. Netzer (2017a) p. 92; Marshak (2015) p. 200; Rozenberg (2017) pp. 204–6, 211.
30. Netzer (2017a) p. 92.
31. For the northern palace, see Yadin (1966) pp. 62–63; Netzer (2017a) pp. 92–94; Richardson and Fisher (2018) p. 258.
32. For a fine, detailed description, see Magness (2019a) pp. 63–64.
33. *War* 7.288.
34. Ben-Tor (2009) pp. 162–65.
35. Cotton and Geiger (1989) nos. 804–16 for the identifying inscriptions (*tituli picti* or labels) of storage amphorae discovered by Yadin; Ecker (2017) p. 67, noting that three more examples of the Philonian labels were found at Masada and six at Herodeion; Richardson and Fisher (2018) pp. 291–92 for discussion.
36. Ecker (2017) pp. 67, 71.
37. For the garum and muria, see Cotton and Geiger (1989) nos. 826, 821; allec, see Cotton, Lernau, and Goren (1996) pp. 223–31; on the garum and its origins, see Berdowski (2006) pp. 239–56; Marshak (2015) pp. 178–80.
38. Cotton and Geiger (1989) pp. 140–67; Ben-Tor (2009) pp. 182–84.
39. *War* 7.295–97
40. *War* 1.286-87.
41. Yadin (1966) pp. 26–29; Ben-Tor (2009) pp. 69–72; Magness (2012) p. 214, (2019a) p. 69; Mason (2016) p. 526.
42. Yadin (1966) pp. 164–67; Magness (2012) pp. 214–15.
43. For debates about the function of the second, see Yadin (1966) p. 134 (swimming pool); Netzer (1991a) pp. 333–34 (*miqveh*); Grossberg (2007) pp. 101–4 (*miqveh*); Eshel (2009) p. 50 (pool); Magness (2019a) pp. 67, 175 (uncertain).
44. Grossberg (2007) pp. 103, 108, 113; Adler (2011) p. 343.
45. Grossberg (2007) pp. 95–126; Mason (2016) p. 552; Magness (2019a) pp. 172–75.
46. Magness (2019a) pp. 172–73 for an excellent, succinct review of the purity rules.
47. Magness (2011b) p. 71, (2019a) p. 176.
48. *War* 7.299.
49. *War* 2.433–34.
50. *War* 7.275; Netzer (2001) pp. 79–97, (2008) pp. 17–41; Ben-Tor (2009); Roller (1998) pp. 187–90; Meyers and Chancey (2012) pp. 75–76.
51. Ben-Tor (2009) pp. 148–207.
52. Eshel (2009) pp. 74–75; Ben-Tor (2009) pp. 212–14; Mason (2016) pp. 548–49.
53. Reich (2001) p. 152; Ben-Tor (2009) pp. 224–26.
54. Reich (2001) p. 162; Magness (2019a) pp. 164, 179–81, arguing that the presence or absence of spindle whorls in individual rooms within the casement wall dwellings at Masada cannot be correlated with the presence of celibate male Essenes, because we know that some Essenes married and the distribution of whorls may also have been affected by other factors, such as looting after the Roman conquest in 70.
55. For the papyrus, see Yadin and Naveh (1989) pp. 9–11; Eshel (1999) pp. 233–34; (2003) p. 94; Magness (2019a) pp. 184–85.
56. *IAA* number 1991-3059; Yadin and Naveh (1989) pp. 32–39; Ben-Tor (2009) pp. 152–54; Eshel (2009) pp. 105–6; Magness (2011b) pp. 19–20; Magness (2019a) p. 186.
57. Ben Tor (2009) pp. 95–96.
58. Ben Tor (2009) p. 79; Magness (2019a) p. 167.
59. Ben Tor (2009) pp. 86–87; Stiebel and Magness (2007) pp. 24–25.

60. Shamir (1994) pp. 265–82.

61. Yadin (1966) pp. 181–87; Magness (2019a) pp. 65–66, 171–72.

62. Yadin (1966) pp. 187–89; Ben-Tor (2009) pp. 198–208; Eshel (2009) pp. 89–90, suggesting that the fragments found were part of a complete version of the Torah (the five books of Moses); Goodblatt (2009) p. 131, reporting 15 Hebrew literary manuscripts, 40–80% of which could be dated to the time of Herod on paleographic grounds.

63. Netzer (1991a) pp. 416–22; Ben-Tor (2009) p. 82; Eshel (2009) pp. 70–82; Magness (2019a) pp. 178–79.

64. Magness (2019a) p. 179.

65. Vanderkam (2001) pp. 171–73 for a comprehensive breakdown of the number of literary and nonliterary texts.

66. Yadin (1966) pp. 172–74; Tov (2004) pp. 300–302.

67. Eshel (2009) pp. 76–79.

68. For the controversies about the dating of the siege, see Eck (1969) pp. 282–89, (1970) pp. 93–111; Jones (1974) pp. 89–90; Bowersock (1975) pp. 180–85; Cotton (1989) pp. 157–62; Cotton and Geiger (1989) pp. 62–67; Ben-Tor (2009) pp. 253–54; G. Davies (2011) pp. 65–66 n. 1; Mason (2016) pp. 561–65; Magness (2019a) p. 6 n. 3. The strength of Legio X at the time has been variously estimated; see Goldsworthy (1996) p. 22 for an estimate of 3,500 based upon the evidence for their tents at Masada. In the absence of explicit evidence for the numbers of legionaries and auxiliaries that Silva brought to Masada, in appendix L I estimated food and liquid requirements for Silva's army at Masada based on what I consider to be the low total of 4,800 for the legion and the high number of 6,000, just as I did for estimates for the armies of Cestius, Vespasian, and Titus. I estimated the number of auxiliaries at 3,200 and also included requirements for military slaves and porters, since water and other supplies needed to be carried to Masada. It was impossible for thousands of legionary soldiers and auxiliaries to live off the land there.

69. Goldsworthy (1996) p. 22; for Camp F, see Magness (2019a) pp. 8–11, 37–38, 189.

70. For Roman military tents, see the classic article of Van Driel-Murray (1990) pp. 109–37; Southern (2007) p. 191; for the walls of Camp F and the tents, see Magness (2019a) p. 9.

71. The remains of the tent units at Masada seem to provide enough space for at most six soldiers (and maybe only four) to be sleeping in them at a time; the hypothesis about their size is that at least two of the other soldiers from the *contubernium* must have had sentry or other duties.

72. Southern (2007) pp. 99–100.

73. For the personal house of Roman commanders, see Keppie (1998) p. 192.

74. Magness (2019a) p. 9.

75. Roth (2012) pp. 57–59.

76. Magness (2012) pp. 218–21; (2019a) pp. 9–10.

77. *War* 7.278; Roth (1995) pp. 93–94.

78. Richmond (1962) p. 153.

79. *War* 7.278; Cassius Dio 65.4.5; Roth (1995) pp. 93–94.

80. Cassius Dio 65.4.5; Roth (2012) p. 121.

81. Ben-Tor (2009) p. 237.

82. For my breakdown of the food and liquid requirements of Silva's army, see appendix L.

83. Richmond (1962) p. 146.

84. Yadin (1966) p. 219; Magness (2019a) p. 9.

85. For the receipt, see Cotton and Geiger (1989) p. 84.

86. *War* 7.305.

87. *War* 7.293.

88. *War* 7.304–5.

89. *War* 7.306.

90. *War* 7.307.
91. Ben-Tor (2009) p. 238.
92. G. Davies (2011) pp. 76–77.
93. *War* 7.309.
94. Gichon (2000) p. 545.
95. Holley (1994) pp. 349–65.
96. *War* 7.309.
97. *War* 7.310.
98. Netzer (1991b) p. 26.
99. *War* 7.311–12. According to the theory of Netzer (1991b), the wood to build these casements was taken from the beams of the western palace complex, which shows no signs of burning from the siege. A different theory, advanced by Gichon (2000) p. 545, is that the earth fill was piled up within the casement wall, which was reinforced with the wooden beams laid against it.
100. *War* 7.313–14.
101. *War* 7.315–19.
102. For interpretations of Josephus's account, see Schulten (1933); Gill (1993) pp. 569–70; (2001) pp. 22–31, 56–57; Roth (1995) pp. 87–110; Arubas and Goldfus (2008) pp. 1937–39, (2010) pp. 19–32.
103. Arubas and Goldfus (2010) pp. 19–32.
104. Magness (2019a) p. 16.
105. For the detailed arguments, see Davies and Magness (2017) pp. 58–60.
106. Mason (2016) p. 574.
107. Davies and Magness (2017) p. 60.
108. Davies and Magness (2017) p. 62.
109. The only other possible source for the measurements would be the seven Jewish survivors of the siege that Josephus reports. Would two older women or five children be likely sources for the length of the Roman-made siege ramp or the platform? Or would Josephus simply have made up the measurements? Again, there were many Roman officers and survivors of the siege who would have taken part in the building of the works. Would Josephus have risked simply inventing the story of the siege ramp and the platform?
110. Diodorus 17.40.4–5.
111. Mason (2016) p. 555, assuming—generously—one fighting man per every seven people on the summit.
112. *War* 7.323–36; translation by H. Thackeray, *Josephus: The Jewish War, Books V–VII* (2006 reprint) pp. 397–401, with modifications.
113. For analyses of the speeches, see Feldman (1984) pp. 763–90; Chapman (1998) pp. 135–68; Mason (2016) pp. 539–45.
114. See Klawans (2012) p. 129 for the argument that the end of the *sicarii* on Masada is presented by Josephus not as martyrdom but as the just end of lives sinfully led.
115. *War* 7.337–39.
116. *War* 7.341–88. See appendix N for a translation of the full speech based upon the Loeb translation with modifications.
117. *War* 7.389.
118. On these speeches, see Rajak (2002) pp. 80–81, 89; Eshel (1999) p. 229, (2009) p. 129; Klawans (2012) pp. 118–19.
119. For analyses of the second speech, see Ladouceur (1980) pp. 245–60; M. Stern (1982) pp. 376–78; especially Luz (1983) pp. 25–43; Klawans (2012) pp. 117–18.
120. Though it was not the decision that Josephus himself chose to make following the Roman capture of Iotapata; for Josephus's deliberate ambivalence about suicide, Eleazar's second speech, and the mass suicide at Masada, see Weitzman (2004) pp. 230–45.

121. *War* 7.389–97.

122. *War* 7.398.

123. *War* 7.401; for the year, see Eck (1969) pp. 282–89, (1970) pp. 93–111 on the inscriptions of Flavius Silva upon which the date of 74 is based; for a critique of Eck's interpretation of the inscription and an attempt to date the siege of Masada to 73, see Bowersock (1975) pp. 180–85; Cotton (1989) pp. 157–62, arguing for 73 on the basis of the papyri found at the site; Mason (2016) p. 565 for what is at stake in the dating controversy. For the characterization of what happened on Masada as a murder/suicide rather than a mass suicide, see Ben-Yehuda (1995) pp. 9, 45–46, 201–4; Klawans (2012) p. 132.

124. Roth (1995) pp. 87–110.

125. *War* 7.399–400.

126. *War* 7.404.

127. *War* 7.406.

128. Yadin (1966) pp. 197–201. Since all the names are written in Hebrew it has been argued that the leaders of the resistance on Masada, at any rate, promoted the use of Hebrew as an ideological statement. For the linguistic issues, see Cotton (1999b) pp. 219–31; Kottsieper (2007) p. 114.

129. *War* 7.395–96; Yadin (1966) p. 201.

130. Ben-Tor (2009) pp. 67, 157–59; 297–99; Eshel (2009) pp. 128–32.

131. Mason (2016) p. 556.

132. Zerubavel (1995); Ben-Yehuda (1995), (2002).

133. Magness (2012) p. 227.

134. Geva (1996) pp. 297–306.

135. For discussion of the nationalist myth, see Silberman (1989) pp. 87–101; Ben-Yehuda (1995), (2002); Zerubavel (1995) pp. 60–76; A. Shavit (2013) pp. 79–97; Rajak (2016) pp. 219–33.

136. Goodman (2007c) p. 246.

137. *War* 6.186–87.

138. Coarelli (2000) p. 191 Plate 147 (XC–XCI/CXIX–CXX), p. 192 Plate 148 (XCI/CXX–CXXI, p. 193 Plate 149 (XCII/CXXI–CXXII).

139. For the inhabitants of Masada as bandits, see *War* 4.504.

140. For the question of the length of the siege at Masada, see Roth (1995).

141. *War* 7.323.

142. Chapman (2007b) p. 88.

143. *War* 7.303.

144. *War* 7.407.

145. *War* 7.407–19.

146. *War* 7.420–21.

147. 2 Maccabees 4.1–34.

148. *War* 1.31–33, 7.420–32; *Antiquities* 12.237–39,12.387–88, 13.62–73, 20.236; for the building, see Hayward (1982) pp. 429–43; Wasserstein (1993) pp. 119–29; Richardson (2004) pp. 165–79; Capponi (2007).

149. *War* 7.433–36; Hayward (1982) pp. 429–43 for the temple; Wasserstein (1993) pp. 119–29.

150. Rives (2005) p. 154. The sacrificial cult of another group of Jews, military colonists who lived on the island of Elephantine opposite Syene (modern Aswan) at the first cataract of the Nile, had been shut down in 410 BCE, when the Temple of Yahu there was destroyed by troops from Syene (at the instigation of the priests of Khnum, the local Egyptian god).

151. For Catullus (not to be confused with the prominent consul L. Valerius Catullus Messalinus), see Cotton and Eck (2005a) pp. 46–48.

152. *War* 7.437–46.

153. *War* 7.447–50; *Life* 424–25.

154. *War* 7.451–53.

CHAPTER 22. THE CAUSES OF THE WAR(S)

1. Rhoads (1976) pp. 12, 56, 175, stating that Josephus placed the blame for the war on misguided revolutionaries; Brunt (1977) pp. 149–53; Rajak (1983) p. 78, writing that the rift was opened up by bad governors and was widened by various criminal or reckless types among the Jews; Goodman (1987) pp. 412–13 against Josephus's explanation, arguing that there was little evidence of Jewish hostility to Rome before 66, (2007c) pp. 393–403; McLaren (1998), arguing that the events narrated (by Josephus) are explained as part of the process that culminated with God punishing the godless generation.
2. Mason (2016) p. 200.
3. Book 1.24–88.
4. The contingent nature of the war undermines the arguments of Justin Martyr, Origen, and Eusebius that the destruction of the Temple and the defeat of the Jews were punishment for the crucifixion of Jesus. Apart from the chronological problem that the Temple was destroyed about 40 years after Jesus's death, the more serious issue for those who do not have a deterministic, theological theory of history is the existence of so many events and choices that had to fall into place for the war to have occurred. Contrary to what Eusebius, for instance, claimed in the *Proof of the Gospel* 6.13, 273a, the Romans did not destroy Jerusalem because of the execution of Jesus or "soon" after it happened but because of the mauling of Cestius's army in 66 and the revolt of Jews against Rome. It is also the case that none of the Jews or Romans who are identified in the Gospels as having been involved in Jesus's execution played roles in the war or its outcome. Eusebius's idea that those who were responsible for Jesus's death were punished between 66 and 70 is simply wrong.
5. Compare the self-immolation of the Tunisian street vendor Mohamed Bouazizi on 17 December 2010 over harassment by municipal authorities that led to protests in Tunisia, the resignation of President Zine El Abidine Ben Ali on 14 January 2011, and then demonstrations in several other countries in the Middle East, the beginning of the "Arab Spring."
6. For the Sadducees' doctrine of free choice, see *War* 2.165.
7. *Antiquities* 20.241.
8. Goodman (2007c) p. 397.
9. *War* 6.312–13.
10. *War* 5.321.
11. *War* 5.458; Brunt (1977) pp. 149–53.

CHAPTER 23. THE COURSE AND OUTCOME OF THE WAR

1. *War* 1.10–12.
2. *War* 4.323.
3. *War* 5.19.
4. *War* 5.412.
5. *War* 6.95–110.
6. *Antiquities* 20.165–66.
7. *War* 2.256.
8. Rajak (2002) pp. 78–103; Klawans (2012) pp. 188–91.
9. This idea in particular is central to the introduction to the *Antiquities,* as Klawans points out; *Antiquities* 1.14–15, 20. See also Gregerman (2016) pp. 140–44, who usefully distinguishes between the corporate theodicy of divine punishment and individual justice. Corporate theodicy is concerned with Israel's sins and fate, not the sins of individuals. Josephus's theodicy seems to blend these ideas, since he faults individuals for leading the Jews to commit greater sins.
10. Grabbe (2004) p. 103; Klawans (2012) pp. 187–91.

11. For example, Deuteronomy 1.26–39, in which the men of the evil generation who doubted the word of God were denied entry into the good land after he freed the people from Egypt. For the Deuteronomistic theology of sin followed by punishment, see VanderKam (2001) p. 68.

12. Isaiah 10.5–6.

13. Arguably Josephus's conception of how and why the Temple was destroyed is therefore consistent with the theocratic interpretation of history promoted by the Deuteronomist(s); the most important substantive difference is that in Josephus's account of the revolt and its outcome, it is the sins of individuals (the tyrants, the *sicarii*) that lead to the mass punishment of Jews, whereas in Deuteronomy and elsewhere in the passages cited earlier God punishes Israel for the sins of Israel. The guilt is corporate, and so is the punishment. The problem with Josephus's modified Deuteronomic theodicy is that it never squarely faces the fact that it was not just a few tyrants and some assassins who caused the war and were willing to fight and die to throw off Roman rule. It was tens of thousands of Jews, as Josephus himself makes clear.

14. For discussion of the compatibility of free will and fate in Josephus, see Klawans (2012) pp. 69–75, 81–91, 189–90.

15. *Life* 363–64.

16. Price (1992) pp. 186–88 for some examples.

17. Klawans (2012) p. 188 argues that Josephus's work presents "a thorough, theological explanation for the destruction of the temple."

18. Deuteronomy 20.1–20.

19. The valor of the "Judaeans" is cited as a literary theme of Josephus's *War* by Mason (2016) pp. 104–6. But in the absence of other evidence that could be used to verify or falsify what Josephus says about the bravery of Jews in specific situations, it is not clear how readers can distinguish between what Josephus tells us about the actions of Jews and his characterizations of their actions. Josephus's Roman readers, including Titus, however, surely must have known that Jews did fight with great courage during the war, and if Josephus fabricated stories such as the one about Castor (*War* 5.317–30) or exaggerated their valor generally, that would have been apparent.

20. Niger the Peraean may be an exception. He has a Latin name, and he might have been a Roman auxiliary soldier, though that is not proved.

21. See Goldsworthy (1996) pp. 8–9, 283–84 on the popular view of the Roman imperial army as a kind of machine that crushed any enemy foolish enough to confront it; and Peters (2012) p. 179.

22. Colville (2002) p. 659.

23. For the Romans' expertise in siege warfare, see Luttwak (1976) pp. 40–41.

24. Payne (2018) p. 28.

25. Price (1992) pp. 281–85 provides a catalog.

26. Magness (2012) pp. 168–69.

27. See Thucydides, 6.63–7.87, on Syracuse; on Napoleon's siege of Acre, see Roberts (2015) pp. 185–205; Mason (2016) pp. 178–80; on the siege during the Third Crusade, see Hosler (2018).

28. Deuteronomy 3.4–5; Joshua 6.15–21.

29. *War* 6.435.

30. *Geography* 5.3.2.7–8.

31. *War* 5.25.

32. For Herod and his commissariat, see Shatzman (1991) p. 188.

33. *War* 1.308.

34. *War* 5.520.

35. It may be that at least some of the inscriptions on stone drums, documenting their fabrication by the Roman army for the "high level" aqueduct from the vicinity of Bethlehem to

Jerusalem, date to the time of the siege; see *CIIP Vol. IV, Part I* (2018) nos. 3231–62 pp. 653–76. In any case, however, the fabrication implies that the aqueduct to Jerusalem built during Herod's reign was not destroyed by the Romans during the siege. That would have been pointless given the abundant water resources within the city.

36. *Antiquities* 15.366–67.
37. Goldsworthy (1996) pp. 79–95, 246–47.
38. *War* 2.517–19, 3.233, 5.54–55, 5.85–97, 5.473–85.
39. On the decisive role of Roman logistics in the war, see McDonnell-Staff (2010).
40. Deuteronomy 1.15.
41. For Josephus's positive assessment of Herod's martial prowess, see *War* 1.430; the one exception was Herod's defeat by the Nabataeans at Canatha, where he seems to have relied upon the advice of younger officers. Herod was no Alexander III of Macedon, but no one else was either. On "Out-Heroding Herod," *Hamlet* III.2; Landau (2006); Vermes (2014) p. 108.
42. For Titus engaged in combat, see *War* 3.487–91, 5.52–66, 5,85–97, 5.486–90; and for the *virtus* expected of Roman commanders, see Goldsworthy (1996) pp. 167–70.
43. These were the qualities that the French general Gamelin told Churchill in May 1940 had allowed the Germans to break through the supposedly unbreakable French lines; see Colville (2002) p. 261. When Churchill asked Gamelin what he intended to do about it, Gamelin shrugged. The Jews in 66 did more than shrug.
44. Klawans (2012) p. 194.
45. I Samuel 23.14, 24.1–3.
46. Deuteronomy 28.7.
47. For historical and comparative studies, see Joes (1996); Arreguín-Toft (2001); Boot (2013).
48. Joshua 2.1–22.
49. Roth (2012) p. 201.
50. Horbury (2014) pp. 325–32.
51. *War* 1.4–5, 6.343.
52. Cassius Dio 66.4.3.
53. For the intervention of Barzapharnes and Pacorus in 40 BCE, for instance, see *War* 1.248–55 and *Antiquities* 14.330–41.
54. *Res Gestae* 29; Cassius Dio 54.8.1–3.
55. *Antiquities* 16.253.
56. Tacitus, *Annals* 14.26.
57. Tacitus, *Annals* 15.25.4–30.2.
58. Mason (2016) pp. 165–66.
59. Boot (2013) p. 113.
60. For the surrender of the Adiabenians in 70, see *War* 6.356–57.
61. *War* 6.357.
62. Saddington (2009) pp. 309–10.
63. Goldsworthy (1996) pp. 38, 114–15.
64. Boot (2013) p. 153.

CHAPTER 24. IN THE BEGINNING WERE THE WORDS

1. Middlemas (2007).
2. 4 Ezra 13.52
3. Schremer (2008) pp. 183–99; Gregerman (2016) pp. 144–45, 148, 191.

APPENDIX A: SOURCES FOR THE WAR

1. *Life* 5.
2. *Life* 1–2; *Against Apion* 2.108; for the 24 priestly courses, see 1 Chronicles 24.1–18; M. Taan. 4.2; and how they came into being, with the drawing of lots in the presence of David and the high priests Sadok and Abiathar, see *Antiquities* 7.366; Safrai and Stern (1976) pp. 587–96. See Rajak (2002) p. 15 for a convincing explanation of how Josephus claimed, on the one hand, to be of royal blood on his mother's side and then goes on to say that his father's grandfather married the daughter of the high priest Jonathan. The explanation for the seeming contradiction is that his great-great grandmother (the daughter of Jonathan) was his family tie to the Hasmoneans.
3. *War* 3.352; later, in his *Life* 80, Josephus nevertheless claims not to have collected the tithes that were due to him as a priest. He probably made this claim to disassociate himself from priests who may have been understood to be living off the work and produce of nonpriestly Jews before the destruction of the Temple.
4. 1 Chronicles 24.1–18; VanderKam (2001) p. 182.
5. *Life* 7–12; Mason (1989) pp. 31–46.
6. *Life* 13–16; for analysis of the story, Rajak (2005) pp. 84–85.
7. *Life* 17–19.
8. *Life* 20–23.
9. *War* 2.568.
10. *War* 3.400–402.
11. *Life* 414.
12. *War* 4.622–29.
13. *Life* 417–21.
14. Although Josephus does not explicitly claim to have been present during the celebration; for the controversy, see Mason (2016) p. 21 and n. 68.
15. *Life* 422–23. Josephus would have to have moved on from the Flavian house on the Quirinal because Domitian had it converted into the Temple of the *gens Flavia* by 94 anyway. We are not sure where he resided afterward.
16. *Life* 424–25; perhaps as compensation for land owned outside Jerusalem but lost during or in the aftermath of the war; see 422.
17. *Life* 414–15, 426–27 for Josephus's marriages.
18. *Life* 428–29.
19. *Ecclesiastical History* 3.9.2.
20. For Josephus's socioeconomic status in Rome, see Cotton and Eck (2005a) pp. 37–52.
21. *Antiquities* 14.68; Rajak (2005) p. 85.
22. A better, descriptive title for the work might be extracted from the first few words of the work, which begins, "Since the war of Jews against Romans" (1.1). The point is not pedantic; from the very first words of his study Josephus makes clear that his work is about a war between Jews—not all Jews, since there is no definite article before Jews—and Romans (but not all Romans). It is not a work about a war between all the Jews and Romans—or others. For the date of composition, see S. Cohen (1979) pp. 87–89, who argues for a Domitianic (81 CE–96) date; S. Schwartz (1986) pp. 375–77, for a date after 93; Rajak (2002) p. 195, the latter part of the reign of Vespasian; Grabbe (2010) pp. 31–32, who dates the completion between 79 and 81; Mason (2016) pp. 91–93. For recent studies accepting the compositional unity of the work and earlier date, see Cotton and Eck (2005a) pp. 37–52; Brighton (2009) pp. 33–41; Siggelkow-Berner (2011) pp. 25–33; and Mason (2016) p. 91, who argues for a date sometime between the dedication of the Temple of Peace in Rome in 75 (which is the last datable event cited in the *War*) and the death of Vespasian on 23 June 79, who is honored in the preface to the work and thus is still implied to be alive.

23. *War* 1.30; *Antiquities* 13.298.
24. *War* 1.3,1.6.
25. Rajak (2002) pp. 180–81.
26. *Life* 364–66.
27. *Life* 358, 342; cf. *Against Apion* 1.56.
28. *Life* 361–62; *Against Apion* 1.50–51.
29. Cotton and Eck (2005a) p. 42, noting that Larcius Lepidus and Iulius Alexander would have been dead by the time the first version of Josephus's account of the war was completed. Other possible candidates for receiving a copy of Josephus's finished version of his war book might have been T. Flavius Clemens and his wife Flavia Domitilla, charged in 95 CE and executed for adopting Judaism (Cassius Dio 67.14.1–2).
30. *War* 3.108.
31. *Antiquities* 20.267 for Josephus's own statements on the connections between the *Antiquities* and his autobiography; for the complicated and intertwined issues related to the dating of the *Antiquities*, the *Life*, and *Against Apion*, see Rajak (2002) pp. 237–38; Mason (2003) pp. xiv–xix; Edmondson (2005) pp. 6–7. On Josephus's use of Nicolaus of Damascus as a source for the reigns of the Hasmoneans and of Herod, see Toher (2001) pp. 427–48; Grabbe (2010) p. 32.
32. *Antiquities* 1.8-9; *Life* 430; *Against Apion* 1.1, 2.1, 2.296.
33. Cotton and Eck (2005a) pp. 50–52, canvassing the possibilities but concluding that the men most frequently suggested, Nero's freedman Epaphroditus, and Epaphroditus, the slave of Modestus, the prefect of Egypt, have to be ruled out: in the first case Nero's freedman Epaphroditus helped the emperor commit suicide, and it is hardly likely that he remained an influential figure in Rome afterward; in the second case, we have no evidence for a Modestus who was prefect of Egypt. If there was no Modestus, then Epaphroditus (if he existed) becomes a lesser figure in Rome, and Cotton and Eck ask why Josephus would have wanted to dedicate three of his works to him. The conclusion from this is that Josephus himself was a rather isolated figure in Rome, not prominent in the social life of Flavian Rome. For a different picture, in which Josephus is presented as one of the main characters in Flavian Rome, among a number of leading representatives from the elites of the world altered by the Jewish war and its outcome (including Berenice and Agrippa II), see Bowersock (2005) pp. 53–62.
34. For Josephus enjoying the support of Domitian and his wife Domitia Longina, see *Life* 429; for Domitian's rigor in the collection of the tax and the persecution of those who embraced Judaism, see Cassius Dio 67.14.2 and Suetonius, *Life of Domitian* 12.2; and for the paradox, see Jones (2005) p. 208.
35. For Josephus's reliance upon the evidence of deserters, see *Against Apion* 1.49. For a concise evaluation of Josephus's sources for the war, see Mason (2016) pp. 130–35.
36. Price (1992) pp. 180–93.
37. Rajak (2002); McLaren (1998).
38. For the controversy over whether Josephus's writings primarily reflected the views and values of his Roman patrons or whether they reveal his own personal outlook on the events of the war and its aftermath, see the works of Lindner (1972); Bilde (1988) pp. 173-234; Mason (1991); (2016); Rajak (2002) pp. 185–222; Barclay (2005); Curran (2007) p. 90; den Hollander (2014).
39. For Titus's role in the *War's* dissemination, see *Life* 363.
40. Klawans (2012) 200–201.
41. *Life* 342, 358; *Against Apion* 1.56.
42. Tacitus, *Histories* 2.4, 5.1–13; Suetonius, *Life of Vespasian* 4.5–6, 5.6, 6.3, 8.1, *Life of Titus* 4.3, 5.2; Dio 65.4–7, 9.2.
43. VanderKam (2001) pp. 138–42 for a summary.

44. Rajak (2002) p. 199.

45. For discussion, see Price (1992) pp. 198–204.

46. Pesachim 57a.

APPENDIX C: THE COSTS OF MUNIFICENCE

1. For a short study, see Gabba (1990) pp. 160–68.

2. *Antiquities* 14.8; from the fact of Antipater's fortune it is inferred that he owned estates in Idumaea. See Richardson (1996) pp. 176–68 on Herod's estates in Idumaea.

3. *War* 1.275; *Antiquities* 14.371.

4. *Antiquities* 17.188–90.

5. 300 talents were worth approximately 1,800,000 drachmas; 15,000,000 denarii equal about 8.3 talents.

6. *Antiquities* 17.305, 17.307.

7. Keddie (2019) p. 120.

8. *Antiquities* 15.5.

9. *War* 1.268; *Antiquities* 14.363.

10. *War* 1.423; *Antiquities* 16.291.

11. For the contributions that were alleged to have been made to Herod by those who contested his will, see *Antiquities* 17.308; for his appointment to the procuratorship, *War* 1.399; and the argument that Herod benefited financially from holding the position, Gabba (1990) pp. 162–63.

12. *Antiquities* 15.380 and in chapter 1. Note Dar (2007) p. 305, citing Warszawski and Peretz (1992) pp. 42–46, estimating that the cost of the building project on the Temple Mount would have been between 3,000 and 4,000 talents. At a minimum that would mean a cost of approximately 18,000,000 drachmas.

13. *Antiquities* 15.107,15.360, 16.128; *War* 1.398–99. Wine could be made from the palm trees, and the sap from the balsam trees was used to treat headaches and eye problems.

14. *Antiquities* 16.179–83.

15. For doubts about Josephus's story of Herod ransacking David's tomb, see Fuks (2002) p. 241; Jacobson (1988) pp. 386–403; Marshak (2015) p. 281.

16. For Hyrcanus's looting of David's tomb, see *War* 1.61; *Antiquities* 13.249.

17. Ariel and Fontanille (2012) p. 13 on the tax revenues from agriculture; Keddie (2019) pp. 120–21 on capitation taxes under Herod.

18. Ariel and Fontanille (2012) p. 14; Udoh (2014) p. 377.

19. *War* 2.4. 2.84–86 for implied taxes; and then lessening taxes at *Antiquities* 15.365; 16.64 and 17.25 on customary forms of obligation; 19.352 for 12 million drachmas annually.

20. For the improvements to infrastructure, especially the water supply system, to accommodate pilgrims, see Amit and Gibson (2014) pp. 9–42; Gurevich (2017) pp. 103–34.

21. Meshorer (1984) p. 177; Broshi (1985) p. 32; Ariel and Fontanille (2012) p. 16.

22. Exodus 30.11–15 for the mandate, once in a lifetime by the children of Israel; in Nehemiah 10.32–33 it is one-third of a shekel yearly for service in the house of God; Mishnah, Mo'ed (Festival) Sheqalim 3.2, 2.2, 2.1 for the appropriations and methods of delivery; 1.1 on 15 Adar, fixing roads and streets and ritual water baths, performing public duties, marking graves; 4.1, bringing the daily burnt offerings, additional burnt offerings, the *omer*, loaves, and other public offerings; 4.2–5, other cult and municipal requirements and needs, including wines, oils, flour, plates of gold, and wages of craftsmen; Ariel and Fontanille (2012) p. 41.

23. Keddie (2019) pp. 46–47.

24. Lapin (2017a) p. 433.

25. For the size of Herod's army, the yearly wage bill, and other costs of maintaining it, see Shatzman (1991) pp. 195–96; Rocca (2009) pp. 10–13; for a summary analysis of Herod's building and administrative expenses, see Ariel and Fontanille (2012) pp. 18–20.

26. Dar (2007) p. 305.

27. Rocca (2008) p. 212 n. 53.

28. Keddie (2019) p. 120, arguing that the exemption dated to after 30 BCE.

29. *Antiquities* 15.299–316; for the scholarly controversies about the date of the famine, see Pastor (1997) pp. 115–26; Ariel and Fontanille (2014) pp. 7, 37–38, who suggest that it was bullion that was send to Egypt for the grain, not coins; Richardson and Fisher (2018) pp. 145–46, for discussion of the dating and the measures Herod took.

30. *Antiquities* 15.365, 16.64–65.

31. An aspect of Herod's overall regime rightly emphasized by Geiger (2009) pp. 162–63.

32. Pastor (1997) p. 97; Udoh (2006) p. 115; Ariel and Fontanille (2012) p. 11; Keddie (2019) pp. 113–14.

33. Ariel and Fontanille (2012) p. 12.

34. See Leibner (2009) for the eastern Galilee and the Golan; Richardson and Fisher (2018) p. 323.

APPENDIX G: THE ROMAN LEGION AROUND 4 BCE

1. Goldsworthy (1996) p. 14; Roth (2012) p. 19.

2. Keppie (1998) pp. 180–82.

3. Goldsworthy (1996) p. 30; Keppie (1998) p. 176.

4. Southern (2007) pp. 125–29.

5. Keppie (1998) pp. 177–78.

6. Tacitus, *Histories* 2.29.2 (Alfenus Varus, prefect of the camp), 3.7 (Minicius Iustus, prefect of the camp); Vegetius, *Epitome of Military Science* 2.10; Keppie (1998) pp. 176–77; Southern (2007) pp. 105, 129, 332.

7. Keppie (1998) p. 178.

8. Goldsworthy (1996) p. 14; Keppie (1998) p. 174. In descending order of seniority the five other centurions were *pilus posterior, princeps prior, princeps posterior, hastatus prior,* and *hastatus posterior.*

9. B. Campbell (1984) p. 102; Goldsworthy (1996) pp. 30–32; Keppie (1998) p. 179; Gilliver (2007) pp. 190–92.

10. Goldsworthy (1996) p. 14; Southern (2007) p. 100.

11. Southern (2007) pp. 101–2. For the figure of the 120 cavalry Vespasian took into the Galilee, see *War* 3.120.

APPENDIX I: CESTIUS'S ARMY, SUMMER 66 CE

1. This total assumes one horse per cavalryman; undoubtedly the Roman auxiliary cavalry must have traveled with herds of extra horses that also needed to be supplied.

2. Roth (2012) pp. 9–13, 42–43, 67, 119, 330, where Roth notes that his estimate of the Roman ration is smaller and lighter than that of other scholars. The adoption of Roth's estimate strengthens the argument made here. If the ration was larger and heavier, that would mean that Roman soldiers and their pack animals had to carry more weight and find more food on their campaigns than is estimated here.

   Recommended caloric and liquid intakes of modern soldiers are also worth considering. According to the recommended dietary allowances of the U.S. Army, which are based upon and adapted from the National Academy of Sciences/National Research Council publication, *Recommended Dietary Allowances* (1980, ninth edition), active-duty soldiers on operations should ingest 3,200 calories per day; it notes that caloric expenditures are increased in hot environments. In extremely hot environments (i.e., above 40 C/104 F) daily energy requirements might be expected to reach 56 kcal/kg of body weight. Special operations soldiers may need up to 4,600 calories ingested per day. Recommended water intake is connected to increased caloric requirements. In temperate climates 1 ml of water is recommended for each calorie expended during moderate activity. But in hot climates water requirements may increase from 50% to 100% during similar levels of activity. For detailed data, see https://www.ncbi .nlm.nih.gov/books/NBK209042/ and https://www.army.mil/article/94874/army_studying _special_operators_nutritional_needs.

Interviews with military scientists at the Military Nutrition Division at the U.S. Army Research Institute of Environmental Medicine who studied the drinking practices of U.S. soldiers serving in the war in Iraq in 2003 support the government studies about liquid consumption needs. Soldiers who expended about 3,000 calories per day drank 3–4 quarts of water or 12 to 16 eight-ounce glasses of water per day, and more active soldiers drank five to six quarts of water. For the interviews, see https://www.washingtonpost.com/archive/lifestyle /wellness/2003/04/08/in-iraq-a-mighty-thirst/0fb42cf3-a463-41d4-93da-7eff54db4c1d/.

My estimates of the caloric and liquid needs of Cestius's soldiers are at the low end of what was probably needed for the soldiers to remain effective over weeks.

3. For the client kings' responsibility for providing for their soldiers, see Roth (2012) p. 239.
4. Roth (2012) p. 114.
5. Roth (2012) pp. 61–67, 198.

APPENDIX K: TITUS'S ARMY, SPRING 70 CE

1. Assuming around 2.85 pounds of food per day and 2.0 liquid liters per legionary.
2. 1,200 slaves per each legion and one pack animal for every three infantrymen.
3. Assuming 2 kg of hard fodder, 6 kg of green fodder, and 20 liters of water per animal.
4. Assuming 2.5 pounds of food and 2 liters of water per cavalryman.
5. One pack animal for every three auxiliaries, each requiring 2 kg of dry fodder, 6 kg of green fodder, and 20 liters of water.
6. 4,000–8,000 horses × 2.5 kg of hard fodder, 7 kg of green fodder, and 20 liters of water. Note that these figures do not include any extra mounts for the cavalry.
7. 4,000 × 2.5 kg of hard fodder, 7 kg of green fodder, and 20 liters of water per day.

APPENDIX N: THE SECOND SPEECH
OF ELEAZAR BEN YAIR

This speech is taken from *War* 7.341–88, translation by H. Thackeray, *Josephus: The Jewish War, Books V–VII* (2006 reprint of original 1928 edition) pp. 402–16 with modifications.

References

Abramson, G. and Parfitt, T. eds. *Jewish Education and Learning* (1994).

Adan-Bayewitz, D. and Aviam, M. "Jotapata, Josephus and the Siege of 67: Preliminary Report on the 1992–1994 Seasons," *JRA* 10 (1997) pp. 131–65.

Adler, Y. "The Archaeology of Purity: Archaeological Evidence for the Observance of Ritual Purity in Erez-Israel from the Hasmonean Period until the End of the Talmudic Era (164 CE–400 CE)," PhD Dissertation, Ban-Ilan University (2011).

Aharoni, Y. ed. *Arad Inscriptions* (1981).

Alföldy, G. "Eine Bauinschrift aus dem Colosseum," *ZPE* 109 (1995) pp. 195–226.

———. "Pontius Pilatus und das Tiberieum von Caesarea Maritima," *SCI* 18 (1999) pp. 85–108.

———. "Nochmals: Pontius Pilatus und das Tiberieum von Caesarea Maritima," *SCI* 21 (2002) pp. 133–48.

Alston, R. "Roman Military Pay from Caesar to Diocletian," *JRS* 84 (1994) pp. 113–23.

Ameling, W., Cotton, H., Eck, W., Isaac, B., Kushnir-Stein, A., Misgav, H., Price, J., and Yardeni, A. eds. with contributions by Daniel, R., Ecker, A., Shenkar, M., and Sode, C. *Corpus Inscriptionum Iudaeae/Palaestinae, Vol. II: Caesarea and the Middle Coast: 1121–2160* (2011).

Ameling, W., Cotton, H., Eck, W., Isaac, B., Kushnir-Stein, A., Misgav, H., Price, J., and Yardeni, A. eds. with contributions by Ecker, A., and Hoyland, R. *Corpus Inscriptionum Iudaeae/Palaestinae, Vol. III: South Coast 2161–2648* (2014).

Ameling, W., Cotton, H., Eck, W., Ecker, A., Isaac, B., Kushnir-Stein, A., Misgav, H., Price, J., Weiß, P., and Yardeni, A. eds. *Corpus Inscriptionum Iudaeae/Palaestinae, Vol. IV: Iudaea/Idumaea Part 1: 2649–3324* (2018a).

———. *Corpus Inscriptionum Iudaeae/Palaestinae, Vol. IV: Iudaea/Idumaea Part 2: 3325–3978* (2018b).

Amit, D. and Gibson, S. "Water to Jerusalem. The Route and Date of the Upper and Lower Level Aqueducts," in Ohlig, C. and Tsuk, T. eds. *Cura Aquarum in Israel II* (2014) pp. 9–42.

Amit, D., Patrich, J., and Hirschfeld, Y. eds. *The Aqueducts of Ancient Israel* (2002).

Andrade, N. "Ambiguity, Violence, and Community in the Cities of Judea and Syria," *Historia: Zeitschrift für Alte Geschichte* 59 (2010) pp. 342–70.

Applebaum, A. "'The Idumaeans' in Josephus' The Jewish War," *JSJ* 40 (2009) pp. 1–22.

Arav, R. "Bethsaida: A Response to Stephen Notley," *NEA* 74 (2011) pp. 92–100.

Arav, R., and Freund, R. eds. *Bethsaida: A City by the North Shore of the Sea of Galilee, Vol. 1* (1995).

———. *Bethsaida: A City by the North Shore of the Sea of Galilee, Vol. 2* (1999).

———. *Bethsaida: A City by the North Shore of the Sea of Galilee, Vol. 3* (2004).

———. *Bethsaida: A City by the North Shore of the Sea of Galilee, Vol. 4* (2009).

Arbel, Y. "The Gamla Coin: A New Perspective on the Circumstances and Date of Its Minting," in Malena, S. and Miano, D. eds. *Milk and Honey: Essays on Ancient Israel and the Bible in Appreciation of the Judaic Studies Program at the University of California, San Diego* (2007) pp. 257–75.

———. "Chapter 6: The Coins Minted in Gamla: An Alternative Analysis," in Syon, D. ed. *Gamla III: The Shmarya Gutmann Excavations 1976–1989, Finds and Studies, Part I (IAA Reports, No. 56)* (2014) pp. 233–38.

Archibald, Z., Davies, J., and Gabrielson, V. eds. *The Economies of Hellenistic Societies, Third to First Centuries BC* (2011).

Arensburg, B. "Analysis of Human Forearm Bones," in Geva, H. ed. *Jewish Quarter Excavations in the Old City of Jerusalem IV* (2010) pp. 288–89.

Ariel, D. "The Coins of Herod the Great," in Jacobson, D. and Kokkinos, N. eds. *Herod and Augustus* (2009) pp. 113–26.

Ariel, D. and Fontanille, J. *The Coins of Herod: A Modern Analysis and Die Classification* (2012).

Arreguín-Toft, I. "How the Weak Win Wars: A Theory of Asymmetric Conflict," *International Security* (2001) pp. 96–98.

Arubas, B. and Goldfus, H. "Masada, the Roman Siege Works," *NEAEHL* 5 (2008) pp. 1937–39.

———. "Masada from the Roman Point of View: The Excavations of the Siege Works," in Yona, S. ed. *Or Le-Mayer: Studies in Bible, Semitic Languages, Rab-*

binic Literature, and Ancient Civilizations Presented to Mayer Gruber on the Occasion of His Sixty-Fifth Birthday (2010) pp. 19–32.

Atkinson, K. "Noble Deaths at Gamla and Masada? A Critical Assessment of Josephus' Account of Jewish Resistance in Light of Archaeological Discoveries," in Rodgers, Z. ed. *Making History: Josephus and Historical Method* (2007) pp. 349–71.

———. *A History of the Hasmonean State: Josephus and Beyond* (2016).

Austin, M. *The Hellenistic World from Alexander to the Roman Conquest: A Selection of Ancient Sources in Translation* (1981).

Avi, G. "'From Polis to Madina' Revisited—Urban Change in Byzantine and Early Islamic Palestine," *Journal of the Royal Asiatic Society* 21 (2011) pp. 301–29.

Aviam, M. "Yodefat/Jotapata: The Archaeology of the First Battle," in Berlin, A. and Overman, A. eds. *The First Jewish Revolt: Archaeology, History, and Ideology* (2002) pp. 121–33.

———. *Jews, Pagans, and Christians in the Galilee* (2004a).

———. "The Archaeology of the Battle of Yodefat," in Aviam, M. *Jews, Pagans and Christians in the Galilee* (2004b) pp. 110–22.

———. "First-Century Jewish Galilee: An Archaeological Perspective," in Edwards, D. ed. *Religion and Society in Roman Palestine: Old Questions, New Approaches* (2004c) pp. 7–27.

———. "Archaeological Illumination of Josephus' Narrative," in Rodgers, Z. ed. *Making History: Josephus and Historical Method* (2007) pp. 372–84.

———. "Yodfat," *NEAEHL* 5 (2008) p. 2077.

———. "Socio-Economic Hierarchy and Its Economic Foundations in First Century Galilee: The Evidence from Yodefat and Gamla," in Pastor, J., Stern, O., and Mor, M., eds. *Flavius Josephus: Interpretation and History* (2011) pp. 29–38.

———. "The Decorated Stone from the Synagogue at Migdal: A Holistic Interpretation and a Glimpse into the Life of Galilean Jews at the Time of Jesus," *NovT* 55 (2013) pp. 205–20.

———. "The Synagogue," in Bauckham, R. ed. *Magdala of Galilee: A Jewish City in the Hellenistic and Roman Period* (2018) pp. 127–33.

Aviam, M. and Bauckham, R. "The Synagogue Stone," in Bauckham, R. ed. *Magdala of Galilee: A Jewish City in the Hellenistic and Roman Period* (2018) pp. 135–59.

Aviam, M. and Richardson, P. "Appendix A: Josephus' Galilee in Archaeological Perspective," in Mason, S. ed. *Flavius Josephus: Translation and Commentary, Vol. 9: Life of Josephus* (2001) pp. 177–201.

Avidov, A. *Not Reckoned among Nations: The Origins of the So-Called "Jewish Question" in Roman Antiquity* (2009).

Avigad, N. *Discovering Jerusalem* (1983).

———. *The Herodian Quarter in Jerusalem* (1989a).

———. "The Inscribed Pomegranate from the 'House of the Lord,'" *Israel Museum Journal* 8 (1989b) pp. 7–16.

Aviram, J., Foerster G., and Netzer, E. eds. *Masada IV: The Yigael Yadin Excavations 1963–65. Final Reports: Lamps (Barag, D. and Hershkovitz M. with contributions by Bailey, D. and Yellin, J.), Textiles (Sheffer, A. and Granger-Taylor, H. with contributions by Koren, Z. and Shamir, O.), Basketry, Cordage, and Related Artifacts (Bernick, K.), Wood Remains (Liphschitz, N.), and Ballista Balls (Holley, A.), Addendum: Human Skeletal Remains (Zias, J., Segal, D., and Carmi, I.)* (1994).

Aviram, J., Foerster, G., Netzer, E., and Stiebel, G. eds. *Masada VIII: The Yigael Yadin Excavations 1963–1965. Final Reports* (2007).

Avi-Yonah, M. *The Jews under Roman and Byzantine Rule* (1976).

Avi-Yonah, M. and Kloner, A. "Mareshah (Marisa)," in Stern, E. ed. *NEAEHL* 3 (1993) pp. 948–57.

Bahat, D. "Jerusalem Down Under: Tunneling along Herod's Temple Mount Wall," *BAR* 21, no. 6 (1995) pp. 31–47.

———. "The Herodian Temple," in Horbury, W., Davies, W., and Sturdy, J. eds. *The Cambridge History of Judaism, Vol. 3: The Early Roman Period* (1999a) pp. 38–58.

———. *The Illustrated Atlas of Jerusalem* (1999b).

———. "The Architectural Origins of Herod's Temple Mount," in Jacobson, D. and Kokkinos, N. eds. *Herod and Augustus* (2009) pp. 235–45.

Bahat, D. and Rubenstein, C. *The Illustrated Atlas of Jerusalem* (1990).

Baltrusch, E. *Die Juden and das römische Reich: Geschichte einer konfliktreichen Beziehung* (2002).

———. "Herodes und das Diaspora-Judentum," in Günther, L. ed. *Herodes und Jerusalem* (2009) pp. 47–59.

Bang, P. "The Roman Empire II: The Monarchy," in Bang, P. and Scheidel, W. eds. *The Oxford Handbook of the State in the Ancient Near East and Mediterranean* (2013) pp. 412–72.

Bang, P. and Scheidel, W. eds. *The Oxford Handbook of the State in the Ancient Near East and Mediterranean* (2013).

Barag, D. "New Evidence on the Foreign Policy of John Hyrcanus I," *INJ* 12 (1993a) pp. 1–12.

———. "King Herod's Royal Castle at Samaria-Sebaste," *PEQ* 125 (1993b) pp. 3–18.

Barclay, J. "The Empire Writes Back: Josephan Rhetoric in Flavian Rome," in Edmonson, J., Mason, S., and Rives, J. eds. *Flavius Josephus and Flavian Rome* (2005) pp. 315–32.

———. *Flavius Josephus: Against Apion: Translation and Commentary* (2013).

Bar-Kochva, B. "Seron and Cestius at Beith Horon," *PEQ* 108 (1976) pp. 13–21.

Bar-Nathan, R. *Masada VII: The Yigael Yadin Excavations 1963–65, Final Reports: The Pottery of Masada* (2006).

Barnes, T. "'The Fragments of Tacitus' *Histories*," *Classical Philology* 72, no. 3 (1977) pp. 224–31.

———. "The Sack of the Temple in Josephus and Tacitus," in Edmondson, J., Mason, S., and Rives, J. eds. *Flavius Josephus and Flavian Rome* (2005) pp. 129–44.

Bartlett, J. ed. *Archaeology and Biblical Interpretation* (1997).

——— ed. *Jews in the Hellenistic and Roman Cities* (2002).

Bauckham, R. ed. *Magdala of Galilee: A Jewish City in the Hellenistic and Roman Period* (2018).

Baumgarten, A. *The Flourishing of Jewish Sects in the Maccabean Era: An Interpretation* (1997).

———. "Herod's Eagle," in Maeir, A., Magness, J., and Schiffman, L. eds. *"Go Out and Study the Land" (Judges 18:2): Archaeological, Historical and Textual Studies in Honor of Hanan Eshel* (2011) pp. 7–21.

Beard, M. *The Roman Triumph* (2007).

Beck, C. "Bernays's Chronicle of Sulpicius Severus," *Christian Examiner* (1862) pp. 22–40.

Belayche, N. *Iudaea-Palaestina: The Pagan Cults in Roman Palestine* (2001).

Ben-Ami, D. ed. *Jerusalem: Excavations in the Tyropoeon Valley (Giv'ati Parking Lot)* (2013a)

———. "Stratigraphy and Architecture," in Ben-Ami, D. ed. *Jerusalem: Excavations in the Tyropoeon Valley (Giv'ati Parking Lot)* (2013b) pp. 7–62.

Ben-Ami, D. and Tchekhanovets, Y. "Has the Adiabenian Royal Family 'Palace' Been Found?," in Galor, K. and Avni, G. eds. *Unearthing Jerusalem: 150 Years of Archaeological Research in the Holy City* (2011) pp. 231–39.

Ben-Dov, M. "Herod's Mighty Temple Mount," *BAR* 12, no. 6 (1986) pp. 40–49.

Benoist, S. ed. *Rome, A City and Its Empire in Perspective: The Impact of the Roman World through Fergus Millar's Research* (2012).

Ben-Tor, A. *Back to Masada* (2009).

Bentwich, N. *Josephus* (1914).

Ben-Yehuda, N. *The Masada Myth: Collective Memory and Mythmaking in Israel* (1995).

———. *Sacrificing Truth: Archaeology and the Myth of Masada* (2002).

Berdowski, P., *"Garum* of Herod the Great (a Latin-Greek Inscription on the Amphora from Masada)," *Analecta Archaeologica Ressoviensia* 1 (2006) pp. 239–56.

Bergmann, M. *Der Koloss Neros: Die Domus Aurea und der Mentalitätswandel im Rom der frühen Kaiserzeit* (1994).

Berlin, A. "Between Large Forces: Palestine in the Hellenistic Period," *BA* 60, no. 1 (1997) pp. 2–51.

———. "The Archaeology of Ritual: The Sanctuary of Pan at Banias/Caesarea Philippi," *BASOR* 315 (1999) pp. 27–45.

———. "Power and Its Afterlife: Tombs in Hellenistic Palestine," *NEA* 65, no. 2 (2002) pp. 138–48.

———. "Jewish Life before the Revolt: The Archaeological Evidence," *JSJ* 36, no. 4 (2005) pp. 417–70.

———. "Herod the Tastemaker," *NEA* 77, no. 2 (2014) pp. 108–19.

Berlin, A. and Overman, A. eds. *The First Jewish Revolt: Archaeology, History, and Ideology* (2002).

Bernays, J. *Ueber die Chronik des Sulpicius Severus: Ein Beitrag zur Geschichte der classischen und biblischen Studien* (1861).

Bernett, M. *Der Kaiserkult in Judäa unter den Herodiern und Römern* (2007).

Bickermann, E. *The Jews in the Greek Age* (1988).

Bilde, P. *Flavius Josephus between Jerusalem and Rome: His Life, His Works, and Their Importance* (1988).

Bishop, M. ed. *The Production and Distribution of Roman Military Equipment: Proceedings of the Second Roman Military Equipment Research Seminar* (1985).

Bishop, M. and Coulston, J. *Roman Military Equipment from the Punic Wars to the Fall of Rome* (1993).

Blenkinsopp, J. "Did the Second Jerusalemite Temple Possess Land?," *Transeu* 21 (2001) pp. 61–68.

———. "The Development of Jewish Sectarianism from Nehemiah to the Hasidim," in Lipschits, O., Knoppers, G., and Albertz, R. eds. *Judah and the Judeans in the Fourth Century B.C.E.* (2007) pp. 385–404.

Bloch-Smith, E. *Judahite Burial Practices and Beliefs about the Dead* (1992).

Blömer, M., Facella, M., and Winter, E. eds. *Lokal Identität im römischen nahen Osten: Kontexte und Perspektiven* (2009).

Bloom, J. *The Jewish Revolts against Rome AD 66–135: A Military Analysis* (2010).

Boffo, L. *Iscrizioni greche e latine per lo studio della Bibbia* (1994).

Bohak, G. *Joseph and Aseneth and the Jewish Temple in Heliopolis* (1996).

Bohrmann, M. *Flavius Josephus, the Zealots and Yavne: Towards a Rereading of the War of the Jews* (1989).

Bond, B. *The Pursuit of Victory: From Napoleon to Saddam Hussein* (1998).

Bond, H. *Pontius Pilate in History and Interpretation* (1998).

Bonnie, R. "From Stadium to Harbor: Reinterpreting the Curved Ashlar Structure in Roman Tiberias," *BASOR* 377 (2017) pp. 21–38.

Boot, M. *Invisible Armies: An Epic History of Guerilla Warfare from Ancient Times to the Present* (2013).

Bourgel, J. "The Destruction of the Samaritan Temple by John Hyrcanus: A Reconsideration," *JBL* 135, no. 3 (2016) pp. 505–23.

Bowersock, G. "Old and New in the History of Judaea," *JRS* 65 (1975) pp. 180–85.

———. "Foreign Elites at Rome," in Edmondson, J., Mason, S., and Rives, J. eds. *Flavius Josephus and Flavian Rome* (2005) pp. 53–62.

————. *Empires in Collision in Late Antiquity* (2012).

Brandon, C. "The Herodian Harbour of Caesarea Maritime: Recent Research and Related Studies," in Ladstätter, S., Pirson, F., and Schmidts, T. eds. *Byzas—19 Harbors and Harbor Cities in the Eastern Mediterranean from Antiquity to the Byzantine Period: Recent Discoveries and Current Approaches* (2015) pp. 45–62.

Brandon, S. "The Defeat of Cestius Gallus: A Roman Legate Faced the Problem of the Jewish Revolt," *History Today* (1970) pp. 38–46.

Braund, D. "Greek and Roman Authors on the Herods," in Kokkinos, N. ed. *The World of the Herods: Volume 1 of the International Conference "The World of the Herods" Held at the British Museum, 17–19 April 2001* (2007) pp. 35–44.

Bresson, A. *The Making of the Ancient Greek Economy: Institutions, Markets, and Growth in the City States* (2016).

Brighton, M. *The Sicarii in Josephus' Judean War: Rhetorical Analysis and Historical Observations* (2009).

Brooke, G. *The Dead Sea Scrolls and the New Testament* (2005).

Broshi, M. "The Expansion of Jerusalem in the Reigns of Hezekiah and Manasseh," *IEJ* 24 (1974) pp. 21–26.

———— ed. *Between Hermon and Sinai: Memorial to Amnon* (1977a).

————. "The Population of Early Jerusalem," in Broshi, M. ed. *Between Hermon and Sinai: Memorial to Amnon* (1977b) pp. 65–74.

————. "Estimating the Population of Ancient Jerusalem," *BAR* 4, no. 2 (1978) pp. 10–15.

————. "The Credibility of Josephus," *JJS* 33 (1982) pp. 379–84.

————. "Basic Lines in the Economy of Eretz Israel in the Period of Herod," in Gross, N. ed. *Jews in Economic Life* (1985) pp. 27–33.

————. "The Role of the Temple in the Herodian Economy," *JJS* 38 (1987) pp. 31–7.

————. *Bread, Wine, Walls and Scrolls* (2001).

Broshi, M. and Finkelstein, I. "The Population of Palestine in Iron Age II," *BASOR* 287 (1992) pp. 47–60.

Broshi, M. and Gibson, S. "Excavations along the Western and Southern Walls of the Old City of Jerusalem," in Geva, H. ed. *Ancient Jerusalem Revealed* (1994) pp. 147–55.

Brousse, P. "La Propagande par le Fait," *Bulletin de la Fédération Jurassienne* (1877) 5 August.

Brunt, P. *Italian Manpower* (1971).

————. "Josephus on Social Conflicts in Roman Judaea," *Klio* 59 (1977) pp. 149–53.

————. "*Princeps* and *Equites*," *JRS* 73 (1983) pp. 42–75.

Büchler, A. "La relation de Josèphe concernant Alexandre le Grand," *REJ* 36 (1898) pp. 1–26.

Buckley, E. and Dinter, M. eds. *A Companion to the Neronian Age* (2013).

Bull, R. "The Excavation of Tell er-Ras on Mt. Gerizim," *BA* 31, no. 2 (1968) pp. 58–72.

Buonfiglio, M., Pergola, S., and Zanzi, G. "The Hemicycle of the Circus Maximus: Synthesis of the Late Antique Phases Revealed by Recent Excavations," *Memoirs of the American Academy in Rome* 61 (2016) pp. 278–303.

Burnett, A. "The Coinage of King Agrippa I of Judaea and a New Coin of Herod of Chalcis," in Huvelin, H., Christol, M., and Gautier, G., eds. *Mélanges de Numismatique offerts à Pierre Bastien à occasion de son 75e anniversaire* (1987) pp. 25–38, pls. 3–5.

Burr, V. *Tiberius Iulius Alexander* (1955).

Burrell, B. "Herod's Caesarea on Sebastos: Urban Structures and Influences," in Jacobson, D. and Kokkinos, N. eds. *Herod and Augustus* (2009) pp. 217–33.

———. "The Legacies of Herod the Great," *NEA* 77, no. 2 (2014) pp. 68–74.

Callwell, G. *Small Wars: A Tactical Textbook for Imperial Soldiers* (1990).

Campbell, B. *The Emperor and the Roman Army: 31 BC–AD 235* (1984).

———. *The Roman Army, 31 BC–AD 337: A Sourcebook* (1994).

———. *War and Society in Imperial Rome, 31 BC–AD 235* (2002).

Campbell, D. "Dating the Siege of Masada," *ZPE* 73 (1988) pp. 156–58.

Capponi, L. *Il tempio di Leontopoli in Egitto: Identità politica e religiosa dei Giudei di Onia* (c. 150 a.C.–73 d.C.) (2007).

Cecconi, G., Testa, R., and Marcone, A. eds. *The Past as Present: Essays on Roman History in Honour of Guido Clemente* (2019).

Champlin, E. *Nero* (2003).

Chancey, M. "The Cultural Milieu of Ancient Sepphoris," *NTS* 47:2 (2001) pp. 127–45.

———. *The Myth of a Gentile Galilee* (2002).

———. *Greco-Roman Culture and the Galilee of Jesus* (2005).

———. "Archaeology, Ethnicity, and First-Century C.E. Galilee: The Limits of Evidence," in Rodgers, Z., Daly-Denton, M., and Fitzpatrick McKinley, A. eds. *A Wandering Galilean: Essays in Honour of Seán Freyne* (2009) pp. 205–18.

———. "Disputed Issues in the Study of Cities, Villages, and the Economy in Jesus' Galilee," in Evans, C. ed. *The World of Jesus and the Early Church: Identity and Interpretation in the Early Communities of Faith* (2011) pp. 53–68.

Chancey, M. and Porter, A. "The Archaeology of Roman Palestine," *NEA* 64 (2001) pp. 164–203.

Chapman, H. "Spectacle and Theatre in Josephus' *Bellum Judaicum*," PhD Dissertation, Stanford University (1998).

———. "Josephus and the Cannibalism of Mary (*BJ* 6.199–219)," in Marincola, J. ed. *A Companion to Greek and Roman Historiography* (2007a) pp. 419–26.

———. "Masada in the 1st and 21st Centuries," in Rodgers, Z. ed. *Making History: Josephus and Historical Method* (2007b) pp. 82–102.

————. "What Josephus Sees: The Temple of Peace and the Jerusalem Temple as Spectacle in Text and Art," *Phoenix* 63 (2009) pp. 107–30.

Charlesworth, J. ed. *Jesus and Archaeology* (2006).

Chepey, S. *Nazirites in the Late Second Temple Period: A Survey of Ancient Jewish Writings, the New Testament, Archaeological Evidence, and Other Writings from Late Antiquity* (2005).

Choi, J. *Jewish Leadership in Roman Palestine from 70 C.E. to 135 C.E.* (2013).

Chrysos, E. ed. *Proceedings of the First International Symposium on Nicopolis (23–29 September 1984)* (1987).

Churchill, W. *The Second World War, Vol. 2: Their Finest Hour* (2000 ed.).

CIIP. See volumes listed under Ameling et al. and Cotton et al.

Coarelli, F. *The Column of Trajan* (2000).

———— ed. *Divus Vespasianus: Il bimillenario dei Flavi* (2009).

Coarelli, F. and Gabucci, A. eds. *The Colosseum* (2001).

Cohen, S. *Josephus in Galilee and Rome: His Vita and Development as a Historian* (1979).

————. "Masada: Literary Tradition, Archaeological Remains, and the Credibility of Josephus," *JJS* 33, no. 1–2 (1982) pp. 385–405.

————. "Alexander the Great and Jaddus the High Priest according to Josephus," *Association for Jewish Studies Review* 7–8 (1982–83) pp. 41–68.

————. "The Significance of Yavneh: Pharisees, Rabbis, and the End of Jewish Sectarianism," *HUCA* 55 (1984) pp. 27–53.

————. "The Conversion of Antoninus," in Schäfer, P. ed. *The Talmud Yerushalmi and Graeco-Roman Culture, Vol. I* (1998) pp. 141–71.

————. *The Beginnings of Jewishness: Boundaries, Varieties, Uncertainties* (1999a).

————. "The Rabbi in Second Century Jewish Society," *CHJ* III (1999b) pp. 922–90.

————. *From the Maccabees to the Mishnah* (2006).

Cohen, S. and Schwartz, J. eds. *Studies in Josephus and the Varieties of Ancient Judaism: Louis H. Feldman Jubilee Volume* (2007).

Cohn, N. *The Memory of the Temple and the Making of the Rabbis* (2012).

Colautti, F. *Passover in the Works of Josephus* (2002).

Collins, A. *Cosmology and Eschatology in Jewish and Christian Apocalypticism* (1996).

Collins, J. *Daniel: With an Introduction to Apocalyptic Literature* (1984).

————. *Beyond the Qumran Community: The Sectarian Movement of the Dead Sea Scrolls* (2010).

Collins, J. and Harlow, D. eds. *The Eerdmans Dictionary of Early Judaism* (2010).

Collins, J. and Manning, J. eds. *Revolt and Resistance in the Ancient Classical World and the Near East: In the Crucible of Empire* (2016).

Collins, J. and Sterling, G. eds. *Hellenism in the Land of Israel* (2001).

Colville, J. *The Fringes of Power: 10 Downing Street Diaries, 1939–1955* (2002).

Cook, E. ed. *Sopher Mahir: Northwest Semitic Studies Presented to Stanislav Segert* (1990).

Cotton, H. "The Date of the Fall of Masada: The Evidence of the Masada Papyri," *ZPE* 78 (1989) pp. 157–62.

———. "Some Aspects of the Roman Administration of Judaea/Syria-Palestina," in Eck, W. and Müller-Luckner E. eds. *Lokale Autonomie und Römische Ordnungsmacht in den kaiserzeitlichen Provinzen vom 1. Bis 3. Jahrhundert. Schriften des Historischen Kollegs Kolloquien 42* (1999a) pp. 75–91.

———. "The Languages of the Legal and Administrative Documents from the Judaean Desert," *ZPE* 125 (1999b) pp. 219–31.

Cotton, H., Di Segni, L., Eck, W., Isaac, B., Kushnir-Stein, A., Misgav, H., Price, J., Roll, I., Yardeni, A. eds. with contributions by Lupu, E. *Corpus Inscriptionum Iudaeae/Palaestinae, Vol. I: Jerusalem. Part 1: 1–704* (2010).

Cotton, H., Di Segni, L., Eck, W., Isaac, B., Kushnir-Stein, A., Misgav, H., Price, J., and Yardeni, A. eds. with contributions by Daniel, R., Feissel, D., Hoyland, R., Kool, R., Lupu, E., Stone, M., and Tchekhanovets, Y. *Corpus Inscriptionum Iudaeae/Palaestinae, Vol. I: Jerusalem. Part 2: 705–1120* (2012).

Cotton, H. and Eck, W. "Josephus' Roman Audience: Josephus and the Roman Elites," in Edmondson, J., Mason, S. and Rives, J. eds. *Flavius Josephus and Flavian Rome* (2005a) pp. 37–52.

———. "Roman Officials in Judaea and Arabia and Civil Jurisdiction," in Katzoff, R. and Schaps, D. eds. *Law in the Documents of the Judaean Desert* (2005b) pp. 23–44.

Cotton, H. and Ecker, A. "Reflections on the Foundation of Aelia Capitolina," in Cecconi, G., Testa, R., and Marcone, A. eds. *The Past as Present: Essays on Roman History in Honor of Guido Clemente* (2019) pp. 681–95.

Cotton, H. and Geiger, J., with a contribution by Thomas, J. *Masada II: The Yigael Yadin Excavations 1963–1965. Final Reports: The Latin and Greek Documents* (1989).

Cotton, H., Hoyland, R., Price, J., and Wasserstein, D. eds. *From Hellenism to Islam: Cultural and Linguistic Change in the Roman Near East* (2009).

Cotton, H., Lernau, O., and Goren, Y. "Fish Sauces from Herodian Masada," *JRA* 9 (1996) pp. 223–31.

Counts, D. and Tuck, A. eds. *Koine: Mediterranean Studies in Honor of R. Ross Holloway* (2009).

Crowfoot, J., Kenyon, K., and Sukenik, E. *The Buildings at Samaria* (1942).

Curran, J. "The Jewish War: Some Neglected Regional Factors," *CW* 101 (2007) pp. 75–91.

Dąbrowa, E. *Legio X Fretensis: A Prosopographical Study of its Officers (I–III C. A.D.)* (1993).

———. *The Governors of Roman Syria from Augustus to Septimius Severus* (1998).

————. *The Hasmoneans and their State: A Study in History, Ideology, and the Institutions* (2010).

————. "The 'Camp of the Assyrians' and the Third Wall of Jerusalem," *Scripta Judaica Cracoviensia* 13 (2015) pp. 19–30.

Dando-Collins, S. *Legions of Rome* (2010).

Dar, S. "The Agrarian Economy in the Herodian Period," in Kokkinos, N. ed. *The World of the Herods: Volume 1 of the International Conference "The World of the Herods" Held at the British Museum, 17–19 April 2001* (2007) pp. 305–11.

Dar, S. and Applebaum, S. "The Roman Road from Antipatris to Caesarea," *PEQ* 105 (1973) pp. 91–99.

Darwall-Smith, R. *Emperors and Architecture: A Study of Flavian Rome* (1996).

David, A. "Second Monumental Arch of Titus Celebrating Victory over Jews Found in Rome," *Haaretz* 21 March 2017.

Davies, G. "Under Siege: The Roman Field Works at Masada," *BASOR* 362 (2011) pp. 65–83.

————. "The Masada Siege—From the Roman Viewpoint," *BAR* 40, no. 4 (2014) pp. 28–36, 70–71.

————. "Prey or Participants? Civilian Siege Experiences during the First Jewish Revolt," in Foote, N. and Williams, N. eds. *Civilians and Warfare in World History* (2018) pp. 67–79.

Davies, G. and Magness, J. "Recovering Josephus: Mason's *History of the Jewish War* and the Siege of Masada," *SCI* 36 (2017) pp. 55–65.

Davies, P. *Death and the Emperor: Roman Imperial Funerary Monuments from Augustus to Marcus Aurelius* (2004).

Davies, P., Brooke, G., and Callaway, P. *The Complete World of the Dead Sea Scrolls* (2002).

Davies, P. and White, R. eds. *A Tribute to Geza Vermes: Essays on Jewish and Christian Literature and History* (1990).

De Groot, A. "Mazar, Tell," *NEAEHL* 3 (1993) pp. 989–91.

De Luca, S. "La città ellenistico-romana di Magdala/Taricheae. Gli scavi del Magdala Project 2007 e 2008: Relazione preliminare e prospettive di indagine," *Studii biblici franciscani liber annuus* 49 (2009) pp. 343–562, 571–72.

De Luca, S. and Lena, A. "The Harbor of the City of Magdala/Taricheae on the Shores of the Sea of Galilee, from the Hellenistic to the Byzantine Times: New Discoveries and Preliminary Results," in Ladstätter, S., Pirson, F., and Schmidts, T. eds. *Byzas 19—Harbors and Harbor Cities in the Eastern Mediterranean from Antiquity to the Byzantine Period: Recent Discoveries and Current Approaches* I (2015a) pp. 113–63.

————. "Magdala/Taricheae," in Fiensy, D. and Strange, J. eds. *Galilee in the Late Second Temple and Mishnaic Periods, Vol. 2: The Archaeological Record from Cities, Towns, and Villages* (2015b) pp. 280–342.

Demandt, A. *Pontius Pilatus* (2012).

den Hollander, W. *Josephus, the Emperors and the City of Rome: From Hostage to Historian* (2014).

Deutsch, R. "Roman Coins Boast 'Judaea Capta,'" *BAR* 36 (1) (2010) pp. 51–53.

———. "Coinage of the First Jewish Revolt against Rome: Iconography, Minting Authority, Metallurgy," in Popović, M. ed. *The Jewish Revolt against Rome: Interdisciplinary Perspectives* (2011) pp. 361–71.

Dirven, L. "The Imperial Cult in the Cities of the Decapolis, Caesarea Maritima and Palmyra: A Note on the Development of Imperial Cults in the Roman Near East," *ARAM* 23 (2011) pp. 141–56.

Dixon, K. and Southern, P. *The Roman Cavalry* (1992).

Domaszewski, A. "Die Dislokation des römischen Heeres im Jahre 66 n. Chr.," *RM* 47 (1892) pp. 207–18.

Donaldson, T. ed. *Religious Rivalries and the Struggle for Success in Caesarea Maritima* (2000).

Duncan-Jones, R. *Structure and Scale in the Roman Economy* (1990).

———. *Money and Government in the Roman Empire* (1994).

Dušek, J. *Aramaic and Hebrew Inscriptions from Mt. Gerizim and Samaria between Antiochus III and Antiochus IV Epiphanes* (2012).

Dyson, S. "Native Revolts in the Roman Empire," *Historia* 20 (1971) pp. 239–74.

Eck, W. "Die *Eroberung* von Masada und eine neue Inschrift des L. Flavius Silva Nonius Bassus," *Zeitschrift für die Neutestamentliche Wissenschaft* 60 (1969) pp. 282–89.

———. *Senatoren von Augustus bis Vespasian* (1970).

———. "Jahres-und Provinzialfasten der senatorischen Statthalter von 69/70 bis 138/139," *Chiron* 12 (1982) pp. 281–362.

———. "Sextus Lucilius Bassus, der Eroberer von Herodium, in einer Bauinschrift von Abu Gosh," *SCI* 18 (1999a) pp. 109–20.

———. "The Bar Kokhba Revolt: The Roman Point of View," *JRS* 89 (1999b) pp. 76–89.

———. "Hadrian, the Bar Kokhba Revolt, and the Epigraphic Transmission," in Schäfer, P. ed. *The Bar Kokhba Revolt Reconsidered: New Perspectives on the Second Jewish Revolt against Rome* (2003) pp. 153–70.

———. *Rom und Judaea: Fünf Vorträge zur römischen Herrschaft in Palaestina* (2007).

———. "The Presence, Role and Significance of Latin in the Epigraphy and Culture of the Roman Near East," in Cotton, H., Hoyland, R., Price, J., and Wasserstein, D. eds. *From Hellenism to Islam: Cultural and Linguistic Change in the Roman Near East* (2009) pp. 13–42.

———. "Die römischen Repräsentanten in Judaea: Provokateure oder Vertreter der römischen Macht?," in Popović, M. ed. *The Jewish Revolt against Rome: Interdisciplinary Perspectives* (2011) pp. 45–68.

Eck, W. and Müller-Luckner, E. eds. *Lokale Autonomie und römische Ordnungsmacht in den kaiserzeitlichen Provinzen vom 1. Bis 3. Jahrhundert. Schriften des Historischen Kollegs Kolloquien 42* (1999).

Ecker, A. "Homer in Herodium: Graffito of Il. 6.264," *ZPE* 183 (2012) pp. 15–20.

———. "Dining with Herod," in Rozenberg, S. and Mevorah, D. eds. *Herod the Great: The King's Final Journey* (2017) pp. 66–79.

Eckhardt, B. "An Idumean, That Is, a 'Half-Jew': Hasmoneans and Herodians between Ancestry and Merit," in Eckhardt, B. ed. *Jewish Identity and Politics between the Maccabees and Bar Kokhba* (2012a) pp. 91–115.

——— ed. *Jewish Identity and Politics between the Maccabees and Bar Kokhba* (2012b).

Edmondson, J. "Introduction: Flavius Josephus and Flavian Rome," in Edmondson, J., Mason, S., and Rives, J. eds. *Flavius Josephus and Flavian Rome* (2005) pp. 1–33.

Edmondson, J., Mason, S., and Rives, J. eds. *Flavius Josephus and Flavian Rome* (2005).

Edwards, D. "Religion, Power, and Power Politics: Jewish Defeats by the Romans in Iconography and Josephus," in Overman, A. and MacLennan, R. eds. *Diaspora Jews and Judaism: Essays in Honor of, and in Dialogue with, A. Thomas Kraabel* (1992) pp. 293–310.

———. "The Social, Religious, and Political Aspects of Costume in Josephus," in Sebesta, J. and Bonfante, L. eds. *The World of Roman Costume* (2001) pp. 153–62.

——— ed. *Religion and Society in Roman Palestine: Old Questions, New Approaches* (2004).

Edwell, P. *Between Rome and Persia: The Middle Euphrates, Mesopotamia and Palmyra under Roman Control* (2008).

Ego, B., Lange, A., and Pilhofer, P. eds. *Gemeinde ohne Tempel, Community without Temple: Zur Substituierung und Transformation des Jerusalemer Tempels und seines Kults im Alten Testament, antiken Judentum und frühen Christentum* (1999).

Elkins, N. *A Monument to Dynasty and Death: The Story of Rome's Colosseum and the Emperors Who Built It* (2019).

Elledge, C. *Life after Death in Early Judaism: The Evidence of Josephus* (2006).

Erdkamp, P. ed. *A Companion to the Roman Army* (2007).

Eshel, H. "Josephus' View on Judaism without the Temple in Light of the Discoveries at Masada and Murabba'at," in Ego, B., Lange, A., and Pilhofer, P. eds. *Gemeinde ohne Tempel, Community without Temple: Zur Substituierung und Transformation des Jerusalemer Tempels und seines Kults im Alten Testament, antiken Judentum und frühen Christentum* (1999) pp. 229–38.

———. "The Dates Used during the Bar Kokhba Revolt," in Schäfer, P. *The Bar Kokhba War Reconsidered: New Perspectives on the Second Jewish Revolt against Rome* (2003) pp. 93–105.

———. *The Dead Sea Scrolls and the Hasmonean State* (2008).

———. *Masada, An Epic Story* (2009).

Esler, P. "Judean Ethnic Identity in Josephus' *Against Apion*," in Rodgers, Z., Daly-Denton, M., and McKinley, A. eds. *A Wandering Galilean: Essays in Honour of Seán Freyne* (2009) pp. 73–91.

Evans, C. "Excavating Caiaphas, Pilate, and Simon of Cyrene: Assessing the Literary and Archaeological Evidence," in Charlesworth, J. ed. *Jesus and Archaeology* (2006) pp. 323–40.

——— ed. *The World of Jesus and the Early Church: Identity and Interpretation in Early Communities of Faith* (2011).

Farhi, Y. "The Bronze Coins Minted at Gamala Reconsidered," *INJ* 15 (2006) pp. 69–76.

Farmer, W. *Maccabees, Zealots, and Josephus: An Inquiry into Jewish Nationalism in the Greco-Roman Period* (1956).

Faulkner, N. *Apocalypse: The Great Jewish Revolt against Rome* (2004).

Feldman, L. trans. *Josephus: Jewish Antiquities, Books 18–20. Vol. IX* (1965).

———. "Masada: A Critique of Recent Scholarship," in Neusner, J. ed. *Christianity, Judaism, and Other Greco-Roman Cults: Studies for Morton Smith at Sixty (Studies in Judaism in Late Antiquity)* (1975) pp. 218–48.

———. *Josephus and Modern Scholarship, 1937–1980* (1984).

———. *Josephus's Interpretation of the Bible* (1998).

———. "Financing the Colosseum," *BAR* 27, no. 4 (2001) pp. 20–31, 60.

Feldman, L. and Hata, G. eds. *Josephus, Judaism, and Christianity* (1987).

———. *Josephus, the Bible, and History* (1989).

Fields, W. *The Dead Sea Scrolls: A Full History, Vol. I* (2009).

Fiensy, D. and Strange, J. eds. *Galilee in the Late Second Temple and Mishnaic Period, Vol. 1: Life, Culture, and Society* (2014).

———. *Galilee in the Late Second Temple and Mishnaic Periods, Vol. 2: The Archaeological Record from Cities, Towns, and Villages* (2015).

Fine, S. *The Menorah from the Bible to Modern Israel* (2016).

———. "From Synagogue Furnishing to Media Event: The Magdala Ashlar," *Ars Judaica* 13 (2017) pp. 27–38.

Firpo, G. "La guerra giudaica e l'ascesa di Vespasiano," in Coarelli, F. ed. *Divus Vespasianus: Il bimillenario dei Flavi* (2009) pp. 42–45.

Fischer, M., Isaac, B., and Roll, I. *Roman Roads in Judaea II: The Jaffa-Jerusalem Roads* (1996).

Fischer, M. and Stein, A. "Josephus on the Use of Marble in Building Projects of Herod the Great," *JJS* 45 (1994) pp. 79–85.

Foerster, G. "Sarcophagus Production in Jerusalem from the Beginning of the Common Era to 70 CE," in Koch, G. ed. *Sarkophag-Studien I. Akten des*

Symposiums "125 Jahre Sarkophag-Corpus," Marburg, 4–7 Oktober 1995 (1998) pp. 295–310.

———. "The Sarcophagi from the Mausoleum Unearthed at Herodium," in Rozenberg, S. and Mevorah, D. eds. *Herod the Great: The King's Final Journey* (2017) pp. 266–77.

Foerster, G. with a contribution by Porat, N. *Masada V: The Yigael Yadin Excavations 1963–65. Final Reports: Art and Architecture* (1995).

Fonrobert, C. and Jaffee, M. eds. *The Cambridge Companion to the Talmud and Rabbinic Literature* (2007).

Foote, N. and Williams, N. eds. *Civilians and Warfare in World History* (2018).

Franke, T. "Review of *Legio X Fretensis: A Prosopographical Study of Its Officers (I–III c. A.D.)* by E. Dąbrowa," *Gnomon* 68 (1996) pp. 236–40.

Freedman, D. and Greenfield, J. eds. *New Directions in Biblical Archaeology* (1969).

Freeman, P. and Kennedy, D. eds. *The Defence of the Roman and Byzantine East: Proceedings of a Colloquium Held at the University of Sheffield in April 1986* (1986).

Frey, J., Schwartz, D., and Gripentrog, S. eds. *Jewish Identity in the Greco-Roman World/Jüdaische Identität in der griechisch-römischen Welt* (2007).

Freyne, S. "Herodian Economics in Galilee. Searching for a Suitable Model," in Esler, P. ed. *Modeling Early Christianity: Social-Scientific Studies of the New Testament in Its Context* (1995) pp. 23–46.

———. "The Revolt from a Regional Perspective," in Berlin, A. and Overman, A. eds. *The First Jewish Revolt: Archaeology, History, and Ideology* (2002) pp. 43–56.

Friedländer, L. *De fonte quo Josephus B. J. II 16,4 usus sit* (1873).

Frova, A. "L'Iscrizione di Ponzio Pilato a Caesarea," *Rendiconti dell'Instituto Lombardo, accademia di scienze e lettere, classe di lettere* 95 (1961) pp. 419–34.

Fuentes, N. "The Mule of a Soldier," *Journal of Roman Military Equipment* 2 (1991) pp. 65–99.

Fuks, G. "Some Remarks on Simon bar Giora," *SCI* 8–9 (1985–1988) pp. 106–119.

———. "Josephus on Herod's Attitude towards Jewish Religion: The Darker Side," *JJS* 53, no. 3 (2002) pp. 238–45.

Gabba, E. "The Finances of King Herod," in Kasher, A., Rappaport, U., and Fuks, G. eds. *Greece and Rome in Eretz Israel: Collected Essays* (1990) pp. 160–68.

———. "The Social, Economic, and Political History of Palestine, 63 BCE–CE 70," in Davies, W. et al. eds. *Cambridge History of Judaism, Vol. III* (1999) pp. 94–167.

Gafni, I. "Rabbinic Historiography and Representations of the Past," in Fonrobert, C. and Jaffee, M. eds. *The Cambridge Companion to the Talmud and Rabbinic Literature* (2007) pp. 295–312.

Galor, K. and Avni, G. eds. *Unearthing Jerusalem: 150 Years of Archaeological Research in the Holy City* (2011).

Galor, K., Humbert, J.-B., and Zangenberg, J. eds. *Qumran, the Site of the Dead Sea Scrolls: Archaeological Interpretations and Debates; Proceedings of the Conference Held at Brown University, November 17–19, 2002* (2006).

Gambash, G. *Rome and Provincial Resistance* (2019).

Gambetti, S. *The Alexandrian Riots of 38 CE and the Persecution of the Jews. A Historical Reconstruction* (2009).

Gannon, M. "Proof of Famine during Roman Siege Unearthed in Jerusalem," https://www.nbcnews.com/science/science-news/proof-famine-during-roman-siege-unearthed-jerusalem-flna6C10486628 (2013) 28 June.

Gardner, G. "Jewish Leadership and Hellenistic Civic Benefaction in the Second Century B.C.E.," *JBL* 126, no. 2 (2007) pp. 327–43.

Garlan, Y. *War in the Ancient World* (1975).

Garnsey, P. *Famine and Food Supply in the Graeco-Roman World: Responses to Risk and Crisis* (1988).

Geiger, J. "Herodes *Philorhomaios*," *AS* 28 (1997) pp. 75–88.

———. "Rome and Jerusalem: Public Building and the Economy," in Jacobson, D. and Kokkinos, N. eds. *Herod and Augustus* (2009) pp. 157–69.

Geiger, J., Cotton, H., and Stiebel, G. eds. *Israel's Land: Papers Presented to Israel Shatzman on His Jubilee* (2009).

Gelb, N. *Herod the Great: Statesman, Visionary, Tyrant* (2013).

Gersht, R. "Representations of Deities and the Cults of Caesarea," in Raban, A., and Holum, K. eds. *Caesarea Maritima: A Retrospective after Two Millennia* (1996) pp. 305–24.

Geva, H. "The Tower of David—Phasael or Hippicus?," *IEJ* 31 (1981) pp. 57–65.

———. "The Temple Mount and its Environs," in Stern, E. ed. *NEAEHL* 2 (1993) pp. 736–44.

——— ed. *Ancient Jerusalem Revealed* (1994).

———. "The Siege Ramp Laid by the Romans to Conquer the Northern Palace at Masada," in Biran, A. et al. eds. *Eretz-Israel* 25 (1996) pp. 297–306.

——— ed. *Jewish Quarter Excavations in the Old City of Jerusalem, Conducted by Nahman Avigad, 1969–1982, I: Architecture and Stratigraphy: Areas A, W and X-2* (2000).

——— ed. *Jewish Quarter Excavations in the Old City of Jerusalem, Conducted by Nahman Avigad, 1969–1982, II: The Finds from Areas A, W and X-2* (2003).

——— ed. *Jewish Quarter Excavations in the Old City of Jerusalem, Conducted by Nahman Avigad, 1969–1982, III: Area E and Other Studies* (2006).

———. "Estimating Jerusalem's Population in Antiquity: A Minimalist View," *Eretz-Israel* 28 (2007) pp. 50–65.

——— ed. *Jewish Quarter Excavations in the Old City of Jerusalem, Conducted by Nahman Avigad, 1969–1982, IV: The Burnt House of Area B and Other Studies, Final Report* (2010a).

———. "Stratigraphy and Architecture in Area B," in Geva, H. ed. *Jewish Quarter Excavations in the Old City of Jerusalem, Conducted by Nahman Avigad, 1969–1982, IV: The Burnt House of Area B and Other Studies* (2010b) pp. 1–90.

———. "Stone Artifacts," in Geva, H. ed. *Jewish Quarter Excavations in the Old City of Jerusalem, Conducted by Nahman Avigad, 1969–1982, IV: The Burnt House of Area B and Other Studies* (2010c) pp. 154–212.

———. "Jerusalem's Population in Antiquity: A Minimalist View," *Tel Aviv* 41 (2014a) pp. 131–50.

——— ed. *Jewish Quarter Excavations in the Old City of Jerusalem, Conducted by Nahman Avigad, 1969–1982, VI: Areas J, N, Z and Other Studies* (2014b).

——— ed. *Jewish Quarter Excavations in the Old City of Jerusalem, Conducted by Nahman Avigad, 1969–1982, Vol. VII: Areas Q, H, O-2 and Other Studies* (2017).

Ghiretti, M. "Lo 'status' della Giudea dall'età Augustea all'età Claudia," *Latomus* 54 (1985) pp. 751–66.

Gibson, S. "The Bethesda Pool in Jerusalem: A New Investigation of Old Excavations," *New Studies on Jerusalem* 14 (2008) pp. 21–29.

Gibson, S. and Jacobson, D. *Below the Temple Mount: A Sourcebook on the Cisterns, Subterranean Chambers and Conduits of the Ḥaram al- Sharīf* (1996).

Gichon, M. "Cestius Gallus' Campaign in Judaea," *PEQ* 113 (1981) pp. 39–62.

———. "Aspects of a Roman Army in War according to the *Bellum Judaicum* of Josephus," in Freeman, P. and Kennedy, D. eds. *The Defence of the Roman and Byzantine East: Proceedings of a Colloquium Held at the University of Sheffield in April 1986* (1986) pp. 287–310.

———. "The Siege of Masada," in Le Bohec, Y. and Wolff, C. eds. *Les légions de Rome sous le Haut-Empire, Vol. 2* (2000) pp. 541–54.

Gill, D. "A Natural Spur at Masada," *Nature* 364 (1993) pp. 569–70.

———. "It's Natural: Masada Ramp Was Not a Roman Engineering Miracle," *BAR* 27, no. 5 (2001) pp. 22–31, 56–57.

Gilliver, K. "The Augustan Reform and the Structure of the Imperial Army," in Erdkamp, P. ed. *A Companion to the Roman Army* (2007) pp. 183–200.

Gleason, K., "The Landscape Palaces of Herod the Great," *NEA* 77, no. 2 (2014) pp. 76–97.

Gleason, K., Burrell, B., Netzer, E., Taylor, L. and Williams, J. "The Promontory Palace at Caesarea Maritima: Preliminary Evidence for Herod's *Praetorium*," *JRA* 11 (1998) pp. 23–52.

Goldstein, I., and Fontanille, J. "A New Study of the Coins of the First Jewish Revolt against Rome, 66–70 C.E.," *American Numismatic Association Journal* 1, no. 2 (2006) pp. 8–32.

Goldsworthy, A. *The Roman Army at War, 100 BC–AD 200* (1996).

———. *Roman Warfare* (2000).

———. *The Complete Roman Army* (2003).

———. *In the Name of Rome: The Men Who Won the Roman Empire* (2016).

Goodblatt, D. *The Monarchic Principle: Studies in Jewish Self-Government in Antiquity* (1994).

———. *Elements of Ancient Jewish Nationalism* (2006).

———. "Dating Documents in Herodian Judaea," in Jacobson, D. and Kokkinos, N. eds. *Herod and Augustus* (2009) pp. 127–54.

Goodman, M. *The Ruling Class of Judaea: The Origins of the Jewish Revolt against Rome, AD 66–70* (1987).

———. "Nerva, the Fiscus Judaicus, and Jewish Identity," *JRS* 79 (1989) pp. 40–44.

———. "Jewish Attitudes to Greek Culture in the Period of the Second Temple," in Abramson, G. and Parfitt, T. eds. *Jewish Education and Learning* (1994a) pp. 167–74.

———. "Sadducees and Essenes after 70 C.E.," in Porter, S., Joyce, P., and Orton, D. eds. *Crossing the Boundaries: Essays in Biblical Interpretation in Honour of Michael D. Goulder* (1994b) pp. 347–56.

———. "A Note on the Qumran Sectarians, Essenes and Josephus," *JJS* 46 (1995) pp. 161–66.

———. "Trajan and the Origins of the Bar Kokhba War," in Schäfer, P. ed. *Bar Kokhba War Reconsidered: New Perspectives on the Second Jewish Revolt against Rome* (2003) pp. 23–29.

———. "Coinage and Identity: The Jewish Evidence," in Howgego, C., Heuchert, V., and Burnett, A. eds. *Coinage and Identity in the Roman Provinces* (2005) pp. 163–66.

———. *Judaism in the Roman World: Collected Essays* (2007a).

———. "The Meaning of 'Fisci Iudaici Calumnia Sublata' on the Coinage of Nerva," in Cohen, S. and Schwartz, J. eds. *Studies in Josephus and the Varieties of Ancient Judaism: Louis H. Feldman Jubilee Volume* (2007b) pp. 81–89.

———. *Rome and Jerusalem: The Clash of Ancient Civilizations* (2007c).

Govaars, M., Spiro, M., and White, L. *The Joint Expedition to Caesarea Maritima Excavation Reports: Field O: The "Synagogue" Site* (2009).

Grabar, O. *The Shape of the Holy: Early Islamic Jerusalem* (1996).

Grabar, O. and Kedar, B. eds. *Where Heaven and Earth Meet: Jerusalem's Sacred Esplanade* (2009).

Grabbe, L. "Josephus and the Reconstruction of the Judaean Restoration," *JBL* 106 (1987) pp. 231–46.

———. *A History of the Jews and Judaism in the Second Temple Period, Vol. 1: Yehud, The Persian Province of Judah* (2004).

———. *An Introduction to Second Temple Judaism: History and Religion of the Jews in the Time of Nehemiah, the Maccabees, Hillel, and Jesus* (2010).

Graetz, H. *History of the Jews* (1949).

Gray, R. *Prophetic Figures in Late Second Temple Palestine: The Evidence from Josephus* (1993).

Gregerman, A. *Building on the Ruins of the Temple* (2016).

Griffin, M. *Nero: The End of a Dynasty* (1984).

———. "Nachwort: Nero from Zero to Hero," in Buckley, E. and Dinter, M. eds. *A Companion to the Neronian Age* (2013) pp. 467–80.

Gross, N. ed. *Jews in Economic Life* (1985).

Grossberg, A. "The *Miqva'ot* (Ritual Baths) at Masada," in Aviram, J., Foerster, G., Netzer, E., and Stiebel, G. eds. *Masada VIII: The Yigael Yadin Excavations 1963–1965. Final Reports* (2007) pp. 95–126.

Gruen, E. *Heritage and Hellenism: The Reinvention of Jewish Tradition* (1998).

———. "Herod, Rome and the Diaspora," in Jacobsen, D. and Kokkinos, N. eds. *Herod and Augustus* (2009) pp. 13–27.

Grüll, T. "A Fragment of a Monumental Roman Inscription at the Islamic Museum of the Haram as-Sharif, Jerusalem," *IEJ* 56, no. 2 (2006) pp. 183–200.

Gurevich, D. "The Water Pools and the Pilgrimage to Jerusalem in the Late Second Temple Period," *PEQ* 149, no. 2 (2017) pp. 103–34.

Guri-Rimon, O. ed. *The Great Revolt in the Galilee* (2008).

Gutmann, S. "The Synagogue at Gamla," in Levine, L. ed. *Ancient Synagogues Revealed* (1981) pp. 30–34.

Hachlili, R. *Jewish Funerary Customs, Practices and Rites in the Second Temple Period* (2005).

———. *Ancient Synagogues—Archaeology and Art: New Discoveries and Current Research* (2013).

Hahn, J. ed. *Zerstörungen des Jerusalemer Tempels: Geschehen-Wahrnehmung-Bewältigung* (2002).

Hall, L. *Roman Berytus: Beirut in Late Antiquity* (2004).

Hanson, K. "The Herodians and Mediterranean Kinship. Part II: Marriage and Divorce," *Biblical Theology Bulletin* 19 (1989) pp. 142–51.

Har-El, M. "Jerusalem & Judea: Roads and Fortifications," *BA* 44 (1981) pp. 8–19.

Harker, A. *Loyalty and Dissidence in Roman Egypt: The Case of the Acta Alexandrinorum* (2008).

Harl, K. "Greek Imperial Coins in the Economic Life of the Roman East," in Nollé, J., Overbeck, B., and Weiss, P. eds. *Nomismata, 1: Internationales Kolloquium zur kaiserzeitlichen Münzprägung Kleinasiens, 27–30 April 1994 in der Staatlichen Münzsammlung München* (1997) pp. 223–29.

Harmand, J. *L'armée et le Soldat à Rome: De 107 à 50 avant notre ère* (1967).

Hartal, M. "The Stadium of Tiberias," *Etmol* 28 (2002) pp. 22–24.

———. "The Material Culture of Northern Golan in the Hellenistic, Roman and Byzantine Periods," PhD Dissertation, Hebrew University (2003).

Hayward, R. "The Jewish Temple at Leontopolis: A Reconsideration," *JJS* 33 (1982) pp. 429–43.

Hendin, D. *Guide to Biblical Coins* (1987).

———. The Metrology of Judaean Small Bronze Coins," *AJN* 21 (2009) pp. 105–121.

Hengel, M. *Judaism and Hellenism: Studies in their Encounter in Palestine during the Early Hellenistic Period* (1974).

———. *The Zealots: Investigations into the Jewish Freedom Movement in the Period from Herod I until 70 A.D.* (1989).

Herr, M. "The Identity of the Jewish People before and after the Destruction of the Second Temple: Continuity or Change?," in Levine, L. and Schwartz, D. eds. *Jewish Identities in Antiquity: Studies in Memory of Menahem Stern* (2009) pp. 211–36.

Herstein, I. and Kaplansky, I. *Matters Mathematical* (1974).

Hezser, C. *The Social Structure of the Rabbinic Movement in Roman Palestine* (1997).

——— ed. *The Oxford Handbook of Jewish Daily Life in Roman Palestine* (2010).

Hilliard, T. "A Mid-1st c. B.C. Date for the Walls of Straton's Tower?," in Vann, R. ed. *Caesarea Papers: Straton's Tower, Herod's Harbour, and Roman and Byzantine Caesarea* (1992) pp. 42–48.

Hirschfeld, Y. *Excavations at Tiberias, 1989–1994* (2004).

Hirschfeld, Y. and Ariel, D. "A Coin Assemblage from the Reign of Alexander Jannaeus Found on the Shore of the Dead Sea," *IEJ* 55 (2005) pp. 66–89.

Hirschfeld, Y. and Galor, K. "New Excavations in Roman, Byzantine, and Early Islamic Tiberias," in Zangenberg, J., Attridge, H., and Martin, D. eds. *Religion, Ethnicity, and Identity in Ancient Galilee* (2007) pp. 207–29.

Hitch, S., and Rutherford, I. eds. *Animal Sacrifice in the Ancient Greek World* (2017).

Hizmi, H. "Archelaus Builds Archelais," *BAR* 34, no. 4 (2008) pp. 48–59, 78.

Hoffman, A. "Topographie und Stadtgeschicte von Gadara/Umm Qais," in Hoffman, A. and Kerner, S. eds. *Gadara-Gerasa und die Dekapolis* (2002) pp. 98–124.

Hoffman, A. and Kerner, S. eds. *Gadara-Gerasa und die Dekapolis* (2002).

Hohlfelder, R. "Building Sebastos: The Cyprus Connection," *IJNA* 28, no. 2 (1999) pp. 154–63.

Hohlfelder, R., Brandon, C., and Oleson, J. "Constructing the Harbour of Caesarea Palaestina, Israel: New Evidence from the ROMACONS Field Campaign of October 2005," *IJNA* 36, no. 2 (2007) pp. 409–15.

Holley, R. "The Ballista Balls from Masada," in Aviram, J., Foerster, G., and Netzer, E. eds. *Masada IV: The Yigael Yadin Excavations 1963–65. Final Reports: Lamps, Textiles, Basketry, Cordage, and Related Artifacts, Wood Remains, and Ballista Balls. Addendum, Human Skeletal Remains* (1994) pp. 349–65.

———. "Stone Projectiles and the Use of Artillery in the Siege of Gamla," in Syon, D. ed. *Gamla III: The Shmarya Guttmann Excavations 1976–1989. Finds and Studies, Part I* (2014) pp. 35–55.

Holum, K. "Temple Platform: Progress Report on the Excavations," in Holum, K., Raban, A., and Patrich, J., eds. "Caesarea Papers 2: Herod's Temple, the Provincial Governor's Praetorium, and Granaries, the Later Harbor, a Gold Coin Hoard, and Other Studies." *Journal of Roman Archaeology Supplementary Series, Number Thirty-Five* (1999) pp. 12–34.

———. "Caesarea's Temple Hill: The Archaeology of Sacred Space in an Ancient Mediterranean City," *NEA* 67, no. 4 (2004) pp. 184–99.

Holum, K., Hohlfelder, R., Bull, R., and Raban, A. *King Herod's Dream: Caesarea on the Sea* (1988).

Holum, K., Raban, A., and Patrich, J., eds. "Caesarea Papers 2: Herod's Temple, the Provincial Governor's Praetorium, and Granaries, the Later Harbor, a Gold Coin Hoard, and Other Studies." *Journal of Roman Archaeology Supplementary Series, Number Thirty-Five* (1999).

Hopkins, K. "On the Probable Age-Structure of the Roman Population," *Population Studies* 20, no. 2 (Nov. 1966), pp. 245–264.

———. *Conquerors and Slaves: Sociological Studies in Roman History, Vol. 1* (1978).

Hopkins, K. and Beard, M. *The Colosseum* (2005).

Horbury, W. *Jewish War under Trajan and Hadrian* (2014).

Horbury, W., Davies, W., and Sturdy, J. eds. *The Cambridge History of Judaism, Vol. 3: The Early Roman Period* (1999).

Horsley, R. "Josephus and the Bandits," *JSJ* 10 (1979a) pp. 37–63.

———. "The *Sicarii*: Ancient Jewish 'Terrorists,'" *Journal of Religion* 59, no. 4 (1979b) pp. 435–58.

———. *Galilee: History, Politics, People* (1995).

———. *Archaeology, History, and Society in Galilee: The Social Context of Jesus and the Rabbis* (1996).

———. "Power Vacuum and Power Struggle in 66–7 C.E.," in Berlin, A. and Overman, A. eds. *The First Jewish Revolt: Archaeology, History, and Ideology* (2002) pp. 87–109.

———. *Jesus and Empire: The Kingdom of God and the New World Disorder* (2003).

———. "Jesus and Empire," in Horsley, R. ed. *In the Shadow of Empire: Reclaiming the Bible as a History of Faithful Resistance* (2008a) pp. 75–96.

——— ed. *In the Shadow of Empire: Reclaiming the Bible as a History of Faithful Resistance* (2008b).

Hosler, J. *The Siege of Acre, 1189–1191: Saladin, Richard the Lionheart, and the Battle That Decided the Third Crusade* (2018).

Houghton, A., Hurter, S., Mottahedeh, P., and Scott, J. eds. *Studies in Honor of Leo Mildenberg: Numismatics, Art History, and Archaeology* (1984).

Howgego, C., Heuchert, V., and Burnett, A. eds. *Coinage and Identity in the Roman Provinces* (2005).

Humphrey, J. ed. *The Roman and Byzantine Near East: Some Recent Archaeological Research* (1995).

Huvelin, H., Christol, M., and Gautier, G., eds. *Mélanges de numismatique offerts à Pierre Bastien à occasion de son 75e anniversaire* (1987).

Hyland, A. *Training the Roman Cavalry: From Arrian's Ars Tactica* (1993).

Iamim, A. "The Missing Building(s) at Sepphoris," *IEJ* 66 (2016) pp. 96–113.

Inbari, M. *Jewish Fundamentalism and the Temple Mount* (2009).

Isaac, B. "Judaea after 70," *JJS* 35 (1984) pp. 44–50.

———. *The Limits of Empire: The Roman Army in the East* (1992).

———. *The Near East under Roman Rule: Selected Papers* (1998).

Isaac, B. and Roll, I. "A Milestone of A.D. 69 from Judaea: The Elder Trajan and Vespasian," *JRS* 66 (1976) pp. 9–14.

———. *Roman Roads in Judaea, I: The Scythopolis-Legio Road* (1982).

Itgenshorst, T. *Tota illa pompa: Der Triumph in der römischen Republik, mit einer CD-ROM, Katalog der Triumphe von 340 bis 19 vor Christus* (2005).

Jacobson, D. "Ideas concerning the Plan of Herod's Temple," *PEQ* 112 (1980) pp. 33–40.

———. "The Plan of the Ancient Haram el-Khalil at Hebron," *PEQ* 113 (1981) pp. 73–80.

———. "King Herod's 'Heroic' Public Image," *RB* 95 (1988) pp. 386–403.

———. "The Plan of Herod's Temple," *BAIAS* 10 (1990–1991) pp. 36–66.

———. "King Herod, Roman Citizen and Benefactor of Kos," *BAIAS* 13 (1993–1994) pp. 31–35.

———. "Sacred Geometry: Unlocking the Secret of the Temple Mount, Part 1," *BAR* 25, no. 4 (1999a) pp. 42–53, 62–64.

———. "Sacred Geometry: Unlocking the Secret of the Temple Mount, Part 2," *BAR* 25, no. 5 (1999b) pp. 54–63, 74.

———. "Geometrical Planning in Monumental Herodian Architecture," *BAIAS* 17 (1999c) pp. 67–76.

———. "Herod the Great Shows His True Colors," *NEA* 64 (2001) pp. 100–104.

———. "Herod's Roman Temple," *BAR* 28, no. 2 (2002a) pp. 19–27, 60–61.

———. "Review Article: Placing Herod the Great and His Works in Context," *PEQ* 134.1 (2002b) pp. 84–91.

———. "The Northern Palace at Masada—Herod's Ship of the Desert?," *PEQ* 138 (2006) pp. 99–117.

———. "Has Herod's Place of Burial Been Found?," *PEQ* 139.3 (2007a) pp. 147–48.

———. "The Jerusalem Temple of Herod the Great," in Kokkinos, N. ed. *The World of the Herods: Volume 1 of the International Conference "The World of the Herods" Held at the British Museum, 17–19 April 2001* (2007b) pp. 145–76.

Jacobson, D. and Gibson, S. "A Monumental Stairway on the Temple Mount," *IEJ* 45 (1995) pp. 162–70.

Jacobson, D. and Kokkinos, N. eds. *Herod and Augustus* (2009).

———. *Judaea and Rome in Coins, 65 BCE–135 CE: Papers Presented at the International Conference Hosted by Spink, 13th–14th September 2010* (2012).

Jacoby, F. *Die Fragmente der Griechischen Historiker* 2A (1926).

Japp, S. *Die Baupolitik Herodes' des Grossen: Die Bedeutung der Architektur für die Herrschaftslegitimation eines Römischen Klientelkönigs* (2000).

———. "Public and Private Decorative Art in the Time of Herod the Great," in Kokkinos, N. ed. *The World of the Herods: Volume 1 of the International Conference "The World of the Herods" Held at the British Museum, 17–19 April 2001* (2007) pp. 227–46.

Jaroés, K. *In Sachen Pontius Pilatus* (2002).

Jensen, M. *Herod Antipas in Galilee: The Literary and Archaeological Sources on the Reign of Herod Antipas and Its Socio-Economic Impact on Galilee,* rev. ed. (2010).

———. "Magdala/Taricheae and the Jewish Revolt," in Bauckham, R. ed. *Magdala of Galilee: A Jewish City in the Hellenistic and Roman Period* (2018) pp. 269–86.

Jensen, W. "The Sculptures from the Tomb of the Haterii," PhD Dissertation, University of Michigan (1978).

Jeremias, J. *Jerusalem in the Time of Jesus: An Investigation into Economic and Social Conditions during the New Testament Period* (1969).

Joes, A. *Guerilla Warfare: A Historical, Biographical and Bibliographical Sourcebook* (1996).

Jones, A. *The Later Roman Empire, 284–602: A Social, Economic, and Administrative Survey* (1964).

Jones, C. "Review of Eck, W. *Senatoren von Augustus bis Vespasian,*" *AJP* 95 (1974) pp. 89–90.

———. "Towards a Chronology of Josephus," *SCI* 21 (2002) 113–21.

———. "Josephus and Greek Literature in Flavian Rome," in Edmondson, J., Mason, S., and Rives, J. eds. *Flavius Josephus and Flavian Rome* (2005) pp. 201–8.

Jongman, W. "The Early Roman Period: Consumption," in Scheidel, W., Morris, I., and Saller, R. eds. *The Cambridge Economic History of the Greco-Roman World* (2013) pp. 592–618.

Jossa, G. "Josephus' Actions in the Galilee during the Jewish War," in Parente, F. and Sievers, J. eds. *Josephus and the History of the Graeco-Roman Period: Essays in Memory of Morton Smith* (1994) pp. 265–78.

Kadman, L. *The Coins of Caesarea Maritima* (1957).

———. *The Coins of the Jewish War of 66–73 C.E.* (1960).

Kamesar, A. ed. *The Cambridge Companion to Philo* (2009).

Kanael, B. "The Historical Background of the Coins 'Year Four . . . of the Redemption of Zion,'" *BASOR* 129 (1953) pp. 18–20.

Kartveit, M. *The Origin of the Samaritans* (2009).

Kasher, A. *Jews, Idumaeans and Ancient Arabs: Relations of the Jews in Eretz-Isrel with the Nations of the Frontier and the Desert during the Hellenistic and Roman Era (332 BCE–70 CE)* (1988).

———. *Jews and Hellenistic Cities in Eretz-Israel: Relations of the Jews in Eretz-Israel with the Hellenistic Cities during the Second Temple Period (332 BCE–70 CE)* (1990).

Kasher, A., Rappaport, U., and Fuks, G. eds. *Greece and Rome in Eretz Israel: Collected Essays* (1990).

Kasher, A. and Witztum, E. *King Herod, a Persecuted Persecutor: A Case Study in Psychohistory and Psychobiography* (2007).

Katzoff, R. and Schaps, D. eds. *Law in the Documents of the Judaean Desert* (2005).

Keddie, A. *Class and Power in Roman Palestine: The Socioeconomic Setting of Judaism and Christian Origins* (2019).

Kelley, N. "The Cosmopolitan Expression of Josephus' Prophetic Perspective in the 'Jewish War,'" *HTR* 97, no. 3 (2004) pp. 257–74.

Keppie, L. *The Making of the Roman Army: From Republic to Empire* (1998).

Klawans, J. "Josephus, the Rabbis, and Responses to Catastrophes Ancient and Modern," *JQR* 100, no. 2 (2010) pp. 278–30.

———. *Josephus and the Theologies of Ancient Judaism* (2012).

Kleiner, D. *Roman Sculpture* (1992).

Kloner, A. and Zissu, B. *The Necropolis of Jerusalem in the Second Temple Period* (2007).

Koch, G. ed. *Sarkophag-Studien I. Akten des Symposiums "125 Jahre Sarkophag-Corpus," Marburg, 4–7 Oktober 1995* (1998).

Kochavi, M. *Aphek-Antipatris: 5000 Years of History* (1989).

Koester, C. "The Origin and Significance of the Flight to Pella Tradition," *Catholic Biblical Quarterly* 51, no. 1 (1989) pp. 90–106.

Kokkinos, N. *The Herodian Dynasty: Origins, Role in Society and Eclipse* (1998).

———. "The City of 'Mariamme': An Unknown Herodian Connection?," *Mediterraneo Antico* 5, no. 2 (2002a) pp. 715–46.

———. "Herod's Horrid Death," *BAR* 28, no. 2 (2002b) pp. 28–35, 62.

———. "The Royal Court of the Herods," in Kokkinos, N. ed. *The World of the Herods: Volume 1 of the International Conference "The World of the Herods" Held at the British Museum, 17–19 April 2001* (2007a) pp. 279–303.

——— ed. *The World of the Herods: Volume 1 of the International Conference "The World of the Herods" Held at the British Museum, 17–19 April 2001* (2007b).

———. *The Herodian Dynasty: Origins, Role in Society and Eclipse*, rev. ed. (2010a).

———. "The Location of Tarichaea: North or South of Tiberias?," *PEQ* 142.1 (2010b) pp. 7–23.

———. "The Prefects of Judaea 6–48 CE and the Coins from the Misty Period 6–36 CE," in Jacobson, D. and Kokkinos, N. eds. *Judaea and Rome in Coins 65 BCE–135 CE* (2012) pp. 85–112.

Kottsieper, I. "'And They Did Not Care to Speak Yehudit': On Linguistic Change in Judah during the Late Persian Era," in Lipschits, O., Knoppers, G., and Albertz, R. eds. *Judah and the Judeans in the Fourth Century B.C.E.* (2007) pp. 95–124.

Krause, A. *Synagogues in the Works of Flavius Josephus: Rhetoric, Spatiality, and First-Century Jewish Institutions* (2017).

Kropp, A. "King-Caesar-God: Roman Imperial Cult among Near Eastern 'Client' Kings in the Julio-Claudian Period," in Blömer, M., Facella, M., and Winter, E. eds. *Lokale Identität im romischen nahen Osten: Kontexte und Perspektiven* (2009) pp. 99–150.

Künzl, E. *Der römische Triumph: Siegesfeiern im antiken Rom* (1988).

Kushnir-Stein, A. "Another Look at Josephus' Evidence for the Date of Herod's Death," *SCI* 14 (1995a) pp. 73–86.

———. "An Inscribed Lead Weight from Ashdod: A Reconsideration," *ZPE* 105 (1995b) pp. 81–84.

———. "The Predecessor of Caesarea: On the Identification of Demetrias in South Phoenicia," in Humphreys, J. ed. *The Roman and Byzantine Near East: Some Recent Archaeological Research* (1995c) pp. 9–14.

———. "Coins of the Herodian Dynasty: The State of Research," in Kokkinos, N. ed. *The World of the Herods: Volume 1 of the International Conference "The World of the Herods" Held at the British Museum, 17–19 April 2001* (2007) pp. 55–60.

Labbé, G. *L'Affirmation de la puissance romaine en Judée (63 avant J.-C.–136 après J.-C.)* (2012).

Ladouceur, D. "Masada: A Consideration of the Literary Evidence," *GRBS* 21, no. 3 (1980) pp. 245–60.

Ladstätter, S., Pirson, F., and Schmidts, T. eds. *Byzas 19—Harbors and Harbor Cities in the Eastern Mediterranean from Antiquity to the Byzantine Period: Recent Discoveries and Current Approaches* (2015).

Lalor, B. "The Temple Mount of Herod the Great at Jerusalem: Recent Excavations and Literary Sources," in Bartlett, J. ed. *Archaeology and Biblical Interpretation* (1997) pp. 95–116.

Lämmer, M. "Griechische Wettkämpfe in Jerusalem und ihre politischen Hintergründe," *Kölner Beiträge zur Sportwissenschaft* 2 (1973) pp. 182–227.

Landau, T. *Out-Heroding Herod: Josephus, Rhetoric, and the Herod Narratives* (2006).

Lapin, H. ed. *Religious and Ethnic Communities in Later Roman Palestine* (1998).

——— *Rabbis as Romans: The Rabbinic Movement in Roman Palestine, 100–400 CE* (2012).

———. "Feeding the Jerusalem Temple: Cult, Hinterland, and Economy in First-Century Palestine," *JAJ* 8 (2017a) pp. 410–53.

———. "Population Contraction in Roman Galilee: Reconsidering the Evidence," *BASOR* 378 (2017b) pp. 127–43.

————. "Temple, Cult, and Consumption in Second Temple Jerusalem," in Tal, O. and Weiss, Z. eds. *Expressions of Cult in the Southern Levant in the Greco-Roman Period: Manifestations in Text and Material Culture* (2017c) pp. 241–53.

Laqueur, R. *Der jüdische Historiker Flavius Josephus: Ein Biographischer Versuch auf Neuer Quellenkristischer Grundlage* (1920).

La Rocca, E., León, P., and Parisi Presicce, C. eds. *Le due patrie acquisite: Studi di archeologia dedicati a Walter Trillmich* (2008).

Le Bohec, Y. *The Imperial Roman Army* (1994).

Le Bohec, Y. and Wolff, C. eds. *Les légions de Rome sous le Haut-Empire, Vol. 2* (2000).

Lee, R. *Romanization in Palestine: A Study in Urban Development from Herod the Great to AD 70* (2003).

Lehmann, C. and Holum, K. *The Joint Expedition to Caesarea Maritima: Excavation Reports: The Greek and Latin Inscriptions of Caesarea Maritima, Vol. 5* (2000).

Leibner, U. *Settlement and History in Hellenistic, Roman, and Byzantine Galilee: An Archaeological Survey of the Eastern Galilee (Texts and Studies in Ancient Judaism)* (2009).

Lemaire, A. "New Aramaic Ostraca from Idumea and their Historical Interpretation," in Lipschits, O. and Oeming, M. eds. *Judah and the Judeans in the Persian Period* (2006) pp. 413–56.

Lena, A. "The Harbor," in Bauckham, R. ed. *Magdala of Galilee: A Jewish City in the Hellenistic and Roman Period* (2018) pp. 69–88.

Leoni, T. "'Against Caesar's Wishes': Flavius Josephus as a Source for the Burning of the Temple," *JJS* 58 (2007) pp. 39–51.

Levick, B. *Vespasian* (1999).

————. "La dinastia flavia," in Coarelli, F. ed. *Divus Vespasianus: Il bimillenario dei Flavi* (2009) pp. 14–23.

Levine, L. "The Jewish-Greek Conflict in First Century Caesarea," *JJS* 25 (1974) pp. 381–97.

———— ed. *Ancient Synagogues Revealed* (1981a).

————. *Jerusalem Cathedra: Studies in History, Archaeology, Geography and Ethnography of the Land of Israel 2* (1981b).

————. *The Ancient Synagogue: The First Thousand Years* (2000).

————. *Jerusalem: Portrait of the City in the Second Temple Period, 538 B.C.E.–70 C.E.* (2002).

Levine, L. and Schwartz, D. eds. *Jewish Identities in Antiquity: Studies in Memory of Menahem Stern* (2009).

Levy, T. ed. *The Archaeology of Society in the Holy Land* (1995).

Lev-Yadun, S., Lucas, D., and Weinstein-Evron, M, "Modeling the Demands for Wood by the Inhabitants of Masada and for the Roman Siege," *Journal of Arid Environments* 74 (2010) pp. 777–85.

Lewin, A. ed. *Gli ebrei nell'Impero romano: Saggi vari* (2001).

Lichtenberger, A. *Die Baupolitik Herodes des Grossen* (1999).

———. "Herod and Rome: Was Romanisation a Goal of the Building Policy of Herod?," in Jacobson, D. and Kokkinos, N. eds. *Herod and Augustus* (2009) pp. 43–62.

Lieberman, S. *Greek in Jewish Palestine, Hellenism in Jewish Palestine* (1994).

Limor, O. and Strousma, G. eds. *Christians and Christianity in the Holy Land: From the Origins to the Latin Kingdoms* (2006).

Linder, A. ed. and trans. *The Jews in Roman Imperial Legislation* (1987).

Lindner, H. *Die Geschictsauffassung des Flavius Josephus im Bellum Judaicum* (1972).

Lipschits, O., Knoppers, G., and Albertz, R. eds. *Judah and the Judeans in the Fourth Century B.C.E.* (2007).

Lipschits, O. and Oeming, M. eds. *Judah and the Judeans in the Persian Period* (2006).

Lutnick, S. *The American Revolution and the British Press, 1775–1783* (1967).

Luttwak, E. *The Grand Strategy of the Roman Empire: From the First Century A.D. to the Third* (1976).

Luz, M. "Eleazar's Second Speech on Masada and Its Literary Precedents," *RM* 126 (1983) pp. 25–43.

Lyautey, H. "Du rôle colonial de l'armée," *Revue des Deux Mondes* (1900) pp. 308–28.

Ma, J. "Relire les Institutions des Séleucides de Bickerman," in Benoist, S. ed. *Rome, A City and Its Empire in Perspective: The Impact of the Roman World through Fergus Millar's Research* (2012) pp. 59–84.

Macalister, R. and Duncan, J. *Excavations on the Hill of Ophel, Jerusalem 1923–1925* (1926).

Maeir, A., Magness, J., and Schiffman, L. eds. *"Go Out and Study the Land" (Judges 18:2): Archaeological, Historical and Textual Studies in Honor of Hanan Eshel* (2011).

Magen, Y. "The Dating of the First Phase of the Samaritan Temple on Mount Gerizim in Light of the Archaeological Evidence," in Lipschits, O., Knoppers, G., and Albertz, R. eds. *Judah and the Judeans in the Fourth Century B.C.E.* (2007) pp. 157–211.

Magen, Y., Misgav, H., and Tsfania, L. *Mount Gerizim Excavations, Vol. 1: The Aramaic, Hebrew and Samaritan Inscriptions* (2004).

Magness, J. "Masada: Arms and the Man," *BAR* 18, no. 4 (1992) pp. 58–67.

———. "The Cults of Isis and Kore at Samaria-Sebaste in the Hellenistic and Roman Periods," *HTR* 94, no. 2 (2001) pp. 157–77.

———. *The Archaeology of Qumran and the Dead Sea Scrolls* (2002a).

———. "In the Footsteps of the Tenth Roman Legion in Judea," in Berlin, A. and Overman, A. eds. *The First Jewish Revolt: Archaeology, History, and Ideology* (2002b) pp. 189–212.

———. "The Arch of Titus at Rome and the Fate of the God of Israel," *JJS* 59, no. 2 (2008) pp. 201–17.

———. "The Pottery from the 1995 Excavations in Camp F at Masada," *BASOR* 353 (2009a) pp. 75–107.

———. "Some Observations on the Flavian Victory Monuments of Rome," in Counts, D. and Tuck, A. eds. *Koine: Mediterranean Studies in Honor of R. Ross Holloway* (2009b) pp. 35–40.

———. "A Reconsideration of Josephus' Testimony about Masada," in Popović, M. ed. *The Jewish Revolt against Rome: Interdisciplinary Perspectives* (2011a) pp. 343–59.

———. *Stone and Dung, Oil and Spit: Jewish Daily Life in the Time of Jesus* (2011b).

———. *The Archaeology of the Holy Land from the Destruction of Solomon's Temple to the Muslim Conquest* (2012).

———. "Arrowheads and Projectile Points," in Syon, D. ed. *Gamla III: The Shmarya Gutmann Excavations 1976–1989. Finds and Studies, Part 1* (2014) pp. 21–33.

———. *Masada: From Jewish Revolt to Modern Myth* (2019a).

———. "Herod the Great's Self-Representation through His Tomb at Herodium," *JAJ* 10, no. 3 (2019b) pp. 258–87.

Mahieu, B. "The Foundation Year of Samaria-Sebaste and Its Chronological Implications," *AS* 38 (2008) pp. 183–96.

———. *Between Rome and Jerusalem: Herod the Great and His Sons in their Struggle for Recognition* (2012).

Malena, S. and Miano, D. eds. *Milk and Honey: Essays on Ancient Israel and the Bible in Appreciation of the Judaic Studies Program at the University of California, San Diego* (2007).

Mantzoulinou-Richards, E. "From Syros: A Dedicatory Inscription of Herodes the Great from an Unknown Building," *Ancient World* 18, no. 3–4 (1988) pp. 87–99.

Ma'oz, Z. "Banias, Temple of Pan: 1993," *Hadashot Arkheologiyot: Excavations and Surveys in Israel* 15 (1996) pp. 1–5.

Marcus, R. trans. *Josephus: Jewish Antiquities, Books IX–XI, Vol. VI* (1937).

——— trans. *Josephus: Jewish Antiquities, Books XII–XIV, Vol. VII* (1943).

Marcus, R. and Wikgren, A. trans. *Josephus: Jewish Antiquities, Books XV–XVII, Vol. VIII* (1963).

Margalit, A. "Josephus vs. Jeremiah: The Difference between Historian and Prophet," *BAR* 38, no. 5 (2012) pp. 53–57, 68.

Marincola, J. ed. *A Companion to Greek and Roman Historiography* (2007).

Marsden, E. *Greek and Roman Artillery: Technical Treatises* (1971).

Marshak, A. "Rise of the Idumaeans: Ethnicity and Politics in Herod's Judaea," in Eckhardt, B. ed. *Jewish Identity and Politics between the Maccabees and Bar Kokhba* (2012) pp. 117–29.

————. *The Many Faces of Herod the Great* (2015).

Marshall, S. *Men against Fire* (1947).

Mason, S. "Was Josephus a Pharisee? A Re-Examination of Life 10–2," *JJS* 40 (1989) pp. 31–46.

————. *Flavius Josephus on the Pharisees: A Composition-Critical Study* (1991).

————. *Flavius Josephus: Life of Josephus* (2003).

————. "Jews, Judaeans, Judaizing, Judaism: Problems of Categorization in Ancient History," *JSJ* 38 (2007) pp. 457–512.

————. *Flavius Josephus: Translation and Commentary, Vol. 1b: Judean War 2* (2008).

————. *A History of the Jewish War: A.D. 66–74* (2016).

Matyszak, P. *The Enemies of Rome: From Hannibal to Attila the Hun* (2004).

Maxfield, V. *The Military Decorations of the Roman Army* (1981).

Mazar, A. *Archaeology of the Land of the Bible, 10,000–586 B.C.E.* (1990).

————. "A Survey of the Aqueducts to Jerusalem," in Amit, D., Patrich, J., and Hirschfeld, Y. eds. *The Aqueducts of Israel* (2002) pp. 211–44.

————. *Excavations at Tel Beth-Shean 1989–1996, Vol. 1: From the Late Bronze Age IIB to the Medieval Period* (2006).

Mazar, B. "A Hebrew Inscription from the Temple Area in Jerusalem," *Qadmoniot* 3, no. 4 (1970) pp. 142–44.

————. *The Mountain of the Lord: Excavating in Jerusalem* (1975).

McCane, B. "Simply Irresistible: Augustus, Herod, and the Empire," *JBL* 127, no. 4 (2008) pp. 725–35.

McDermott, W. "Flavius Silva and Salvius Liberalis," *CW* 66, no. 6 (1973) pp. 335–51.

McDonnell-Staff, P. "A War of Logistics: The Siege of Jerusalem, 66 A.D.," *Ancient Warfare* 4, no. 2 (2010) pp. 36–41.

McGing, B. "Population and Proselytism: How Many Jews Were There in the Ancient World?," in Bartlett, J. ed. *Jews in the Hellenistic and Roman Cities* (2002) pp. 88–106.

McGing, B. and Mossman, J. eds. *The Limits of Ancient Biography* (2006).

McLaren, J. *Power and Politics in Palestine: The Jews and the Governing of their Land, 100 BC–AD 70* (1991).

————. *Turbulent Times? Josephus and Scholarship on Judaea in the First Century CE* (1998).

————. "The Coinage of the First Year as a Point of Reference for the First Jewish Revolt (66–70 CE)," *SCI* 22 (2003) pp. 135–52.

Mendels, D. *The Rise and Fall of Jewish Nationalism: Jewish and Christian Ethnicity in Ancient Palestine* (1992).

Merritt, B. "Greek Inscriptions," *Hesperia* 21 (1952) pp. 340–80.

Meshorer, Y. "A Stone Weight from the Reign of Herod," *IEJ* 20 (1970) pp. 97–98.

————. *Ancient Jewish Coinage, Vol. 1: Persian Period through Hasmonaeans* (1982).

————. "One Hundred Ninety Years of Tyrian Shekels," in Houghton, A., Hurter, S., Mottahedeh, P., and Scott, J. eds. *Studies in Honor of Leo Mildenberg: Numismatics, Art History, and Archaeology* (1984) pp. 171–80.

————. *City-Coins of Eretz-Israel and the Decapolis in the Roman Period* (1985).

————. *The Coinage of Aelia Capitolina* (1989).

————. *A Treasury of Jewish Coins: From the Persian Period to Bar Kokhba* (2001).

Meyers, E. ed. *The Oxford Encyclopedia of Archaeology in the Near East. Vols. I–V* (1997).

————. "Sepphoris: City of Peace," in Berlin, A. and Overman, A. eds. *The First Jewish Revolt: Archaeology, History, and Ideology* (2002) pp. 110–20.

Meyers, E. and Chancey, M. *Alexander to Constantine: Archaeology of the Land of the Bible, Vol. III* (2012).

Middlekauff, R. *The Glorious Cause: The American Revolution, 1763–1789* (2005).

Middlemas, J. *The Templeless Age: An Introduction to the History, Literature, and Theology of the "Exile"* (2007).

Millar, F. *The Roman Near East: 31 B.C.–A.D. 337* (1993).

————. "Last Year in Jerusalem: Monuments of the Jewish War in Rome," in Edmondson, J., Mason, S., and Rives, J. eds. *Flavius Josephus and Flavian Rome* (2005) pp. 101–28.

————. *Rome, the Greek World and the East, Vol. 3: The Greek World, the Jews, & the East,* ed. Cotton, H. and Rogers, G. (2006).

Miller, N. "Patriarchal Burial Site Explored for the First Time in 700 Years," *BAR* 11, no. 3 (1985) pp. 26–43.

Miller, S. *Ancient Greek Athletics* (2004).

Modrzejewski, J. *The Jews of Egypt from Rameses II to Emperor Hadrian* (1997).

Mommsen, T. *The Provinces of the Roman Empire from Caesar to Diocletian,* trans. W. Dickson, 2 vols. (1887).

Montevecchi, O. "Vespasiano acclamato dagli Alessandrini: Ancora su P. Fouad 8," *Aegyptus* 61 (1981) pp. 155–70.

Mor, M., Pastor, J., Ronen, I., and Ashkenazi, Y. eds. *For Uriel: Studies in the History of Israel in Antiquity Presented to Professor Uriel Rappaport* (2005).

Morgan, G. *69 A.D.: The Year of Four Emperors* (2006).

Murdoch, A. *Rome's Greatest Defeat: Massacre in the Teutoburg Forest* (2006).

Nagy, R. ed. *Sepphoris in Galilee: Crosscurrents of Culture* (1996).

Nahman, A. *Discovering Jerusalem* (1983).

Naveh, J. "The Ossuary Inscriptions from Giv'at ha-Mivtar, Jerusalem," *IEJ* 20 (1970) pp. 33–37.

————. "The Aramaic Ostraca from Tel-Arad," in Aharoni, Y. ed. *Arad Inscriptions* (1981) pp. 153–76.

Nelson, M. *The Temple Complex at Horvat Omrit, Vol. 1: The Architecture* (2015).

Netzer, E. "Herod's Family Tomb in Jerusalem," *BAR* 9, no. 3 (1983) pp. 52, 55, 59.

———. "Herod the Great's Contribution to Nikopolis in Light of his Building Activity in Judea," in Chrysos, E. ed. *Proceedings of the First International Symposium of Nicopolis (23–29 September 1984)* (1987) pp. 121–28.

———. *Masada III: The Yigael Yadin Excavations 1963–1965. Final Reports: The Buildings, Stratigraphy and Architecture* (1991a).

———. "The Last Days and Hours at Masada," *BAR* 17, no. 6 (1991b) pp. 20–32.

———. "Floating in the Desert—A Pleasure Palace in Jordan," *Archaeology Odyssey* 2 (1999) pp. 46–55.

———. *The Palaces of the Hasmoneans and Herod the Great* (2001).

———. *The Architecture of Herod, the Great Builder* (2006).

———. "The Ideal City in the Eyes of Herod the Great," in Kokkinos, N. ed. *The World of the Herods: Volume 1 of the International Conference "The World of the Herods" Held at the British Museum, 17–19 April 2001* (2007) pp. 71–91.

———. *The Architecture of Herod, the Great Builder*, 2nd ed. (2008).

———. "Palaces and the Planning of Complexes in Herod's Realm," in Jacobson, D. and Kokkinos, N. eds. *Herod and Augustus* (2009) pp. 171–80.

———. "In Search of Herod's Tomb," *BAR* 37, no. 1 (2011) pp. 37–48, 70.

———. "Herod, Master Builder," in Rozenberg, S. and Mevorah, D. eds. *Herod the Great: The King's Final Journey* (2017a) pp. 80–117.

———. "The Main Features of Herod's Architecture," in Rozenberg, S. and Mevorah, D. eds. *Herod the Great: The King's Final Journey* (2017b) pp. 162–65.

Netzer, E. with Porat, R., Kalman, Y., and Chachy-Laureys, R. "Herodium," in Rozenberg, S. and Mevorah, D. eds. *Herod the Great: The King's Final Journey* (2017a) pp. 126–61.

———. "The Tomb Complex at Herodium," in Rozenberg, S. and Mevorah, D. eds. *Herod the Great: The King's Final Journey* (2017b) pp. 240–55.

Neusner, J. ed. *Christianity, Judaism, and Other Greco-Roman Cults: Studies for Morton Smith at Sixty (Studies in Judaism in Late Antiquity)* (1975).

Newman, H. *Proximity to Power and Jewish Sectarian Groups of the Ancient Period: A Review of Lifestyle, Values, and Halakha in the Pharisees, Sadducees, Essenes, and Qumran* (2006).

Nicols, J. *Vespasian and the Partes Flavianae* (1978).

Nollé, J., Overbeck, B., and Weiss, P. eds. *Nomismata, 1: Internationales Kolloquium zur kaiserzeitlichen Münzprägung Kleinasians, 27–30 April 1994 in der Staatlichen Münzsammlung München* (1997).

Notley, R. "Et-Tell Is Not Bethsaida," *NEA* 70, no. 4 (2007) pp. 220–30.

Notley, R. and Garcia, J. "Queen Helena's Jerusalem Palace—in a Parking Lot?," *BAR* 40, no. 3 (2014) pp. 28–40, 62, 64.

Noy, D., Panayotov, A., and Bloedhorn, H. eds. *Inscriptiones Judaicae Orientis, Vol. 1: Eastern Europe* (2004).

Nusseibeh, S. "The Haram Al-Sharif," in Grabar, O. and Kedar, B. eds. *Where Heaven and Earth Meet: Jerusalem's Sacred Esplanade* (2009) pp. 366–73.

Ohlig, C. and Tsuk, T. eds. *Cura Aquarum in Israel II* (2014).

Overman, A. and MacLennan, R. eds. *Diaspora Jews and Judaism: Essays in Honor of, and in Dialogue with, A. Thomas Kraabel* (1992).

Overman, A., Olive, J., and Nelson, M. "A Newly Discovered Herodian Temple at Khirbet Omrit in Northern Israel," in Kokkinos, N. ed. *The World of the Herods: Volume 1 of the International Conference "The World of the Herods" Held at the British Museum, 17–19 April 2001* (2007) pp. 177–96.

Painter, R. "The Origins and Social Context of Mithraism at Caesarea Maritima," in Donaldson, T. ed. *Religious Rivalries and the Struggle for Success in Caesarea Maritima* (2000) pp. 205–25.

Panzram, S. "Der Jerusalemer Tempel und das Rom der Flavier," in Hahn, J. ed. *Zerstörungen des Jerusalemer Tempels: Geschehen-Wahrnehmung-Bewältigung* (2002) pp. 166–82.

Parente, F. and Sievers, J. eds. *Josephus and the History of the Greco-Roman Period: Essays in Memory of Morton Smith* (1994).

Parisi Presicce, C. "L'Arco di Tito al Circo Massimo: Frammenti inediti della decorazione scultorea," in La Rocca, E., León, P., and Parisi Presicce, C. eds. *Le due patrie acquisite: Studi di archeologia dedicati a Walter Trillmich* (2008) pp. 345–54.

Parker, S. "The Byzantine Period: An Empire's New Holy Land," *NEA* 62, no. 3 (1999) pp. 134–80.

Parrot, A. *Samaria: The Capital of the Kingdom of Israel* (1958).

Pastor, J. *Land and Economy in Ancient Palestine* (1997).

Pastor, J., Stern, P., and Mor, M. eds. *Flavius Josephus: Interpretation and History* (2011).

Patrich, J. "A Sadducean Halacha and the Jerusalem Aqueduct," *Jerusalem Cathedra* 2 (1982) pp. 25–39.

———. "Herod's Theater in Jerusalem: A New Proposal," *IEJ* 52 (2002) pp. 231–39.

———. "Herodian Caesarea: The Urban Space," in Kokkinos, N. ed. *The World of the Herods: Volume 1 of the International Conference "The World of the Herods" Held at the British Museum, 17–19 April 2001* (2007) pp. 93–129.

———. "Caesarea," *NEAEHL* 5 (2008) pp. 1673–80.

———. "The Date of the Foundation of Caesarea as a Colony," in Geiger, J., Cotton, H., and Stiebel, G. eds. *Israel's Land: Papers Presented to Israel Shatzman on His Jubilee* (2009a) pp. 135–56.

———. "Herodian Entertainment Structures," in Jacobson, D. and Kokkinos, N. eds. *Herod and Augustus* (2009b) pp. 181–213.

———. "Revisiting the Mausoleum at Herodium: Is It Herod's Tomb?," *PEQ* 147, no. 4 (2015) pp. 299–315.

Patrich, J. and Arubas, B. "'Herod's Tomb' Reexamined: Guidelines for a Discussion and Conclusions," in Stiebel, G., Peleg-Barakat, O., Ben-Ami, D., Weksler-Bdolah, S., and Gadot, Y. eds. *New Studies in the Archaeology of Jerusalem and Its Region* (2013) pp. 287–300.

Payne, K. *Strategy, Evolution, and War: From Apes to Artificial Intelligence* (2018).

Pearlman, M. *The Zealots of Masada: Story of a Dig* (1967).

Pekáry, T. "*Seditio*: Unruhen und Revolten im römischen Reich von Augustus bis Commodus," *AS* 18 (1987) pp. 133–50.

Peleg-Barkat, O. *The Temple Mount Excavations in Jerusalem 1968–1978, Directed by Benjamin Mazar. Final Reports, Vol. V: Herodian Architectural Decoration and King Herod's Royal Portico* (2017).

Persico, T. "Why Rebuilding the Temple Would be the End of Judaism as We Know It," *Haaretz* (2014, 13 November).

Peters, F. *Jerusalem: The Holy City in the Eyes of Chroniclers, Visitors, Pilgrims, and Prophets from the Days of Abraham to the Beginnings of Modern Times* (1985).

Peters, R. *Cain at Gettysburg* (2012).

Pfanner, M. *Der Titusbogen* (1983).

Pipes, D. "The Muslim Claim to Jerusalem," *Middle East Quarterly* 8, no. 4 (2001) pp. 49–66.

Pollard, N. *Soldiers, Cities, and Civilians in Roman Syria* (2000).

Popović, M. "The Jewish Revolt against Rome: History, Sources and Perspectives," in Popović, M. ed. *The Jewish Revolt Against Rome: Interdisciplinary Perspectives* (2011a) pp. 1–25.

——— ed. *The Jewish Revolt against Rome: Interdisciplinary Perspectives* (2011b).

Porat, R., Chachy, R., and Kalman, Y. *Herodium: Final Reports of the 1972–2010 Excavations Directed by Ehud Netzer, Vol. I: Herod's Tomb Precinct* (2015).

Porat, R., Kalman, Y., and Chachy, R. "Excavation of the Approach to the Mountain Palace-Fortress at Herodium," *JRA* 29 (2016) pp. 142–64.

Porath, Y. *Caesarea Maritima, Vol. I: Herod's Circus and Related Buildings, Part 1: Architecture and Stratigraphy* (2013).

———. *Caesarea Maritima, Vol. I: Herod's Circus and Related Buildings, Part 2: The Finds* (2015).

Porten, B. *The Elephantine Papyri in English: Three Millennia of Cross-Cultural Continuity and Change* (1996).

Porter, S., Joyce, P., and Orton, D. eds. *Crossing the Boundaries: Essays in Biblical Interpretation in Honour of Michael D. Goulder* (1994).

Prawer, J. and Ben-Shammai, H. eds. *The History of Jerusalem: The Early Muslim Period, 638–1099* (1996).

Price, J. *Jerusalem under Siege: The Collapse of the Jewish State 66–70 C.E.* (1992).

———. "The Failure of Rhetoric in Josephus' *Bellum Judaicum,*" *Ramus* 36, no. 1 (2008) pp. 6–24.

Pucci Ben Zeev, M. *Jewish Rights in the Roman World: The Greek and Roman Documents Quoted by Josephus Flavius* (1998).

———. *Diaspora Judaism in Turmoil, 116/117 CE: Ancient Sources and Modern Insights* (2005).

Pummer, R. *The Samaritans* (1987).

———. *The Samaritans in Flavius Josephus* (2009).

Raban, A. "In Search of Straton's Tower," in Vann, R. ed. *Caesarea Papers: Straton's Tower, Herod's Harbour, and Roman and Byzantine Caesarea* (1992) pp. 7–22.

Raban, A., Artzy, B., Goodman, B., and Gal, Z. eds. *The Harbour of Sebastos (Caesarea Maritima) in Its Roman Mediterranean Context* (2009).

Raban, A. and Holum, K. eds. *Caesarea Maritima: A Retrospective after Two Millennia* (1996).

Rajak, T. "Justus of Tiberias," *CQ* 23 (1973) pp. 345–68.

———. *Josephus: The Historian and His Society* (1983).

———. "Was There a Roman Charter for the Jews?," *JRS* 74 (1984) pp. 107–23.

———. "The Hasmoneans and the Uses of Hellenism," in Davies, P., and White, R. eds. *A Tribute to Geza Vermes: Essays on Jewish and Christian Literature and History* (1990) pp. 261–80.

———. *Josephus: The Historian and His Society,* 2nd ed. (2002).

———. "Josephus in the Diaspora," in Edmondson, J., Mason, S. and Rives, J. eds. *Flavius Josephus and Flavian Rome* (2005) pp. 79–100.

———. "The Herodian Narratives of Josephus," in Kokkinos, N. ed. *The World of the Herods: Volume 1 of the International Conference "The World of the Herods" Held at the British Museum, 17–19 April 2001* (2007) pp. 23–34.

———. *Translation & Survival: The Greek Bible of the Ancient Jewish Diaspora* (2009).

———. "Josephus, Jewish Resistance and the Masada Myth," in Collins, J. and Manning, J. eds. *Revolt and Resistance in the Ancient Classical World and the Near East: In the Crucible of Empire* (2016) pp. 219–33.

Rankov, B. "Roman Military Forces in the Late Republic and the Principate," in Sabin, P., van Wees, H., and Whitby, M. eds. *The Cambridge History of Greek and Roman Warfare, Vol. 2: Rome from the Late Republic to the Late Empire* (2007) pp. 30–75.

Rappaport, U. "Jewish-Pagan Relations and the Revolt against Rome in 66–70 C.E.," in Levine, L. ed. *Jerusalem Cathedra: Studies in History, Archaeology, Geography and Ethnography of the Land of Israel* 2 (1981) pp. 81–95.

———. "John of Gischala: From Galilee to Jerusalem," *JJS* 33, no. 1–2 (1982) pp. 479–93.

———. "Who Minted the Jewish War's Coins?," *INR* 2 (2007) pp. 103–16.

———. "The Great Revolt: An Overview," in Guri-Rimon, O. ed. *The Great Revolt in the Galilee* (2008) pp. 9–13.

———. *John of Gischala: From the Mountains of Galilee to the Walls of Jerusalem* (2013).

Rathbone, D. "Military Finance and Supply," in Sabin, P., van Wees, H., and Whitby, M. eds. *The Cambridge History of Greek and Roman Warfare, Vol. 2: Rome from the Late Republic to the Late Empire* (2007) pp. 158–76.

Reed, J. *Archaeology and the Galilean Jesus: A Re-Examination of the Evidence* (2000).

Regev, E. *The Sadducees and their Halakhah: Religion and Society in the Second Temple Period* (2005).

———. "Herod's Jewish Ideology Facing Romanization: On Intermarriage, Ritual Baths, and Speeches," *JQR* 100, no. 2 (2010) pp. 197–222.

Reich, R. "Women and Men at Masada: Some Anthropological Observations Based upon Small Finds (Coins, Spindles)," *ZDPV* 117 (2001) pp. 149–62.

———. "Baking and Cooking at Masada," *ZDPV* 119 (2003) pp. 140–58.

———. "The Distribution of Stone Scale Weights from the Early Roman Period and Its Possible Meaning," *IEJ* 59 (2009) pp. 175–84.

———. "A Note on the Population Size of Jerusalem in the Second Temple Period," *RB* 121, no. 2 (2014) pp. 298–305.

Reich, R. and Shukron, E. "Jerusalem, Gihon Spring," *Hadashot Arkheologiyot* 108 (1998) pp. 136–37.

———. "Jerusalem, Gihon Spring," *Hadashot Arkheologiyot* 109 (1999) pp. 77–78.

———. "The Pool of Siloam in Jerusalem of the Late Second Temple Period and Its Surroundings," in Galor, K. and Avni, G. eds. *Unearthing Jerusalem: 150 Years of Archaeological Research in the Holy City* (2011) pp. 241–55.

Reid, B. ed. *Military Power: Land Warfare in Theory and Practice* (1997).

Reisner, G., Fisher, S., and Lyon, D. *Harvard Expeditions at Samaria, 1908–1910, Vol. 1* (1924).

Rhoads, D. *Israel in Revolution: 6–74 C.E.: A Political History Based on the Writings of Josephus* (1976).

Rich, J. and Shipley, G. eds. *War and Society in the Roman World* (1995).

Richards, K. ed. *Society of Biblical Literature Seminar Papers* (1982).

Richardson, P. *Herod: King of the Jews and Friend of the Romans* (1996).

———. *City and Sanctuary: Religion and Architecture in the Roman Near East* (2002).

———. *Building Jewish in the Roman East* (2004).

Richardson, P. and Fisher, A. *Herod: King of the Jews and Friend of the Romans* (2018).

Richmond, I. "The Roman Siege-Works of Masada, Israel," *JRS* 52 (1962) pp. 142–55.

Ritmeyer, K. and Ritmeyer, L. "Reconstructing Herod's Temple Mount in Jerusalem," *BAR* 15, no. 6 (1989) pp. 23–24, 26–27, 29, 32, 35–37, 40, 42.

Ritmeyer, L. *The Quest: Revealing the Temple Mount in Jerusalem* (2006).

Rives, J. "Flavian Religious Policy and the Destruction of the Jerusalem Temple," in Edmondson, J., Mason, S., and Rives, J. eds. *Flavius Josephus and Flavian Rome* (2005) pp. 145–66.

———. "Animal Sacrifice and Political Identity in Rome and Judaea," in Tomson, P. and Schwartz, J. eds. *Jews and Christians in the First and Second Centuries: How to Write Their History* (2014) pp. 105–25.

Roberts, A. *Napoleon: A Life* (2015).

———. *Churchill: Walking with Destiny* (2018).

Rocca, S. *Herod's Judaea: A Mediterranean State in the Classical World* (2008).

———. *The Army of Herod the Great* (2009).

———. "Herod's Eagle: An Iconographic Study," *Mediterraneo Antico* 21, no. 1–2 (2018) pp. 477–508.

Rodgers, Z. "Justice for Justus: A Reexamination of Justus of Tiberias' Role in Josephus' Autobiography," in McGing, B. and Mossman, J. eds. *The Limits of Ancient Biography* (2006) pp. 169–92.

——— ed. *Making History: Josephus and Historical Method* (2007).

———. "Monarchy vs. Priesthood: Josephus, Justus of Tiberias, and Agrippa," in Rodgers, Z., Daly-Denton, M., and Fitzpatrick McKinley, A. eds. *A Wandering Galilean: Essays in Honour of Seán Freyne* (2009) pp. 173–84.

Rodgers, Z., Daly-Denton, M., and Fitzpatrick McKinley, A. eds. *A Wandering Galilean: Essays in Honour of Seán Freyne* (2009).

Rogers, G. *Alexander: The Ambiguity of Greatness* (2004).

———. *The Mysteries of Artemis of Ephesos: Cult, Polis, and Change in the Graeco-Roman World* (2013).

Roller, D. "The Problem of the Location of Straton's Tower," *BASOR* 252 (1983) pp. 61–68.

———. *The Building Program of Herod the Great* (1998).

———. "New Insights into the Building Program of Herod the Great," in Kokkinos, N. *The World of the Herods: Volume 1 of the International Conference "The World of the Herods" Held at the British Museum, 17–19 April 2001* (2007) pp. 313–20.

Romanoff, P. "Jewish Symbols on Ancient Jewish Coins (Continued)," *JQR* 34, no. 3 (1944) pp. 299–312.

Rosenfeld, B. and Menirav, J. *Markets and Marketing in Roman Palestine* (2005).

Roth, J. "The Size and Organization of the Roman Imperial Legion," *Historia* 43 (1994) pp. 346–62.

———. "The Length of the Siege of Masada," *SCI* 14 (1995) pp. 87–110.

———. *Roman Warfare* (2009).

———. *The Logistics of the Roman Army at War (264 BC–AD 235)* (2012).

Roussel, P. "Nikanor d'Alexandrie et la porte du temple de Jérusalem," *REG* 37, no. 169 (1924) pp. 79–82.

Rozenberg, S. "Interior Decoration in Herod's Palaces," in Rozenberg, S. and Mevorah, D. eds. *Herod the Great: The King's Final Journey* (2017) pp. 166–223.

Rozenberg, S. and Mevorah, D. eds. *Herod the Great: The King's Final Journey* (2017).

Rutgers, L. "Some Reflections on the Archaeological Finds from the Domestic Quarter on the Acropolis of Sepphoris," in Lapin, H. ed. *Religious and Ethnic Communities in Later Roman Palestine* (1998) pp. 179–95.

Sabin, P., van Wees, H., and Whitby, M. eds. *The Cambridge History of Greek and Roman Warfare, Vol. 2: Rome from the Late Republic to the Late Empire* (2007).

Saddington, D. *The Development of the Roman Auxiliary Forces from Caesar to Vespasian (49 B.C.–A.D. 79)* (1982).

———. "Client Kings' Armies under Augustus: The Case of Herod," in Jacobson, D. and Kokkinos, N. eds. *Herod and Augustus* (2009) pp. 303–24.

Sadler, J. and Serdiville, R. *Caesar's Greatest Victory: The Battle of Alesia, 52 BC* (2016).

Safrai, S., Stern, M., eds. with Flusser, D. and van Unnik, W. *The Jewish People in the First Century: Historical Geography, Political History, Social, Cultural and Religious Life and Institutions, Vol. 2* (1976).

Saldarini, A. "Varieties of Rabbinic Response to the Destruction of the Temple," in Richards, K. ed. *Society of Biblical Literature Seminar Papers* (1982) pp. 437–58.

———. *Pharisees, Scribes, and Sadducees in Palestinian Society* (2001).

Samuelsson, G. *Crucifixion in Antiquity: An Inquiry into the Background and Significance of the New Testament Terminology of Crucifixion* (2011).

Sanders, E. *Jesus and Judaism* (1985).

———. *Judaism: Practice and Belief, 63 BCE–66 CE* (1992).

Sartre, M. *The Middle East under Rome* (2005).

Satlow, M. *How the Bible Became Holy* (2014).

Savage, C. *Biblical Bethsaida: An Archaeological Study of the First Century* (2011).

Schäfer, P. *Der Bar Kokhba-Aufstand: Studien zum zweiten jüdischen Krieg gegen Rom* (1981).

———. *The History of Jews in Antiquity* (1995).

——— ed. *The Talmud Yerushalmi and Graeco-Roman Culture, Vol. I* (1998).

——— ed. *The Bar Kokhba War Reconsidered: New Perspectives on the Second Jewish Revolt against Rome* (2003a).

———. *The History of the Jews in the Greco-Roman World* (2003b).

Schalit, A. *König Herodes: Der Mann und sein Werk* (2001).

Scheidel, W. *Measuring Sex, Age, and Death in the Roman Empire: Explorations in Ancient Demography* (1996).

Scheidel, W., Morris, I., and Saller, R. eds. *The Cambridge Economic History of the Greco-Roman World* (2013).

Schick, R. "Palestine in the Early Islamic Period: Luxuriant Legacy," *NEA* 61, no. 2 (1998) pp. 74–108.

Schiffman, L. *From Text to Tradition: A History of Second Temple and Rabbinic Judaism* (1991).

Schiffman, L., Tov, E., and VanderKam, J. eds. *The Dead Sea Scrolls Fifty Years after Their Discovery 1947–1997: Proceedings of the Jerusalem Congress, July 20–25, 1997* (2000).

Schiffman, L. and VanderKam, J. eds. *Encyclopedia of the Dead Sea Scrolls, Vols. 1 and 2* (2000).

Schmid, K. "The Late Persian Formation of the Torah: Observations on Deuteronomy 34," in Lipschits, O., Knoppers, G., and Albertz, R. eds. *Judah and the Judeans in the Fourth Century B.C.E.* (2007) pp. 237–51.

Schofield, A. and Vanderkam, J. "Were the Hasmoneans Zakokites?," *JBL* 124, no. 1 (2005) pp. 73–87.

Schremer, A. "'The Lord Has Forsaken the Land': Radical Explanations for the Military and Political Defeat of the Jews in the Tannaitic Literature," *JJS* 59 (2008) pp. 183–99.

———. *Brothers Estranged: Heresy, Christianity and Jewish Identity in Late Antiquity* (2010).

Schulten, A. *Masada: Die Burg des Herodes und die römischen Lager, mit einem Anhang: Beth-Ter* (1933).

Schumer, N. "The Memory of the Temple in Palestinian Rabbinic Literature," PhD Dissertation, Columbia University (2017a).

———. "The Population of Sepphoris: Rethinking Urbanization in Early and Middle Roman Galilee," *JAJ* 8, no. 1 (2017b) pp. 90–111.

Schürer, E. *Lehrbuch der neutestamentlichen Zeitgeschichte* (1874).

———. *The History of the Jewish People in the Age of Jesus Christ (175 B.C.–A.D. 135), Vols. I–III*, ed. Vermes, G., Millar, F., and Goodman, M. (2014).

Schwartz, D. *Agrippa I: The Last King of Judaea* (1990).

———. "Herodians and *Ioudaioi* in Flavian Rome," in Edmondson, J., Mason, S., and Rives, J. eds. *Flavius Josephus and Flavian Rome* (2005) pp. 63–78.

———. "Herod in Ancient Jewish literature," in Kokkinos, N. ed. *The World of the Herods: Volume 1 of the International Conference "The World of the Herods" Held at the British Museum, 17–19 April 2001* (2007a) pp. 45–53.

———. "'Judaean' or 'Jew'? How Should We Translate *Ioudaios* in Josephus?," in Frey, J., Schwartz, D., and Gripentrog, S. eds. *Jewish Identity in the Greco-Roman World/Jüdische Identität in der griechisch-römischen Welt* (2007b) pp. 3–27.

———. "One Temple and Many Synagogues: On Religion and State in Herodian Judaea and Augustan Rome," in Jacobson, D. and Kokkinos, N. eds. *Herod and Augustus* (2009a) pp. 383–98.

———. "Philo, His Family, and His Times," in Kamesar, A. ed. *The Cambridge Companion to Philo* (2009b) pp. 9–31.

———. "Introduction," in Schwartz, D. and Weiss, Z. eds. *Was 70 CE a Watershed in Jewish History? On Jews and Judaism before and after the Destruction of the Second Temple* (2012) pp. 1–19.

———. "Herod the Great: A Matter of Perspective," in Rozenberg, S. and Mevorah, D. eds. *Herod the Great: The King's Final Journey* (2017) pp. 34–43.

———. *Judeans and Jews: Four Faces of Dichotomy in Ancient Jewish History* (2014).

———. "Herodium in History," in Porat, R. Chachy, R., and Kalman, Y. *Herodium: Final Reports of the 1972–2010 Excavations Directed by Ehud Netzer, Vol. I: Herod's Tomb Precinct* (2015) pp. 1–14.

Schwartz, D. and Weiss, Z. eds. *Was 70 CE a Watershed in Jewish History? On Jews and Judaism before and after the Destruction of the Second Temple* (2012).

Schwartz, J. "Once More on the Nicanor Gate," *HUCA* 62 (1991) pp. 245–83.

———. "Bar Qatros and the Priestly Families of Jerusalem," in Geva, H. ed. *Jewish Quarter Excavations in the Old City of Jerusalem, Conducted by Nahman Avigad, 1969–1982, IV: The Burnt House of Area B and Other Studies, Final Report* (2010) pp. 308–19.

Schwartz, J., Amar, Z., and Ziffer, I. eds. *Jerusalem and Eretz Israel: The Arie Kindler Volume* (2001).

Schwartz, S. "The Composition and Publication of Josephus' *Bellum Iudaicum* Book 7," *HTR* 79 (1986) pp. 373–86.

———. *Josephus and Judaean Politics* (1990).

———. "Herod, Friend of the Jews," in Schwartz, J., Amar, Z., and Ziffer, I. eds. *Jerusalem and Eretz Israel: The Arie Kindler Volume* (2001a) pp. 67–76.

———. *Imperialism and Jewish Society, 200 B.C.E. to 640 C.E.* (2001b).

———. "Conversion to Judaism in the Second Temple Period: A Functionalist Approach," in Cohen, S. and Schwartz, J. eds. *Studies in Josephus and the Varieties of Ancient Judaism: Louis H. Feldman Jubilee Volume* (2007) pp. 223–236.

———. "Sunt Lachrymae Rerum," *JQR* 99, no. 1 (2009) pp. 56–64.

———. *Were the Jews a Mediterranean Society? Reciprocity and Solidarity in Ancient Judaism* (2010).

———. "Jewish States," in Bang, P. and Scheidel, W. eds. *The Oxford Handbook of the State in the Ancient Near East and Mediterranean* (2013) pp. 180–98.

———. *The Ancient Jews from Alexander to Muhammad* (2014).

Sebesta, J. and Bonfante, L. eds. *The World of Roman Costume* (2001).

Segal, A., and Eisenberg, M. "Sussita-Hippos of the Decapolis: Town Planning and Architecture of a Roman-Byzantine City," *NEA* 70, no. 2 (2007) pp. 86–107.

Seigne, J. "Gerasa-Jerasch-Stadt der 1000 Säulen," in Hoffman, A. and Kerner, S. eds. *Gadara-Gerasa und die Dekapolis* (2002) pp. 6–22.

Shamir, O. "Loomweights from Masada," in Aviram, Y., Foerster, G., and Netzer, E., eds. *Masada IV: The Yigael Yadin Excavations 1963–65. Final Reports: Lamps, Textiles, Basketry, Cordage, and Related Artifacts, Wood Remains, and Ballista Balls. Addendum, Human Skeletal Remains* (1994) pp. 265–82.

Shanks, H. "Was Herod's Tomb Really Found?," *BAR* 40, no. 3 (2014) pp. 40–48.

Sharon, N. "The Title *Ethnarch* in Second Temple Period Judea," *JSJ* 41 (2010) pp. 472–93.

———. "Setting the Stage: The Effects of the Roman Conquest and the Loss of Sovereignty," in Schwartz, D., and Weiss, Z. eds. *Was 70 CE a Watershed in Jewish History? On Jews and Judaism before and after the Destruction of the Second Temple* (2012) pp. 413–45.

———. *Judea under Roman Domination: The First Generation of Statelessness and Its Legacy* (2017).

Shatzman, I. *The Armies of the Hasmoneans and Herod* (1991).

———. "On the Conversion of the Idumaeans," in Mor, M., Pastor, J., Ronen, I., and Ashkenazi, Y. eds. *For Uriel: Studies in the History of Israel in Antiquity Presented to Professor Uriel Rappaport* (2005) pp. 213–41.

———. "Jews and Gentiles from Judas Maccabaeus to John Hyrcanus according to Jewish Sources," in Cohen, S. and Schwartz, J. eds. *Josephus and the Varieties of Ancient Judaism: Louis H. Feldman Jubilee Volume* (2007) pp. 237–65.

Shavit, A. *My Promised Land: The Triumph and Tragedy of Israel* (2013).

Shavit, Y. *Athens in Jerusalem: Classical Antiquity and Hellenism in the Making of the Modern Secular Jew* (1997).

Shaw, B. "Tyrants, Bandits and Kings: Personal Power in Josephus," *JJS* 44, no. 2 (1993) pp. 176–204.

Sherk, R. *The Roman Empire: Augustus to Hadrian* (1988).

Shimron, A. and Peleg-Barkat, O. "New Evidence of the Royal Stoa and Roman Flames," *BAR* 36, no. 2 (2010) pp. 56–62.

Shroder, J., Jol, H., and Reeder, P. "El Araj as Bethsaida: Spatial and Temporal Improbabilities," in Arav, R. and Freund, R. eds. *Bethsaida: A City by the North Shore of the Sea of Galilee, Vol. 4* (2009) pp. 293–309.

Sicker, M. *Between Rome and Jerusalem: 300 Years of Roman-Judaean Relations* (2001).

Siegelmann, A. "The Identification of Gaba Hippeon," *PEQ* 116, no. 2 (1984) pp. 89–93.

Siggelkow-Berner, B. *Die jüdischen Feste im Bellum Judaicum des Flavius Josephus* (2011).

Silberman, N. *Between Past and Present: Archaeology, Ideology, and Nationalism in the Modern Middle East* (1989).

———. *A Prophet from amongst You: The Life of Yigael Yadin, Soldier, Scholar, and Mythmaker of Modern Israel* (1993).

————. *Heavenly Powers* (1998).

Simon, M. *Verus Israel: A Study of the Relations between Christians and Jews in the Roman Empire AD 135–425* (1986).

Sivan, R. and Solar, G. "Excavations in the Jerusalem Citadel, 1980–1988," in Geva, H. ed. *Ancient Jerusalem Revealed* (1994) pp. 168–76.

Sly, D. "The Conflict over *Isopoliteia*: An Alexandrian Perspective," in Donaldson, T. ed. *Religious Rivalries and the Struggle for Success in Caesarea Maritima* (2000) pp. 249–65.

Smallwood, E. *Philonis Alexandrini Legatio ad Gaium* (1970).

————. *The Jews under Roman Rule: From Pompey to Diocletian, A Study in Political Relations* (1981).

Smith, R. and Day, L. *Pella of the Decapolis 2: Final Report on the College of Wooster Excavations in Area IX, the Civic Complex, 1979–85* (1989).

Sorek, S. *The Jews against Rome: War in Palestine AD 66–73* (2008).

Southern, P. *The Roman Army: A Social and Institutional History* (2007).

Stamper, J. *The Architecture of Roman Temples: The Republic to the Middle Empire* (2005).

Steinmann, A. "When Did Herod the Great Reign?," *NovT* 51, no. 1 (2009) pp. 1–29.

Stern, E. ed. *The New Encyclopedia of Archaeological Excavations in the Holy Land, Vols. I–IV* (1993).

Stern, E. and Magen, Y. "The First Phase of the Samaritan Temple on Mt. Gerizim: New Archaeological Evidence," *Qadmoniot* 33, no. 120 (2000) pp. 119–24.

————. "Archaeological Evidence for the First Stage of the Samaritan Temple on Mount Gerizim," *IEJ* 52 (2002) pp. 49–57.

Stern, M. *Greek and Latin Authors on Jews and Judaism I–III* (1976–1984).

————. "The Suicide of Eleazar ben Jair and His Men at Masada, and the 'Fourth Philosophy,'" *Zion* 47, no. 4 (1982) pp. 367–98.

Stern, S. *Time and Process in Ancient Judaism* (2003).

Stevenson, G. *Roman Provincial Administration till the Age of the Antonines* (1939).

Stiebel, G. "Military Equipment," in Syon, D. ed. *Gamla III: The Shmarya Gutmann Excavations 1976–1989. Finds and Studies, Part I (IAA Reports, No. 56)* (2014), pp. 57–107.

Stiebel, G. and Magness, J. "The Military Equipment from Masada," in Aviram, J., Foester, G., Netzer, E., and Stiebel, G. eds. *Masada VIII: The Yigal Yadin Excavations 1963–65. Final Reports* (2007) pp. 1–94.

Stiebel, G., Peleg-Barakat, O., Ben-Ami, D., Weksler-Bdolah, S., and Gadot, Y. eds. *New Studies in the Archaeology of Jerusalem and Its Region, Vol. VII* (2013).

Stieglitz, R. "Stratonos Pyrgos—Midgal Sar—Sebastos: History and Archaeology," in Raban, A. and Holum, K. eds. *Caesarea Maritima: A Retrospective after Two Millennia* (1996) pp. 593–608.

Strange, J. "Herod and Jerusalem: The Hellenization of an Oriental City," in Thompson, T. ed. *Jerusalem in Ancient History and Tradition* (2003) pp. 97–113.

Strobel, A. "Das römische Belagerungswerk um Machärus: Topographische Untersuchungen," *ZDPV* 90 (1974) pp. 128–84.

Strugnell, J. "Quelques inscriptions Samaritaines," *RB* 74 (1967) pp. 555–80.

Syme, R. "Domitius Corbulo," *JRS* 60 (1970) pp. 27–39.

———. "Governors Dying in Syria," *ZPE* 41 (1981) pp. 125–44.

———. *The Augustan Aristocracy* (1989).

Syon, D. "Gamla: Portrait of a Rebellion," *BAR* 18, no. 1 (1992) pp. 20–37, 72.

———. "The Coins from Gamala—An Interim Report," *INJ* 12 (1992–93) pp. 34–55.

———. "'City of Refuge': The Archaeological Evidence of the Revolt at Gamla," in Guri-Rimon, O. ed. *The Great Revolt in the Galilee* (2008) pp. 53–65.

———. "Chapter 5: Coins," in Syon, D. ed. *Gamla III: The Shmarya Gutmann Excavations 1976–1989. Finds and Studies, Part I (IAA Reports, No. 56)* (2014a) pp. 109–223.

——— ed. *Gamla III: The Shmarya Gutmann Excavations 1976–1989. Finds and Studies, Part I (IAA Reports, No. 56)* (2014b).

Syon, D. and Yavor, Z. "Gamala," *NEAEHL* 5 (2008) pp. 1739–42.

Szkolut, P. "The Eagle as Symbol of the Divine Presence and Protection in Ancient Jewish Art," *Studia Judaica* 5 (2002) pp. 1–11.

———. "Symbol Orla w Sztuce Judaizmu Okresu Rzymskiego I Wczesnobizantyjskiego," PhD Dissertation, University of Lodz (2004).

Tal, O. and Weiss, Z. eds. *Expressions of Cult in the Southern Levant in the Greco-Roman Period: Manifestations in Text and Material Culture* (2017).

Talmon, S., Newsom, C., Yadin, Y., Qimron, E., and Martinez, F. *Masada VI: The Yigael Yadin Excavations 1963–65. Final Reports: Hebrew Fragments from Masada, Songs of the Sabbath Sacrifice, the Ben Sira Scroll from Masada, with Notes on the Reading, Bibliography* (1999).

Taylor, J. "Khirbet Qumran in Period III," in Galor, K., Humbert, J.-B., and Zangenberg, J. eds. *Qumran, the Site of the Dead Sea Scrolls: Archaeological Interpretations and Debates; Proceedings of the Conference Held at Brown University, November 17–19, 2002* (2006a) pp. 133–46.

———. "Pontius Pilate and the Imperial Cult in Roman Judaea," *NTS* 52, no. 4 (2006b) pp. 555–82.

Thackeray, H. trans. *Josephus, The Life, Against Apion, Vol. I* (1926).

——— trans. *Josephus: The Jewish War, Books I–II, Vol. II* (1927a).

——— trans. *Josephus: The Jewish War, Books III–IV* (1927b).

——— trans. *Josephus: The Jewish War, Books V–VIII* (1928).

——— trans. *Josephus: Jewish Antiquities, Books I–IV, Vol. IV* (1930).

Thackeray, H. and Marcus, R. trans. *Josephus: Jewish Antiquities, Books V–VIII, Vol. V* (1934).

Thomas, J. *The Epistrategos in Ptolemaic and Roman Egypt, Part 2: The Roman Epistrategos* (1982).

Thompson, T. ed. *Jerusalem in Ancient History and Tradition* (2003).

Toher, M. "Nicolaus and Herod in the *Antiquitates Iudaicae*," *HSCP* 101 (2001) pp. 427–48.

———. "Herod, Augustus, and Nicolaus of Damascus," in Jacobson, D. and Kokkinos, N. eds. *Herod and Augustus* (2009) pp. 65–82.

Tomson, P. and Schwartz, J. eds. *Jews and Christians in the First and Second Centuries: How to Write Their History* (2014).

Tov, E. *Scribal Practices and Approaches Reflected in the Texts Found in the Judean Desert* (2004).

Toynbee, J. *The Flavian Reliefs from the Palazzo della Cancelleria in Rome* (1957).

Trebilco, P. "I 'timorati di Dio,'" in Lewin, A. ed. *Gli ebrei nell'Impero romano: Saggi vari* (2001) pp. 161–93.

Tsafrir, Y. "The Location of the Seleucid Akra in Jerusalem," *RB* 82 (1975) pp. 501–21.

———. "The Walls of Jerusalem in the Period of Nehemiah," *Cathedra* 4 (1977) pp. 31–42.

Tucci, P. *The Temple of Peace in Rome, Vol. I: Art and Culture in Imperial Rome* (2017).

Turner, E. "Tiberius Iulius Alexander," *JRS* 44 (1954) pp. 54–64.

Tuval, M. "Doing without the Temple: Paradigms in Judaic Literature of the Diaspora," in Schwartz, D. and Weiss, Z. eds. *Was 70 CE a Watershed in Jewish History? On Jews and Judaism before and after the Destruction of the Second Temple* (2012) pp. 181–239.

Udoh, F. *To Caesar What Is Caesar's: Tribute, Taxes, and Imperial Administration in Early Roman Palestine 63 B.C.E.–70 C.E.* (2006).

———. "Taxation and Other Sources of Government Income in the Galilee of Herod and Antipas," in Fiensy, D. and Strange, J. eds. *Galilee in the Late Second Temple and Mishnaic Periods, Vol. 1: Life, Culture, and Society* (2014) pp. 366–87.

Ussishkin, D. "The Rock Called Peristereon," *IEJ* 24, no. 1 (1974) pp. 70–72.

———. "The 'Camp of the Assyrians' in Jerusalem," *IEJ* 29, no. 3–4 (1979) pp. 137–42.

VanderKam, J. *An Introduction to Early Judaism* (2001).

———. *From Joshua to Caiaphas: High Priests after the Exile* (2004).

———. *The Dead Sea Scrolls Today* (2010).

VanderKam, J. and Flint, P. *The Meaning of the Dead Sea Scrolls: Their Significance for Understanding the Bible, Judaism, Jesus, and Christianity* (2002).

Van Driel-Murray, C. "The Production and Supply of Military Leatherwork in the First and Second Centuries AD: A Review of the Archaeological Evidence," in

Bishop, M. ed. *The Production and Distribution of Roman Military Equipment: Proceedings of the Second Roman Military Equipment Research Seminar* (1985) pp. 43–81.

———. "New Light on Old Tents," *Journal of Roman Military Equipment Studies* 1 (1990) pp. 109–37.

Van Henten, J. "The Honorary Decree for Simon Maccabee (1 Macc 14:25–49) in Its Hellenistic Context," in Collins, J. and Sterling, G. eds. *Hellenism in the Land of Israel* (2001) pp. 116–45.

Vann, R. ed. *Caesarea Papers: Straton's Tower, Herod's Harbour, and Roman and Byzantine Caesarea* (1992).

Vardaman, J. "A New Inscription Which Mentions Pilate as Prefect," *JBL* 81, no. 1 (1962) pp. 70–71.

——— ed. *Chronos, Kairos, Christos II: Chronological, Nativity, and Religious Studies in Memory of Ray Summers* (1998a).

———. "Were the Samaritan Military Leaders, Rufus and Gratus, at the Time of Herod's Death, the Later Roman Judaean Governors Who Preceded Pontius Pilate?," in Vardaman, J. ed. *Chronos, Kairos, Christos II: Chronological, Nativity, and Religious Studies in Memory of Ray Summers* (1998b) pp. 191–202.

Vermes, G. *The True Herod* (2014).

Vervaet, F. "Domitius Corbulo and the Senatorial Opposition to Nero," *AS* 32 (2002) pp. 135–93.

———. "Domitius Corbulo and the Rise of the Flavian Dynasty," *Historia* 52, no. 4 (2003) pp. 436–64.

Villing, A. "Don't Kill the Goose that Lays the Golden Egg: Some Thoughts on Bird Sacrifices in Ancient Greece," in Hitch, S. and Rutherford, I. eds. *Animal Sacrifice in the Ancient Greek World* (2017) pp. 63–102.

Vogel, M. *Herodes: König der Juden, Freund der Römer* (2002).

Vörös, G. "The Herodian Fortified Palace Overlooking the Dead Sea in Transjordan," *Liber Annuus* 60 (2010) pp. 349–61.

———. "Machaerus: Where Salome Danced and John the Baptist Was Beheaded," *BAR* 38, no. 5 (2012) pp. 30–41, 68.

———. *Machaerus I: History, Archaeology and Architecture of the Fortified Herodian Royal Palace and City Overlooking the Dead Sea in Transjordan. Final Report of the Excavations and Surveys, 1807–2012* (2013).

———. "Anastylosis at Machaerus," *BAR* 41, no. 1 (2015a) pp. 52–61.

———. *Machaerus II: The Hungarian Mission in the Light of the American-Baptist and Italian-Franciscan Excavations and Surveys. Final Report, 1968–2015* (2015b).

———. "Machaerus: A Palace-Fortress with Multiple Mikva'ot," *BAR* 43, no. 4 (2017) pp. 30–39, 60.

Walsh, J. *The Great Fire of Rome: Life and Death in the Ancient City* (2019).

Warszawski, A. and Peretz, A. "Building the Temple Mount: Organization and Execution," *Cathedra* 66 (1992) pp. 3–46.

Wasserstein, A. "Notes on the Temple of Onias in Leontopolis," *Illinois Classical Studies* (1993) pp. 119–29.

Weber, F. *Herodes—König von Roms Gnaden? Herodes als Modell eines römischen Klientelkönigs in spätrepublikanischer und augusteischer Zeit* (2003).

Weber, W. *Josephus und Vespasian: Untersuchungen zu dem Jüdischen Krieg des Flavius Josephus* (1921).

Weiss, Z. "Josephus and Archaeology on the Cities of the Galilee," in Rodgers, Z. ed. *Making History: Josephus and Historical Method* (2007) pp. 385–414.

———. "From Roman Temple to Byzantine Church: A Preliminary Report on Sepphoris in Transition," *JRA* 23, no. 1 (2010) pp. 196–218.

———. "Buildings for Mass Entertainment in Herod's Kingdom," in Rozenberg, S. and Mevorah, D. eds. *Herod the Great: The King's Final Journey* (2017) pp. 224–39.

———. *Public Spectacles in Roman and Late Antique Palestine* (2014).

Weitzman, S. "Josephus on How to Survive Martyrdom," *JJS* 55, no. 2 (2004) pp. 230–45.

Welch, K. *The Roman Amphitheatre: From Its Origins to the Colosseum* (2007).

Wellesley, K. *The Long Year A.D. 69* (1975).

White, L. *Building God's House in the Roman World: Architectural Adaptation among Pagans, Jews, and Christians* (1990).

Whitehead, D. *Aineias the Tactician: How to Survive under Siege* (1990).

Wilker, J. *Für Rom und Jerusalem: Die herodianische Dynastie im 1. Jahrhundert n. Chr.* (2007).

Will, E. "Antioche sur l'Oronte, Métropole de l'Asie," *Syria* 74 (1997) pp. 99–113.

Wilson, J. *Caesarea Philippi: Banias, The Lost City of Pan* (2004).

Wilson, J. and Tzaferis, V. "A Herodian Capital in the North: Caesarea Philippi (Panias)," in Kokkinos, N. ed. *The World of the Herods: Volume 1 of the International Conference "The World of the Herods" Held at the British Museum, 17–19 April 2001* (2007) pp. 131–43.

Wolters, R. "Bronze, Silver, or Gold? Coin Finds and the Stipendium of the Roman Army," *Zephyrus* 53–54 (2000–2001) pp. 579–88.

Yadin, Y. *Masada: Herod's Fortress and Zealot's Last Stand* (1966).

———. *Bar-Kokhba: The Rediscovery of the Legendary Hero of the Second Jewish Revolt against Rome* (1971).

Yadin, Y., and Naveh, J., "The Aramaic and Hebrew Ostraca and Jar Inscriptions," in Yadin, Y., Naveh, J. and Meshorer, Y. *Masada I: The Yigael Yadin Excavations 1963–1965. Final Reports: The Aramaic and Hebrew Ostraca and Jar Inscriptions. The Coins of Masada* (1989) pp. 1–68.

Yadin, Y., Naveh, J., and Meshorer, Y. *Masada I: The Yigael Yadin Excavations 1963–1965. Final Reports: The Aramaic and Hebrew Ostraca and Jar Inscriptions. The Coins of Masada* (1989).

Yarden, L. *The Spoils of Jerusalem on the Arch of Titus: A Re-Investigation* (1991).

Yona, S. ed. *Or Le-Mayer: Studies in Bible, Semitic Languages, Rabbinic Literature, and Ancient Civilizations Presented to Mayer Gruber on the Occasion of his Sixty-Fifth Birthday* (2010).

Zangenberg, J., Attridge, H., and Martin, D. eds. *Religion, Ethnicity, and Identity in Ancient Galilee: A Region in Transition* (2007).

Zapata-Meza, M. and Sanz-Rincón, R. "Excavating Mary Magdalene's Hometown," *BAR* 43, no. 3 (2017) pp. 37–42.

Zerubavel, Y. *Recovered Roots: Collective Memory and the Making of Israeli National Tradition* (1995).

Zias, J. "Whose Bones? Were They Really Jewish Defenders? Did Yadin Deliberately Obfuscate?," *BAR* 24, no. 6 (1998) pp. 40–45, 64–65.

———. "Human Skeletal Remains from the Southern Cave at Masada and the Question of Ethnicity," in Schiffman, L., Tov, E., and VanderKam, J. eds. *The Dead Sea Scrolls Fifty Years after Their Discovery, 1947–1997: Proceedings of the Jerusalem Congress, July 20–25, 1997* (2000) pp. 732–39.

Zias, J. and Gorski, A. "Capturing a Beautiful Woman at Masada," *NEA* 69, no. 1 (2006) pp. 45–48.

Zias, J., Segal, D., and Carmi, I. "Addendum: The Human Skeletal Remains from the Northern Cave at Masada—A Second Look," in Aviram, J., Foerster G., and Netzer, E. eds. *Masada IV: The Yigael Yadin Excavations 1963–65. Final Reports: Lamps, Textiles, Basketry, Cordage, and Related Artifacts, Wood Remains, and Ballista Balls* (1994) pp. 366–67.

Index